Europe and the People Without History

EUROPE AND THE PEOPLE WITHOUT HISTORY

ERIC R. WOLF

**Cartographic Illustrations
by Noël L. Diaz**

University of California Press
Berkeley Los Angeles London

University of California Press
Berkeley and Los Angeles, California

University of California Press, Ltd.
London, England

Copyright © 1982 by The Regents of the University of California

Library of Congress Cataloging in Publication Data

Wolf, Eric Robert, 1923–
  Europe and the people without history.

  Bibliography: p. 427
    1. Europe—History—1492–   .   2. Europe—Economic
conditions.   3. Europe—Social conditions.   4. Social
change.   I. Title.
D208.W64   940.2   81-24031
                       AACR2

Printed in the United States of America

    2   3   4   5   6   7   8   9

FOR SYDEL

Contents

Preface

In 1968 I wrote that anthropology needed to discover history, a history that could account for the ways in which the social system of the modern world came into being, and that would strive to make analytic sense of all societies, including our own. Such an analytic history was needed, I believed, to counter the ascendancy in the human sciences of a formal rationality that no longer inquired into the causes of human action but sought merely technical solutions to problems conceived primarily in technical terms. Our methods were becoming more sophisticated, but their yield seemed increasingly commonplace. To stem a descent into triviality, I thought, we needed to search out the causes of the present in the past. Only in this way could we come to comprehend the forces that impel societies and cultures here and now. This book grew out of these convictions.

It was clear to me from the start that such an analytic history could not be developed out of the study of a single culture or nation, a single culture area, or even a single continent at one period in time. It was necessary to return to the insights of an older anthropology and to recover the inspiration that guided anthropologists such as Alfred Kroeber and Ralph Linton in their efforts to develop a global culture history. They understood, as we seem to have forgotten, that human populations construct their cultures in interaction with one another, and not in isolation.

That older anthropology had little to say, however, about the major forces driving the interaction of cultures since 1492—the forces propelling Europe into commercial expansion and industrial capitalism. Yet the cultural connections that these anthropologists sought to delineate can be rendered intelligible only when they are set in their political and economic context. The insights of anthropology therefore have to be rethought in the light of a new, historically oriented political economy.

Such rethinking must transcend the customary ways of depicting Western history, and must take account of the conjoint participation of Western and non-Western peoples in this worldwide process. Most of the groups studied by anthropologists have long been caught up in the changes wrought by European expansion, and they have contributed to these changes. We can no longer be content with writing only the history of victorious elites, or with detailing the subjugation of dominated ethnic groups. Social historians and historical sociologists have shown that the common people were as much agents in the historical process as they were its victims and silent witnesses. We thus need to uncover the history of "the people without history"—the active histories of "primitives," peasantries, laborers, immigrants, and besieged minorities.

To that end, this book strives to cross the lines of demarcation that separate the various human disciplines from one another, and to abrogate the boundaries between Western and non-Western history. It was written in the belief that a better understanding of our human condition is now within our grasp.

The project for this book emerged from the intellectual reassessments that marked the late 1960s. It was carried forward during a year's research in England in 1973–1974, made possible by the grant of a senior fellowship from the National Endowment for the Humanities. I acknowledge the support of the Endowment with abiding gratitude.

I began to write this book in the spring of 1974; the final draft was completed in 1981. Several friends read it with a critical eye. I am grateful for this to Roderick Aya, Richard Fox, Ashraf Ghani, Shirley Lindenbaum, Rayna Rapp, Roger Sanjek, Jane Schneider, and Peter Schneider. Samuel Bowles and Sidney Mintz took time to correspond about various ideas. Where I have not followed their counsel, the responsibility is mine alone. I am grieved that my friend Angel Palerm died before he could read this work; I miss his penetrating comments.

I owe thanks for advice on sources to Anne Bailey, Mario Bick, Charles Bishop, Warren DeBoer, Ashraf Ghani, Herbert Gutman, Shirley Hune, Herbert Klein, Carol Kramer, Hermann Rebel, Roger Sanjek, Gerald Sider, Juan Villamarín, Elizabeth Wahl, and Frederick Wyatt. I received advice and help on pictorial materials from Anna Roosevelt, James G. E. Smith, and Donald Werner of the Museum of the American Indian, Heye Foundation; from Robert Carneiro, Barbara Conklin, and Gordon Ekholm of the American Museum of Natural History; from William Sturtevant of the Smithsonian Institution; as well as from Lambros Comitas, June Finfer, Fred Popper, Lucie Wood Saunders, Bernard B. Shapiro, and Archibald Singham. Noël L. Diaz and Caryl Davis drew excellent maps. I am indebted to all. I am also most grateful to The School of Oriental and African Studies and to The London School of Economics and Political Science, University of London, for granting me access to their library holdings. Throughout my labors, Herbert H. Lehman College of the City University of New York, and the Ph.D. Program in Anthropology, The Graduate School and University Center, City University of New York, provided me with an unusually stimulating setting for research, teaching, and the exchange of ideas. I want to express my thanks for this opportunity.

None of these efforts would have come to fruition, however, without the advice, editorial skill, and unfailing encouragement of Sydel Silverman, my helpmate, wife, and foremost anthropological critic. "Di tante cose quant' i'ho vedute, dal tuo podere e dalla tua bontate riconosco la grazia e la virtute" (*Paradise*, XXXI). To her, in love and admiration, this book is dedicated.

E. R. W.

Caravan leaving Aleppo. Copper engraving by Theodore de Bry, 1599. (Courtesy of the Rare Books and Manuscript Division, The New York Public Library. Astor, Lenox, and Tilden Foundations)

Part One
Connections

1 Introduction

The central assertion of this book is that the world of humankind constitutes a manifold, a totality of interconnected processes, and inquiries that disassemble this totality into bits and then fail to reassemble it falsify reality. Concepts like "nation," "society," and "culture" name bits and threaten to turn names into things. Only by understanding these names as bundles of relationships, and by placing them back into the field from which they were abstracted, can we hope to avoid misleading inferences and increase our share of understanding.

On one level it has become a commonplace to say that we all inhabit "one world." There are ecological connections: New York suffers from the Hong Kong flu; the grapevines of Europe are destroyed by American plant lice. There are demographic connections: Jamaicans migrate to London; Chinese migrate to Singapore. There are economic connections: a shutdown of oil wells on the Persian Gulf halts generating plants in Ohio; a balance of payments unfavorable to the United States drains American dollars into bank accounts in Frankfurt or Yokohama; Italians produce Fiat automobiles in the Soviet Union; Japanese build a hydroelectric system in Ceylon. There are political connections: wars begun in Europe unleash reverberations around the globe; American troops intervene on the rim of Asia; Finns guard the border between Israel and Egypt.

This holds true not only of the present but also of the past. Diseases from Eurasia devastated the native population of America and Oceania. Syphilis moved from the New World to the Old. Europeans and their plants and animals invaded the Americas; the American potato, maize plant, and manioc spread throughout the Old World. Large numbers of Africans were transported forcibly to the New World; Chinese and Indian indentured laborers were shipped to Southeast Asia and the West Indies. Portugal created a Portuguese settlement in Macao off the coast of China. Dutchmen, using labor obtained in Bengal, constructed Batavia. Irish children were sold into servitude in the West Indies. Fugitive African slaves found sanctuary in the hills of Surinam. Europe learned to copy Indian textiles and Chinese porcelain, to drink native

American chocolate, to smoke native American tobacco, to use Arabic numerals.

These are familiar facts. They indicate contact and connections, linkages and interrelationships. Yet the scholars to whom we turn in order to understand what we see largely persist in ignoring them. Historians, economists, and political scientists take separate nations as their basic framework of inquiry. Sociology continues to divide the world into separate societies. Even anthropology, once greatly concerned with how culture traits diffused around the world, divides its subject matter into distinctive cases: each society with its characteristic culture, conceived as an integrated and bounded system, set off against other equally bounded systems.

If social and cultural distinctiveness and mutual separation were a hallmark of humankind, one would expect to find it most easily among the so-called primitives, people "without history," supposedly isolated from the external world and from one another. On this presupposition, what would we make of the archaeological findings that European trade goods appear in sites on the Niagara frontier as early as 1570, and that by 1670 sites of the Onondaga subgroup of the Iroquois reveal almost no items of native manufacture except pipes? On the other side of the Atlantic, the organization and orientations of large African populations were transformed in major ways by the trade in slaves. Since the European slavers only moved the slaves from the African coast to their destination in the Americas, the supply side of the trade was entirely in African hands. This was the "African foundation" upon which was built, in the words of the British mercantilist Malachy Postlethwayt, "the magnificent superstructure of American commerce and naval power." From Senegambia in West Africa to Angola, population after population was drawn into this trade, which ramified far inland and affected people who had never even seen a European trader on the coast. Any account of Kru, Fanti, Asante, Ijaw, Igbo, Kongo, Luba, Lunda, or Ngola that treats each group as a "tribe" sufficient unto itself thus misreads the African past and the African present. Furthermore, trade with Iroquois and West Africa affected Europe in turn. Between 1670 and 1760 the Iroquois demanded dyed scarlet and blue cloth made in the Stroudwater Valley of Gloucestershire. This was also one of the first areas in which English weavers lost their autonomy and became hired factory hands. Perhaps there was an interconnection between the American trade and the onset of the industrial revolution in the valley of the Stroud. Conversely, the more than 5,500 muskets supplied to the Gold Coast in only three years (1658–1661) enriched the gunsmiths of Birmingham, where they were made (Jennings 1977: 99–100; Daaku 1970: 150–151).

If there are connections everywhere, why do we persist in turning dynamic, interconnected phenomena into static, disconnected things? Some of this is owing, perhaps, to the way we have learned our own history. We have been taught, inside the classroom and outside of it, that there exists an entity called the West, and that one can think of this West as a society and civilization independent of and in opposition to other societies and civilizations. Many of us even grew up believing that this West has a genealogy, according to which ancient Greece begat Rome, Rome begat Christian Europe, Christian Europe begat the Renaissance, the Renaissance the Enlightenment, the Enlightenment political democracy and the industrial revolution. Industry, crossed with democracy, in turn yielded the United States, embodying the rights to life, liberty, and the pursuit of happiness.

Such a developmental scheme is misleading. It is misleading, first, because it turns history into a moral success story, a race in time in which each runner of the race passes on the torch of liberty to the next relay. History is thus converted into a tale about the furtherance of virtue, about how the virtuous win out over the bad guys. Frequently, this turns into a story of how the winners prove that they are virtuous and good by winning. If history is the working out of a moral purpose in time, then those who lay claim to that purpose are by that fact the predilect agents of history.

The scheme misleads in a second sense as well. If history is but a tale of unfolding moral purpose, then each link in the genealogy, each runner in the race, is only a precursor of the final apotheosis and not a manifold of social and cultural processes at work in their own time and place. Yet what would we learn of ancient Greece, for example, if we interpreted it only as a prehistoric Miss Liberty, holding aloft the torch of moral purpose in the barbarian night? We would gain little sense of the class conflicts racking the Greek cities, or of the relation between freemen and their slaves. We would have no reason to ask why there were more Greeks fighting in the ranks of the Persian kings than in the ranks of the Hellenic Alliance against the Persians. It would be of no interest to us to know that more Greeks lived in southern Italy and Sicily, then called Magna Graecia, than in Greece proper. Nor would we have any reason to ask why there were soon more Greek mercenaries in foreign armies than in the military bodies of their home cities. Greek settlers outside of Greece, Greek mercenaries in foreign armies, and slaves from Thrace, Phrygia, or Paphalagonia in Greek households all imply Hellenic relations with Greeks and non-Greeks outside of Greece. Yet our guiding scheme would not invite us to ask questions about these relationships.

Nowhere is this myth-making scheme more apparent than in school-book versions of the history of the United States. There, a complex orchestration of antagonistic forces is celebrated instead as the unfolding of a timeless essence. In this perspective, the ever-changing boundaries of the United States and the repeated involvements of the polity in internal and external wars, declared and undeclared, are telescoped together by the teleological understanding that thirteen colonies clinging to the eastern rim of the continent would, in less than a century, plant the American flag on the shores of the Pacific. Yet this final result was itself only the contested outcome of many contradictory relationships. The colonies declared their independence, even though a majority of their population—European settlers, native Americans, and African slaves—favored the Tories. The new republic nearly foundered on the issue of slavery, dealing with it, in a series of problematic compromises, by creating two federated countries, each with its own zone of expansion. There was surely land for the taking on the new continent, but it had to be taken first from the native Americans who inhabited it, and then converted into flamboyant real estate. Jefferson bought the Louisiana territory cheaply, but only after the revolt of the Haitian slaves against their French slave masters robbed the area of its importance in the French scheme of things as a source of food supply for the Caribbean plantations. The occupation of Florida closed off one of the main escape hatches from southern slavery. The war with Mexico made the Southwest safe for slavery and cotton. The Hispanic land-owners who stood in the way of the American drive to the Pacific became "bandits" when they defended their own against the Anglo-phone newcomers. Then North and South—one country importing its working force from Europe, the other from Africa—fought one of the bloodiest wars in history. For a time the defeated South became a colony of the victorious North. Later, the alignment between regions changed, the "sunbelt" rising to predominance as the influence of the industrial Northeast declined. Clearly the republic was neither indivisible nor endowed with God-given boundaries.

It is conceivable that things might have been different. There could have arisen a polyglot Floridian Republic, a Francophone Mississippian America, a Hispanic New Biscay, a Republic of the Great Lakes, a Columbia—comprising the present Oregon, Washington, and British Columbia. Only if we assume a God-given drive toward geopolitical unity on the North American continent would this retrojection be meaningless. Instead, it invites us to account in material terms for what happened at each juncture, to account for how some relationships gained ascendancy over others. Thus neither ancient Greece, Rome, Christian Europe, the Renaissance, the Enlightenment, the industrial revolution, democracy, nor even the United States was ever a thing propelled toward its unfolding goal by some immanent driving spring, but rather a temporally and spatially changing and changeable set of relationships, or relationships among sets of relationships.

The point is more than academic. By turning names into things we create false models of reality. By endowing nations, societies, or cultures with the qualities of internally homogeneous and externally distinctive and bounded objects, we create a model of the world as a global pool hall in which the entities spin off each other like so many hard and round billiard balls. Thus it becomes easy to sort the world into differently colored balls, to declare that "East is East, and West is West, and never the twain shall meet." In this way a quintessential West is counterposed to an equally quintessential East, where life was cheap and slavish multitudes groveled under a variety of despotisms. Later, as peoples in other climes began to assert their political and economic independence from both West and East, we assigned these new applicants for historical status to a Third World of underdevelopment—a residual category of conceptual billiard balls—as contrasted with the developed West and the developing East. Inevitably, perhaps, these reified categories became intellectual instruments in the prosecution of the Cold War. There was the "modern" world of the West. There was the world of the East, which had fallen prey to communism, a "disease of modernization" (Rostow 1960). There was, finally, the Third World, still bound up in "tradition" and strangled in its efforts toward modernization. If the West could only find ways of breaking that grip, it could perhaps save the victim from the infection incubated and spread by the East, and set that Third World upon the road to modernization—the road to life, liberty, and the pursuit of happiness of the West. The ghastly offspring of this way of thinking about the world was the theory of "forced draft urbanization" (Huntington 1968: 655), which held that the Vietnamese could be propelled toward modernization by driving them into the cities through aerial bombardment and defoliation of the countryside. Names thus become things, and things marked with an *X* can become targets of war.

The Rise of the Social Sciences

The habit of treating named entities such as Iroquois, Greece, Persia, or the United States as fixed entities opposed to one another by stable internal architecture and external boundaries interferes with our ability to understand their mutual encounter and confrontation. In fact, this tendency has made it difficult to understand all such encounters and confrontations. Arranging imaginary building blocks into pyramids called East and West, or First, Second, and Third Worlds, merely compounds that difficulty. It is thus likely that we are dealing with some conceptual shortcomings in our ways of looking at social and political phenomena, and not just a temporary aberration. We seem to have taken a wrong turn in understanding at some critical point in the past, a false choice that bedevils our thinking in the present.

That critical turning point is identifiable. It occurred in the middle of the past century, when inquiry into the nature and varieties of human-kind split into separate (and unequal) specialties and disciplines. This split was fateful. It led not only forward into the intensive and specialized study of particular aspects of human existence, but turned the ideological reasons for that split into an intellectual justification for the specialties themselves. Nowhere is this more obvious than in the case of sociology. Before sociology we had political economy, a field of inquiry concerned with "the wealth of nations," the production and distribution of wealth within and between political entities and the classes composing them. With the acceleration of capitalist enterprise in the eighteenth century, that structure of state and classes came under increasing pressure from new and "rising" social groups and categories that clamored for the enactment of their rights against those groups defended and represented by the state. Intellectually, this challenge took the form of asserting the validity of new social, economic, political, and ideological ties, now conceptualized as "society," against the state. The rising tide of discontent pitting "society" against the political and ideological order erupted in disorder, rebellion, and revolution. The specter of disorder and revolution raised the question of how social order could be restored and maintained, indeed, how social order was possible at all. Sociology hoped to answer the "social question." It had, as Rudolph Heberle noted, "an eminently political origin. . . . Saint Simon, Auguste Comte, and Lorenz Stein conceived the new science of society as an antidote against the poison of social disintegration" (quoted in Bramson 1961: 12, n. 2).

These early sociologists did this by severing the field of social relations from political economy. They pointed to observable and as yet poorly studied ties which bind people to people as individuals, as groups and associations, or as members of institutions. They then took this field of social relations to be the subject matter of their intensive concern. They and their successors expanded this concern into a number of theoretical postulates, using these to mark off sociology from political science and economics. I would summarize these common postulates as follows:

1. In the course of social life, individuals enter into relations with one another. Such relations can be abstracted from the economic, political, or ideological context in which they are found, and treated sui generis. They are autonomous, constituting a realm of their own, the realm of the social.

2. Social order depends on the growth and extension of social relations among individuals. The greater the density of such ties and the wider their scope, the greater the orderliness of society. Maximization of ties of kinship and neighborhood, of group and association, is therefore conducive to social order. Conversely, if these ties are not maximized, social order is called into question. Development of many and varied ties also diminishes the danger of polarization into classes.

3. The formation and maintenance of such ties is strongly related to the existence and propagation of common beliefs and customs among the individuals participating in them. Moral consensus, especially when based on unexamined belief and on nonrational acceptance of custom, furthers the maximization of social ties; expectations of mere utility and the exercise of merely technical reason tend to weaken them.

4. The development of social relations and the spread of associated custom and belief create a society conceived as a totality of social relations between individuals. Social relations constitute society; soci-

ety, in turn, is the seat of cohesion, the unit to which predictability and orderliness can be ascribed. If social relations are orderly and recurrent, society has a stable internal structure. The extent of that structure is coterminous with the intensity and range of social relations. Where these grow markedly less intense and less frequent, society encounters its boundary.

What is the flaw in these postulates? They predispose one to think of social relations not merely as autonomous but as causal in their own right, apart from their economic, political, or ideological context. Since social relations are conceived as relations between individuals, interaction between individuals becomes the prime cause of social life. Since social disorder has been related to the quantity and quality of social relations, attention is diverted from consideration of economics, politics, or ideology as possible sources of social disorder, into a search for the causes of disorder in family and community, and hence toward the engineering of a proper family and community life. Since, moreover, disorder has been located in the divergence of custom and belief from common norms, convergence in custom and consensus in belief are converted into the touchstone of society in proper working order. And, finally, the postulates make it easy to identify Society in general with a society in particular. Society in need of order becomes a particular society to be ordered. In the context of the tangible present, that society to be ordered is then easily identified with a given nation-state, be that nation-state Ghana, Mexico, or the United States. Since social relations have been severed from their economic, political, or ideological context, it is easy to conceive of the nation-state as a structure of social ties informed by moral consensus rather than as a nexus of economic, political, and ideological relationships connected to other nexuses. Contentless social relations, rather than economic, political, or ideological forces, thus become the prime movers of sociological theory. Since these social relations take place within the charmed circle of the single nation-state, the significant actors in history are seen as nation-states, each driven by its internal social relations. Each society is then a thing, moving in response to an inner clockwork.

Economics and Political Science

This severance of social relations from the economic, political, and ideological contexts in which they are embedded and which they activate was accompanied by the assignment of the economic and political aspects of human life to separate disciplines. Economics abandoned its concern with how socially organized populations produce to supply their polities and became instead a study of how demand creates markets. The guiding theory of this new economics was

> a theory of markets and market interdependence. It is a theory of general equilibrium *in exchange*, extended almost as an afterthought, to cover production and distribution. It is not a theory of a social system, still less of

economic power and social class. Households and firms are considered only as market agents, never as parts of a social structure. Their 'initial endowments,' wealth, skills, and property, are taken as *given*. Moreover, the object of the theory is to demonstrate the tendency towards equilibrium; class and sectoral conflict is therefore ruled out almost by assumption. [Nell 1973: 77–78]

Stated in another form, this new economics is not about the real world at all (Lekachman 1976). It is an abstract model of the workings out of subjective individual choices in relation to one another.

A similar fate befell the study of politics. A new political science severed the sphere of the political from economics and turned to consideration of power in relation to government. By relegating economic, social, and ideological aspects of human life to the status of the "environment," the study of politics divorced itself from a study of how the organization of this environment constrains or directs politics, and moved instead to an inquiry into decision making. The political process is one in which demands are aggregated and translated into decisions, much as in the market model of economics the interplay of demands issues in the production of supplies. As in the market model, such an approach easily slips into the assumption

that the organized private power forces of the society balance one another so as to preclude concentrated irresponsible rule. . . . wise public policy is assumed to prevail, explained by a mystique not unlike Adam Smith's invisible hand. [Engler 1968: 199]

Ultimately, in such a model, the willingness to abide by the rules of the political market is necessarily determined not by the market itself but by the orientation and values of the participants, aspects of what political scientists have come to call their "political culture." Much of political science thus focused on the study of decisions, on the one hand, and the study of orientations, understood as constituting together the autonomous political system of a given society, on the other.

Underlying all these specialties is the concept of an aggregate of individuals, engaged in a contract to maximize social order, to truck and barter in the marketplace, and to provide inputs for the formulation of political decisions. Ostensibly engaged in the study of human *behavior*, the various disciplines parcel out the subject among themselves. Each then proceeds to set up a model, seemingly a means to explain "hard," observable facts, yet actually an ideologically loaded scheme geared to a narrow definition of subject matter. Such schemes provide self-fulfilling answers, since phenomena other than those covered by the model are ruled out of the court of specialized discourse. If the models leak like sieves, it is then argued that this is either because they are merely abstract constructs and not expected to hold empirical water, or because troublemakers have poked holes into them. The specialized social sciences, having abandoned a holistic perspective, thus come to resemble the Danae sisters of classical Greek legend, ever condemned to pour water into their separate bottomless containers.

The Development of Sociological Theory

We have seen how sociology stemmed from an attempt to counteract social disorder by creating a theory of social order, by locating order and disorder in the quantity and quality of social relations. An important implication of this approach is that it issues in a polarity between two types of society: one in which social order is maximized because social relations are densely knit and suffused with value consensus; and another in which social disorder predominates over order because social relations are atomized and deranged by dissensus over values. It is only a short step from drawing such a polarity to envisioning social process as a change from one type of society to the other. This seemed consistent with the common view that modern life entails a progressive disintegration of the lifeways that marked the "good old days" of our forebears. In nineteenth-century Europe, where older social ties in fact disintegrated under the twin impact of capitalism and industrialization, such a temporal interpretation of the sociological polarity carried the conviction of experience. Ferdinand Tönnies saw this movement as one from "community," or Gemeinschaft, to "society," or Gesellschaft. Sir Henry Maine phrased it as a shift from social relations based on status to social relations based on contract. Emile Durkheim conceived it as a movement from a kind of social solidarity based on the similarity of all members to a social solidarity based on an "organic" complementarity of differences. The Chicago school of urban sociology saw it as the contrast between a cohesive society and the atomized, heterogeneous, disorganized city. Finally, Robert Redfield drew the various formulations together into a polar model of progression from Folk to Urban Society. In this model the quantity and quality of social relations again were the primary, independent variables. Isolation or paucity of social interaction, coupled with homogeneity or similarity of social ties, generated the dependent variables: orientation toward the group, or "collectivization"; commitment to belief, or "sanctity"; and "organization," the knitting together of understandings in the minds of men. In contrast, contact, or high frequency of contact, coupled with heterogeneity or dissimilarity of social ties, was seen as producing the dependent variables of "individualization," "secularization," and "disorganization." In sum, increases in the quantity and diversity of social interaction caused "the moral order" of the folk to give way to "the technical order" of civilization.

Sociology thus took its departure from a sense that social order was threatened by the atrophy of community. As the twentieth century wore on, however, it gradually came to be taken for granted that society was headed toward increased size and differentiation, and hence also toward the growth of utilitarian and technical relations at the expense of sacred and moral ties. Society was evidently moving toward what Max Weber, using Tönnies's terms, had called *Vergesellschaftung*. By this he meant the expansion of relations resting on

> rationally motivated adjustment of interests or a similarly motivated agreement, whether the basis of rational judgement be absolute values or reasons of expediency. It is especially common, though by no means inevitable, for the associative type of relationship to rest on a rational agreement by mutual consent. [1968: 10)]

Although Weber himself used the term with ambivalence and misgivings, his latter-day followers embraced the prognosis with enthusiasm. Whereas "traditional society" had fitted people narrowly into inherited positions, and then bound them together tightly in particularistic positions, "modern society" would sever people from inherited ties and allocate the newly mobile population to specialized and differentiated roles responding to the changing needs of an overarching universal society. Such an emerging society would also require a mechanism for setting social goals and a machinery for implementing them. The way the modernizers saw it, goal setting would come out of enlarged popular participation. Implementation of the goals, such as economic development, in turn would require the creation of bureaucracy, defined as organizations capable of marshalling resources rationally and efficiently toward stated goals. Finally, public participation in setting and meeting goals would require a psychic reorientation that could sustain the enactment of such technical and rational norms. Those capable of generating such new arrangements would find themselves launched into modernity. Those incapable of doing so would find their society arrested at the point of transition or mired in traditionalism. In the succession from Max Weber to Talcott Parsons, therefore, *Vergesellschaftung* was transfigured into "modernization" through a simple change of signs. If Gesellschaft had once seemed problematical, after the mid-twentieth century it came to be seen as desirable and forward-looking. The negative pole of the polarity was now allocated to "traditional society," slow to change, inflexible, and lacking in psychic drive toward rational and secular achievement.

Thus, in a reversal of sociology's original critical stance toward the workings of nineteenth-century society, "modernization theory" became an instrument for bestowing praise on societies deemed to be modern and casting a critical eye on those that had yet to attain that achievement. The political leaders of the United States had pronounced themselves in favor of aiding the development of the Third World, and modernization theorists seconded that pronouncement. Yet modernization theory effectively foreclosed any but the most ideologically charged understanding of that world. It used the term *modern*, but meant by that term the United States, or rather an ideal of a democratic, pluralistic, rational, and secular United States. It said *traditional*, but meant all those others that would have to adopt that ideal to qualify for assistance. As theory it was misleading. It imparted a false view of American history, substituting self-satisfaction for analysis. By casting such different entities as China, Albania, Paraguay, Cuba, and Tanzania into the hopper of traditional society, it simultaneously precluded any study of their significant differences. By equating tradition with stasis and lack of development, it denied societies marked off as traditional any significant history of their own. Above all, by dividing the world into modern, transitional, and traditional societies, it blocked effective understanding of relationships among them. Once again each society was defined as an autonomous and bounded structure of social relations, thus discouraging analysis of intersocietal or intergroup interchanges, including internal social strife, colonialism, imperialism, and societal dependency. The theory thus effectively precluded the serious study of issues demonstrably agitating the real world.

Anthropology

If these social sciences have not led to an adequate understanding of the interconnected world, what of anthropology? Anthropology, ambitiously entitled The Science of Man, did lay special claims to the study of non-Western and "primitive" peoples. Indeed, cultural anthropology began as world anthropology. In its evolutionist phase it was concerned with the evolution of culture on a global scale. In its diffusionist phase it was interested in the spread and clustering of cultural forms over the entire face of the globe. The diffusionists also saw relations between populations exhibiting the same cultural forms—matriliny, blackening of teeth, or tailored clothing—as the outcome of intergroup communication by migration or by copying and learning. They were not much concerned with people, but they did have a sense of global interconnections. They did not believe in the concept of "primitive isolates."

Such interests and understandings were set aside, however, as anthropologists turned from a primary concern with cultural forms to the study of "living cultures," of specified populations and their lifeways in locally delimited habitats. Fieldwork—direct communication with people and participant observation of their ongoing activities *in situ*—became a hallmark of anthropological method. Fieldwork has proved enormously fruitful in laying bare and correcting false assumptions and erroneous descriptions. It has also revealed hitherto unsuspected connections among sets of social activities and cultural forms. Yet the very success of the method lulled its users into a false confidence. It became easy for them to convert merely heuristic considerations of method into theoretical postulates about society and culture.

Limitations of time and energy in the field dictate limitations in the number and locations of possible observations and interviews, demanding concentration of effort on an observable place and on a corps of specifiable "informants." The resulting observations and communications are then made to stand for a larger universe of unrealized observations and communications, and used to construct a model of the social and cultural entity under study. Such a model is no more than an account of "descriptive integration," a theoretical halfway house, and not yet explanation. Functionalist anthropology, however, attempted to derive explanations from the study of the microcosm alone, treating it as a hypothetical isolate. Its features were explained in terms of the contribution each made to the maintenance of this putatively isolated whole. Thus, a methodological unit of inquiry was turned into a theoretical construct by assertion, a priori. The outcome was series of analyses of wholly separate cases.

There were three major attempts to transcend the boundaries of the microcosm. One of these, that of Robert Redfield, had recourse to sociological theory. It applied the polarity of Gemeinschaft and Gesellschaft to anthropological cases by using "communities" as representations or exemplifications of such "imagined types of societies." Thus the communities of X-Cacal and Chan Kom in Yucatan were made to exemplify the folk end of a universal folk—urban continuum of social relations and cultural understandings. The two locations illuminated the theory, but the theory could not explicate the political and economic processes that shaped the communities: X-Cacal as a settlement set up by Maya-speaking rebels during the Caste Wars of the nineteenth century; Chan Kom as a village of cultivators released from the hacienda system by the Mexican Revolution, settling as newcomers in a frontier area with the support of the Yucatecan Socialist Party. Thus, like Gemeinschaft-Gesellschaft theory in general, Redfield's concepts led only in one direction, up to the theory but not back down from it.

A second attempt to generate a theoretical construct for understanding the microcosm studied in a larger context was Julian Steward's concept of levels of sociocultural integration. The concept, derived from the philosophy of "emergent evolution," was meant to suggest that units of the same kind, when subjected to integrative processes, could yield novel units that not only subsumed those of the lower level but also exhibited qualitatively different characteristics at the higher, emergent level. Steward initially used the concept to counter arguments that treated "the community" as a small replica of "the nation," as if these were qualitatively identical structural phenomena. He then proceeded, however, to construct a conceptual edifice in which units at the family level became parts of a community level, units at the community level became parts of a regional level, and units at the regional level became parts of the level of the nation.

Although the term *integration* suggests a process, the concept is not processual but structural. It suggests an architecture of a whole and its parts, which remain to be specified substantively only after the fact. The model is thus a "hollow" representation of societal complexity, theoretically applicable to all complex sociocultural wholes. Yet it makes no statement about any processes generating the structure, or about the specific features that integrate it, or about the content of any of its parts. Knowledge about processes does not flow from the model but must be added to it. Thus, when Steward turned to the study of "contemporary change in traditional societies," the model remained silent about the penetration of capitalism, the growth of a worldwide specialization and division of labor, and the development of domination by some populations over others. Steward was forced back, unhappily, to the comparative study of separate cases and the unsatisfactory concepts of tradition and modernization.

The third attempt to go beyond the microscopic study of populations in specified locations took the form of a revival of evolutionism. Evolutionary thinking in anthropology, so prominent in the nineteenth century, had been halted by the assertion that "the extensive occurrence of diffusion . . . lays the axe to the root of any theory of historical laws" (Lowie 1920: 434). Evolutionists and diffusionists were not so much opposed as interested in quite different phenomena. The evolutionists had recognized the facts of diffusion, but had felt justified in abstracting from these facts to their model of successive stages of social and cultural development. The diffusionists, in turn, sidestepped the problem posed by major inequalities in the technology and organization of different populations to focus instead on the transmission of cultural forms from group to group. Whereas the evolutionists disclaimed an interest in the history of particular societies and cultures, the diffusionists disclaimed any interest in the ecological, economic, social, political, and ideological matrix within which the cultural forms were being transmitted in time and space. The two schools of thought thus effectively talked past each other. The functionalists, in turn, rejected altogether the "conjectural history" of the diffusionists in favor of the analysis of internal functioning in putatively isolated wholes.

When Leslie White reintroduced the evolutionary perspective into American anthropology in the forties and fifties, he did so by reasserting the validity of the earlier model proposed by Tylor, Morgan, and Spencer. To this model of universal or unilineal evolution, Julian Steward opposed a multilineal model that depicted evolution as a process of successive branching. Subsequently Sahlins and Service sought to unify the two approaches by counterposing general and specific evolution as dual aspects of the same evolutionary process. General evolution was defined by them as "passage from less to greater energy exploitation, lower to higher levels of integration, and less to greater all-round adaptability" (Sahlins and Service 1960: 22–23). Specific evolution they defined as "the phylogenetic, ramifying, historic passage of culture along its many lines, the adaptive modification of particular cultures" (1960: 38). Though cognizant of convergence as an aspect of cultural as opposed to biological phylogeny, they defined it in old-fashioned diffusionist terms as the diffusion of culture traits, and not as the outcome of multifaceted relationships between interacting culture-bearing populations. When they turned to the detailed analysis of specific evolution, they thus emphasized adaptation as "specialization for the exploitation of particular facets of the environment" (1960: 50). They understood that environment included both the physical and the sociocultural matrices of human life, but they laid primary stress on adaptation to different physical environments. In the sixties and seventies, the study of particular ecological "systems" became increasingly sophisticated, without, however, ever transcending the functional analysis of the single case, now hypothesized as an integral, self-regulating ecological whole. Thus, despite its theoretical effort, evolutionary anthropology turned all too easily into the study of ecological adaptation, conducting anthropology back to the comparative study of single cases.

The ecological concentration on the single case is paralleled by the recent fascination with the study and unraveling of what is "in the heads" of single culture-bearing populations. Such studies turn their back on functionalism, including what was most viable in it, the concern with how people cope with the material and organizational problems of their lives. They also disregard material relationships linking the people with others outside. Instead, their interest lies in the investigation of local microcosms of meaning, conceived as autonomous systems.

This turn toward the study of meaning has been influenced strongly by the development of linguistics, notably by de Saussure's structural theory of language as a superindividual social system of linguistic forms that remain normatively identical in all utterances. Such a view relates linguistic sign to linguistic sign without reference to who is speaking to whom, when, and about what. It was originally put forward to oppose the position that a language consisted of an ever-changing historical stream of individually generated utterances, a perspective associated with the names of Humboldt and Vossler. De Saussure, instead, wholly divorced language (*langue*) from utterance (*parole*), defining signs by their mutual relation to one another, without reference to any context external to them. In the same way, meanings were defined in terms of other meanings, without reference to the practical contexts in which they appear.

Clearly, the opposition between the two views requires for its resolution a relational, dialectical perspective, as Vološinov noted fifty years ago. He called into question de Saussure's view of the static linguistic system carried by a faceless and passive collectivity, noting instead that in reality such a collectivity consisted of a population of speakers with diverse "accents" or interests, participating in a historical stream of verbal utterances about diverse, concrete contexts. Contexts should not be thought of as internally homogeneous and externally segregated. For Vološinov, they constituted instead intersections between "differently oriented accents . . . in a state of constant tension, of incessant interaction and conflict" (1973: 80). Neither sign nor meaning could be understood without reference to what they are about, their theme in a given situation. The trend within anthropology to treat systems of meaning as wholly autonomous systems threatens to reverse this insight by substituting for it the study of solipsistic discourses generated *in vacuo* by the human mind.

While some anthropologists thus narrow their focus to the ever more intensive study of the single case, others hope to turn anthropology into a science by embarking on the statistical cross-cultural comparisons of coded features drawn from large samples of ethnographically known cases. A good deal of attention has been paid to the methodological problems of how to isolate discrete cases for comparison and how to define the variables to be coded and compared. Are the hundreds of Eskimo local groups separate cases? Are they instances of larger, self-identified clusters such as Copper, Netsilik, and Iglulik? Or do they constitute a single Eskimo case? Other questions deal with the nature of the sample. Can one be sure that the cases are sufficiently separated historically and geographically to constitute distinct cases? Or is the sample contaminated by spatial or temporal propinquity and communication? All the answers to these questions nevertheless assume the autonomy and boundedness of the cases that are selected in the end. Whatever sample is finally chosen, it is interpreted as an aggregate of separate units. These, it is held, either generate cultural traits independently through invention, or borrow them from one another through diffusion. We are back in a world of sociocultural billiard balls, coursing on a global billiard table.

What, however, if we take cognizance of *processes* that transcend separable cases, moving through and beyond them and transforming them as they proceed? Such processes were, for example, the North American fur trade and the trade in native American and African slaves. What of the localized Algonkin-speaking patrilineages, for example, which in the course of the fur trade moved into large nonkin villages and became known as the ethnographic Ojibwa? What of the Chipeweyans, some of whose bands gave up hunting to become fur trappers, or "carriers," while others continued to hunt for game as "caribou eaters," with people continuously changing from caribou eating to carrying and back? What of the multilingual, multiethnic, intermarrying groups of Cree and Assiniboin that grew up in the far northern Plains of North America in response to the stimulus of the fur trade, until the units "graded into one another" (Sharrock 1974: 96)? What of the Mundurucú in Amazonia who changed from patrilocality and patriliny to adopt the unusual combination of matrilocality and patrilineal reckoning in response to their new role as hunters of slaves and suppliers of manioc flour to slave-hunting expeditions? What, moreover, of Africa, where the slave trade created an unlimited demand for slaves, and where quite unrelated populations met that demand by severing people from their kin groups through warfare, kidnapping, pawning, or judicial procedures, in order to have slaves to sell to the Europeans? In all such cases, to attempt to specify separate cultural wholes and distinct boundaries would create a false sample. These cases exemplify spatially and temporally shifting relationships, prompted in all instances by the effects of European expansion. If we consider, furthermore, that this expansion has for nearly 500 years affected case after case, then the search for a world sample of distinct cases is illusory.

One need have no quarrel with a denotative use of the term *society* to designate an empirically verifiable cluster of interconnections among people, as long as no evaluative prejudgments are added about its state of internal cohesion or boundedness in relation to the external world. Indeed, I shall continue to use the term in this way throughout this book, in preference to other clumsier formulations. Similarly, it would be an error to discard the anthropological insight that human existence entails the creation of cultural forms, themselves predicated on the human capacity to symbol.

Yet the concept of the autonomous, self-regulating and self-justifying society and culture has trapped anthropology inside the bounds of its own definitions. Within the halls of science, the compass of observation and thought has narrowed, while outside the inhabitants of the world are increasingly caught up in continent-wide and global change. Indeed, has there ever been a time when human populations have existed in independence of larger encompassing relationships, unaffected by larger fields of force? Just as the sociologists pursue the will-o'-the-wisp of social order and integration in a world of upheaval and change, so anthropologists look for pristine replicas of the precapitalist, preindustrial past in the sinks and margins of the capitalist, industrial world. But Europeans and Americans would never have encountered these supposed bearers of a pristine past if they had not encountered one another, in bloody fact, as Europe reached out to seize the resources and populations of the other continents. Thus, it has been rightly said that anthropology is an offspring of imperialism. Without imperialism there would be no anthropologists, but there would also be no Dené, Baluba, or Malay fishermen to be studied. The tacit anthropological supposition that people like these are people without history amounts to the erasure of 500 years of confrontation, killing, resurrection, and accommodation. If sociology operates with its mythology of Gemeinschaft and Gesellschaft, anthropology all too frequently operates with its mythology of the pristine primitive. Both perpetuate fictions that deny the facts of ongoing relationships and involvements.

These facts clearly emerge in the work of anthropologists and historians who have specialized in what has come to be known as ethnohistory. Perhaps "ethnohistory" has been so called to separate it from "real" history, the study of the supposedly civilized. Yet what is clear from the study of ethnohistory is that the subjects of the two kinds of history are the same. The more ethnohistory we know, the more clearly "their" history and "our" history emerge as part of the same history. Thus, there can be no "Black history" apart from "White history," only a component of a common history suppressed or omitted from conventional studies for economic, political, or ideological reasons.

These remarks echo those made by the anthropologist Alexander Lesser who, in a different context, asked years ago that "we adopt as a working hypothesis the universality of human contact and influence"; that we think "of human societies—prehistoric, primitive, or modern— not as closed systems, but as open systems"; that we see them "as inextricably involved with other aggregates, near and far, in weblike, netlike connections" (1961: 42). The labors of the ethnohistorians have demonstrated the validity of this advice in case after case. Yet it remains merely programmatic until we can move from a consideration of connections at work in separate cases to a wider perspective, one that will allow us to connect the connections in theory as well as in empirical study.

In such a perspective, it becomes difficult to view any given culture as a bounded system or as a self-perpetuating "design for living." We thus stand in need of a new theory of cultural forms. The anthropologists have shown us that cultural forms—as "determinate orderings" of things, behavior, and ideas—do play a demonstrable role in the management of human interaction. What will be required of us in the future is not to deny that role, but to understand more precisely how cultural forms work to mediate social relationships among particular populations.

The Uses of Marx

If we grant the existence of such connections, how are we to conceive of them? Can we grasp a common process that generates and organizes them? Is it possible to envision such a common dynamic and yet maintain a sense of its distinctive unfolding in time and space as it involves and engulfs now this population, now that other?

Such an approach is possible, but only if we can face theoretical possibilities that transcend our specialized disciplines. It is not enough to become multidisciplinary in the hope that an addition of all the disciplines will lead to a new vision. A major obstacle to the development of a new perspective lies in the very fact of specialization itself. That fact has a history and that history is significant, because the several academic disciplines owe their existence to a common rebellion against political economy, their parent discipline. That discipline strove to lay bare the laws or regularities surrounding the production of wealth. It entailed a concern with how wealth was generated in production, with the role of classes in the genesis of wealth, and with the role of the state in relation to the different classes. These concerns were common to conservatives and socialists alike. (Marx addressed himself to them when he criticized political economists for taking as universals what he saw as the characteristics of historically particular systems of production.) Yet these concerns have been expunged so completely from the repertory of the social sciences that the latest *International Encyclopedia of the Social Sciences* does not even include entries under "political economy" and "class." Today, concern with such matters is usually ascribed only to Marxists, even though Marx himself wrote in a letter to a friend (Joseph Weydemeyer, March 5, 1852):

> no credit is due me for discovering the existence of classes in society nor yet the struggle between them. Long before me bourgeois historians had described the historical development of this class struggle and bourgeois economists the economic anatomy of the classes. [quoted in Venable 1945: 6, n. 3]

It is likely that it was precisely the conception of political economy as a structure of *classes* that led the nascent social sciences to turn against the concept of class. If social, economic, and political relations were seen to involve a division into antagonistic classes, endowed by the structure of the political economy itself with opposing interests and capabilities, then the pursuit of order would indeed be haunted forever by the specter of discord. This was what led James Madison, in his tough-minded *Federalist Papers*, to define the function of government as the regulation of relations among antagonistic classes. The several social science disciplines, in contrast, turned their back on political economy, shifting instead to the intensive study of interaction among individuals —in primary and secondary groups, in the market, in the processes of government. They thus turned away also from concern with crucial questions about the nature of production, class, and power: If production is the condition of being human, how is production to be understood and analyzed? Under what conditions does production entail the rise of classes? What are the implications of class division for the allocation of resources and the exercise of power? What is the nature of the state?

Although these questions were abandoned by the social sciences, they persist as their hidden agenda. Because Marx raised these questions most persistently and systematically, he remains a hidden interlocutor in much social science discourse. It has been said, with reason, that the social sciences constitute one long dialogue with the ghost of Marx. If we are to transcend the present limits and limitations of the specialized disciplines, we must return to these unanswered questions and reconsider them.

Marx is important for this reconsideration in several ways. He was one of the last major figures to aim at a holistic human science, capable of integrating the varied specializations. Contrary to what is all too often said about him, he was by no means an economic determinist. He was a materialist, believing in the primacy of material relationships as against the primacy of "spirit." Indeed, his concept of production (*Produktion*) was conceived in opposition to Hegel's concept of *Geist*, manifesting itself in successive incarnations of spirit. For him, production embraced at once the changing relations of humankind to nature, the social relations into which humans enter in the course of transforming nature, and the consequent transformations of human symbolic capability. The concept is thus not merely economic in the strict sense but also ecological, social, political, and social-psychological. It is relational in character.

Marx further argued—against those who wanted to universalize Society, or the Market, or the Political Process—the existence of different modes of production in human history. Each mode represented a different combination of elements. What was true of one mode was not true of another: there was therefore no universal history. But Marx was profoundly historical. Both the elements constituting a mode of production and their characteristic combination had for him a definable history of origin, unfolding, and disintegration. He was neither a universal historian nor a historian of events, but a historian of configurations or syndromes of material relationships. Most of his energy was, of course, spent on efforts to understand the history and workings of one particular mode, capitalism, and this not to defend it but to effect its revolutionary transformation. Since our specialized disciplinary discourse developed as an antidote to revolution and disorder, it is understandable that this ghostly interrogator should have been made unwelcome in the halls of academe.

Yet the specter has vital lessons for us. First, we shall not understand the present world unless we trace the growth of the world market and the course of capitalist development. Second, we must have a theory of that growth and development. Third, we must be able to relate both the history and theory of that unfolding development to processes that affect and change the lives of local populations. That theory must be able to delineate the significant elements at work in these processes and their systemic combinations in historical time. At the same time, it ought to cut finely enough to explain the significant differences marking off each such combination from all the others—say, capitalism from other historically known combinations. Finally, theoretically informed history and historically informed theory must be joined together to account for populations specifiable in time and space, both as outcomes of significant processes and as their carriers.

Among those who have contributed to a theoretically informed history of the world to which capitalism has given rise, two names stand out, both for the trenchancy of their formulations and the scope of their research effort. One of these is Andre Gunder Frank, an economist, who began to question the modernization approach to economic development in the early 1960s. Frank clearly articulated the heretical proposition that development and underdevelopment were not separate phenomena, but were closely bound up with each other (1966, 1967). Over the past centuries, capitalism had spread outward from its original center to all parts of the globe. Everywhere it penetrated, it turned other areas into dependent satellites of the metropolitan center. Extracting the surpluses produced in the satellites to meet the requirements of the metropolis, capitalism distorted and thwarted the development of the satellites to its own benefit. This phenomenon Frank called "the development of underdevelopment." The exploitative relation between metropolis and satellite was, moreover, repeated within each satellite itself, with the classes and regions in closer contact with the external metropolis drawing surplus from the hinterland and distorting and thwarting its development. Underdevelopment in the satellites was therefore not a phenomenon sui generis, but the outcome of relations between satellite and metropolis, ever renewed in the process of surplus transfer and ever reinforced by the continued dependency of the satellite on the metropolis.

Similar to Frank's approach is Immanuel Wallerstein's explicitly historical account of capitalist origins and the development of the "European world-economy." This world-economy, originating in the late fifteenth and early sixteenth centuries, constitutes a global market, characterized by a global division of labor. Firms (be they individuals, enterprises, or regions) meet in this market to exchange the goods they have produced in the hope of realizing a profit. The search for profit guides both production in general and specialization in production. Profits are generated by primary producers, whom Wallerstein calls proletarians, no matter how their labor is mobilized. Those profits are appropriated through legal sanctions by capitalists, whom Wallerstein classifies as bourgeois, no matter what the source of their capital. The growth of the market and the resulting worldwide division of labor generate a basic distinction between the core countries (Frank's metropolis) and the periphery (Frank's satellites). The two are linked by "unequal exchange," whereby "high-wage (but low-supervision), high-profit, high-capital intensive" goods produced in the core are exchanged for "low-wage (but high-supervision), low-profit, low-capital intensive goods" produced in the periphery (see Wallerstein 1974: 351). In the core, goods are produced mainly by "free" wage-remunerated labor; in the periphery goods are produced mainly by one kind or another of coerced labor. Although he adduces various factors to explain this difference, Wallerstein has recourse to what is basically a demographic explanation. He argues that the growth of free wage labor in the core area arose in response to the high densities of population that made workers competitive with one another and hence willing to submit to market discipline, while in the periphery low population densities favored the growth of labor coercion. We shall have occasion to look critically at some of these propositions. Yet what is important about both Frank's and Wallerstein's work is that they have replaced the fruitless debates about modernization with a sophisticated and theoretically oriented acount of how capitalism evolved and spread, an evolution and spread of intertwined and yet differentiated relationships.

Both Frank and Wallerstein focused their attention on the capitalist world system and the arrangements of its parts. Although they utilized the findings of anthropologists and regional historians, for both the principal aim was to understand how the core subjugated the periphery, and not to study the reactions of the micro-populations habitually investigated by anthropologists. Their choice of focus thus leads them to omit consideration of the range and variety of such populations, of their modes of existence before European expansion and the advent of capitalism, and of the manner in which these modes were penetrated, subordinated, destroyed, or absorbed, first by the growing market and subsequently by industrial capitalism. Without such an examination, however, the concept of the "periphery" remains as much of a cover term as "traditional society." Its advantage over the older term lies chiefly in its implications: it points to wider linkages that must be investigated if the processes at work in the periphery are to be understood. Yet this examination still lies before us if we wish to understand how Mundurucú or Meo were drawn into the larger system to suffer its impact and to become its agents.

This book undertakes such an examination. It hopes to delineate the general processes at work in mercantile and capitalist development, while at the same time following their effects on the micro-populations studied by the ethnohistorians and anthropologists. My view of these processes and their effects is historical, but in the sense of history as an analytic account of the development of material relations, moving simultaneously on the level of the encompassing system and on the micro-level. I therefore look first at the world in 1400, before Europe achieved worldwide dominance. I then discuss some theoretical constructs that might allow us to grasp the determining features of capitalism and the modes that preceded it. Next I turn to the development of European mercantile expansion and to the parts played by various European nations in extending its global sway. Following the global effects of European expansion leads to a consideration of the search for American silver, the fur trade, the slave trade, and the quest for new sources of wealth in Asia. I then trace the transition to capitalism in the course of the industrial revolution, examine its impact on areas of the world supplying resources to the industrial centers, and sketch out the formation of working classes and their migrations within and between continents. In this account, both the people who claim history as their own and the people to whom history has been denied emerge as participants in the same historical trajectory.

2 The World in 1400

In the year 1271 the Venetian merchants Niccolo and Maffeo Polo, together with Niccolo's son Marco, left the eastern shore of the Mediterranean and traveled through Iran to Hormuz on the Persian Gulf. From there they set off northeastward to Kashgar, where they took the old Silk Road and went on to Peking. After long travels through China and South Asia, the Polos set sail for Europe, arriving in Venice in 1295. Some forty years later, Ibn Battutah, a scholar-official from Morocco, embarked on a pilgrimage to Mecca, and went on through Iran, Anatolia, and the Crimea to Constantinople. From there he traveled to Central Asia and India, spending some years in government positions in Delhi and the Maldive Islands. After visiting southern China and Sumatra, he went home to Morocco in 1349. Three years later he accompanied Moroccan merchants across the Sahara to the kingdom of Mali in the Western Sudan and returned to Fez to dictate his travel story to a scribe. Between 1405 and 1433 the Chinese admiral Cheng-ho sailed seven times to southern Asia, reaching as far as the Red Sea and the East African coast. In 1492 a Genoese sea captain in the employ of the Queen of Aragon got his first glimpse of the New World, where he sighted the Bahamas and thought he had arrived in Japan.

These voyages were not isolated adventures but manifestations of forces that were drawing the continents into more encompassing relationships and would soon make the world a unified stage for human action. In order to understand what the world would become, we must first know what it was. I shall therefore follow an imaginary voyager in the year 1400 and depict the world that he might have seen.

In this effort at global anthropology, I will go beyond the portrayal of distinctive tribes, culture areas, and civilizations to delineate the interlocking networks of human interaction that extended across each of the two still separate hemispheres—the "Old World" of Europe, Asia, and Africa, and the "New World" of the Americas. These networks grew up and spread out in time as well as space. To account for them—to follow their growth and spread—means also to trace the historical itineraries of populations that history written from a Western point of view has tended to ignore or to caricature. Like the anthropologist's "primitive contemporaries," they have been treated as people without a history of their own.

These wide-ranging linkages among populations before European expansion were outcomes of identifiable material processes. One of these processes was the build-up of contentious hegemonic political and military systems. Each of the two hemispheres witnessed, separately, the rise of empires, which drew toward themselves the surpluses produced by varied and manifold groups. A second process at work was the growth of long-distance trade, which everywhere connected zones of supply with centers of concentrated demand, and which opened up specialized roles for the peoples who sat astride the routes of commerce. Empire building and trade, in turn, created extensive grids of communication, which bound together different populations under the aegis of dominant religious or political ideologies. Together these processes shaped the world that Europe would soon reorganize to answer to requirements of its own.

Political Geography of the Old World

To understand this world of 1400, we must begin with geography. A map of the Old World reveals certain physical constants. One of these is the great chain of mountains running in an east—west direction across the Eurasian landmass. Rising up from the rugged ranges of southern and western China, the chain ascends to the heights of the Kunlun, Himalayas and Pamir, "roof of the world," and reaches across the Elburz Range to the Caucasus, the Carpathians, the Alps, and finally the Pyrenees. Sometimes these mountains retarded contact between north and south. At other times, gaps in the chain encouraged population movement and attacks. In northern China, the Han had to build their big wall to keep the Chinese in and the Mongols and Turks out. In Turkestan, roads led southward into Iran and India. In the west, raiders could move up the valley of the Danube into the heart of Europe.

An endpaper map shows us a second constant, the distribution of major climatic zones. These encourage different covers of natural vegetation and, hence, favor different kinds of human habitation. The map immediately shows us a major belt of dry country running east and west from the Sahara and the Arabian deserts across the plateau of Iran into Turkestan and Mongolia. This is the country of pastoral populations, driving their herds over the pasture available along desert margins and on the steppe. Cultivation is possible only around permanent water sources in oases. South of the dry zone of desert and steppe lie warm and moist tropical and subtropical forest and savanna, often favorable to cultivation, as in West Africa, the Gangetic Plain, the peninsulas and islands of Southeast Asia, and southern China. To the north of the dry zone extends the forest. West of the Ural Mountains, the forest country is rainy and experiences a longer growing season; hence, when cleared, it makes good farming country. To the east of the Urals, the forest is drier and colder. It becomes taiga, cold-weather coniferous forest, and—together with the treeless, lichen-covered belt of circumpolar tundra—the predilect habitat of forest hunters. Here cultivators ventured only rarely, and herders found it difficult to keep their animals alive.

When we compare the distribution of cultivable and improvable agricultural land with that of desert and steppe, a significant contrast emerges. The distribution of the dry belt is continuous; that of the cultivable landscape is spotty and archipelagic. The pastoral corridor facilitated centrifugal movement; the compartmentalized arable zones oriented people centripetally toward the grounds of their home village. This dichotomy between steppe and sown shaped much of the course of human action in the Old World, sometimes dividing pastoralist and villager, at other times prompting them into interaction.

Cultivation in northwestern Africa is confined mainly to the Mediterranean vertient north of the Atlas, and is impeded to the south and east by steppe and desert. Wheat raised in the Sus Valley and the Rharb of Morocco, in the plains of Shelif and Mitidja in Algeria, and in the Medjerda Plain of Tunis was important in sustaining local courts and elites. East of Tunis lies the oasis of Tripoli, and beyond that Egypt, the great oasis formed by the Nile. Its grain had fed Rome during the days of the Roman Empire, and thereafter it played the same role for Byzantium, for the Arabs at Damascus, and—after 1453—for the Ottomans. Byzantium and the Ottoman Empire also drew increasingly on the lands of the lower Danube and the shores of the Black Sea for their grain supply. (See map at back of book.)

Small islands of cultivation could be sustained on terraced hillsides in Palestine, and there were major agricultural oases at Antioch (now Antakya) and Damascus. The Syrian steppe, farmed in Roman times and again in the twentieth century, is ecologically marginal and long lay abandoned to occupation by pastoral nomads. In Anatolia agriculture is possible along the shores of the Mediterranean and the Black Sea and in occasional patches on the mountainous plateau, but the rest is steppe, and to the southeast the desert again supervenes. Iraq—the land between the Tigris and the Euphrates—was once enormously productive. Surplus production, aided by hydraulic works, had underwritten state formation since Akkadian times; construction of waterworks of all kinds reached a climax here under the Sassanid dynasty of Iran (A.D. 226–637). But with the Islamic conquest of the area and the concomitant growth of Baghdad into a capital with over 300,000 inhabitants, agricultural wealth and human resources were increasingly sacrificed to the city. This led to a decline in agricultural output and a steady decrease in the amount of tribute obtained (Adams 1965: 84 ff.). A final blow to productivity was delivered by the Mongol invasion in the mid-thirteenth century, when the Mongol khan Hulägu destroyed the irrigation works of the lower valley.

Beyond the mountain chain of the Zagros lies the Iranian plateau. Most of it is covered by steppe and desert, with cultivation possible only in favored spots along a belt of alluvial fans extending around the inside rim of the mountain chain. On occasion cultivation has been extended into the drier zone by means of underground tunnels (*qanats*), which carry water by gravity flow along the water table to outlying fields. Waste and desert again restrict cultivation in Afghanistan and Baluchistan to the east.

Despite the prevalence of inhospitable desert and steppe throughout this area, a string of urbanized oases based on irrigation agriculture furnished rest stops and supply stations for caravans moving east and west. The most important of these caravan routes was the Silk Road. It began at Antioch in northern Syria, ran through Rai (near Teheran), then passed through Merv and Balkh (Bactria) to Kashgar. At Kashgar the road forked, conducting travelers both north and south of the Taklamakan (southern Gobi) Desert. The northern fork led to Kucha and Karashahr, the southern one through Yarkand and Khotan. Both forks met again at Tunhwang in Chinese Kansu, whence roads led on into China. Kashgar—which Marco Polo praised for its gardens and vineyards—was thus a major hub of long-distance commerce, inhabited, in Polo's words, by people "who travel and trade all over the world." From Kashgar another route led northward to Samarkand and on to Sarai on the lower Volga, from which point one could reach Azov and the Black Sea. All along the northern escarpment of the great Eurasian mountain chain, too, there were pockets of arable land that could be cultivated if the herders, with their demand for pasture and water, could be kept at bay.

Thus, a chain of widely spaced cultivated regions formed a great arc extending from the Moroccan Atlas Mountains to the very gates of China in Kansu. The agricultural regions were connected by routes of traffic and trade. This long chain was unified, both politically and religiously, only once in history, when the armies of Islam fanned out from the Arabian peninsula east and west in the course of the seventh and eighth centuries A.D. After that the links of the chain ripped apart and were never reassembled. Political separation was further exacerbated by religious sectarianism, each kind of segmentation reinforcing the other.

Renewed segmentation weakened many of the links in the long chain. Separate agricultural regions generated separate polities, limited internally by the circumscribed resources at their command and exposed to incursions and takeovers across unprotected boundaries. What held this beadlike geopolitical structure together were connections of trade and religious faith. These proved capable of transcending the limitations of each separate component and could aggregate resources on a wider scale; yet in the absence of a politically unified force to defend them, these linkages, too, were exposed to repeated interference and rupture.

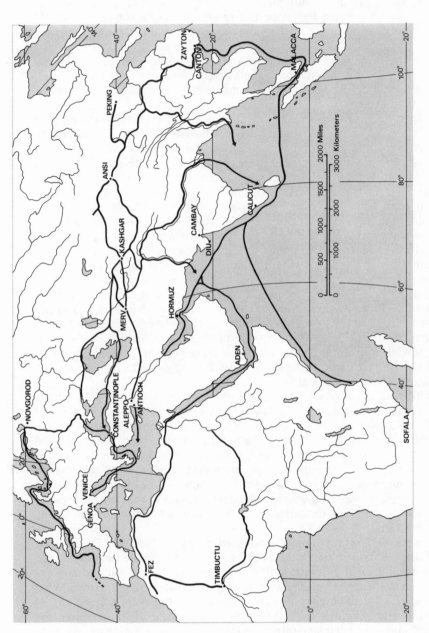

The Old World in 1400: major trade routes.

North of the Eurasian mountain chain lay the steppe, forming a vast corridor from the Mongolian steppe in the east, through the Kirghiz and Russian steppes, to the Hungarian steppe close to the heart of Central Europe. These were the predilect traveling grounds of pastoral nomads. The conversion of the southern Russian prairie to permanent cultivation had to await the defeat of the pastoralists and their khans by the Russians in the seventeenth century A.D.

Westward beyond the Russian prairie lay the European peninsula, a zone of temperate forests that could be cleared and farmed. The development of this peninsula beyond the confines of the Roman Mediterranean was, however, very slow. Almost completely surrounded by bodies of water—the Baltic Sea, the North Sea, the Atlantic, and the Mediterranean—this proximity to water could be turned into a major asset only when the shores could be held and defended against sea marauders from both north and south. This task was not realized completely until the ninth century A.D. At the same time, the clearing of the European forest took millennia. Not until A.D. 1000 did the balance between forest and farm tilt in favor of the cultivators. Secure cultivation in favored and militarily defensible core areas developed then in the belt between forest and sea, often where some major river furnished an outlet for coast-bound shipping. Such favored regions of high productivity were the Low Countries, the Seine basin, the drainage of the Middle Rhine, the Thames Valley in England, the valley of the Tejo in Portugal, and the Po Valley in Italy. The agricultural surpluses of these regions fed the growth of political power, becoming strategic bases of supply for developing states.

At the eastern end of the Silk Road, in Kansu, the trans-Eurasian route extended into China, a political-economic world very different from that of both Europe and Islam. Europe was confined to the outliers of a peninsula, its geopolitical core areas consolidating along the perimeter of the land. The Islamic world lay stretched out longitudinally across the Eurasian spine, with extensions into western and eastern Africa. China, instead, developed into a compact unit, huge in comparison with the polities of the west. This development took place only gradually. State formation was first underwritten by agricultural expansion in the north, the areas of the Ching and Wei rivers in Shansi, the Fen River in Shansi, and the lower valley of the Yellow River. Millet was the main crop in this region, although wheat came increasingly to the fore after A.D. 700. This older political center of gravity was then brought into relationship with the rice-growing Yangtze Valley, and the two areas were connected by big canals at the beginning of the seventh century. Somewhat later a third key area developed south of the Yangtze. Migration by ethnic (Han) Chinese into the fertile deltas and basins of this area began in the third century A.D. but speeded up greatly in the seventh and eighth centuries, supported by a more sophisticated rice-growing technology based on improved tools, seeds, and irrigation techniques.

A state structure influenced by both Chinese and Hindu models, and sustained by irrigated rice, arose in the Mekong Delta as early as the first century A.D. The formation of hydraulic cores in adjacent regions and islands during the first millennium A.D., however, followed primarily Hindu prototypes. Among these were the Khmer kingdom of Angkor and kingdoms of central Java and Ceylon. In India itself an earlier core area lying on the Indus River had once supported the state systems of Mohenjo-Daro and Harappa; but these had been destroyed in 1200 B.C., probably by Indo-European invaders. After that the dry Indus Valley never recovered its previous key role, except as a staging area for armed incursions from Central Asia. When states formed thereafter, they originated in the valley of the Ganges, especially in the region of Bihar and Bengal. Rice was here the main crop, grown with supplementary irrigation where annual rainfall reached only forty to eighty inches, and defended against floods with dams and dykes in the areas receiving more than eighty inches a year.

The advance of irrigation agriculture in eastern and southern Asia displaced populations employing less intensive modes of cultivation. Intensive cultivators in India pressed against hill tribes engaged in slash-and-burn agriculture, such as the Mundas and the Oraons of Bihar. In China the Han people assumed their historical identity as their irrigation-based political economy developed after 700 B.C. To the south of them were non-Han "barbarians"—Mong (Miao), Yu Mien (Yao), and Tai-speakers. As the Han advanced across the Yangtze River into "barbarian" territory, they incorporated some of the groups with agricultural and political patterns similar to their own, while pushing back the slash-and-burn cultivators into more mountainous or inhospitable regions. Elsewhere the migratory cultivators withdrew to protect their kin-ordered societies from the pressures of political and economic exactions. As a result, remnant populations of non-Han minorities have existed in the mountains of southwestern China and adjacent Burma, Thailand, Laos, and Vietnam since the twelfth and thirteenth centuries. The same processes were repeated on a smaller scale wherever nuclei of irrigation agriculture developed in the lowlands, while the hill dwellers resorted to extensive slash-and-burn cultivation to farm the mountainous and inaccessible hinterlands.

Trade

In making his way across the heights and fastnesses of the Old World in 1400, our imaginary observer would have followed in the footsteps of innumerable traders, who, for millennia, had labored to construct far-flung commercial networks between widely separate regions. Indeed, the archipelagic distribution of agricultural areas put a premium on connecting routes, whether by sea or by land. Such routes, whether short- or long-distance, required servicing and defense against attack. At the same time, any group that seized control of a major connecting link could insert itself into the transport grid to its own benefit, or else cut off connections together, accentuating the compartmentalization of the cultivable archipelagos. Thus, the history of the Old World could be written not only in terms of the strategic agricultural areas but also in terms of the links among them.

One of the great advantages possessed by the European peninsula of Eurasia was its proximity to water routes all along its perimeter, from the Gulf of Finland and the Baltic Sea to the eastern Mediterranean. From the northeasternmost pole of this maritime network, people could portage across to the Volga, and—like the Vikings—sail down to the Caspian. This route, however, was interrupted by the steppe nomads and not reopened until the middle of the sixteenth century. From the ports of the eastern Mediterranean, the Silk Road led toward Kashgar and on into China. A second route from the Mediterranean led from Aleppo on to the Persian Gulf, and thence by ship to India and Southeast Asia. A third route involved portage across the isthmus of Suez and maritime transport through the Red Sea and the Gulf of Aden to East Africa and India beyond. From the southern Mediterranean littoral, caravan routes using camels, the "ships of the desert," crossed the Sahara to converge upon the cities of Gao and Timbuctu on the bend of

The European Peninsula: proximity to waterways.

the Niger River. From there, river transport and pack donkeys carried goods deep into the West African heartland. Southeast Asia, in turn, was traversed by innumerable routes of raiding and trading, from Malaya to the Philippines and Japan.

The existence of such routes reminds us that long-distance exchanges possess ancient roots. Merchants have long moved goods from areas of surplus production to deficit areas, and obtained a return for their service. As long as transport facilities were limited—as long as burdens had to be borne overland by human or animal carriers, and across the seas in the hold of ships of low tonnage—the movement tended to favor luxury goods, that is, goods that yielded a high profit per unit sold. To the extent that trade in elite goods predominated, trade exchanges tended to move in two different spheres. There was the sphere of local trade and exchange, in which goods for everyday use moved among villages and towns within restricted regions; and the sphere of long-distance trade in valuables, produced for consumption by elites and serving to underline their positions of political and economic domination.

Pastoral Nomads

In traversing the Old World dry belt from Africa to the far reaches of Asia, traders and other travelers entered the predilect habitat of populations specialized in its use, the pastoral nomads. These were not merely herders; they also sat astride most of the routes that connected oasis with oasis, core area with core area, region with region. Equipped with cavalry, they could interdict movement across strategic points and could mass attacks against hubs of trade in oases and towns. Today the tables have turned against the pastoralists, who increasingly have been deprived of their ability to wage war on their own behalf. Before the Europeans opened up the sea route to the Orient, however, the pastoralists played a major role in the transcontinental caravan trade, exacting tribute in return for promises of safe conduct. The ability to impose such "protection rents," in F. C. Lane's phrase, furnished a lucrative income. Niels Steensgard has estimated the financial loss to the Levant resulting from direct European trade with Asia—by sea around the Cape of Good Hope—at 3−4 million piasters (1973: 175).

In A.D. 1400 the caravan trade was still in its heyday, as were the pastoral nomads who patrolled it. It is not that pastoralists could survive in independence of the settled zone. Although pastoralists were specialists in livestock keeping, moving with their herds in search of pasture and water, they usually depended upon cultivators to furnish them with grain and artisan products. Pastoralists and cultivators were thus often linked by necessary exchanges. The terms of these exchanges depended upon the distribution of power between the exchanging populations. Where pastoral nomads possessed horses, they frequently held the advantages of surprise, mobility, and superior impact in dealing with settled populations. Pastoralists organized into segmentary and ranked lineages also held strategic advantages. Lineages that ordinarily operated on their own could be brought together through appeals to a common genealogical charter, the massing body led by lineages of higher rank.

This does not mean that pastoralists always stood ready to attack settled populations. There were many kinds of pastoralists who lived in pacific symbiosis with settled villages. There were also many pastoral populations who carried on some cultivation during the course of the annual migratory cycle or delegated tasks of permanent tillage to a subgroup of their federation. There were numerous factors that affected the rates of exchange between pastoral and agricultural products; certain shifts caused pastoralists to abandon herding in favor of tillage, while other shifts led cultivators to abandon their fields and become full-time raisers of livestock. The question that must be asked, and which has no easy answer, concerns the precise conditions under which pastoral nomads chose the alternative of aggressive war, rather than strategies of accommodation or symbiosis.

Our observer of A.D. 1400 would undoubtedly have thought of pastoral nomads as "scourges of God." For the better part of 400 years, they had unleashed attack after attack against the centers of cultivation. The reasons for this are not wholly clear. Owen Lattimore has traced the source of movements in the history of the steppe to those border zones where cultivators and nomads competed for land that could serve either as arable or as pasture (1951). Such areas were also political shatter-belts, where the interest of those who ruled over cultivators lay in setting the nomads at each other's throats, while at the same time the nomads acquired a knowledge of the strengths and weaknesses of the settled areas. The impact of pastoral nomads—whether Turk, Mongol, Arab, or Berber—reached an intensity and scope in the four centuries before our observer's trek that set this time span off from others before or since.

The ability to mass large mobile fighting forces under effective command served the nomads well in times of war, but it created problems in times of peace. It rendered difficult the continuous administration of conquered populations without attendant loss of their fighting effectiveness. "The empire was created on horseback, but it cannot be governed on horseback," the Sinicized Khitan Ch'u-ts'ai is supposed to have said to Jenghiz Khan's successor, Ögödai (Grousset 1970: 257). To consolidate their gains, therefore, the pastoral conquerors usually adopted the administrative models of the peoples that they had overcome. In practice this meant that the nomads of the western steppe followed Islamic prototypes, while those of the eastern steppe and desert borrowed the models of the Han Chinese. This step had further consequences. Concentration on the skills of routine administration tended to weaken the skills that supported military prowess. At the same time, success in improving the tax base, on which the splendor of settled court life depended, invited rivals—still nomadic—to challenge the conquerors (Lattimore 1951: 76–77). The result was a constant turnover of ruling elites, often accompanied by violent depreciation or destruction of the prizes won in war, including the decimation of the surplus-producing population and of the technological base upon which their production depended.

The pastoralists not only interacted with the zones of intensive cultivation; they also interacted with one another. Pastoralists invaded pasture grounds of other groups and disputed control of the vital pressure points of trade. According to Frederick Teggart (1939), for instance, each defeat at the great wall of China sent pastoralists reeling backwards against other pastoral populations, transmitting the pressure until migratory invaders were sent crashing against the Roman *limes* in the west. While Teggart's description probably exaggerates the synchronization of the process, the continuous movement of pastoralists along the dry belt—Mongol- and Turkic-speakers in the north and Arabic-speakers in the south—turned the corridor into an area of dense interaction, as well as a staging area of conflict.

The Near East and Africa

Turks

In 1400 our voyager would have encountered large pastoral populations in movement all along the trail of the old Silk Road. To the east of Kashgar, these were mainly Mongol-speakers; west of Kashgar were mainly speakers of Turkic languages. Since the year 1000, Turkic-speakers had come into increasing contact with town dwellers and cultivators, notably in the northern borderland of Iran and the adjacent belt of steppe. There agriculture and the power of the agrarian class waned as the steppe warriors gained ascendancy. Converting to Sunna Islam and merging their warrior ideology with the role of the *ghazi* frontier fighter for the faith, the Turks were able to recapture some of the ideological energies of early, expansionist Islam. From the eleventh century on, Turks increasingly replaced others as mercenaries and military bondsmen in the service of Near Eastern rulers. Indeed, in two areas—central Anatolia and northwestern India—they consolidated their own rule in the eleventh century, and in the mid-thirteenth century a Turkish and Circassian elite of military bondservants (*mamluk*) replaced a ruling group of Kurdish descent in Syria and Egypt.

In the course of the thirteenth and fourteenth centuries, most Turkish groups were swept up in the conquests of Jenghiz Khan and his Mongols, initially joining with the Mongols and later benefiting from their retreats. In Iran, for example, a dynasty of Seljuk Turks fell before the Mongol onslaught in the first third of the thirteenth century, but a hundred years later competition beween Mongol and Turkic rivals reopened. This contest was won first by a Turk from Transoxeania, the terrible Timur (Tamerlane). In 1400 his domain stretched from the Black Sea to the gates of Kashgar, but it would soon begin to crumble after his death in 1405. A century later the Timurid heartland in Transoxeania would fall to Uzbek conquest, led by a khan descended from Jenghiz. Then the religious leaders of the Shiite Safawi order would mobilize the pastoralist Turkoman, defeat the Sunnic Uzbeks to the east, and unify Iran against the pressure of the Sunnic Ottoman Turks encroaching from the west.

The Ottomans themselves were descendants of an Oghuz clan holding grazing grounds around the city of Merv, and led by a Persian-speaking Seljuk Turkish elite. They became the nucleus of what McNeill has called "a freebooters' frontier principality" (1963: 499). From A.D. 1300 on, they raided and pillaged Byzantine settlements from a base in northwestern Anatolia, expanding rapidly into the Balkans in the second half of the fourteenth century. By 1400 they had reduced the once powerful Byzantines to enclaves at Constantinople and Salonica and in the southeastern Peloponnesus, and they were readying their final attacks on these targets when Timur routed them at Ankara (1402). Surviving their rivalries with Timur, the Ottomans would resume expansion in the fifteenth century, conquering Constantinople in 1453 and establishing an empire that would last until the end of World War I.

Our observer, then, would have encountered the Ottomans just before their defeat by Timur. He would have noted the power of the ghazi ideology, which inspired Ottoman expansion against the infidels under the slogan of the *jihad*, or holy war; but he would have seen little as yet of the system the Ottomans would construct to hold and administer their conquests. This massive empire would for over three centuries dominate the Near East, block direct European access to the Orient, and deflect European expansion westward toward the Americas and the sea routes around the Cape of Good Hope. It is therefore worth looking ahead briefly to the imperial structure that would develop.

The Ottoman polity was centered upon the *sultan* with his imperial household, consisting of his military bondsmen or slaves—the famous janissaries. These slaves were usually recruited among non-Moslems, war captives or children received in payment of tribute imposed upon conquered populations. Raised in allegiance to the sultan, they owed loyalty only to him, not to any kin group that crosscut the machinery of the state. In this way the Ottomans attempted to obviate the problems of divisiveness and competition usually posed by the segmented social organization of the pastoral nomads. (This pattern was not original with the Ottomans. It is attested as early as the eighth century among the Abbasid caliphs of Baghdad, who recruited mostly Turks from the nearby steppes, and among the Umayyad caliphs of Córdoba in Spain, who favored Slavs.)

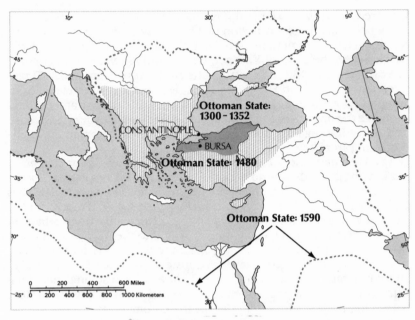

Ottoman expansion.

The military bondservants were sent out to govern the provinces and to collect their surpluses, which fed the Ottoman army and guaranteed the food supply of the core region. In return the military bondsmen received grants to shares of the tribute for their lifetime (*iq ta*). Actual title to land was retained by the sultan and not given as property, thus inhibiting the growth of a European form of feudalism, in which bodies of kinsmen came into hereditary possession of land and labor. The Ottoman state also established domination over the *ulema*, the Islamic teachers of the sacred law. Contrary to prior Islamic practice, they organized the ulema into a hierarchy answerable to the state and charged with standardizing the law against the centrifugal influences of local religious variants. The military bondsmen and the ulema together formed the class of *askeri*, soldiers. All others were classified as subjects (*raeya*), who sustained the state and its officialdom with tribute.

The Ottoman economy was, however, based on the extensive use of money. Tributary surpluses, together with the produce of peasants and the craft products of artisan guilds, were sold in local, regional, and inter-regional marketplaces. Thus, both revenue collection and revenue valorization depended upon a stratum of merchants, whose activities were necessary to the state and yet always threatened to escape state control. Merchants were officially licensed by the state, and market sales were closely scrutinized and taxed by state officials. In the late sixteenth century, however, trade within the Ottoman realm came to be increasingly linked to trade with Venice, Genoa, and Florence, and with the commercial emporia along the Black Sea. Much of this trade was in contraband, and indeed "contraband carried the day" (Islamoğlu and Keyder 1977: 41). At the same time, the state—increasingly unable to collect revenues—moved from the remuneration of its officials with tribute to tax farming. The tax farmer furnished revenue to the state in exchange for the rights to collect tribute and taxes locally and to dispose of them at a profit. Diminishing control by the state led, in turn, to the rise of a class of local notables, the *ayans*, who accumulated local power and commercial influence as the power of the palace and its representatives waned.

North and West Africa

Further west, in North Africa, nomadic populations also held a strategic role in 1400. Here each city or caravan emporium stood within a ring of surrounding fields and palm groves, separated one from the other by desert or steppe. The towns were linked by wide-ranging routes of trade, but their caravans had to ply these lanes of traffic across inhospitable ground held by seminomads and nomads in pursuit of their own interests.

While the geography and settlement pattern of the area suggest sharp contrasts between the steppe and the sown, and between cities and their rural hinterlands, the societies of Muslim North Africa bridged these gaps by ties of "horizontal solidarity" (Laroui 1976: 35). Cities were not set off from the surrounding countryside as independent and self-ruling entities. Each city contained quarters that housed groups separated from one another by ethnic, religious, or occupational distinctions; these groups had their counterparts in towns and villages. Cities, towns, and villages thus formed "geographical and ecological, as well as social composites including territories and populations who were neither exclusively urban nor exclusively rural, but a combination of the two" (Lapidus 1969: 73–74). Each regional composite was dominated by an elite of intermarrying families, comprising landowners, merchants, state officials, heads of guilds, and the religious leaders of mosques, schools, and charitable foundations (*ulama*). At the same time, ties of common interest connected such elites across regional boundaries. Long-distance trade wove a network of commercial relations among merchant communities and drew into alliance the leaders of pastoral groups involved in guaranteeing the wide-ranging caravan traffic. Moreover, the religious elite of the ulama was found throughout the Muslim world, linking different regions as leaders and interpreters of religion and law. Strategic centers and strong-points, finally, were in the hands of political-military elites, usually composed of the slave soldiery of a paramount sultan, who taxed and ruled in conflict or accommodation with members of the regional elites.

The maintenance of power in these polities depended on keeping control of the region through its elite, and on effective alliances with pastoral groups able to defend the caravan routes and oases in the hinterland. Contesting control meant forming alliances with disaffected tribal segments and enlisting the cooperation of disgruntled urban merchants and artisans. The result was a constant seesaw in which the allied dissidents would test the limits of the ruler's control until the road was clear for their takeover. After a seizure of power the cycle would recommence.

This continuous process of building up and tearing down of alliances was brilliantly analyzed in the fourteenth century by the Berber courtier Ibn Khaldun, who saw in it a continuous alternation between the kinship solidarity of the nomad and the diversification of interests attendant on sedentary life. The process has its own logic, as Ibn Khaldun showed. Yet in North Africa it was the consequence also of a larger context, that of trans-Saharan trade, on the one hand, and of relations with economic and political forces in Iberia and Italy, on the other.

The trans-Saharan trade with West Africa was of strategic importance to North Africa, the Near East, and even to Europe. The trade routes reached across the desert into the trans-African savanna belt, and beyond that into the zone of tropical forest. The gold mines of West Africa, in Bambuk and Buré, played a vital role in the bullion supply of the Old World. In the late Middle Ages, this area furnished about two-thirds of

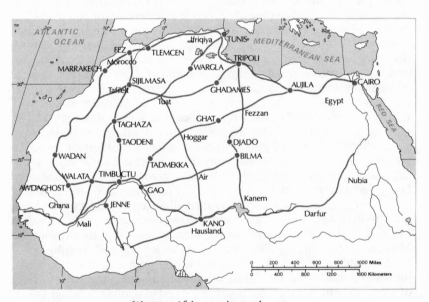

Western Africa: major trade routes.

the gold circulating in the economy of the hemisphere (Hopkins 1973: 82). The forest zone also furnished large numbers of slaves for the Near East. In addition, this zone exported cloth, ivory, pepper, and kola nuts (prized as a stimulant in areas where Islam forbade the use of alcohol) and received, in return, horses, brass, copper, glassware, beads, leather, textiles, tailored clothing, and preserved foodstuffs from North Africa, as well as salt from the mines of the Sahara. The trade routes through the western Sahara to Morocco and Algeria lay mainly in the hands of Mande-speaking Dyula traders, who had expanded southward from Jenne (located on the Bani, a tributary of the Niger) to Begho, the major collecting point for gold and forest products on the edge of the forest zone. The eastern trade routes to Tunisia and Libya connected up with the commercial network of the Hausa, who traded south toward the forest from the city of Kano in northern Nigeria and from other Hausa towns.

This external network, of course, had political implications. Control of the transfer points between forest and savanna and between savanna and desert placed power in the hands of those able to achieve and hold control. The interface between the three zones also proved to be critical for state formation in West Africa. The earliest of these polities, dating from before A.D. 800, had been Aukar, pivoted on market centers in the grasslands north of the upper Niger and Senegal. This state, probably founded by Soninke and usually called Ghana after the title of its ruler, controlled the trade in gold from the placers at Bambuk and used its monopoly to obtain needed goods from Morocco through a colony of Muslim traders. The kingdom had fallen in the eleventh century to Mauritanian Berbers, the Al-Murabitun, who thus seized control of its northward trade. Then, in the thirteenth century, a former dependency of Ghana had risen to become the Malinke-dominated polity of Kangaba (Mali). Once again this power was founded on control of the gold trade and on hegemony over the routes from Timbuctu.

In 1400 Kangaba was in decline. In the course of the century, it would give way to Songhay, with its capital at Gao. Songhay carried on trade with the north through Muslim Lemtuna Berber merchants from the oases to the north. Songhay would subsequently fall to Moroccan invasion from the north. Further state formation would take place along the southern and eastern peripheries of former Songhay. To the south there would emerge, toward the end of the sixteenth century, the several states of the Mossi, controlling the route from Jenne to the forest land of the Asante and the savanna region of the lower Volta. To the east the polity of Kanem-Bornu, straddling the trade routes to Tunisia and Libya and to the Middle Nile, would be pushed into the background by the Hausa states, centered upon Katsina and Kano, the two leading eastern market towns. From these centers the Hausa entered into contact with the Yoruba-speaking peoples and their neighbors of the West African forest.

Thus, Africa south of the Sahara was not the isolated, backward area of European imagination, but an integral part of a web of relations that connected forest cultivators and miners with savanna and desert traders and with the merchants and rulers of the North African settled belt. This web of relations had a warp of gold, "the golden trade of the Moors," but a weft of exchanges in other products. The trade had direct political consequences. What happened in Nigerian Benin or Hausa Kano had repercussions in Tunis and Rabat. When the Europeans would enter West Africa from the coast, they would be setting foot in a country already dense with towns and settlements, and caught up in networks of exchange that far transcended the narrow enclaves of the European emporia on the coast.

We can see such repercussions at the northern terminus of the trade routes in Morocco and Algeria. Here one elite after another came to the fore, each one dependent on interaction with the Sahara and the forest zone. Each successive elite was anchored in a kin-organized confederacy, usually mobilized around a religious ideology. We have already referred to the Al-Murabitun who destroyed Ghana. They were members of a religious movement, which had arisen in the eleventh century among the pastoral Sanhaja Berber confederations when their resource base was threatened by Arab Bedouin moving into the Mauritanian Sahara. From their military-religious hermitages (ribat, the root of their name), they preached return to a purified Islam. One branch of the Al-Murabitun went south to lay hold of the gold of Ghana; another branch moved north to conquer Morocco and Spain. Under their Hispanicized name—the Almoravids—they ruled Al-Andalus between 1090 and 1110. They were replaced in the twelfth century by the Al-Muwihiddin (Hispanicized as Almohades), or Unitarians, of the Masmuda confederacy. The Al-Muwihiddin were succeeded in the thirteenth century, in turn, by the Beni Marin, pastoralists from the desert near the trading emporium of Sijilmassa, who then excluded both Sanhaja and Masmuda from power in favor of their own confederacy, the Zanata. Subsequently the Beni Marin fought a two-front war, one against remnants of the Al-Muwihiddin in Tunis, the Hafsids, and another against a section of their own confederation, the Zayanids of western Algeria, who disputed their control over Sijilmassa. Hafsids and Zayanids traded with the European shore, especially with Aragón in eastern Spain, attempting to counteract Marin power and to compensate for the impoverishment of their own hinterlands by nomad depredations. After the fall of Moslem Granada to the kingdom of Castile in 1492, Hafsids and Zayanids would seek Ottoman protection, which would come in the shape of a pirate fleet, making piracy the main source of revenue from then on (Abun-Nasr 1971: 167).

In 1400 our traveler would have encountered the Beni Marin still in control of Morocco. Increasingly, however, they would lose support. In the sixteenth century rulership would pass to the leaders of a religious movement who claimed descent from the Prophet Mohammed. The movement originated among the Berbers of the Sus Valley and preached holy war against the Portuguese. These Sa'dians would strive to regain control of the gold of the Sudan by invading and destroying Songhay toward the end of the sixteenth century, but they would merely succeed in driving the gold trade away from the western caravan routes toward the east. In due course, like their counterparts in Algeria and Tunis, these rulers of Morocco also would turn to piracy as a way of tapping the wealth moving over the new sea-lanes created by the Europeans.

East Africa

East Africa, too, was involved in the network of overland routes and sea-lanes, the consequences of which would have been evident to an observer in 1400.

This area was inhabited largely by Bantu-speaking populations. While their history remains to be fully unraveled, present evidence from archaeology, comparative linguistics, and ethnohistory indicates that they originated in the central Cameroons. From there two streams of populations moved outward, in different directions. The first stream moved eastward through the Sudanic belt, taking up cereal production, animal raising, and ironwork by the second millennium B.C. By 1000 B.C. clusters of populations belonging to this eastern stream had reached the Rift Valley and the highlands of Tanzania and southern Kenya. Around 500 B.C. this stream turned southward, crossing the belt of tropical forest in the vicinity of Lake Victoria. From this point of entry, populations of Bantu-speaking cultivators and herders moved southward toward Transvaal and southwestward into central Zambia, Zimbabwe (Rhodesia), and on into Angola. The southward movement crossed the Limpopo River into Transvaal about A.D 400.

A second stream of migrations carried Bantu-speakers from the Cameroons southward, along coastal and riverine routes to the mouth of the Congo. In contrast to the stock-raising and ironworking cultivators of the eastward movement, the populations of this second stream long remained stone-tool-using cultivators of root crops. Around the beginning of the Christian era, the populations of these two movements came together, probably in northern Angola. By A.D. 500 they were expanding eastward into Zambia and southeastern Zaire, setting in motion some of the state-making processes still evident in historic times. Their advance displaced hunting-and-gathering populations; their Khoisan-speaking predecessors were driven into the inhospitable African Southwest, where they still survive as Khoi-Khoi("Hottentot") cattle raisers and San ("Bushmen") food collectors.

These expanding Bantu came increasingly into contact with Near Eastern and Asian traders. Arab trading stations existed in East Africa at least by the tenth century, if not before; they exported slaves, ivory, iron, rhinoceros horn, tortoise shell, amber, and leopard skins to India and beyond. Chinese sources mention slaves from Zenj (Black Africa) as early as the seventh century, and by 1119 most of the wealthy people of Canton were said to have possessed Black slaves (Mathew 1963: 108). It seems possible that the traders involved in this early export trade were Malays from the kingdom of Sriviyaya in Sumatra, which controlled the trade between India and China from the eighth to the eleventh centuries. Although Zanzibar may have been occupied by Arabs since the eighth century, the first port of major importance in East Africa appears to have been Kilwa, in control of the trade in gold from southern Rhodesia from the eleventh century on. Other important depots were Mogadishu, Kisimani Mafia, and Malindi. As the trade routes

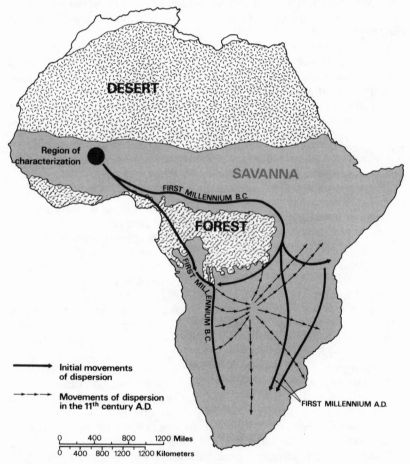

The migrations of the Bantu-speaking peoples. (After Phillipson, 1977; courtesy of the author)

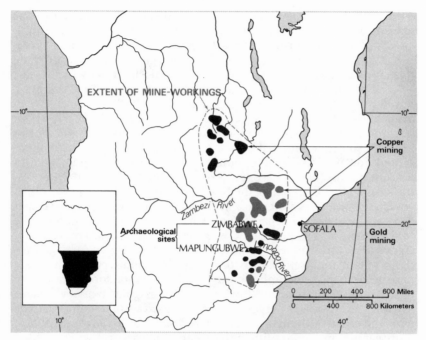

Prehistoric mining in eastern Africa.

connecting Anatolia with the Persian Gulf and the Indian Ocean took precedence in the thirteenth century over the continental routes sponsored by the Mongols, the East African trade in gold, ivory, copper, and slaves increased heavily. East Africa thus became part of the trade network of the southern seas. In return for its exports, East Africa received Indian beads and cloth, as well as Chinese porcelain (mostly Ming) and wares from Burma and Vietnam.

The gold trade had a major impact on the hinterland. By the ninth century, mining of gold deposits (sometimes more than 100 feet deep) was in full swing in the area between the Zambezi and the Limpopo. It is "very probable that immense quantities of gold were exported" (Summers 1961: 5). The miners were iron-using cattle keepers and possibly cultivators as well. About A.D. 1000 they came under the domination of newcomers, probably Shona-speakers, who established themselves among the miners in stone-built headquarters and ceremonial centers, the best known of which is represented by the ruins of Zimbabwe. Their chiefs took over the gold trade with the coastal Arabs, and tapped the ivory and copper of the Limpopo River valley. Their influence in the hinterland can be seen in the rich burials at Ingombe Ilede on the Zambezi River, which clearly reveal an extensive trade in copper, iron, and gold.

In 1400 the Shona of Zimbabwe were ruled by a Rozwi dynasty, the Mwene Mutapa, whose polity was described by early Portuguese travelers and in later oral-historical accounts of the area (Abraham 1966). What we know of them affords us an unusual glimpse into a case of state formation predicated upon entry into the hemispheric network of trade, as well as some insight into the political economy and ideology of a developing African kingdom. In these accounts the Shona emerge as an association of patrilineages, organized into a number of "tribes," or kinship corporations. Each corporation was associated with *midzimu*, or ancestor spirits, dominated by one or more *mhondoro* spirits who represented and perpetuated the founder of the tribal chieftaincy and his descent group. Above these spirits of chiefly ancestors stood the ancestral spirit of the royal clan of the Nembire, who linked the clan with god, *mwari*. Zimbabwe was at one and the same time the ceremonial center dedicated to mwari, the pan-Shona deity, and the political center of the Mbire ruler, whose praise title was Mwene Mutapa. Ultimate sovereignty over the land lay with the supreme ruler. He, in turn, granted rights to land to the chiefs of associations of patrilineages, who would in time become the senior mhondoro spirits in the mhondoro hierarchy. In return, the ruler received from the grantees gold, ivory, weapons, livestock, and hoes. These goods were then used as commodities in trade with the coast. Although the centralized polity of the Mwene Mutapa disintegrated in the mid-fifteenth century, the various successor chiefdoms would play a vital role in the burgeoning Portuguese trade with the East. "East African gold and ivory," says Malyn Newitt (1973: 32), "purchased the Indian spices which were Portugal's main quest in the east. Without control of this trade the Portuguese would never have competed with the Muslims in the Indian market."

South and East Asia

Eastward, across the Indian Ocean and beyond, lay the vast spheres of India and China and the Southeast Asian archipelago. Ocean-borne trade in spices and gold between India and the West, which was extensive during the early Roman Empire, had weakened after the second century A.D. (see Wheeler 1955). This had reoriented Indian trade toward Southeast Asia (Coedès 1964: 44–49), and Arabs and Persians had taken over the routes to the east. In the fourth century and again in the early seventh century, there were colonies of Arab merchants in Canton (Leur 1955: 111). Until the tenth century the Chinese shipped their goods abroad in Arab or Iranian bottoms, and in the ships of non-Han seafaring peoples of South China and the China seas. Thus, there had been long-standing connections of trade among the core regions of southern, eastern, and western Asia.

Yet the development of both India and China depended, in the last instance, more on the expansion of cultivation and the surpluses afforded by it than on any linkages created by external trade. In the course of this expansion, India and China each developed distinctive economic and political arrangements linking surplus takers to surplus producers. Each of these needs discussion in its own right. We shall then turn to Southeast Asia, an area where the roads between China and India intersected.

India

Our observer, traveling through the India of 1400, would have found many cities in ruin. In 1388 Timur had invaded northern India and destroyed the armies of the Turko-Afghan sultans. In 1398 he sacked Delhi, massacred its inhabitants, and carried the treasure of the sultans home to Transoxeania. Political conditions in northern India remained chaotic for a long time thereafter, even though a new Afghan dynasty began to reconsolidate a measure of power in the mid-fifteenth century.

If he had moved through the villages of India, our traveler would have been struck by the enduring division of the population into heredi-tary castes. The Macedonian ambassador to the court of Chandragupta Maurya reported some of the features of caste as early as 300 B.C.; at the beginning of the sixteenth century, the Portuguese Duarte Barbosa, who accompanied Magellan on his trip around the world, would de-scribe caste at length. (Indeed, the very word has come down to us from the Portuguese *casta*.) Caste has thus had a long history in India, and it has shaped relationships among the peoples of the subcontinent, both before and after the advent of the Europeans. We therefore need to examine caste in some detail—but we need to do so processually, for if caste has influenced the course of change, it has also been affected by change in turn.

The root of the Indian word for caste is *jati*, from *jan*, to give birth; it carries the connotation of descent from a common ancestor. This notion of common descent can be invoked at various levels—that of the ex-tended family, the lineage, lineages related at the local level, the cluster of lineages operating in a region, as well as the supercategory of *varna*, which classifies all the units in four hierarchical ranks, set off from the great negative category of Outcastes, or Untouchables. The level that will be invoked depends on the interests at issue in a given context. Levels may be merged to facilitate commonality and alliance under one set of circumstances; their separation may be reasserted as circum-stances change (Béteille 1969: 157). While segments are continuously dividing and merging, they are also mutually ranked. The idiom of caste rank is the idiom of purity or pollution, which renders the caste order "consistent and rational to those who live in it" (Dumont 1970: 44).

To constitute a caste, a group of people connected by kinship must adhere to certain customs, such as food habits and styles of dress, and perform common rituals. Should one caste segment wish to separate from another, it must develop distinctive customs and rituals. Should two segments merge, their merger is announced by a merger of custom and performance. While the guiding ideology of the system pretends that its arrangements are static, a great deal of flexibility and mobility is actually possible within it. Since caste membership is related to economic and political power, the actions of any segment affect all the adjacent segments. The mobility of any one caste may therefore be hindered by the countervailing efforts of other castes. Yet some segments have demonstrably risen in the caste hierarchy, while other segments have fallen. Finally, the system allows outsiders to take up positions in it. Characteristically, new conquerors are allowed to move in near the top of the hierarchy of segments, as *kshatriya*, or warrior castes; and non-Hindu ethnic groups can be brought into the system by being assigned to a category of caste.

To understand how caste works concretely, one must, however, look beyond kinship organization and ritual idiom to the political economy of caste. In any given province, clusters of lineages hold positions of command and domination; at the center of these stands a chiefly lineage. The dominant lineages intermarry, reinforcing their commanding position throughout the province. Such a cluster of lineages exhibits its position ritually, but its domination is political as well as ritual. In each village, segments of the dominant caste control economic and political life both as landholders and as warriors. At the level of the province, the dominant caste furnishes the ruler, or *raja*, constituting the province politically as a "little kingdom" (Dumont 1957). Such a little kingdom was often part of a still larger encompassing state. An increase in the political standing of a provincial raja within such a state enhanced the influence of the dominant caste in the province; a decline threatened the standing and solidarity of the dominant caste and of its segments down to the village level.

In ideal terms, highest rank in the caste order rests with the kinship clusters of the priests, or *Brahmins*. They are the bearers of *dharma*, or universal order, values, and norms (Dumont 1970: 68). Embodying the highest degree of ritual purity, they pollute none below them but can be polluted by all others. They officiate at religious events and are arbiters of the proper standards of behavior according to the ancient Sanskrit texts. Hence castes and caste segments lower on the ladder of purity but wishing to climb it would model their customs and ritual on Brahmin patterns and would seek certification of their success from Brahmin priests. The result was a spread of Brahmin models down the ranks of caste segmentation (Srinivas, 1961: Chap. 1). Imitation of the priesthood was not, however, the only means of achieving higher status; there was also imitation of warrior and merchant models.

Whereas Brahmin rank certified ritual purity, kshatriya or warrior rank signified power. In contrast to the priestly dharma, the warrior realm was that of *artha*—of force, gain, and self-interested advantage (Dumont 1970: 66). But since force creates power, it was ultimately artha that cemented together the order of ranking and segmentation. Within a village or a cluster of related villages, the locally dominant caste segment fulfilled warrior functions. In ideological terms, the dominant lineage represented the royal function at the village level (Dumont 1970: 66). Thus, kshatriya power was the real linchpin of the system, and whoever in a given locality was able to exercise or usurp that power functioned as kshatriya (Jayawardena 1971: 118). Under certain circumstances, however, where merchant groups became more important than kshatriyas, lower castes might aspire to merchant status instead (Sinha 1962). Caste categorization could thus adjust to changed circumstances of power and influence; in particular, local or provincial lineages could manipulate it to reinforce or expand their standing over a wider area. At the level of the state, the king could even reassign caste statuses himself (Hutton 1951: 93−97). In the towns, caste often became less significant than membership in artisan guilds (Lehman 1957: 523). Even in the villages, the hold of the dominant caste was not absolute. Where the dominant caste exhibited special relationships with service castes through feasting, exchanges, and ritual, other lower-status castes might counter by emulating Brahmin-like comportment, thus signifying their opposition to the dominant caste (Heesterman 1973: 101).

The strongest suit in the hands of the locally dominant caste segment was its control of village lands. Several forms of landholding prevailed until the British initiated land reforms in the eighteenth century. One was *bhaiacharya* tenure, in which land was held by the segment as a whole and redistributed periodically among its households according to fluctuations in household size and need; the segment paid rent to the raja as a group. Another form of tenure was *pattidari*: the land was divided among the households of the dominant caste segment according to their genealogical position, but rent was still paid as a unit. A third form was *bighadam*, in which landholdings were unequal in size and landholders paid rent according to the size of their holding. In pre-British India these forms of tenure and revenue arrangements were not mutually exclusive, but constituted changing points on a continuum. Continued land fragmentation over time or the pressure of a strong state could weaken kinship ties, and could lead to a change from tenure based on genealogical rank to a share-out by household needs. The reverse could occur if the head of an ascendant lineage became powerful. Underlying these tenure arrangements were kinship rights and obligations, including claims to support and leaders' claims to the labor and loyalty of kinsmen. Hence, rights to land shifted as these other claims waxed and waned. When the British took over, they interpreted these fluctuating relationships between people as fixed types of property on the European model, instituting what they saw as a liberal regime of property law but in fact abrogating the adaptive capacity of former arrangements.

The villages also contained two categories of people without rights to land. The first consisted of caste groups that furnished services to the landowning group as artisans or barbers. They could be associated with a particular landowning household, or they could work in the service of the landholding caste as a whole. Such village servants owned the tools of their trade and obtained something of a "guaranteed living." This distinguished them sharply from a stratum of people who owned neither the tools of their trade nor any lineage-based claims to land (Meillassoux 1974: 102–103; Newell 1974: 487). These were either landless laborers or tenants-at-will of landholders; some might also be part-time leather workers or drummers. These people constituted a pool of labor available at the behest of the dominant village stratum (Mencher 1974). They made up the so-called Untouchable castes, whose low position was reinforced by taboos governing their relations with the higher castes. The distribution of such untouchable castes was related to ecological factors. Untouchable castes were concentrated mainly in the densely populated irrigated regions of the Indo-Gangetic Plain of the north and in the fertile stretches of coast in the south, where they were mostly agricultural laborers. In drier and more mountainous districts, the landowners cultivated the land themselves, and artisans were frequently drawn from the poorer households of the landowning segment itself. Indeed, with shrinking resources the village landowners on occasion drove the Untouchable laborers from their villages (Newell 1974: 487–488). Where they remained, they worked primarily at the behest of village landowners and were subject to their dictation.

The overall architecture of Indian society—at once cellular and segmented and yet able to generate links between different cells and segments—is best understood against the backdrop of India's political ecology. There are at least three Indias: the India of the plain formed by the River Ganges; the India of the coastal littoral; and the India of the Deccan, the central mountain plateau. Gangetic India is an area of high rainfall and of most intensive rice cultivation. Historically, it has been the central area of Indian state formation; this is where the Maurya polity of 322–185 B.C. had its center and where the Guptas exercised sovereignty between A.D. 300 and 600. India of the littoral embraces a series of river deltas and coastlands, such as Andrah and Tamilnad along the Coromandel coast in the east, and Kerala (on the Malabar coast), Konkan, and Gujarat in the west. Ports along these coasts have long been prominent in long-distance overseas trade. The third India—the Deccan—is separated from the other two Indias by chains of hills and mountains. It is cut off from the Gangetic Plain to the north by a mountainous area still inhabited by speakers of Austro-Asiatic languages and from the coastal lowlands by two mountain ranges, the Western and the Eastern Ghats. The Deccan itself is a dry plateau; its natural vegetation is scrubland, and the predominant crops, such as millet, are adapted to dry-zone conditions. Rice and other crops can be grown by irrigation with water drawn from scattered ponds or "tanks," but these tend to go dry when water is most needed, making the plateau a zone of periodic food shortages.

The Indian peninsula is today one of the most densely populated areas in the world, but concentrated settlement and the agricultural intensification that made it possible advanced only slowly and discontinuously, leaving intervening districts in the hands of food collectors and swidden cultivators. When centralized states emerged, they used their power to sponsor land clearance, irrigation, deep mining, and frontier colonization by guilds of settlers or Brahmin organizations. Yet political centralization was achieved only rarely, under the Maurya and Gupta, and then only in the Gangetic Plain. At other times and places, the prevalent political unit remained the "little kingdom," a province ruled by the raja of the ranking lineage, which generally lacked the power to mobilize its people for agricultural expansion. In the Deccan, moreover, irrigation was possible only by scattered tanks, leading to population dispersal rather than concentration around a hydraulic core. Colonization and the scattering of settlements into favorable but isolated ecological niches further intensified dispersal and decentralization. The intervals between settled areas frequently remained in the hands of kin-ordered groups hostile to the encroaching states. The expansion of the Indian culture sphere thus exhibited a quite different modality from that of China. China advanced by expanding a homogeneous hydraulic core, displacing slash-and-burn cultivators into the southwestern mountains. India, in contrast, developed by incorporating diverse populations through assigning them different positions in the larger network of caste.

The Brahmins provided a countervailing force to this recurrent fragmentation. Each separate local unit of landowners, artisans, and servants was held together by the local rituals and cults of a "little" tradition, supported by reference to the sacred Sanskrit texts. Acephalous ethnic groups could become part of the larger cultural network through certification of their chiefs as warriors, through giving their women to Brahmins in marriage, and through adoption of Sanskritic ritual practices—processes that still operate today when members of "tribes" become Hindus by accepting Brahmin jurisdiction. (The Austro-Asiatic-speaking "scheduled tribes" of the hilly ranges are precisely those remaining ethnic groups that have refused, to date, to grant "to the Brahmin (the priest), rather than to its own members, primacy as a religious interpreter and instructor" [Cohn 1971: 19].) Frequently, the Brahmins also introduced new agricultural techniques, such as plow agriculture and new crops, and furnished links with wider networks of trade and markets. Kings and aspiring rulers would invite Brahmins to settle in their villages and would grant them land (Kosambi 1969: 171–172).

Brahmin dominance and the replication of the caste model throughout rural districts and villages can thus be understood as a response to ecological and political decentralization. It simultaneously furnished organizational links between members of the top castes—priests, warriors, and merchants—and connected the local caste segments of these strata to local clusters of artisans and dependents. It was, in Heesterman's words, "the poor man's solution to empire" (1973: 107). Frederic Lehman has argued that the caste model served to build organizational services and cultural skills into the structure of the Indian countryside, counteracting protracted periods of disorder owing to "long-term breakdowns in effective central authority" (1957: 151–152).

The rural infrastructure, based on caste, withstood the repeated onslaught of foreign conquerors over the centuries. One after another, contingents of prospective rulers descended on the Indian plain from the belt of steppe to the north of the sheltering mountains, always following the route that led from Balkh (Bactria) over the passes into the Punjab. The East-Iranian-speaking Sakas and Kushnan of the first three centuries A.D. were followed by the Mongol-Turkish Epthalites (Ye-Tai) in the fifth and sixth centuries, one contingent of which, the Gujaras, remained behind to become the Rajput (literally, "King's sons"). They were followed by Persianized Turks (the Ghaznavids) in the eleventh century, by Afghans from Herat (the Ghorids) in the twelfth, by a dynasty of Turkish Ghorid bondsmen and Mongol invaders at the beginning of the thirteenth, by Timur's Persianized Turks in the late fourteenth, and by Afghans in the fifteenth.

In 1525 Babur, a descendant of Timur, having abandoned Transoxeania to the conquering Uzbeks, moved to conquer India. Winning out over Afghan and Hindu Rajput opposition, he established himself as the first of a line of rulers that would unify most of the Indian subcontinent and rule it until its takeover by the British. This Mughal (Mongol) dynasty was, however, but the latest in a series of elites originating in the pastoral belt of Central Asia. Far from representing "traditional India," as they have been characterized, they rested their newly won power on social constellations older and more solid than their own.

China

At the eastern end of the old Silk Road in China, our voyager would have witnessed another major phase in the continuing interaction between the nomads of the north and the settled cultivators to the south of the Great Wall. In the preceding centuries China had come under repeated attack by the northern "barbarians." Early in the eleventh century, a Mongol-speaking elite from Jehol, the Khitan (Liao), had occupied China north of the Hwai River. Only a few years later, the Khitan were replaced by the Tungusic Jurchen from the forest belt of what is today the maritime province of the Soviet Union; these Jurchen pushed the frontier of their realm to the shores of the Yangtze. By the end of the century the Mongols of Jenghiz Khan had overrun both the

Jurchen in the north and the Chinese Sung dynasty still ruling south of the Yangtze, and were riding over the southern mountain ranges to the gates of Bhamo in Burma and Hanoi in Vietnam. Soon, however, the Mongol princes fell to attacking each other. By 1370 the Chinese founder of the Ming dynasty had succeeded in driving the Mongols back into Mongolia, putting a decisive end to Mongol rule in China. The year 1400 would thus have seen this Chinese resurgence under the early Ming.

Although repeatedly invaded from the north, China constituted a cultural sphere marked by strong continuities—Hegel called it the land of the recurrent principle. A strategic condition of this continuity lay in the importance of waterworks to the operations of the Chinese state, as Karl Wittfogel has demonstrated. These hydraulic works were basically of two kinds: canals and irrigation ditches to deliver water to the fields, and great dams and sluices to defend the areas of settlement against floods. These were supplemented by the development of transport canals permitting the movement of grain over wider areas. The first great waterworks known were built in the period of the declining Chou (ca. 500–250 B.C.), when political domains began to compete fiercely with one another. The most important were the hydraulic complexes that irrigated the Chengtu Plain in Szechwan (serving 3,500 square miles) and the Wei-pei Plain of Shensi (serving 1,000 square miles).

Planting irrigated rice, Szechwan province, China. Photograph by Bruno Barbey, 1960. (Barbey, Magnum)

These complexes predate the rise of the unified Chinese empire under the Ch'in dynasty (221–207 B.C.), and they may have been instrumental in furnishing the basis for its consolidation. Transport canals were also begun under the Ch'in, although their greatest expansion came later, in the seventh century A.D. The maintenance and expansion of such hydraulic works came to constitute one of the major tasks, if not the major task, of the Chinese state. Marshalling labor and taxes for this purpose remained a primary consideration, and the decline of dynasties is associated with their inability to channel resources to that end (Wang 1936).

From the seventh century on, the wealth of China was increased through further agricultural colonization of the area south of the Yangtze River. Significant innovations in the growing of irrigated rice— not only the introduction and expansion of hydraulic works but also improved tools and techniques for preparing the soil and more intensive use of fertilizer—took place in southern Kiangsu and Chekiang. Irrigated rice cultivation spread south from there. This diffusion was sponsored by the Sung dynasty, which had lost control of the area north of

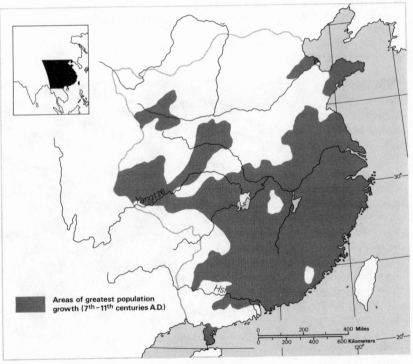

Areas of greatest population growth (7th–11th centuries A.D.)

Han expansion into South China. (Adapted from Elvin, 1973; courtesy of the author)

the Yangtze and therefore had an interest in increasing the productivity of its reduced land. Greater output led to a vast increase in population, and output was in turn facilitated by the greater numbers. Population in the south more than doubled between A.D. 606 and 742, and doubled again between 742 and 1078 (Elvin 1973: 206, 208). In the process, the Chinese (who referred to themselves as Han, in contrast to other ethnic groups) absorbed non-Han populations south of the Yangtze, or pushed them into zones where intensive rice cultivation proved difficult. Thus, the Miao, once found on the lower middle Yangtze, were pushed into Yunnan, Szechuan, and Kweichow; the Yao, who once occupied the mountainous east coast provinces, were displaced into their present habitat in Kweichow. In these areas, where intensive cultivation and Chinese bureaucratic organization could not be supported, localized chiefships and slash-and-burn agriculture prevailed (Fried 1952).

It must not be thought that all irrigation systems were built under the auspices of the state. Most of the hydraulic works of the lower Yangtze region, for instance, were constructed by wealthy landowners. Nevertheless, it is reasonable to suppose that the specific hydraulic requirements of Chinese agriculture influenced the development of the characteristic Chinese bureaucracy. Clearly, many of the tasks sponsored by the state, including control of the hydraulic complexes, transcended the ability of local or regional aristocrats or associations. In creating a manpower pool of potential bureaucrats, the state assured itself of a supply of functionaries who could carry out state-level tasks and stave off the centrifugal influence of local power holders.

This bureaucracy is sometimes referred to as the mandarinate. The mandarins were selected from the gentry class. Their Chinese title is *shen-shih,* or sash-bearing scholar. The sash marked tenure of an imperial office; *scholar* meant acquaintance with the Chinese classics. Tenure in office was theoretically for one lifetime only and could not be inherited. During that lifetime, however, the incumbent was exempt from corvée and taxes, was free of judicial control by the local magistrate, and was permitted to take part in imperial religious ceremonial. Training in etiquette and ideology was based on the study of the classics—especially the sayings and writings of Kung-tse (Confucius), who preached the maintenance of proper social relationships embodied ultimately in the ideal of the "gentleman." Written at a time when the aristocracy was yielding power to rising commoners, the Confucian texts portrayed an aristocratic style of comportment, which could yet be adopted by commoners of merit as well as by nobles. Men trained in such comportment would adhere to religiously sanctioned custom (*li*), and would adjudicate conflict by reference to custom rather than to positive law, *fa.*

Although this class of imperial servants goes back to the first Ch'in emperors and perhaps earlier, it rose to prominence only during the seventh to ninth centuries under the rule of the T'ang, who used it to counteract the power of noble lineages. By the year 1000 the sash bearers were well on the way to gaining economic and political power in their own right. Many of them became large and powerful landowners, farming their estates with serf labor, enjoying exemption from taxation, and handing on their bureaucratic offices to their descendants through the hereditary privilege of *yin*. Just as the aristocrats of earlier periods had fortified their position through the creation of ancestor-based lineages, so the sash-bearing gentry began to create powerful lineage domains managed by an elite of successful members. These patrilineages controlled ancestral halls, lands, and graveyards, and adjudicated internal disputes. They defended common interests against outsiders and enlarged their spheres of influence through marital alliances and political ties. Such lineages were especially prominent in the Chinese South, where they often acted as agents of colonization. Most powerful Chinese lineages, in fact, go back to Sung times, the strategic period of agricultural expansion south of the Yangtze River (Hu 1948: 12–13). It is therefore not surprising that much of the effort of the Ming and Ch'ing emperors, after the restoration of Chinese rule at the end of the fourteenth century, was directed at containing and rolling back the increasingly independent power of the sash bearers. This was attempted first in Ming times through the revocation of the yin privilege and through the institution of mandatory imperial examinations for all applicants for bureaucratic positions. Only in the eighteenth century, however, would the Ch'ing—the Manchu dynasty—attempt to weaken the gentry's hold over the land by liquidating serfdom as an institution.

It should thus be evident that the sash-bearing literati constituted neither a class of philosopher-kings dedicated only to the higher ideals embodied in the state, nor simply a class of local landowners. They served to mesh institutions operating at the level of the state with local and regional arrangements. Inevitably, their position was contradictory and subject to change, depending on whether the encompassing state or local interests gained the upper hand.

If the role and character of the class of sash-bearing literati changed over time, so also did the role and character of the peasantry. The state of Ch'in, which unified China for the first time in 221 B.C., also pioneered legislation that made peasants owners of their land, in return for taxes, corvées, and military service paid directly to the state rather than to some intervening noble (Wittfogel 1931: 50–51; Lattimore 1951: 441–442). Lattimore has pointed out that this also created a category of landless men, who constituted a body of mobile manpower always at the behest of the state (1951: 441–442). This policy of enlarging the free peasantry was continued under the Han, Sui, and early T'ang dynasties, all of which relied on a peasant militia as the backbone of the army. Large estates were often confiscated, and legislation favoring more equitable distribution of land was frequent.

From the mid-eighth century on, however, such legislation lapsed, and large estates increased apace. The peasant militia declined, and peasant exemptions from taxes were lifted. As a result, many peasants either had to seek protection from taxation by binding themselves to a landlord, or sell their land to make ends meet. Others became bound laborers through coercion. While there was also some slavery, it never involved more than a small percentage of the population (Wilbur 1943: 174; Elvin 1973: 74, n.1). Bound labor took two forms. First, there were tenant-serfs, bound to the service of a particular person; their status was heritable, and they could be bought and sold. In theory only sash bearers were allowed to own serfs, but in practice landowners without the sash managed to acquire serfs through the use of the legal fiction of adoption. In addition, there were tenants who were bound to the soil and subject to sale along with the piece of land they cultivated. In 1400 the manor cultivated by bound labor was the dominant form of estate (Balazs 1964: 125; Elvin 1973: 79–80). Only much later, in the 1730s under the Manchu Ch'ing, would serfdom finally be abolished. Declining returns from agriculture in the sixteenth and seventeenth centuries and rising opportunities for profit elsewhere would cause the landowners to relocate their investments. As a result, landowning by peasants would again increase, but under circumstances different from those that had prompted the establishment of a free peasantry during the early Chinese dynasties.

Around 1400 China's relations with the outside world began to change. At earlier times, links of trade and religion had created connections between the Heavenly Kingdom and its neighbors. Under the T'ang (A.D. 618–906) there had been growing contacts with India, and China had opened its doors to the influence of Buddhism approaching from the south. At the time of the Sung (A.D. 960–1279), there had been a great expansion of trade with the southern seas. Under the Mongols (A.D 1280–1367) China had made contact with the West by reopening the old silk routes and bringing Moslem, Christian, and Jewish traders into China. (The Chinese admiral Cheng-ho, who sailed the imperial fleet into the Indian Ocean and to the coast of Africa, was a Moslem.) The Mongol rulers, moreover, preferred Uigur and Nestorian Christians as scribes and advisors, diminishing in the process the role of the Confucian sash bearers.

The expulsion of the Mongols in 1367 and the seizure of power by the Ming reversed the processes that were tying China more strongly to the outside. China folded in on itself and closed off external connections. Perhaps this was due to the nativistic character of the Ming themselves, who sought a return to Chinese roots after 400 years of foreign invasion. Such a reaction was favored by the sash bearers, whose influence had suffered under the Mongols and who stood to gain by a reversal of foreign policy. Certainly China was experiencing economic difficulties; the population sank to a low after the high reached before the Mongol invasions. Perhaps, as Mark Elvin (1973: 298 ff.) has argued, the reversal was the result of an onset of technological stagnation, prompted by the fact that techniques and organization had already reached the limits of productivity possible before the industrial revolution. Certainly the new dynasty put its efforts into ensuring the safety of China's northern frontiers, mobilizing huge armies and constructing the Grand Canal linking south and north to supply the troops. This strategy emphasized the use of internal waterways to the detriment of coastal waterways, now also assailed by Japanese pirates and their Chinese collaborators. Thus, under the Ming China withdrew and abandoned innovation and exploration in favor of stability. Only in the seventeenth century would this pattern change. A coalition of Tungusic Jurchen clans from Manchuria would enlist Mongol help and Chinese collaboration to establish Manchu rule as the last imperial dynasty, the Ch'ing.

Southeast Asia

Where the Indian Ocean and the China Seas converge lie the peninsulas and islands of Southeast Asia, one of the points of intersection of the Indian and Chinese culture spheres. In 1400 this region showed both Indian and Chinese influences. These influences had been superimposed upon an earlier cultural base resting on slash-and-burn or swidden cultivation of unirrigated, dry rice. Such cultivation is still practiced by the "hill people" on the mainland of Southeast Asia and by "tribal" groups in the Indonesian Outer Islands, and it supports their genealogically related and ranked communities. Our voyager would have seen such *ladang* cultivators, who continued alongside the colonists who introduced irrigated rice cultivation and Indian or Chinese cultural forms around the beginning of the Christian era.

Indian influence in the area preceded that of China. The bearers were probably Indian traders. They came accompanied by Brahmins who, with their ritual powers, could induct local chieftains into the caste of rulers, or *kshatriyas*. By bestowing such ritual powers, they created a political infrastructure, much as they had done on the Indian subcontinent itself.

From 200 B.C. to A.D 200 such colonizing groups had settled in mainland Southeast Asia, as well as on the major islands of Sumatra and Java. They grew gradually into more powerful elites, focused upon royal courts and drawing resources from intensive rice cultivation or from trade. The form of the royal court was everywhere quite similar. At its center stood a divine god-king, housed in a palace that was simultaneously temple and redoubt. Associated with the palace were the armed retainers of the king, his kinship group, artisans, and ritual specialists. The court was at once the apex of power and the symbolic core of the universe. Beyond the core lay a world of vassals and allies, contributing the resources that enabled the center to reward its followers and strengthen its base of support. Surpluses were enlarged through the construction of hydraulic works, through the marshalling of labor in corvées, and through colonization. Much of the expanded surplus was invested in building large temple complexes to reinforce the cosmic connection between royal power and the supernatural, such as the Borobudur of central Java (eighth century) and the capitals of Angkor Thom and Angkor Wat in Cambodia (ninth and twelfth centuries). In spite of these efforts to strengthen the royal charisma—and perhaps because of the outlays they involved—such states were frequently unstable and subject to disintegration through dynastic rivalries, rebellion by local lords, and decline in royal power.

The Dutch sociologist J. C. van Leur has contrasted such "inland" states with what he called "harbor principalities," trading ports located on seacoasts and at river mouths. These did not depend on irrigation and labor corvées, but on commerce. Some of their food was obtained from nearby estates worked by slaves; the rest came from the slash-and-burn fields of the "tribal" population, who furnished crops to the commercial emporia through the agency of their chiefs, vassals of the sea king. Merchants played a strategic role in these principalities. They were mostly foreigners, who settled in separate quarters according to their ethnic provenience, each represented politically and commercially by a spokesman. Although some merchants were influential in court circles, they did not come to constitute an independent class, perhaps because of their foreign provenience and cosmopolitan commitments. They remained subject to the prince and his retinue, and modeled their comportment on that of the royal entourage.

The reality was often more complex and hybrid than van Leur's dichotomous ideal types. At least twice, "inland" kingdoms and harbor principalities had come to be organized into larger structures that encompassed both. One such case was the state of Sriviyaya. It expanded between the seventh and tenth centuries from Palembang in eastern Sumatra, which faced on the key commercial route leading through the Straits of Malacca. Clearly a sea power, Sriviyaya occupied Sumatra and much of Java, and in the eighth century it placed a member of its royal dynasty on the Khmer throne of Cambodia. A second instance was the fourteenth-century state of Madjapahit, whose core lay in eastern Java. This was an inland kingdom in structure, but it was widely engaged in trade with China, India, and mainland Southeast Asia. In the course of time it came to occupy Java, Sumatra, the southern Malay peninsula, Borneo, and much of the Philippines. By 1400 Madjapahit was in full decline because of dynastic quarrels and popular rebellions against its exactions, a pattern characteristic of inland states. At the same time, its maritime endeavors were curtailed by Chinese incursion into southern waters, and—more significantly—by the expanding influence of Islam in the commercial world of the Indian Ocean and the China Sea. The disintegration of Hindu-Buddhist Madjapahit was accompanied by the rapid conversion of traders and rulers to Islam in harbor principalities all along the Southeast Asian coasts.

In 1400 the city of Malacca was in ascendance. It had been founded around 1380 by a band of pirates from Sumatra led by a prince from Sriviyaya, who were in rebellion against Madjapahit. Toward the end of the century, the prince converted to Islam, attracting to Malacca the rich Muslim trading community of Pasai in Sumatra. His companions became the chief officials of the new emporium, furnishing the war leader, the collector of customs, and the joint post of treasurer, chief justice, and master of royal ceremonies. There were four major trading communities in the city, each headed by a representative: the Gujaratis, the Kalingas and Bengalis, the traders from the archipelago, and the Chinese. The Portuguese Tomé Pires, writing of Malacca a century later, estimated a population of 40,000 to 50,000, with sixty-one "nations" represented in its trade. It was, he said, of "such importance and profit that it seems to me it has no equal in the world. Whoever is lord of Malacca has his hands on the throat of Venice."

Islam provided a ready-made ideological link among the Muslim trading emporia that ranged from the ports of the Indian Ocean to the Sulu islands of the Philippines. Wandering Sufi preachers carried the message into the hinterland, where Islamic mysticism entered into a syncretic mix with the beliefs in personalized forces held by the population. Above all, Islam imparted ideological legitimacy to the new harbor princes or pirate chiefs, who, as Muslim sultans, could act as "shadows of God upon earth." The religious conversion of the ports reopened, in a new way, the antagonism between inland states and harbor principalities, this time to the clear advantage of the lords of trade. Eventually Islam would come to dominate the inland areas as well. Only in Bali would a group of Hindu-Buddhist refugees maintain intact the older ideological cult of the island world.

The New World

No Ibn Battuta, Marco Polo, or Cheng-ho has left us a record of travels in the New World. It is possible, however, to use archaeological, linguistic, and ethnohistorical evidence to reconstruct what a voyager might have seen in the Americas in A.D. 1400.

Such evidence makes interconnections among different cultural regions of the Western Hemisphere highly probable, and—in some cases—virtually certain. Archaeologists have come to speak of areas that exhibit strong internal resemblances as "interaction areas," on the grounds that the wide diffusion of similar tools, architectural forms, and art styles within the areas are probable indicators of contact, and hence of social relationships. In 1400 there were two interaction orbits of "high contour," as archaeologist Gordon Willey has put it. These two areas are characterized archaeologically by the remains of intensive cultivation, including irrigation; large and densely populated settlements, including cities built around impressive works of architecture, such as temples or palaces; craft products, such as pottery or weaving, clearly made for high-status elites; and massive evidence of an ideological superstructure through which the goals of these elite-ruled orbits were manifested to the population at large. One such interaction area of high contour was the Central Andes, in what is today Peru and Bolivia. This area would form, in the course of the fifteenth century, the heartland of the Inca empire; but in 1400 the Inca were still a group of rustic parvenus occupying a small polity whose capital was the highland town of Cuzco. The other area was Mesoamerica, located in the highlands of present-day Mexico and Guatemala and in the adjacent lowlands. This was the area inhabited at the time of the Spanish Conquest by the Aztecs and the Maya. In 1400, however, our traveler would hardly have noticed the Aztecs, then a minor group of mercenaries in the service of a larger state, while the Maya were engaged in internecine quarrels among epigonal elites disputing the heritage of a more glorious past.

South America

The strategic arena for agricultural intensification and for the rise of overarching political systems in South America was the Andean belt of mountains extending along the continent's western flanks. The Andes consist of great longitudinal ranges, with peaks of 15,000 to 20,000 feet rising above the upland basins, and plains that formed the arenas of human habitation. From the western cordillera the mountains descend to the Pacific coast, a narrow desertlike strip transected at intervals by small river valleys reaching down from the mountain slopes to the sea. Both the desert and the mountainsides have been in cultivation for millennia—the desert by means of canal irrigation, the mountains through the construction of massive terraces and spillways.

It is characteristic of the Andean area that the coast, the piedmont, the altiplano highlands, and the tundra steppe (puna) afford very different environments and resources, and hence require and enable different human activities. People on the coast could raise cotton in favored oases and gather the dung of seabirds as fertilizer. The piedmont could produce maize and peppers. The highlands furnished potatoes and quinoa. In the puna shepherds herded llamas for meat and wool and gathered salt. On the eastern vertient of the Andes people grew coca and could acquire honey, lumber, feathers, and other products of the forest. At the same time, the activities of different zones often interdigitated. Thus, the altitudinal limits of crops could be raised by fertilizing them with dung accumulated by llama herders. Digging ponds and drainage ditches at lower altitudes not only aided agriculture, but the increased water supplies and fodder crops also allowed herding to expand into lower altitudes (Orlove 1977). It has been argued (Murra 1972) that such close proximity of altitudinal levels and their interdigitation placed a premium on the social organization of productive activities. This has led Andean populations at all levels of social complexity—hamlet, village, region, kingdom, empire—to attempt to control the widest possible range of ecological zones at different elevations. It has favored, moreover, the systematic concentration of the resources of these zones by some superordinate authority that could then reassign them among the zones. This, Murra has argued, underlies the Andean proclivity to organize exchange systems through reciprocity and redistribution, rather than through open exchanges by private parties and markets. Compared to other areas of the world with intensive systems of cultivation and state systems, where resources were usually traded in markets, the Andes showed a tendency to channel the movement of goods through the hands of hierarchically organized representatives of political groups.

At the time the Spaniards arrived, the whole area from north of Manta in Ecuador to the Maulé River in Chile was under the sway of the Inca, but in 1400 their expansion had barely begun. The period preceding Inca domination, between A.D. 1000 and 1476, was in fact a period of political fragmentation. It is classified by archaeologists as the Late Intermediate, because it occurred between an earlier period of unification and the later Inca unity. There was an effort at political consolidation between A.D. 800 and 1200. Archaeological sites show two widely ranging art styles, each connected with a city: Tiahuanaco in the southern basin of Lake Titicaca, and Wari in the Ayacucho Valley of the Central Andes. Tiahuanaco motifs, such as the "gateway god" with jaguar mouth and serpent-ray headdress (a prototype of the Inca god Viracocha) and a feline god, dominate in the Titicaca Basin and southward into the Cochabamba region, as far as the arid southern Atacama rim. Willey has suggested that this style was carried by actual colonists, perhaps by colonizing elites. The city of Wari to the north was located in the basin of the Mantaro River. Its early growth was probably stimulated by Tiahuanaco. Its sphere of influence was marked especially by multicolored pottery bearing the emblems of the Tiahuanaco mythological figures and animals. This style was probably carried by dominant elites that established themselves in local political and religious centers reaching from the Urubamba Basin to the middle Marañón, and from Ocono to Chicama on the coast. Later Wari settlements were made up of planned compounds, a pattern possibly derived from the coast and an early evidence of the modes of planning that marked later Andean polities. Such planning involved food distribution from state-managed storehouses on a territorial basis, as well as the placing of control stations along highways and near important settlements.

By A.D. 1250 these two larger political systems had broken up into several distinct polities. A number of states fought for control of the highlands. Other states dominated sections of the coast. The most important of these was Chimu, which ruled the northern coast from Chira to Supe. Its capital, Chanchan, was located in the Moche Valley; covering a site of at least six square miles, it was divided into ten separate

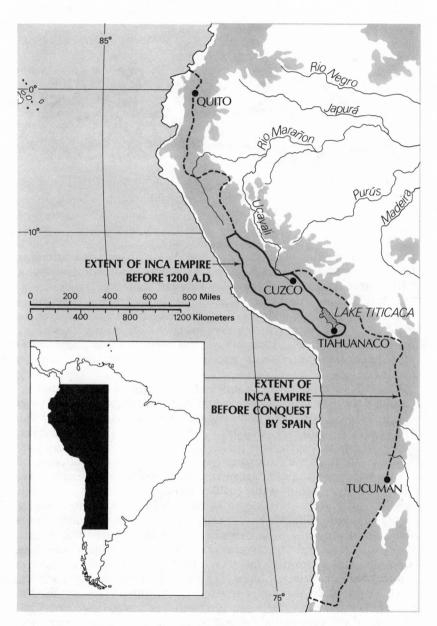

The Andean Area.

Warfare, depicted on painted pottery, Moche style, North Coast Peru, c. A.D. 400. (Courtesy of Christopher Donnan, Museum of Cultural History, Los Angeles)

walled quadrangles, each containing residential structures, courtyards, sunken reservoirs, and tombs. Beyond this elite center were provincial administrative towns and numerous hamlets. There is evidence of massive fortifications throughout the Chimu domain, and a large multi-valley canal system supplied forts and centers with water. Traffic moved over major highways, which served to carry on trade and to reinforce political control over several valleys. It is likely that this Chimu polity provided or transmitted some of the patterns of control later utilized by the Inca.

The Inca in 1400 formed a statelet in the upper reaches of the Urubamba Basin; the Inca dynasty would then have been about 200 years old. It was only with the ninth dynastic ruler, Pachacuti Inca Yupanqui (1438–1471), however, that Inca expansion began. Inca expansion would be spearheaded by a professional army; conquests were consolidated through the construction of highways and control points.

Inca society during its phase of imperial growth can be described as a hierarchy organized into the godlike Inca dynasty, carrier of the state religion; an aristocracy made up of relatives of the dynasty, as well as local rulers who submitted to Inca rule; a category of local men of rank standing at the head of landowning endogamous patrilineal descent groups (*ayllus*); and the members of the descent groups themselves. Men paid tribute through labor on public works, in agriculture, or in military service. Women spent much of their time weaving, and the cloth so produced was concentrated in Inca storehouses and used to remunerate faithful subjects; woven cloth was charged with extraordinary ritual and ceremonial value. The state undertook to colonize new agricultural lands, especially in areas lying along the piedmont of the mountain ranges where maize could be grown. The state also maintained irrigation works and roads, as well as an extraordinary postal system, which employed runners to speed messages from one end of the realm to the other. Anyone who submitted peacefully to Inca demands was assured of a place within this hierarchical and well-organized scheme of things; but refusal was answered with war, and rebellious groups were relocated far from their places of origin.

North of Peru the Andes continue into Ecuador and then descend in ramifying mountain chains to the coastal lowlands. The highland basins of Ecuador are neither as large nor as productive as those in Peru, but their climate resembles that of the Central Andes, and the major crops were the Andean potato and quinoa. Further north, however, where the mountains enter the subtropics and the tropics, the major crop came to be maize. This zone is characterized by an extraordinary variability in local microclimates, which were exploited in highly variable ways through slash-and-burn cultivation, soil selection, terracing, and canal irrigation. The scale of these activities was always narrow and environmentally circumscribed.

This northern rim of the Andean heartland was characterized by small-scale political domains under local rulers, or by federations of such domains under a paramount. In southern Ecuador the most important of these federations was the Canari. The Inca subdued them without difficulty in the 1450s, but only sixty years later they would ally themselves with the Spaniards to shake off the Inca yoke. In northern Ecuador the Cara federation, organized under hereditary chiefs, offered greater resistance to the Inca.

On the Ecuadorian coast a league of seagoing towns had formed under a paramount whose capital was at Manta. A dense population was supported here by intensive cultivation of the terraced hillsides, as well as by extensive trade. The people of Manta were excellent navigators, using balsa and log rafts, and probably entertained important trade relations with Mesoamerica. The scale of trade in this area is attested to by the Spanish capture, soon after their arrival, of a large balsa raft equipped with sails and cabin, manned by a crew of twenty, and laden with thirty tons of luxury merchandise.

In Colombia, to the north, the most important polities were those of the Chibcha and the Tairona. The Chibcha occupied highland basins in the areas of present-day Cundinamarca and Boyacá. There were two major Chibcha states, headed by rulers known as the Zipa and the Zaque, and several minor independent polities. At the time of the Spanish Conquest the Zipa dominated, having consolidated his own realm against several rivals in the fifteenth century and established ascendance over the Zaque in the early sixteenth century. The Zipa domain, controlling a population of between 120,000 and 160,000 (Villamarín and Villamarín 1979: 31), was organized hierarchically. Groups of households formed captaincies, which in turn formed semi-autonomous communities each owing loyalty to the Zipa. The Zipa's capital has been identified with a large site near modern-day Funza and appears to have been a highly concentrated town of thatch-roofed temples, palaces, warehouses, and residences. Economically, the state was supported by the production of maize, potatoes, and quinoa on ridged fields and hillside terraces. The aristocracy who managed the state drew tribute in kind and labor from the population of commoners, and traded produce and textiles to the lowlands for the gold they needed for ritual and for conspicuous consumption. There is evidence that the Chibcha elite exercised wide-ranging cultural hegemony through the development of a religious cult based on the privileged acquisition of esoteric supernatural knowledge.

The Tairona were located to the north of the Chibcha in the Sierra Nevada de Santa Marta, a block of mountains close to the Caribbean Sea. Their political organization seems to have resembled that of the Chibcha, with several semiautonomous communities forming a domain under a paramount ruler. These rulers lived in large centers, of which the Buritaca 200 site furnishes an example. The site, which was occupied A.D. 1360 to 1635, spreads out over a thousand acres along the ridge of the steep Corea Mountain on the northern slope of the Sierra. The center consists of elaborate constructions in stairways, ditches, roadways, retaining walls, and terraces, arranged in different zones for residential use, work, public functions, and religious ritual. Intensive cultivation of terraced hillsides, making use of irrigation and crop rotation, furnished the subsistence base of maize, beans, manioc, sweet potatoes, and chili. Excavations of burials at the site have yielded fine pottery and gold work.

The Chibcha, Tairona, and other populations of Colombia were involved in incessant warfare. This warfare was ceremonial and a means of gaining status, but it had economic functions as well. As Reichel-Dolmatoff has noted, those populations in Colombia inhabiting regions of low rainfall and producing only a single harvest of maize tended to invade more fertile territories with two or three annual harvests, making the eighty-inch isohyet "practically a military frontier" (1961: 86). Warfare also provided slaves for field labor and domestic service, and for sacrifice and culinary cannibalism.

The pattern whereby local communities with their own heads were organized into larger domains under paramount rulers characterized a number of other areas: the Caribbean lowlands, the islands of the Greater Antilles, and the Mojos Plain in southern Bolivia. In the Venezuelan lowlands and the Caribbean islands, such domains were built upon the cultivation of maize and bitter manioc, together with maritime resources. The polities of the Mojos Plain grew sweet manioc and maize on riverine savannas that were ridged to control flooding. This area was in contact with the Andean highlands. We know, for instance, that Mojo merchants traveled to the Aymara country to exchange cotton cloth and feathers for metal tools and ornaments. It was by this route that Andean precious metals and copper passed down as far as the upper Paraguay River, where the first conquistadores learned of a fabulous kingdom to the west called the Realm of the Great Mojo. Inca gold ornaments also passed down the Ucayali River as part of intergroup trade in the tropical Montaña.

East of the Andes lies the tropical rain forest of interior South America. It was populated largely by slash-and-burn cultivators, who grew bitter (poisonous) manioc and obtained protein by hunting and fishing. The population was generally organized into large coresidential units, which recruited their members through rules of exogamy and post-marital residence. The network of kin relations thus extended across local groups. Leaders might organize warfare, redistribute food and other goods, and aid in the resolution of conflicts through the management of consensus. They lacked, however, any institutionalized apparatus for applying sanctions. Relations between humans and nonhumans, as codified in myth, were conceptualized as relations between various kinds of forces, and these were managed by shamans who made contact with the supernatural through the use of hallucinogens. Upon the arrival of the Europeans, tropical-forest populations would be subject to decimation by illness, slave raiding, surplus extraction, and outright genocide; it is therefore likely that in A.D. 1400 their numbers were considerably higher than in historic times.

There were apparently important connections between the peoples of the tropical forest and those of the Andes. The tropical forest was probably the source of a number of the crops successfully cultivated on the arid Pacific coast, such as the sweet potato, sweet manioc, and peanuts. Throughout Andean history, products of the eastern slopes, such as coca, feathers, jaguar skins, fish poisons, and medicines, were exchanged for highland produce and crafts. The Inca were, however, unable to subdue populations in the tropical forest. A war against the head-hunting Jívaro, whose land was rich in placer gold, failed. Similarly, Inca efforts to advance southeastward into the lowlands was halted in the area occupied by the Mosetene.

Southward from the Central Andes, highland cultural patterns had been carried into the arid belt of northern Chile and Argentina, first in Tiahuanaco times and later under the Inca. Llama herding became extensive in this area, but crops were also grown on terraces and by means of irrigation. The Atacameño were known for their far-flung carrying trade, by means of which coastal products like fish and salt were exchanged for highland commodities such as llama wool and tobacco. The Diaguita were renowned for their metallurgy; but what the Inca sought in their expansion into Diaguita territory, as in Picunche terrain farther south, were the precious metals themselves—gold, silver, and copper. The Inca also incorporated the Araucanian-speaking Picunche into their empire, but the Araucanian-speakers to the south—the Mapuche and Huilliche—proved unconquerable. These people were potato cultivators and llama herders organized in autonomous localized lineages loosely federated under war chiefs. In the wet beech and cedar forests south of the Bío-Bío River, Andean ecological and political patterns encountered their southern limit, and Inca attempts to penetrate farther failed.

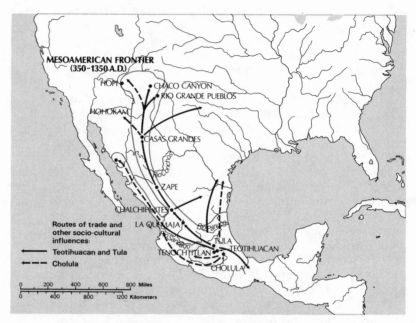

Mesoamerica. (Adapted from Weigand, 1978; courtesy of the author)

Mesoamerica

In Mesoamerica our observer in A.D. 1400 would have encountered a scene of even greater political fragmentation than in the Andean area at that time. Teotihuacan, a major center in the Valley of Mexico, had in the first century A.D. established its hegemony over wide areas reaching at least as far south as Kaminaljuyu, near present-day Guatemala City, and Tikal, in the heart of the forested Petén. At its height the city of Teotihuacan concentrated within its precinct an estimated 150,000 to 200,000 people, nearly depopulating the surrounding areas. The agricultural technology that supported it probably included canal irrigation and intensive drainage of the nearby alluvial lakeshores. The city controlled major obsidian mines and contained numerous workshops that produced obsidian tools. Yet by A.D. 700 the far-flung Teotihuacano system had disintegrated.

The reasons for this collapse are not well understood. It is likely that the religious and political mechanisms for control of the population failed as agricultural productivity reached a critical limit of expansion. Thereafter, people moved back into the rural areas in large numbers to smaller settlements closer to their home fields. At the same time, there appears to have been a massive failure in the system of trade. This is suggested by the outward movement of warlike bands northward toward the source of turquoise and southward toward the lands of precious feathers, gold, and cacao beans, then the major medium of monetary exchange.

The fall of Teotihuacan brought in its wake the decline of the Maya cities in the tropical forests of the Petén. Perhaps they too encountered some critical limit in the expansion of their drained−field agriculture. Conceivably, they too had overconcentrated the population of urban complexes. Or, as Rathje has suggested, the producers of obsidian and basalt on the periphery of the Maya area may no longer have been willing to supply these items (which the Maya centers lacked) in return for religious indulgences; instead, they may have attempted to take into their own hands the exchange networks involving precious goods.

After the fall of Teotihuacan, various warlike elites, flourishing different symbols of political legitimacy, appropriated the city's patrimony. These successor states contested one another's spoils and spread out in various directions in search of new horizons. For a brief time the center of gravity within the Mesoamerican heartland shifted northward, apparently to Tula in Hidalgo, outside the Valley of Mexico. Tula became the capital of a Toltec domain, less an integrated "empire" than an epicenter of groups of warriors, traders, cultivators, and priests employing the Toltec name and symbols as charters for conquest and colonization. Some groups migrated farther northward, expanding cultivation into the arid zone north of the Mexican plateau. Toltec colonists or traders in search of turquoise, alum, salt, incense, and raw copper

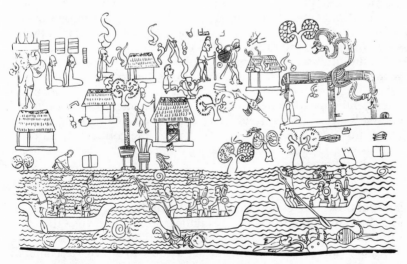

Mural from the Temple of the Warriors, Chichén Itzá, Yucatan, c. A.D. 1200, depicting warriors in boats, villagers pursuing daily tasks, and an offertory (upper right). (Courtesy of the American Museum of Natural History, New York)

may have reached as far as the present southwestern United States.

Other groups moved southward to conquer Nicaragua, highland Guatemala, and Yucatán. In Yucatán a war band of Chontal-speaking Putún from lowland Tabasco assumed control in the twelfth century, establishing a capital at Chichén Itzá. This move may have been an attempt to dominate the trade that carried salt, cotton cloth, honey, copal incense, and slaves from Tabasco to Honduras, returning with cacao, gold, jade, and obsidian from Central America. These Putún appear to have been allied with the highland Toltecs at Tula. When Tula declined after A.D. 1200 Putún-controlled Chichén Itzá declined as well. A Putún splinter group moved to a new center at Mayapan, until that city too collapsed in the middle of the fifteenth century and gave way to a multitude of warring statelets.

In the Valley of Mexico itself, the Mesoamerican heartland, our visitor of 1400 would have witnessed conflict and strife among five distinctive city-states, each dominated by an independent ruling elite. One of these city-states, Azcapozalco, ruled by a group of Otomí-speaking Tepanec, was then clearly gaining in power. It is unlikely, however, that anyone could have predicted at that time the destruction of that city only thirty years later at the hands of the Aztec (or, as they are properly called, Colhua-Mexica), then a mere band of mercenaries in service to the Tepanec.

North America

Two streams of Mesoamerican influence were carried into North America after A.D. 1000. One of these may have been brought by "Toltec" colonists and traders into the arid Southwest. There the newcomers influenced the Hohokam, who lived on irrigated farmlands in the Gila River Basin, and the Anasazi of the Colorado Plateau, known for their large multihousehold complexes supported by intensive cultivation with irrigation and terracing. Most of the characteristic Southwestern ceremonial art derives from the end of the Toltec period (about A.D. 1300) and appears to be a fusion of the Mesoamerican cult of the rain god with local religious traditions (Kelley 1966: 107–108). Soon afterward, however, the frontiers of sedentary life contracted sharply, as increasing aridity and warfare made it more difficult to occupy marginal agricultural areas.

The extension of Mesoamerican influence northwest into the desert was paralleled by a spread northeast into the warm and humid woodlands and riverine embayments near the confluence of the Mississippi, Missouri, and Ohio rivers. The resulting culture is known as the Mississippian. In contrast to the arid west, where the route of Mesoamerican influence can now be reconstructed, the route by which Mesoamerican prototypes of settlement pattern, architecture, and ceremonial art styles reached the Mississippian coast remains unknown. The great terraced earthen platforms, arranged around plazas and bearing temples, elite residences, and other buildings, show a generic relationship to features found in Mexico, as do the striking artistic depictions—weeping and winged eyes, human hands with eyes or crosses on them, and human skulls and long bones—associated with the so-called "Southern cult." Precise parallels, however, occur only in ceramic techniques and dental mutilations. Contact with Mesoamerican long-distance traders, like the Aztec *pochteca*, has been suggested as an explanation of the Mesoamerican-like traits, but it is unclear what such merchants might have been seeking in the eastern woodlands.

The Mississippian superseded an older culture complex known as Burial Mound. Burial Mound takes its name from the practice of burying the dead under mounds with elaborate, status-ranked grave goods obtained from regions as widely separated as Wyoming and the East Coast. These grave goods bespeak the presence of a stratum of high rank, which communicated over wide areas through a common system of symbols. Despite this wide-ranging interaction, local food systems were highly variable, including wild fauna and flora and local cultigens (like sunflower and sumpweed), as well as maize.

The Mississippians, in contrast, relied heavily on the cultivation of maize, squash, and beans. This subsistence base supported a pattern of settlement focused on large towns with temple mounds and plazas, which were surrounded by smaller towns with mounds, ringed about in turn by moundless villages. Colonies of Mississippians moved outward from the center around Cahokia (near modern St. Louis) as far away as Wisconsin and Georgia. This migration carried with it the Southern cult, which like the earlier Burial Mound focused on lavish disposal of the dead, but gave special emphasis to prowess in warfare. The cult may have had important political functions. Spiro Mound in Oklahoma, one of its major sites, seems to have been a "headquarters from which the politically significant descendants of the honored dead drew their ideological power" (Brown 1975: 15). The raw materials for this mortuary art, such as copper and shells, were drawn from a wide radius extending from north of Lake Superior to the Florida shoals.

Spreading out centrifugally from the Central Mississippi Valley, the Mississippians encountered and affected cultures of the Burial Mound type all around them. When the Mississippian power declined after A.D. 1300, perhaps due to intensified warfare, these regional cultures re-emerged. These cultures were antecedents of several of the groups that met the incoming Europeans: the Iroquois at the headwaters of the Ohio; the Cherokee in the southern Appalachians; the Natchez on the lower Mississippi; and the Pawnee, Mandan, and other "village Indians" on the Missouri, who combined village-centered cultivation with annual summer bison hunts. The Iroquois and the "village Indians" would become conspicuous participants in the fur trade (chapter 6), and the Cherokees would be displaced in the development of the Cotton South (chapter 9). The Natchez, however, would pass from

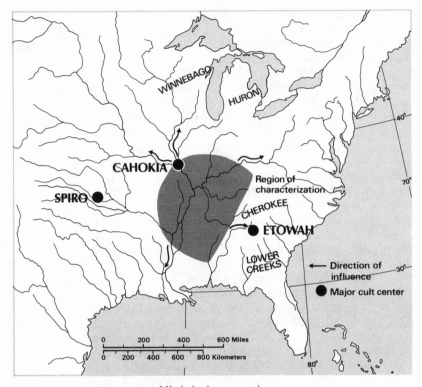

Mississippian expansion.

view. Their complex system of stratification—into a royal lineage of "Suns" pivoted upon a Great Village, two collateral ranked lineages of nobles, and a category of commoners called "stinkards"—seems to have been the outcome of contact between the Mississippians and an earlier Caribbean-like Gulf tradition. The French would decimate the Natchez in the eighteenth century, selling many into slavery in the West Indies; remnants would join the Creek and Cherokee. They would live on in the European imagination, however, through Chateaubriand's fanciful novel *Atala*.

Our voyager of A.D. 1400 would thus have witnessed great political fragmentation in the two areas of "high contour" in the Americas, as well as rampant warfare among the polities surrounding the zones of Andean and Mesoamerican influence. Beyond the belt of war-making statelets and federations adjacent to the two core areas lay still other zones of horticultural occupation, in the tropical forests of South America and in the northeastern woodlands of North America.

When slash-and-burn cultivators expanded into these zones, they impinged on hunters and gatherers, who retreated into marginal areas.

These food collectors varied greatly in their use of resources available in such environments. Along the ocean shores of both Americas, such groups as the hunters of the Arctic circumpolar belt, the fishermen and sea-mammal hunters of the North American Pacific coast, and the shellfish gatherers of the Chilean archipelago exploited maritime resources. In the mountains and steppes not utilized by cultivators, other groups foraged for game and wild plants, as did the hunters of the northern Boreal forest, the acorn-and-seed gatherers of Arid America from montane California down to the Mesoamerican frontier, and the guanaco and rhea hunters of the South American Chaco and pampa. Sometimes expanding into cultivable zones where they challenged the cultivators, as in Arid America after the fall of Teotihuacan, sometimes exploiting zones not amenable to cultivation with the agricultural technologies then available, they maintained themselves in these habitats until the advent of the Europeans.

* * *

Everywhere in this world of 1400, populations existed in interconnections. Groups that defined themselves as culturally distinct were linked by kinship or ceremonial allegiance; states expanded, incorporating other peoples into more encompassing political structures; elite groups succeeded one another, seizing control of agricultural populations and establishing new political and symbolic orders. Trade formed networks from East Asia to the Levant, across the Sahara, from East Africa through the Indian Ocean to the Southeast Asian archipelago. Conquest, incorporation, recombination, and commerce also marked the New World. In both hemispheres populations impinged upon other populations through permeable social boundaries, creating intergrading, interwoven social and cultural entities. If there were any isolated societies these were but temporary phenomena—a group pushed to the edge of a zone of interaction and left to itself for a brief moment in time. Thus, the social scientist's model of distinct and separate systems, and of a timeless "precontact" ethnographic present, does not adequately depict the situation before European expansion; much less can it comprehend the worldwide system of links that would be created by that expansion.

In following our traveler on his voyage, we have not as yet taken him to Europe, which was then about to launch its great expansion overseas. For a long time Europe was of little account in the affairs of the wider world, "the land of the Franks on the western seas" to the Arabs. The Portuguese, the first Europeans to reach Asia, became known as *Feringhi* in Malaya and *Fo-lang-ki* in China. Only gradually did the Chinese learn to distinguish between the Portuguese and the Jesuits from "I-ta-li" who were at Portuguese Macao, and between the Dutch (*Ho-lan*) and the English. On the other side of the world, the Aztec ruler would wonder whether the arriving Spaniards were gods or men, although an empirically minded Tlaxcaltec war leader solved the problem by holding a Spanish prisoner under water until he died like any other mortal. In the Pacific the incoming Europeans came to be known as Cookies, after Captain Cook. The speed and intensity with which these "red-haired, high-nosed external barbarians" imposed themselves on different parts of the world demands that we take a special look at Europe. We do so in chapter 4.

3 Modes of Production

In our survey of the world in 1400 we let our imaginary traveler roam among the populations of four continents. We sketched out, in the process, the different social systems and varied cultural understandings that Europe would later encounter in the course of its expansion. To grasp the strategic features of this variability analytically as well as descriptively, we will employ the Marxian concept of the "mode of production." We will first discuss the premises of the concept, and then delineate the modes that will allow us to point to the central processes at work in the interaction of Europeans with the majority of the world's peoples.

Production and Social Labor

In formulating the mode of production concept, Marx began with two axiomatic understandings of the human condition. Both are also axioms of modern anthropology. The first sees the species *Homo sapiens* as a part of nature; the second defines *Homo* as a social species, its individual members always linked to others in social relationships. The human species is an outgrowth of natural processes; at the same time, the species is naturally social.

The human species is, however, not merely a passive product of natural processes; it has also, in the course of evolution, acquired the ability to transform nature to human use. If humanity stands to nature as part to whole, then that part has acquired the ability to oppose the whole that encompasses it; or, as Marx phrased it, man "confronts the material of nature as one of her own forces. . . . [By] changing it, he at the same time changes his own nature" (quoted in Schmidt 1971: 77–78). This active relation of the species to nature, while rooted in biological characteristics, is put into effect by the exosomatic means of technology, organization, and ideas. Man rises up against nature by means of what we would today call culture.

Marx's second axiom emphasizes the sociality of humankind. Human beings exist in organized pluralities. Moreover, the way they are organized socially governs the way they confront and transform nature, and nature thus transformed affects, in turn, the architecture of human social bonds. In Marx's words, "the restricted relation of men to nature determines their restricted relation to one another, and their restricted relation to one another determines men's restricted relation to nature" (quoted in Colletti 1973: 228).

Is there a concept that allows us to grasp this complex connection between a socially interrelated humanity and nature? Marx found such a concept in his notion of labor. Humankind adapts to nature and transforms it for its own use through labor. Thus, "the labor process . . . is the general condition for the metabolism between men and nature; it is the everlasting nature-imposed condition of human existence" (quoted in Schmidt 1971: 136). Yet labor is always social, for it is always mobilized and deployed by an organized social plurality. Marx therefore drew a distinction between work and labor. Work represents the activities of individuals, singly or in groups, expending energy to produce energy. But labor and the labor process was for him a social phenomenon, carried on by human beings bonded to one another in society.

This concept of labor as a social process carried on by an organized plurality could not be imagined as long as different kinds of work—cultivating, spinning, praying—were thought of as qualitatively different. Only when different kinds of work could be subsumed under the common denominator of money did "labor-in-general" become conceivable. Marx credited Adam Smith with the first formulation of this concept, noting that this "immense step forward" occurred precisely when different kinds of labor had become interchangeable (*Gr.* 1973: 104), that is, after the onset of capitalism. The utility of the concept, however, transcends its particular historical origins. Once one can talk about labor-in-general, one can begin to visualize how any organized human society activates this process and shares out its products.

Understanding how humans transform nature to their use thus does not stop with the description and analysis of techno-environmental interaction. The laborer, the direct producer, is never an isolated Robinson Crusoe but is someone who always stands in relationship to others, as kinsman, serf, slave, or wage laborer. Similarly, the controllers of social labor are not to be thought of as technicians who guide the technical operations of work. They are assigned to their positions by the system of deploying social labor, which casts them in the role of elder kinsman, chief, seignorial lord, or capitalist. It is this conception of social mobilization, deployment, and allocation of labor that allows us to understand how the technical transformation of nature is conjoined with the organization of human sociality.

Marx adopted the term *production* for this complex set of mutually dependent relations among nature, work, social labor, and social organization. We shall use the term in this sense in the present work. Because modern usage often restricts it exclusively to technology, it is important to be aware of the background that evoked it. The concept of production was employed by Marx to contrast his perspective with Hegel's conception of *Geist* ("Spirit"). It thus carries overtones of Marx's confrontation with Hegelian idealism. For Hegel the various human transformations of nature represented successive concretizations of Spirit or Mind ("models of" and "models for"). Marx's use of *production* also contrasts with Feuerbach's contemplative materialism. Feuerbach had criticized Hegel for treating thought as transcendental rather than as an attribute of natural humankind. Yet he took account neither of human sociality nor of the human confrontation with nature. Marx, in contrast, stressed the activity of socially organized humankind in a double sense—active in changing nature, and in creating and re-creating the social ties that effect the transformation of the environment. The term *production* expressed for him both this active engagement with nature and the concomitant "reproduction" of social ties.

It is also important to note that Marx's concept of production incorporates his insistence that the human species produces with both hand and head. In contrast to other animals, humans conceptualize and plan the labor process. Labor thus presupposes intentionality, and therefore information and meaning. Just as labor is always social labor, information and meaning are always social. As Marx put it, thought does not descend from on high into the real world; thought and language "are only manifestations of actual life" (quoted in Coletti 1973: 225). Social labor with both hand and head is deployed to cope with nature; the deployment of social labor, in turn, reproduces both the material and the ideational ties of human sociality.

Modes of Production

The concept of social labor thus makes it possible to conceptualize the major ways in which human beings organize their production. Each major way of doing so constitutes a mode of production—a specific, historically occurring set of social relations through which labor is deployed to wrest energy from nature by means of tools, skills, organization, and knowledge.

What modes of deploying social labor are there? Marx himself spoke of a number of different modes: an original, primitive, communitarian mode, conceived after Morgan's model of primitive communism; the slaveholding mode of classical European antiquity; a Germanic mode, supposedly characteristic of the Germanic peoples in their early migrations; a Slavonic mode, said to characterize the early Slavs; a peasant mode; a feudal mode; an Asiatic mode; and a capitalist mode. Not all of these are based on equivalent criteria. Some may never have constituted primary modes in their own right, but may have been only accessory or supplementary modes; others represent extrapolations from historical interpretations now adjudged to have been erroneous.

For the purposes of this book, it is immaterial whether Marx was right or wrong—whether he should have postulated two or eight or fifteen modes of production, or whether other modes should be substituted for those suggested by him. The utility of the concept does not lie in *classification* but in its capacity to underline the strategic relationships involved in the deployment of social labor by organized human pluralities. Since we want to deal with the spread of the capitalist mode and its impact on world areas where social labor was allocated differently, we shall construct only those modes that permit us to exhibit this encounter in the most parsimonious manner. For this purpose we shall define but three: a capitalist mode, a tributary mode, and a kin-ordered mode. No argument is presented here to the effect that this trinity exhausts all the possibilities. For other problems and issues it may be useful to construct other modes drawing further distinctions, or to group together differently the distinctions drawn here.

Nor is there any intention, in the present context, to argue that these three modes represent an evolutionary sequence. While we shall explore certain historical relations between modes, it is a major argument of this book that most of the societies studied by anthropologists are an outgrowth of the expansion of Europe and not the pristine precipitates of past evolutionary stages. This position extends the caveats already introduced by other writers against the uncritical equation of the bands, tribes, or chiefdoms described by observers since 1400 with the societies existing before European expansion and even before the rise of the state (Service 1968: 167; Fried 1966, 1975). Fried has stated resolutely that the "tribe" is "a secondary sociopolitical phenomenon, brought about by the intercession of more complex ordered societies, states in particular" (1975: 114). I believe that all human societies of which we have record are "secondary," indeed often tertiary, quaternary, or centenary. Cultural change or cultural evolution does not operate on isolated societies but always on interconnected systems in which societies are variously linked within wider "social fields." One of the utilities of the concept of mode of production lies precisely in that it allows us to visualize intersystemic as well as intrasystemic relationships. We shall use the concept to reveal the changing ways in which one mode, capitalism, interacted with other modes to achieve its present dominance. In this process Iroquois, Asante, Tamil, and Chinese are as much participants as Barbadians, New Englanders, and Poles. The process linked victims and beneficiaries, contenders and collaborators.

The three modes that we employ should not be taken as schemes for pigeonholing societies. The two concepts—mode of production and society—pertain to different levels of abstraction. The concept of society takes its departure from real or imputed interactions among people. The concept of mode of production aims, rather, at revealing the political-economic relationships that underlie, orient, and constrain interaction. Such key relationships may characterize only a part of the total range of interactions in a society; they may comprehend all of a society; or they may transcend particular, historically constituted systems of social interaction. Used comparatively, the concept of mode of production calls attention to major variations in political-economic arrangements and allows us to visualize their effect. The use of the concept enables us, above all, to inquire into what happens in the encounters of differently constituted systems of interaction—societies—predicated upon different modes of production.

We shall begin our exposition with the capitalist mode, despite the fact that it developed later than the others, in the course of the eighteenth century. It was in the analysis of this mode that Marx developed his general concepts, and we follow him in his conviction that an understanding of how this mode works provides the key to the understanding of others.

The Capitalist Mode

Marx spent most of his life on the analysis of the capitalist mode of production. He did so, of course, to understand it in such a way that he could help put an end to it. What, according to him, were its salient characteristics?

For Marx, the capitalist mode came into being when monetary wealth was enabled to buy labor power. This specific capability is not an inherent attribute of wealth as such; it develops historically and requires the installation of certain prerequisites. Labor power is not in itself a commodity created in order to be offered for sale in a market. It is an attribute of human beings, a capability of *Homo sapiens*. As long as people can lay their hands on the means of production (tools, resources, land) and use these to supply their own sustenance—under whatever social arrangements—there is no compelling reason for them to sell their capacity to work to someone else. For labor power to be offered for sale, the tie between producers and the means of production has to be severed for good. Thus, holders of wealth must be able to acquire the means of production and deny access, except on their own terms, to all who want to operate them. Conversely, people who are denied access to the means of production must come to those who now control the means and bargain for permission to operate them. In return they receive wages that will allow them to pay for what they need to sustain themselves.

Indeed, in the capitalist mode production determines distribution. Those who detain the means of production can also detain the commodities produced. Those who produce the commodities must buy them back from the owners of the means of production. Means of production, in turn, circulate only among those with capital to acquire them. Those who lack capital and must sell their labor power also lack the means of production. Hence, the way in which the mode commits social labor to the transformation of nature also governs the way the resources used and obtained are distributed among producers and non-producers. Streams of resources, including income, are not—as an ecologically oriented anthropologist wrote recently (Love 1977: 32)— the human analogue of the way biological organisms capture energy. Between people and resources stand the strategic relationships governing the mode of allocating social labor to nature.

The holders of wealth who now detain the means of production, however, would have no reason to hire laborers if they produced only enough to cover the costs of their wage package. In the course of a working day, the laborers in fact produce more than the cost of their wages; they produce a surplus. This surplus, under the conditions of the capitalist mode, belongs to the holder of wealth, the capitalist, whose means of production the workers put into operation. The greater this surplus, the greater the rate of profit obtained by the capitalist when he measures it against his outlays for plant, resources, and labor.

There are two ways in which capitalists can increase this surplus. One way is to keep wages low, or to reduce them to the lowest possible point that is biologically or socially feasible. The other way is to raise the level of the surplus produced, above and beyond the amount that has to be paid for labor power, through raising the output of workers during any given period of work. Such increases in productivity require improvements in the technology and organization of production. These imperatives produce relentless pressures, spurring capitalists to ever-increased accumulation of capital and renewal of technology. The greater the capital at their command, the greater their ability to raise technological productivity; hence the greater their ability to accumulate additional surplus to further expand production, as well as to outproduce and undersell competitors who fail to invest in new technology and who attempt to meet competition through placing greater burdens on their laborers.

The capitalist mode thus shows three intertwined characteristics. First, capitalists detain control of the means of production. Second, laborers are denied independent access to means of production and must sell their labor power to the capitalists. Third, the maximization of surplus produced by the laborers with the means of production owned by the capitalists entails "ceaseless accumulation accompanied by changes in methods of production" (Sweezy 1942: 94; Mandel 1978: 103–107).

These characteristics, however, must be understood not only synchronically but also historically, as developing facets of a mode that had determinate origins in time and that develops over time. The point is crucial. Wealth in the hands of holders of wealth is not capital until it controls means of production, buys labor power, and puts it to work, continuously expanding surpluses by intensifying productivity through an ever-rising curve of technological inputs. To this end capitalism must lay hold of production, must invade the productive process and ceaselessly alter the conditions of production themselves. As long as wealth remains external to the process of production, merely skimming off the products of the primary producers and making profits by selling them, that wealth is *not* capital. It may be wealth obtained and engrossed by overlords or merchants, but it has not yet entered what Marx called "the really revolutionary road" of appropriating and transforming the means of production themselves (*Cap.* III, 1967: 334). Only where wealth has laid hold of the conditions of production in the ways specified can we speak of the existence or dominance of a capitalist mode. There is no such thing as mercantile or merchant capitalism, therefore. There is only mercantile wealth. Capitalism, to be capitalism, must be capital-ism-in-production.

The capitalist mode of production, so conceived, is necessarily based on a division of classes. It initiates a division between segments of the population who produce surpluses and segments of the population who control the means of production, and it continuously re-creates that differentiation. At the same time, it differentiates each class internally. In the race for higher productivity, the owners of the means of production are differentiated into victors and losers. In the continuous move-ment between the genesis of new sources of surplus production and renewed recession, the labor force shuttles among full employment, underemployment, and unemployment. The two processes of differen-tiation are in fact linked, as the shareholders in capital are continuously driven to seek new pools of cheap and tractable labor, or else to replace costly or intractable labor with machines.

The growth of this capitalism-in-production is a historical, develop-mental process, originating in certain areas of the European peninsula. It expanded from there to envelop areas beyond Europe. It grew through its own internal ability to reproduce itself on an ever-widening scale; it grew also by entering into working arrangements with other modes, siphoning off wealth and people and turning them into capital and labor power. The capitalist mode thus always exhibited a dual character: an ability to develop internally and branch out, implanting its strategic nexus of relations across the face of the globe; and an ability to enter into temporary and shifting relations of symbiosis and competi-tion with other modes. These relations with other modes constitute part of its history and development. Indeed, as we shall see, the internal dynamic of the capitalist mode may predispose it to external expansion, and hence to interchanges with modes other than itself.

The Tributary Mode

In the world in 1400 the major agricultural areas traversed by our imaginary traveler were held by states based on the extraction of sur-pluses from the primary producers by political or military rulers. These states represent a mode of production in which the primary producer, whether cultivator or herdsman, is allowed access to the means of production, while tribute is exacted from him by political or military means. Marx characterized the key attributes of this mode as follows:

> It is furthermore evident that in all forms in which the direct laborer remains the "possessor" of the means of production and labor conditions necessary for the production of his own means of subsistence, the property relationship must simultaneously appear as a direct relation of lordship and servitude, so that the direct producer is not free; a lack of freedom which may be reduced from serfdom with enforced labor to a mere tributary relationship. The direct producer, according to our assumption, is to be found here in possession of his own means of production, the necessary material labor conditions required for the realization of his labor and the production of his own means of subsistence. He conducts his agricultural activity and the rural home industries connected with it independently. . . . Under such conditions the surplus-labor for the nominal owner of the land can only be extorted from them by other than economic pressure, whatever the form assumed may be. [*Cap.* III, 1967: 790−791]

In other words, social labor is, under these conditions, mobilized and committed to the transformation of nature primarily through the exercise of power and domination—through a political process. Hence, the deployment of social labor is, in this mode, a function of the locus of political power; it will differ as this locus shifts position.

It is possible to envisage two polar situations: one in which power is concentrated strongly in the hands of a ruling elite standing at the apex of the power system; and another in which power is held largely by local overlords and the rule at the apex is fragile and weak. These two situations define a continuum of power distributions.

A ruling elite of surplus takers standing at the apex of the power system will be strongest when it controls, first, some strategic element in the process of production, such as waterworks (Wittfogel 1931), and second, some strategic element of coercion, such as a standing army of superior military capability. Rulers will then be able to deploy their own tribute gatherers without need of assistance from local power holders. They will be able to loosen the grip of local overlords over resources and hence over the primary producers of surplus, and render the overlords dependent on revenues tendered by the rulers. If the rulers are successful in this, they can also induce the local overlords to fight among themselves for privileged positions at the source of revenue. Such rulers will also be able to curtail the power of traders, keeping them from access to the primary producers in the countryside and preventing them from financing potentially rebellious overlords on their own behalf. Finally, such a strong central power will be able to place limits on translocal "grass-roots" organization, be they guilds, estates, leagues, or religious sects. At the same time, strong central rule often finds support among surplus-producing peasantries, since central rulers and peasants are linked by a common antagonism against power-holding and surplus-taking intermediaries.

Conversely, the central power will be weak and local power holders strong where strategic elements of production as well as means of coercion are in the hands of local surplus takers. Under such conditions local figures can intercept the flow of tribute to the center, strengthen their grip over land and the population working it, and enter into local or regional alliances on their own. Such local alliances, however, are frequently directed not only against the center but also against members of their own class, with the result that factional struggles will ramify throughout the countryside, thus weakening their class position. Factional struggles, in turn, may allow the elite at the center to survive by stratagems of divide-and-rule. Paradoxically, internecine faction fights also weaken the position of the primary producers, since in the absence of strong central control they must seek protectors against unrest and predation.

In broad terms, the two situations we have depicted correspond to the Marxian concepts of the "Asiatic mode of production" and the "feudal mode of production." These are usually treated as enduring and unchanging opposites. One term is usually ascribed to Europe, the other to Asia. The preceding exposition should make clear, however, that we are dealing rather with variable outcomes of the competition between classes of nonproducers for power at the top. To the extent that these variable outcomes are all anchored in mechanisms exerting "other than economic pressure," they exhibit a family resemblance to each other (Vasiliev and Stuchevskii 1967; Töpfer 1967). This resemblance is best covered by a common term for this mode—*tributary mode of production*—used by Samir Amin (1973b).

Reification of "feudalism" into a separate mode of production merely converts a short period of European history into a type case against which all other "feudal—like" phenomena must be measured. The concept of the Asiatic mode of production, in which a centralized state bureaucracy dominates unchanging village communities of hapless peasants, similarly suffers from an ahistorical and ideological reading of Asian history. It has long been customary in the West to counterpose Western freedom with Eastern despotism, whether this was done by Herodotus with reference to the Greek city-states in their struggles with Persia, or by Montaigne and Voltaire counterposing societies based on the social contract with societies characterized by multitudes groveling under despotic rule. Our portrayal should permit us, rather, to specify the politically relevant variables that distinguish one tributary situation from another. Thus China, with a strongly concentrated hydraulic component, clearly represents a set of tributary relationships different from those in India, with its reliance on dispersed "tank" irrigation, or in Iran, with its irrigation by means of underground wells and canals.

Moreover, strongly centralized "Asiatic" states frequently break down into political oligopolies resembling feudalism; and more feudal, dispersed controls by local power holders yield to more centralized and concentrated power over time. To reify the weak phases of the Sassanian, Byzantine, or T'ang Chinese states into a feudal—like mode of production, and the strong phases of these same states into an Asiatic mode, wrongly separates into two different modes of production oscillations within the continuum of a single mode.

If variation within the tributary mode depends on the organization of power in particular states, the operation of the mode is at least in part determined by whether that state is weak or strong in relation to other polities. Shifts of power within the states of North Africa and of western, central, and eastern Asia, for example, were intimately connected with the military and political expansion and contraction of pastoral-nomadic populations, and with the widening and narrowing of surplus transfer through overland trade. If it is true that noncapitalist, class-dependent modes utilize "other than economic means" for the extraction of surplus, it follows that successful surplus extraction cannot be understood in terms of an isolated society alone; rather, it is a function of the changing organization of the wider field of power within which the particular tributary constellation is located.

Historical societies predicated upon the tributary mode may thus tend toward centralization or fragmentation, or oscillate between these two poles. They also exhibit variation in the ways tribute is gathered up, circulated, and distributed. Only in the rarest cases, where a surplus taker and his retinue consume all the surplus obtained *in situ*, is there no role for processes whereby surpluses are circulated either socially or geographically. Similarly rare are cases where all surpluses are siphoned upwards and redistributed downward through the echelons of a hierarchically organized elite without the participation of commercial intermediaries or merchants. The Andean Inca polity appears to have approximated this form most closely, but even there some evidence exists for the operation of merchants in restricted areas of the Peruvian and Ecuadorian coasts. Much more frequently, surpluses are transferred and exchanged through the transactions of commercial intermediaries.

Civilizations

The larger social fields constituted by the political and commercial interaction of tributary societies had their cultural counterparts in "civilizations"—cultural interaction zones pivoted upon a hegemonic tributary society central to each zone. Such hegemony usually involves the development of an ideological model by a successful centralizing elite of surplus takers, which is replicated by other elites within the wider political-economic orbit of interaction. Although one model may become dominant within a given orbit, as did the Confucian model carried by the Chinese scholar-gentry, the civilizational orbit is also an arena in which a number of models coexist or compete within a multiple array of symbols, which find their differential referents in the shifting relationships among the tributary societies comprising the orbit.

A hallmark of these models is that they not only underline the status of the surplus takers and the social distance separating them from other people, but they also claim supernatural origins and validation. The Chinese emperor was the holder of the mandate of Heaven, ensuring the balance of Heaven and Earth; the Confucian sash-bearing scholars activated that mandate by enacting the proper hierarchical relationships. The *kraton*, or palace, of the Southeast Asian ruler was more than the center of government; it was also the site of religious ritual carried on by the king-god and his noble entourage. The Islamic caliph is *emir el-mominin*, the Commander of the Faithful, the guardian of the law, and the one who "orders Good and prohibits Evil" (Koran III: 106). Among the Shona the ancestral spirits of the royal clan of the Nembire link the clan with god, *mwari*. Elsewhere the relation of superordinate power to the supernaturally instituted order is less direct, and it may be mediated through priests. The Hindu *raja* follows *arta*, the principle of self-interest and utility, but he requires the services of the Brahmin to institute *dharma*, the principle of proper supernatural order. In Christendom, the king is ruler by divine right, but he shares rule with the other Coordinate Power, the Church. Whether monolithic or bifurcate, domination is in all these cases inscribed into the structure of the universe.

These ideological models paralleling the tributary mode have certain common characteristics. Typically they show a hierarchical representation of the cosmos, in which the dominant supernatural order, working through the major holders of power, encompasses and subjects humanity. At the same time, the ideological model displaces the real relation between power-wielding surplus takers and dominated producers onto the imagined relation between superior deity and inferior "subject" (see Feuchtwang 1975). The problem of public power is thus transformed into a problem of private morality, and the "subject" is invited to win merit by maintaining order through the regulation of his own conduct. The displacement also embodies a contradiction. If public power falters and justice is not done, the ideological ties linking subject and supernatural are also called into question. The rulers lose legitimacy; the mandate of Heaven may pass to alternate contenders, or people may begin to assert the claims of their segmental morality against the official apparatus of mediation. Yet the arguments proffered in support of these claims will center upon the nature of the imaginary tie between subject and supernatural, not upon the nature of domination anchored in "other than economic means."

Mercantile Wealth

If the tributary mode points to key relationships through which surpluses are extracted, one must also ask how these surpluses are distributed after extraction. In nearly all instances some part of the surplus is placed into circulation and exchanged. Long before 1400 merchants were transferring commodities over wide areas by caravan and sailing ship, reaping profits from their sale and accumulating great stocks of wealth. Especially where tributary societies existed in a wider field created by competition or symbiosis among contending polities, long-distance trade in elite goods or luxuries was a frequent and highly developed phenomenon. Such goods embodied the ideological models through which superiority was claimed, and therefore they had an important political referent. As Jane Schneider has phrased it:

> The relationship of trade to social stratification was not just a matter of an elevated group distinguishing itself through the careful application of sumptuary laws and a monopoly of symbols of status; it further involved the direct and self-conscious manipulation of various semiperipheral and middle level groups through patronage, bestowals, and the calculated distribution of exotic and valued goods. [1977: 23]

Yet this trade in luxury goods often went hand in hand with long-distance transactions in bulky staples, especially where access to waterways lowered the energy costs of transport, as in the areas of the Mediterranean, the Black Sea, the Indian Ocean, and the China seas. When the European sea traders intruded into other continents, therefore, they often found long-standing networks of commercial relationships that involved principles and operations with which they were wholly familiar.

If tributary relationships and mercantile activity have long existed side by side, often to their mutual benefit, such mutualism also entailed conflicts. A merchant is a specialist in exchange, buying and selling goods to obtain a profit. To increase profits merchants strive to enlarge the sphere of exchange, drawing subsistence or prestige goods produced within the kin-ordered or tributary mode into the channels of commodity exchange, the market. This transformation of use values into commodities, goods produced for exchange, is not neutral in its consequences. It can seriously weaken tributary power if it commercializes the goods and services upon which that power rests. Granted too much latitude, it can render whole classes of tributary overlords dependent upon trade, and reshuffle social priorities to favor merchants over political or military chieftains. Thus, societies predicated on the tributary mode not only gave impetus to commerce but also repeatedly curtailed it when it grew too strong. Depending on time and circumstance, they have taught merchants to "keep their proper place" by subjecting them to political supervision or to enforced partnerships with overlords; by confiscating their assets, instituting special levies, or exacting high "protection" rents; by denigrating merchant status socially, supporting campaigns against commerce as sinful or evil, or even delegating mercantile activity to despised and powerless out-groups. The position of merchants is thus always defined politically as well as economically, and is always dependent on the power and interests of other social classes.

While defensive mechanisms were invoked whenever tributary power felt threatened by mercantile encroachment, it seems that the European polities that developed after A.D. 1000 granted merchants greater independence and privileges than did most other political systems. This may have been due to the very backwardness of the peripheral European peninsula, as compared to the stronger, wealthier, and more centralized tributary structures of the Middle East and the Orient. Sovereigns striving to consolidate power in the European core regions often needed the aid of merchants to gain access to funds, and they frequently lent support to merchant groups in order to check the demands of rival power seekers. Given the political fragmentation of the European periphery, moreover, merchants were better able to resist political and social pressures, through the creation of their own wide-ranging networks of trade and finance.

The European merchants also enjoyed locational and technological advantages over merchants on other continents. Europe's proximity to the sea permitted an early growth of river and ocean shipping. Water transport not only entailed lower energy costs than transportation overland; it also permitted a closer integration of local and translocal commerce, and avoided the heavy protection costs that burdened the transcontinental caravan trade. An expanding orbit of commercial transactions deployed over a widening grid of transportation, in turn, speeded up the turnover time of money-begetting money, allowing a given sum to earn repeated profits.

Some scholars have seen in these medieval European merchants the direct ancestors of capitalism. In this view the change from merchant wealth to capital is continuous, linear, and quantitative; the development of capitalism is thus envisioned merely as an expansion of processes already at work in the tributary mode. This is essentially the position taken by Weber, Wallerstein, and Frank. If, however, the change from merchant wealth to capital is seen as entailing not merely quantitative growth but rather a major alteration in the determinant processes, then capitalism appears as a qualitatively new phenomenon, a new mode of mobilizing social labor in the transformation of nature. That was the position taken by Marx. From this viewpoint the history of money-begetting money was but "the prehistory of capital." Mercantile wealth did not function as capital as long as production was dominated by either kin-ordered or tributary relations. What was not consumed by producers or tribute takers might be taken to market and exchanged for surplus products elsewhere, allowing the merchants to feed off the price differentials obtained in the carrying trade.

The growth of trade after A.D. 1400 greatly enlarged the scale of the market, but it did not automatically lead to the installation of the capitalist mode. The tributary mode remained dominant until the capitalist mode unfolded and began to threaten it from within in the course of the eighteenth century. During this long period, tributary surpluses continued to be the mainstay of a class of overlords, together with their retinues and servants. Tribute also continued to furnish the sinews of the state: it paid for its armies and navies, supplied its quartermaster corps, and remunerated its officials. The continued extraction of tribute thus set the terms under which mercantile activity could operate and thrive. Yet, by dint of its very success, mercantile wealth began to multiply the channels of commodity exchange, rendering tribute takers increasingly dependent upon it. It generated ever larger amounts of money-begetting money and invested that wealth so as to increase the flow of commodities to the market. In the process it drew producers in different parts of the world into a common web of exchanges, adjusting existing relations of production to embrace commodity exchange, or subsidizing coercive arrangements for the production of commodities.

The European merchants engaged in overseas operations brought surpluses into mercantile exchange in a number of different ways. Sometimes they favored one alternative to the exclusion of the others; under certain circumstances they utilized all of them together. None of these ways of turning goods into commodities was new; all had analogues in other tributary systems. They grew directly out of the operations of the tributary mode and long remained intertwined with it.

One way involved the sale of tributary surpluses. Merchants bought stocks of surplus from tributary overlords and state agencies, and supplied goods in return. Their commodities underwrote the life-style of the tributary class; their goods supplied the armies of the state and stocked its magazines. On occasion the merchants also participated in booty taking and plunder themselves, and then sold the spoils.

A second way in which merchants drew goods into the circuits of trade was to open exchanges with primary gatherers and producers. The merchants offered goods that were cheap for them yet desirable to the natives, in return for articles of little value to the producers yet capable of fetching high prices in distant markets. In the course of such exchanges, the native producers received use values that they treasured. If pursued over time, however, such exchanges rendered the target populations dependent upon the merchant. Intensified production of the strategic valuable usually entailed diminution or abandonment of other important economic activities. As producers grew more specialized in furnishing one kind of object, they came to rely increasingly upon the merchant for tools, household articles, prestige goods, and even food. Where the producers proved reluctant to enter or to continue the exchange, merchants sometimes had recourse to forcible sales of commodities, which the producers were then obligated to repay. At other times merchants smoothed the course of exchange with liquor or tobacco, which rendered the producer somatically dependent on the donor, thus guaranteeing the resumption of exchange. In time, such unequal exchange, now extended temporally through a system of advances, could produce a kind of peonage in which the primary producer was constrained by his needs to commit himself to production of the same valuable in the future.

A similar process of increasing specialization and dependence marked the development of "putting-out" systems under mercantile control. Such systems usually originated with the production of specialized commodities by households, which then sold their product to merchants for resale. Gradually, however, the merchants extended their control over the labor process by advancing tools or raw materials, receiving the finished product in repayment for the factors of production advanced.

Both commodity peonage and putting-out bordered on capitalism, but they were not yet governed by capitalist relations. Both forms of employing labor developed in mercantile terms, with the merchant as agent of exchange advancing subsistence and manufactured goods and receiving specialized commodities. By means of advances the merchant could develop a long-term lien on labor, be it the labor of a kin-ordered group or of a craft shop operating on the edges of a tributary domain. He might even take the further step of advancing tools and raw materials—powder, shot, and traps, or looms and textile fibers—and thus outfit that labor with complex tools. Such a merchant, however, did not yet buy labor power in a market in which workers compete for available jobs, and he did not yet control the actual labor process. Surplus was not extracted as surplus value but through unequal exchange within the framework of monopolistic and quasi-tributary relationships. The process of production was still governed from the demand end, from the requirements of merchants exchanging in a market, rather than flowing from the orchestration of labor power and machines within the process of production itself. As long as this was the case, merchants also remained limited in their ability to control the productive process and to alter it in the face of new demands.

A third way in which merchants obtained surpluses for exchange was to expand slavery. Slave labor has never constituted a major independent mode of production, but it has played a subsidiary role in providing labor under all modes—kin-ordered, tributary, and capitalist. Slavery has been employed repeatedly in large-scale agricultural and mineral production, where output is dependent on a maximization of labor, with minimal deployment of tools and skills. The use of slaves in such production has a continuous history in Europe since classical antiquity, and the option of using slaves to raise commodities for exchange was thus available from the beginnings of the European expansion overseas. The later American growth of slavery represents but an overseas reincarnation of a process already going on in Crete, Sicily, Madeira, the Azores, the Canaries, and the islands of the Gulf of Guinea.

As in the systems of advances initiated with primary producers and processors, slavery too required a heavy infusion of commodities to set it in motion. Merchants advanced commodities to African suppliers of slaves, thus placing slaves into the circuits of exchange as one kind of commodity among others. Merchants also advanced money and commodities to planters who purchased slaves for work on plantations. As a system of coerced labor, slavery entailed inherent costs, frequently covered through mercantile advances. Slaves had to be broken in and supervised; high productivity entailed high costs of coercion. Since most slave populations did not reproduce, new slaves had constantly to be acquired and paid for. Slaves had to be maintained by their owners, and the costs ate into plantation profits. If the slaves were allowed to supply their own needs on plantation "provision grounds," their increased autonomy decreased owner control. Effective control thus often depended on the importation of foodstuffs and other requisites. Merchants were not the only participants in the system; planters often brought with them inherited tributary wealth and reinvested profits in their own plantations. Yet merchants played an ever-expanding role in financing slavery, in furnishing needed commodities, in providing product markets, and in repatriating profits to the home country.

In the process of European expansion, mercantile wealth pioneered routes of circulation and opened up channels of exchange. Its source of gain lay in the maintenance of price differentials—enabling it to buy cheap and sell dear—and it defended itself against price leveling through alliances with any power that could impede the development of a "free" market. It relied on political and military power to seize zones of supply, to gain privileged access to suppliers, to bar interloping competitors in trade, and to ensure maximal profits through monopolistic controls over sales. Aiming for power over persons in order to increase and to diversify output, it did not create a labor market. Thus, mercantile wealth did not alter the mode of mobilizing social labor and remained wedded to the tributary mode. That dependence would not be severed until new political and economic circumstances promoted the rise of industrial capitalism.

The Kin-Ordered Mode of Production

If the areas of intensive agricultural production in 1400 were occupied by societies predicated on the tributary mode, on the peripheries of these areas all around the world were social groups organized differently. Such populations are usually called "primitive" in the anthropological literature. The term is misleading if it leads one to think of Iroquois or Crow or Lunda as one's "contemporary ancestors," or as people who have not yet aspired to the heights of civilization. It is also analytically problematical, since it refers to a beginning which it does nothing to portray. Claude Meillassoux has rightly argued that to characterize such populations by an absence of features, calling them "classless," "acephalous," or "stateless" tells us nothing about what they *are*.

It is common to describe these populations as bound together by "kinship," but less common to inquire into what kinship is. Empirically, populations vary in the extent and intensity of their kinship ties. Some people have "a lot of kinship," others much less. Coresidence is often more significant than genealogy; many local groups include people who are relatives but also others who are not. Tasks may be carried out by teams of nonrelatives, and products of the hunt or of other activities may be shared out among nonkin as well as kinfolk. Indeed, many anthropologists have seen residence as more critical than kinship in understanding how people organize themselves. Thus, both Kroeber and Titiev have argued that coresidence underlay the formation of lineages (Kroeber 1952: 210; Titiev 1943). Leach, similarly, has enjoined anthropologists to "start from a concrete reality—a local group of people—rather than from an abstract reality—such as the concept of lineage or the notion of kinship system" (1961: 104). Even Meyer Fortes, whose major contribution lies in the analysis of wider kinship systems and their jural and political implications, has noted:

> A lineage cannot easily act as a corporate group if its members can never get together for the conduct of their affairs. It is not surprising therefore to find lineage in African societies is generally locally anchored, but is is not necessarily territorially compact or exclusive. A compact nucleus may be enough to act as the local center for a group that is widely dispersed. [1953: 36]

Particular populations also vary greatly in how far they "extend" patterns of kinship found within familial entities to more distantly related families. They differ, further, in the degree to which the extended or replicated patterns of familial kinship are made to bear the burden of jural and political obligations among groups. In other words, kinship rules may govern filiation (ties between individual parents and offspring) and marriage (ties between particular spouses), but little more. Such rules, moreover, may furnish people with only a vocabulary of kinship "names," without at the same time involving them in jural and political obligations. Among other populations, however, kinship looms large. Patterns of kinship may be used to expand the scope of social and ideological linkages, and such linkages may become major operative factors in the jural and political realm.

Kinship can thus operate at two levels, that of the family or the domestic group and that of the political order. Yet such statements still suggest what kinship *does* and not what kinship *is*. Indeed, if we cannot define kinship, by the same token we cannot define nonkinship. It may come as something of a surprise to the nonanthropological reader that anthropologists by no means agree about what kinship is. They divide, generally, into three groups with respect to this issue. First, there are those analysts who assume that the facts of kinship are an outgrowth of human biology. Human beings are sexually dimorphous and engage in sexual relations; as a result, human females bear offspring. The biological facts of sex relations and procreation are seen as basic to the human institutions of marriage and descent. In this view kinship is a matter of tracing pedigrees. Second, taking a stand against this position, other anthropologists have argued that kinship is not merely a matter of the social control of sex and procreation, but involves cultural definitions of the marriage bond and cultural constructs that allow offspring to be allocated to parental consorts. In this view kinship is a distinctive cultural domain with its own content, which consists of symbolic constructs of descent and affinity. These symbols will vary from culture to culture. Finally, there are anthropologists who argue from a third position, which holds that kinship is merely an "idiom" in which economic, social, political, and ritual relations are discussed. In this perspective kinship is a metaphor; its real content lies elsewhere. The facts of kinship are explained when the relations it serves to "express" are explained.

Those anthropologists who see kinship as the social regulation of biology (sex and procreation) put their emphasis on the way in which rights and obligations, including rights to resources and support, are shared out among biologically produced actors. In their view kinship forms or patterns are cultural epiphenomena serving the task of such allocation. Generally speaking, their concept of kinship has been primarily jural: kinship serves to assign people born into the group to jural positions. The cultural symbolists, in contrast, see kinship as a domain of symbolic constructs connected with other symbolic constructs of the culture. The function of kinship constructs is seen as moral, as a contribution to the ideological ordering of the symbolic universe of the culture bearers. In practice, the symbolists view the elementary family as a kind of storehouse of symbols of the culture and trust that inquiry into domains other than the familial will reveal identical or parallel symbolic constructs (see Schneider 1972).

In a larger sense these two positions are complementary. Given that people—unlike snapping turtles—are not hatched from eggs, deposited in a safe spot, and then abandoned, but are born and socialized through the operations of the incest taboo, kinship names and categories are symbolic constructions *ab ovo*. The human institution of the incest taboo depends for its very operation upon a differentiation between those people with whom we share some kind of substance, symbolized by a commonality of blood or bone, with whom we may not mate, and those people with whom we can mate, who do not share our symbolic substantial heritage. Although explanations for the origins of the incest taboo are still incomplete, Claude Lévi-Strauss has rightly made it the point of departure of his study of kinship. Just as the initial categories of kinship set up by the taboo are symbolic constructs, so are all the other basic kinship categories, such as gender, absolute and relative age, descent, and affinity. Since symbolism thus enters into the very definition of human sociality, human beings everywhere have also brought these basic constructs of human "nature" into connection with their constructs of encompassing nature and supernature. (In view of this, the third position in kinship studies sketched above, which denies all but metaphorical status to kinship symbols, appears unsatisfactory, short-circuiting inquiry into phenomena with which it does not want to deal.)

It is possible to combine these two approaches into an operational view of kinship that allows us to see kinship in the context of political economy. Kinship can then be understood as a way of committing social labor to the transformation of nature through appeals to filiation and marriage, and to consanguinity and affinity. Put simply, through kinship social labor is "locked up," or "embedded," in particular relations between people. This labor can be mobilized only through access to people, such access being defined symbolically. *What* is done unlocks social labor; *how* it is done involves symbolic definitions of kinsmen and affines. Kinship thus involves (a) symbolic constructs ('filiation/marriage; consanguinity/affinity') that (b) continually place actors, born and recruited, (c) into social relations with one another. These social relations (d) permit people in variable ways to call on the share of social labor carried by each, in order to (e) effect the necessary transformations of nature.

If kinship is a particular way of establishing rights in people and thus laying claim to shares of social labor, it is also true that the ways in which such rights and claims are established vary widely among different culture-bearing populations. Anthropologists have come to recognize that kinship works in basically different ways in two kinds of situations, those in which resources are widely available and open to anyone with the ability to obtain them, and those situations in which access to resources is restricted and available only to claimants with a "kinship license." In the first case, the ties of kinship grow out of the give-and-take of everyday life and link people who are in habitual interaction with one another. In the second case, the circle of kinship is drawn tightly around the resource base by means of stringent definitions of group membership.

This contrast defines two variants of the kin-ordered mode, for social labor is deployed differently in the two. The first variant is best exemplified in the anthropological literature by food-collecting "bands." Such populations do not transform nature, but gather up and concentrate for human use resources naturally available in the environment. The natural environment is not a means for humanly controlled organic transformations, as in cultivation or herding; it is "the object of labor" but not its "instrument" (Marx, *Cap.* I, 1977: 284–285). Under such circumstances the aggregation or dispersion of people, each embodying a share of social labor, follows ecological constraints and opportunities. Upper limits to pooled social labor are set by the interaction of the technology with the local environment, as well as by the group's ability to manage conflict through consensus formation and informal sanctions. Kinship then works primarily to create relations among persons—partnerships among shareholders in social labor—through marriage and filiation. Such partnerships extend in reticulate fashion from particular participants to others. Having no defined boundary, they can attach newcomers or exclude them, as the interests of the interlinked partners permit or require.

The deployment of social labor works differently in the second variant of the kin-ordered mode. Where nature is subject to transformation through social labor, the environment itself becomes a means of production, an instrument on which labor is expended. A segment of nature is transformed by a set of people—equipped with tools, organization, and ideas—so as to produce crops or livestock. In such a society, social labor is distributed in social clusters that expend labor cumulatively and transgenerationally upon a particular segment of the environment, accumulating at the same time a transgenerational corpus of claims and counterclaims to social labor. Where conditions tend toward ecological closure, relations among these clusters need to be more closely defined and circumscribed, and the clusters readily become exclusive groups.

Under these conditions the idiom of filiation and marriage is used to construct transgenerational pedigrees, real or fictitious. These serve to include or exclude people who can claim rights to social labor on the basis of privileged membership.

Such groups are typically equipped with mythical charters defining culturally selected and certified lines of kin connection. These charters fulfill a number of functions. First, they allow groups to claim privileges on the basis of kinship. Second, they serve to permit or deny people access to strategic resources. Third, they organize the exchange of persons between pedigreed groups through their definition of ties of affinity; marriage, instead of being a relationship between bride and groom and their immediate relatives only, becomes a tie of political alliance between groups. And fourth, they allocate managerial functions to particular positions within the genealogy, thus distributing them unevenly over the political and jural field—whether this be as elders over juniors, as seniors over cadet lines, or as lines of higher over lower rank. In this process kinship on the jural-political level subsumes and organizes kinship on the familial-domestic level, making interpersonal relations subject to charters for categorical inclusion or exclusion.

The "extension" of kinship is therefore not the same as kinship on the level of filiation and marriage; it is concerned with jural allocation of rights and claims, and hence with political relations between people. On the level of filiation and marriage, kinship sets up individuated linkages among shareholders in social labor; extended kinship, in contrast, organizes social labor into labor pools and places controls over the transfer of labor from one pool to another.

The persistence of the idiom of kinship in the jural-political realm, however, poses a problem. Kinship nomenclature always involves a symbolic process. In the escalation of kinship from a set of interpersonal relations to the political order, kinship becomes a governing ideological element in the allocation of political power. But why should the language of kinship persist in this different setting? Meyer Fortes is one of the few to have dealt with this question.

> Why descent rather than locality or some other principle forms the basis of these corporate groups is a question that needs more study. It will be remembered that Radcliffe-Brown [1935] related succession rules to the need for unequivocal discrimination of rights *in rem* and *personam*. Perhaps it is most closely connected with the fact that rights over the reproductive powers of women are easily regulated by a descent group system. But I believe that something deeper than this is involved; for in a homogeneous society there is nothing which could so precisely and incontrovertibly fix one's place in society as parentage. [1953: 30]

While this explanation is not wholly satisfactory, Fortes does point to two major sources of power in the kin-ordered mode: control over the reproductive powers of women, and parentage. Both operate transgenerationally; both allocate people differentially to positions of power and influence. The first grants rights over the social labor embodied in females, offspring, and affines; the second defines not only descent but also collaterality—the genealogical range of mobilizable allies. The terminology of marriage and filiation is thus used to convey information about differential capacities to mobilize labor for work and support—information that is, about the shifting distribution of social labor among contending groups.

Where the symbolic constructs of kinship are thus extended, the relations among the bearers of social labor in competition for resources are structured monopolistically or oligopolistically, with social groups vying for precedence and dominance. At the same time, the tendency to maximize external oppositions vis-à-vis other groups goes hand in hand with a multiplication of internal oppositions. First, there are oppositions between men and women. Some complementary equilibrium between gender roles can perhaps be maintained as long as kinship is but one ordering element among others in a situation of open resources. With the emergence of pedigreed groups into the political field, however, affinal relations become political relations, and women lose status in relation to men as they become tokens of alliance. There is also the opposition of elders and juniors, with elders in characteristic positions of managerial command inside and outside the group. Some juniors may come to be seniors and take their place; but others will never succeed to any position of importance. We know that this opposition can break out into open conflict. We shall see, for example, rebellion of "boys" against their elders in the expansion of horse pastoralism on the Great Plains (chapter 6) and in the formation of slave-raiding groups in Angola (chapter 7).

Finally, internal ranking creates oppositions between original settlers and newcomers, between senior and junior lines of descent from the same ancestor, and between lines rising to prominence and those in a state of decline. Oscillations of rise and decline may be due to demographic ascendancy or failure; to successful or unsuccessful management of alliances, people, or resources; to success or failure in war. Leaders effective in contracting politically strategic marriages or in the judicious redistribution of subsistence and luxury goods to followers gain at the expense of less apt contenders. With the passage of time, such gains can be translated into genealogical claims, and pedigrees modified to exhibit the change.

The fact that leaders can rise to prominence in this way constitutes one of the Achilles' heels of the kinship mode, one of its diagnostic points of stress. For as a chief or other leader draws a following through judicious management of alliances and redistributive action, he reaches a limit that can only be surpassed by breaking through the bounds of the kinship order. He can manipulate bridewealth to acquire women who will produce offspring owing loyalty primarily to him; he can invite outsiders to settle in his group's domain, in the hope of attracting a personal following; he can acquire pawns and slaves to labor under his personal control. Yet as long as such strategies can be checked by his kinsmen and their allies, his radius of action is curtailed. One way in which a chief may try to expand his grasp on surpluses is by making war. Yet the fruits of warfare remain limited, since booty may be only occasional and impermanent, and it must be shared with others. To break through the limitations of the kin order, a chief must gain independent access to reliable and renewable resources of his own.

While kin ordering thus sets upper limits to internal differentiation, under conditions of closed resources it appears more likely to produce inequalities than an egalitarian distribution of life chances. Distinctions of gender, age, and prescriptive and acquired power work so as to create oppositions that disrupt the kinship order from within. In addition, disruptions are caused by conflicts between individuals or groups, by the assertion of conflicting claims over people on the part of different kinsmen, and by the nonperformance of normative kinship obligations among close or extended kin. All these forces and factors threaten the continuance of the kinship order. What, then, prevents its disintegration? How do kin-ordered units cohere at all over time?

The ability of the kin-ordered mode to regenerate itself may lie in the absence of any mechanism that can aggregate or mobilize social labor apart from the particular relations set up by kinship. The oppositions as they are normally played out are particulate, the conjunction of a particular elder with a particular junior of a particular lineage at a particular time and place, and not the general opposition of elder and junior as classes. In everyday life the kin-ordered mode contains its oppositions by particularizing tensions and conflicts.

In myth and ritual, however, the very oppositions fraught with danger in everyday life are dramatized on the level of universality. Whereas in everyday life generality is dissolved into particularities, in myth and ritual particularities are dissolved into generalities, conveying messages about the nature of the universe. Explanations, if offered, take the form of universalized verities. One may speculate that such projection of particular conflicts upon the screen of universal mythic events and meanings can serve to defuse those conflicts. The effectiveness of such a mechanism would seem to depend on the degree to which real conflicts can be kept particularized and segmented. A continuous accumulation of conflicts of the same kind, in the same direction, may place the myth-ritual system under cumulative stress and diminish its efficacy.

Conflicts within and between kin-ordered units may also be dampened by a fear of the high cost of massing support. Seeking allies means calling in past promises of aid and pledging support to allies in the future. Any escalation of conflict thus threatens to extend the conflict temporally as well as spatially. Nevertheless, when the stakes are high enough, escalation may well become desirable, with an attendant increase in gift giving and in exchanges of women to cement alliances. The story of the North American fur trade can be read as the gradual extension of supportive alliances among "English Indians" against "French Indians." Such alliances may also be stabilized and reinforced through the elaboration of myth and ritual, as in the case of the Iroquois league, which attempted to curb internal conflicts by directing energies outward against common enemies.

Yet conflict resolution in the kin-ordered mode encounters an ultimate limit in the structural problems of the mode itself. Cumulative conflict often exceeds the capacity of kin-based mechanisms to cope with them. Groups will then break up and fission. Such occurrences are not only frequent but are, in fact, important sources of change. Because we have tended to conceptualize societies as if they existed in a timeless ethnographic present and in isolation from one another, we have been misled into seeing the breakup and fission of kin-ordered groups as merely replicating the ordering of the parent group. In reality, fissioning groups can rarely escape into unoccupied terrain to avoid competitors, and they are likely to experience pressures from societies in the tributary and capitalist modes. Replication is thus probably exceptional. It is more likely that fissioning groups began to change as soon as they encountered limits to free movement.

Social clusters built up on kinship, therefore, are in no way exempt from internal differentiation and external pressures for change. Differential allocation of shares of social labor can favor the emergence of influential managers; at the same time, contact with other groups can lend importance to persons able to deal with differences of interest and with possible conflict. These tendencies toward inequalities in function are greatly enhanced when kin-ordered groups enter into relationships with tributary or capitalist societies. Such relationships afford opportunities for the seizure and transfer of surpluses beyond those available within the kin-ordered mode. Chiefs can then employ these external resources to immobilize the workings of the kinship order. This is why chiefs have proved to be notorious collaborators of European fur traders and slave hunters on two continents. Connection with the Europeans offered chiefs access to arms and valuables, and hence to a following outside of kinship and unencumbered by it.

The Problem of Chiefdoms

The term *chief* has come into common parlance to denote the recognized leader or head (from the Latin *caput*) of a socially organized population. In practice, the term was usually bestowed by Europeans upon any native person of influence who was in a position to forward or to hinder their interests. As such, references to chiefs cover different kinds of recruitment and degrees of authority, and are of little analytic utility. The actual ability of any such personage to command social labor and to influence the development of intergroup relations depends upon his assets in the game of power; the size and strength of the population under his jurisdiction; the nature of the resources held by that population and their importance to outsiders; and his war-making potential, his capacity both to defend resources and to interfere with the operations of opponents. A Northwest Coast *tais* had less potential power than a Zulu *induna*, an *induna* less than a Mongol *khan*. These differences also affected the ability of a chief to break through the limitations of the kin-ordered mode of production and to become a partner in tributary or capitalist relations.

Such variation among "chiefs" throws some light on the long-standing anthropological problem of "the chiefdom." In efforts to establish an evolutionary ordering of cultures, the chiefdom was conceptualized as a type of society intermediate between kin-ordered tribes and class-divided states. In this view of the chiefdom, status and power are allocated by differential rank within a common genealogy, yet without entailing differential access to the means of production. The chief and his high-ranking lineage are seen as acting on behalf of a social whole in coordinating specialized activities, planning and supervising public works, managing redistribution, and leading in war. Chiefdoms are thus "redistributional societies with a permanent agency of coordination" (Service 1962: 144). While genealogical rank differentiates people by the functions they perform, the society as a whole appears to be laced together through common interests, common descent, and general redistribution. All are kinsmen, as it were; only some are more so than others.

The concept of mode of production, however, shifts attention from the form and idiom of interaction between high-ranking chiefs and commoners in a given society to inquire instead into the ways social labor is deployed. In this perspective the societies classified as chiefdoms appear to be of two rather different kinds; those based on the kin-ordered mode, in which the chief and his followers are still embedded in kinship arrangements and bound by them, and those in which the form and idiom of kinship may be maintained even as a dominant group transforms divisions of rank into divisions of class—in fact, using kinship mechanisms to strengthen its own position. In this second kind of chiefdom, the chiefly lineage is in fact an incipient class of surplus takers in the tributary mode.

The growth of such a class may involve a number of different processes. Population increase can enhance the relative importance of the chiefly families. Such growth of the chiefly lineage allows it "numerous connections of different kinds with other lineages" (Service 1962: 149). The pursuit of affinal strategies requires that the chiefly lineage concentrate wealth from marriage exchanges in its own hands. This implies, in turn, control over exchangeable women and the interdiction of access to elite women by members of the lower ranks. Such control over women can be expanded downward, so as to widen elite control over affinal exchanges in general. Affinal strategies, furthermore, entail strategies of inheritance. Who gets what is circumscribed by membership in the privileged stratum; goods strategic in the matrimonial exchanges and in the inherited wealth of the aristocracy may therefore not pass into general redistribution.

At the same time, growing chiefly lineages may expand by a "budding off of families" (Service, 1962: 166), both within the habitual zone of interaction and beyond it. Such territorial proliferation of high-ranking personnel may create a plurality of power centers in place of a single apex of decision making. Members of the chiefly lineage can become contenders for the chiefship, or create new domains of their own by separating from the parent body. Competition for power feeds back, in turn, upon the processes of accumulation and redistribution. Contenders for power must accumulate adequate "funds of power" and redistribute them selectively to gain followers, rather than open resources to general redistribution.

Seen in this light, therefore, redistribution appears as a set of strategies in class formation, rather than as a general characteristic of chiefdoms as "redistributional societies." Polanyi, to whom anthropology owes the introduction of the concept of redistribution, allowed us to visualize mechanisms of exchange beyond those covered by "reciprocity" or "market" exchange. It is, however, necessary to qualify the concept of redistribution in three ways. First, the different kinds and spheres of redistribution must be specified. Redistribution through feasting is not identical with the redistribution of supplies for public works or warfare, or with the redistribution of specialized resources through the agency of the chief. Second, it is important to be precise about what gets redistributed, how much, and—most importantly—to whom. Feasting with the general participation of all can go hand in hand with the privileged accumulation of strategic goods by the elite. Banquets for war veterans can honor the military contribution of the entire army even as captured people and resources are allocated differentially to nobles and to commoners. Third, redistribution can also serve to "buy" allies and to pacify potential rivals by drawing them and their resources into the hierarchically managed flow of prestations. In this light, redistribution appears not as a kind of normative altruism characteristic of a type of society, but rather as a recurrent strategy in a process of class formation.

In such chiefdoms of the second kind, therefore, the function of kinship changes from that of ordering similarly organized groups in relation to one another to that of drawing a major distinction between one stratum and another. There is now an aristocracy that utilizes and exhibits kin-ordered ties as a mark of its distinctiveness and separateness, leaving to the commoner stratum only residual claims. The aristocratic class thus constitutes itself by radically altering the bonds of kinship in order to promote social distance between rulers and ruled. They may claim differential descent from the gods, or privileged possession of mana; they may strive to subvert the kin ties of their subjects through the punishment of adultery and incest (see Cohen, 1969), even while setting themselves off as a separate stratum through the practice of class endogamy; and they may invoke special rights over the disposition of war booty, including conquered populations not included in their charter of kin relationships.

Aristocracies of the kind just described frequently bud off to conquer and rule foreign populations. In such fission and spread, the aristocracy characteristically maintains its separate kinship ties as a source of class solidarity and as a way of setting itself off from the body of the ruled. This may conceivably happen peacefully, as it did when non-Alur ethnic groups invited the members of Alur chiefly lineages, who were bearers of rainmaking and conflict-resolving powers, to settle among them as their rulers (Southall, 1953). More frequently, however, warlike and migratory aristocracies invoke supernatural entitlements to impose their models of domination upon subject populations. Examples of such predatory aristocracies are the Toltecs who spread outward from Tula to the frontiers of Mesoamerica; the Luba and Lunda elites fanning out from their home in central Africa (see chapter 7); and the many Mongol, Turkic, and Arab aristocracies that imposed themselves on agricultural populations along the dry-belt corridor of the Old World.

Our discussion should make it clear that the deployment of social labor has both an economic and a political dimension. The kin-ordered mode inhibits the institutionalization of political power, resting essentially upon the management of consensus among clusters of participants. Moreover, the ties of kinship set limits to the amount of social labor that can be mobilized for collective purposes. Social labor can be aggregated through the temporary convergence of many separate ties, but it is dispersed again when changing conditions require a rearrangement of commitments. At the same time, the extension and retraction of kin ties create open and shifting boundaries of such societies.

A chief can become a pivot of the power of his kinship group; but if he is sometimes able to incarnate the kin order, he is also its prisoner. Chiefs who want to break through the limitations of the kin order must lay hold of mechanisms that can guarantee them independent power over resources. Such chiefs must either allocate some of the labor under their control to another mode, or enter into the relations of that mode directly, be it as tributary overlords or as participants in capitalist production. To effect such change requires new political instruments of domination, whether controlled directly by the chiefs or applied by others on their behalf. Failing this, the people they strive to mobilize may well rebel or secede, leaving them as chiefs only "over the pumpkins."

In contrast to the kin-ordered mode, both the tributary and the capitalist modes divide the population under their command into a class of surplus producers and a class of surplus takers. Both require mechanisms of domination to ensure that surpluses are transferred on a predictable basis from one class to the other. Such domination may involve, at one time or another, a wide panoply of sanctions based on fear, hope, and charity; but it cannot be secured without the development of an apparatus of coercion to maintain the basic division into classes and to defend the resulting structure against external attack. Both the tributary and the capitalist modes, therefore, are marked by the development and installation of such an apparatus, namely the state.

In the case of the tributary mode, the mode itself is constituted by the mechanisms of domination that extract tribute from the producers by "other than economic pressure" (see p. 80). Politics in a tributary state may affect the concentration and distribution of tribute among contending categories of surplus takers, but it remains anchored in the direct extractive relationship, no matter what the organizational form of the state.

The capitalist mode, in contrast, appears to be economically self-regulating. As long as means of production are owned by capitalists and denied to laborers, the laborers are continuously forced back into the employment of capitalists after each cycle of production reaches completion, and the cycle starts anew. Yet the state has a strategic role both in the genesis of the mode and in its maintenance. To set the mode in motion it was first necessary to stockpile money-begetting money, to convert it into capital, and to create a class of laborers offering their labor power for sale as a commodity. In these twin processes of "original accumulation," the state played a vital part. Once the mode was installed, the state had to deploy its power further to maintain and guarantee the ownership of the means of production by the capitalist class, at home and abroad, and to support the regimes of work and labor discipline required by the mode. In addition, the state had to provide the infrastructure of technical services—such as transportation and communication—required by the mode. Finally, it fell to the new state to arbitrate and manage conflicts between competing cohorts of capitalists within its jurisdiction, and to represent their interests in the competition between states—by diplomacy when possible, by war if required.

The three modes of production I have outlined constitute neither types into which human societies may be sorted nor stages in cultural evolution. They are put forth as constructs with which to envisage certain strategic relationships that shape the terms under which human lives are conducted. The three modes are instruments for thinking about the crucial connections built up among the expanding Europeans and the other inhabitants of the globe, so that we may grasp the consequences of these connections.

4 Europe, Prelude to Expansion

An observer looking at the world in A.D. 800 would barely have taken note of the European peninsula. Rome had fallen, and no effective centralized power had taken its place. Instead, a host of narrow-gauged tributary domains disputed rights to the shattered Roman inheritance. The center of political and economic gravity had shifted eastward to the "new Rome" of Byzantium, and to the Muslim caliphate. Six hundred years later, in A.D. 1400, an observer would have noted a very different Europe and a marked change in its relation to neighboring Asia and Africa. The many petty principalities had fused into a smaller number of effective polities. These polities were competing successfully with their neighbors to the south and east and were about to launch major adventures overseas. What had happened?

If we want to answer that question, we must consider at least three interrelated problems. First, there were shifts in long-distance trade, which changed the position of Europe from that of a dependent fringe of Asia into a key area of commercial development. What was the nature of these shifts? Second, the numerous small and scattered tributary principalities of A.D. 800 had grown into politically and militarily consolidated kingdoms. What was involved in that consolidation? Finally, several of the consolidated states sought out new frontiers, in a collaboration between war-making rulers and the merchant class. What were the forces driving these states toward expansion, and what was the nature of the collaboration in each case?

The Shift in Patterns of Long-Distance Trade

The western Mediterranean region and southwest Asia had long-standing connections. Periodically the balance of power shifted from the western sector to its eastern counterpart, and then shifted back again. The archaeological record supports a picture of Asian pre-eminence in surplus production, state formation, craft specialization, city building, and long-distance commerce. Proliferation of Egyptian and Mesopotamian development into the Aegean in the second millennium B.C. triggered the growth of trade with western Europe, which supplied the eastern sector with needed resources and transferred valued articles to the chieftains of the West in return. Aegean traders were followed by Phoenicians and Carthagenians. Then there was a turning of the tide. Greek expansion opened the doors, in the third century B.C., to "an almost uninterrupted stream of peoples from southeastern Europe [who] poured into Syria, Babylonia, and Iran, augmented from Asia Minor and even Syria" (Ghirshman 1954: 225). Roman expansion followed the same course, turning Egypt into the granary of Rome.

Then came the prolonged fall of the Roman Empire. Gradually the countryside won out over the cities. Economically, the various parts of the empire grew increasingly self-sufficient after A.D. 100. Food production could not support the cities, and urban crafts left the towns to relocate in the hinterland. The remarkable political and legal structure of Rome, which had "concentrated on organizing overwhelming power by inexorably exacting order and obedience in a limited sphere of life" (Deutsch 1954: 10), grew less and less effective. Provincial armies became nearly autonomous, and the marginal provinces of the empire gained ascendancy over the imperial center.

When a minor chieftain, Odoakar the Herulian, delivered the final blow to a Roman army in the west, Rome "fell," but only in its western orbit. It survived, indeed, for a thousand years in its eastern dominions, Byzantium—the new Rome. Byzantium maintained its course on the grounds staked out by Greek expansion, with Roman institutions and law, a developed town life, a common religious loyalty to Eastern Christendom, and gold coinage that remained the envy of the West until the eleventh century. In the sixth century it also developed a powerful navy, which sealed off western and southern access to Byzantium and allowed the state to expand into the borderlands of the Black Sea, whence it drew ample supplies of wheat, timber, and slaves. It became, in effect, more a Hellespontine power than a Mediterranean one, abandoning most of the Mediterranean to other claimants.

The major part of the Mediterranean region was divided between Islam and Western Christendom. Islam expanded quickly from its center in the caravan city of Mecca, and in the course of the seventh century A.D. it overran North Africa. During the second decade of the eighth century, Muslim armies occupied most of the Iberian peninsula; in the ninth century Sicily fell to the Muslims. When the capital of the Islamic caliphate moved from Damascus to Baghdad in the mid-eighth century, however, the Islamic center of gravity moved eastward away from the Mediterranean, in a movement parallel to the eastward shift of Byzantium. Trade with the Caucasus, Inner Asia, Arabia, India, and China grew more important than trade connections with the western

Mediterranean. This Mediterranean trade, now marginal, continued to be carried on by merchants from Syria and—above all—by Jews, such as the merchants known as Radanites or Al-Radhaniya (perhaps from the Persian *rah dan*, meaning "knowing the way"), who connected "the lands of the Franks" with Egypt, and Egypt with China.

The economic history of the Muslim world is still poorly known, but it is possible to outline some of its major aspects. Beginning with the eighth century, the Islamic countries underwent an agricultural revolution that entailed changes in plants and plant strains, in farming practices, and in hydraulic technology. This revolution issued in a great expansion of colonization and recolonization. The agricultural sector yielded increasing surpluses, which were plowed back into agricultural intensification and underwrote an expansion of commerce and town life. From the ninth century on, the Islamic world achieved a virtual monopoly over the gold of the Sudan and the treasures of Egypt and Iran. All this increased enormously the scale of Muslim trade relations and craft production, both for internal elites and for external consumers of luxury products.

Islam and Eastern Christendom had thus parceled out much of the Mediterranean littoral between them; yet both turned their backs upon the sea. The shattered inheritance of western Rome fell to Western Christendom, then a congeries of tributary polities headed by Teutonic chieftains supported by their bodyguards. No cities survived in Western Christendom comparable to Constantinople with at least 200,000 inhabitants (Russell 1958), Baghdad with about 400,000 (Adams 1965: 115), or Cordoba with 90,000 (Russell 1972: 178). Although urban crafts had become established in the countryside, the rural zones of Europe had relapsed into subsistence agriculture and localized exchange. European merchants involved in long-distance trade had not disappeared (Vercauteren 1967), but their activities were overshadowed from the sixth to the eighth centuries by Syrians and Jews who connected the Levant with the European peninsula, an area "exploited for the benefit of Syria, Alexandria, and Constantinople" (Lewis 1951: 14). Europe furnished mainly slaves and timber, receiving some luxury goods in return.

European slaves reached the Near East not only across the sea-lanes of the Mediterranean but also, along with precious furs and other products, down the Russian rivers into the Black Sea. They were brought by the Varangian Rus, a branch of the seafaring and sea-raiding peoples who had fanned out from their *viks*, or inlets, in Scandinavia to harass the European littoral and to carry off slaves to Near Eastern markets. In the ninth century they also began to subdue and colonize lands in England and Normandy, in Sicily, in the Baltic littoral, and in Russia. It is thus possible to conceive of the European peninsula at this stage as a land area surrounded by water on three sides, dominated by a long-distance trade whose center was in the Hellespont and the Levant.

The Rise of the Italian Ports

In the course of the ninth century, new competitors intruded into this commerce. These came from the port cities maintained as Byzantine enclaves along the coastline of Italy. The most important were Venice, at the head of the Adriatic, and Amalfi, on the Gulf of Salerno. They were at first but minor intermediaries in a trade that was of no great importance to the powers that ruled over the Levant. Building upon their initial positions as minor middlemen, however, both cities benefited by the gradual intensification of commerce.

Amalfi was described by the Arab merchant Ibn Hawqal in A.D. 977 as "the most prosperous town in Lombardy, the most noble, the most illustrious, on account of its conditions, the most affluent and opulent" (quoted in Lopez and Raymond 1955: 54). Nevertheless, it soon lost out to predatory neighbors. Venice, in contrast, moved increasingly to the fore, exchanging Western iron, timber, naval stores, and slaves for Eastern silks, spices, and ivories, to which it added salt from its lagoons and the products of its glass industry.

In the tenth century two other Italian Lombard ports embarked on a career of commercial and military expansion. These were Pisa and Genoa, on the Tyrrhenian Sea. Reacting to Muslim raiding by converting their fishing boats into naval craft, they counterattacked successfully in Corsica, Sardinia, and on the North African littoral.

Through their success in trade and war, these Italian towns began to tilt the balance of exchange between the western and eastern halves of the Mediterranean in favor of the West. Largely deprived of an agrarian hinterland of their own, their frontier of expansion lay in sea-borne commerce. They were thus in a position to become the main beneficiaries of the new conjuncture of power and influence in the Mediterranean after the year A.D. 1000. By then, Byzantium had initiated a policy of military consolidation on land, relying on its armed peasantry to defend it against growing attacks on all sides. Venice became virtually the commercial agent of Byzantium and engrossed most of its sea-borne trade.

Political Consolidation

While the Italian port towns were assuming increased importance in the Mediterranean region, the rural hinterlands south and north of the Alps were independently caught up in processes of economic and political consolidation. These processes operated on two levels: one local, the other regional. We have noted that the decline of Rome in the western Mediterranean involved a collapse and dismantling of the Roman legal and political superstructure, as well as a simultaneous retreat of urban crafts into the countryside. Growing ruralization and the diffusion of artisan technology together provided the technical basis for the development of a new form of political-economic organization. This form grouped cultivators around the stronghold of a superordinate "lord" (from the Anglo-Saxon *hlafweard*, or loaf warden, one who feeds dependents). Cultivators were tied to lords in arrangements of dependency, which varied widely in their origins and precise characteristics, defining in different ways the transfer of tribute from surplus producers to surplus takers. Such arrangements underwrote the political and military power of any given surplus taker in his relations to his fellows, as well as the power of surplus takers as a class.

After A.D. 1000 the surpluses so produced grew considerably, as a result of both intensification and extension of cultivation. This was particularly true of areas north of the Alps, where the introduction of triennial rotation by means of the heavy horse-drawn plow resulted in an absolute increase of the surplus product. Clearing of the dense forest cover of continental Europe and plowing up of the European plain expanded the arable from which surpluses could be taken. Both processes took place under the aegis of tribute-taking overlords, and both, in turn, increased the political power of the dominant class. Increased production of surpluses further enhanced the military capability of this class, which rested upon the ability to sustain the high cost of war horses and armor.

The movement toward political consolidation under a central kingship depended upon the combined ability to extract tribute in order to pay for war and to develop a war-making potential commensurate with the scale of the political task. There were, in essence, three ways in which this could be accomplished. One was to expand externally, against enemy powers, and seize surpluses from external enemies. Another was to discover resources, either home-grown or acquired as booty, to sell to merchants in exchange for needed goods or credit. A third way was to enlarge the royal domain, the area from which the king could draw direct support without the interference of intermediaries. The developing polities of Europe followed all three strategies, in a different mix at different times, and with different results.

War Abroad

Seizure of external resources was the main strategy followed by the Iberian powers of Portugal, León-Castile, and Aragón in their *Reconquista* of Muslim Spain. Another attempt to use this strategy took the form of the Crusades, carried on by the kings of France and England not long after their initial consolidation of power (1096–1291). The announced motivation for the Crusades was the reconquest of the Holy Land from the infidels. On another level, however, the Crusades were efforts to consolidate still incipient political systems through an attack against greatly weakened enemies. Byzantium was withdrawing into its territorial core area, yielding up its commerce to the Venetians. The Abbasid caliphate in Baghdad was wracked by internal rebellions and by nomad attacks from outside, perhaps because the very success of its long-distance trade had overtaxed its tribute-producing peasantry (see Anderson 1974: 509). The Crusades failed in the end and, in any event, did not produce direct benefits for the northwestern European kings.

The real beneficiaries of the Crusades were the Italian port-cities, which profited by the carrying services they had performed, marketed most of the plunder obtained, and were able, in the aftermath of the wars, to set up extraterritorial colonies in both Byzantium and the Muslim Levant. As the French and English withdrew, the Italian merchants—now reinforced in numbers and influence by the growing participation of the inland cities of Italy as well—were able to launch their great expansion in commerce and finance "from Greenland to Peking," as Robert Lopez put it. In expanding, this Italian trade network also vaulted the Alps, initiating contacts with the South German towns and, by way of the Rhineland, with Flanders and England.

Still another attempt at expanding royal resources through external seizure was initiated by the German Holy Roman Emperor. Hampered within the original German home provinces (*Urdeutschland*) by powerful competitors, the only strategy available to him in expanding royal resources lay in conquest abroad. This strategy involved, especially, an attempt to seize Italy for the German imperial crown. The attempt failed in 1176, when the Italian Lombard city-states leagued together to defeat the emperor at Legnano. This also put an end to the centralizing aspirations of the German kings.

Commerce

A second strategy—commercialization of products grown or won in war—developed alongside the other means of securing surpluses. Trade and warfare necessarily fed upon each other; at the same time, they involved different principles of organization. Trade led to the formation of merchant companies and federations of merchants. Warfare put a premium on the development of military specialists, who had to be fed and supplied by a secure base of tribute payers. Sometimes the merchants and the military cooperated; at other times they were at loggerheads. As Edward W. Fox had put it:

> If feudalism, as a system, was nourished by the agricultural production of endless individual manors, it was loosely bound together by the circulation of messages and men in the practice of military protection. The commercial society depended for its existence on the circulation of goods, by water transport when possible, and on messages, in the form of orders and payments. These are really very different operations, and there is a good deal of traditional evidence to indicate that they do not ordinarily mix. [1971: 57]

To some extent, one can visualize the growth of states during the European Middle Ages as a contest between political blocks that rested upon agricultural cores and military power, on the one hand, and mercantile networks along riverine and maritime routes of traffic, on the other. The fate of the Champagne fairs furnishes a telling example. These fairs, visited by Italian traders who came to exchange Mediterranean goods for northern products, were accessible from the Mediterranean over the trough formed by the Rhone and Saône rivers. They flourished as long as they remained independent of the Kingdom of France and the Holy Roman Empire of the German Nation. When the French kingdom took over the region in 1285, the fairs soon declined in the wake of increased taxation, growing warfare, and restrictions on the importation of English wool and Flemish cloth.

Commerce then shifted to the coastwise maritime route and to the overland routes between northern Italy and the valley of the Rhine. Along the maritime route there was a growth of autonomy-seeking merchant corporations and leagues, such as the *consolats* of Catalonia, the Brotherhood of the Marismas of the Cantabrian ports, and trading brotherhoods, or Hansa, which extended from Cologne and the Rhineland toward Lübeck and Hamburg in the thirteenth century. Along the routes over the Alps and up the Rhine, there formed pass states intimately linked with the movement of wares over the mountains, such as the Swiss Confederation and the Tyrol. Along the Upper Danube and the Rhine, the thirteenth and fourteenth centuries witnessed a burgeoning of merchant houses in the South German towns and of merchant confederations like the Swabian League, the Rhenish League, and the Brotherhood of the Seventeen Towns of Flanders and Brabant. Although none of these mercantile federations remained independent of land-based military overlords, "the cities of the trade-route belt from the Mediterranean to the North Sea and the Baltic were for centuries strong enough to thwart all efforts of military-administration" (Rokkan 1975: 576).

Enlarging the Royal Domain

The third strategy toward political consolidation, the expansion of a central domain, was followed in the regions that would become France and England. This was a very different route from that followed in the Iberian peninsula. Portugal and Castile were, in the main, predatory states, living off the resources of Muslim Spain. The embryo of the Portuguese state was the armed military brotherhood of the Knights of Aviz, whose Grand-Master became the first Portuguese king in 1384. The Castilian state rested, similarly, upon the religious-military orders of Calatrava, Alcántara, and Santiago, all founded in the twelfth century. In contrast, France and England were formed around the personal domains of their kings.

The nucleus of future France was the direct domain of the Capetian dynasty; this area, called Francia, straddled the valleys of the Seine and the Loire. Its agricultural importance is attested by the fact that the first documentary evidence for triennial crop rotation and modern means of harnessing draft animals refers to this region. From this initial base, the French kings proceeded to enlarge their direct domain through war, clerical aid, and matrimonial strategies. By 1328 the royal domain and the fiefs of the French crown together encompassed nearly all of France.

England was formed when a group of Frenchified Vikings from Normandy created, by force of arms, an "English Normandy" (Douglas 1969: 29) across the Channel. The core of this English Normandy was created by William the Conqueror when he shared out fiefs among his followers but assured to himself a direct domain, within each shire, larger than that of any vassal. English and French domain building soon collided. The kings of France and England fought for centuries over possession of western and southern "France." Until the thirteenth century, the "English" controlled the better part of "France," and they were not finally expelled until 1453.

All the European states grew slowly, as composites of many different segments and accretions. Their boundaries might well have been drawn differently, creating a map of Europe quite different from the arrangement of countries that we think of today as inalienable national entities. The map might have shown a sea-based empire, comprising Scandinavia, the northern seacoast of Europe, and England; a polity comprising western France and the British Isles; a union of eastern France and western Germany, or a state comprising the valleys of the Rhone and the Rhine intervening between Germany and France; a union of Germany and northern Italy; a state uniting Catalonia and the south of France; an Iberian peninsula divided into a northern Christian tier of kingdoms and a southern Muslim tier. Each of these represents a possibility that in fact existed at some time, and each suggests that the geopolitical boundaries segmenting Europe today require explanation and should not be taken for granted.

State Making and Expansion

External warfare, trade, and internal consolidation created new states in Europe and reversed the relationship between dominant East and impoverished West that had characterized earlier days. Around the year A.D. 1300, however, the pace of European growth seemed to slacken again. Agriculture ceased to grow, perhaps because the available technology reached the limits of its productivity. The climate worsened, rendering the food supply more precarious and uncertain. Epidemics affected large numbers of people debilitated by a poorer diet. Yet the ecological predicament appears to have been but an aspect of a wider crisis, sometimes referred to as "the crisis of feudalism." To pay for war and expansion, the military tribute takers stepped up the extraction of surpluses, producing in turn a rising tide of peasant resistance and rebellion.

The way out of this crisis lay in the discovery of new frontiers. Economically, this was necessary in order to generate additional surpluses. In practice, it meant moving into still newer areas to grow more food, as well as finding new food preservatives. It meant the possibility of luxury goods at lower prices, or alternatively, more gold and silver to pay for them. It also meant the hope of stanching the outflow of bullion to the East, a problem that had worried even the Romans and by A.D. 1200 had become critical. The solution to the crisis required an increase in the scale and intensity of war: an increase in the production of armaments and ships, in the training of soldiers and sailors, and in the financing of military operations and outposts.

Economically, the crisis of feudalism was solved by locating, seizing, and distributing resources available beyond the European frontiers. The movement to the New World, the establishment of forts and trading posts along the coasts of Africa, the entry into the Indian Ocean and the China seas, and the spread of the fur trade through the boreal forests of America and Asia all represent ways in which these goals were sought and fulfilled. New goods entered the circuits of exchange: tobacco, cacao, potatoes, tulips. African gold and American silver, as Braudel has said, enabled Europe to live beyond its means.

Yet it was not enough to add to the stock of wealth circulating in Europe and to multiply the variety of its forms. "Primitive accumulation" required not only the seizure of resources but also their concentration, organization, and allocation. These operations soon outgrew the capacity of any single merchant firm or merchant guild, or of any single body of soldiers and officialdom. Their pursuit favored the emergence of overarching organizations that could focus such large-scale expansionist and mercantile efforts, and that could rally the surplus-producing populace to such goals.

The overarching organizations that developed were states characterized by a high degree of concentration of command, whether placed in the hands of a single ruler and his clientele, as in Portugal and Spain, or in a committee of the ruling oligarchy, as in the United Provinces of the Netherlands. Such states can best be understood as a political coalition between the centralizing executive and the merchant class. The state bought arms and ships. Goods won by force of arms paid for the hiring of mercenaries, for the manufacture of guns and cannon, and for the construction of more ships. The armed merchants foraging overseas needed the state to shield them against competitors and to provide the officialdom capable of holding and consolidating the newly won areas. At the same time, the state needed the merchants to lend money to the Crown or to the captains of expeditions; to collect, ship, and sell the goods obtained abroad; and—increasingly—to acquire and export the goods needed in the far-flung outposts of the realm. Different authors have stressed now the bureaucratic character of the expansionist state, now its basis in surplus production by rural power holders, now its tie to merchants bent on overseas plunder and easy profits. The emerging states were all of these things, although the constituent elements were differently combined in each.

The key states that carried forward the expansion overseas were Portugal, Castile-Aragón, the United Provinces, France, and England. Each was the outcome of distinctive circumstances and of distinctive strategies to meet them. Each developed a variant array of classes arranged around the pivot of the state. Each committed people and resources to the task of conquest and commerce, and each set its seal upon some part of the globe, affecting large populations in turn. Each sought to oust the others from access to resources at home and abroad, and to reduce the ability of its competitors to continue in the game of expansion. We shall take a look at each of these political formations to show how each developed, used the resources of war and mercantile expansion, and then reached the limit of a political economy based on mercantile wealth.

Portugal

Portugal was the first of the European polities to develop into a center of expansionist activity in the search for wealth. It is also perhaps the least understood of the polities involved in expansion. It was a poor country, populated by no more than a million inhabitants at the end of the European Middle Ages. It soon acquired colonies as far away as Brazil in the Americas, Mozambique in Africa, and Malacca in Southeast Asia. In 1725 the Archbishop of Goa could still dream of a Portuguese empire, built on God's "infallible promises for the subjugation of the whole globe" (quoted in Boxer 1973a: 376). Yet by 1800 it had declined to the status of a second-rate power. What seems all the more extraordinary in retrospect is the power and fervor of its initial expansion, predicated upon so narrow a base of ecological resources.

Portugal began as a border fief of Spanish León. Like León, it grew gradually, as marauding bands of knights and settlers moved southward into the lands of Moslem Iberia. Yet, unlike Spain, it achieved political definition early. In 1147 Lisbon was taken from the Moslems; in 1249 Silves, the last remaining Moslem stronghold, fell to the Portuguese soldiery. In 1385 the new kingdom successfully routed the Castilians, maintaining its integrity under a dynasty founded by the Grand-Master of the religious-military order of Aviz.

Although Portuguese were later to sail to the far reaches of the globe, the country remained heavily dependent on agriculture throughout the course of its history. This was true even though much of the land is too steep or stony to be cultivated at all, rainfall is scant and irregular, and crops are consequently meager. Nevertheless, the bulk of the population worked the land, most of them under rental agreements that secured long-term occupance for the cultivators through payments in kind or money (covering from one-tenth to one-half of the annual produce), and through the rendering of two or three days per week of unremunerated labor.

The reliance on agriculture also oriented the country inland, away from the sea. There was fishing in the cool current that runs off Portugal and the west coast of Africa, but it had to contend with hostile tides and winds and with a lack of sheltered ports. Despite its maritime exploits, Portugal never had a very large seafaring population and never enough sailors for its oceangoing ships. Nor did the Portuguese have many ships. There was little timber within Portugal suitable for shipbuilding, and much of the timber and naval stores had to be imported. Even at the height of its power, Portugal possessed only 300 ocean-going ships (Boxer 1973a: 56). After the expansion overseas, most Portuguese ships were built at Goa in India, where timber was cut from the teak forests of the western coast, and at Bahia, where Brazilian hardwoods were used. To make up for the lack of Portuguese seamen, the Portuguese increasingly recruited other Europeans, Asians, and African slaves.

At home, agricultural rents and labor dues supported a military nobility exempt from taxes and protected against arbitrary arrest, as well as a large clerical establishment. A decline of population in the wake of the Black Death in the fourteenth century created pressures for lower rents in the countryside, but it also drew rural folk to the towns through the promise of higher wages. The scarcity of agricultural labor probably prompted the rentier nobility to take up arms in search of alternative sources of labor abroad. Of the 150,000 African slaves secured by the Portuguese between 1450 and 1500 (Boxer 1973a: 31), some were sent to the newly occupied sugar- and wheat-producing islands of Madeira and the Azores; others were sold in Italy and Spain. Many, however, were taken to Portugal, where they furnished a new source of bound labor. At the same time, the military nobility lost a great deal of its political power after the war with Castile in 1385, when a majority of the "old nobility" was killed or exiled for having sided with the Castilians. This made way for "new" nobles who supported the dynasty of Aviz, and it also increased the relative importance of the merchant class.

The merchants grew more prominent in the late fourteenth century, especially in Lisbon and Oporto. They dealt in agricultural products, trading first grain and later olive oil, wine, cork, and dyestuffs for English cloth. From the salt pans of Setúbal, they also supplied Europe with much of the salt it needed to preserve meat and fish.

Despite these gains, it is doubtful whether one should speak of a growing emancipation of the mercantile stratum from tributary controls, as some scholars have done. The greatest merchant of them all was to be the Crown, set upon this course through the activities of the Infante Dom Henrique (commonly known as Prince Henry the Navigator). Dom Henrique has gone down in history for his interest in navigation and map-making, but he also financed his activities with income from trade in West Africa and in the Atlantic islands, from fishing rights off the Algarve, from the importation of dyes and sugar into Portugal, and from control of soap-making at home—all this in the face of repeated protests in the Portuguese assembly. He was also the architect of the Portuguese seizure in 1425 of Ceuta, one of the terminal points in the gold trade across the Sahara, and he benefited from the capture and sale of slaves obtained in the course of the voyages along the African west coast. Subsequently, the Crown reserved for itself the monopoly over the import of gold, slaves, spices, and ivory, as well as all rights of export and re-export. The merchants profited from all this activity through concessions and contracts, but they never gained the power necessary to alter the class structure of the country in any significant way.

Castile-Aragón (Spain)

The other power in the Iberian peninsula was Spain, which achieved political unity with the union of the crowns of Castile and Aragón in 1469. When Germanic invasions from the north and Moslem invasions from the south shattered the administrative unity of the Roman province of Hispania, small remnant states survived in the north. These consolidated themselves gradually into the dual polities of the Crown of Castile and the Crown of Aragón, which included the Principality of Catalonia and the Kingdom of Aragón.

In the fourteenth century the union between these two polities was by no means assured. Castile, advancing against Moslem Al-Andalus, became locked into a military role, distributing conquered land in large latifundia to the military nobles who captained the conquest. This produced in the late fifteenth century a pattern of land ownership in which two or three percent of the population owned ninety-seven percent of the land, most of it in the hands of a few families (Elliott 1966: 111). The dominant pursuit in Castilian terrain came to be livestock keeping, notably the pasturage of sheep for the production of merino wool, to be finished into cloth in the Netherlands.

The lands of the Crown of Aragón, in contrast, were colonized gradually by settlers who created small communities in which the land was more evenly distributed than in Castile. At the same time, the Crown of Aragón had brought together the commercially oriented Principality of Catalonia and a primarily rural Aragón. Catalonia was, in the thirteenth and fourteenth centuries, a prosperous commercial state with maritime trade connections far into the Levant. In the fifteenth century, however, it lost out to Genoese competition. Genoa not only reduced Catalan influence in the Mediterranean but bypassed it by entering into commercial and financial relations with Castile. This coalition of Genoese financiers and noble Castilian wool producers effectively throttled Catalan mercantile growth and undermined the effectiveness of Catalan textile production and export. In the late fourteenth and fifteenth centuries, Catalonia was further undermined economically through a series of fierce uprisings by the peasantry against tributary ("feudal") dues and through open conflicts in the towns between the mercantile patriciate and the smaller merchants and artisans.

The union between Castile and Aragón yoked together two very unequal partners and ensured the dominance of Castile over Aragón, then "a society in retreat" (Elliott 1966: 42). It granted a leading role in the new Iberian polity to the noble owners of enormous sheep herds. They were organized in a powerful sheep-owners' association, the Mesta, which was able to promote their social and political interests with the state in exchange for paying taxes to the Crown. The export of Castilian wool through the northern ports tied this Cantabrian periphery to the interests of the Castilian military nobility.

The decisive Castilian shift toward a pastoral economy not only throttled industrial development in the Spanish realm, but it also reduced the ability of other classes to challenge the dominion of the military tribute takers. Warfare and seizure of people and resources, rather than commercial and industrial development, became the dominant mode of social reproduction. In this perspective the conquest of the New World represents but a prolongation of the Reconquista within the Iberian peninsula itself. The influx of silver from the New World from the sixteenth century on still further reduced Spanish industrial development through rising prices and inflation, rendering it uncompetitive with the industrial products of the Netherlands.

The silver of the New World, however, also enhanced the revenues of the Crown. Together, Spanish sheep and American silver underwrote large-scale Spanish military operations in Europe and the growth of a royal bureaucracy far beyond the ultimate capabilities of the Spanish economy. Deficit spending was made up by loans from foreign financiers only too happy to lend against future imports of silver or against taxes to be raised on the sale of wool. Spain thus never developed a coherent economic policy; the imperial bureaucracy acted simply as a conduit of wealth into Italian, South German, and Dutch coffers. The expulsion of 250,000 unconverted Moslems from southern Spain between 1609 and 1614 further weakened Spanish agriculture by halting rent payments to overlords, who then could not repay their mortgages. In the mid-seventeenth century even Spanish wool exports began to lose out to English competition. Shipping declined, and by the end of the sixteenth century Spanish shipbuilders could no longer compete effectively with the new techniques of North European dockyards. Capital began to flow increasingly into private loans and government bonds, which earned better rates of interest than investment in direct productive pursuits. The Spain of 1600 was already that spectral world of decay and disenchantment which Miguel Cervantes portrayed so masterfully in his *Don Quixote*. The Spanish economy had become a mere throughput of mercantile wealth for other economies, a "mother of foreigners, a step-mother of Spaniards."

The International Circuits of Mercantile Wealth

In both Portugal and Castile-Aragón, therefore, foreign merchants came to play a strategic role in managing the economy. Portugal sought and found needed wealth and mercantile support in the Italian city of Genoa, then fighting Venice for control of the trade with the Levant and more than willing to sponsor Portuguese trade as a way of breaking out of the constraining limits of the Mediterranean. Genoese merchants appeared in Portugal in the thirteenth century, and by the early fourteenth century Lisbon had become a major center of Genoese commerce. The Genoese also settled in Seville in the fifteenth century, where they helped finance the Spanish voyages to the Western Hemisphere in the fifteenth and sixteenth centuries. Major participants in this process were the families of Spinola, Centurioni, Giustiniani, and Doria. It is surely no accident that Columbus worked for the Centurioni in Lisbon in 1477, and in 1478 spent his honeymoon sailing to Madeira to purchase sugar for them (Pike 1966: 154, n. 58; 206, n. 2). Funds for Columbus's first and second voyages were contributed by Francisco Pinelo (Italian, Pinelli). The Genoese financiers were soon joined by the Fuggers and Welsers of Augsburg in southern Germany, whose growing prosperity from the mid-fifteenth century drew on South German trade with Venice and on mining operations throughout the Alps and the Carpathians.

Genoese and Bavarian financial growth together underwrote the rise of the city of Antwerp, located on the estuary of the Scheldt River in Brabant. It was still a minor port in the early fifteenth century, but between 1437 and 1555 it grew from an estimated 17,000 inhabitants to more than a hundred thousand (Russell 1972: 117; Smith 1967: 395). Accessible to the sea-lanes, it was the terminus of the overland route from Venice to the Rhine and a link in the chain of Hansa cities in the northern seas. When the Duke of Burgundy, within whose realm Antwerp was located, became the Emperor Charles V, the city's network grew to embrace the routes of the silver fleet from the Western Hemisphere as well. Antwerp thus became, in the first half of the sixteenth century, the hub of an international system of credit and payments. Genoese and Bavarian bankers soon held mortgages on the American silver fleet and on the tax income of Castile, obtained through loans advanced to the imperial Crown; in this way, silver flowed northward to Antwerp and into its international conduits.

Yet the predominance of Antwerp and its sponsors proved short-lived. The Spanish Crown experienced its first bankruptcy in 1550. Soon after, in 1566, the Netherlands rose in revolt; the rebellious "sea-beggars" sealed off Antwerp from the sea, and Spanish troops sacked it in 1576 in lieu of receiving their back pay. In 1575–1576 the Spanish Crown experienced its second bankruptcy, taking the Bavarian merchant houses with it. The Genoese, however, held their course and tightened their hold on the imperial resources, which now flowed increasingly into Genoa. They became, as a result, "the masters of international payments, of the fortunes both of Europe and of the world, the not unchallenged but well-entrenched masters of the political silver of Spain, from 1579 and perhaps even from 1577 on" (Braudel 1972: 393).

But the Genoese too were displaced in their turn, early in the seventeenth century, by Amsterdam and the Dutch cities allied with it. Amsterdam now became the center of Europe's international system of payments, taking in Spanish silver and Portuguese gold in exchange for goods manufactured in northern Europe. An important role in this ascendancy fell to Portuguese "New Christians," baptized or crypto-Jews, who had emigrated to Amsterdam to avoid economic and religious persecution in Iberia. They had played a leading role in the Portuguese trade in slaves and sugar in the New World, and they now put their capital and knowledge at the disposal of the Dutch.

The United Provinces

As Portugal and Spain both wrestled with the problems of their expanded empires, they encountered a new rival in the shape of the seafarers and fishermen of the Dutch Netherlands. The Dutch had come to the fore in the course of the fifteenth century in the sea-borne trade between the Baltic and western Europe, carrying Baltic grain and timber as well as Swedish metal on their trips to the west, and taking salt and cloth to the northern littorals on their trips east. After the herring migrated from the Baltic into North Sea waters in 1452, moreover, they intensified their fishing, their "principal gold mine." This Baltic trade always remained economically more important than the Dutch trade with Asia and the West Indies. Dutch expansion into other seas continued this commitment to sea-borne commerce.

To finance these undertakings abroad, the Dutch at first relied on foreign capital, provided mainly by Italian and South German bankers. When Charles V incorporated the Netherlands into his transoceanic empire, he also granted their merchants the privileges enjoyed by Spanish merchants in Spanish ports. The Dutch merchants thus benefited also from the flow of bullion coming in through Lisbon and Seville, and were amassing sufficient capital to engage in business transactions independently of foreign financiers.

The onset of the Reformation and the Dutch conversion to Protestantism led to a rupture with Catholic Spain, and to an eighty-year war between the Dutch United Provinces and the Iberians. Paradoxically, the United Provinces emerged from this prolonged warfare more powerful not only militarily but also financially. The revolt cemented an alliance among several Dutch towns, each governed by its local elite of merchant oligarchs, as well as an alliance between these maritime elites and the tributary lords of the landward provinces. Welcoming religious dissenters from Wallonia and Flanders, as well as Portuguese and Spanish Jews, the new Republic greatly added to its stock of capital and skills. Whereas before 1585 Dutch ships had appeared but rarely in the Mediterranean, they were frequent visitors thereafter. Direct Dutch trade with Brazil increased until the Dutch controlled between half and two-thirds of the carrying trade between Brazil and Europe by 1621. Throughout the prolonged war, moreover, Dutch merchants continued to trade with the enemy. The Spanish and Portuguese navies needed the timber and naval stores that the Dutch brought from the Baltic; taxes paid by Dutch merchants for permits to trade with the enemy were the chief source of Dutch revenue for carrying on the war (Boxer 1973b: 23–24). In the seventeenth century, as a result of such far-flung trade, Amsterdam became the center of the European trade in bullion, a role it would retain for 200 years.

During the second half of the seventeenth century, however, Dutch hegemony reached its zenith and then began to decline. Baltic grain grew less important in the markets of Europe; this diminished Dutch influence (Glamann 1971: 42–44). At the same time, the United Provinces began to suffer from competition with England, which increased its grain exports in response to depression and began to tax Dutch goods, thus spurring import substitution by English industries at home. Costly wars also affected the Dutch economy, as taxes rose to pay for them.

Why, then, did the United Provinces not turn toward industrial development? There are several reasons. First, shipping, shipbuilding, and the activities connected with them continued to be important and remunerative. Second, the returns on mercantile activity remained high, indeed higher than on investment in textile production. Third, agriculture in the United Provinces was already capital-intensive and specialized, and it paid high wages; there was therefore no poor rural populace to furnish industrial labor at low rates, as was the case in England. Fourth, the entire Dutch development was ultimately predicated on their ability to capitalize on skills and services, rather than on a strong resource base of their own. The population of the United Provinces was small. It had risen from 275,000 in 1514 to 883,000 in 1680; it fell back to 783,000 in 1750. In fact, manpower was scarce even in shipping, and increasing numbers of Scandinavians and North Germans were hired to man Dutch ships in the eighteenth century. Moreover, the United Provinces possessed neither coal nor iron, with which England was plentifully endowed. Finally, the Republic had always been a polity made up of nearly autonomous city-states, each with its own mercantile oligarchy. What had given them a common direction was the predominance of Amsterdam and their common success during the phase of Dutch ascendancy. In a period of growing difficulties, intensifying faction fights interfered with the ability of the various partners to the Dutch alliance to formulate and carry out common policy. After 1688, therefore, Dutch capital began to flow increasingly to England, where it was invested in the English East India Company, the Bank of England, and the British national debt, as well as in newly developing industries. In this, the Netherlands paid "the penalty of the commanding lead." Dominance passed into the hands of her chief rival.

France

The case of France represents still another response to the crisis of feudalism. This was the home of classic political feudalism, which utilized the legal form of ties between lords and vassals to build a vast edifice of graded relationships, with the king standing at the apex of the edifice. Here the main thrust of political consolidation was to convert the feudal pyramid, headed by the king, into a network of patron-client relations extending throughout France and controlled by the king through his control of superior resources (see Koenigsberger 1971: 6). This transformation was accomplished in France through the concentration of domestic agricultural surpluses rather than through expansion overseas. At the same time, the French Crown avoided—to a much greater extent than did the rulers of Portugal or Castile-Aragón— dependence on foreign financiers and the resulting international entanglements.

We have seen how the France-to-be grew outward from a small but fertile core region that controlled the rivers of the Seine and the Loire in their middle courses. At first the king was but *primus inter pares* among a number of other powerful feudatories, but he gained increasing power by expanding the direct royal domain in all directions, until by 1328 it covered half of what is now France. The other half was held in fiefs of the Crown. In this process of expansion, however, not only did the French king oust the English and their feudal tenants, but he also gained ascendancy over potential rivals in Aquitaine to the west and Occitania in the south. This put additional agricultural resources at the disposition of the Crown, and it subjected to the political center at Paris the maritime margins of the west and south, including the commercial cities of Nantes, Bordeaux, and Toulouse. From the fifteenth century on, the economic and political exigencies of the land-based core of the French monarchy controlled and limited mercantile activity along the Atlantic fringe, with major implications for the participation of France in the course of European expansion (Fox 1971).

Although the king consolidated his control over France, he could not and did not challenge outright the rights of the nobility to draw surpluses from the peasantry. The peasantry received the right to pay rents in money or in kind, rather than in labor on a tribute taker's home farm or demesne. It was the peasantry who carried on production, the lords taking their share of the crops as tribute to sell on the market. In this regard, the king was simply the topmost noble, living off his own domain. The large extent of his domain made him correspondingly powerful, but since the nobility remained exempt from taxation, the financial resources of the Crown were limited. The king attempted to capitalize on trade and credit relations with the Italian cities, but their decline affected his ability to obtain funds.

In the end, the king attempted to solve this problem by creating a nobility of his own—the nobility of the robe as contrasted with the nobility of the sword—by selling offices and noble status to merchants and professionals. Among the new nobility were tax farmers who advanced money to the Crown in return for the right to collect and retain taxes. The taxes were paid ultimately by the peasantry and by mercantile and manufacturing entrepreneurs. Income obtained by taxes was huge—ten times, for example, that obtained in England (Finer 1975: 128)—but its very size depressed agriculture and throttled trade and industry as well. The peasantry was overburdened; the bourgeoisie, too, was under pressure to survive (Wallerstein 1974: 297).

This set of relations obtaining between the king, the old nobility, the new nobility, and the peasantry was shattered in the French Revolution of 1789. The revolution was made by peasants rising to shake off their noble rentiers, by poor artisans and journeymen of Paris, and by bourgeoisie "under pressure to survive." It was a revolution against the aristocracy in that it freed the peasantry from the payment of tribute and cleared the road to office for members of the Third Estate. It was not, however, a revolution that cleared the road toward capitalist development. The "bourgeoisie" it set free was not a class of industrial capitalists, but a "petty" bourgeoisie of artisans, shopkeepers, small merchants, and small-scale entrepreneurs. Heavy industrialization in France had to await the second half of the nineteenth century.

The Limits of Mercantile Circulation

We have seen how three European states—Portugal, Spain, and the United Provinces—underwent a phase of mercantile expansion overseas, only to experience a downturn in their affairs in the aftermath. A fourth polity, France, directed its energies toward domestic consolidation, curtailing the activities of its maritime fringe through the centralization of power in Paris.

The alliance of state and merchants that made possible the ascendancy of Portugal began in the early fifteenth century, acquired momentum in the sixteenth, and declined in the seventeenth. The Methuen treaty of 1703, which permitted the entry of English textiles into Portugal in exchange for the import of port wine into England, merely formalized that decline. Spain, the union of polities led by the rulers of Castile, expanded in the sixteenth century to create an empire ranging from Florida to Chile, and from the Caribbean islands to the Philippines. Yet by the beginning of the seventeenth century, Spain was in decline and began to live out fantasies of past greatness in the midst of decaying realities. Even the hardheaded attempts of the Bourbon dynasty, in the eighteenth century, to stem that decline through measures of an "applied enlightenment" proved fruitless. The United Provinces, in turn, rose successfully against Spain in 1566 and expanded overseas in the sixteenth and seventeenth centuries; but they reached the limits of their power in the late seventeenth century, when they came under increasing pressure from the successful English. France attempted in the course of the eighteenth century to oust England from India and North America. Having retarded the growth of its industry and its naval capability, however, it faced this task essentially as a land power unable to match the navy and industry of England.

The seventeenth century played a decisive role in these affairs of state. States that had proved successful in overcoming "the crisis of feudalism" in the fifteenth century found themselves dragged down by economic depression and political difficulties in the seventeenth. This was especially clear in the Iberian peninsula. There, whatever surpluses had been generated were used up in the military and political activities of the state and in the conspicuous consumption of the court. Continuous warfare and pillage favored the persistence of tributary lords and even a growth in their power. The continuation of the Reconquista in the Americas strengthened the military and social power of the king and nobles, while inducing economic stagnation in the towns and countryside. At the same time, the rising costs of war burned up resources or handed them over to the creditors of the Crown. In France surpluses were concentrated in the hands of the king and were used to crush or buy off opposition at home and to further war abroad, to the detriment of economic and political alternatives. In the Dutch polity government was more modest in its demands, and conspicuous expenditures were less marked. Yet worldwide commercial expansion accentuated the middleman role of the Dutch merchants, even while it furthered the development of manufactures accessory to trade and shipping, such as shipbuilding and the provision of naval stores. The Dutch case demonstrates that it was not the costly expenditures of war or court life as such that generated the crisis, but rather the inability to convert the gains of war and mercantile activity into new surplus-producing activities. This ability depends on the conversion of mercantile wealth into capital.

Behind the economic and political crisis of the seventeenth-century state lay a larger crisis, caused by the inability of mercantile wealth to alter and transform the ways of committing labor to the creation of new resources. We have already drawn the distinction between capitalism and the employment of wealth to gain a profit. The merchants of Europe did indeed make money and pile up wealth. They traded in furs, spices, slaves, gold, and silver. They developed regional specialization through the development of the staple trade, exchanging grain grown here for salt produced there, cloth woven in one place for iron smelted in another. They created commercial networks that made it possible to aggregate men and tools and thus to produce commodities in ever larger quantities for centralized sales. They affected and transformed the sites and routes of circulation. They carried on *commerce*, as understood by Ibn Khaldun, the Berber sociologist of the fourteenth century, who wrote:

> One must know that commerce is the search for gain by increasing the initial fund when one buys commodities at a favorable price and resells them at a higher price, whether these commodities consist of slaves, cereals, animals, or textiles. This increase is called profit. This profit is obtained by storing the commodity and awaiting a fluctuation in the tendency of the market to rise, which produces a great profit; or by transporting the commodity mentioned to another region where the demand for it is stronger, which also produces a great profit. [quoted in Rodinson 1966: 47]

The European merchants even altered, here and there, the organization of work and the conditions of labor employed in producing a commodity for sale. What they did *not* do, however, was to use their wealth as capital to acquire and transform means of production and set them in motion through the purchase of labor power offered for sale by a class of laborers.

England

Only England would take the step from accumulation and distribution of mercantile wealth to a thoroughgoing capitalist transformation. Yet if one looks at England before 1400, it would seem an unlikely candidate for its later predominance. It was eccentric in its geographical position off the coast of Europe, and the course of its development appears idiosyncratic when compared with that of the continental states. Its conquest by the French-speaking descendants of Norwegian Vikings in 1066 had imposed a unified fiscal and judicial system on the island, under the aegis of the king. This system relied for its operation less on an elaborate and centralized bureaucracy of the French type, and more on the cooperation of local notables. The costs of government were thus reduced. Furthermore, the burdens of taxation were distributed more equitably than in France. English nobles paid taxes, while the French nobility remained exempt from taxation until the Revolution of 1789. Because of its insular position, England was relatively immune to attacks from the continent, and after the English kings were pushed out of France the country was spared the large expenditures for war on land and sea that plagued its later continental rivals.

Until the end of the fourteenth century, England was in the main an agricultural country, looking inward and not yet drawn to the sea

(Graham 1970: 14). Two characteristics, however, distinguished the English economy from developments on the continent. The first was the gradual abrogation, during the fourteenth and fifteenth centuries, of heritable peasant tenure held from an overlord, in favor of rents renegotiable at intervals with terms set by the prevailing economic situation. This made possible, over time, the conversion of "customary" dues into variable money rents. In France, in marked contrast, the peasantry was able to strengthen its grip on the land through increased guarantees of perpetual inheritance. The overlord could attempt to increase tribute due him by multiplying dues receivable; but he was not able to alter in any fundamental way the conditions of land management and cultivation. Thus, the English peasantry was surprisingly weak in comparison with that of France. The use of land to yield profit in the form of variable money rent placed in the hands of the overlord the power to reallocate land to tenants who could maximize profits. It was, therefore, easier for the English tribute taker than for his French counterpart to turn land itself into a commodity. In the course of the sixteenth century, then, English landowners began to pursue commodity production as "improving landlords."

The second important characteristic of the English economy lay in the early role of England as a producer of raw wool, perhaps the finest in Europe. In the thirteenth and fourteenth centuries much of its wool was sold abroad, especially to feed the woolen industry of Flanders. The wool trade soon became a mainstay of royal income. The export of wool turned England into a kind of colony of the Flemings, "content", as Pirenne says,

> to supply them with the raw material. They were to the Flemish cloth industry what the Argentine Republic and Australia are to the cloth industry of Europe and America today. Instead of competing with them, they devoted themselves to producing more and more wool for which there was always a sale. [1937: 153]

Not only was this wool destined for foreign markets but it was mostly foreigners, notably the Hansa, who carried it to its destination on the other side of the Channel.

Yet at the end of the fourteenth century, the English turned from the export of wool to the manufacture of cloth on their own account. Several interlinked aspects facilitated this changeover. As cloth production increased, it became economically feasible for English woolens to compete in foreign markets. At the same time, the fourteenth-century crisis of feudalism rendered such an alternative attractive, especially in agricultural areas attempting to cope with the prevailing depression. The manufacture of woolen cloth was thus able to move from the towns into rural areas, where it could take advantage of water power to run the fulling mills and where it could find cheap labor untrammeled by the restrictions on employment maintained by urban guilds. Such alternative employment of rural labor, together with the expansion of sheep ranges at the expense of cultivation, intensified the use of land as a marketable commodity and as an instrument in commodity production.

Expanding cloth manufacture invited the support of the state. Home industry was protected against foreign imports. The construction of English ships was encouraged, and the new maritime technology was used to build "round" sailing ships equipped with guns. State-chartered commercial organizations, such as London Mercers' Company in the fourteenth century and the Company of Merchant Adventurers in the fifteenth, were created to further the export of English cloth. The organizations of traders abroad soon multiplied: the Russia Company, in 1553; the Spanish Company, in 1577; the Eastland Company, set up in 1578 to trade in Scandinavia and the Baltic; the Levant Company, established in 1592; the East India Company, in 1600; the Virginia Company, in 1606; the English Amazon Company (1619–1623); and the Massachusetts Bay Company, in 1629. Still later, in 1660, came the Royal Adventurers into Africa, to be replaced twelve years later by the more efficient Royal African Company. These companies and their successors soon widened the scale of English commercial operations. This spurred the development of crafts and manufactures to supply the new routes and sites of circulation.

The path of expansion was cleared by the political upheavals of 1640 and 1688. The Glorious Revolution arrayed profit-taking landlords, manufacturers, and commercial agents against the privileges held and defended by the court, the high nobility, and the merchant monopolists. It destroyed royal absolutism, streamlined the government, and changed the tax base, doing away with levies on manufacturing monopolies and royal tributary dues in favor of the excise (a tax on commodities in general use) and the assessment, a tax on landed estates. It set up a national army and navy and prepared them for military competition with the United Provinces and France. It accelerated the growth of agricultural commodity production by encouraging further enclosures of land and commons. It supported the development of domestic industry, employing the labor of displaced cultivators or landless households.

In the course of the revolution power shifted from one class to another, from court-based power holders who still relied on the arrangements of a tributary mode to coalitions of provincial entrepreneurs. The revolution, however, did not obliterate the losers. Instead, it took them into partnership (see Hill 1949: 126). Indeed, the English preserved many institutions of their tributary tradition—such as monarchy, peerage, church, parliament, and common law—and adapted them to new functions. They also maintained the ideology and etiquette of nobility as the form, if not the content, of class rule: the profit-taking landlord and the rising manufacturer and putting-out merchant adopted the symbolic forms of traditional squirearchy.

In many ways, then, the English case appears unique. England began as a marginal and colonial country, lying off a continent populated by more powerful neighbors, wealthier and equipped with more elaborate institutions than its own. Yet it achieved an early unity under the Norman kings, who unified its administration and obliterated internal barriers to the circulation of goods and people, barriers that still bedeviled many of its continental neighbors well into the nineteenth century. Its peasantry proved surprisingly weak juridically and was easily uprooted. The growth of its cloth trade—which underwrote its entry into wider markets and political orbits—proved a success story, benefiting by a series of fortunate conjunctures. Finally, its mode of governance—with its mixture of old and new, but above all low in cost—was remarkably successful in establishing and maintaining the distribution of class forces upon which successful capitalist industrialization depended. England, too, would come to pay "the penalty of the retarding lead," but only a century after it had staged the breakthrough into a new mode of production.

The centuries after A.D. 800 saw Europe transformed from a marginal frontier of the Old World into a hub of wealth and power. The European thrust was carried forward by two classes in alliance: a class of military overlords bent on enlarging their tributary domains, and a class of merchants hoping to convert tributary surpluses into money and profit. Political and military consolidation gave rise to territorial states that transferred power from autonomous overlords to paramount rulers. In the process the tributary aristocracy lost its ability to form independent alliances across state boundaries and yielded increasingly to guidance from a political center, gaining in exchange political guarantees of its tributary rights. At the same time, the growth of trade multiplied opportunities for the conversion of tributary surpluses into both strategic and prestige-conferring commodities. Sponsorship of commerce thus enabled the new political systems to widen the range of resources at their disposal. Yet commerce also posed a potential threat: unfavorable exchanges could weaken the state, "consume a nation's heart," much as favorable exchanges could strengthen it. The new centralizing political systems had also to define their relation to trade and to its ambivalent promise.

Two Iberian powers, Portugal and Castile, emerged as successful organizations of tribute takers in the course of wars against the Muslim states of the peninsula. In both kingdoms royal control of commerce enhanced the power of the kingship and provided a tribute-taking elite with wealth to purchase goods abroad without altering the tributary structure at home. Yet in both countries that wealth did not suffice to cover the costs of administration and war. Royal bankruptcies and debts transferred control of exchequer and trade to foreign merchant-bankers, turning the two countries into "the Indies of the Genoese" (Suárez de Figueroa 1617, quoted in Elliott 1970: 96). France, in contrast, avoided this fate, achieving political centralization without dependence on foreign credit. It granted priority to the production of home-grown agricultural surpluses over the interests of commerce, underwriting, in the process, the development of "classic" land-based tributary feudalism. While France thus did not fall victim to foreign indebtedness, it also curtailed for a long time to come its ability to compete effectively in commerce abroad.

While the Iberian powers fell prey to foreign commerce and France eschewed it, the United Provinces of the Netherlands and England adapted to it successfully. The United Provinces developed as a federation of merchant oligarchies. Dependent since early times on sea-borne commerce, the Dutch maximized its possibilities at the cost of securing a sizable territorial base in their hinterland. They became the "Italians of the North," like the trading cities of Genoa and Venice investing their major efforts in the expansion of long-distance trade. England, in contrast, was long a territorial power, dominated by a military aristocracy of tribute takers until the fifteenth century, when it had to abandon its predilect battlefields in France. Thrown back upon its island, the English aristocracy destroyed itself in civil wars, clearing the field for the emergence of a new aristocracy more attuned to the commercial opportunities of sheep raising, the manufacture of woolen cloth, and overseas commerce. At the same time, the new English Crown proved less powerful than its continental counterparts; although no less bent on centralization than the continental kings, the English monarchy was successfully checked by both landowning gentry and merchant groups. Crown, landowners, and merchants were thus forced into partnerships with one another, producing flexible coalitions that redounded to the profit of all partners.

The United Provinces and England differed in their development, but they shared—in contrast to the other European powers—a willingness to turn commerce into an outright instrument of political competition. England had early freed itself from the stranglehold of Italian and Hansa merchants over its foreign commerce; the Dutch had won independence from Spain by carrying economic and political war to their enemies. This common experience led them both to use commerce, rather than be used by it, as "a politique secret war" (John Hagthrope Gent 1625). In the hands of the Dutch and English ruling oligarchies, commerce and warfare abroad became alternate means toward the same end, the successful accumulation of treasure, "the very body and blood of kings" (Gerard Malynes 1623).

In Dutch and English overseas expansion, therefore, the three means of building state power that had underwritten political consolidation within Europe were fused into a unitary policy, one aimed at maximizing the possession of bullion in the hands of the state. To accomplish this

"Sanguinification of the Common-wealth," as Thomas Hobbes called it, it was necessary to augment the flow of bullion toward the national treasuries and to impede its outward flow. For the Netherlands and for England this meant drawing as much gold and silver as possible out of Portugal and Spain and their American possessions, and using this wealth to organize and monopolize commerce in the Orient. Asia, since the Roman era a purveyor of valued goods for the tribute-taking classes of Europe, had for as long a time drained Europe of precious metals. Expanding conquest and trade in Asia thus promised to reverse the asymmetrical relation between debtor and creditor, and to give the European sea merchants unimpeded access to the treasures of the East. Whoever controlled that trade, wrote Charles Davenant in the seventeenth century, would be able to "give law to all the commercial world."

Washing gold. Copper engraving by Theodor de Bry, 1590. (Courtesy of the Rare Books and Manuscripts Division, The New York Public Library. Astor, Lenox, and Tilden Foundations)

Part Two
In Search
of Wealth

The expansion of Europe overseas began with a minor event in 1415: the seizure by the Portuguese of the Muslim port of Ceuta on the African side of the Straits of Gibraltar. The Portuguese sought only to take "the key to the Mediterranean" but the invasion of the North African coast would lead them to the Atlantic islands and the African coast. In thus opening up the routes of the southern Atlantic to European ships, the Portuguese acted as an advance guard of the European thrust. We have seen how diminishing surpluses drove the Europeans to seek resources abroad, especially as increased wealth was required to finance the emergent states. Such wealth could be found in the Levant of Byzantium and Islam, but the road to riches through the eastern Mediterranean was barred—on the one hand, by Byzantium, the Seljuk Turks, and after 1453 by the Ottoman Turks, and on the other hand, by Venice and Genoa, the agents of European trade with the Orient. The new Atlantic route opened by the Portuguese promised to bypass the Turkish roadblock to the treasures of Asia.

The Portuguese quickly followed the seizure of Ceuta with settlement of Madeira in 1420, construction of a fort and warehouse on Arguin Island off Mauritania in 1448, and a second fort at Elmina (Mina) in the Bight of Benin in 1482. A year later they reached the mouth of the Congo River, and in 1487 they rounded the Cape of Good Hope. The road to India thus lay open, and in 1497 Vasco da Gama initiated his voyage around the Cape to East Africa and to the Indian Malabar coast. In 1505 the Portuguese built an advance base at Sofala in East Africa, and four years later they launched their conquests of the key strongpoints of the south Asian seas. The Portuguese also crossed the Atlantic, beginning with Cabral's landing in Brazil in 1500. By 1502 a *converso* from Lisbon was authorized to ship brazilwood to Portugal. In the 1520s sugar cultivation began in the Brazilian northeast, and after 1530 African slaves started to arrive in the new colony. Thus, the spice trade came to link Lisbon with Asia; sugar connected the Portuguese capital with America; and the slave trade forged a chain across the southern Atlantic.

From this time on, all struggles for dominance within Europe would take on a global character, as the European states sought to control the oceans and to oust their competitors from points of vantage gained in Asia, America, or Africa. From then on, too, events in one part of the globe would have repercussions in other parts. The several continents would be drawn into one worldwide system of connections.

The Portuguese expansion was soon followed by Castile-Aragón. In 1492 Columbus, sailing for Castile, reached the islands of the Caribbean. Penetration of the mainland proceeded rapidly. Balboa crossed the Isthmus of Panama to reach the Pacific in 1513; Cortés began his conquest of Mexico in 1519; in 1530 Pizarro set out from Panama to conquer Peru. A Spanish expeditionary force sailing from Mexico occupied the Philippines in 1564, extending the Spanish sway into the

Pacific. In 1580 the Spanish king succeeded to the Portuguese throne as well, tying Portugal to Spain until 1640.

The Dutch, then fighting their prolonged war against Spain, thus found an excuse and an opportunity to oust the Portuguese from their holdings in Asia and America. The Dutch East India Company was founded in 1602 in order to break the Portuguese monopoly over the spice trade. In 1621 a Dutch West India Company was created as well. Twenty years later, the Dutch had taken most of the Portuguese strongholds along the Atlantic coast of Africa, seized Brazil, occupied Curaçao and several other Caribbean islands, and established settlements in North America at New Amsterdam, on Long Island, and in Delaware. But while the Dutch seizure of the East Indies proved successful, they were unable to hold most of their new western possessions. Brazil rose in rebellion, ousting the Dutch in 1654; the Portuguese regained many of their African strongholds; and the English captured New Amsterdam in 1644.

The English expansion overseas was at first in the shadow of Dutch power. The English East India Company had been chartered in 1600, but it took second place to the Dutch Company until the latter part of the seventeenth century. While the English had raided in the Americas during their struggle with Spain in the sixteenth century, they established themselves in the Spanish Caribbean only in 1624, with the settlement of Barbados, followed by the seizure of Jamaica in 1655. They had founded a number of settlements along the North American coast in Virginia, Maryland, and New England, consolidating these in the face of Dutch competition; in the course of the global struggle between the English and the Dutch in the second half of the seventeenth century, these English possessions in America gained as Dutch power receded. The organization of a new English company to trade in Africa in 1660 allowed England to make further inroads on Dutch trade.

Yet as the Dutch threat receded, the English found themselves face to face with French competition in North America. French colonization had begun there early in the sixteenth century. In 1608 Quebec was founded; in 1642, Montreal. As the fur trade expanded westward along the St. Lawrence River into the Great Lakes, it gave rise to a prolonged struggle in which the English strove to choke off the French advance. This struggle would end only the capture of Canada by Britain in 1763. On the other side of the globe, the English East India Company would face the fierce competition of the French India Company (founded in 1664). This competition, too, was resolved in favor of England, when ruinous war debts drove the French Company into bankruptcy in 1769.

In less than two centuries, therefore, the European powers expanded the scope of their trading activities to all the continents and made the world their battleground. The quest for American silver, the fur trade, the trade in slaves, and the search for Asian spices drew people into new and unforeseen interdependencies and profoundly changed their lives.

5 Iberians in America

In 1493 Columbus returned from his first voyage to the Caribbean, in the belief—which he maintained until his death—that he had reached islands lying off the eastern coast of Asia. A year later, Castile-Aragón and Portugal signed a treaty at Tordesillas staking out their claims to the newly found lands. They drew a dividing line 370 leagues west of the Cape Verde Islands. Castile, believing that it now controlled a direct route to the Orient, claimed all lands west of the line—and thereby acquired the major part of the Western Hemisphere. Portugal, intent mainly upon keeping the Spaniards out of the South Atlantic, took all lands to the east of the line and thus came into possession of Brazil. Portugal, occupied with establishing its hegemony over the South Atlantic and Monsoon Asia, was slow to consolidate its claims in the New World. Castile-Aragón, however, moved rapidly to secure the fabled treasures of the "Indies."

Two decades after the discovery of the Americas, the Castilians had already consolidated their bases in the Great Antilles and along the Isthmus of Panama. Cortés's conquest of Mexico was completed in 1521 with the destruction of the Mexica capital of Tenochtitlán. Pizarro captured the Inca capital of Cuzco in 1533. By 1541 the Castilians had laid the foundations of the new city of Santiago in Chile. These Indies belonged to the Crown of Castile and were administered by direct representatives of the Castilian king sitting in Mexico City, center of the Viceroyalty of New Spain, and in Lima, center of the Viceroyalty of Peru.

In this realm created by conquest, the prizes of victory were fame and fortune—both dependent, it was thought, on the labor of the native populations. The new society thus came to be divided from the outset into "the natives of the land" (*naturales de la tierra*) and Spaniards. The natives were categorized together under the cover term *Indian*, in spite of marked differences in their languages and cultures. Above the natives stood the Spaniards—the conquerors, their descendants, and all the later arrivals who aspired to their status—who came to define themselves as "men of reason" (*gente de razón*). Not that these men of reason

Spain and Portugal in the New World.

were all of one kind. The conquerors included nobles and commoners, rich and poor. After the conquest they rapidly divided further into various and often antagonistic layers: the captains of real wealth and power; the men of moderate means, skill and influence; an array of hungry followers who depended upon others for their "bread and water" (*paniaguados*); and hosts of vagrants, who lived along the margins of the developing networks of social relations. Yet they all shared an interest in maintaining their common superiority as conquerors over the conquered. They formed the dominant element in the towns, which enmeshed the conquered countryside in a network of Spanish control, constituting the foundation of Spanish power in the Indies. These towns were all laid out along the same grid-pattern plan, pivoted upon a central square containing mayoralty and church, site at once of the regular market and the emergency call-up of military forces. Each town, with its oligarchic *cabildo* (town council) of *vecinos* (citizens eligible to attend council meetings), represented a microcosm of Spanish control in a sea of "Indians."

It was ultimately these Indians whom the colonists hoped to control. Yet this basic resource underwent an immediate and catastrophic decline.

The Great Dying

The "great dying" first affected the islands of the Caribbean. It then spread to the mainland shores and to the Middle and South American lowlands in general. Finally, it made inroads into the highlands, which had supported the great polities of the Aztec, Chibcha, and Inca. Thus, Española (Santa Domingo) had about a million inhabitants in 1492, when first contacted by Columbus; by the end of the 1520s only insignificant numbers survived (Sauer 1966: 65–69, 200–204). A primary cause of the population decline was the spread of Old World pathogenic organisms to which New World populations were not immune. The impact of smallpox and measles, often complicated by respiratory ailments, was perhaps decisive over wide areas. There were as many as fourteen major epidemics in Mesoamerica and perhaps as many as seventeen in the Andean region between 1520 and 1600 (Gibson 1964: 448–451; Dobyns 1963: 494). Other illnesses had more localized effects. On the Mesoamerican coast, malaria—probably introduced by Spanish merchants and soldiers from Italy—caused regional havoc and then spread through the tropical lowlands.

The advent of pathogens, however, does not in itself furnish an adequate explanation of what happened. One must ask also about the social and political conditions that permitted the pathogens to proliferate at so rapid a rate. On the islands and in the borderlands of the Caribbean, these conditions clearly included the profligate use of Indian labor in the search for gold, and (after 1494) the massive intensification of slave raiding and slavery. Nicaragua alone lost, in the first half of the sixteenth century, an estimated 200,000 inhabitants to slave raiders, who sold their prey in the Caribbean islands, Panama, and Peru (MacLeod 1973: 52). Portuguese settlement in Brazil also brought large-scale Indian slavery. By the 1560s there were 40,000 native Americans laboring as slaves in the Brazilian Northeast (Hemming 1978: 143). During the last third of the sixteenth century, native social relations had grown sufficiently deranged to cause the Indians of Bahia to rise up in a great millenarian movement, the *Santidade*, in which people ceased to grow food for themselves in the hope that God would free them from slavery and make the Europeans their slaves instead. In all, the slave-raiding *bandeirantes* of São Paulo are thought to have furnished the Brazilian Northeast with 350,000 native American slaves during the period of Brazilian slavery. Since most of the populations of the lowlands were organized according to kin-ordered modes, such massive drains of manpower severely curtailed their ability to enforce and reproduce the rights to people that made their survival possible.

In Mesoamerica and in the Andean areas, large-scale populations had supported complex tributary systems, such as the Aztec confederation and the Inca domain. In these areas the catastrophic population decline contributed to the fragmentation of existing polities. The pre-Hispanic population of Mesoamerica has been estimated at 25 million, that of the Inca domain at anywhere between 6 million (Rowe) and 30 million (Dobyns). Whatever the baseline figure, the decline decimated the population. In Mesoamerica the population count fell to a low point of 1.5 million by 1650, recovering slowly thereafter. The number of inhabitants of the Spanish audiencias of Lima and Charcas, in Lower and Upper Peru respectively, declined from 5 million at the time of the Conquest to less than 300,000 in the 1780s and 1790s (Kubler 1946: 340).

In these highland areas malnutrition probably increased the virulence of the new diseases (see Feinman 1978). Food supplies both in Mesoamerica and the Andes depended, in the first instance, on highly organized and intensive systems of land use. Any dislocation of these systems—through warfare, foreign encroachment, or death by illness of some part of the labor force—threatened the survival of the remaining population. The disruption of hydraulic works and the interruption of exchanges between zones specializing in different products set off ramifying consequences. Both regions were also dependent on a finely calibrated system of food transfers—through the concentration and redistribution of tribute in the Andes, through both tribute redistribution and marketing arrangements in Mesoamerica. When these mechanisms were destroyed, available surpluses could not reach populations in need; many undoubtedly died as a result. Finally, these ordering mechanisms depended, in turn, on the political and ideological role of the ruling classes; the dislocation of the native elite and the imposition of Spanish norms of government and religion severely undermined this role.

Within a short time the Europeans also began to appropriate land and water for their own farms, mills, and pasture grounds, and to draft native populations for work. In many parts of Mesoamerica, as in Spain, sheep began to "eat" men. In the Andes the parallel development of European agriculture on the coast and mining in the interior highlands upset the synchronized ecological relationships between coast, piedmont, highland, and puna (see chapter 2). The new agriculture and pastoralism made use of crops brought in from the Old World—such as wheat—in addition to the native crops of maize or potatoes, and introduced herd animals that had not existed in the Americas before the Conquest, such as horses, cattle, sheep, goats, and pigs. Yet the new system of food production was not as intensive as the hydraulic horticulture of the pre-Hispanic populations, even where dams were built, canals dug, and land irrigated. Decreased intensity and integration of cultivation required a smaller labor force, and thus the decline in population could be weathered. An agriculture of clean-tilled fields and open pasture range replaced a horticulture based on the meticulous cultivation, drainage, and terracing of small plots.

The Wealth of Spanish America

The Search for Silver

What the Iberians sought in the New World was, above all else, treasure in the form of bullion. At first this meant gold. Placer gold was found in the Antilles, but "the productive districts were few, of small extent, and slight depth" (Sauer 1966: 198). The native population was soon sacrificed in its extraction. The auriferous deposits of the Central American isthmus proved ephemeral. Only Colombia—"Castilla de oro," as it was soon called—became a significant gold producer. It contributed most of the 185,000 kilograms of gold shipped to Seville between 1503 and 1660, an amount that increased European gold supplies by a fifth (Elliott 1966: 180). Yet it was silver production that finally became the mainstay of Spanish wealth, and thus the major indicator of the strength or debility of royal control.

Silver deposits were first discovered by the Spaniards in 1545, when an Indian prospector located the 2,000-foot-high silver mountain of San Luis Potosí, in what is now Bolivia. This was followed by a succession of strikes in the western mountain chains of Mexico: at Zacatecas in 1546, Guanajuato in 1548, Taxco in 1549, Pachuca in 1551, Sombrerete and Durango in 1555, Fresnillo in 1569. Potosí, especially, became synonymous with the notion of wealth beyond the dreams of avarice. Its coat of arms proclaimed it to be "treasure of the world, king of all the mountains, envy of all the kings." By 1611 it was the largest and wealthiest city of the Americas, with a population of 160,000 inhabitants. It was located in a high-altitude environment (13,000 feet) so inhospitable that all food had to be imported, and the wives of Spaniards had to move to lower-lying valleys to raise their children. To mine the ores of the magic mountain, the lords of the mines called on the native American population. At Potosí in 1603, there were 58,800 Indian workers. Most of these, 43,200, were free day laborers; 10,500 were *mingas*, or contract laborers. The remainder, 5,100, were *mitayos*, or labor draftees, most of whom were employed in the perilous work of carrying the baskets of ore over treacherous ladders to the mouth of the mine. A rotational, obligatory labor draft (*mita*) had existed in Inca times; the Spaniards extended it to service in the mines. Institutionalized in 1570, it required every village to make available annually a seventh of its adult male population for work in the mines or on public projects. The laborers were suppose to work for no more than eighteen weeks every seven years and be paid wages, working under conditions to be supervised by royal inspectors. The wages received would also allow the miners to pay their tribute, now rendered payable in silver.

Actual practice, however, proved rather harsher than theory. At the end of the sixteenth century, for instance, the province of Chuicuito on the shores of Lake Titicaca sent 2,200 adult males each year to the mines of Potosí. Since these draft laborers went accompanied by their families, the 300-mile, two-month-long journey was negotiated by 7,000 people in all, as well as by 30,000 to 50,000 llamas to carry their belongings and provide sustenance on the way. In Potosí the mitayo spent four months in the mines and two months in additional compulsory service. If he survived the six months of arduous labor, the return to Chuicuito would require another two months. Once back home, he had to depend on his neighbors until he could again harvest his own crops and raise a new herd of llamas. At the same time, he was subject in his home village to other mitas for domestic work, transportation, mail service, innkeeping (*tambos*), and road work (Kubler 1946: 372–373). In the seventeenth and eighteenth centuries, moreover, villagers could be forced to produce artisan goods and to supply food, fodder, and wood to the cities (Villamarín and Villamarín 1975: 73). Resident villagers (*hatunrunas*) also had to pay tribute.

During the period of sharp population decrease, service and tribute quotas remained constant. Local authorities thus had to impress men into service more often than stipulated by law, exact higher contributions from those remaining in the villages, or hire contract laborers (*mingas*) to stand in for absentees. Many labor draftees refused to return to their communities when they had completed their turn of duty, attempting in this way to avoid further tribute and mita obligation. Some remained in the mining centers, swelling the number of free laborers. Others took service with Spaniards as serfs, or *yanaconas*, until there were nearly as many serfs as tribute-paying villagers (Villamarín and Villamarín 1975: 76; Kubler 1946: 377–378). Still other mitayos

Wooden beaker (kero) *of pre-Conquest style, Cuzco region, depicting a hunting scene with Spanish riders. (Photograph courtesy Museum of the American Indian, Heye Foundation)*

became migrants, *forasteros*. Although the colonial records do not always distinguish between village-affiliated cultivators, who migrated regularly between various ecological zones in traditional Andean fashion, and nonaffiliated migrants, outright movement was frequent and extensive (Rowe 1957: 180; Santamaría 1977: 255–257). Finally, some highlanders simply fled into the tropical forest (Rowe 1957: 175).

While the mita in Potosí and Upper Peru was not abolished until 1823, in Mexico the use of rotational labor in the mines disappeared soon after the beginning of the seventeenth century. On the one hand, rotational labor was needed for public work projects, such as the drainage of the Valley of Mexico. On the other hand, by 1600 there already existed a sizable free, wage-paid labor force in the mining districts. It was made up of Indians, who quickly lost their cultural and linguistic connections with their home villages, or poor Spaniards, and of Africans, both slave and free. Mining was carried out on a basis analogous to sharecropping. The mine owner would contract with an independent miner (a *buscón,* or prospector), who either worked on his own behalf or hired others to dig for him. The owner furnished the prospector with implements and powder, receiving one-half of the product in return. The prospector paid for lighting in the shaft and for transporting the ore to the mouth of the mine, receiving thereupon the other half of the product. This he could sell either to the owner of the mine or directly to the smelter. But, the extraction of silver ore with mercury, a process entailing the hazards of mercury poisoning and silicosis, was usually assigned to slaves, first Indians and later Africans. This labor system—combining free labor in mining and slave labor in processing—served the Mexican mines until the very end of the eighteenth century, when the great mines at Guanajuato more than made up for the decline of silver output in Potosí.

The Flow of Silver

To channel the flow of silver to Spain, the Crown turned travel and trade with the Indies into a royal monopoly. The agency created by the Crown to control the flow of specie, commodities, and people was the House of Trade (*Casa de Contratación*) in Seville. The Casa licensed both ships and merchants for the trade, issued permits to move passengers and goods, and received the precious silver from the Indies. In the second half of the sixteenth century, a system of regular annual sailings

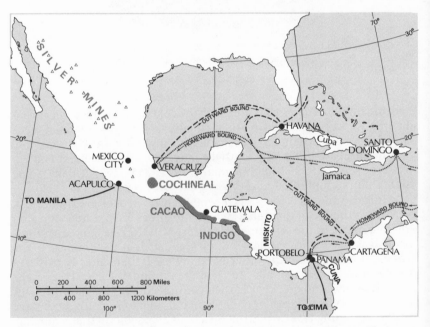

The maritime approaches to the Spanish dominions in the New World.

by massed fleets was organized to safeguard the Atlantic crossing against external attack. After 1560 two fleets left each year from Cadiz or Seville to sail to the Americas. The first, the New Spanish fleet, landed at Veracruz in Mexico. The second, the Peruvian fleet, sailed for Cartagena in Colombia or for Portobelo on the Isthmus of Panama. From Cartagena mule trains carried the European goods across Andean paths to Upper Peru. From Portobelo other mule trains took their cargoes to the Pacific coast, for coastwise transshipment to Lima. On their return trips, the mule trains carried silver and American goods to the fleets wintering in their American ports before the voyage home. The new Spanish fleet loaded again at Veracruz, the Peruvian fleet at the Colombian and Panamanian ports. The two fleets converged at Havana, stopping at Antillean ports on the way, and then set sail for the mouth of the Guadalquivir in Spain.

Between 1503 and 1660 more than seven million pounds of silver reached Seville from America, tripling the European supply of the metal (Elliott 1966: 180). The Crown received about 40 percent of this amount, either in settlement of American taxes or in payment of the royal fifth levied on all silver production. Even so, all the silver of the Americas could not stave off the bankruptcy of the Spanish Crown, so heavily was it overextended in its military pursuits in Europe and all around the globe. Until the 1550s the Emperor Charles V received 200,000 to 300,000 ducats of American silver a year, but he spent about a million, and in thirty-seven years he ran up a debt of 39 million ducats, mostly to foreign creditors. Philip II, more parsimonious than his father, received about 2 million ducats of silver from America by the 1590s, in addition to almost 8 million in taxes raised from Castilian and ecclesiastical revenues. Yet by that time he was spending over 21 million ducats a year (Elliott 1966: 203, 282−283). Simultaneously, the inflow of silver drove up prices in a home economy already weakened by a decline in domestic food production, by a rise in wood exports to pay for cheaper foreign imports, and by a heavy increase in the importation of foreign manufactured goods for use both in Spain and in the Indies. The advent of American silver thus did little to relieve the financial problems of the Crown, while it did much to exacerbate the decline of Spanish industry in favor of Spain's competitors.

Spain witnessed a massive, general rise in prices, which increased the costs of commodities both to the Crown and to the people. Contemporary witnesses of this "price revolution" and later economic historians alike saw its primary cause in the heavy influx of bullion. A greater supply of money may certainly have played a significant role, but it cannot account for the economic crisis in its entirety. Increased demand for European goods in the Americas may have driven up prices in the sixteenth century; there was also an increased demand for goods at home. When the American dependencies grew more self-sufficient in goods and services, this perhaps had an adverse effect on the home country. Most silver, however, did not stay in Spain: at the end of the sixteenth century, for instance, three-fifths of all the bullion that entered Spain went abroad in settlement of royal and private debts. Again, as the American traffic developed, it absorbed ever larger sums in ships, supplies, and protection. Spanish reliance on the export of primary products such as wool, wine, and olive oil in order to acquire naval stores, tin, linen, fish, and cereals created a balance of payments problem, which was met, in turn, by larger exports of silver.

Secondary Exports: Dyestuffs and Cocoa

Silver was the main export of the Spanish Americas, but cochineal, indigo, and cacao all assumed a measure of importance. Cochineal is a red dye produced from an insect that feeds on cactuses. As many as 70,000 dried insects are required to produce one pound of cochineal dye. Native American communities, especially in the province of Oaxaca (Mexico), were pressured into gathering and processing these insects by *encomenderos* and royal *corregidores*. Cochineal grew in importance as an export in the second half of the sixteenth century, becoming, after silver, the most significant export of New Spain. Indigo, another dyestuff, produces a blue dye of great natural fastness. It is obtained by steeping the leaves of a shrub and allowing the resulting sludge to settle into cakes. It was first produced through the use of seasonal native labor, on the same Pacific coast of Central America that had first produced cacao. In the seventeenth century, increased transportation costs favored the relocation of the indigo industry to the Mexican lowlands, where Yucatan in particular remained a significant producer until the nineteenth century.

Cacao had been grown in pre-Hispanic times along the Pacific vertient of Central America. Under the Spanish, the native American population was forced to pay cacao in tribute and to settle advances in goods extended by royal officials. Officials and encomenderos even demanded cacao deliveries from highland cultivators, who had to descend to the coast to labor in the cacao stands in order to pay their tribute. High mortality rates, however, limited the production of cacao, and Central America increasingly yielded priority in its production to slave plantations of the tropical shorelands of Ecuador and Venezuela.

The Siphon of External Trade

Spain took silver, gold, cacao, cochineal, and indigo from the New World, and returned high-priced manufactured and luxury goods. A large share—perhaps most—of these goods originated outside Spain, mainly in northwestern Europe; they were priced to yield taxes and customs duties to the state, as well as to produce monopolistic profits for the sellers. Exchange was in the hands of merchants who were organized at the European end in the merchant guild, or *consulado*, of Seville and at the American end in the twin guilds of New Spain and Lima. On the European side the guild dovetailed with the royal House of Trade, the major government agency charged with supervising ships, people, and goods traveling to and from the Indies and with collecting taxes and customs for the royal coffers. The trade was purposefully confined to narrow channels, intended to be carried on exclusively by monopolistic agencies using Spanish ships and Castilian agents. It was not created by the free working principles of demand and supply; it was rather—in Carmagnani's phrase—"constrained trade," constrained by demand on the European side (1975: 31).

This constrained trade involved, in fact, two different cycles of transactions. One was transatlantic, the other intra-American. To activate the transatlantic cycle, European merchants bought commodities with money and sent them to their factors or agents (*habilitadores*) in the New World, in the hope of getting repaid with American commodities that could be sold at high monetary profits. There was an investment of money at the European start of the cycle of transaction, and a conversion of commodities into money and profits in Europe at the end of the cycle. Within the Americas, however, there was no exchange of money for money, but only an exchange of commodities for commodities. The American factors advanced European commodities to mine owners or cochineal entrepreneurs, who had to settle their accounts with their factors by delivering American commodities. As prices for manufactured goods rose in Europe, the exchange values of American silver and other commodities declined. This disproportion then put pressure on American producers to keep down or to reduce the costs of production. We shall see how this cycle contributed to the resurgence of tributary domination in New World agriculture and livestock ranching. It also led to a great deal of fraud and coercion in the putting-out systems through which cochineal and indigo were obtained from the native producers.

New Systems of Supply

As silver mining assumed a pivotal role in the economy of the Castilian Indies, it came to dominate and reshape the structure of the Castilian domains of the New World. Reliance on mining shifted the key economic areas of the realm away from the zones of intensive pre-Hispanic horticulture and settlement to the silver veins of the arid Sierra Madre of New Spain and of the forbidding Bolivian *altiplano*. It produced major changes in the production of foodstuffs and raw materials. It entailed a shift in government policies from an initial concern with ensuring royal control of both conquerors and conquered to policies aimed primarily at maximizing mining and securing its supplies. These shifts created a new geography and altered the ecological, economic, and political conditions of the conquered populations.

These changes were closely interconnected. The diminution of the native American population and the destruction of the political controls basic to intensive native horticulture called for new ways of producing foodstuffs and livestock products for the mines and towns. Mining created a heavy demand for food and drink to supply men and working animals, skins and hides for ropes and containers, tallow for candles and fatwood torches to light the mine shafts, mercury for the extraction of silver from ore, blasting powder, wood to fuel smelters, and large numbers of draft animals for work and transportation. The new agricultural economy also had to feed the Spanish towns, which supported the grid of Spanish control, the ecclesiastical establishments in towns and countryside, and the stopping places along the traffic routes linking mining locations, towns, and ports of call. The needs of the mines and the requirements of urban conspicuous consumption demanded, moreover, that products be made available as cheaply as possible.

The Crown assisted the growth of this support system in a number of ways. Since mercury was an essential ingredient in the processing of silver ore, and constituted a major cost in mining, the Crown strove to guarantee the supply of the metallic element at low prices. Mercury production and sale was a royal monopoly; Peruvian miners received it from the royal mine at Huancavelica, the miners of New Spain from the Spanish mine at Almadén. The Crown also pursued a policy of ensuring food supplies to the mines and towns at regulated prices through public granaries. Above all, royal policy increasingly transferred both land and labor to agricultural entrepreneurs, thus abandoning early attempts by the Crown to maintain its own sovereign control of the Indian population.

It had been the initial intention of the Crown to deny the incoming conquerors any direct control of land and of Indian hands to work it. It wanted to inhibit the development of an independent class of tributary overlords in the Indies, and thus insisted at first on granting the services of native Americans only on its own terms. This was done by the issuing of temporary grants of trusteeship (*encomienda*). An encomienda permitted the recipient to employ stipulated amounts of Indian tribute and labor in his own service, in return for Christianizing their pagan souls. A grant of encomienda did not, however, bestow on the *encomendero* (trustee) rights over Indian land or unlimited rights to Indian services. These rights the Crown reserved to itself. The Crown hoped for the emergence of a society dichotomized into a sector of conquerors and a separate Indian sector. Thus, it strove to interpose its royal officials between Spanish employers of Indian labor power and the Indians themselves.

After 1542 encomenderos were required to petition a royal official if they wanted to have native laborers assigned to them for specific tasks. The official was supposed to receive such petitions, establish priorities among them, assign laborers on a rotational basis, and ensure that they be paid wages at a stipulated rate. This mode of labor allotment came to be known officially as the *repartimiento*. In Mesoamerica, however, it continued to be referred to by the Aztec word for obligatory labor on public works, *cuatequitl*, and in the Andes it continued to be called by the Quechua term *mita*.

Another means used to cut off the Spaniards from the Indian population was the formal abolition of Indian slavery in 1542. Indian slavery was declared illegal everywhere, except in frontier zones where rebellious populations refused to accept Spanish sovereignty. This meant that Araucanians from southern Chile could be taken prisoner and enslaved until the 1680s. This was also true on the northwestern frontiers of Mexico, where Apache, Navaho, and Shoshoni continued to be enslaved well into the nineteenth century (Bailey 1966). Yet in the core areas of Spanish occupation, Indian slavery was abolished, or at least significantly curtailed. This prohibition of slavery did not extend, however, to Africans, who were imported in large numbers to replace the declining native American population, particularly in the lowlands.

The Hacienda

Gradually the trusteeships were superseded by *haciendas*, landed estates worked by laborers settled upon them and directly dependent upon the estate owners. The Crown did not possess enough personnel or resources to stem their growth, while agrarian entrepreneurs in full control of land and labor were better able than trustees, dependent on royal officialdom, to respond to the demands of town and mine. Yet the development of haciendas did not everywhere take the same form or follow the same rhythm. They appeared earlier in underpopulated areas where livestock could be raised with few hands. They developed later where either native villages or royal corregidores interested in native labor and tribute opposed hacienda claims to land and manpower. Thus, in the Peruvian highlands hacienda building appears to have been a phenomenon of the eighteenth century, not before. Elsewhere, encomenderos who obtained their grants in the sixteenth century became owners of haciendas only a century later. Legally, a grant to an encomienda could not produce a hacienda: encomienda grants were royal donations that neither gave rights to land nor permitted the grantee to set the terms of native labor services or tribute. The hacienda, in contrast, rested squarely on the legal ownership of land, and upon the ability of the owner to negotiate the terms of the laboring contract directly.

Most of the hacienda workers were recruited among native Americans. Sometimes hacienda owners obtained workers by depriving native settlements of their land. At other times they attracted migrants who had left their tribute-laden villages to settle elsewhere. The hacienda owners also offered to pay the tribute on their workers' behalf, or to extend credit in other forms. Outright enserfment through debt, including the establishment of heritable debt, seems to have developed in later centuries.

Usually the worker was given access to a portion of hacienda land in return for stipulated services and crop deliveries to the owner. The owner reserved for himself the *casco* (center) with the processing machinery, the strategic supply of water, and the land most suitable for growing the major commodity crop, leaving to his laborer-tenants the poorer and more peripheral lands of his estate. The hacienda thus came to be based on a dual structure of commercial crop farming and predial servitude by serf-tenants. Over time there was an alternation between direct management by the owner and cash cropping by serf-tenants. An enlargement of the market favored expansion of the owner's sector at the expense of the serf-tenants; a decline of the market favored the tenants.

Haciendas could serve different purposes. Those held by owners of mines or workshops provided the necessary products for these operations at little or no cost. Other haciendas produced for a regional market created by the demand of nearby towns, mining centers, or ports. Some geographical zones became specialized in producing food for such markets. The Central Valley of Chile grew wheat for Peru; the agricultural valleys of Cochabamba and Sucre fed Upper Peru (Bolivia); the Valley of Mexico and the Bajío region provided Mexico City and the mining centers with grain. The dry Mexican northland raised cattle for towns and mines, as did the drainage of the Rio de la Plata. Some lowland zones specialized in the production of sugar and distilled liquor for internal markets; the Mexican uplands grew century plants and manufactured agave beer (*pulque*); the tropical vertient of the Andes produced coca leaf. Everywhere there were also haciendas that were owned by ecclesiastical establishments or upper-class family clusters, which included clients and dependents. Sometimes haciendas changed their function, shifting from supplying a town granary to supplying a mine, or changing from a marketing orientation to subsistence. They were also responsive to changing markets and could grow or contract their operations as demand fluctuated.

Despite the adaptability of the haciendas, their potential growth was limited by the size of effective demand as much as by difficulties of transport. They seemed to function most profitably where they could sell in a secure but restricted local or regional market, in which relative scarcity guaranteed price levels. This was true, for instance, of haciendas producing a European staple like wheat, for which there was a small but secure market of European consumers. It was also the case in those situations where obligatory sales to the public granary forestalled price competition from native American communities that could often produce more cheaply.

In general, haciendas were not very profitable enterprises. Most of them incurred debts and then often passed into the hands of new owners, among whom ecclesiastical organizations were the most frequent and the most successful. David Brading probably described general conditions in the Hispanic Americas when he characterized the Mexican hacienda as

> a sink through which drained without stop the surplus capital accumulated in the export economy. The fortunes created in mining and commerce were invested in land, there to be slowly dissipated or to be gradually transferred into the coffers of the Church. In consequence, a continuous replacement in the hacendado class occurred. [1977: 140]

Indian Communities

Towns and mines came to be ringed about by haciendas; the haciendas were in turn surrounded by settlements of the surviving native populations. This settlement pattern was oriented toward the mines; yet it was not merely geographic or ecological. It was organized by the political economy it embodied, in which each lower level yielded surplus to the level above it. Miners sold to merchants, who extracted high prices for European manufactured goods. Mine owners then pressed upon hacienda owners or managers to supply them with foodstuffs and raw materials at low prices. Hacienda owners and managers pressed upon the native communities, drawing their members either into dependent serf-tenancy on the estates or into seasonal employment at low wages. Within this hierarchy, the emerging Indian communities came to occupy the lowest rung.

These *repúblicas de indios*, as the Spaniards called them, have often been treated by anthropologists as if they were repositories of a pre-Hispanic past untouched by three centuries of Castilian domination. Yet these communities were given organizational form by the colonial bureaucracy, as integral components of the Hispanic state and its economic system. In setting up these units, the Crown followed a double purpose: to break up the pre-Conquest apparatus of power, and to ensure the separation and fragmentation of the resulting jurisdictions. While the destruction of the overarching Inca, Mexica, or Chibcha polities permitted the re-emergence of some older claims to rule and loyalty, in general the outcome was the replacement of pre-Conquest states by small tributary lordships and local communities.

The higher Indian nobility was formally assimilated into the Spanish nobility and confirmed in their claims to tribute, property, and pensions, but they were deprived of any access to the commanding levers of power. Conversion of this stratum to Christianity also ensured its severance from pre-Conquest sources of ideological influence and integrated it into the ongoing activities of the Church. The lower orders of the Indian nobility—*principales* in Mesoamerica, *kurakas* in the Andes— were charged with the supervision of local communities. Like the African chiefs installed three centuries later by the British to rule over African populations in "indirect rule," this local nobility came to mediate between conquerors and conquered. They represented their constituencies to the external authorities, while striving to maintain their jurisdiction internally through the exercise of traditional claims and loyalties.

The communities over which they were installed were not the same as those that had existed before the Conquest. Many pre-Conquest communities had been nearly wiped out by the ravages of the Great Dying, and new communities were formed through the aggregation of population remnants brought together for closer administrative and ecclesiastical control. This general Spanish policy of resettlement and concentration redefined the nature of local constituencies not only demographically but also economically and administratively. Each new community was given legal identity, with its own administrative local council, or *cabildo*, and ecclesiastical identity, with its local chapel or church dedicated to a patron saint. It was also redefined economically, receiving rights over village lands and resources, as well as obligations to furnish tribute. These exactions included tribute in specie to the Crown, tribute in goods and services to the Spanish trustee, or encomendero, tribute to the recognized Indian lord, and obligatory labor on government projects, such as the construction of dams or roads.

Royal officials, *corregidores de indios*, watched over the Indian administrative sector made up of these communities. Special Indian courts were set up to attend to legal cases brought by local representatives. This administrative structure was inspired by the original intention of the Crown to keep Indians and Spaniards separate. Yet the Indian courts were soon swamped by complaints against Spanish conquerors and entrepreneurs who strove to incorporate native lands and water courses into their haciendas. Moreover, the local Indian elite of principales or kurakas, charged with managing community resources and obligations, often enlarged the scope of their own power in the villages by entering into collusion with outside Spanish power holders. The corregidores, in turn, were in a privileged position to benefit commercially from their administrative offices. They could, as in Peru, collect tribute, sell it at auction, buy it back at half its market value up to the amount due for tribute, and then resell it at the market rate (Rowe 1957: 163). They could buy goods cheaply from merchants in town and force their Indians to buy them at high prices., or they could buy products from the Indians to sell more dearly elsewhere. They could, finally, become entrepreneurs in their own right. Thus, in western Guatemala a corregidor could buy raw cotton on the coast, force Indian women in his district to spin and weave it, and then sell the cloth back to the Indians or to colonists at a handsome profit (see MacLeod 1973: 316).

Such Indian leaders and royal officials rallied to the defense of the native communities if they saw their own sources of power and profit threatened by outside interests. At the same time, confronted with an increasing demand for labor by industrial and agricultural entrepreneurs in the face of a decreasing native population, many were persuaded to reduce the level of their zeal as public defenders. The Crown, too, discovered that its interest in maximizing monetary returns through taxes or emoluments often ran counter to its role of protecting the native Americans. If a colonist used labor and resources in some combination that promised to yield surplus for the Crown, political or moral considerations were frequently set aside. This was especially true as entrepreneurs shifted from stocking up the goods that were valued in the pre-Hispanic past—such as cacao, precious feathers, and cotton textiles—to rearranging land and labor in order to grow wheat, mine silver, produce woolen cloth, collect cochineal, or raise sheep for wool. When money began to talk, it spoke Spanish rather than Nahuatl or Quechua.

Finally, this rearrangement of resources to produce goods for mines and towns gave rise to new groups who were not part of Indian communities. These included artisans, laborers, and servants who worked in or about the new settlements, and middlemen who moved goods from one location to another. This growing population of Indians and *mestizos* soon filled the social and economic interstices between the communities and the formal tributary pyramid, and began to connect people in localities with activities and interests beyond. Repeated complaints by royal officials that outsiders were entering Indian communities in pursuit of their own interests, and that members of Indian communities were leaving their assigned jurisdictions to join the mestizo or *cholo* outsiders, demonstrate that community boundaries were often permeable and negotiable.

The communities, moreover, were not internally unitary and undifferentiated. At one point in time, a community might unite under a principal of its own against the encroachment of Spanish hacienda owners or entrepreneurs. At another time, that principal—having become like a hacienda owner or entrepreneur himself in his dealings with the people entrusted to him—might join the Spaniards or be accused of doing so by his followers. Elsewhere, merchants and cultivators grown well-to-do within a community might enter into conflict with superordinate authorities, including their own Indian overlord, and represent themselves as spokesmen for their community against tyranny. These same merchants and cultivators, drawn into the market through the production of cochineal or cotton cloth, might then close off the community against the outside, in order to maintain an internal monopoly of jurisdiction over labor.

In both viceroyalties communities were allowed and expected to manage their internal affairs through a hierarchy of local officials, endowed with Spanish titles and based on Hispanic prototypes. At the same time, the Church installed ecclesiastical organizations, on the pattern of Spanish sodalities, to stage the rituals connected with the annual Catholic calendar. In the larger Spanish and Hispanicizing settlements these two sets of organizations, civil and religious, remained quite distinct, but in the Indian communities they were generally merged into common civil-religious hierarchies, in which tenure of a secular political office alternated with sponsorship of a religious event. Such sponsorship usually involved large outlays for fireworks, decorations, incense and candles, musicians, and for food and drink to be distributed among the participants. This usually meant that only the better-off members of a community could advance to the higher and more costly positions of religious and political authority, which demanded a great deal of economic redistribution. Conversely, such redistribution came to play an important part in the economy of recipient households, rendering them economically as well as politically and religiously dependent on the operations of the sacralized officialdom. The civil-religious hierarchies thus installed a system of elite domination within the communities, while at the same time allowing that elite to represent the community as a whole before external power holders and authorities.

The hierarchy also carried on the rituals relating the community to the supernatural. These rituals characteristically came to bear a dual character, part Christian and part pagan. Christianity is less concerned with defining sacred space than sacred time; while it takes cognizance of sacred sites, such as Jerusalem, Rome, Assisi, or Lourdes, it places central emphasis upon the cumulation of time through the Fall, Redemption, Judgment, and Resurrection. In contrast, the pre-Hispanic religions were strongly organized in spatial terms, using segments of space to demarcate segments of time, attributes of social groups, aspects of nature, and cohorts of supernaturals. The fusion of the Christian liturgical calendar with pre-Hispanic devotions connected the time frame of Christian salvation with the ecological referents of pre-Christian traditions. In pre-Hispanic times these local ecological referents formed part of an encompassing ideological organization of sacred space, organized and maintained by the overarching Inca, Mexica, or Chibcha polity. The Conquest destroyed this larger ideological framework and substituted the Christian economy of salvation for it. At the same time, this dominant liturgy was joined to local belief and practice by missionaries attempting to anchor it in local understandings and by local practitioners striving to render it expressive of local interests. The outcome was the development of religious structures that varied from community to community and that paralleled in their ideological localocentrism the political separateness of communities.

The Indian communities were thus dependent parts of a larger political and economic system, and changed as that system changed. They constituted neither "tribal" remnants of the pre-Hispanic past, nor a static type of peasant community characterized by a set of fixed attributes. They grew up in the tug of war between conquerors and conquered, and were subject to the interplay of external and internal interests. The Hispanic state granted them rights to land and revenue, yet obliged them to deliver tribute and labor as part of their political obligations. Often they proved defenseless against predatory landowners, officials, and churchmen. At times, heavy exactions drove them to rebellion, noncooperation, or flight. The communities were allowed to govern themselves through their civil-religious hierarchies. These local officials might defend the community against external authorities and competitors, but they might also aggrandize themselves at the expense of their fellow villagers or betray their interests to outside power holders.

From the perspective of the larger Hispanic colonial order, the Indian communities did not constitute its primary foundations but rather its secondary, lateral supports. The center of the order consisted of the mining economy and the activities that supplied it. The Indian communities, in turn, acted as reservoirs of labor and as sources of cheap agricultural and craft products. Where the Indians had to pay tribute in money, they had to hire themselves out for wages or produce for a market. Alternatively they worked off tribute obligations through payments in kind. Subject to labor drafts by the public authorities, moreover, they could be made to work on public-works projects or for private interests that the royal corregidores deemed of public importance. They thus paid with their poverty for the system of imperial extraction.

Brazil and the Caribbean

While the Spaniards were erecting their realm of the Indies upon a highland base of silver, the Portuguese initiated the production of sugar on plantations set up in the tropical lowlands of the Brazilian littoral. Hispanic agriculture in New Spain and Peru was geared to supplying the internal needs of the colonies, but the new Portuguese enterprises were organized from the start to raise a crop for export. What silver was to Spanish America, sugar would long to be to Brazil and Portugal. Yet in the course of the seventeenth century, sugar growing also spread to the islands of the Caribbean, and the Dutch, English, and French came to rival Portuguese production of the crop. Whereas the agriculture of the Hispanic mainland faced away from Europe toward the towns and mining camps of the interior, the developing plantation belt of tropical America was linked directly to European markets.

In planting sugar on the clayey black soil (*massapé*) of the Brazilian Northeast, the Portuguese transferred to the New World an agricultural complex of long standing in the European Mediterranean, where the Arabs had introduced it toward the end of the first millennium A.D. During the centuries preceding the conquest of the New World, sugar growing had diffused steadily westward across the Mediterranean islands. In the last quarter of the fifteenth century, the Portuguese began to grow sugar on Madeira, and soon afterward on São Tomé in the Gulf of Guinea, using slaves purchased on the nearby West African coast. In 1500 an India-bound Portuguese fleet first sighted The Land of the True Cross—soon to be called Brazil after the red dyewood that grew along its shores. A quarter-century later, duty was being paid on Brazilian sugar at the Lisbon customs house. Portuguese plans to expand sugar production in Africa were thwarted by African resistance, which restricted the Portuguese to the coast; instead, they intensified production in Brazil. By 1570 there were already sixty mills in Brazil producing 180,000 *arrobas* of sugar a year, and in that same year production in the Brazilian regions of Pernambuco, Bahia, and Rio de Janeiro matched the levels of Madeira and São Tomé. After 1570 Brazilian sugar production increased exponentially, reaching more than a million arrobas after 1627 (see Barrett and Schwartz 1975: 541).

The focus of production in the Brazilian countryside was the grinding mill, the *engenho*. It ground both sugar produced on its own land and sugar raised on freeholds by *lavradores de cana*, the latter accounting for perhaps half the crop. Slave labor, first by Brazilian Indians and later by Africans, was important, but free wage labor was also significant. The largest mill in Brazil in the sixteenth and seventeenth centuries, Sergipe do Conde in Bahia with a grinding capacity of about 180 tons of cane, owned 259 workers in 1600, but it also paid wages to 270 laborers. It is estimated that the 20 freeholders delivering cane to Sergipe may have owned another 200 slaves (Barrett and Schwarts 1975: 547).

While production was in Portuguese hands, processing and financing came to be controlled by Flemings and Dutchmen. From the beginning, much of the sugar produced by the Portuguese was shipped to the Low Countries. First Antwerp, and after 1590 Amsterdam, became the main center for sugar refining as well as for financing of the Portuguese sugar trade. Even during the period from 1580 to 1640, when the kingdom of Portugal was joined to the Crown of Castile, the Dutch managed to retain their Portuguese contacts through Portuguese intermediaries. The Dutch made an abortive attempt in 1624–1625 to seize Bahia outright; simultaneously they moved in central Africa, to take hold of the profitable source of slaves in Luanda. In 1629 they invaded Pernambuco, occupying the sugar districts for fifteen years. In 1645, however, the population of Dutch Brazil, led by the debt-ridden Luso-Brazilian planters, rose against their overlords. Although the Dutch had native American allies in some groups of Potiguar and Gê-speaking Tapuia, other Potiguar and the Maranhao Tobajara backed the Portuguese. In the ensuing guerilla warfare, the Luso-Brazilians came to control the countryside, and the Dutch were increasingly forced into the coastal cities. They held on to Recife until 1654, when they were forced to capitulate there, too. The guerilla tactics used against them had taken their toll. At the same time, the Netherlands had become embroiled in their first commercial war with England. The decisive factors, however, were that much of the sugar industry of Brazil had been physically destroyed, that the effort of founding an enduring Dutch sugar colony in Brazil had cost too much, and that the stockholders of the Dutch West Indies Company were beginning to grumble about costs and losses.

Beset by difficulties in Brazil, the Dutch shifted their activities to the Caribbean. English-owned islands like St. Kitts, Nevis, and Barbados had begun to grow tobacco on small farms in the second quarter of the seventeenth century. By 1639 the European markets were glutted with the leaf, and many islanders migrated elsewhere in search of better opportunities. In the early 1640s, Dutch from Brazil introduced English settlers in Barbados to the raising of sugar cane. They extended the English credit so they could acquire African slaves, as well as the boiling pans and cooling pots needed to transform cane juice into sugar, and they offered to sell the product in Europe. Sugar quickly transformed the economic and political scene of the islands. The tobacco-raising small holders became "poor whites" and, rapidly displaced by the large plantations worked by African slaves, they migrated elsewhere. In 1655 the English invaded Jamaica, driving out the last Spaniards five years later.

Cane cultivation in the islands grew rapidly thereafter. It soon surpassed in scale the Luso-Brazilian sugar industry and proved able to accumulate capital even in the face of ever-declining world sugar prices. The rate of profits on known sugar plantations was continuously positive—perhaps as much as 20 percent on capital invested before 1700, at least 10 percent between 1750 and 1775, and about 7.5 percent around 1790 (Craton 1974: 139). Much of the life of Bristol and Liverpool in England came to depend on Jamaica and Barbados; at the end of the eighteenth century, William Pitt the Younger estimated that four-fifths of the British incomes drawn from overseas derived from the West Indies. Nantes and Bordeaux in France were similarly supported by the productivity of French-held Saint Domingue (Haiti). When the Haitian slaves rose in rebellion against their overlords in 1791, they demolished a structure that had absorbed two-thirds of French foreign commercial interests.

Contraband

One of the consequences of the spread of sugar cultivation to the Caribbean islands was to create a series of advance bases for the European Atlantic powers at the very gates of entry into the Castilian realm of the Indies. This Dutch, English, and French advance came at a time when Spanish power was on the decline. While the remittances of silver to Spain rose steadily throughout the sixteenth century, they peaked in the century's last decade and declined thereafter. Yet although the amount of silver shipped to Spain decreased, the production of silver in the New World did not fall appreciably. The silver now stayed in the Americas, or it sought outlets through other channels. Some of it paid for better defenses against foreign encroachment and

Europeans building a caravel on the Caribbean shore of Panama (Veragua). Copper engraving by Theodor de Bry, 1590. (Courtesy of the Rare Books and Manuscript Division, The New York Public Library. Astor, Lenox, and Tilden Foundations)

competition. Much of it, however, went into contraband dealings with the enemies of the Spanish Crown—the Dutch West Indies Company and the English sea traders.

As Spanish power grew weaker, these competitors and antagonists increasingly sought access to the riches of the Spanish possessions in the New World. Growing numbers of foreigners bought the privileges of naturalization, which allowed them to trade with the Indies. The number of foreign vessels taking part in the transatlantic fleets rose, until they comprised one-third of all craft crossing the Atlantic in 1630. From then on, contraband increased to unprecedented heights.

Cut off from access to Iberian salt by Spain's occupation of Portugal and by the Spanish seizure of Setúbal, the Dutch initiated regular voyages into the Caribbean in 1594, seizing the salt island of Araya in 1599. They began to trade directly with the Spanish colonists of the Venezuelan and Colombian coast, exchanging North European merchandise and African slaves first for salt, later for tobacco and hides, and then for ever larger quantities of cacao. The English seizure of Jamaica opened another lucrative trade in slaves and European contraband with the Spanish possessions. As Venezuela increased its production of cacao, it also began to exchange cacao for Spanish silver from Mexico. The Dutch and the English were thus able to tap the flow of Spanish silver through the open veins of the Caribbean. At the end of the seventeenth century, the amount of Spanish silver drawn off through the Jamaican trade alone is estimated at 200,000 pounds sterling a year, or about half the amount of bullion exported annually to the Far East by the British East India Company (Lang 1975: 57). Goods from northwestern Europe also entered the Western Hemisphere through Brazil, where the Portuguese traded overland with the Spanish holdings in Potosí and Upper Peru. To pay for these goods the Spaniards used silver, and it is estimated that this Brazilian trade succeeded in drawing off as much as a quarter of Potosí's silver production during the seventeenth century (Lang 1975: 56). When England gained the right to supply the Spanish colonies with African slaves as a result of the Treaty of Utrecht in 1730, the flow of contraband to the Spanish Caribbean increased along with the sale of slaves.

Yet Spanish silver did not go only toward Europe; it also moved westward, across the Pacific. In the second part of the sixteenth century, a multilateral trade network—much of it in contraband—grew up around the main commercial axis connecting Acapulco in Mexico with Manila in the Philippines. In 1564 the Spaniards—taking advantage of diminishing Portuguese strength in the South Asia seas—had initiated their conquest of the Philippine Islands. Yet even after Portugal lost its claim to the islands, the Portuguese merchants of Macao on the China coast continued to trade at Manila. In 1573 the first Manila galleon carried Chinese silks, satins, porcelain, and Far Eastern spices to Acapulco, returning to Manila with Spanish silver from the New World. From then on, Manila became the hub of a trade network that drew the Chinese into the Philippine orbit and that created a commercial circuit in which Chinese textiles were exchanged for New World silver. Manila became not only a Spanish city but a Chinese one as well. In the last two decades of the sixteenth century, the Chinese became so numerous in Manila that a special quarter (*Parian*, i.e., market) was created for them. By the middle of the seventeenth century, Manila boasted 42,000 inhabitants, supported by rice, timber, and labor furnished as tribute by the inhabitants of neighboring Luzon and Pampanga through the intermediation of native *principales*.

At Acapulco goods were loaded on muleback for transshipment to Mexico City. Peruvian merchants, however, also arrived in large numbers, bringing Peruvian silver to exchange for Chinese goods. This illegal Peruvian trade in Acapulco and along the coast of Nicaragua soon became a source of great concern to the Spanish Crown, which tried to limit it. Yet the trade continued, despite governmental prohibitions and despite increased Dutch raiding in the South Asian seas; in the eighteenth century it attracted not only increasing participation of the Chinese through Canton but also Indian traders via Manila (Chaunu

Acapulco. Copper engraving by Theodor de Bry, 1590. (Courtesy of the New York Public Library, New York)

1960; Bertin et al. 1966). In the course of the eighteenth century, in fact, there developed two circuits of Chinese trade: one moving in a westerly direction and exchanging Chinese tea for Indian opium, and another in the opposite direction, exchanging Chinese textiles for American silver. This Chinese–South American trade lasted until the end of Spanish rule in South America (Cheong 1965).

The scale of this commerce was large indeed. In 1597, admittedly an exceptional year, the bullion sent from Acapulco to Manila reached 12 million pesos, a sum larger than all that involved in transatlantic shipments. In the last decades of the sixteenth century, bullion exports usually ran between 3 and 5 million pesos, of which two-thirds probably came from Peru (Parry 1973: 119). Between 1570 and 1780 an estimated 4,000 to 5,000 tons of silver were exported to the Far East (Konetzke 1971: 310).

Pirates, "Colonial Tribes," and Maroons

In the wake of contraband, slave raiding, and slaving, there grew up—in the borderlands of the Caribbean—a number of populations that inhabited the margins of constituted society and lived off the flotsam and jetsam of its resources. The mountainous and dissected Caribbean environment, its many islands and inlets, and the density of cover provided by its tropical vegetation furnished hide-outs for smugglers and runaway slaves, and commercial or military opportunities for the allies of both.

One element in this unstable world were the buccaneers. The majority were French; some were English. They began as hunters of feral cattle left behind by the Spaniards on Santo Domingo, taking their name from the *boucan*, the wooden grill used to dry meat by smoking; they sold meat and hides to the crews of passing ships. Ejected by the Spaniards, they began to combine their hunting with piracy. When the Spaniards attempted to stop their activities, they expanded their freebooting, allying themselves alternately with the English governor of Jamaica and the French governor of Saint Domingue, first against the Spaniards, later against the Dutch. Half pirates, half mercenaries, they launched attacks on major Spanish towns and ports, while trading with people along the coast and in the hinterland. In the last quarter of the seventeenth century, their activities became so threatening to the growth of commerce in the area that the major European powers in the Caribbean took serious steps to oust them from the region. Some of them thereupon took up slaving and logwood cutting along the coast of British Honduras. Others moved their base of operation to Sierra Leone in West Africa, and from there to Madagascar. In Madagascar they set up the Pirate Republic of Libertalia, a veritable "market of the Jolly Roger" (Toussaint 1966: p.146). Dispersed by a powerful French fleet, they then sought refuge with the slave-trading state of the Betsimisaraka on the eastern coast of Madagascar, continuing their piracy in alliance with the native population until the beginning of the nineteenth century.

A second element in the circum-Caribbean mix were the groups that Mary Helms has dubbed "colonial tribes." The best known of these are the Miskito of the Mosquito shore in Honduras and Nicaragua, and the Cuna of Panama and Colombia. The Miskito were a kin-ordered native American population that absorbed large numbers of runaway African slaves and buccaneers. Equipped by the buccaneers with guns and ammunition, the Miskito began to raid and trade with their neighbors inland. They obtained cacao, gold, tobacco, indigo, and—later—cattle from the inland producers and then traded these goods, along with their own canoes, paddles, tortoise shells, skins, gum, and hammocks, to the incoming English for manufactured goods. The Miskito also raided for slaves, and they were used by the English to hunt down the rebellious maroons in Jamaica (Campbell 1977: 395, 411–412).

The Cuna were a Chibchan-speaking population that had sustained, before the advent of the Europeans, a much more complex technology and organization than the Miskito. The Cuna were organized into class-divided tributary polities with ruling dynasties, and they were known for their elaborate metallurgy and for their specialization in long-distance trade. In the wake of the conquest, they lost their complex social and political organization, gave up metalwork, and turned increasingly to food collecting for subsistence, thus becoming one of Steward and Faron's classic cases of "historic deculturation." Like the Miskito, they proved hospitable to runaway slaves and allied themselves with the buccaneers, from whom they received guns and ammunition. Using their newly acquired weaponry, they began in the seventeenth century a fierce expansion across the Atrato River into Colombia, burning Montería on the Sinú River in 1779 and forcing the Spaniards to secure passage on the Sinú with flotillas of dugouts (Fals Borda 1976: 18). They were not brought under Colombian control until the nineteenth century.

The prominence of runaway slaves among the Miskito and Cuna calls attention to a third population element in the circum-Caribbean vortex, the runaway slaves, or maroons. The term *maroon* comes from the Spanish *cimarrón*, initially applied to escaped feral Spanish livestock, then to runaway Indian slaves, and finally—in the 1530s—to African runaways. Frequently the runaways joined together for mutual support, defense, and raiding. They formed bands and, where environmental conditions aided them, more enduring communities. *Marronage*, as the French called this phenomenon of escape, proved to be a constant and significant feature of plantation life, a kind of slow and ongoing hemorrhage of the plantation system. Rebel communities of runaway slaves sprang up everywhere. One of the first was the rebel community formed at the Bursia mines near Barquisimeto (Colombia). Other early ones appeared in Cuba in the 1530s. Eventually there were many such groups in out-of-the-way recesses of the Caribbean and Isthmian littorals, along the Pacific coast of Colombia and Ecuador, and in the mountain fastnesses of some Caribbean islands. Such groups frequently engaged in smuggling and piracy to supplement their subsistence agriculture, and they often lent their support to armed raiders probing the defenses of the Spanish Main.

Thus, the "inland sea" of the Caribbean constituted the soft underbelly of the Spanish dominions in the New World. Here passed the strategic lines of transport connecting the dominions with the metropolis in Spain, but it was an area of military vulnerability, the point of entry for the enemies of Spain. It was also a region of political and economic weakness, where contrabandists, cash-cropping plantation owners, and free-lancing entrepreneurs of violence penetrated the monopolistic structure of the Spanish empire and drained its strength to the benefit of the external international economy.

The beginning of the sixteenth century saw the expansion of the two Iberian kingdoms into the Americas, the Spanish conquering Nuclear America and consolidating their hold over the mainland, while Portugal occupied the Atlantic littoral of Brazil.

In the highlands of Hispanic America, the Castilian Crown erected a new colonial order upon the ruins of the pre-Hispanic tributary polities. That order was based upon the extraction of precious metals, and a new European-run system of food production was called into being to furnish the mining enterprises with needed supplies. Lines of constrained trade linked the silver economy with the outside world, but the system supplying foodstuffs and raw materials faced inward, away from the sea, toward the mining locations of the hinterland. To control the native American populations, the new order fashioned their communities into institutions of indirect rule, their autonomy always determined by the workings of the Spanish sector. To that sector the Indians supplied cheap labor and commodities, and from it they purchased goods, often under duress. Within their own communities, the Indian populations were permitted to build up their own hierarchies of officeholders. These officials represented the communities to the outside, while ordering their internal affairs through the operations of civil-religious ranking, through economic redistribution, and through the management of religious symbols that combined Christian and local cultural forms. Within the larger Hispanic system, the Indian sector—broken up into a multitude of local entities—constituted a reserve of labor and products.

In the plantation belt of the lowland littorals and islands, European planters and their descendants broke the resistance of the pre-existing kin-ordered and tributary societies and replaced them with platoons of African slaves working under a system of forced regimented agriculture. The system operated to produce a cash crop for export, but it also cordoned off the plantation frontiers against native American intruders from the interior and against escape to the frontier by laborers on the littoral. The production of export crops tied the zone firmly to European markets, while the constant need for new slaves integrated Plantation America directly with the expanding tricontinental commerce in slaves. Thus, African slaves and their descendants became the dominant population along the Atlantic coast of Brazil, on the Caribbean isles and littoral, and along the coast of Colombia, Ecuador, and Peru. Here they wrought, on the plantations and in the redoubts of runaway slaves, their own modes of adaptation and rebellion, in a history that is just beginning to be explored.

6 The Fur Trade

Until the end of the sixteenth century, Iberian fleets dominated the Atlantic, curtailing the expansion of other Europeans into North America. As Iberian power waned, however, northern European settlement along the coast proceeded rapidly, and along with it came the unfolding of the North American fur trade. In the European search for wealth, furs were not items of highest priority: gold, silver, sugar, spices, and slaves were all more desirable and profitable. Nevertheless, the quest for furs was to have a profound impact upon the native peoples of North America and their modes of life, constituting one of the most dramatic episodes in the history of European mercantile expansion.

History of the Fur Trade

The fur trade already had a long and remunerative history in Europe and Asia at the time that the first European fur traders began their activities on the North American continent. Scandinavia had provided ancient Rome with furs, along with amber, sea ivory, and slaves, receiving gold, silver, and treasures in return (Jones 1968: 23). In the late ninth century A.D. seignorial traders, such as Ottar from the Norwegian fjords near modern Tromsö, took marten, reindeer, bear, and otter furs in tribute from Lapp hunters and sold them in Norway, Denmark, and England (Jones 1968: 161–162). In the early tenth century, the Viking Rus delivered sable, squirrel, ermine, black and white fox, marten, beaver, and slaves to Bulgar on the bend of the Volga; in A.D. 922 the Arab Ibn Fadlan described graphically the voyage of the Rus merchants down the Volga with sables and slave girls for the markets of the Islamic Levant. After the Vikings, the North German League of the Hanse tapped the fur trade in the northland. From a trading post at Bergen they mercilessly exploited the Norwegians, forcing them to deliver and clean large quantities of fur and fish in return for payments advanced, thus operating a kind of "international debt peonage" (Wallerstein 1974: 121).

In what is today Russia, the operations of the Viking Rus prompted the development of the polities of Kiev and Novgorod in the ninth and tenth centuries. For these states, as for all their successors, fur became "the most valuable single item of trade from the very earliest beginnings to the eighteenth century and beyond" (Kerner 1942: 8). Indeed, the entire course of Russian expansion has been portrayed as one extended quest for "domination of successive river basins by the control of portage between them, the speed of expansion being determined by the exhaustion of fur-bearing animals in each successive basin" (Kerner 1942: 30). The Russians, like Ottar before them, collected furs through tribute (*iasak*) imposed on native populations as a body, and through a tithe on all furs obtained by individuals. Indeed, furs so obtained later constituted a major item in the income of the Russian state, rising from 3.8 percent of all state revenues in 1589 to 10 percent in 1644. Only when Peter the Great launched Russia on its road to industrialization did the fur tribute decline in importance. Even so, it remained the main contribution of Siberia to the Russian economy until the nineteenth century.

The fur trade was thus not a North American but an international phenomenon. The connecting link between the Old and the New World was the Dutch West Indies Company. Until the British conquest of Canada, Amsterdam received a large percentage of furs obtained in North America, and it re-exported beaver fur to Russia for further processing as part of its Baltic export trade. The international network of re-exports often prevented gluts on European markets, especially during the wars of the seventeenth century, and kept prices steady throughout the international system (see Rich 1955). In the nineteenth century, beaver grew less important, and it was replaced by sea otter and seal exported mainly from North America to China. Russia, too, lost its dominant role in the European fur market by the end of the seventeenth century, and sought outlets for its furs in China and elsewhere in Asia (Mancall 1971: 12).

The main target of the North American trade was the beaver, especially after the decline of the animal in Europe by the end of the sixteenth century. It was sought not for the pelt but for fur-wool, the layer of soft, curly hair growing next to the skin, which had to be separated from the pelt and from the layer of longer and stiffer guard-hairs. This fur-wool was then felted for cloth or hats. The use of beaver fur-wool for hats became especially important. In England, for example, Spanish and Dutch immigrants popularized the habit of wearing hats in place of woolen caps early in the sixteenth century. Thereafter, no amount of sumptuary legislation could stem the decline of cap making. Wearing caps became a hallmark of the lower classes. For those of higher status, shape and type of hat became a barometer of political allegiances. The Stuarts and their followers favored the high-crowned, broad-brimmed, and squarish "Spanish beaver." The Puritans introduced the plain conical felt or beaver hat. The Restoration fancied the

Small copper beaver effigy from Hudson's Bay, used as a token in the early fur trade. Its value was one beaver fur. (Photograph courtesy Museum of the American Indian, Heye Foundation)

broad-brimmed, flattish, slouch hat of the French court, decorated with a feather. The Glorious Revolution brought on the low-crowned, broad-brimmed "clerical shovel," which yielded to the three-cornered cocked hat. This style held out until the French Revolution, which produced the "high hat." Only in the early nineteenth century did the beaver hat go out of fashion, in favor of hats made of silk and other materials.

Initially, however, it was not the search for fur but for fish that drove European sailors to move into the waters of the North Atlantic. Fish was one of the strategic commercial items in medieval Europe: dried and salted, it furnished essential proteins during the days of obligatory fast and through the bitter winters. In the fifteenth and sixteenth centuries the harvests of herring in the Baltic declined, and fishermen began to explore the cod-filled banks off Labrador, Newfoundland, and New England. Portuguese fishermen were perhaps the first, and they laid official claim to the entire coastline, although they could not defend that claim against the ever-growing number of competitors from Normandy, Brittany, and the English West Country. At first, landfalls were sporadic, and sailors would return to their home ports with fresh fish ready for the market. Later, however, the fishermen began to go ashore for the summer, to mend their nets and to preserve their fish by drying and smoking. Thus, "the beaches of the Newfoundland coast became the regular seasonal camp-sites of a tough and independent cosmopolitan fishing community" (Parry 1966: 69).

The North American fur trade began when these fishermen started to barter for fur with the local Algonkins. The possibility of exploiting the "new-found lands" for fur was not lost on the royal agents and settlers who explored the coasts of North America. Effective colonization of the coast by northern Europeans, however, had to await the demise of Iberian maritime hegemony in the Atlantic, which came with the death of Philip II in 1603. Soon thereafter several settlements were established: Jamestown, founded by the English-based Virginia Company in 1608; Quebec, base of the Company of New France established in the same year; Fort Nassau at Albany in 1614, and New Amsterdam in 1624, both founded by the Dutch West Indies Company; New Plymouth in 1620; and Massachusetts Bay in 1630.

Among these settlements Quebec and New Amsterdam would play a pivotal role in the growth of trade. Each of these towns was located athwart a major route to the inland riches of the fur country. Quebec controlled the course of the St. Lawrence River, which led to the chain of the Great Lakes and their successive portages. New Amsterdam controlled the Hudson River to Albany and the route westward to Oswego on Lake Ontario. Thus, the northern route was long controlled by French interests, while the southern access was held first by the Dutch and—after 1644—by the English. From the beginning, therefore, the fur trade was carried on in the context of competition between two states. This competition affected not only the European traders but also the native American populations that provided them with fur.

One of the signal features of the trade was its rapid movement westward as one beaver population after another was hunted out, and the fur hunters had to push farther inland in search of untapped beaver grounds. This meant, inevitably, that people who had felt the first impact of the fur trade were left behind in its wake, while new groups sought to enter it. Everywhere, the advent of the trade had ramifying consequences for the lives of the participants. It deranged accustomed social relations and cultural habits and prompted the formation of new responses—both internally, in the daily life of various human populations, and externally, in relations among them. As the traders demanded furs from one group after another, paying for them with European artifacts, each group re-patterned its ways around the European manufactures. At the same time, the demands of the Europeans for fur increased competition among the native American groups— competition for new hunting grounds to meet the rising European demand, and competition also for access to the European goods, which soon became as much essential components of native technology as markers of differential status. The fur trade thus changed the character of warfare among Amerind populations and increased its intensity and scope. It led to the decimation of whole populations and the displacement of others from their previous habitats. Nor were furs the only item furnished by the Indians. The growing trade also required supplies, and as the commerce in furs expanded westward it altered and intensified the patterns through which food was produced for hunters and traders alike.

A consideration of the fur trade as a whole, therefore, entails several dimensions. Frenchmen and Englishmen interacted with one another and with various groups of Indians. Successive Amerind populations, in

Routes of the North American fur trade

turn, found themselves under pressure to make new adjustments to the Europeans, and to one another. The target of all these conflicts and accommodations was the profit to be made from trapping a small fur-bearing animal weighing about 1½ pounds.

Northeastern Populations

Abenaki

Among the first native American populations with whom the Europeans entered into sustained trading for furs were the Algonkin-speaking Eastern Abenaki of the Maine coast. Their case demonstrates two recurrent effects of such contact. One was the precipitous decrease of the native population. The other was a shift in the mix of economic activities carried on by the indigenous groups, and the resultant changes in their social relations. In the first years of the seventeenth century, the Eastern Abenaki occupied more than twenty villages, each under a chief, with a total population of 10,000 people. By 1611 only 3,000 survived, the others succumbing to European-borne diseases to which the native Americans were not immune. The survivors became more involved in taking beaver for exchanges with the Europeans. They continued to grow some maize, but with the short growing season and frequent crop failures they were eager to trade furs for food, as they did with the Plymouth Colony after 1625. They abandoned the coast, where they had previously fished and hunted waterfowl, and carved out small family hunting territories inland, making hunting by small family groups a mainstay of their new adjustment (Snow 1976).

In this development of the family hunting territory, the Abenaki are by no means alone. It is quite possible that before the advent of the Europeans native hunters favored particular hunting grounds where they hunted in the winter. Yet the hunting territory, held and defended exclusively by small family groups against other possible users, was a consequence of the new individualized exchange relationship between trapper and trader (see Leacock 1954). The Catholic missionaries who followed in the wake of the first explorers also benefited from this splitting up of larger groups, since it made conversion easier as each family took "its own territory for hunting without following in the track of its neighbors" (Jesuit Relations 1632, quoted in Bailey 1969: 89).

Huron

Traveling up the St. Lawrence, the French explorers and traders soon established relations with the Iroquoian-speaking Huron. The Huron (French from *hure*, meaning boar, ruffian, savage), who called themselves Wendar, formed a confederation of 20,000 to 30,000 people of multiple origins, established perhaps as early as the fifteenth century. Originally strongly committed to horticulture, they had settled on the shores of Georgian Bay in Lake Huron and opened trade with the hunters-and-gatherers to the north of them; they exchanged maize, tobacco, and Indian hemp for furs, skin clothing, fish, copper, and hunting and traveling gear. The Huron were thus in a strategic position to carry the expanding fur trade to the inhabitants of the north woods.

As their commitment to the trade grew, they also lessened their involvement in horticulture, drawing ever larger supplies of maize from their allies, the Petuns (Tiontati), to the west of them and the Neutrals (Attiwandaron, meaning "those who speak a slightly different language") on the land bridge between lakes Ontario and Erie. From the inhabitants of the north woods they took over the efficient birchbark canoe, which became the preferred means for transporting large quantities of furs downriver to annual fairs at Montreal. For a time the Huron language became the lingua franca of the Upper Great Lakes and the Canadian Shield. Until their destruction by the Iroquois in 1648, they were the main agents and beneficiaries of the French trade with the interior, and the mainstay of French military operations in the area.

There were several reasons for Huron success in this role. They occupied a strategic location for exchanges between the biotic zone to the south, which favored crops like maize, beans, squash, and tobacco, and the zone to the north, occupied by hunters and fishermen. These exchanges predate contact with the Europeans by several centuries, perhaps dating back to the stimulus provided by horticulture around A.D. 1200 (McPherron 1967). When the fur trade entered the area, there already existed mechanisms that permitted and facilitated exchanges of goods, to which beaver and other furs could now be added. Father Jean de Brebeuf, writing in 1636, suggests that certain circuits or lines of exchange were held by particular family lines and had to be activated by a "master," whose role was heritable.

Transactions of all kinds were accompanied by exchanges of gifts as tokens of friendship, and gift giving was a part of curing ceremonies and diplomatic feasts (see Wright 1967). Most notably, large-scale gift exchanges accompanied the Feast of the Dead, which was held every decade or so to bury the remains of those who had died since the last feast. On such occasions the successors to the dead chiefs were installed, and the names of the dead transferred to them. The rituals thus served to ensure continuity in the leadership of local descent groups, while at the same time providing occasions for gift exchanges between the chiefs of such groups. They underlined the separate identity and distinctiveness of such groups, while simultaneously establishing links of alliance between them. These occasions could bring together members of different linguistic and political groups, as in the feast witnessed by the French missionary Lalemant in 1641 at Georgia Bay, when the local Nipissing invited 2,000 people from as far west as the Sault and as far east as Huronia. The quantity of valuables offered in furs, robes, beads, and hardware was considerable. On that occasion, Lalemant says, "the presents that the Nipissirians gave to the other Nations alone would have cost in France forty or even fifty thousand francs" (quoted in Hickerson 1960: 91). Such gift exchanges, incarnating ties of alliance and recognition of chiefly status, became a widespread concomitant of the fur trade as it spread inland from the Huron. Adopted first by the Algonkin speakers of the Great Lakes, it spread from them to the Cree west of Lake Superior, and from the Cree into the Great Plains at the end of the seventeenth century (Nekich 1974).

Iroquois

The Dutch at New Amsterdam, and the English who took over from them in 1644, encountered in the upper drainage of the Hudson River another Iroquoian-speaking population of horticulturalists, who came to be known to Europeans as "Iroquois"—the French version of an Algonkin word meaning "real adder." The Iroquois were organized into a confederacy, which they called *Ganonsyoni* ("The Lodge Extended Lengthwise"). The five "nations"—or named clusters of matriline-ages—comprising the confederacy were: the Mohawk (from an Algon-kin word for "cannibal"), who called themselves *Ganiengehaga*, or "Flint People"; the Oneida; the Onondaga; the Cayuga; and the Seneca (after *Sinneken*, a mistaken Dutch rendering of a Mahican version of the Iroquoian name for the Oneida). Early in the eighteenth century, the Oneida permitted entry into the confederacy by the Tuscarora. To outsiders the confederacy became known as the "Six Nations," al-though the Tuscarora never had the right to sit in confederate councils. The available evidence indicates that the Iroquois have long resided in this region. In historic times, each of the five nations controlled its own settlement cluster, fields, forests, and hunting territories. Though linked in one political organization, there were cultural and linguistic differ-ences among them. The languages of the various clusters were mutually unintelligible, and the business of the confederacy was carried on by multilingual chiefs.

The Iroquois confederacy had probably come into being in the course of the fifteenth century, as a means for reducing conflict and warfare among the clusters. Soon, however, the growing fur trade gave the various clusters an overriding convergent interest. While the beaver was uncommon in Iroquois country and quickly grew even scarcer in response to increased hunting, the Iroquois soon realized that their separate and collective future depended on the beaver. To increase their own access to furs, however, they had first to reduce or eliminate the competition of their neighbors. Backed by the Dutch, and later on by the English, they unleashed a series of destructive wars against their French-backed rivals. After an epidemic of smallpox weakened the Hurons in 1640, the Iroquois attacked and destroyed Huronia as a separate entity in 1648. In 1656 they destroyed the Neutral Nation and the Erie. In 1675 the Mohawk fell upon the Algonkin confederacy, which had formed to oppose the English colonists in New England. In the same year the Seneca, in league with the English settlers of Maryland and Virginia, ended the threat of the Susquehannock, who controlled the central valley of Pennsylvania. In 1680 the Five Nations opened war on the Illinois to prevent French contact with them.

Despite the scale of Iroquois military operations, the actual number of warriors fielded in the course of these actions was not very great. In 1660 a Jesuit father estimated that the Mohawks could mobilize 500 warriors, the Oneida fewer than 100, the Onondaga 300, the Cayuga 300, and the Seneca less than 1,000 (quoted in Trelease 1960: 16). What lent the Iroquois their military capability was increased access to firearms, traded to them mainly by the Dutch and the English. By 1660 each warrior probably had his own musket, and superior firepower, together with reliance on individual prowess in guerilla-like warfare, granted them superiority over their neighbors (Otterbein 1964).

Entry into the fur trade and intensified warfare brought on other changes in Iroquois ecology and social organization. The economic basis of Iroquois life before the growth of the fur trade was horticulture and the hunt. Horticulture was largely in the hands of women, although the men helped in clearing land during the slash-and-burn cycle. The social composition of the clearing group remains unknown, but other tasks of cultivation were carried out by the women of the village as a whole, under the guidance of the head matron of the dominant lineage and with the matrons of other family lines acting as lieutenants. Rights to use land, as well as the tools used in cultivation and food processing, passed through the female line. Distribution of produce was similarly in the hands of women. The weight of these economic roles granted women considerable authority, since they could use their ability to provide food and moccasins to exercise a veto over the activities of war parties of which they did not approve (Randle 1951: 172). It also placed in their hands the dispensation of hospitality in feasting, an important activity in cementing alliances within and among the clusters (Brown 1975: 247–248; Rothenberg 1976: 112). Furthermore, women owned the multifamily dwellings and exercised the right to nominate councilors to sit in the Council of the Lodge Extended Lengthwise.

Hunting and warfare, in contrast, were the work of men, and these activities grew increasingly important as the Iroquois became more involved in the fur trade, and more dependent upon it. European trade goods, presumably exchanged for fur, appear in Iroquois sites as early as 1570, and a century later the Iroquois had come to rely almost completely upon trade and diplomatic gifts in order to obtain arms, metal tools, kettles, clothing, jewelry, and liquor. The beaver was largely extinct in Iroquois country by 1640, and the Iroquois thus had to range farther and farther into the lands of neighbors and enemies to obtain the resources that paid for the European commodities, or to carry on warfare in order to recompense diplomatic gifts made to them. The separation of male and female roles increased with the growth of the fur trade and the intensification of foreign involvements; the men were often away for years in pursuit of fur and enemies, while the women were tied more closely to the sites of their fields and gardens. It is possible that the Iroquois became increasingly matrilocal after the early seventeenth century (Richards 1957), in response to this growing bifurcation of activities.

It also seems likely, as Richards argues, that women gradually assumed the right to adopt captives into the local matrilineages, a function that grew vital as the Iroquois sought replacements for men killed in warfare. In 1657 the Seneca were said "to contain more foreigners than natives of the country." In 1659 the Jesuit Lalemant said: "If one should compute the number of pure-blooded Iroquois, he would have difficulty in finding more than 1,200 of them in all the Five Nations, since they are, for the most part, only an aggregation of different tribes whom they have conquered." Two-thirds of the Oneida were Algonkin and Huron in 1669. The Jesuits even complained that it became difficult to preach to the Iroquois in their own language. (See Quain 1937: 246−247.)

This evidence has some striking implications. It points to the possibility that in the course of fur trading and enhanced warfare the forms of kinship affiliation remained the same, but their meaning and function underwent a major change. When the Europeans first arrived, the Lodge Extended Lengthwise was primarily a league of local groups adjudicating local interests in cultivated land and other resources, as well as impeding the escalation of local quarrels into feuds and warfare. Yet increasingly the Iroquois confederacy found itself acting as an association of fur traders and warriors, sometimes of quite different origins, in relation to the translocal imperatives of the fur trade and of the political struggles between rival European state systems. William Fenton has spoken of the League as a "kinship state," thus linking two concepts that are often treated as incompatible. The Iroquois confederacy is perhaps better characterized as an association that tried to use the forms of kinship in the pursuit of associational functions. It might even be seen as a native American parallel to the structure of the European trading companies, which also combined economic and political functions. In this characteristic the Iroquois invite comparison with the Aro in the area of the lower Niger in West Africa, who also utilized kinship mechanisms and ritual to organize and dominate the local slave trade (see chapter 7). Like the Aro, the Iroquois were not a state but an association predicated on kinship affiliations that developed in response to translocal political and economic pressures.

The continuing kinship basis of the confederacy was the source at once of its strength and of its weakness. We have seen that the Iroquois women held the right to nominate male members of their matrilineages to positions on the Council at Onondaga. These positions were associated with fifty titles or names, which were owned or controlled by matrilines. It is important to note that the councilors always gave strong voice to local interests and sentiments, and that when they spoke in Council they spoke not in their own names but in the interest of their local kin-based constituencies. The confederacy was thus never a monolithic political instrument. It functioned mainly to reduce infighting and feuds among the constituent village clusters and gained some jurisdiction over negotiations with foreign ambassadors and agents. It could declare war on behalf of the confederacy as a whole, but decisions had to be unanimous. A case over which there was disagreement had to be set aside and resolved by the actions of one or another cluster. Many of the activities of the confederacy were ceremonial, such as the condolence councils during which dead councilors were mourned and new councilors installed. Through such ritual the titles and the unity of the Council were perpetuated on the ideological plane, even when divergent interests came to divide the constituents over economic, social, political, and religious issues.

Divisiveness within the Council increased as warfare grew more intense. As Quain noted,

> when warfare, under the stimulus of European contact, became a part of the daily routine, war leaders turned military popularity to their own political advantage and assumed the principal governmental role. The balance of power between sachems and war chiefs, which seems formerly to have been strongly weighted in favor of the sachems, was shifted so that the cooperative motives of sachem government were no longer significant. [1937: 267]

Ultimately, no mechanism existed to cancel out actual or potential dissidence. Thus, relations between the Mohawk in the east and the Seneca in the west were often strained, even to the point that warfare between the two threatened in 1657. The Seneca and the Onondaga often cheered on French attacks on the Mohawk, and the Mohawk in turn refrained from aiding the Seneca and Cayuga in their wars with the Susquehanna. One or another group of villages would on occasion sign agreements with French or English representatives separately from the others in the cluster. Only rarely was there any united action by the confederacy, and for this reason it could not play a unified game of balancing off the French against the English. As Allen Trelease has said (1960: 342), the difficulty was that the councilors "lacked either the decision or the power to follow it consistently." The same inability to formulate and to follow a common policy also bedeviled the Iroquois during the American Revolution. The Mohawk and the Onondaga split internally, some throwing their support to the American rebels, others to the pro-British loyalists. The Cayuga and the Seneca supported the British, while the Oneida and the Tuscarora aided the Americans, in spite of official declarations of neutrality.

One must not, therefore, overemphasize the political unity of the Iroquois confederacy, or assign to it any concerted strategy for monopolizing the fur trade. Access to beaver was, of course, of primary importance to the Iroquois, but they gained this access either by occupying the hunting grounds of their neighbors or by capturing peltry collected and transported by others. Although they ousted the Huron from their middleman position in the trade, they were unable to prevent the passage of that role to the Ottawa, the Hurons' western neighbors. Their military potential was considerable, but it might not have sufficed to stem a European invasion had not the French and the English shared a strong interest in allowing the Iroquois to play the role of a buffer between them. By arming the Iroquois, the English could impede access of the French to the Ottawa and to the hunting grounds of the Great Lakes. In turn, the French saw that it was to their interest "to weaken the Iroquese, but not to see 'em entirely defeated;" as Baron de Lahontan said around 1700 (quoted in Trelease 1960: 246, n. 44). The relation between the French and the Iroquois was richly paradoxical in that

> although the Iroquois constituted the greatest economic and military threat to Canada they were also the only factor keeping Albany from opening direct relations with the Ottawa and thus crippling the Canadian fur trade. [Trelease 1960: 246]

Indeed, had a direct route opened up between Albany and the west, New France could not have competed with New York. The English had the advantage of lower manufacturing and shipping costs, lower rates of taxation, higher-quality merchandise, and access to cheap rum from the West Indies. In 1689 it took five beaver skins to obtain a gun at Montreal, but only one beaver skin to get one at Albany; two beaver skins to get a red or white blanket at Montreal, but only one at Albany. One beaver skin sold in Albany got an Indian six full quarts of rum, while in Montreal that skin would fetch not even a quart of brandy (Trelease 1960: 217, n. 27). The same differential was still at work in the eighteenth century, when Cadwallader Colson summed it up by saying "that the Traders of New-York may sell their Goods in the Indian Countries at half the Price the People of Canada can, and reap twice the Profit" (see Washburn 1964: 153). The Iroquois presence thus protected French commerce with the West, despite the fact that they were usually enemies.

Conversely, the Iroquois could play off the French and the English against each other. Yet this diplomatic game rarely took place at the level of the confederacy. Rather, some clusters backed now the French, now the English. Only the Mohawk consistently supported the English cause. Others, like some of the Seneca, even fought for the French in the mid-eighteenth century and took part in the French-supported rising of Pontiac against the English (1763–1764).

These differential foreign involvements, however, took their toll on Iroquois unity. The American War of Independence set cluster against cluster. Factions within each cluster also opposed kinsmen to one another. This left the confederacy weak and divided; it continued on a ceremonial basis, but with the American victory it lost its major military and political functions. The pro-British Iroquois moved to Canada, where their descendants still reside.

The Iroquois confederacy thus revealed its essential weaknesses. It was able to adjudicate conflicts among clusters only as long as these did not grow insurmountable. It was able to play off the interests of contending foreign powers and their Indian allies against one another, but it could not develop a concerted strategy in the face of a dominant adversary. The bonds that tied it together were those of kinship and of ceremonial. In installing the ritual of the condolence councils it made use of the pattern—widespread among neighboring tribes—of celebrating the demise of dead chiefs and announcing their successors. For the Huron, the Feast of the Dead served this same purpose, tying the participants into relations of alliance. We shall meet this pattern again among the Ojibwa and allied groups. In all such cases, cohesion was created by ritual means. Ritual could create politically viable ties as long as political interests worked in a common direction. It could not, however, furnish these populations involved in the contradictions of fur trade and politics with any mechanism for making the temporary consensus binding for all parties. Sophisticated as they were in council and warfare, the Iroquois had not succeeded in creating a state, and in competition with more centralized political entities they found themselves at a disadvantage.

Populations of the Great Lakes

Although the Iroquois were never able to monopolize the fur trade west of the lower St. Lawrence, they had an enormous effect on the populations of the Great Lakes region. The Hurons who were not killed or absorbed by the Iroquois fled westward. The Iroquois also drove the prairie-dwelling, corn-planting Potawatomi, Sauk, Fox, Kickapoo, Mascouten, and sections of the Illinois from their lands. These populations were pushed from the area of lower Michigan and Ohio north of the Ohio River to the western side of Lake Michigan. There they entered the fur trade through Potawatomi and Ottawa middlemen at the French trading post established at Green Bay in 1634. None of these people were native to this area, nor did any settle there (as has been suggested) primarily to take advantage of the occurrence of wild rice. The magnet that drew them to Green Bay was the fur trade; the force pushing them out of their original habitat was the Iroquois (Wilson 1956).

The middleman role of the Huron, however, was taken over mainly by the Ottawa, so-called after the Algonkin term *adave*. This term, familiar to many Algonkin-speakers of diverse affiliation, served as a cover name for a congeries of Algonkin-speaking groups who abandoned their own subsistence activities for involvement in trade, moving westward to the fur-trapping grounds as far as Chequamegon Bay by 1660. By 1683 two-thirds of all peltries reaching the French passed through Ottawa hands (Peckham 1970: 6).

Other groups also began to move westward after fur. As early as 1620, groups of Algonkin speakers bearing animal names like Bear or Crane began to converge upon the Sault Sainte Marie River, which links Lake Huron with Lake Superior over rapids. The French called these rapids the Sault, and the people of the rapids the Saulteurs or Salteaux. The region was an ideal meeting place for fur traders, since it furnished an abundant and easily accessible food resource, the whitefish. Soon the Saulteur groups were joined by refugees from the Iroquois and by contingents of people identified variously as Potawatomi, Cree, Algonkin, and Winnebago. Gradually the term *Salteurs* yielded to the name of one of the local groups, *Outchibous*, or Ojibwa.

These fusions and changes of identity are instances of a more general process set off by the intensification of the fur trade in the eastern subarctic. Small local groups, with localized names,

became dislocated, mostly westward, in their search for furs; intergroup conflicts increased, and groups became intermixed. In time they lost their identity and became subsumed under larger group names. The names for these larger groups sometimes seem to have been derived from one of the former small local groups such as *Saulteurs* (Salteaux) or "Outchibons" (Ojibwa). There was no large group known as Ojibwa or Saulteaux at the time of the French. Furthermore, the establishment of trading posts in place of mission stations perhaps encouraged the formation of larger groups of diverse origins from the surrounding areas. [Rogers, 1969: 38]

One such point of fusion was the village of Chequamegon on the southern shores of Lake Superior. This village was occupied by Ojibwa in 1679, when they entered into an agreement with the Dakota—who hunted and grew maize west of the lake—to allow them access to their hunting territories in exchange for trade goods obtained from the French. Chequamegon, producing maize and other crops, attained a population of about 750 to 1,000 by 1736, when the arrangement with the Dakota was abrogated and gave way to violent war between the former treaty partners.

The Midewiwin

Such processes of fusion and alliance among groups that had previously entertained separate local identities had important ideological repercussions. The Feast of the Dead was replaced as the major ritual of exchange and alliance by new religious forms, the best known of which is the

Midewiwin. This cult probably originated at Chequamegon around 1680. The Feast of the Dead had celebrated local group identity and succession to local leadership, at the same time that it strengthened alliances and exchanges among similar local groups. The Midewiwin, in contrast, was directed more toward the individual and his integration into a hierarchical association that transcended locality and descent group.

In the ceremony of the Midewiwin, individual power gained through direct contact with the supernatural was conveyed by a white shell, or *megis*. Each member of a Mide lodge owned a "medicine" bag of religious artifacts which contained such a shell. A person was initiated by being "shot" with "rays" emanating from these shells. Each megis was a repository of supernatural power, and it replicated within each settlement the power of the association as a whole. At the same time, the founding myth of the association declared that it was formed before any of the descent group emblems or totems, and thus had priority over any particular local descent group. The association itself was graded, and members advanced from lower to higher grades and from lower to higher levels of sacred knowledge by paying the officers in charge.

Wealth was thus a prerequisite for advancement in the association; ascribed leadership yielded to achievement in war and fur trading. Moreover, the society was translocal in scope. The leaders and priests of the association were at once the bearers of the highest kind of sacred knowledge and the arbiters of social and jural relations in the newly compounded settlements. They also dealt with outsiders—traders, government officials, and missionaries. In the wake of the fur trade, the distinctive symbols of descent groups thus yielded to the development of a translocal "church," providing a mechanism for the social and ideological control of large aggregate populations that congregated during the winter months.

Expansion Westward

Up to the final third of the seventeenth century, North American furs reached Europe primarily over the two routes of the St. Lawrence and the Hudson. In 1668, however, a new trade route opened up—this time through the north—when The Governor and Company and Adventurers of England trading into Hudson's Bay built a fort at the estuary of Rupert's River, which flows into James Bay. The fort came to be known as Rupert's House, the company as the Hudson Bay Company. Other posts quickly followed, attracting the Cree and the Siouan-speaking Assiniboin, who had previously been at war with the Cree but who now threw their lot in with them against their own kin, the Yanktonai. The great attraction offered by the Hudson Bay Company was guns, more than 400 of which were traded annually between 1689 and 1694 (Ray 1974: 13). Even though many of the weapons proved useless once they broke down, their possession gave the Cree and the Assiniboin a decided advantage over their competitors—the Dakota Sioux to the south, the Gros Ventre and the Blackfoot to the southwest, and the Athabascan speakers to the north.

The French, now fearing encirclement from Hudson's Bay as well as from New York and New England, began a fierce war for possession of the forts along the bay and tried to set the Dakota against the English trading posts. In 1713, however, the Treaty of Utrecht granted the bay to England, and equipped with English guns the Cree and Assiniboin now increased their pressure on the Dakota. The French, in turn, began to push their trading posts and missions westward, as much to enter into direct contact with native American populations in new hunting territories as to counteract the advance of the Hudson Bay Company from the north and the movement of traders from the Louisiana colony to the south. In this, however, the French merely aroused the suspicions of the Ojibwa that they were about to lose their role as middlemen for the Dakota. The Ojibwa, including those from Chequamegon, thus joined the Assiniboin and Cree in sanguinary warfare against the Dakota, driving them from their area of settlement in Minnesota and northern Wisconsin. The Cree and Assiniboin, in turn, expanded into Athabascan territory as far as the Churchill River, until the opening of Fort Churchill in 1717 allowed the Athabascans access to guns of their own.

The conflicts between the Dakota and the Ojibwa, Cree, and Assiniboin were not merely disputes among native American populations but were a North American manifestation of the global conflict between France and England. In India the French East India Company and the English East India Company carried on undeclared war, until the outbreak in 1756 of the Seven Years' War (known in America as the French and Indian War) brought outright confrontation between the two states and their allies. In the Treaty of Utrecht England had retained Hudson Bay, but in the interval between 1713 and 1756 the French had strengthened their position by cementing alliances with native groups, founding New Orleans to open the Mississippi River to shipping by sea, and building Fort Duquesne at Pittsburgh to consolidate their hold over Ohio. An attempt by the English in 1755 to take the fort failed miserably. During the ensuing seven years of war, however, the English decisively defeated the French on three continents. In India, Clive routed the French and their allies at Plassey in 1757. In 1758 the English took Fort Duquesne, calling it Fort Pitt after the British prime minister. In 1759 the British navy crippled the French navy off the coast of France. In 1760 the English took the city of Quebec. In the Treaty of 1763 France yielded Canada to Britain and the Upper Missouri region to Spain.

Changes in the Fur Trade

In the course of the second half of the eighteenth century, the fur trade spread into the drainage of the Saskatchewan. This brought on a series of linked changes. There was a change in the logistics of the trade itself.

There were, in consequence, changes in the internal structure of the native American groups involved in the trade, and changes in the relationships between traders and trappers. Before this time, the routes of the fur trade had followed the natural lines of penetration from the eastern coast up the rivers, along chains of lakes, and over inland seas. The major inland trading posts and forts had been set up at the head of these maritime or riverine routes. Now there were efforts to drive routes overland beyond the divide between the Atlantic and Pacific drainages. These attempts also left behind the supply bases of the lower St. Lawrence and the fishing grounds and maize-producing littorals of the Great Lakes, to enter country that required new sources of transport.

Along with these new ecological exigencies came organizational changes in the trade. Until the middle of the eighteenth century, the trading companies had been content to rely for the delivery of furs on the cooperation of native American middlemen. This cooperation, however, only partly met the needs of the companies, for as long as the middlemen groups were autonomous the companies could exercise only marginal control over their social and political relations, including their alliances and conflicts. The companies thus sought to remove the middlemen by going directly to the primary "producer," the hunters and collectors of the furs themselves. Increasingly, therefore, the traders penetrated directly into the hinterland to tap the supply of furs at its source.

Pontiac's Revolt

These changes in the trade, coinciding with the French–English war, issued in a major native American uprising, Pontiac's revolt in 1763. Pontiac was an Ottawa, a member of the leading middleman group on the Great Lakes. By the mid-eighteenth century, the Ottawa had come to depend heavily on the European traders for the continuation of their role as intermediaries and for their supply of European manufactures. At the same time, the direct penetration of the hinterland by European fur traders was threatening their privileged position. It was becoming clear that the Europeans were there to stay—no longer as guests of the native Americans but as permanent lodgers ready to take over the entire abode. This "double-bind," dependence on the very agents who were also undermining their chances of survival, produced among the native American populations of the eastern woodlands strong currents of ideological resistance. Prophets preached moral reform, coupled with appeals to drive out the encroaching colonizers. The Pontiac uprising was at once a mystical response to the message of the Master of Life and a military response to the decision of the English that the Ottawa would from then on "have to support their families by an 'industrious way of life' without other assistance" (Jacobs 1972: 81; see also Peckham 1970; Wallace 1970: 120–121). The revolt was joined by Shawnees, Ojibwa, Huron, Miami, Potawatomi, and Seneca. After initial successes, the movement failed when the rebels were unable to take the major British forts at Detroit, Niagara, and Pittsburgh. Insufficiently provided with arms and ammunition, and deserted by the French, who made a separate peace with England that year, the rebellion fell prey to internal dissension and defections.

Northwestern Athabascans

While middleman groups were being excluded from their strategic role in the fur trade, new populations living west of Hudson Bay were drawn directly into the trade. The fur traders contacted the Athabascan-speaking Chipeweyans between Fort Churchill and the Great Slave and Athabasca lakes. Chipeweyan bands, now armed with guns, began to drive Beaver and Slave populations from the region of Lake Athabasca and the Slave River, and to exact furs from the northern Yellowknife and Dogrib. There was also friction between the Chipeweyans and the woodland Cree to their south and east; the Cree, previously middlemen, were now losing that position. Some Cree and Assiniboin bands gradually moved into the border zone between the subarctic forest and the prairie, where they began to hunt the bison. They acquired horses after 1730 and became fully specialized horse pastoralists thereafter.

The fur traders now attempted to carry the trade to the trappers, rather than letting the trappers carry the trade to them. The demands of hunting caribou and fishing were at odds with the tasks of trapping beaver. The fur traders, therefore, tried increasingly to convert "caribou eaters" into "carriers" (the distinction drawn by the Chipeweyans) by advancing food, guns and ammunition, traps, cloth, blankets, liquor, and tobacco both to "chiefs" and to individual Indians. In the course of the eighteenth century, advances of food staples such as flour, lard, and tea led to a decline in the autonomous hunting activities of the trapping populations. As people came to rely less on the large-scale caribou drive and on group fishing, the "great man whom we all follow," who organized the large caribou-hunting bands, lost his function. The fur traders now hired hunters to provide their forts with meat, or dealt with "trading chiefs," who gained a measure of influence over their followers by drawing on advances of hunting equipment and staples from the trading posts. Some kin-based groups began to hunt and trade on their own, especially when competition among traders for furs multiplied both the number of chiefs eager to enter into alliance with them, and the conflicts between such chiefs. Thus the relationship of trader and trapper became individualized, favoring the formation of small bands, based on interlinked conjugal pairs, over the larger hunting aggregates of earlier times.

New Companies

In 1797 the Hudson Bay Company faced a new competitor in the Northwest Company, which was sponsored by displaced fur merchants from Albany who had remained loyal to the British Crown during the American War of Independence. It built upon the expertise acquired by the French fur traders, and employed mostly French-Canadian *voyageurs* and Scottish veterans who had fought in the British conquest of Canada or against the Americans. The new company promoted exploration and trade with great vigor all across the lakes and portages to the Rocky Mountains and beyond. Its men were often the first Europeans in the new territories of the interior Northwest.

The westward expansion of the two Canadian-based companies spurred competition from the Americans, who wanted to assure control of the continent for the newly formed republic. In 1803 the United States acquired the Louisiana Territory, and in 1804–1806 Lewis and Clark explored the West on behalf of the U.S. Congress. In 1808 John Jacob Astor incorporated the American Fur Company with President Jefferson's tacit approval, and in 1811 the company established Fort Astoria at the mouth of the Columbia River. Although Astoria was surrendered to the British two years later, the American Fur Company was able to displace the older French companies operating out of St. Louis and to compete successfully with the Canadian companies until it went bankrupt in 1842.

Horse Pastoralists on the Plains

Throughout the areas west of the Great Lakes, the fur traders relied increasingly for their food supplies on meat furnished them by the horse-riding buffalo hunters of the Plains. The development of horse pastoralism in this area was a recent historical development, following upon the introduction of the horse by the Spaniards during the conquest of Mexico in 1519. The first native Americans to mount horses were the food-collecting "Chichimecas" on the northern frontiers of New Spain, who captured or stole them from the Spanish outposts. Successive populations then obtained horses, using them to raid weaker neighbors for prisoners to sell to the French and Spaniards as slaves.

The Apache acquired horses from the Chichimecas around 1630; the Ute and Comanche got them from the Apache around 1700. The eastern Shoshoni of eastern Wyoming and Montana—including the Snake— became mounted in the first third of the eighteenth century, and the Snake soon became the main traffickers in horses and the leading slave catchers in the northern plains. The Shoshoni, in turn, supplied horses to the Blackfoot. Another route in the diffusion of the horse led northeastward. The Comanche supplied them to the Kiowa to their north around 1730; the Kiowa were probably the main source of horses for the horticultural Pawnee, Arikara, Hidatsa, and Mandan.

The horse endowed its new owners with enhanced military capabilities. It also improved their capacity to hunt the buffalo and to transport gear and supplies. Greater mobility, in turn, permitted increased involvement in the widening trade networks, and trade soon brought access to a new military resource, the gun.

The first native Americans to combine horse riding with the use of the gun were the Dakota. As we have seen, the Dakota had been pedestrian horticulturalists and hunters in the woodland and prairie west of Lake Superior until the 1730s, when they were faced with the advance of Cree, Assiniboin, and Ojibwa, who were supplied with guns by the Hudson Bay Company. The Dakota, in turn, obtained guns from the French, who wanted to hold back the allies of the English. Still on foot, they used these guns to ward off attacks from the north, to displace other people (such as the Cheyenne), and to raid the horticultural villages along the Missouri River for slaves to sell to the Europeans. The villagers, however, who had acquired horses from the Kiowa, turned cavalry on the Dakota, until the Dakota were able to obtain horses of their own from the Arikara around 1750. By 1775 the Dakota were the horse-riding and gun-toting lords of the northeastern plains. They opened direct trade relations with the European merchants at St. Louis, thus bypassing the Mandan who had come to engross much of the trade between the Plains and the towns on the Mississippi River. The Dakota defeated the Cheyenne, cut off the Kiowa from the Arikara, and interrupted contacts between the Crow and the Mandan.

In the northwestern plains a similar role came to be occupied by the Blackfoot. Food collectors who had been pushed out of their former habitat to the west of Hudson Bay by advancing Cree and Assiniboin, the Blackfoot obtained horses around 1730 and guns in the second half of the eighteenth century. They were soon successful in rolling back their main competitors, the Snake, as well as the Kutenai and Flathead—none of whom had access to guns.

The advent of the horse not only altered military patterns and increased mobility; it also permitted far more effective access to the buffalo, which could now be hunted in large numbers in tribal surrounds. The lure of the new life led many populations to become full-time buffalo hunters. Marginal horticulturalists abandoned their fields; some examples are the Gros Ventre, the Dakota, the Cheyenne, and the Arapaho. In other instances, splinter groups broke off from horticultural populations, as did the Crow, an offshoot of the Hidatsa.

Even the permanent horticultural villages of the Mandan, Arikara, Hidatsa, and Pawnee along the Missouri and Platte rivers felt the impact of these new opportunities. These large villages were based on the cultivation of maize, carried on by women on lands held by matrilineages. The men made war and hunted, but gardening and horticultural ritual dominated the annual cycle, which included an annual bison hunt. The matrilineages were stratified into elite and commoner households. One lineage furnished the village chief, another the ceremonial leader. The village chief kept order within the village and controlled warfare; the ceremonial leader, together with other members of the elite, cared for the sacred bundles of the matrilineages, keeping them in a lodge that occupied a central place in each village. The elite drew surpluses from the highly productive horticulture; they also received gifts offered during ceremonies, fees paid for entrance into the hierarchically graded men's associations, and goods from the surrounding food collectors in exchange for horticultural products. Wealth so obtained was redistributed according to the differential statuses of the recipients. The general configuration appears to have been predicated on the kinship mode. While the prestations were based on kinship and ceremonial participation, it is possible that they were taking on tributary characteristics, as the elite began to use surplus maize to enter into widening exchanges with the Assiniboin (who traded firearms and manufactures obtained from the Hudson Bay Company) and with European traders.

The new opportunities for individual enterprise offered by the bison hunt had the effect of calling into question elite control over warfare, associational activity, and the acquisition of supernatural powers. As young male warriors or "boys" attempted to hunt, trade, and carry on warfare on their own, they began to challenge the authority of their village leaders. Thus, when members of the Young Dog Society among the Pawnee stole sacred meat while policing the village, they defended their action by saying that they had been out west where people shared alike (Holder 1970: 133). Among the Arikara, "bad young men" who sided with the Sioux had to be expelled (Holder 1970: 129).

Most importantly, the enhanced ability to kill buffalo furnished a major new article for trade with the Europeans. When the fur trade expanded into the Mackenzie Basin in the second half of the eighteenth century, fur traders could now obtain a new source of food from the horse pastoralists. This was pemmican—bison meat cut into slices, dried in the sun or over a fire, pounded with a maul, and mixed with melted fat, marrow, and a paste made from dried chokecherries. The mixture was packed into hide bags weighing about 90 pounds. It has been estimated that a voyageur in the fur trade required an average of 1½ pounds of pemmican per day; thus each bag was capable of supplying a French voyageur for 60 days (Merriman 1926: 5, 7). In 1813 the Northwest Company required 58,059 pounds of pemmican, or 644 bags, to supply its 219 canoes (Ray 1974: 130, 132). The Plains nomads became the chief purveyors of pemmican for the posts of the Woodland, the Barren Grounds, and the Churchill, Columbia, and Frazer rivers. They also began to supply them with horses, needed for transport in the north country beyond the canoe anchorage at Fort Edmonton. The buffalo yielded other commodities as well. There developed a lively trade with St. Louis in buffalo tongues and tallow, and—as the beaver declined in importance after the first quarter of the nineteenth century—buffalo robes became a major article in the fur trade. Between

Nez Percé woman preparing pemmican. Photograph by William Henry Jackson, 1871. (National Anthropological Archives, Smithsonian Institution)

1841 and 1870, 20,000 buffalo robes were gathered at Fort Benton in the Blackfoot country alone (Lewis 1942: 29).

Thus, the combination of horse and gun, in the context of expanding relations of commerce, set the stage for the emergence of the Plains Indian configuration in the course of a few brief years. This configuration was adopted in short order by pedestrian hunters-and-gatherers and cultivators alike. Moreover, these diverse populations came to resemble one another socially and culturally, despite their varied origins. Some of the reasons for this convergence inhered in the new mode of ecological adaptation. The bison herd dispersed during the winter, moving in small groups to shelter in the mountains; in spring the animals moved back to the grassy plains, massing again in a large herd during their mating season in July and August. Bison hunting had to accommodate itself to this rhythm. People dispersed in small bands or family groups during the winter, then massed again for the great annual summer surround. Camp sites also had to be chosen to meet the needs of the horse herds for pasturage and for protection.

Other reasons for the convergent development of Plains culture stemmed from the requisites of large bands, which had to be brought together and held together for hunting and raiding, while retaining flexibility in adapting to changing seasonal demands. The great annual surround required that dispersed and often distinct groups come together in a common camp circle. In response to this requirement, the horse pastoralists borrowed organizational forms with centripetal functions from adjacent sedentary horticulturalists such as the Mandan and the Pawnee. Among such forms were male sodalities, which served as dancing clubs, military associations, and "buffalo police" coordinating the annual bison hunt. Another unifying mechanism lay in the use of symbols that could bind together the different bands, such as the tribal medicine bundle of the Pawnee, the sacred arrows of the Cheyenne, and the sacred pipe and wheel of the Arapaho. Of particular importance in this regard was the great annual Sun Dance ceremonial, which originated among previously horticultural groups such as the Arapaho, Cheyenne, and Dakota. Particular elements of this ritual have prototypes or analogues among the Mandan, Arikara, and Pawnee, but in its adoption by the horse pastoralists the unifying functions of the collective ritual were combined with the pattern of individual merit making. The event was usually held in conjunction with the annual bison hunt. It centered upon individual self-torture, but it invoked a promise of world renewal for all. This new ceremonial spread from the northeastern Plains to virtually all the populations that moved into the Plains.

Whereas in the villages land, privileges, and medicine bundles had been owned by matrilineages or clans, on the Plains corporate kinship units became attenuated or disappeared altogether. Ownership of means of production, such as horses and weapons, as well as rights to medicine bundles, song, dances, and names, was individualized. Kinship terminology associated with descent lines gave way to a more bilateral emphasis, stressing filiation through both parents of an individual; moreover, the extension of terms for *brother* to nonrelatives strengthened the egalitarian unity of the warrior set at the expense of the unity of descent lines. In the villages, leadership had been the hereditary prerogative of elite households who exacted obedience from the entire village population. Among the horse pastoralists, however, leadership came to depend primarily upon achievement in war and trade, and the leader now received his major support from his own band rather than from the tribe as a whole. Thus, while the Plains configuration drew centripetal elements from the horticultural villages, it also loosened the bonds of kinship and authority.

The decentralization of decision making and the enhanced mobility of mounted groups on the Plains also had their roots in the requisites of expanding trade. To obtain more guns and ammunition, kettles and metal tools, woolens, tobacco, and liquor, the horse pastoralists had to obtain more pemmican and horses to sell to the fur traders. There was thus a rising demand for horses and a concomitant increase in horse raiding and rustling. This, in turn, intensified the need for horses to use in both offense and defense. The number of horses required in bride price grew, further increasing the demand for horses, since access to horses permitted men to acquire more wives and thereby to enlarge the work force for preparing pemmican.

The greater the amount of pemmican a man could funnel into trade, the greater was his ability to acquire the weapons and gear to equip a war party, and the greater also his ability to free his male kin and dependents for warfare. Thus, the more successful entrepreneurs and chiefs—those who had links to trading posts—also became successful war leaders. The result was a concentration of horses and valued goods in the hands of the wealthy and successful, producing a differentiation between richer and poorer, between chiefs and their dependents. Since the achievement of social position required liberal distributions of wealth, fees for entry and advancement in associations, payments for medicine bundles and dance prerogatives, and expenditures of bride price, access to horses and guns ultimately spelled success in social and supernatural relations as well. Even the development of graded associations among the Blackfoot, Arapaho, and Gros Ventre may not have been the result of borrowing old elements from the village tribes. This development was probably late, dating from around 1830. The associations provided "an ideal mechanism for expressing and channelizing the vertical mobility which came with the increase in wealth" (Lewis 1942: 42).

The Red River Métis

The Plains Indians did not long remain the only providers of pemmican to the fur trade, nor did the Plains Indian ecological adaptation remain exclusive to Indians. At the beginning of the nineteenth century, Scottish immigrants settled in the Red River country in Manitoba and soon turned to hunting to supplement a meager agriculture. They were joined, in turn, by so-called métis—mixed European and native Americans, many of whom were displaced as trappers and middlemen by the rationalization of the fur trade—as well as by Cree and Ojibwa bands. When the Northwest Company sought to equip its Saskatchewan and Athabascan brigades, they turned to these Red River hunters and trappers as suppliers of pemmican. Along the Red River, therefore, there arose a cycle of activities not unlike that of the Missouri villagers. The Red River people would live in stable settlements, in log cabins near their farms, for most of the year, drawing advances from the companies. In the running season they would move into tents, riding out after the buffalo and bringing back their kills in two-wheeled carts capable of bearing 900 pounds of buffalo meat. On occasion they would fight the Dakota. During a two-month hunt in 1840, the Red River métis obtained nearly a million pounds of buffalo meat. It was sold to the Company to settle debts and to buy household goods; but many hunters had to go out again for a second or third time that year to obtain enough meat to last their own families throughout the winter. When the Canadian government granted reservations to native American groups and to half-natives affiliated with such groups, the métis were excluded. Their dissatisfaction issued in two major rebellions, in 1869 and 1885, under the leadership of Louis Riehl.

Northwest Coast

In the last quarter of the eighteenth century a new frontier opened up for the fur trade on the Northwest Coast of North America. Captain Cook's ships, the *Resolution* and the *Discovery*, landed in 1778 at Nootka Sound, where they acquired several sea-otter skins. When these were sold in China, the best skins fetched $120. News of this spread, and by 1792 there were twenty-one European vessels engaged in the effort to obtain more sea-otter pelts. The maritime trade reached its apogee between 1792 and 1812. Soon after its beginnings, fur traders of the Northwest Company reached the coast overland, and the first fur-trading post west of the Rockies was established in 1805. By the end of the British-American War of 1812, the Northwest Company had full control of the Pacific slope. Only when the Northwest Company merged with the Hudson Bay Company in 1821, however, did systematic land-based trading begin. The most important forts of the Company came to be Fort Simpson, built among the Tsimshians near the "grand mart" at the mouth of the Nass River in 1831, and Fort Rupert, established among the Kwakiutl in 1849.

The Siberian Fur Trade

As the Europeans entered the waters of the Northwest Coast, their trading ships encountered the Russians, who had begun to explore the coast in the 1730s. We noted earlier that the Russians had begun to search for furs as early as the tenth century. Their search gained momentum with the Russian victories over the Mongol-Turkish khanates of the Volga Basin in the mid-sixteenth century. By 1581 a host of Cossacks in the employ of the merchant house of Stroganov crossed the Urals and destroyed the khanate of Sibir. From there the Cossacks pushed on until they reached the Pacific shore in 1638. By 1690 there were permanent settlements in Kamchatka, and in the 1730s and 1740s the Kuriles and Aleutians were explored. In 1797 a state trading company was organized to explore the fur resources of the Far Northeast; it set up a base on Kodiak Island and founded colonies along the coast as far south as California. In 1839 the Hudson Bay Company leased the mainland coast from Mt. Fairweather to the Portland Canal, in exchange for providing supplies to the northern Russian forts. Alaska passed into the hands of the United States through purchase in 1867.

In contrast to the North American trade, which involved the exchange of commodities for fur, the Russian fur trade relied mainly on tribute—that is, payments in fur made as tokens of political subjugation. Thus, when Sibir was conquered, an annual tribute was immediately imposed, which was to be paid in sables and silver foxes. Boris Godunov, better known as the czar who inflicted serfdom on the Russian peasants, set the terms of the fur tribute at ten sables for each married man, five sables for each bachelor, plus one-tenth of all other skins hunted. The Rusian term for the fur trade was *iasak*, from a word common to both Mongols and Turks, meaning "to regulate" or "to fix" (Grousset 1970: 586 n. 106)—a legacy of Mongol state making. The imposition of fur tribute went hand in hand with expansion in Siberia. The ethnographic map (*Remezoff Atlas*) made for Peter the Great in 1673 showed the distribution of iasak in relation to settlements and social groups (Baddeley 1919, I: cxxxvi). The furs were initially collected by military commanders; later this became the task of "sworn men" who received no salary but were licensed to distill alcohol and operate taverns, and who often took furs in payment for drink. While private merchants had only a restricted role in earlier periods, in the eighteenth century they increasingly came to the fore, as they began trading furs to China in exchange for Chinese tea, silks, linen, and rhubarb. In these endeavors the merchants were backed by Buriat, Tungus, and Yakut clan and tribal chiefs, whom the Russians coopted by turning them into hereditary nobles. They were given Russian titles and privileges, and—after the 1760s—the right to collect the iasak themselves (Watrous 1966: 75).

As in North America, however, the expansion of hunting in order to meet the requirement of the iasak led to wholesale decimation of fur-bearing animals. In the fifteenth century, sables had roamed as far west as Finland; by 1674 they were limited to Siberia, and by 1750 to southeastern Siberia. In the eighteenth century, the focus of trade shifted from sables to the sea otter, which was prized in China, especially among the Manchu nobility. Russian expansion into the north Pacific was prompted by the search for sea otters.

The spread of the Russian trade into the Pacific orbit required a major logistic effort. The center of the trade was in Irkutsk; supplies had to be drawn from as far west as Yeniseisk. The local Yakuts were called on not only to provide cattle but also to furnish horses to transport grain and other supplies to the seaboard and peninsulas. Large numbers of horses with Yakut guides were brought together by chiefs (*toions*) who acted as outfitters; individual Yakuts were subject to requisition. The small and sturdy animals they used were the famous "fish-eating" horses of the Yakut; they were fed on fresh fish in addition to pasture, bark, and willow twigs (Gibson 1969: 191). During the winter, transportation was by dog team, and local fishing had to be intensified greatly to provide the large amount of fish needed to feed the six dogs required by each man.

Just as the Russians had to rely on the local population to supply them with fish, they also needed their maritime skills to hunt the sea otter. They first employed Kamchadal, but the sea otter was hunted out in Kamchatka by 1750. In the 1750s the Russian traders moved on to the Aleutians, imposing compulsory service in sea-otter hunting on the Aleut. The Aleut population was reduced to a twentieth of its number in the course of seventy years, and the sea otter grew rare in the Aleutian Islands by 1789. Most of the sea-otter trade shifted thereafter to the Northwest Coast of North America, a trade that was mainly in the hands of British and Boston-based American ships, and from which the Russians were largely excluded.

Populations of the Northwest Coast

In reaching the coast, the Europeans entered an environment very different from that of boreal North America. The climate is temperate; warm moist air rises from the Japanese Current and condenses as rain and fog on the coastal ranges. The heavy rainfall supports thick stands of conifers—fir, spruce, cedar, yew, and redwood. The inhabitants of the Northwest Coast were primarily fishermen, depending in large measure on ocean-living salmon and herring, harvesting them during their annual runs upriver in search of fresh-water spawning grounds. The harvest was supplemented by fishing in coastal waters, by hunting wild fowl, and by gathering shellfish and edible roots. One group, the Nootka, specialized in whaling. Food resources on the coast were plentiful, although spells of bad weather and annual fluctuations in the number of spawning fish caused occasional shortages.

The first recorded meeting of European navigators and the inhabitants of the coast took place in 1774, when the Spanish ship *Santiago* traded with a group of Haida, giving them clothes, beads, and knives in exchange for otter furs, blankets, and carved wooden boxes, and other artifacts. It was four years later that Captain Cook's ships landed and traded for sea-otter pelts at Nootka Sound.

The newcomers quickly realized that they were dealing with trade partners as astute and calculating as any they had encountered on their voyages. They had, in fact, entered an area of extensive native trade. Since resources in the Northwest Coast area were often localized, there had long been trade between islanders and mainlanders, as well as between coast dwellers and inland populations. Thus, olachen ran only in restricted areas, such as the Nass and certain rivers and inlets along Queen Charlotte Sound; people came from far away with goods to trade for olachen oil, a monopoly held by the groups with rights over the fishing tracts. Hunting for land animals was especially important in the upriver communities. The northern Tlingit made the Chilkat blankets woven with mountain-goat wool and cedar bark, but since cedars do not grow in their habitat, bark and cedar wood had to come from the south. Copper was brought from the Copper River area to the Chilkat, and taken south from there. The Haida and the Nootka were known especially for their fine canoes, and yellow cedar-bark robes produced by Nootka and Kwakiutl, as well as Salish robes of mountain-goat wool, dog hair, and the down of wild fowl, were traded up and down the coast. The islanders supplied the mainlanders with dried venison, seal oil, dried fish, shellfish, greenstone for tools, cedar bark, cedar-bark baskets, cedar wood for ceremonial artifacts, and yew wood for bows and storage boxes. The mainlanders furnished the islanders with hides and furs, cloth and clothing, olachen and olachen oil, cranberries, horn spoons, baskets of spruce roots, and Chilkat blankets.

Although the native trading voyages did not involve travel on the open ocean but mainly hugged the coast, they sometimes covered great distances. Tlingit groups traveled 300 miles to trade with Haida or Tsimshian. The mainlanders also traded with the Athabascan speakers of the interior, bringing cedar-bark baskets, fish oil, iron, and shell ornaments to them and returning with hides, moccasins, thongs, and placer copper (Drucker 1963; Oberg 1973: 107−108). One population located along the lower Columbia River, the Chinook, filled an important role as middlemen in the trade along the coast and between coast and interior. They traded slaves from California down the Columbia to the coast (see French 1961: 363−364), in exchange for Nootka canoes and dentalium shells. Their language, incorporating Chinook and Nootka structural features and English vocabulary, became the Chinook "jargon," the trade language of the Northwest Coast.

What the Europeans sought on the coast was, above all, sea-otter pelts. Between 1785 and 1825, some 330 recorded vessels visited the coast, nearly two-thirds of them trading in two seasons or more (Fisher 1977: 13). Sea-otter skins were obtained, at first, in return for iron and other metals; later for cloth, clothing, and blankets; still later for rum, tobacco, molasses, and muskets. The native American traders were mostly "chiefs" who mobilized their followers and personal contacts to deliver the otter skins, and whose power grew concomitantly with the development of the trade.

These chiefs occupied the apical positions in the kinship units of the area. Among the populations north of the Douglas channel—the Tlingit, the Haida, and the Tsimshian—the basic units were matrilineages. South of the channel—notably among the Nootka and Kwakiutl—the units were ambilaterally extended families, or "houses." Each of the lineages or clusters of houses formed a local grouping that held rights, as a body, to resources such as fishing grounds, hunting territories, shellfish beds, and berry patches, as well as possessing ceremonial prerogatives. The rights to manage these resources were vested in certain titled positions; the occupants of these positions were chiefs, called *tais* by the Spaniards and *tyee* in Chinook jargon. As organizers of group resources, these chiefs also became the main agents of the fur trade. The best known of them is the Nootka chief bearing the title of Maquinna, who was first contacted in 1791. He controlled a trade network of populations living on the east coast of Vancouver Island, and he soon became recognized as the leading trader in the area. By 1803 he was wealthy enough to offer in a giveaway 200 muskets, 200 yards of cloth, 100 shirts, 100 looking glasses, and 7 barrels of gunpowder (Jewitt 1815, quoted in Fisher 1977: 18). There were other such chiefs as well. They not only committed their own people to intensified sea-otter hunting but drew into their trade networks groups of people elsewhere, whose furs they re-exported.

Entry into the fur trade must have appealed to these men, because it offered an immediate way of enlarging the scale of resources at their disposal. As Joyce Wike has pointed out (1957: 309), "In most sectors the more accessible resources of importance or value seem already to have been owned or divided up to such an extent that it may have been impossible for one group to expand except at the expense of others." The increasing availability of European arms prompted a rise in warfare, both for territorial acquisition and for slaves. At the same time, the local chiefs must also have seen the new trade as a way of enhancing their position within their societies. Since their accession to office was not automatic but required the expenditure of resources in public giveaways, participation in the fur trade promised to enlarge the stock of wealth on which their status depended.

Where people were grouped into matrilineages, each such group shared a common genealogy and a stock of ceremonial titles. The incumbent to the chiefship was supposed to derive from the senior line of descent, yet the rule specified only those eligible, not the actual heir. Selection of the successor depended upon a man's ability to validate the inheritance through giveaways, in which gifts were presented to guests drawn from actual or potential affinal lineages. Such giveaways were known as *potlatches*, from a Chinook word meaning "to give." While the assumption of all titles involved some form of giveaway, the strategic potlatch among the northerners was the one that announced succession to the chiefship (a function reminiscent of the Feast of the Dead among

Walrus-hide armor decorated with Chinese coins, Tlingit. (Photograph courtesy Museum of the American Indian, Heye Foundation)

the Huron and the Great Lakes Algonkin). As a result of the fur trade, the scope of these giveaways was greatly enlarged. Before the advent of the Europeans, the items given were mostly food and skin clothing. After the onset of the fur trade, they ran the gamut of imported European commodities, as well as native foods and artisan products obtained through trade in such commodities.

Among the southern groups, the ambilateral extended "houses" were ranked with respect to one another, but claimants to high rank had to develop a "portfolio" of titles on both their father's and their mother's side. The road to success among these people was therefore not heirship in the senior line of descent, but the accumulation of titles bilaterally through various rites of passage. The most significant of these was marriage. Each rite of passage was accompanied by a giveaway, with potlatches at marriage playing a determinant role in setting up the title portfolio for a would-be chief.

The members of a matrilineage or an ambilaterally extended house were, of course, linked by kinship, yet they were divided by rank. In the north, descendants of the senior line, and in the south, the "well-born" incumbents to titles, formed a distinctive stratum of "nobles" distinguished through dress, comportment, and ritual prerogatives from a stratum of "commoners." The northern nobility reinforced their special position through cross-cousin marriage, thus keeping purity of descent and potlatching wealth within restricted lines. In the south, where status climbing and potlatch giving were more open in theory, the strategic high-ranking titles were in fact preempted by each generation of title holders for the benefit of their immediate descendants. Possession of titles carried advantages: the nobility received between one-fifth and one-half of the food produced by the commoners (Ruyle 1973: 615). The noble stratum furnished the administrators of lineage resources, the war leaders, the entrepreneurs in trade, and the organizers of ceremonial exchanges, and received all the prerequisites that attended such offices.

The nobility, furthermore, owned and traded slaves. Slaves were mainly war captives, or men and women traded in from Puget Sound or northern California. The percentage of slaves in different groups is variously estimated at one-seventh to one-fourth of the population (Ruyle 1973: 613–614). The Nootka chief Maquinna had nearly 50 slaves, according to Jewitt (1815), who was Maquinna's slave for three years. Roderick Finlayson, clerk to the Hudson Bay Company, says that two Tlingit chiefs at Fort Stikine had 90 to 100 slaves each, mostly purchased from the Haida (Hays 1975: 45). Slaves could be ransomed by their kin groups, an option likely to be taken up if the captors lived close by or if the captive was an important person. Among the Tlingit in the first decade of the nineteenth century, the ransom consisted primarily of sea-otter skins (Langsdorff 1817, quoted in Gunther 1972: 181). The more distant the captive was from his group of origin, the less likely it was that he would be ransomed.

Slavery was hereditary. Slaves were tied to their owners and could not leave, unlike commoner lineage members who might break away to form new settlements. Slaves could be sacrificed or given away in gift exchanges. They could also be put to work. They often did menial household work, and as the fur trade intensified, they were put to the arduous labor of drying and stretching sea-otter pelts in preparation for the market. We do not know how much a slave was worth in contact times. The Tlingit chiefs at Fort Stikine around 1840, however, were willing to sell slaves for $10 apiece. In the 1870s the Chilkat Tlingit rented their slaves to the whites at $9 to $12 a load (Hays 1975: 96). Oberg's old informants reported in 1931 that when they were young (presumably in the last quarter of the nineteenth century) one slave was worth four Chilkat blankets or one breech loading gun; ten to fifteen slaves could buy a large canoe (1973: 111–112).

The chiefs thus used their pivotal positions in the fur trade to accumulate potlatch wealth, to augment their affinal connections through auspicious marriages, to extend their trading networks, and to reinforce their social prerogatives. Some chiefs used the labor of their slaves to increase the production of wealth objects. The basic deployment of social labor in the societies of the Northwest Coast nevertheless remained predicated on the kinship mode. The chief occupied his leading position as the executive of his kin group. Households contributed goods for his prestations by virtue of their kin connections, and in the expectation of returns through redistribution. The frequency with which "worthless people" appear in ethnographic accounts makes it likely that the contributions of kinsmen to a chief—in the form of labor or potlatch wealth—were not always automatic. If dissatisfied with the chief, people could and did secede and move elsewhere. Finally, if a chief mismanaged the resources of the group, he could be killed.

As the civil authorities of Columbia began to interfere with native warfare, the political functions of the potlatch in rivalry and alliance making probably intensified, "stopping up rivers of blood with rivers of wealth." The growing economic utility of slaves diminished ceremonial killing, while contributing at the same time to the successful rise to prominence of parvenu entrepreneurs. The chiefs, however, could not make themselves independent of the potlatch system. If the potlatch constituted a kind of banking, as suggested by Chief Maquinna of Nootka in 1896 in a letter to the *Daily Colonist* (Hays 1975: 88), it consisted in the banking of kin-ordered relations, not of tributary wealth or capital.

By the 1830s the sea otter had become scarce, and trade shifted from the islanders to the mainlanders, whose main concern was to establish and maintain control over fur supplies from the mountainous hinterland. The Tlingit at Wrangell, under Chief Shakes, monopolized the trade with the Athabascans at the head of the Stikine River. The Tlingit at Taku controlled the trade up and down the Taku River, the Tlingit at Chilkat the valley of the Chilkat River. The inhabitants of Milbanke Sound dominated the routes between Ft. McLoughlin and the interior Chilkat. The Tshimshian under Chief Legaic at the Hudson Bay Company's Fort Simpson engrossed the trade on the upper Skeena with the Gitskan, who in turn controlled trade with the Sekani; the Bella Coola played the same role in relation to the Alkatcho Carrier. When the Hudson Bay Company established Fort Rupert in 1849, the Kwakiutl who moved there controlled the trade with other populations.

In these relations between coastal groups and groups in the hinterland, kin ties often structured the partnership of asymmetrical trade. The Bella Coola, for example, integrated the Alkatcho Carrier into their network of trade partners by accepting Alkatcho men as sons-in-law. These Alkatcho affinals were recruited from "the successful hunters, the shrewd and energetic traders, the lucky gamblers" (Goldman 1940: 344)—those who were able to furnish their Bella Coola fathers-in-law with furs. In turn, they obtained noble Bella Coola wives, as well as titles and big names from the wife-giving lineage. As a result, there developed an Alkatcho "aristocracy," which became enmeshed in the Bella Coola potlatch system. The most important Alkatcho "noble" of a village became its potlatch chief and its agent in inter-village potlatches. The real authority of such figures remained limited, however. The Alkatcho subsistence base was too restricted to permit any but minor potlatch exchanges; "an ordinary exchange involved some ten blankets" (Goldman 1940: 347). Property was destroyed among the Bella Coola, but among the Alkatcho it was only symbolically "thrown into the fire." Potlatching increased the productivity of the extended families that participated and led some Alkatcho entrepreneurs to collect furs from neighboring Carrier and Chilcotin, but the restricted productive base ultimately set limits to the escalation of potlatching. The Alkatcho, furthermore, did not take over the elaborate secret society complex of their wealthier affinals. The failure to adopt these forms may have been, in part, the result of difficulty in supporting such events with the humble resources of the Alkatcho villages. At the same time, the Bella Coola guarded these ceremonials and the associated ritual prerogatives as ways of impressing their neighbors, who also remained fearful of Bella Coola sorcery.

The dominant trading populations were not loath to defend their monopolies. In 1834, when the Hudson Bay Company wanted to build a fort on the Stikine to intercept the Tlingit fur trade with the Russians the Tlingit threatened to destroy it. (It was, in fact, built in 1839 with Russian consent.) In 1854 the Chilkat Tlingit sent a war party 300 miles inland to the Yukon Valley to destroy the Hudson Bay Company's Fort Selkirk, which they felt interfered with their trade.

Such forceful control over the channels of trade benefited the coastal intermediaries at the expense of interior groups. In the 1930s some Tlingit still recalled with pleasure how they acquired flintlock rifles from a European trader in return for a pile of furs equal to the height of a gun, and then traded the same gun to the Athabascans for a pile of furs twice its height (Oberg 1973: 10). There was also a great increase in raiding for slaves and in slave trading. Early possession of guns by the people to the north of Puget Sound gave them an advantage over the coastal Salish, who were still fighting with bow and arrow. Slave raids became so prevalent that up river people were soon afraid to come down to the ocean front in the course of their annual cycle (Collins 1950: 337). Fort Simpson, as well as The Dalles, became a major market for slaves.

At Fort Simpson and at Fort Rupert, moreover, significant new political developments took place among the Tsimshian and Kwakiutl. Fort Simpson was set up in Tsimshian country. Nine of the fourteen Tsimshian groups or clusters, with salmon-fishing tracts on the lower Skeena and olachen grounds on the Nass, formed a common winter settlement at Metlakatla Pass (near modern Prince Rupert). These groups had already developed a system of ranking the lineages within each cluster, granting top rank to the chief of the highest lineage. In forming a

Counting blankets in preparation for a potlatch, Fort Rupert. Photograph by Franz Boas, 1894. (Courtesy of the American Museum of Natural History, New York)

confederacy, they faced the problem of ranking the nine lineage clusters with respect to one another. The four groups of Kwakiutl that moved to Fort Rupert in 1849 formed a confederacy, in turn, and came to be known as the "Fort Ruperts." These are the people first described in detail by Franz Boas; they were characterized by an extraordinary efflorescence of their potlatch. Far from constituting an area-wide pre-contact phenomenon, the competitive potlatch "properly belongs to the realm of acculturation studies, not primitive economics" (Ruyle 1973: 625). Philip Drucker has pointed out (1955: 137–140) that the competitive potlatch is especially marked among these two groups, which faced identical problems. The Fort Ruperts had no precedent for ranking the chiefs of the four constituent groups of the new confederacy, and competitive potlatching developed as a way of establishing their rank. The Tsimshian at Fort Simpson did the same, using the potlatch to rank the nine clusters within the confederacy. In these two places, therefore, the competitive potlatches "reached their highest development—or perhaps one should say their peak of bitterest rivalry" (Drucker 1963: 137).

Competitive potlatching involved not only an escalation in bitterness but also an increase in the quantity of goods given away. Helen Codere, writing of the pre-1849 potlatches, points out that

during the six generations before 1849, each of about twenty years (there is no record of the potlatches many years before this or until the fabulous

first three generations of the account), five of the ten potlatches men-
tioned are 170–220 blankets in size, in a size range of 75–287 blankets,
and there is no trend toward increasing the size; the two relatively small
potlatches of the account were given in the later years. [1961: 443]

Thereafter, the number of blankets distributed increased by leaps and
bounds. A potlatch held in 1869 featured 9,000 blankets, one in 1895
over 13,000 blankets, and the last Kwakiutl potlatch in 1921 over
30,000 blankets (1961: 467), as well as other goods.

Some of this wealth was derived from the fur trade; Fort Rupert
earned an estimated 6,000 pounds sterling through fur trading in 1850
(Codere 1961: 457). But from 1858 on, the boom town of Victoria
offered opportunities to Kwakiutl men as day laborers, and Kwakiutl
women began to earn money as laundresses and prostitutes. A growing
number of canneries also employed men in fishing and women in
canning. At the same time, there was a catastrophic decrease in population, much of it brought on by European diseases such as syphilis and
smallpox. The Southern Kwakiutl, who numbered 7,500 to 8,000 in
1835, declined to 2,300 in 1881 and to 1,200 in 1911, a sixth of their
number only 75 years before (Codere 1961: 457). Thus, as the volume
and circulation of money increased, the number of incumbents to
crests, titles, and prerogatives decreased. This furnished novel opportunities to the socially and economically mobile. A commoner was able
to take advantage of the demise of houses and heirs in the late nineteenth century to acquire high titles by employing money drawn from
prostitution and informants' fees (Wike 1957: 311; see Boas 1921:
1113–1117).

In 1858 the native American populations of the area received a final
setback when the news that gold had been discovered in the Fraser
River reached California. Within months thousands of gold miners
arrived, to be followed soon afterward by settlers eager to establish
themselves on land they claimed was "lying waste without prospect of
improvement" (quoted in Fisher 1977: 104). The consequences were
clear to a native Vancouver Islander when he said, in 1860, "that more
King-George-men will soon be here, and will take our land, our firewood, our fishing ground; that we shall be placed on a little spot, and
shall have to do everything according to the fancies of the King-George-
men" (quoted in Fisher 1977: 117).

For more than three centuries the fur trade thrived and expanded in
North America, drawing ever new native American groups into the
widening circuits of commodity exchange that opened up between the
incoming Europeans and their native partners in trade. The trade first
touched the food collectors and horticulturists of the eastern woodlands
and subarctic. Then, with the expulsion of the French and the partition

of the north country between British Canada and the United States, it reached beyond the Great Lakes into the western subarctic, creating at the same time a new zone of supply in the area of the Plains. Finally, at the conclusion of the eighteenth century, the trade established a beachhead in the Pacific Northwest, eventually linking up, across the coastal mountains, with the advancing inland trading posts.

Wherever it went, the fur trade brought with it contagious illness and increased warfare. Many native groups were destroyed, and disappeared entirely; others were decimated, broken up, or driven from their original habitats. Remnant populations sought refuge with allies or grouped together with other populations, often under new names and ethnic identities. A few, like the Iroquois, expanded at the expense of their neighbors.

Some groups, strategically located or strong militarily, became primary beneficiaries of the trade in furs. They prospered, and elaborated new cultural configurations that combined native and European artifacts and patterns. Such cultural elaboration was made possible by the flow of new and valued European goods into a still self-regulating native economy. As long as the native Americans were able to direct most of the social labor available through kin-ordered relations to the task of guaranteeing their subsistence, the goods attained by part-time fur hunting supplemented rather than replaced their own means of production.

Until the end of the eighteenth century, moreover, native American groups were sought as allies by the rival European powers engaged in political and military competition. The Indians were still independent military and political agents—"nations," in the parlance of the time— whose support had to be gained with supplies of goods, including weaponry. As a result, the exchange of goods and services between Indians and Europeans resembled the giving of gifts more than an exchange of commodities, signaling relations that transcended the merely material. As Marcel Mauss pointed out, the exchange of gifts embodied an invitation to friendship and alliance, or the cessation of feuds and war.

Access to European goods and gifts soon altered patterns of interaction both within and between groups. In kin-ordered social groups, an increased ability to obtain such goods and to distribute them among kinsmen and followers gave prominence to salient "big men" or war leaders, or enhanced the influence and scope of redistributing chiefs. Gifts and goods phrased as gifts also created alliances between Indian groups, as well as between Europeans and Indians. Such exchanges played an important part in the formation of new groups and in the development of wider-ranging ethnic identities. Sometimes such larger ethnic entities or confederations grew out of the amalgamation of previously distinct local groups around a European stronghold or trading emporium. At other times, such alliances or confederacies were formed in an effort to gain control of new hunting grounds or strategic routes of access to the trade. Many of the Indian "nations" or "tribes" later recognized as distinct ethnic entities by government agents or by anthropologists took shape in response to the spread of the fur trade itself, a process in which the native Americans were as much active participants as the traders, missionaries, or soldiers of the encroaching Europeans. Thus, the history of these supposedly history-less peoples is in fact a part of the history of European expansion itself.

To bind these new ethnic entities together, the native Americans developed overarching collective forms and rituals. Sometimes they imparted new functions to traditional cultural forms, as in the transformation of the Algonkin Feast of the Dead into the "trade ritual," in the elaboration of shamanic contests into the Midewiwin "church," or in the use of the Northwest Coast potlatch to cement trade partnerships or to coordinate competing groups. At other times, wider solidarities were created through novel combinations of cultural forms of diverse origins, as when the peoples of the Plains developed in the Sun Dance a group ritual suited to their more mobile way of life.

Yet as the European traders consolidated their economic and political position, the balanced relation between native trappers and the Europeans gave way to imbalance. The decline of international warfare diminished the politically motivated flow of goods from European authorities to native American allies. The native Americans themselves came to rely increasingly on the trading post not only for the tools of the fur trade but also for the means of their own subsistence. This growing dependence pressured the native fur hunters and pemmican suppliers to commit ever more labor to the trade in order to repay the goods advanced to them by the trader. Abandoning their own subsistence activities, they became specialized laborers in a putting-out system, in which the entrepreneurs advanced both production goods and consumption goods against commodities to be delivered in the future. Such specialization tied the native Americans more firmly into continent-wide and international networks of exchange, as subordinate producers rather than as partners.

7 The Slave Trade

In South America the search for wealth centered on gold and silver. In North America it was the beaver that was sought, "the beloved" of the Europeans, as the native Micmac called the animal. In Africa the main commodity came to be "black ivory"—people, to be sold primarily in the Americas.

Trade in people was not a new phenomenon, nor was it confined to the Americas. The European peninsula had long supplied slaves, first to Byzantium and later to the Islamic world; in the Mediterranean, in Cyprus and Sicily, slave labor was employed to grow sugar cane and to work in the mines as early as the twelfth century. At that time slavery was clearly color-blind. The Europeans also made use of slaves in Asia. In the seventeenth century the Dutch, for instance, drew slaves from as far away as Madagascar and Mindanao to work in the settlements on the Cape of Good Hope in Africa and in the nutmeg groves of the Banda Islands. The town of Batavia in Java, newly established by the Dutch, was peopled with slaves brought from the Bay of Bengal (Boxer 1973b: 268–269). As the slave trade unfolded during the fifteenth century, however, slaves were increasingly drawn from Africa, and as time wore on they were destined in ever larger numbers for transportation to the Americas. America provided the major demand, Africa the major supply.

The Course of the Slave Trade

This American demand underwent various changes of phase. It grew gradually, during the sixteenth century, in response to a Spanish demand for labor in the silver mines and on plantations, and a Portuguese demand for cutters and millers of sugar cane in the Brazilian Northeast. Some 275,000 slaves were sent to America and Europe between 1451 and 1600. In the course of the seventeenth century, slave exports from Africa quintupled to an estimated total of 1,341,000, primarily in response to the development of sugar cane cultivation on the islands of the Caribbean. (This Antillean boom compensated to some extent for the economic depression of the seventeenth century in Western Europe.) The middle of that century marks a watershed in agricultural production in the Caribbean islands. Before 1650 most of the islands grew tobacco, a crop then mainly in the hands of European settlers working small farms. After 1650 the islands turned to sugar production on slave plantations, while tobacco, too, came to be raised increasingly with slave labor on large estates on the North American mainland, mainly in Virginia and the Carolinas.

The eighteenth century proved the golden age of slaving, with over 6 million people being forcibly exported from Africa between 1701 and 1810. The principal centers of production were British-owned Jamaica and French-owned St. Domingue; two-thirds of the slaves shipped to the Caribbean worked on sugar plantations. In 1807 Britain abolished the slave trade; yet almost 2 million more slaves were transported from Africa between 1810 and 1870, many of them destined for Cuba, the major Caribbean sugar producer in the nineteenth century. Clearly the eighteenth century and the first half of the nineteenth century witnessed the height of the slave trade; 80 percent of all slaves to reach the New World came between 1701 and 1850.

The initiators of the trade along the western coast of Africa were the Portuguese, who had extended their colonization of the Atlantic islands southward. Madeira, already known to map-makers in the fourteenth century, was settled by Portuguese in 1402. The Canary Islands had been seized by Castile in 1344, but in the second quarter of the fifteenth century Portugal began to settle some of the islands, fighting—as had their Castilian counterparts—against the Guanche, the white natives of the islands. The Portuguese enslaved the Guanche and took them to Madeira, using them to construct the irrigation works that soon transformed Madeira into "a veritable agricultural paradise" of wheat and sugar-cane fields (Greenfield 1977). The Azores were first occupied by Portuguese in the 1430s. The first Portuguese trading post (*feitoria*) was established at Arguin off the coast of Mauritania in 1445. There followed the discovery of the islands of São Tomé and Príncipe in the Gulf of Guinea in 1470, and of Fernando Po at the mouth of the Niger in 1471. Soon afterward, in 1482, the second major coastal trading post was established at Elmina in the Bight of Benin, followed by one at Axim in 1503. In 1483 Diogo Cão sailed up the mouth of the Congo River and initiated a period of "friendly relations" between the kingdom of the Congo and the king of Portugal.

Early Portuguese commerce in West Africa did not concentrate on the recruitment of slaves. It was the search for gold and spices that prompted the early Portuguese voyages, and the traders shipped home gold, pepper, ivory, dyewoods, gum, beeswax, leather, and timber, as well as slaves. During the reign of Don Manuel I (1496–1521), the gold shipped to Portugal from Elmina alone amounted to an annual average of 170,000 *dobras*, or gold coins (Boxer 1973a: 29). In return, the

Portuguese brought to Africa textiles from England, Ireland, France, and Flanders; wheat from Morocco, the offshore Atlantic islands, and northern Europe; brass utensils and glass beads from Germany, Flanders, and Italy; and oyster shells from the Canaries. They were thus mostly re-exporters of other peoples' goods. Brazilian tobacco, however, soon became famous in Africa and gained the Portuguese a commodity that continued to be marketable for the duration of the African trade.

While the Portuguese thus carried on commerce in many commodities, the trade in slaves proved lucrative from the beginning. Between 1450 and 1500 the Portuguese may have acquired as many as 150,000 slaves, shipping many of them to Portugal (Boxer 1973a: 31). The slave trade escalated further when it was discovered, around 1500, that São Tomé and Príncipe, previously uninhabited, were ideal for growing sugar cane. Thereafter the influx of African slaves increased, although other people—such as Jewish children deported from Portugal—were settled there as well. São Tomé became one of the sparkplugs of the burgeoning trade in sugar and slaves. Between 1500 and 1530 its production of sugar increased thirtyfold. By 1520, however, sugar planting had begun in Brazil, which soon became the greatest consumer of slaves.

If the Portuguese were the major purveyors of the slave trade in the fifteenth and sixteenth centuries, the Dutch West Indies Company began to encroach on Portuguese preserves, and soon they dominated the trade. The advent of the Dutch on the African shores must be seen in conjunction with their attempt to wrest control of the Brazilian sugar coast from the Portuguese between 1624 and 1654. Moving into East Africa, the Dutch attacked the Portuguese in Mozambique in 1607 and 1608; in West Africa, they captured Elmina, Axim, and Shama on the Gold Coast in 1637, and occupied the coast of Angola between 1641 and 1648. By 1654, however, they lost their last stronghold in Brazil and thereafter abandoned the effort to obtain outright territorial control both in Brazil and in Africa. They did, however, maintain their grip on the offshore islands of Curaçao and Aruba in the Caribbean.

Instead of carrying on primary production of sugar themselves, the Dutch turned to supplying Caribbean sugar producers with capital and skills, and to trading in slaves. Much of the Brazilian sugar destined for Europe would still reach Amsterdam, since the Portuguese processed their sugar in Dutch mills. By 1660, however, the Dutch faced the first organized English competition, in the shape of the so-called Royal Adventurers into Africa and their more efficient successors, the Royal Africa Company. Beginning in 1664 the French also chartered a number of companies to trade in the South Atlantic.

Like the Portuguese before them, the English did not at first come to Africa to trade only for slaves. Gold was the most important item of the goods handled by the Royal Africa Company at the end of the seventeenth century. Indeed, it is estimated that the Gold Coast exported gold amounting to a value of 200,000 pounds sterling per year between 1500 and 1700 (Bean 1974: 353). Yet from the beginning of the eighteenth century slaves constituted the main commodity of the African trade, and the English dominated that trade. Between 1701 and 1810, England exported from West Africa over 2 million slaves, about two-thirds of the total number shipped by the three major powers in the slave trade; the other two, France and Portugal, transported about 600,000 slaves each during the same period. By 1710 the Royal Africa Company, based in London, had given way to private merchantmen operating out of Bristol, and by mid-century Bristol yielded predominance to Liverpool. Liverpool became the leading slave port in Europe until the trade was abrogated in 1807; that city was favored in this role by its close connection with an increasingly industrial hinterland, which furnished capital and cheap industrial goods for exchanges with the suppliers of slaves in Africa. The main French slaving port was Nantes, which after 1763 was joined by other French ports trying to compensate for the loss of the Canadian fur trade to the English.

While the number of slaves transported to America grew steadily, the rate of profit obtained in the slave trade is a matter of dispute. Individual traders earned profits of up to 300 percent (Craton 1974: 120); many others, however, went bankrupt. Slavers had to pay fees and taxes to local African authorities, hire local labor, absorb the costs of delays in loading, and face losses of crews and slaves in Middle Passage. Overall, however, the trade was certainly profitable. Malachy Postlethwayt, the British mercantilist who wrote in defense of the interests of the Royal Africa Company, claimed that "the Negroe-Trade and the natural Consequences resulting from it, may be justly esteemed an inexhaustible Fund of Wealth and Naval Power to this Nation" (quoted in Davis 1966: 150). The slave trade, he wrote, was "the first principle and foundation of all the rest, the mainspring of the machine which sets every wheel in motion" (quoted in Craton 1974: 120). In 1700 the Royal Africa Company expected to sell slaves at four times the value of trade goods paid for them, while private traders expected a return of six to one. Craton estimates the total return between 1620 and 1807 at approximately 12 million pounds, with perhaps half that sum accruing between 1750 and 1790 (1974: 117). Klingberg estimated the annual profit of the trade in the eighteenth century at 24 percent (in Davis 1966: 155, n. 60); according to Anstey, however, between 1769 and 1800 profits were lower, ranging from 8 to 13 percent annually (1977: 84).

The trade had indirect effects on the European countries engaged in it. The commodities traded for slaves on African coasts had to be produced or paid for in the home country. Thus, between 1730 and 1775 the value of British exports to Africa rose by some 400 percent. Manufacturers, provisioners, and sailors all benefited by the trade and at various times petitioned for its continuance. Moreover, the plantations worked by slave labor were profitable, and much of the profit returned to the home country. West Indian sugar plantations earned approximately 20 percent annual profit before 1700, at least 10 percent between 1750 and 1775, and about 7.5 percent in 1790 (Craton 1974: 139). Craton concludes that

> it is thus quite reasonable to assume that profits on all West Indian plantations were never lower throughout the eighteenth century than the rate of 8 to 12 per cent of the market value of the slaves deduced from sugar plantations. [1974: 140]

In his book *Capitalism and Slavery* Eric Williams argues that the slave trade and its adjuncts, in fact, provided the capital that allowed England to take off into the industrial revolution. Williams probably underestimates the growth of the domestic market and overestimates the role that Africa and the Americas played in generating capital for English growth. The home market was important, and English exports to Europe exceeded in value those going to Africa and the Americas in the seventeenth and eighteenth centuries. Yet the growing demand of the English plantations in the second half of the seventeenth century did furnish "a market in which English manufacturers were protected, in which they had little native competition, and which had an absorptive

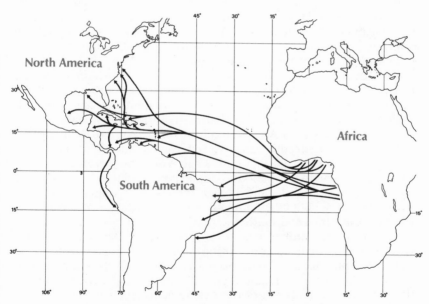

Sources and destinations of the Atlantic slave trade.

capacity rapidly expanding as colonial exports grew" (Davis 1954: 154). Moreover, English exports to Africa and the Americas increased tenfold during the eighteenth century, while the amount going to Europe remained stationary. "The principal dynamic element in English export trade all the middle decades of the eighteenth century was, therefore, colonial trade" (Davis 1962: 290). The Williams thesis may thus be rephrased to suggest not that English industrial development was predicated mainly on the Atlantic trade, but that the Atlantic trade furnished English industrial development with a "principal dynamic element."

Over the course of the trade, the source of demand for slaves changed, as old plantation areas and mining districts were superseded by new ones; the zones providing slaves shifted, too, with the changing fortunes of traders and suppliers. During the initial period of Portuguese ascendancy in the trade of the fifteenth century, slaves came predominantly from the region extending south of the Senegal River to Sierra Leone, an area easily reached from the Cape Verde Islands and called by the Portuguese *Guinea of Cape Verde* (Curtin, 1969: 96). In the sixteenth century, Senegambia remained a major area of supply, furnishing numerous captives taken in the wars that followed the collapse of the Jolof state. At the same time, the area south of the Congo River grew more important, with Portuguese penetration of the kingdom of Ndongo (Curtin 1969: 101–102). By the mid-seventeenth century, the great majority of slaves exported into the Iberian sectors of the New World were "Angolas."

During the seventeenth century, Brazil received 42 percent of the slaves shipped and Spanish America received 22 percent, but the British Caribbean now took 20 percent of the supply and the French Caribbean another 12 percent. The slaves bought by the English, however, came increasingly from a new area of supply—from West Africa between Cape Mount and the Gap of Benin, comprising the Grain Coast, the Ivory Coast, the Gold Coast, and the Slave Coast. Around 1675, 64 percent of all slaves traded by the Royal Africa Company came from this region (Curtin 1969: 122). This change in distribution probably had its effects on the new Afro-American cultures of the Western Hemisphere.

During the eighteenth century, Senegambia and Sierra Leone receded further into the background, while West Africa became the major source of supply. In this period, about 60 percent of the slaves exported by Portuguese, English, and French traders were drawn from West Africa (some 3,234,000), while 40 percent (2,228,000 people) came from central Africa and southeastern Africa (Curtin 1969: 211). Within West Africa, the number of slaves supplied from different areas varied with changing circumstances. During the first decade of the century, the Bight of Benin, or Slave Coast, played a major role in the trade through the strategic port of Whydah. From 1730 to 1750, a period marked by the rise and consolidation of the Asante polity, the Gold Coast was a prominent source of supply. In the 1740s and again in the 1760s, slaves came in large numbers from the Windward Coast, especially from the area of modern Liberia, where the Kru began to play a role as slavers and seafarers. By 1740 the Bight of Biafra—the region of the Niger Delta—also began to furnish slaves in large numbers. From then until the end of the century, this area exported more than 100,000 slaves in each decade; in the 1760s and again in the 1790s the number rose to about 140,000. This increase in slave exports is related to the growth of efficient slave-capturing and delivery organizations in areas previously marked by kin-ordered populations. In the 1780s the Slave Coast again became an important source of supply, exporting more than 120,000 slaves; this was the time when the kingdom of Oyo intensified its participation in the trade.

During the eighteenth century, the slave trade went on apace in central Africa as well. Although in the 1710s and 1720s the Portuguese drew the majority of their slaves from the Bight of Benin, in each decade from the 1730s until the end of the slave trade they never exported fewer than 120,000 slaves from central Africa and Mozambique, and the number from this area exceeded 180,000 in the last decade of the century. The British also relied on this region, receiving from it over 100,000 slaves during each of the decades between 1781 and 1810 and the French bought some 130,000 slaves from this region during the 1780s (Curtin 1969: 211). These figures bespeak a vast expansion of the trade in central Africa, with major sociopolitical implications for this area.

Although the British decision to abolish the slave trade in 1807 ended the flow to the British Caribbean and greatly reduced slave imports into the United States, more than 600,000 slaves still went to the Spanish dominions of the New World in the nineteenth century, 550,000 of them destined for Cuba. The French Caribbean acquired almost 100,000 slaves between 1811 and 1870, and Brazil as many as 1,145,000. The Brazilian supply came mostly from the catchment area in the Congo and in Angola. Ever larger numbers, however, came from Mozambique in East Africa, where the Yao operated at the eastern end of the great lane of slave traffic that had been forged through the middle of central Africa.

Why Africa?

Why did Africa become the main source of slaves for the Western Hemisphere? Indeed, why did Africa become the source of slaves for Europeans rather than Europe itself? The answer is by no means clear, but some pieces of the puzzle are becoming apparent. We have seen that in the first millennium A.D. Europe did indeed furnish slaves to the Moslems and the Byzantines. During the centuries of the Crusades, Moslems enslaved Christians and Christians enslaved Moslems, a pattern that continued in the Iberian peninsula until the end of the fifteenth century. In the thirteenth century the Genoese and the Venetians began to import Turkish and Mongol slaves through Tana on the Black Sea, while most of the slaves imported into Europe during the fourteenth century were Slavs and Greeks. In the fourteenth and fifteenth centuries slaves from these areas formed a significant proportion of the population of Tuscany and of Catalonia-Aragón. Much of the wealth of Venice came to depend on the trade in slaves. Although slaves could not be sold at public auctions in Venice after 1386, they continued to be sold by private contract throughout the sixteenth century. Slave trading also formed a large part of the activities of pirates on both sides of the Mediterranean well into the seventeenth century. Slavery in Europe, however, was not entirely a Mediterranean phenomenon. Coal miners and saltpan workers in Scotland were still enslaved in the seventeenth and the eighteenth centuries, some even made to wear collars marked with their owners' names (John Millar 1781, quoted in Davis 1966: 437; Mantoux 1928: 74—75). In addition, Scottish and Irish prisoners of war were sent into servitude (though not lifetime slavery) in the New World.

The English, furthermore, relied heavily on indentured servitude to provide labor for the New World colonies. Indenture was a contractual relationship in which "parties are upon certaine termes or conditions for a certaine time onely under the power of a man" (Baynes 1641–1643, quoted in Jordan 1968: 62). In practice, indentured servitude differed little from slavery. Indentured servants were often bought and sold while contractually bound; they were harshly punished for breaches of discipline, and many did not outlive the period of their bondage—much like the African slaves imported into the Caribbean area, who had a notoriously short life span. Of every ten indentured servants in English North America between 1607 and 1776, only two attained the status of independent farmer or artisan after their term of servitude. Most of them died before their contracts expired; the rest became day laborers or paupers (Smith 1947: 297—300). Indenture in North America reached its high point at the end of the eighteenth century. Indentured servitude may have offered certain advantages to employers, for the cost of an indentured servant was less than that of a slave. At the same time, indenture was limited in time, hedged about with customary and legal restrictions, and subject to the relative ease with which servants could escape. In any case, the force of legal or ideological constraints upon the enslavement of Europeans should not be overestimated. The question of why Europeans were not legally enslaved still remains open. Perhaps mercantilist notions about conserving domestic manpower played a part, whenever appeals to Christian equality proved insufficient. In the context of the New World, the distinction between European limited-time bondservants and African lifetime slaves separated Whites from Blacks in numerous legal and social contexts.

Why, then, did the Europeans not make more extensive use of native

American slaves? The Spaniards had no compunctions about enslaving Indians, especially during the first phase of their colonization in the Caribbean. They raided not only the Central American mainland for slaves, but also the Atlantic and Gulf coasts of North America. In 1520 Lucas Vásquez de Ayllón carried off fifty Indians from the North American mainland to the West Indies (Nash 1974: 110). In Brazil the Portuguese began in the sixteenth century to use native labor in the sugar districts of Bahía, and in the course of the sixteenth and seventeenth centuries slave raiders operating out of São Paulo are said to have enslaved as many as 350,000 Indians (Curtin 1977: 6).

In North America, in what was later South Carolina, English settlers obtained Indian slaves—captured in war—as well as deerskins from the native populations, rewarding the slave-hunting groups with European commodities. As Gary Nash has put it, the English "subcontracted war" to Indians (1977: 117). They set the Westos against the people of the interior; the Shawnee against the Westos; the Creek against Timucua, Guales, and Apalachees (10,000 people of these groups being exported as slaves in the year 1704); the Catawba against the Shawnee; the Catawba, Congarees, and Shawnee against the Cherokee; and the Cherokee against everybody else. The Indian slave trade in the Carolinas reached its peak in the Yamasee war of 1715−1717 and declined thereafter.

A reason often given for the preference for African slaves over native Americans is the claim that Africans were better and more reliable workers. By the 1720s Africans fetched higher prices than Indians (see Perdue 1979: 152 n. 5). The main factor, however, seems to have been that Indian proximity to their native groups encouraged rebelliousness and frequently, escape. The English colonists also feared that Indian slavery would alienate native American allies in the wars against the Spaniards and the French. Finally, native American groups could be enlisted to aid in returning runaway African slaves to their masters. In 1730, for instance, the Cherokee signed an agreement to seize and return runaway slaves, upon the promise of a gun and matchcoat for each slave delivered (Perdue 1979: 39).

Whereas white bondsmen and native American slaves were able, to some degree, to enlist the aid of their own groups, African slaves were forcibly deprived of such support. Sale or capture at the African terminus of the trade divorced them from kinsmen and neighbors; upon arrival in American ports, slaves of different ethnic and linguistic origin were then deliberately mixed to inhibit solidarity. Once assigned to owners, their segregation from white bondsmen and native Americans was confirmed by legal discrimination and fostered by the growth of racist sentiment. If they ran away, their skin color served as a mark of identification for every "patroller" bent upon reaping a reward. The enslavement of Africans thus offered the possibility of a labor force that could be set to work in arduous and continuous operations under an owner's direction, with restraints of law and custom reduced to a minimum. It foreclosed alternatives open to the other laboring populations in the New World. Why then Africa? In the Mediterranean there was a high level of trade in slaves at the time of the Portuguese and Spanish exploration of the Atlantic. The western Mediterranean, however, was soon cut off from the source of slaves in the eastern Mediterranean and around the Black Sea by the Ottoman seizure of Constantinople in 1453 and the ensuing Turkish blockade of trade routes to the east. Portuguese slaving along the western coasts of Africa had already begun by then; the Dutch, French, and English merely followed in the wake of Portuguese pioneers. On his first voyage in 1562, John Hawkins heard in the Canaries "that Negroes were very good merchandise in Hispaniola" (quoted in Jordan 1968: 59). The notion that "some gaines" could be obtained in this trade undoubtedly inspired his crest, which featured a "demi-Moor captive and bound."

The African Background

While Hawkins was informed that "store of Negroes might easily be had upon the coast of Guinea," Africa was not, in fact, an area burgeoning with population. The population of West Africa, from the northern boundaries of Senegal to the eastern border of modern Nigeria, is estimated at about 11 million in 1500; west-central Africa (Equatoria, Zaire, and Angola) had about 8 million inhabitants at that time (McEvedy and Jones 1978: 243, 249). The introduction of American food crops, such as maize and manioc, probably contributed to an increase in the population of these regions to about 20 million and 10 million, respectively, by 1800. The ability of this area to sustain a large-scale trade in people thus seems surprising, as does the rapid development of the delivery system that linked European demand and African supply. This development combined European initiative with African collaboration. Europeans financed and organized the trade. Capture, delivery, and control and maintenance of captives while waiting for ocean transport remained mostly in African hands. Ocean transport, "seasoning"—the process of habituating the captives to their new conditions—and sale at the point of arrival, in turn, were carried out by Europeans.

This new trade was engrafted upon societies with a similar ecological base in slash-and-burn cultivation of tubers, bananas, millets and sorghums, and—where possible—in livestock raising. (The raising of cattle and horses was inhibited in much of the forest belt by the prevalence of the tsetse fly.) Ironworking craftsmen furnished iron-headed hoes and axes, as well as spearheads and swords. There was much interchange of craft products and localized resources—such as iron ore, copper, salt, and palm products—through extensive networks of exchange and market places. Access to land and other resources was controlled by lineages, which represented continuous corporations of ancestors and descendants. These lineages were managed by elders, who were also charged with implementing alliances among lineages through the exchange of bridewealth for rights over the reproductive capabilities of women and over their offspring. The scarce factor in this adaptation was not land but labor; rights to labor were locked up in kinship arrangements manipulated by the elders as lineage representatives.

While such interacting lineages tended to form autonomous social and economic systems, overarching polities sometimes came into being under the rulership of "divine kings," who embodied in their person and status the attributes of the supernatural. Where such ritual kingship came to be combined with royal control over strategic resources—such as gold, iron ore deposits, salt, and slaves—and with jurisdiction over long-distance trade, more complex "pyramidal" political structures emerged. These polities trace their origins through mythical charters that derive their ruling lineages from major centers of supernatural power, but their formation is probably closely connected with the shifting political relationships among the populations that lived along the trade routes from the forest zone of Africa to the Mediterranean littoral (see chapter 2). Political consolidation through warfare and involvement in long-distance trade underwrote the development of warring and trading elites, which could draw together a number of local lineages around a royal center. The resulting political "pyramids" rested

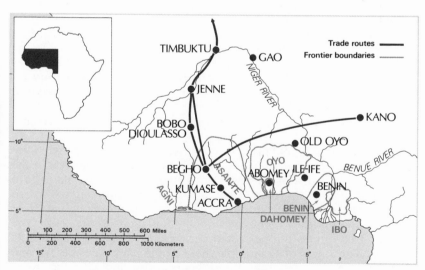

State formation and trade routes in West Africa.

upon a relatively autonomous agricultural base, but a ruling stratum aggregated military and economic resources, concentrating them at a royal court. The localized kin-organized lineages retained a large measure of control over land and labor, while yielding to the royal center in matters of war and trade. This distribution of power also allowed the interests of the "elders," who operated the local economy of land and bridewealth, to fuse with the wider-ranging concerns of the ritual and trading elite of the royal lineage. (This convergence is perhaps reflected in the regnant ideology, according to which authority is not so much delegated as participated in and shared.) The development of key monopolies, the intensification of warfare, and the expansion of long-distance trade could enlarge the sociopolitical pyramid; foreign encroachment or secession could reduce it again. Alternatively, such pyramidal systems were subject to conquest or to infiltration from the outside.

Contact with the Europeans, bringing in metal, hardware, firearms and powder, textiles, rum, and tobacco, affected such pyramidal systems at two points: first, in the circulation of prestige goods governing marital alliances and the allocation of offspring; second, at the point of elite consumption—the apex of relationships involving long-distance trade. One might say, therefore, that European expansion dovetailed with pre-existing African circuits of exchange, not altering their basic structure but merely adding to the flow of goods through them. There is, however, another aspect to this encounter, and it soon affected not only circulation as such but also the allocation of labor power. As long as the Europeans wanted only pepper or gold or alum, the issue of slavery remained secondary; but soon the demand for people in return for imports affected the very nature of productive relations.

Inevitably, the burgeoning slave trade had political repercussions in the areas of supply, especially since only in the rarest of instances did the Europeans engage in hunting slaves themselves. They relied instead, as the French factor Jean Barbot wrote in the late seventeenth century, on African "kings, rich men, and prime merchants" (quoted in Davidson 1966: 213). African collaboration, in turn, strengthened existing states and spurred state formation in areas where no states had existed before European impact.

Two areas that would play an important part in the slave trade were already under the command of African states upon the arrival of the Europeans. The first of these was the Kingdom of Kongo, said to have been founded in the second part of the fourteenth century, when several ranked kinship groups originating from north of the River Congo superimposed themselves upon populations to the south. The second area of pre-European state formation was Benin, in southern Nigeria. The rulers of Benin, like those of the later states of Oyo and Dahomey in this area, traced their genealogical origins to the sacred Yoruba city of Ile-Ife, which may have had ties to the area of the Niger farther east and north.

In two other areas, state formation postdates European contact. One of these, to the east of Kongo, had its center around Lake Kisale, in the region of the Upper Congo River. This was the heartland of Luba-Lunda expansion after the beginning of the seventeenth century, which was probably set in motion by "the economic stimulus provided by the Portuguese opening of the Atlantic coast" (Oliver and Fage 1962: 129). The second area of state formation postdating the European arrival was the Gold Coast, where a number of smaller polities gave way to the growth of the Asante power in the late seventeenth century.

Mechanisms of Enslavement

Who were the slaves, and by what means were they drawn into slavery? Before the advent of the Europeans, there existed three mechanisms that might turn a free man into a potential slave: the institution of pawnship, the judicial separation of a person from the protection of his lineage, and warfare for captives.

The first of these mechanisms, pawnship, was widespread. It was used to settle debts, placing a person in the possession of another in payment of a debt. This transferred to the receiver all rights over the person's labor, reproductive activities, and progeny for the period of the pawn. People might also pawn themselves or their relatives in case of famine, exchanging rights in persons for access to food.

The second mechanism for creating potential slaves operated through the judicial process. In brief, infractions against the kinship order and the lineage structure were seen as directed not merely against living people but also against the ancestors, and hence the supernatural. When a crime was punished by severing a person from his lineage, not only was such an individual cut off from the support of his kin but he was declared to be at odds with the supernatural order. In a sense, the kinship order protected itself by putting persons who challenged it outside its domain. Such people could be sold as slaves. Sometimes such a slave might be blamed for crimes when either the owner's lineage or his affinals wielded enough power to avoid standing accused themselves (Balandier 1970: 338–339).

A third mechanism was capture in war. In effect, like the other mechanisms, this meant the victim was severed from his native lineage and deprived of supporting kin. Thus, potential slaves in general— whether pawns, criminals, or captives—were all obtained by cutting their ties from kin and transferring the victim to the owner's kinship group.

It is important to recognize that once in the possession of his owner's lineage, a pawn or slave could become a functioning member of the domestic group, even if denied linkage with the owner's lineage. Pawnship and slavery could thus have relatively benign consequences, without any of the attributes of chattel slavery, which became characteristic of the Western Hemisphere. Nevertheless, both pawns and slaves lacked the rights of lineage members and were thus open to manipulation by their owners. Mary Douglas has pointed out how this capacity to manipulate pawns was especially significant in matrilineally organized social constellations:

> A pawn woman produces lineage segments of other clans who can be expected to reside in his [the owner's] village and remain under his control. He can offer her daughters to his young clansmen as wives and so build up his local clan section. Her sons, who will also be his pawns, he can persuade to live in his village. By offering them wives from his own clan he can counteract the tendency for men to join their mother's brothers. Pawn owners can also make elaborate alliances between their pawns of different clans. [1964: 303]

Under conditions of polygyny, moreover, pawnship could put additional power into the hands of lineage elders, who controlled the allocation of women and bridewealth (see Douglas 1964: 310).

All of these mechanisms worked differently at the level of the cultivating domestic group and at the level of elite management. Pawns, criminals, and captives acquired by chiefs and by the paramount ruler did not become members of domestic groups, but instead were put to work in the chief's gardens, in the royal gold mines, or in the transport of goods in long-distance trade. Merchants also used slaves to raise food for the caravan stops along trade routes and to act as bearers. For the military, judicial, and commercial elites, therefore, slave labor furnished a considerable proportion of the surpluses on which they relied for their support, as well as the goods and services commensurate with elite status. Hence, warfare and judicial control together were used to enlarge the class whose labor underwrote elite privileges (Terray: 1975).

All three mechanisms were employed to furnish slaves for the trade. In this way, pre-existing institutions were placed in the service of European mercantile expansion. African societies became specialized in the delivery of slaves, and in the backward and forward linkages that the trade carried with it. To examine the ramifications of the trade and its impact on local populations, we shall focus on the two areas that furnished the bulk of slaves exported to the Western Hemisphere: West Africa (particularly the Gold Coast, the Slave Coast, and the Niger Delta) and central Africa, the source of the "Angolas" and the "Congos" of the slave registers.

Areas of Supply: West Africa

The Gold Coast

The advent of the slave trade immediately unleashed a series of political upheavals on the Gold Coast. During the second half of the sixteenth century, a number of small states emerged along the tropical forest belt, taking advantage of the new commercial opportunities. Some of these formed around "big men," men powerful enough, in fact, to switch their support from one group of European traders to another as their own interests demanded. Examples of such big men were the Akrosan brothers, who wielded power at Fetu in the mid-seventeenth century. After the death of the elder brother in 1656, the younger one—known to Europeans as John Claessen—became "the most powerful man on the whole of the Guinea coast" (Daaku 1970: 109). His power was reinforced by his possession of a fleet of war canoes and 2,000 soldiers armed with muskets. Maneuvering between the Dutch at Elmina and the Swedish Company, he was in a position to turn down the bribes of both. Although offered the kingship of Fetu, he turned it down, because ritual prohibitions against the king coming into contact with the sea would have kept him from his negotiations with the Europeans. Another such big man was Akomani of Akwamu, whose possession of cannon allowed him to take and hold Christiansborg Castle at will.

The most famous of these coastal entrepreneurs, however, was Johnny Kabes of Komenda. Born around 1640 or 1650, he died in 1722. Johnny Kabes became one of the main middlemen between the English and the Asante, while maintaining his independence of both. He controlled vital salt pans and maize plantations that furnished food for the slavers setting out on the Middle Passage, provided labor and raw materials for the construction of forts and trading posts, and maintained flotillas of canoes for hire. Although acknowledging the sovereignty of the ruler of Egufo, he kept his own army. A contemporary of Johnny Kabes was Johnny Konny of Pokoso in Ahanta. He also acted as an intermediary with the Asante, expecially in their trade in gold. Anti-Dutch, he favored the Brandenburg Company. The Dutch and English actually made an alliance to rid themselves of him, but they failed in the effort (see Daaku 1970; Henige 1977).

That such early entrepreneurs maintained their own military forces signals the advent of a new political factor, firearms. The impact of firearms as such should not be overestimated, since in the tropical forest environment early forms of firepower were often not fully effective. These new weapons acquired momentum only when they came into the hands of organizations that could make effective use of them. The state of Benin developed in this area before European arms were introduced; the dynasty ruling this forest state had come into existence in the early fourteenth century, before the advent of the Portuguese (Bradbury 1964: 149; Kea 1971: 185–186).

The use of firearms and the skills associated with them were not introduced into this area exclusively by Europeans. In the belt of savanna to the north of the forest, the use of guns and gunpowder followed Near Eastern models rather than European ones. While metal guns came into use first in Western Europe and in Scandinavia in the early fourteenth century, by the end of that century cannon had spread to the Balkans and reached the Ottoman Turks. Hand guns became widespread in the early fifteenth century, and by the middle of the fifteenth century cannon and arquebus had wrought a revolution in Ottoman warfare. In 1590 Moroccan troups—consisting of arquebus-carrying Spanish Muslims and Portuguese and Spanish prisoners of war—destroyed Songhay; and by the end of the sixteenth century, the ruler of Bornu was training a corps of musketeers with Turkish instructors imported from Tripoli (Goody 1971: 52; Davidson 1966: 139). Guns were therefore already known on the northern fringes of the forest zone at the time of European contact.

It is clear, however, that the large-scale possession of firearms by people in the forest greatly altered the balance of political power and speeded up the formation of new polities. The Portuguese, to protect their forts, distributed firearms to "friendly natives" around Elmina, and in 1610 the English began selling firearms. By 1660 there was a thriving trade in guns with "Akany" (Akan) traders. The quantity of firearms in the area increased sharply after the middle of the seventeenth century, when the English East India Company began to sell arms freely. Between 1658 and 1661, the East India Company sold 5,531 muskets and powder on the Gold Coast. In 1700 the Dutch trader William Bosman wrote from Elmina:

> The main military weapons are muskets or carbines, in the use of which these African are wonderfully skillful. . . . we sell them very great quantities, and in doing so we offer them a knife with which to cut our own throats. But we are forced to do this. For if we did not do it, they would easily get enough muskets from the English, or from the Danes, or from the Prussians. And even if we governors could all agree to stop selling firearms, the private traders of the English or the Dutch would still go on selling them. [quoted in Davidson 1966: 217]

By 1730 the annual imports of guns into West Africa had reached the figure of 180,000; between 1750 and 1807 gun imports oscillated between 283,000 and 394,000 per annum (Inikori 1977; Richards 1980). In meeting the heavy demand for arms, the flintlock proved crucial. It enhanced the military capability of its owners and furnished the means of violence for political organizations capable of utilizing it.

The new opportunities for trade and warfare prompted the emergence of small states, all of them based—as Kea has said (1971: 201)— "on the firearm." One of the earliest of these states was Denkyira on the Oda River. Drawing strength from the Dutch at Elmina, who furnished them with firearms, Denkyira was able to shake off its former overlord, Adanse, and become an independent state. Farther east, the Akwamu federation along the Birim River broke through to the coast in 1677, subduing the Ga towns—especially Great Accra—and establishing direct contact with the English, Dutch, and Danes. Aided by the Europeans, Akwamu expanded farther until it included the Fante polity of Agona in the west and all of the eastern Gold Coast up to Whydah (1702). In 1729–1730, however, Akwamu was destroyed by its northern neighbor, Akyem, which controlled rich gold mines and organized the short-lived state of Akyem Abuakwa.

The maneuvers of all these groups were cut short by the rapid expansion of Asante. The Asante, who dominated the Gold Coast in the eighteenth and nineteenth centuries, emerged as a distinct political entity only toward the end of the seventeenth century. In the earlier decades of that century, some Twi-speaking matrilineages began to move out of the Adanse region. By mid-century, some of these—notably the Ekuono and Oyoko *mmusua*—came into political prominence, probably in connection with the acquisition of guns through the coastal trade in firearms (Wilks 1975: 110). In the 1660s and 1670s these lineages engaged in a struggle for control of the Kwaman area around the old gold mart of Tafo. At first they were subject to the state of Denkyira, which exacted gold and slaves from them to pay for guns and other goods at Elmina. They rose against Denkyira in 1699, however, destroyed its power in 1701, and then took its place in exchanges with the Europeans.

The power of the royal stool, which became the symbol of Asante

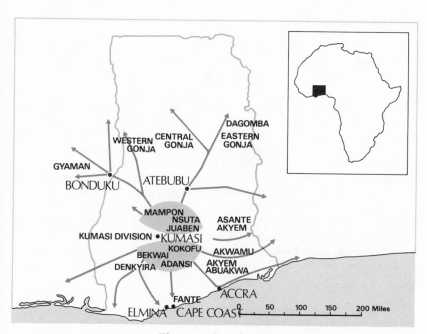

The expansion of Asante.

kingship, seems to have been based squarely on the ability of the Asantehene (the Asante ruler) to acquire guns from the Europeans and to control trade—that is, on a centralization of military and commercial functions. The golden stool of the Asante also symbolized judicial sovereignty, as well as the common tie of all the Asante with the supernatural. At the same time, matrilineages under their chiefs remained quite autonomous, even in military organization; and the Asante state was more a compound of lineages than a centralized polity.

The district of Kumasi was the locus of the Asantehene, seated on his golden stool; it was also a region of dense settlement, containing a sizable town (12,000–15,000 in 1817) and large numbers of cultivators who raised food for the chiefs and their families. It constituted the most powerful military unit within the Asante army. It furnished 60,000 soldiers in 1817; the next largest district, Dwaben, furnished 35,000, while three other districts provided 15,000 men each. As long as the slave trade prospered, however, all the territorial clusters within the state had a common interest in the expansion of Asante overlordship, for it furnished access to new trade routes and to slaves.

Equipped with muskets furnished initially by the Dutch, the Asante expanded in all directions. They overran Western Gonja (1722–1723), Eastern Gonja (1732–1733), Accra (1742), Akyem Abuakwa (1744), and Mamprussi (1744–1745). At the beginning of the nineteenth century, they broke the alliance between the coastal Fante and the English. The dates of the military successes of the first half of the eighteenth century are mirrored in the large number of slaves exported from the Gold Coast at that time. With each victory, the Asante acquired slaves in the form of war captives and tribute. In 1751 the king of Kpembe acknowledged Asante overlordship and promised to pay an annual tribute of 1,000 slaves. When in 1772 the Asante seized the ruler of Dagomba, his sons ransomed him with 1,000 slaves (Wilks 1975: 22). It would seem that as long as the slave trade prospered, the military orientation of the Asante state received strong reinforcement. Merchants remained under state control, and an independent class of traders was not allowed to develop.

The decline of the slave trade in the nineteenth century weakened the influence of the military, producing in turn a new political coalition. It linked the commercial entrepreneurs (asikafo) with the lower class (ahiafo), which was composed of slaves (mostly of northern origin), Asante pawned in payment of debt, and officials stripped of their position. This coalition took form specifically around the issue of military conscription (Wilks 1975: 701–720).

Oyo and Dahomey

The Asante polity had expanded from a core in the forest country to embrace provinces both on the southern coast and in the inland savanna. Another polity, the Yoruba kingdom of Oyo, expanded from a core of open parkland both northward, to draw tribute from Nupe on the Niger River, and southward, to make contact with the Europeans in the new ports. Between the western forest country of the Asante and the eastern forests extending to the Niger River, a broad band of open savanna reaches down to the coast. Here the Oyo state was able to deploy cavalry in ways not possible in the forest zone. Buying horses from the Hausa to the north of them, the rulers of Oyo began around 1550 to expand militarily and politically, coming to dominate the savanna corridor.

The Oyo rulers, or *alafins*, were members of a Yoruba-speaking dynasty, which traced its genealogy back to Odua, believed to be the creator of the earth and the first king of the holy city of Ile-Ife. Even today, this belief serves as a mythical charter for the kingship among most Yoruba subgroups, and the order of precedence among the kings is argued in terms of genealogical connections with the sixteen sons of Odua (see Bascom 1969: 9–12). While the alafins were endowed with divine descent, in practice they faced the power of the Oyo nobles, all of whom controlled cavalry. They sought to check the nobles through the recruitment of court officials from former slaves. Reliance on the horse proved a source at once of strength and of weakness for Oyo. Local horse breeding was hampered by the prevalence of the tsetse fly, and horses had to be imported continuously from the north, along with grooms to take care of them. To pay for the horses, the alafins had to ensure the flow of goods northward. With the advent of the Europeans, the items most desired were trade goods brought by the sea merchants, who in turn had to be compensated in the form of slaves. The Oyo kingdom, therefore, became a major purveyor of slaves. Diminution of the slave trade in the nineteenth century eventually upset this pattern of exchange, bringing on endemic conflicts between nobles and king.

Oyo, however, did not cover its requirements of slaves solely from its own resources; it also received slaves and trade goods as tribute from other states. One such state was Dahomey, organized by the Alladaxonu clan among the Fon in the second half of the seventeenth century. The Alladaxonu, like the alafins of Oyo, claimed descent from Odua. Like other branches of the descendants of Odua, they had assumed control over local populations, establishing themselves on the Abomey plateau (whence the name Dahomey) within the savanna gap.

The Dahomey polity, ruled over by the Onidada, or king of the Fon, is often represented as if it were a wholly autonomous state, carrying on slave raiding and trading on its own account. It was, in fact, a tributary of Oyo, following its defeat by Oyo in 1712. Oyo reinforced this claim by sending its cavalry against Abomey at least five times between 1724 and 1730. The annual tribute, the *agban*, was paid almost continually for a century. Among the items tributed were some 1,700 guns per year. The attacks of Oyo upon Abomey were directed not only at obtaining tribute but also at interdicting Fon control of the coast. In 1725 the Fon had attacked Ardrah, then a kingdom under Oyo hegemony controlling a number of coastal ports. The Fon seized some of these ports themselves, such as Whydah (1727), Savi (1728), and Jakin (1732); but they soon relinquished control of Ardrah and Jakin (or Porto Novo) to Oyo. After trying to interest the English in taking over Whydah on an exclusive and permanent basis (see Polanyi 1966: 29–30), the Fon acceded to an agreement made between the ruler of Savi and the Europeans in 1704 to open the port to all comers thereafter. By seizing Whydah the Fon were able to systematize the slave trade. Until 1772, however, they faced numerous local rebellions, aided either by Oyo or by various foreign agents and companies. Thus Whydah, far from being an asset to Dahomey, became "an open wound to the body politic" (Polanyi 1966: 33).

Despite its external difficulties, which continued until Oyo disintegrated around the beginning of the nineteenth century, the Dahomey state was highly centralized and cohesive internally. The basic units of the state were landholding patrilineages, headed by elders. A number of such patrilineages formed a village, which maintained its own organization for communal labor, the *dokpwe*. The village headmanship was subject to certification by the king. The new state, however, was more than an organization in which a royal patrilineage ruled over other patrilineages. It possessed a standing army equipped with muskets, including a royal bodyguard of 2,500 women soldiers. In addition, there was general conscription in case of war. The state also had an efficient tax system, collecting a basic tax on agricultural produce assessed against each village; taxes on livestock, salt, and artisan products; and tolls on goods taken to market. Censuses of people and production were kept and checked by ingenious methods. The kingship exercised strong judicial control. If a chief committed a crime, his compound was destroyed, his property confiscated, the female members of his household sold as slaves, and his male descendants impressed into the army. Secret associations, which were common in the West African forest belt, were outlawed in Dahomey to inhibit countervailing sources of power. Instead, there was a state cult run by priests who controlled initiation. To further inhibit challenges to the state, members of the royal patrilineages were not allowed to hold public office, and only sons born to the king by commoner women could accede to the kingship. State officials were usually commoners, drawn into state service with the offer of gifts and with permission to wed females of the royal clan. They were kept from consolidating any power because they served at the behest of the king, their positions were not heritable, and their work was closely supervised by a female of the royal clan, called "mother" of the official in her charge.

External trade was also strongly controlled by the state. Whenever a ship arrived at Whydah, it would be greeted by the king's representatives, and local porters would be assigned to carry trade goods to the depot in town. The Europeans would reside in town while conducting their business, and they would be given servants and attendants. Trade was under the direction of a royal official. Prices for goods and slaves were set by the king. The Europeans were not allowed to leave Whydah, except with permission of the king. At the same time, slave traders from the north were not allowed to visit Whydah and deal directly with the Europeans, but had to sell their captives to Dahomean factors. No guns or ammunition were allowed to pass beyond Dahomey to the states to the north.

Possession of slaves was permitted only through a public grant of slaves from the king; no one was allowed to own or trade in slaves independently. However, certain officials could hunt for slaves with armies of their own, and they were allowed to keep the slaves taken by their soldiers upon payment of a tax to the state. When a town was taken in war, the victorious officer was entitled to monopolize the town's trade, subject to taxes. He was required, however, to work through licensed trading officials who were independent of the military.

Benin

Probably the only state in coastal West Africa that preceded European control was Benin, in eastern Guinea. Like the *alafin* of Oyo and the *onidada* of Abomey, the rulers, or *obas*, of Benin also traced their descent back to Odua of Ile-Ife, the holy city of the Yoruba. This dynasty established control over the Edo-speakers of the Benin area in about 1400, perhaps in connection with trade on the Niger River. In contrast to Oyo, where the alafin had to contend with a hereditary nobility, the Benin state was marked by a plethora of associations that allowed commoners to advance in status. These associations, which resemble those found in the Niger River region to the east, were organized bodies of titleholders and traders (Bradbury 1964). While Benin prospered, these associations probably amplified the basis of support for the kingship among the native population.

Selling first pepper and then slaves to the Portuguese, Benin was the first power on the Slave Coast to obtain firearms. The rulers of Benin employed muskets to expand as far as Bonny in the east and Eko (Lagos) in the west. During the seventeenth century Benin became a major source of slaves. By the end of the century, however, intensified competition from other Yoruba towns raised the cost of slaves shipped out of Benin, and caused the Europeans to seek cheaper slaves in Whydah and Calabar. As Benin's economic decline continued, internal conflict increased. The oba continued to serve as the sacred center of Benin, but around him swirled conflicts among hereditary noblemen, men holding titles in the different association of palace retainers, ritual representatives of the commoners, and members of the trading associations that controlled routes between the Slave Coast and the inland markets. Such divergent interests led to internal revolt, until by the end of the eighteenth century Benin had lost much of its power.

The Niger Delta

The states of the Gold Coast and the Slave Coast—Asante, Oyo, Dahomey, Benin—had their bases inland, from which they reached out to the coast to take control of the vital points of embarkation and import. In the region west of Benin, comprising the delta of the Niger River, centers of the slave trade developed instead along the coast and waterways. Great ports like Bonny, New Calabar, and Old Calabar arose, serving as points of entry for European goods and influence and as embarkation points for slaves from the hinterland. In contrast to the Gold and Slave coasts, where the commerce in slaves was carried on by tributary states, in the Niger Delta the trade took root in a social context dominated by kinship corporations.

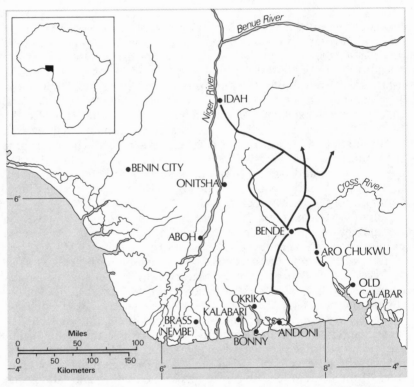

The Niger Delta. (Aro trade routes after Ottenberg, 1958; courtesy of the author)

Benin had already pioneered in the Niger Delta, sending out colonists led by relatives or retainers of the oba. These colonist had formed small satellite kingdoms with variable ties to Benin. One such kingdom was Aboh, located strategically at the point where the Niger forms three branches on its way to the sea. Another satellite of Benin was Idah, to the north, in the kingdom of the Igala. From Idah, the Igala ruler, or ata, sent out titled chiefs to colonize still farther inland, tapping this tributary region for slaves, ivory, and other products, which they traded downriver to Aboh in exchange for salt and European manufacturers.

The mangrove swamplands of the delta below Aboh were inhabited by Ijaw-speaking people, organized in autonomous villages made up of extended-family "houses" (*wari*). The Ijaw fished and collected salt, exchanging their products for the crops, poultry, and livestock of the satellite kingdoms to the north. Ijaw-produced salt and fish was then traded farther along the Niger for yams, palm products, livestock, camwood, ivory, and potash.

When the Europeans contacted the coast, the Ijaw were in a strategic position to exploit the routes that led from the new ports, over the creeks and branches of the delta, to the cities upriver. In the early sixteenth century, the northern kingdoms began to trade with the Ijaw villages giving them—in return for salt—slaves, produce, and livestock, which the Ijaw in turn sold to the Europeans for copper bracelets. By the end of the seventeenth century, the Ijaw communities of Kalabari, Andoni, Bonny, Okrika, and Brass (Nembe) had become important centers in the exchange of slaves for European manufactured goods. In the eighteenth century, as firearms became generally available, Ijaw war leaders armed their fifty-man canoes with cannon and competed for control of the growing trade. In the course of trading and fighting, the Ijaw extended-family houses turned into "canoe houses"—corporations made up of kinsmen and assimilated slaves, which engaged in extensive commerce and warfare geared to obtaining slaves.

By the eighteenth century, canoe houses armed with large numbers of cannon-equipped canoes had developed in Aboh as well. Aboh, in fact, became the major source of such canoes for the delta as a whole. Most of the slaves acquired by Aboh came, in turn, from the Igala of Idah to the north, who drew slaves and ivory from the region where the Niger and Benue rivers converge, and traded them southward in exchange for salt and European goods. These slave-trading activities polarized the populations of the area into *olu* and *igbo*—slave-hunting riverine populations headed by kings (olu), and upland people who were raided for slaves (igbo). The term *igbo* thus was originally applied to the victims of the trade; only gradually did it become the name of an ethnic category, the present-day Ibo (see Henderson 1972: 40−41). As a result of these struggles, Brass, Kalabari, and Bonny emerged as the major centers of the eastern Delta.

Another such center of the slave trade grew up in Old Calabar on the

A party of Englishmen being escorted to Aboh. Sketch by William Allen, who surveyed the Niger for the British Admiralty, 1832–33, from his Picturesque Views of the River Niger, *1840. (Courtesy of the General Research Division, The New York Public Library. Astor, Lenox, and Tilden Foundations)*

Cross River, among the coastal Ibibio-speaking peoples. Here, too, populations lived primarily by fishing, salt making, and trading their products northward to Ibo areas in exchange for yams. In the late sixteenth century, a group of Ibibio-speaking fishermen and traders moved from their home village to what came to be known as Creek Town (Etunko). At the beginning of the seventeenth century, a segment of the Creek town dwellers hived off, forming Old Town (Obutong); then, in the 1620s or 1630s, a lineage section breaking off from Old Town established Duke Town (Atakpa). These several towns constituted Old Calabar. The trade in slaves began here in the middle of the seventeenth century; an estimated 250,000 slaves were exported between 1650 and 1841, when the external slave trade ended (Latham 1973: 22–23). The European goods received in return were at first iron, copper, hardware, and cloth; firearms were added in 1713.

Soon slaving became big business in Old Calabar. As among the Ijaw-speakers, where slaving had transformed the extended-family houses into "canoe houses," so also among the Ibibio-speaking Efik did the slave trade undermine the patrilineages and the councils formed of lineage chiefs. Taking the place of the patrilineages were seven wards, each made up of various extended families and lineage segments grouped around an important trader and his slave following. Some of these wards prospered and grew at the expense of others. "It was those wards," says A.J.H. Latham,

> most successful in trade which expanded fastest because they accumulated most retainers. Certain wards grew more quickly than others, for the Europeans traded and gave credit to those who paid their debts promptly and honestly. In the course of time, bad debtors lost their access to credit, and only the credit-worthy were supported. The more trust they were allowed, the bigger their organizations and reserves became, and the more they were able to justify being given further credit. [1973: 51]

In contrast to the Ijaw-speakers, the Efik did not incorporate slaves into their extended families and lineages. They maintained and intensified their solidarity as an upper stratum, in part through the cult of a common tutelary deity, *Ndem Efik*. They did, however, open the road to entrepreneurs of non-Efik ancestry by allowing them to participate in the secret Ekpe sodality, named after a forest spirit. Ekpe (known to the Europeans as Egbo), which came to the fore early in the eighteenth century, was open to all males, free and slave. Membership was by purchase. The sodality was graded, the top four grades theoretically attainable only by freemen, although a man born as a slave is known to have become a vice-president. Each grade had a master (*obong*); at the head of Ekpe stood a president (*eyamba*) and a vice-president (*ebunko*). Masterships, the presidency, and the vice-presidency usually went to members of the dominant wards. The members of the top grade made up the decision-making council; the second grade carried out the decisions.

This sodality had various functions. On one level, it was a social club where the men of important wards could meet to talk or feast together. On another level, it exercised legal authority; it made and enforced the law. It could fine people, arrest them or order house arrests, and execute offenders. It could declare boycotts. It could confiscate or destroy a man's property, or place a taboo on its use. Most importantly, the sodality had an economic function. It had the power to enforce the repayment of debts. It was "this power to insist on the repayment of credit which lay behind the spread of the Ekpe societies among the other peoples further inland up the Cross River, for by adopting Ekpe they made themselves credit-worthy in the eyes of the Efik, and therefore could avail themselves of Efik credit" (Latham 1973: 39). As a result, several European traders joined Ekpe.

While the Efik took charge of the slave trade at the point of embarkation, most of the slaves in their markets were supplied by an inland group known as the Aro. The Aro consisted of people of diverse origins, who were brought together by Okoyong mercenaries from Akankpa near Creek Town. The pattern of hiring mercenaries for trade or war was common, but the Aro represent a special development of this pattern. They first established themselves near the Cross River, just to the east of the major slave market at Bende. Their settlements consisted of nine primary villages, each housing an original patrilineage, and ten secondary villages, made up of segments of these lineages. The head of the central patrilineage in the village of Otusi was also head of the Aro chiefly lineage. The nine patrilineage heads, together with representatives of the secondary villages, made up the Aro council. Following a pattern widespread among Ibo populations, they set up at Aro Chukwu an oracle and pilgrimage center (later to be known among the British as Big Juju).

From their center at Aro Chukwu, the Aro sent out colonies among other peoples, which ranged from small posts along Aro trade routes to major settlements dominating a market or village cluster. These colonies often housed a local oracle to which people could bring trouble cases— disputes over land and inheritance, feuds, theft, witchcraft, sorcery, and murder. Those disputes that could not be resolved locally were referred to the major oracle at Aro Chukwu for resolution. Any individual Aro was empowered to refer people to an Aro oracle. In doing so, he would also collect information for the oracle keepers, to be used in making judgments. People found guilty by the oracles could be fined, killed, or sold into slavery.

The Aro also advanced credit to non-Aro individuals, gaining their gratitude or, in case of inability to pay, forcing them to sell themselves or a member of their family into slavery. The Aro also acquired slaves by buying them in local slave markets or by hiring mercenaries to catch them. Backing up Aro judicial, supernatural, and economic functions was their control of firearms, obtained in quantity through their connections in Calabar.

The Aro did not establish a true state. They never developed a centralized hierarchy of command, nor were they interested in political domination as such. Nevertheless, they came to carry out some of the functions associated with states, as a kind of economic mafia with an aura of religious legitimacy. In these characteristics they bear closer resemblance to the Iroquois confederacy, and to the Varangian Rus who came down the Volga with slaves and amber in the ninth century, than to the centralized West African states of Asante, Dahomey, or Benin.

Areas of Supply: Central Africa

The Kingdom of Kongo

When the Portuguese sailed up the Congo River in 1483, they came face to face with one of the largest African polities, the kingdom of the Bakongo, whose capital was at Mbanzakongo (the later San Salvador).

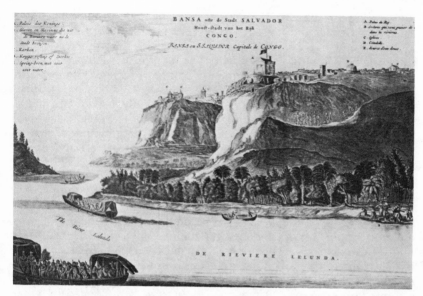

Mbanza or Salvador, chief city of the Kingdom of Congo. Copper engraving published by Olfert Dapper, 1676. (Courtesy of the General Research Division, The New York Public Library. Astor, Lenox, and Tilden Foundations)

This Kongo kingdom had grown to be among the most important of a number of states along the upper Congo River and its two tributaries, the Kasai and the Sankuru. All of these states appear to trace their origin to a founding kingdom north of the area of Stanley Pool. Farther east, above the impenetrable Stanley Falls, lay a second area of state formation, on the upper reaches of the Congo River and its tributaries. Its center was located around Lake Kisale. This was the point of origin of the Luba and Songye elites that became increasingly active in state building, as the influence of the slave trade penetrated inland to the shores of the Lualaba River (see Vansina, Mauny, and Thomas 1964: 96–97).

The Kongo kingdom was large, covering an area of about 60,000 square miles extending from the Congo River southward to the River Dande and from the Atlantic coast eastward to the Kwango River. This area was inhabited by an estimated 2.5 million people at the time of European contact. The social organization of the kingdom was based on matrilineal descent, coupled with avunculocal residence. The basic social units were matrilineages; these were ranked, with the royal matrilineage at the apex. Each matrilineage gave its women in marriage to the next higher-ranking one, receiving in return bridal compensation and gifts. It also received from the wife-taking matrilineage any sons born to these marriages. The sons would take up residence with the wife-giving matrilineage in the compounds of their mothers' brothers. The royal lineage did not exchange women but retained them. Their women could marry commoners and slaves; both the women and their offspring stayed within the royal lineage. A corollary of this system was that the royal lineage was also the initiator of the chain of bridewealth and gifts moving to lower-ranking matrilineages (Ekholm 1977). Since the royal matrilineage did not receive gifts but only made them, one of the basic prerequisites of the entire set of marriage exchanges was royal access to resources not available to any other groupings.

In pre-European times, these resources were copper, salt, and *nzimbu* shells from the royal fishery of Luanda Island, which Pigafetta called "the money mine used by the king of the Congo and the people of the surrounding regions" (quoted in Balandier 1968: 130). Units of this shell money were standardized: one *kofo* (20,000 big shells) represented twice the value of one *lufuku* (10,000 big shells), and one lufuku was equal to ten *funda* (1,000 big shells). Nzimbu shells formed the main part of pre-European tribute payments and constituted the coin of the realm, the chief instrument of public finance. For private transactions, the use of standardized sizes of cloth was common; toward the end of the seventeenth century 100 napkin-sized *mpusu* corresponded to 4,000 Portuguese *reis* or one slave (Balandier 1968: 129–132). It thus seems clear that the royal power would have welcomed the advent of new resources from abroad so as to extend its fund of power at home.

The Portuguese were therefore eagerly received by the *mani kongo*, the ruler of Kongo. Yet they demanded slaves and ivory in exchange for their goods. Hence, any increment in exchanges with the Portuguese also increased slaving and intensified pre-existing forms of slavery. For a time, indeed, the Kongo kingdom was an ally of the Portuguese. The Portuguese sent missionaries to instruct the Bakongo court in Christianity and to baptize its members. King Nzinga Nvemba (1506–1543) converted and became Dom Afonso I, abandoning in the process the sanctions of divine kingship as understood by Bakongo. The Portuguese offered what we would today call technical assistance, perhaps because their supply of manufactured goods was quite limited. Skilled laborers, artisans, and even instructors in domestic economy were sent from Lisbon to Mbanzakongo to teach their skills to the Bakongo. Some young Bakongo were also sent to Portugal for study abroad.

Yet the expanding slave trade increasingly subverted these efforts. By 1530 the annual export of slaves from the Kongo was estimated at between 4,000 and 5,000 *peças de Indias*. One *peça* (or piece) was equal to a young able-bodied male, with females and slaves of other ages counted at less than a peça. At first the slaves were obtained from regions beyond the Bakongo kingdom, by barter from the Teke and Mpumbu to the northeast, or by warfare or trade with the Mbundu to the south. As time passed, however, the Portuguese increasingly sought slaves from Kongo itself. Portuguese artisans, merchants, priests, ship's officers and sailors, and royal officials entered the slave trade on their own behalf. This wholesale participation by the Portuguese also meant that European trade goods and guns no longer flowed only through the hands of the royal lineage but became available to local chiefs or strongmen who could deliver slaves. Thus, the sociopolitical organization of the Kongo kingdom collapsed, along with its hierarchical arrangement of matrilineages and its flow of women and prestations. With this collapse went the power of kingship itself. Furthermore, as local chiefs began to raid for slaves themselves, matrilineal reckoning gave way to patrilineal clusters, because chiefs needing manpower to field a slave-hunting force began to claim the children they produced with their own slave women.

To enlarge their area of capture, the Portuguese extended their trade to the Mbundu kingdom of the Ndongo, south of the River Dande, setting up Kongo chiefs as overlords over Mbundu chieftains and exacting slaves from them. This trade was initiated by private entrepreneurs from São Tomé, who shipped out slaves from the mouth of the Kwanza River despite attempts by the Crown to channel all slave traffic through the Kongolese port of Mpinda. After the mid-sixteenth century, however, the Crown took an increasing interest in intensifying its control over the state of Ndongo and in containing, on the eastern fringes of the area, raiders who had been taking advantage of the weakness of the Kongo state to engage in slave hunting on their own account. Toward the end of the sixteenth century, Portuguese royal troops advanced systematically into Angola, taking slaves as captives, imposing tribute in the form of slaves on Mbundu chiefs, and sending out Euro-African traders, or *pombeiros*, to buy slaves in the *pombos*, fairs of the hinterland. The term *pombo* stems from the name of one of the most important of these fairs, held among the Hum at Stanley Pool. Gradually this term was extended to African captains of slave-buying expeditions. Slaves were bought and sold for Portuguese wine and brandy, Brazilian rum and tobacco, European and Indian cloth, and fine African palm cloth, which was obtained from the forest dwellers along the northern border of Kongo in exchange for salt and sea shells from the coast. As a result of this expansion of the slave trade, 13,000 to 16,000 slaves were shipped out of Angola by mid-seventeenth century. The decline of the kingdom of the Kongo itself was demonstrated by Portuguese seizure of the *nzimbu* fisheries in the mid-seventeenth century. The act, in effect, transferred the royal treasury of the Kongo to the authority of King João of Portugal.

Whereas the slave trade, coupled with trade in commodities, had first attracted populations to the coast, now the ravages of the trade caused people to move eastward away from the coast. This withdrawal was in part an attempt to escape the slave hunters. In part it was prompted by

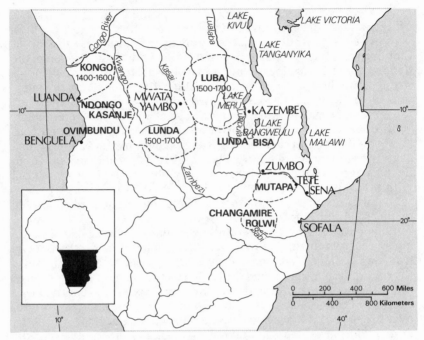

State formation in Central Africa.

the desire of slave-hunting chieftains to improve their own terms of exchange with the Portuguese by monopolizing the trade farther inland.

Imbangala

The decline of Kongo hegemony and the expansion of the trade inland unleashed a chain of events in areas far removed from direct Portuguese influence. One locus of these new developments was in the savanna between the Upper Lualaba and the Kasai rivers, where major political shifts occurred after 1500. The changes may have owed little to external influence at the outset; yet they soon became enmeshed with processes originating in the slave trade.

These changes were first felt within the area of Portuguese influence when slave hunters appeared on the eastern confines of Kongo and Ndongo. Taking advantage of the increasing disorder in Kongo, which set subchiefs and chiefs against one another in contests for the kingship, armed bands from farther inland overran tributary groups of the larger kingdoms and established slave-trading polities of their own. For two centuries the rulers of these polities played an important role as slave raiders and traders for the Portuguese, while at the same time impeding further European advances inland. They generally go by the name of Imbangola or Imbangala, although some Imbangala segments have gone down in history as the Jaga—people depicted in fictitious Portuguese tales as cannibals who killed their own children when they proved a hindrance (Miller 1973). The appearance of the Imbangala on the eastern borders of Kongo and Ndongo may have resulted, in part, from the expansion of the Luba and Lunda farther to the east; it no doubt also resulted from the potential for slave trading. A string of states was set up by the Imbangala in the regions of Kwango, Ambaka, Kasanje, and the Benguela highlands; Kasanje soon became the most important slave market for the coast (Vansina 1968: 145, 202). Farther to the north, the Yaka kingdom of Kwango terrorized the people of the middle Kwango-Kasai river basin. The major Yaka trading center was Matamba, whose trade was in the hands of local Ambaka, other Africans, and Portuguese. The kingdoms that the Imbangala set up among the Ovimbundu in the Benguela highlands also began to raid inland, selling captives to traders from Ndongo. In the eighteenth century, all these kingdoms were major participants in the slave trade (Vansina 1968: 199).

Luba-Lunda

The appearance of the Imbangala along the frontiers of Kongo and Ndongo may have been the product of a wider political process, whose roots were farther to the east, around Lake Kisale. This process, a radiation of political-military aristocracies, resulted in the development of the Luba and Lunda kingdoms.

The Luba emerged initially as a set of patrilineages that imposed domination over a large number of local groups. These Luba patrilineages thus became an elite of invaders, the *balopwe*. This elite furnished the king, whose rule was conceptualized as the exercise of *bulopwe*—a supernatural power transmissible in the male line. The elite also provided the chiefs who supervised the conquered groups. Native chiefs were retained, their power conceptualized as that of the "ritual owners of the land." The Luba then expanded farther by sending out colonies under chiefs, answerable to the center, who would settle among adjacent populations. Luba sovereignty, however, remained limited, in that the balopwe elite and the "owners of the land" were kept as distinct categories. The owners of the land did not fuse with the Luba ruling elite but remained only tribute collectors, and hence often became sources of local dissidence. At the same time, the power of the kingship was checked by the power of balopwe patrilineages who had furnished wives to the royal line, and who could throw their support to competing royal heirs. This pattern appears to characterize the main Luba kingdom between the Lwembe and Lualaba rivers, as well as the smaller Luba kingdoms of Kikonja to the east and of Kalundwe and Kaniok to the west.

Some lineages of Luba balopwe settled in the valley of the Nkalaany River, becoming the core of the Lunda kingdom. In contrast to the Luba, among whom the balopwe lineages always remained apart from the native groups, the Lunda developed a political model that maintained kinship ties among the Lunda elite while permitting the incorporation of non-Lunda through kinship fictions. This model involved the twin principles of positional succession and perpetual kinship (Vansina 1968: 80−83). Positional succession meant that the incumbent to an office inherited not only the office but also the resources and social identity of his predecessor, including his name and kinship connections. Thus, genealogical descendants of two brothers, separated by great kinship distance, could be identified with the two ancestors and conceptualized as brothers. Successive incumbents to offices would assume the identity of the original ancestors present at the founding of the kingdom. At the same time, non-Lunda local chieftains could be assimilated by appointment as village headmen and given social identities within the scheme of Lunda perpetual kinship.

According to the Lunda model, villages were governed by such headmen, whose position was hereditary within the matriline, and who were backed by a council of elders. The headmen of the fifteen oldest villages held special ritual positions at court. The villages were grouped together according to the ties of perpetual kinship recognized among their headmen; groups of villages formed districts supervised from the center but ruled by chiefs nominated by the headmen. The main function of such chiefs was to collect tribute.

At the center of this hierarchy stood the king, Mwaant Yaav. Surrounding him were religious titleholders, including the headmen of the oldest villages; "father" officials, whose "sons" collected the tribute paid by the district chiefs; and the representatives of non-Lunda chiefs in the countryside, who were "children" of the king. "Traveling chiefs" went out to the non-Lunda periphery of the kingdom to gather tribute and to execute orders.

The Lunda kingdom was not a bounded entity but a sphere of power, most strongly concentrated at the center and diminishing outward from the capital. The capital, Mussamba, was supported by tribute and trade. Tribute flowed toward it in the form of salt, copper, food, and slaves. A major center of commerce, its main trade partner from the seventeenth century on was the Imbangala kingdom of Kasanje to the west, which was linked to the Mwaant Yaav by ties of kinship and ritual. Slaves and ivory moved from Mussamba to Kasanje and then to the coast, while guns and cloth traveled in the reverse direction. This was also the route by which American food crops diffused inland. Maize had arrived on the coast in the second half of the sixteenth century, and manioc was introduced around 1600 (Vansina 1968: 21). These crops may have contributed to the consolidation of Lunda power. Slaves were used at Mussamba to work in manioc gardens, which probably strengthened the productive base of the kingdom. Clearly the Lunda structure rested on slaving and on the ability of the warrior aristocracy to deliver slaves to the center (Vellut 1972: 77, 83–84).

Lunda warrior elites also carried this political model toward the south and east. Among those who moved southward toward the headwaters of the Zambezi River was a warrior chief, Kanongesha. He divided his newly won lands among relatives and members of his retinue, in return for tribute that was passed on, in part, to the Mwaant Yaav. In time, the chiefs of the new lands became increasingly autonomous and were joined by other newcomers with their retinues. Among the people brought under Lunda hegemony through this process of elite colonization were the Ndembu, known to anthropologists through the work of Victor Turner. Although the tie between the rulers of the Ndembu and the Lunda center at Mussamba grew increasingly tenuous over time, they still identified themselves to Turner in the 1950s as the "people of Mwaant Yaav" (Turner 1967: 3).

Other Lunda chiefs moved eastward into the area between the Luabala and the Luapula rivers. This time the extension of the Lunda domain was rapid, supported by the possession of guns. Again, a ritual tie with the Mwaant Yaav was maintained, as the chiefs of the new domain grew increasingly independent politically. Toward the end of the eighteenth century, one of these Lunda chiefs with the title of Kazembe became dominant, and he organized chiefships owing tribute payments to him over a wide area extending beyond Lake Mweru. He opened trade on his own account with the Portuguese at Tete, and his capital became a regular stop on the route to Lake Nyasa and on to Kilwa. Nevertheless, the Kazembe never relinquished trade relations with the Mwaant Yaav, sending slaves to Mussamba in return for fine woolens, cowrie shells, necklaces of blue pearls, *velorio* beads, looking glasses, and tea sets (Cunnison 1961: 65). Maize, manioc, and the raffia palm also traveled this route eastward (Vansina 1969: 173).

Thus, by the end of the eighteenth century a major transcontinental trade route linked the Atlantic shore with the littoral of the Indian Ocean. It operated through the Ibangala middlemen of Kasanje in the west, and through the Bisa in the east. The Bisa—whose home lay in the area between Lake Bangweulu and the Bemba plateau—had been organized by Lunda chieftains who acknowledged Kazembe hegemony. They were famed as long-distance traders. A Portuguese visitor to Kazembe's capital on the Luapula River in 1806 met a Bisa who was familiar with Angola (Cunnison 1961: 65).

Ivory and Slaving in Eastern Africa

In the late eighteenth and early nineteenth centuries, the eastern borderlands of the Kazembe domain experienced the pressures caused by a rising demand for ivory and slaves. East Africa had long furnished elephant tusks for Asian markets, but the eighteenth century saw the

Europeans introduced to Chinese and Indian tastes in art and their desire fanned for ivory carvings, inlay work, fans, billiard balls, and piano keys. At the same time, there developed a new demand for slaves. The French sought slaves for their new plantations on the Indian Ocean islands of Réunion and Mauritius; they bought them in rising numbers from the slave-hunting kingdoms of Madagascar and from slave traders in the Muslim ports of the East African coast. British interference with West African sources of supply after the abolition of the slave trade in 1807 led Brazilian and Cuban slave traders to look to East Africa for new slaves. At the same time, Omani Arabs set up clove plantations in Zanzibar, purchasing slaves for their new operations on the African coast nearby.

The dual demand for ivory and for slaves was met by a number of populations in the East African interior that had already begun to carry ivory to the coast by 1700. A major group of such traders were the Bisa, who linked Kazembe's capital on the Luapula with Kilwa on the coast; alternatively, they traded with the Yao, the main suppliers of ivory to the Portuguese. The Yao, who occupied the area east of Lake Malawi (formerly Lake Nyasa), now began to expand their trade network northward to include Kilwa and Zanzibar, as well as the Portuguese settlements along the Zambezi River. As Kazembe and the Bisa lost their former dominance over the trade, the Yao intensified their involvement in slaving, as did another group of people, the Chikunda, who began to raid westward along the Zambezi River. These Chikunda were of mixed ethnic origins, but they grew into a "new" tribe—with a distinctive language and ethnic identity—in the course of their involvement in the trade. In the area north of Lake Malawi, the slaving and trading role was assumed by the Nyamwezi, organized into distinct groups under *ntemi* (decision-making) chiefs who combined ritual and judicial functions with entrepreneurial roles in the caravan trade between the interior and the coast.

These new commercial opportunities not only spurred the entry of interior groups into the trade in ivory and slaves; they also attracted Omani Arabs from Zanzibar and Muslim Swahili traders from the coast. These newcomers organized armed caravans and set up forts and trading stations in the interior. Increasingly equipped with firearms, they set themselves up as local potentates, sometimes in alliance with African chiefs, sometimes in open conflict with them. Growing political competition, along with the ever-expanding slave trade, brought on a rising tide of armed conflict. As some polities declined, others—more attuned to military escalation—came to the fore. Among these ascendant groups was one known as the Bemba.

The Bemba

The Bemba define their identity through common recognition of a line of chiefs drawn from the crocodile clan and bearing the perpetual title of *chitimukulu*. They think of themselves as descendants of the followers of the first Luba balopwe, who founded the Lunda kingdom. (Chitimu-kula—Chiti the Great—is the praise title of this Luba—Chiti Maluba, or Chiti the Luba.) The Bemba reached the Upper Lualaba River around the middle of the eighteenth century, following the Lunda pattern of setting up chiefships among the local populations they overran. By the end of the eighteenth century, they had begun to collect tribute in ivory and to hunt elephants themselves. From 1800 to the 1830s, they grad-ually subjected the Bisa. Now strategically located between Lake Nyasa and Kilwa on Lake Meru, the Bemba were able to control the growing trade in ivory and slaves with the Swahili coast.

Around 1840 a Bemba district chief, who had grown rich in the ivory trade through control of Bisa middlemen, seized the Bemba kingship and centralized control in his hands. He organized a standing army, and at the same time made ivory trading a royal monopoly. Exchanging ivory for guns, he expanded his sway over the ivory trade and raided his neighbors for slaves. Allying himself with the incoming Arabs, this Bemba paramount was for a time able to ward off all competitors, even the Ngoni, thus establishing the Bemba reputation for military prowess, which still persists. Once again, then, we witness the rapid development of a predatory and militaristic state in connection with the external trade in slaves, ivory, and guns. When the British abolished the trade in slaves and brought elephant hunting to an end, the Bemba were forced into shifting cultivation on poor land, and into labor migration to the mines of the copper belt (see Stevenson 1968: 114).

For 500 years, from Senegambia in the west to the Swahili-speaking coast in the east, the slave trade sent millions of people coastward for transport overseas, principally to the New World. Slaving gave rise to a division of labor in which the business of capture, maintenance, and overland transport of slaves was in African hands, while Europeans took charge of transoceanic transport, the "seasoning" or breaking in of slaves, and their eventual distribution. Responding to American de-mand, the trade rested upon the active collaboration of buyers of people with their suppliers, and upon a sophisticated orchestration of activities on both sides.

This basic point needs emphasis because a history written by slavers and their beneficiaries has long obliterated the African past, portraying Africans as savages whom only the Europeans brought into the light of civilization. That history denied both the existence of a complex political economy before the advent of the Europeans and the organizational ability exhibited by Africans in pursuit of the trade once begun. More recently, another approach to African history—with the signs re-versed—has been put forward to deny the participation of African military and commercial elites in the enslavement of their fellows. Yet the task of writing a realistic account of African populations is not to justify one group as against another, but to uncover the forces that brought Europeans and Africans (and others) into connection with one another in the construction of the world. The human costs of the slave trade remain incalculable; but the economic and political causes and consequences for all participants are ascertainable.

In West Africa the trade strengthened some existing states, such as Benin, and prompted the emergence of others, such as Asante, Oyo, and Dahomey. In the Niger Delta, it underwrote the transformation of kin-ordered patrilineages into fighting and trading organizations captained by entrepreneurial figures. Along the shores of the Niger, the trade augmented the power of local tributary rulers who became engaged in slaving, while in the hinterland it led to the formation of the slave-hunting lineage federation of the Aro. In the Congo, the slave trade weakened an earlier state structure and produced throughout central Africa a proliferation of tributary military and commercial elites that fanned out eastward in trade and war.

In these commercial and military operations there were victors and losers; the losers were frequently enslaved or pushed into fringe areas, where some of them have survived to the present day. Such was the case with LoDagaa, "Grunshi," Tallensi, and Kokomba in the borderland between the Upper Volta and Ghana. The Tallensi, of anthropological fame, were formed from a fusion of original inhabitants of the country with immigrants headed by slave-taking chiefs, who were part of a hierarchy of chiefs tributing slaves to the Asante. Another shatter zone created by slaving was the Nigerian Middle Belt, a favorite slaving ground both for the Islamic emirates to the north and for slave traders from the coast who sought slaves among its kin-ordered populations. To the southeast of this belt lay *igbo* country, where common subjection to slave raiding from the coast imparted an "ethnic" commonality to the localized kin-based clusters that became the modern Ibo. Still another target zone of slave raiders was the borderland between modern Angola, Zaire, and Zambia, inhabited by the Southern Lunda, of whom the Ndembu have become best known in the anthropological literature. Here epigonal chiefs of a Lunda elite gained new economic and political life in the second half of the nineteenth century by becoming slave-raiding agents for Ovimbundu slave traders.

While Africa had long formed an integral part of the political and economic system of the Old World, European expansion after 1400 drew the continent into a traffic of global scale. The demand for African slaves reshaped the political economy of the entire continent. It gave rise, in one common process, to new tributary states and specialized organizations of slave hunters, and it turned societies described by anthropologists as "acephalous, segmented, lineage-based" into the predilect target populations of slavers. These different configurations cannot, therefore, be understood as typologically separable states or "tribes" of people without history. They are, rather, the variable outcomes of a unitary historical process. Nor can one understand Europe without a grasp of the role Africa played in its development and expansion. Leading participants in that growth were not only the European merchants and beneficiaries of the slave trade but also its African organizers, agents, and victims.

8 Trade and Conquest in the Orient

The voyages of European explorers and merchants to America and Africa grew out of the search for routes to Asia, the imaginary treasure house of unlimited wealth. In 1291, the year that Marco Polo returned to Venice to tell of his travels to the Orient, the Vivaldi brothers set out from Genoa to seek a "westward" sea route to the "Indies." They were never heard from again, but attempts to reach Asia by the western ocean never ceased. Columbus thought he had embarked for Marco Polo's Cipangu (Japan). The Venetian Giovanni Caboto (John Cabot) believed that by sailing westward in high latitudes, where the world might be narrower, he could reach Cipangu from the north. Even the fur trader Jean Nicolet, upon contacting the Winnebago Indians on the western shore of Lake Michigan in 1638, donned a Chinese robe he had brought with him in expectation of meeting the Great Khan of China.

Overland routes to China were known to the Europeans from the time of Marco Polo's voyages. In the early fourteenth century the Tuscan Pegolotti wrote, in his *Practice of Commerce*, detailed instructions for making the journey from Azov to Cathay. The possibility of an eastern sea route to Asia—contrary to Ptolemy's declaration that the Indian Ocean was landlocked—was suggested by a map of the Venetian Fra Mauro in 1459, a copy of which came into the hands of the Portuguese Prince Henry the Navigator. Portuguese mariners soon turned that possibility into reality. They followed the African coastline, not only in quest of Guinea gold but also to search for Prester John, a mythical potentate ruling somewhere in the fabled Indies. In 1487 Bartholomeu Dias proved Ptolemy wrong by sailing around the Cape of Good Hope. Ten years later, Vasco da Gama rounded the Cape, picked up an experienced Arab navigator in Malindi, and reached Calicut in India. The eastward route to the Orient stood open.

When the European sea merchants began to expand trade in Asia during the sixteenth century, the landmass was in the hands of big and powerful tributary states—larger, more densely populated, and often more productive than their European counterparts. The sea-lanes around Asia, however, lay open to intruders able to marshall sufficient military and organizational resources to push aside the Turkish coastal fleet and to penetrate the waters of the Indian Ocean. The Portuguese, trading for their king and on their own behalf, were the first to accomplish this feat. The Dutch East India Company followed soon after, disputing primacy with the Portuguese in the southern seas. Next came the English. The East India Company licensed by the English Crown challenged its predecessors for control of sea-lanes and trade. For the better part of three centuries, these European powers could not engage the Asian territorial polities outright. They established "factories"— points of settlement and commerce—around the maritime periphery of the continent, thus confining themselves "in most of Asia to precarious footholds on the tidal margins" (Murphey 1977: 13). Only in the late eighteenth century did England move to take over a land-based empire, the Mughal polity, and begin to combine tax revenues with the profits of commerce.

Superior naval power and commercial organization allowed the Europeans to seize the sea-lanes, dominating ocean-borne traffic and encroaching on the extensive and lucrative carrying trade operated by

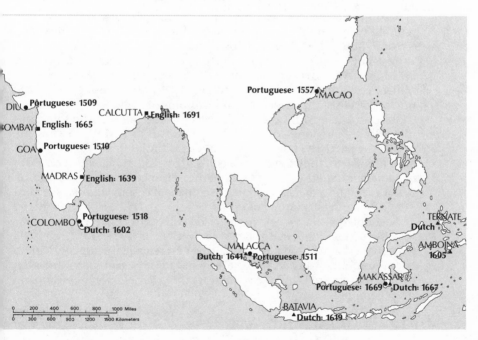

Portuguese, Dutch, and English bases in Asia, 1500–1700.

Arab, Gujarati, Malay, and Chinese merchants among the coastlines and islands of the Indian Ocean and the China Sea. Yet the Europeans were unable to dominate production and commerce as decisively as they had done in the Americas and, through the slave trade, in Africa. The different European trading groups remained long dependent on the good will of local rulers and subject to shifts in political alliances. They fought one another for control of naval stations and markets but could not establish clear hegemony over major polities. At the same time, they found themselves engaged in a struggle with rivals from another cultural realm—that of Asian Islam, created by an earlier Muslim expansion.

Islam in South Asia

In the ninth century A.D., ships from the Persian Gulf had begun to range up and down the East African coast, tapping the hinterlands of "Zenj" through trading posts established on offshore islands. The Muslim traders imported cloth, pottery, and glass, and they exported ivory, ambergris, leopard skins, turtle shells, gold, and slaves. The number of slaves obtained must have been large, judging from the scale of Zenji slave revolts in Iraq during the ninth century. Many of the luxury goods were re-exported to China, where Arab trading colonies had been set up as early as the seventh century, possibly before.

Around the end of the eleventh century, the first stable Muslim polities were established in northern India. After 1200 Bengal and Gujarat, both with important ports opening on the southern seas, were in Muslim hands. Late in the thirteenth century, the pivotal area of Southeast Asian trade along the Malay Straits became Muslim, with Malacca established as the major trade emporium and stronghold on the northern side of the straits. By the beginning of the fourteenth century, India was under Muslim control, with the exception of the southernmost Hindu kingdom of Vijanagar. With the straits in Muslim hands, the rest of the ports and harbor principalities of the islands followed suit. In adopting Islam, they took over a cultural model that preached religious egalitarianism in the face of the inherited distinctions of rank and caste; Islam carried, at the same time, the appeal of cosmopolitan trade connections. At the beginning of the sixteenth century, the rulers of inland Java adopted Islam as well, perhaps to keep control over the peasantry, to which Islam had begun to spread (Wertheim 1973: 13). Only Bali, located on the periphery of the trade routes, remained staunchly Hindu. Islam and trade thus went hand in hand in the Asian seas. When the Europeans entered these seas, therefore, they also entered the domain of hegemonic Islam.

The Portuguese in Asia

The Portuguese arrival on the Swahili coast of East Africa brought them into immediate contact with this expanding Muslim trade network in

The market and merchants' houses in Portuguese Goa. Copper engraving by Theodor de Bry, 1598. (Courtesy of the General Research Division, The New York Public Library. Astor, Lenox, and Tilden Foundations)

southern Asia. Alffonso de Albuquerque, the Portuguese admiral, quickly grasped the nature of this network and located the strategic pressure points within it. In rapid succession, the Portuguese seized the major Muslim strongholds along the Asian shores. These were Goa, on the Konkan coast of India in the kingdom of Bijapur; Hormuz, a wealthy point of transshipment between India and Persia, located on a barren island at the entrance to the Persian Gulf; and Malacca, the opulent city of 50,000 inhabitants and emporium of the spice trade with the Moluccas. Goa was taken in 1510; Hormuz in 1515; Malacca in 1519. Occupation of these key bases was followed by the construction, all along the coasts from Sofala in Southeast Africa to Ternate in the Moluccas, of *feitorias*, Portuguese forts and trading posts. Finally, settlements were planted in zones controlled by other sovereign powers, such as São Tomé de Meliapor on the Coromandel coast, Hughli in Bengal, and Macao on the China coast.

The instrument that enabled the Portuguese and other Europeans thereafter to expand into Asia was the gun-bearing sailing ship. Around A.D. 1400, European shipbuilders had begun to combine the square rig of their own traditional models with the lateen rig of the Arabs. The square rig on the foremast gave the ship an advantage when sailing close-hauled; the Arab-style lateen sail on main and mizzen masts granted it speed when running. A further achievement was to equip ships with cannon. Cannon had come into wide use in both Europe and Asia during the fourteenth century, but in the fifteenth century European gunsmiths began to out-produce Asian competitors in both the quantity and quality of their weapons. After 1500, moreover, it became common in Europe to install guns not only on the upper deck and castles but also on the main deck, by cutting gun ports in the ship's hull. The result was the galleon—half warship and half merchantman—a powerful sailing vessel equipped with guns. The prizes in naval war no longer went to the captain who rammed or boarded his opponent, but to the naval artilleryman who knew how to maneuver his ship into position and to fire broadside. Thus at Diu, in 1509, Albuquerque destroyed the joint Egyptian Mamluk and Gujarati fleet and opened the sea routes of the southern seas to Portuguese expansion.

What the Portuguese sought was mainly spices, especially pepper, "the substance of the Indies," as the Viceroy was reminded by Lisbon in 1587. The demand for pepper grew out of a European need for spices of all kinds. Spices were necessary as preservatives for meat and fish, in part because European cattle could not be kept stall-fed over the long winters, and the meat of animals slaughtered in the fall had to be salted and pickled for adequate storage. Another factor was the influence of Eastern cooking, which introduced Europeans to unfamiliar spices. Pepper became the most important spice; ginger was a close second. A great deal of the European demand for pepper was supplied by the Portuguese trade in malaguette from West Africa. Large quantities of this product were traded, but the profits it yielded could not match those for pepper from South and Southeast Asia. Indeed, pepper came to serve as money in parts of Europe. Like gold, it was durable and easily divisible, and it was often demanded in payment of taxes.

The spice trade from Asia to Europe has an ancient history, going back to classical times. At the time of Portuguese intrusion, the eastern terminals of the trade were in the hands of Chinese, who collected the cloves, nutmeg, and mace of island Southeast Asia and brought them to Malacca. From Malacca, Muslim merchants added Ceylonese cinnamon and Indian pepper, and carried the goods to the ports of the Malabar coast and Gujarat. Here they were received by the factors of Muslim merchants based in East Africa, Arabia, or Egypt and transported to the ports of the Red Sea and the Persian Gulf. From there the spices traveled overland to ports in the eastern Mediterranean. In Alexandria and along the Syrian coast, Venetian traders would then buy the produce at high prices for resale throughout Europe. The Portuguese effectively cut into this trade and for a while dominated it by offering pepper at lower prices. Yet they never achieved a complete monopoly over the trade. Instead, they chose to control shipping in the Asian seas, by making ship captains carry a Portuguese license, or *cartaz*, and pay customs at Portuguese strongholds. Consequently, "Portuguese shipping in this region was merely one more thread in the existing warp and woof of the Malay–Indonesian interport trade" (Boxer 1973a: 49). When the Portuguese attempted to expand their beachhead in China by force in 1521, they were decisively defeated by the Chinese coastguard fleet. From then on, they made use of their foothold in Macao to acquire a share of the China trade, but it was on the terms of the Chinese emperor.

Thus, there were limits to Portuguese power. The Portuguese had succeeded against politically and militarily disunited sea kings and merchant colonies because they followed a unified political strategy, opening up economic opportunities to their friends and agents and denying them to their enemies. They laid hold of the major sea-lanes and tapped the networks of the Asian carrying trade, but they never established domination over any continental hinterland. They organized maritime ports of call and used them to increase their participation in trade between various Asian shores. They profited from access to pepper and other spices, as long as they remained unchallenged in their control of the Indian Ocean. Yet by the 1630s it was clear that they were not strong enough to blockade the Persian Gulf against competitors who wanted to ship spices through the gulf, now guarded by the increasingly powerful Turks. As a result, the Portuguese settlements in the East began to see the prospects for their survival as resting in Asia rather than in relations with the home country, "encrusting themselves," in the phrase of Godinho (1969: 783), "in the world of the Orient."

The Dutch in Asia

By 1600 the Portuguese began to feel the competition of the Dutch. The Dutch effort in the Indies at the close of the sixteenth century was initially carried forward by separate and competitive companies, but in 1602 the States-General chartered the Vereenigte Oost-Indische Compagnie (VOC), the Dutch East India Company. It differed markedly from its Portuguese counterparts. The Portuguese king maintained a monopoly over the spice trade, but private individuals could invest in the trading effort. Private trade in nonmonopolized commodities was carried on alongside the spice trade, making use of Asiatic traders. The Dutch Company, in contrast, gained a complete monopoly over the entirety of Dutch trade. It received the right to make war against local sovereigns and to conclude peace; to build forts and to organize local administration. While its home office was run by a board of directors, the Gentlemen Seventeen, the governor-general who represented the Company in the East had a great deal of latitude in formulating tactics and in carrying out decisions on the spot. The principal goal of the organization was to establish an early and complete dominance over the production and distribution of spices.

Dutch attacks on Portuguese strongholds in the Asian ocean began with the capture of Tidore and Amboyna in the Moluccas in 1605. Realizing that these forts were too remote from the hub of Asian trade, the Dutch Company attempted to seize Malacca in 1606, but—failing in this attempt—instead wrested the little Javanese port of Jakarta from the Sultan of Bantam. Here they constructed their main stronghold of Batavia, which they successfully defended from an attack by the Javanese state of Mataram in 1628–1629. In 1638 they initiated their campaign against the Portuguese in Ceylon, winning by 1658 control of the island and of its cinnamon production. In 1641 they dislodged the Portuguese from Malacca, and in 1662 they drove off the Spaniards, who had come to aid the Portuguese. Their conquest of Malacca granted the Dutch a whip hand over the kingdom of Mataram, which exported rice to the Malay peninsula. By 1677 they had defeated that state, following this up in 1684 with the conquest of Bantam in Java. Since the Portuguese had already lost Hormuz to the Persians in 1622, only Goa and Macao remained in Portuguese hands.

Among the most prized possessions in the southern seas were the Moluccas, the source of cloves, nutmeg, and the nutmeg fleece called mace. The main producer of cloves was the island of Amboyna; mace and nutmeg were produced on the island of Banda. The formal ruler of these islands was the Sultan of Ternate. From him the Dutch Company obtained the right to exercise monopoly control over these spices, in return for a promise to protect him from the Spaniards in the Philippines. The Dutch then entered into formal contracts for exclusive deliveries of the spices with local headmen in both Amboyna and Banda, the so-called *orang kaya* (literally, "rich men").

Neither the sultan's formal grant nor the contracts with the local headmen, however, could prevent other traders—both Asian and European—from buying the commodities, or the natives from selling them. To ensure control, therefore, the Dutch proceeded to limit competition ruthlessly. In 1621 the people of Banda were killed or deported to Batavia, to be replaced by Dutch colonists (*perkenier*) who were granted land tracts planted with nutmeg trees, together with the services of Company slaves for cultivation. Control of clove production was achieved by destroying all clove tree plantings except on Amboyna and a few neighboring islands. The Sultan of Ternate was compensated for his loss of income by payments that appear as "extirpation money" on the Company books. From 1625 on, periodic expeditions of armed outriggers began to visit unauthorized clove-producing areas to cut down unlicensed clove trees. The labor supply in Amboyna was increased further by the forcible relocation of 12,000 people from West Ceram in 1651. With the final subjugation of Macassar in 1669, the Dutch put an end to all illegal transactions in spices. They also gained control of a harbor that had become a refuge for disgruntled Muslim traders from other areas.

Various factors account for Dutch superiority over the Portuguese in the battle for the Indies. First, the United Provinces possessed vastly larger numbers of ships than did the Portuguese; these were lighter, better built, and more maneuverable than Portuguese craft and were equipped with better long-range cannon. With bases in the islands, the Dutch could stay out at sea longer and could more easily undertake local initiatives than could the Portuguese based at Goa. Second, the Dutch had no difficulty finding sailors and soldiers for their undertakings, if not at home, then by hiring French, German, Scandinavian, and—before 1652—English mercenaries. The Portuguese were hampered by a paucity of seagoing mariners; they were so hard-pressed for men to become soldiers in the Indies that they recruited prisoners from Portuguese jails. Third, the Dutch commanders had better mastery of naval tactics, relied more on a trained soldiery, and had greater leeway in deploying their ample resources than their Portuguese counterparts. The Portuguese still carried on naval warfare by boarding and entering; still charged to the cry of *"Santiago e a elles!"* ("St. James and at them!") in land battles; and were subject to an inefficient and centralized command in their operations. In addition, the Portuguese depended heavily on religious motivations, while the Dutch understood that their main concern was trade and "knew better than to endanger it through the preaching of their doctrine" (Meilink-Roelofz 1962: 181). Yet the major factor was undoubtedly that the Netherlands were rich, while the Portuguese were growing increasingly poorer. The difference in their wealth was, in turn, the outgrowth of the wide-ranging mercantile activities of the Dutch commercial oligarchy, whereas Portugal soon fell prey to the poverty of its home base and to its need to import cereals, cloth, and manufactured goods. In the contest between the Dutch and the Portuguese, a mercantile bourgeoisie defeated an elite of sea-trading aristocrats.

Yet in spite of Dutch successes against the Portuguese, their victory in the East proved hollow. The Company made profits but at heavy costs, the chief of these being the cost of war. Moreover, just when the Dutch consolidated their hold over the spice trade, the spices themselves began to lose their market appeal in Europe. Attempting to hold on to its monopoly at great expense, the Dutch Company throttled the activities of Asian merchants and deranged the trade of kingdoms and harbor principalities. Malacca never regained its former position. Mataram on Java, which had supplied rice to Malacca, consequently lost its connection with the island trade. The trade of Bantam in northeastern Java— once a great emporium supplying rice and slaves to the spice islands as well as to the ports of Malaya and Java—was redirected toward Batavia. The harbor principalities fell into decline; the rice-producing kingdoms became Company satellites. The inhabitants of the islands where clove trees had been extirpated turned to sago as their main source of food. Thus, the activities of the Dutch Company upset the trade networks of the southern seas in favor of a narrow commitment to the production of a few valued commodities for a distant market.

The English in India

The English, like the Portuguese, initially were at a disadvantage in relation to the Dutch; yet they were soon able to turn this disadvantage to their favor. The English East India Company was not as tightly centralized as the Dutch Company. Its monopoly was always less stringent than that of the Dutch Company, and many private British "country merchants" traded alongside the Company. The English also had less capital and less ready money than the Dutch; the Dutch Company started out with a stock of capital eight times larger than that of the English Company. In fact, the English often had to borrow money from native princes and notables (Meilink-Roelofz 1962: 194). The Dutch also had nearly twice as many ships at the beginning of the seventeenth century.

The English soon conceded the Dutch hold on the spice trade, especially after an English attempt to seize Banda forcibly failed in 1619. Having set up trading posts in Siam and Japan in 1612 and 1613, they closed them down again in 1623. The execution of English merchants by the Dutch on Amboyna further hastened the English retreat from overextended positions. Indonesian trade remained important to the English until the last third of the seventeenth century, but they gradually shifted their attention from Indonesia to India.

In entering the Indian subcontinent, the English came neither as religious crusaders, like the Portuguese, nor in search of outright political power, like the Dutch. Theirs was not a moral or political choice, but an economic one. They had neither the organization nor the capital to build new forts and to man warships. Moreover, they were well aware of Dutch superiority at sea. Making a virtue of necessity, they accepted the sovereignty of local rulers. They relied on negotiations to win advantages in trade, and often used their host governments to protect them against their Portuguese and Dutch rivals. Thus, they established a factory at Masulipatam in Golconda (1611), and one at Surat on the western frontiers of the Mughal polity (1612). They acquired Madras in 1639 from a minor Hindu chief, and administered it as the representatives of Indian rulers. Not until 1665 did Bombay become an English colony, passing to Charles II as part of the dowry of the Portuguese Catherine of Braganza. Charles, in turn, ceded the colony to the East India Company in exchange for a loan. In 1690 the Company established a modest settlement at Calcutta.

For the better part of a century, the English traders depended on the good will of the Mughal rulers. Their early settlements at Surat, at Madras, and elsewhere on the coast had to be accommodated to pre-existing conditions. The English could strive to alter these conditions through economic or social manipulation, but not by means of force. Trading at Surat, they made use of the chief port of the Mughal state, which exported textiles and indigo drawn from a wide hinterland. Surat was also the chief port of embarkation for the *haj*, the pilgrimage to Mecca. Shipping was in the hands of Muslims who traded with the Arab ports on the Red Sea; brokerage, commerce, and money lending were dominated by powerful lineages of Hindu merchants. The brokers, in turn, were in contact with village headmen in the areas of primary production. Each broker drew produce from his own zone of supply. These tight controls left the English little room for maneuver. Only in the eighteenth century, when the power of the Mughals waned and the warlike Marathas seized much of Surat's hinterland, did some of the local merchant families seek the protection of the Company. At that point, rebellion and political disorder began to interfere with trade from Surat to the West, and the English, followed by their Parsi trade partners, removed to Bombay.

As Surat and the Western trade declined, commerce with the East— China, the Philippines, and Indonesia—increased. The English traders were especially welcome on the Coromandel coast of southeastern India. On this coast, which was beyond Mughal range, they were not blocked by powerful merchant clans as in Surat, and they could enter into relations with many small merchants to tap the flourishing textile production of the hinterland. In addition, mutually beneficial arrangements allowed Englishmen to serve as naval officers on Indian ships, and Indian hiring agents and freight masters to work for the British.

Madras, which became the main British base, affords us a glimpse into the ways that relations between the foreign traders and the local population were structured. The town, dominated by the British-built Fort St. George, consisted of a "White" town and a "Black" town. White Town housed fifty European employees of the East India Company, twenty-five European free merchants, and sixty European sea captains, along with nine Armenian and six Jewish households, three or four upper-class Eurasian households, and an occasional Indian merchant. White Town was garrisoned by 200 European private soldiers and 400 non-European foot soldiers and artillerymen. Black Town, with more than 10,000 inhabitants, sheltered the local population. In the port of Madras, ships from Europe brought in silver and coral jewelry produced especially for the Eastern trade by Jews in Leghorn; they took away Chinese tea, Indonesian pepper, Spanish silver dollars from the Philippines, and textiles from Coromandel. By the end of the seventeenth century, however, Madras in turn lost out to Calcutta with its rising export trade to China.

The Mughal Empire

At Calcutta the English again faced the Mughals. They were subject to Mughal dominance when the Mughal empire was at its height, and they were caught up in the vicissitudes of its decline. It has become common to speak of Mughal India as "traditional" India, but the Mughal polity was itself but a recent political phenomenon. It was created by Timurid Turks from Turkestan, who had begun to raid into India at the beginning of the sixteenth century and who, in 1527, made their chief, Babur, the first Mughal emperor. As the Mughal system crystallized under Babur's grandson Akbar, it institutionalized a Turkish Central Asian pattern that granted predominant positions of power to soldiers, who were ranked according to the number of troops under their command. This military elite, the *mansabdars*, also furnished the top bureaucrats. At the time of Akbar, about a third of these military officeholders

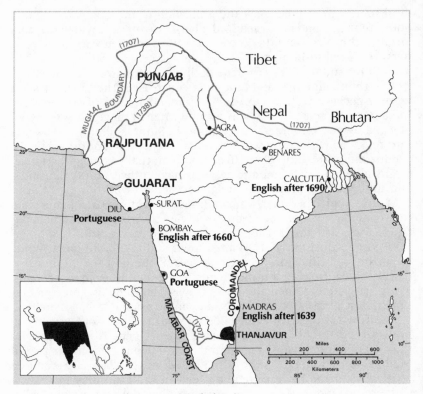

Mughal India.

were recruited from the original force that had crossed from Turkestan into India; a third was made up of Persian, Jagatai, and Uzbek Muslims; and another third comprised local Hindu (mainly Rajput) and Muslim chieftains. In time, the proportion of local chieftains increased.

These mansabdars formed a cosmopolitan elite and created a cosmopolitan court culture, exemplified by fine armor and weaponry, costly textiles and carpets, and palaces with luxurious gardens and interiors. Their artistic tastes, their styles of dress (trousers, shirt, and a coat prototypic of the modern "Nehru jacket"), their penchant for poetry, calligraphy, and miniature painting, and their use of Persian and a Persianized Hindi (Urdu) served as models for the lower orders of power holders within the realm. Court and palace life, in turn, generated artisan and craft production in palace towns and in whole regions that became specialized in crafts. Since they received their emoluments in money, the members of the elite also furthered commerce both in subsistence goods and in luxuries. This, in turn, gave rise to a class of merchants, who also lent the money the elite needed to pay for its luxurious way of life.

The members of this mansabdar elite were rewarded with grants (*jagirs*) to tribute drawn from particular areas. These grants were held during the lifetime of the grant holder, or *jagirdar*, and were not heritable. In this they followed the pattern of the Turkish *iqta* and the Spanish *encomienda*. Moreover, the area from which revenue was drawn would often shift during a jagirdar's lifetime as he moved to serve as mansabdar over different areas of the realm.

Between the mansabdar elite and the population at large stood the *zamindars*. These were usually chiefs of leading lineages, who held hereditary patrimonial rights to receive tribute from given areas. The lineages from which zamindars were drawn belonged to the dominant caste of the region. As heads of the central lineage, they drew tribute from other lineage members and passed on some of the surplus obtained in money payments to the Mughal government. As intermediaries between the central power and their lineages, the zamindars gained or lost in influence as the tie between state and lineages grew stronger or weaker. When the tie was weak, the chieftains of the central lineage, backed by their multitudinous kin, became more powerful and rose in influence with the state bureaucracy. When the state was strong, it would expand its tribute-taking power so as to bypass the central lineage and collect directly from local lineage segments, or it would create new settlements entirely by mixing lineage segments from different lineage systems. The distribution of power was thus fluid. Moreover, zamindari rights were transferable through sale (Habib 1964: 43). Jagirdars converted their jagirs into zamindari tenure when the central state was unable to interfere. Conversely, zamindari rights could be converted into jagirs through coercion when the state was strong. A potential conflict thus existed between the state and the zamindars, a conflict that constituted a major weakness in the edifice of the Mughal polity.

Another source of weakness in the Mughal polity was religious dissent. Anti-Muslim opposition was maintained in part by the Hindu kingdom of Vijayanagar, which had been founded by refugees from the Deccan who had fled from Muslim incursions in the early fourteenth century; the kingdom survived into the seventeenth century. Another source of opposition were various eclectic cults that drew on Hindu mysticism and Muslim Sufism, preaching *bhakti*, the participant devotion of the individual to one god, and turning against ritual and caste. The teachers of the cults addressed their followers in the vernacular. Many of these leaders were artisans and even low-caste; the most famous of them, Kabir (1440–1518), was a weaver. Another leader, Nanak (1469–1539), the founder of Sikhism, preached the unification of religions and the abolition of social distinctions among the Jat cultivator castes of the Punjab. Still another sect was the Satnamis, who attracted peasants, artisans, and petty traders.

The Mughal rulers were at first accepting of religious differences, since a dead infidel paid no taxes. In time, however, they grew increasingly intolerant. Aurangzeb, who ascended to the throne in 1658, was a fanatic who destroyed Hindu temples and imposed special taxes on non-Muslims. His religious persecutions drove many zamindars and their peasant followers into open rebellion, which became ever more serious as the regime weakened. In 1647 the Marathi-speaking populations of the western Deccan, under their leader Sivaji, rose against the Mughals in an attempt to restore the Hindu faith violated by the Muslim rulers. Organized as the Maratha confederacy, these people became a dominant influence in the Deccan. Similarly, the Mughals lost the support of the Hindu lineages of the central Gangetic Plain (the area that is today known as Uttar Pradesh). Finally, as Mughal rule waned, Mughal officials in outlying areas began to expand their own power and to trade with the incoming Europeans on their own behalf. By the end of the seventeenth century, the stage was thus set for the intrusion of the English into Indian affairs.

The Development of English Rule

The settlement of the English at Calcutta (1690) was strategically placed to benefit from Mughal decline. The province of Bengal, relatively isolated from the wars and crises that beset the rest of India, now entered a period of commercial florescence, exporting not only fine silks and cottons but also sugar, rice, saltpeter, indigo, and opium. Although the French and the Dutch also had trading stations in the area, the English East India Company soon carried on trade in more than 150 "factories." Dealing through powerful Indian merchant-bankers who tax farmed for the *navab* (the semi-independent Mughal provincial governor or ruler, anglicized as "nabob") and who often advanced huge credits to the English, the Company was able to expand its contracts with weavers who produced textiles for its trade. Bengal now witnessed a growing struggle between the navab and the zamindars, many of whom were colonizing new land without passing on the obligatory revenues to the ruler. In this conflict, the English supported the zamindars against the navab. Backed by the merchant-bankers and in secret alliance with many zamindars, the Company provoked the navab into open warfare. Supplied with funds advanced by the chief bankers of Bengal, it defeated the navab's troops conclusively at Plassey in 1757.

In the wake of its victory, the East India Company plundered the state treasury of Bengal to the tune of over 5 million pounds sterling. It also set up a monopoly over export and import trade. Setting prices to its own benefit, it ousted the local mechant class and reaped, between 1775 and 1780, another 5 million pounds in profit. Using Indian go-betweens, who often bought their positions from the Company, it gained direct control over 10,000 Bengali weavers, whose contracts forced them to deal exclusively with the Company. By 1765 the Company had also become the official *diwan*, or civil administration, in Bengal. It quickly moved to rationalize the taxation system, increasing the direct yield in land revenue from nearly 15 million rupees in 1765 to 30 million rupees in 1776–1777. The increased tax burden proved ruinous to large numbers of Bengali cultivators and artisans. There were major famines in 1770 and 1783.

Having gained a foothold in Bengal and aided by increasing political strife, the East India Company was able to expand its territorial sway rapidly and effectively. Continuous warfare required the Company to develop an ever more effective army; continuous "intervention" in the civil affairs of territorial rulers furthered the development of a territorially based Company bureaucracy. The Company took over some areas of India directly, leaving others to be administered through local rulers under its sponsorship. In the years after 1765, therefore, the Company changed its character from that of a chartered trading organization, operating under the rules set by another government, to that of a military and bureaucratic arm of the British government.

This transformation in the character of the Company, and hence in the nature of English rule in India, also entailed a major change in English aspirations. Before the victory at Plassey, the characteristic Englishman in India was a merchant who, through life in his "factory" and trade dealings in the hinterland, acquired a sense of equality with the members of the Indian elite with whom he dealt. The merchant, or the Company merchant acting as official, often lived like the Indian notables, with an Indian mistress, or *zenana*, and surrounded by Parsi or Muslim servants, Portuguese or Goanese cooks, and Malabari or Malagassy slave butlers. Paradoxically, as Spear has noted,

> the days of corrupt Company officials, of ill-gotten fortunes, of oppression of ryots [peasants], of zenanas and of illicit sexual connexions, were also the days when Englishmen were interested in Indian culture, wrote Persian verses, and foregathered with Pandits and Maulwis and Nawabs on terms of social equality and personal friendship. [1963: 145]

Whereas before Plassey the English merchant dealt with Indian merchants on an equal footing, after their victory the English began to use their newly gained political power to control their Indian competitors along with the traders of other European companies. Before Plassey the English had worked through local intermediaries, called *dubash* or *modeliar* in Coromandel and Malabar, and *dadni* in Bengal. The term *dadni* (sing., *dadan*) stood for advances at interest made to merchants in the interior who, in turn, made advances to local cultivators or artisans against future deliveries. Such intermediaries not only fulfilled a financial and organizing function; but they also dealt with local political authorities and craft organizations and were, at one and the same time, "courtier, negotiator, interpreter, formulator of contracts . . . serving also as guarantor and expert" (Dermigny 1964, I: 783). These intermediaries were now replaced with *gomastas*, or salaried clerks, who handled the Company's business, issuing trading permits. At the same time—as we shall see below—this did not make the English independent of Indian capital. The thrust of English activities, both by the Company and by private entrepreneurs, was to use Indian resources and labor to produce goods for the trade with China. Much of the wealth that financed this growing trade came from Indian bankers and moneylenders.

The role of the English trader underwent an essential change, from that of a trade partner of Indians to a socially distant superior. This paralleled the change in the political realm, as the establishment of order and the routinization of administration gave precedence to the soldier-administrator, who tended to despise "the soft Bengalee," and who looked down upon Indians from a pinnacle of moral righteousness, wishing to rule them by English example and to reform their un-English habits.

The English success at Plassey opened the door to a takeover of the Indian peninsula. The moves towards English domination did not follow a master plan, but occurred as successive responses to regional crises and wars. The Mughal polity disintegrated into a number of warring successor states, such as the Maratha federation in the western Deccan, Hyderabad in the uplands between the Krishna and Godavari rivers, and Mysore, uniting the inland plateau with the coastal area north of Kerala. These new polities constituted a real threat to the English presence in Bombay, Madras, and Calcutta. They also enlisted French or Afghan help for their shifting alliances, thus tending to escalate regional wars into international conflicts. At the same time, their internal disunity and their inability to forge a common alliance allowed the English to divide them from one another and to defeat them separately. The English defeated Hyderabad in 1789, Mysore in 1799, and the Maratha federation between 1816 and 1818.

These many-sided wars for control proved enormously destructive of wealth and resources. For half a century, all sides taxed and pillaged to obtain funds for sustained political and military competition. English success in war, however, granted the East India Company and its officials the means to subordinate Indian resources to the process of accumulation in the home country. Large private fortunes, obtained by plunder, were repatriated and invested in England. Tribute that had previously sustained local rulers could now be "transferred to stockholders in Europe through the medium of unrequited exports" (Fieldhouse 1967: 159). Conquest of political sovereignty also allowed England to reorganize Indian land tenure and land taxation to make India pay for the expenses of warfare and to cover the cost of continued English occupation. Finally, land and tax reform could be used to reorient Indian agriculture toward the production of profitable commodities, such as raw cotton and opium, as strategic means for enhancing England's commerce with China.

New Patterns of Land Tenure and Taxation

The Mughal polity had operated essentially in the tributary mode, allowing jagirdars and zamindars to pump surplus out of cultivators over whom they exercised either personal domination or domination by virtue of their office. The critical difference from the later English practice was that these rights were not, properly speaking, rights of property in land, but rather claims on people's labor and the products of that labor. In the Permanent Settlement that the English introduced in Bengal in 1793, however, the zamindars were turned into outright property owners, required to turn over to the British administration nine-tenths of the tribute received from their peasants, and retaining one-tenth for their personal use. The English thus created, at one stroke, a class of 3,000 Indian landlords who held the same property rights as English landlords, including the right to sell, mortgage, and inherit land.

As a result of the work of Bernard S. Cohn, a great deal is known about the impact of the new English land law and tax assessment in one region affected by the Permanent Settlement, the region of Benares. Cohn's studies furnish the historical background to the work carried out by American anthropologists in the 1940s and 1950s in Jaunpur district, which formerly constituted a part of the Rajadom of Benares. In this region in the eighteenth century, rights over people and tribute were held by corporate lineages, mostly Rajput, by petty chiefs or rajas, and by holders of service grants, or *jagirs*. All these local tribute takers owed obligations to the Raja of Benares, himself subordinate to the Navab of Oudh, who in turn owed loyalty to the Mughal ruler. The holders of service grants received tribute but paid no taxes. All others owed tribute to their several superiors, although actual tribute payment varied with the political and military capability of tribute payers and receivers. There were numerous conflicts over resources among the various groups through arbitration and compromise.

English rule at one fell swoop converted all of these group and status rights over persons and tribute into rights to private property. Landed estates became the properties of registered tribute payers, who undertook to pay the taxes stipulated in return for private rights of ownership, inheritance, and disposal. Since taxes were fixed permanently, they were not affected by changes in land prices or in the value of crops grown. Underassessed estates became especially valuable as sources of and authorities, which were settled by force or mediated profitable investment. The actual work of assessing and collecting taxes was delegated to a body of Indian officials, who found themselves in a position to benefit from fraudulent assessments and forced sales of estates that defaulted on their taxes. Some of these officials doubled as money lenders, merchants, or bankers, or entertained relations with such money-managing notables.

Such officials benefited further by their knowledge of English legal procedure. English law superseded Indian legal practice, which was based on considerations of what Sir Henry Maine called "status," as opposed to "contract." Indian legal procedure considered that contesting parties to a dispute were not discrete individuals but were connected to others by complex and multiple social, political, and ritual ties. It recognized the existence of socially, politically, and ritually unequal corporate lineages and castes, and understood cases of conflict as moments in ongoing relations among such groups. Now, however, members of corporate lineages were to be treated as individuals. English law insisted on defining plaintiffs and defendants as equal and individual partners to a contract, and on dealing only with the case before the judge, to the exclusion of the social matrix that had spawned the case. Indian legal practice had avoided final decisions and solutions, in favor of continuous negotiation. English legal procedure, in contrast, insisted on resolving a case brought before the court by a clear-cut decision. The result was that Indian plaintiffs and defendants conspired to circumvent the British process of legal adjudication by ingenious means, illegal in the eyes of the court but practiced in self-defense by the contestants. "It is likely," concludes Cohn (1959: 90), "that most of the cases that went into courts were fabrications to cover the real disputes." The imposition of the new legal codes, intended to be just and fair, thus favored those best able to take advantage of the law.

As a result of the new systems of landed property, tax assessment, and legal procedure, a new class of landlords arose in the Benares region, recruited mainly among Indian civil servants, bankers, and merchants. These new landlords were often absentee, managing their estates through agents rather than through the older system of rights over persons and tribute. By the middle of the nineteenth century, this class would control nearly half of all the land in the region, while many unsuccessful zamindars declined to the status of peasants.

In still other areas, as in parts of northern and western India, a reform settlement was put into effect in 1833, which ousted revenue-collecting overlords and—in the belief that Indian villages were egalitarian republics of co-sharers in a corporate body—granted the land to corporate village groups or "cultivating brotherhoods."

Throughout India, all the new property holders came under stronger pressure to produce crops for the market, whether sugar, tobacco, spices, cotton, jute, or indigo. Although there developed a few mono-crop plantations under European auspices, much of this agricultural output was obtained through a kind of agrarian putting-out system in which crops were passed from producer to buyer through a chain of middlemen (Moore 1966: 356). Everywhere moneylenders—already well-established figures in the Indian countryside—enlarged the scale and scope of their activities, advancing money at high interest rates to help peasants make their crop and meet the demand for revenue. Everywhere, also, zamindars who could not compete with their more affluent fellows, local notables who had revenues taken away from them, and chieftains who had fought English encroachment combined to form cliques of disgruntled critics of the new order, which had stripped them of their resources and titles and destined them to downward social mobility. The number of landless laborers also increased, especially when English machine-produced cottons began to flood the Indian market after 1814, effectively ruining the high-quality textile crafts of the Indian towns and their suppliers in the countryside.

The new situation also reinforced the position of a stratum of rural power holders who were able to withstand and even benefit from the radical and destructive changes that had occurred. These were the "strong men" (Thorner and Thorner 1962: 16–17; Thorner 1964: 64–66), who used the mechanisms of local lineage and caste to maintain and expand their hold over agricultural laborers and tenants forced by hunger to work for a minimal livelihood. At the same time, these power holders used local ties of kinship and marriage to deflect the power of absentee zamindars and state officials. Legal claims against them could not be enforced effectively, and even powerful zamindars and merchants were forced to enter into bargains with them in order to obtain revenue and produce. Such strong men, powerful within local lineage segments, kept control in their hands through advances of credit, seed, and food to their fellow villagers, through their role in the management of conflicts within the village, and—in the last instance—through their control of the means of local violence, ranging from physical intimidation of their opponents to the destruction of crops and the denial of land and housing in the village (Srinivas 1959: 15; Cohn 1971: 85). The outcome was the development of a rural oligarchy mediated by kinship and caste constraints. Such rural oligarchs maintained tributary relationships in the countryside even when, in relation to the market, they filled the role of entrepreneurs.

A New Army and Bureaucracy

The English dominion had two other consequences for the conquered population. One was the creation of an army under English jurisdiction, officered by Englishmen and staffed by Indian *sepoys*—Brahmins, Rajputs, and Muslims—who were hired as mercenaries and paid by the English government. This effectively ended the Mughal pattern in which tribute-taking notables also had the right to maintain troops and the obligation to furnish them to the ruler. It placed the means of violence in the hands of the new European rulers. Another consequence was the creation of an officialdom exclusively European at the highest levels, which worked through a vast and growing army of subordinate clerks.

These subordinate officials were recruited mostly in Bengal, among the numerous interpreters, brokers, junior administrators, and small traders and landholders who had served as junior partners with the English Company and with private merchants (Mukherjee 1970: 48). Many of them had served the Mughals before the English. They now switched their allegiance and took advantage of the new political and economic opportunities created by the English presence. Most of them had their origins in the Brahmin, Baidya, and Kayastha high castes, and they used their appointments to strengthen their position as bearers of an elite culture pattern; yet they also permitted recruitment of the lower-caste men.

These new professionals called themselves *bhadralok* ("respectable people"), substituting for an identity defined in terms of caste new criteria, such as English language education, control of a literate Indian tradition, and professional and clerical employment. They were thus not just Westernizers but also innovators of a distinctive pattern of their own. They combined skills sought by the Europeans with a strong sense of their own mission. They envisioned a return, under their own auspices, to a great Bengali past before the true Brahmanic virtues had become corrupted by Buddhism and by the emotional Hinduism of the *bhakti* movement (see Broomfield 1966: 63–64). Similar regional elites developed in Madras in the southeast and in Maharashtra in the west; and the English recruited employees from such groups for service upcountry, as new areas came under their control. Inevitably, such supporters of English rule encountered the hostility of previous elites. As English and literate education spread to other segments of the population, such as Muslims and low-caste Hindus, the bhadralok came under increasing pressure even in their home regions.

In southern India, as in Madras in 1812, there were no zamindars, and a different model was put into effect. In the hope of creating a vigorous self-reliant peasantry, the English granted land in *ryotwari* tenure to individual peasants, who were required to pay revenue directly to the state. One example of the changes wrought by the new rules of property and taxation is furnished by Kathleen Gough's study (1978) of Thanjavur District (called Tanjore by the British) near Madras, now part of Tamil Nadu. Before the advent of the British, each Thanjavur village was dominated by a managerial Brahmin or Vellala caste. Such a caste acted collectively to distribute fixed shares of the grain harvest among village cultivators, sharecroppers, and servants, and was collectively responsible for paying tribute to the state. The new English administration made each household individually responsible for its cultivating tenants and for the payment of taxes, and after the middle of the nineteenth century issued individual title deeds to shares of village lands. The cultivators, required to pay taxes in cash, increasingly became indebted to money lenders, who previously had been allowed to take only houses, crops, and jewelry as collateral for loans but now were enabled to attach land as well. As a result, many people lost their land, while the properties of some grew in size. Agriculture shifted from a main emphasis on provisioning household needs to the production of rice for export to the plantations of South Asia, while the hereditary share-tenants of the past became increasingly insecure tenants working on annual contracts. Thanjavur District thus became one of the main supply zones of indentured laborers seeking employment abroad (see chapter 7).

Rebellion

As the nineteenth century approached the halfway mark, English policies affected ever-widening geographic areas. The various land settlements and tax reforms altered the nature of economic and political hierarchies. Indian textiles, until the end of the eighteenth century a major export, were banned from British markets, while India was required to admit the entry of English manufactures duty free. This led to the rapid destruction of specialized Indian textile handicraft production. The spread of machine-made goods disrupted village crafts, reducing the number of artisans who derived their living from producing pottery, tanned skins, dyed cloth, oil, and jewelry. Shipbuilding and railroad construction in the 1840s and 1850s speeded up the growth of commercial crop production in the countryside, prompting exports of wheat from the Punjab, cotton from Bombay, and jute from Bengal, as well as a shift from the production of food crops to industrial crops such as cotton, peanuts, sugarcane, and tobacco. Moneylending at high interest rates expanded steadily as peasants began to buy foodstuffs on the market, as money was needed to spur cash-crop production, and as land prices rose after mid-century. There was a rising tide of dissatisfaction, fanned by former power holders and their retinues, who were increasingly edged out and threatened by English land and tax reforms. That discontent became manifest in violent outbreaks in northern India, which the English designated as the Great Mutiny of 1857.

The ostensible reason for this outbreak was word that the cartridges for the new Lee-Enfield rifle had to be heavily greased with tallow made from cow and pig fat. To load the cartridges they had to be bitten open at the end, releasing the powder. Killing cows was anathema to Hindus, contact with pork products taboo to Muslims. In May the sepoys mutinied, touching off armed rebellion over wide areas. The mutiny was only the spark that ignited the tinder, which had long been fueled by discontent. Former dignitaries now relegated to the margins, local notables hoping to restore Mughal or Maratha power, villagers under economic and political pressure, adherents of religious causes opposed to the intrusive Christians—all of these and more rallied to the cause of rebellion. The mutiny was defeated, at a great cost in human life. For the English, the sudden realization that India could slip out of their control altered their attitudes toward their subjects. After the mutiny, the English rulers abandoned the idea of reforming India through the application of English liberal ideas, and strove instead to strengthen what they regarded as Indian traditions. There arose what Hutchins has called the myth of the "real India."

> This "real India" consisted of the ancient India of the countryside; and of retainers and dependents of British power, of princes, peasants, and minority groups. Indians who lived in cities, engaged in business and the professions, who were not dependent on British favor, without an interest in preserving for themselves a privileged position guaranteed by British might, were designated "unrepresentative." [1967: 156]

The English paid renewed attention to the distinctions of caste, separating regiments from one another on the basis of their religious and caste status and shoring up the privileges of kshatriya groups. At work was undoubtedly a desire to divide and rule and to reinforce the constraints of caste and privilege against the mobility and assertiveness of "new" men, both as individuals and as groups.

The members of the English community drew together as a new quasi-caste of rulers, separate and distinct from the inhabitants of the country. There was a growing tendency to call Indians "niggers" (Hutchins 1967: 108), indeed to see the lower classes at home and the Indians as similarly inferior. There was a growing tendency, also, to live up strenuously to an ideal of hard work, masculinity, authoritative bearing, denial of comfort, and the pursuit of sports in order to develop moral qualities; and at the same time to project upon the Indians the opposites of these traits—to see them as slothful, physically weak and cowardly, effeminate, deceitful, wasteful, and immoral (Hutchins 1967: 29–78). Their new role as rulers—guardians, as Woodruff has called them—also justified their pursuit of an elite life well above the manner to which they were accustomed in England. "India's function was to turn Englishmen into 'instant aristocrats' " (Hutchins 1967: 107–108), and the adherence of Englishmen to these new standards was in inverse proportion to the realities of their station at home.

From India to China

Political and economic consolidation within India went hand in hand with England's expansion of trade with China. The resources of India were mobilized to gain entrance to the treasure house of the East. "Everything took place," says Louis Dermigny of the English, "as if they had made the peninsula into a vassal in order to orient it towards China" (1964, I: 781).

In gaining access to the markets of China, however, the English faced a formidable obstacle in the unwillingness of the Chinese state to engage in any trade with the "red-haired barbarians." With the advent of the Tungusic Manchu dynasty to rule in Peking as the Ch'ing (1644), imperial control over foreign trade was tightened. Such renewed control served both to stamp out the protagonists of the preceding Ming

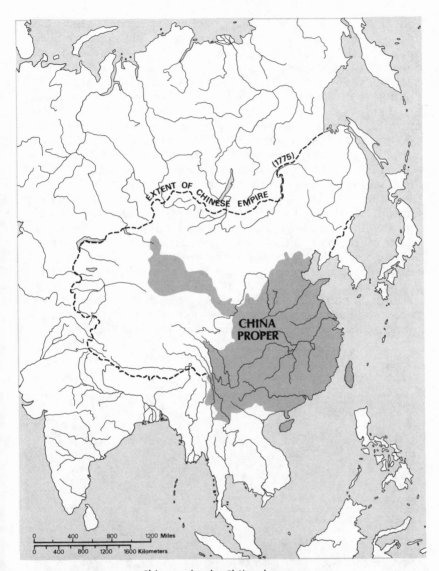

China under the Ch'ing dynasty.

dynasty and to contain foreign influence on the China coast. The major Ming supporter in the south was Chen Ch'eng-kung (Coxinga), who came to dominate Fukien province and who nearly conquered Nanking. He entertained extensive contacts with the Europeans, having worked in Macao and Manila for the Portuguese and Spaniards, in

Taiwan for the Dutch, and in Japan, where he married. When he was driven from the mainland, he sought refuge in Taiwan, where he held out until 1683. Although Coxinga was the best-known and most powerful of the challengers to Manchu rule, there were others as well (Dermigny1964, I: 97, 132). On the advice of a former lieutenant of Coxinga's, the Manchu emperor cleared the coast entirely, hoping through the creation of a no-man's land to diminish the possibility of uncontrolled contact between seafarers and the inland population.

With the re-establishment of imperial control, foreign traders were again welcomed at Chinese ports. The English East India Company was the main beneficiary of this renewed opportunity. From 1685 to 1760 the English were allowed to trade a number of ports in Fukien and Chekiang provinces. However, they increasingly took their trade to Canton, where they found a foreign trade guild (the Cohong), which was wealthy enough to stock large supplies of goods in advance, and where the customs official (the Hoppo) acted in direct representation of the emperor, independent of the local gentry. When the emperor again restricted foreign trade in 1760, Canton remained the only port open to foreign trade.

During the first years of their China trade, the English bought silks, porcelain, and medicines. They tried to pay in English woolens, but found no takers among the Chinese. They sold some English lead, used

European trade headquarters at Canton, seen from the harbor. Oil on canvas by George Chinnery (1774–1852). (Courtesy of The New York Historical Society, New York City)

to line chests, some tin, rattan from the Malay Straits, and pepper, saltpeter, and rice from Java and the Philippines; but as the Chinese emperor wrote to George III in 1793, "there is nothing we lack . . . nor do we need any more of your country's manufactures" (quoted in Teng and Fairbank 1961: 19). Ultimately the English had to pay in silver, payments that constituted a continuous drain on their supply of bullion. The payment deficit increased even further when, in the course of the eighteenth century, the Company added to its list of desired commodities the serrated leaves of the tea shrub.

Opium for Tea

Tea drinking, introduced into Europe by the Dutch, had begun in England in 1664, when a quantity of two pounds, two ounces was imported. By 1783 the amount sold by the East India Company alone was nearly 6 million pounds, and two years later it came to more than 15 million (Greenberg 1951: 3). An additional amount perhaps as great was smuggled into England by private traders attempting to avoid taxes. (When the Crown could not collect tea taxes in Europe, it tried to do so in Boston, turning Americans into rebels and coffee drinkers at the same time.) All this tea had to be paid for in silver, causing silver to flow to the East in "a chronic hemorrhage" (Dermigny 1964, I: 724). China drew silver both from Japan and Manila. In 1600 the flow of silver from Japan to China amounted to 200,000 kilograms, but around that same year the annual flow of silver from Manila into China came to 8 million kilos (Rawski 1972: 76). China became "the tomb of American treasure." Dermigny estimates the amount of silver flowing into China between 1719 and 1833 at between 306 and 330 million piasters, representing one-fifth of all the silver produced in Mexico during this time, and perhaps as much as 20 percent of all European stocks of silver (1964, I: 740).

In this bullion drainage, the English inherited an ancient problem. Even in Roman times, southern India had sent spices, muslins, and precious stones to the Mediterranean, receiving in turn Roman gold. Roman *aurei* or *denarii* have been found in quantity in hoards of Roman coins in India (Wheeler 1955: 164–166). The amount of bullion drained from the Mediterranean was considerable. Pliny remarked that "in no year does India absorb less than fifty million sesterces" (quoted in Wheeler 1955: 167). Nor did the outflow cease with the fall of the Roman Empire. The Middle Ages witnessed a steady outflow of gold and silver through Italy to Byzantium and the Muslim world, and from there on to India (Lopez, Miskimin, and Udovitch 1970). In the early modern period, Braudel writes,

> the Mediterranean as a whole operated as a machine for accumulating precious metals, of which, be it said, it could never have enough. It hoarded them only to lose them all to India, China, and the East Indies.

The great discoveries may have revolutionized routes and prices, but they did not alter this fundamental situation. [1972, I: 464]

By the seventeenth century, the same problem faced northwestern Europe.

All this commercial activity had, of course, repercussions within China itself. In the sixteenth century along the southern coast of China, expanding Portuguese and Spanish trade had prompted the specialized production of sugar, textiles, porcelain, and metal wares for the overseas market. In turn, the Iberians brought tobacco, sweet potatoes, and peanuts from the New World. The new food crops were eagerly adopted by the Chinese peasantry, and they appear to have been instrumental in its rapid population growth (Ho 1965). Tobacco became a major cash crop in the course of the seventeenth century, spreading inland from the coast to Yunnan, to northwestern China, and to the valley of the lower Yangtze. Rawski (1972) has traced the chain of consequences of this commercialization in rising land values, heightened competition for land, greater investment in land improvements, rising productivity, and higher rents and interest rates. Increasing demand for tea intensified this cycle, as advances began to flow from the East India Company to the

The China Tea Trade. Oil on canvas, China Export School, c. 1800. The leaves are grown on the hillside (upper left), dried, roasted, trampled, packed, and weighed. Foreigners buy the tea (bottom left) and take it to their ships (far right). (Courtesy, Berry-Hill Galleries, New York)

Cohong, and from the Cohong to tea wholesalers in Fukien, Chekiang, Kiangsi, and Anhwei. The tea wholesalers advanced the money to family-sized "hill households," who gradually moved from tea-shrub raising as a subsidiary occupation to full-time specialization in tea. This tea had to be paid for, and the East India Company faced an ever-growing deficit in its balance of payments. It was already in serious debt to the English Crown for monies lent in the course of the conquest of India. To meet its obligations, it borrowed money from rich Parsi bankers, like Jagath Seth, while its officials—trading as private parties— often incurred debts with Indian moneylenders. The money went into growing cotton in India and shipping it to China. There developed a complex triangular trade whereby private agency houses of "country traders," run mostly by Parsi and Scottish merchants, would take Indian cotton to Canton and sell it there for silver. With this silver they would buy East India Company bills of credit, redeemable in London. The Company, in turn, used the silver obtained through the sale of its bills of credit to buy tea.

In the course of these transactions, many of the English country traders and Company officials dealing on their own behalf laid the basis of considerable private fortunes, which they parlayed into influence and political representation at home. In Parliament their influence, combined in what William Pitt called "the Bengal squad," soon outweighed that of the West Indian interests.

Yet even though the English sold an annual average of 27 million pounds of raw Indian cotton between 1785 and 1833, the sums obtained still did not suffice to buy all the tea they wished to ship to England. To add to the stock of specie, the English India Company had to import it from the Spanish possessions in the New World. In 1776, however, the American Revolution cut England off from the supply of Mexican silver. At the same time, cotton from northern China began to flow into Chinese textile production at prices lower than those of Indian cotton. The answer to the Company's financial prayers was opium from India.

The sale of opium had already constituted a major source of Mughal revenues. In 1773 the East India Company had established a monopoly over opium sales, and in 1797 it extended its monopoly to cover production. The factors at Patna and Ghazipur near Benares gave their names to the opium they produced—Patna and Benares. Later the principality of Malwa on India's west coast joined the producers. Patna and Benares opium, packed in mango-wood boxes holding about 145 pounds each and representing the production of five or six acres, was auctioned off to agency houses on Tank Square in Calcutta. Malwa opium reached Canton through Parsi merchants from Bombay. Americans joined the trade as well, shipping increasing quantities of opium from Turkey to New York, and from there to China.

The opium trade was covert and illegal, and enormously profitable.

The agency houses dealing in opium soon handled quantities worth four times the value of all the goods the Company brought to Canton in its own ships. Armies of henchmen and corrupt officials moved the opium inland. By the end of the nineteenth century, one out of every ten Chinese is thought to have become an addict. The Europeans, however, finally had something to sell to the Chinese. During the first decade of the nineteenth century, China still showed a trade surplus of 26 million silver dollars. In the third decade, 34 million dollars left China to pay for opium (Wakeman 1975: 126). The outflow of silver from China soon affected the country at large. The government set tax quotas in silver; the peasants paid in copper cash. As silver grew scarce and rose in price, ever larger amounts of copper were required to meet taxes. Opium thus did more than undermine the health of Chinese addicts; it began to subvert the social order in the countryside.

Trade in the Pacific

Opium was by far the most important import into China, but the Europeans also strove to locate other resources of interest to the Chinese. One of these was sandalwood, which furnished an oil used by the Chinese in making incense. Early in the development of the sandalwood trade, a ship "sandalwooding" out of Sydney, Australia, could make a profit of 25 percent (Furnas 1947: 221). Various Pacific islands were exploited to obtain sandalwood, often to the point of depletion. Fiji was cut over in the years between 1804 and 1810, the Marquesas between 1804 and 1818, Hawaii between 1811 and the mid-1830s. The Hawaiian king traded an annual $300,000 in sandalwood, receiving in return hardware, cloth, clothing, rum, guns, and even a luxury yacht built in Salem, Massachusetts. By 1826, however, the chiefs were in arrears in their deliveries, and American traders exacted instead a contract according to which each male Hawaiian was to be taxed for one picul (about 140 pounds) of sandalwood at four Spanish dollars to cover the debt (Furnas 1947: 120).

Around mid-century, natives were hired on contract to obtain sandalwood in New Caledonia and the New Hebrides, and the use of native labor became common during the 1850s, when the Australian gold rush depleted the supply of European labor. In payment the natives received iron tools and hardware, cloth, tobacco and pipes, as well as muskets and powder. At the same time, the traders also paid in the native products of other islands, thus intensifying inter-island exchanges. Fiji, Lifu, and Tana furnished pigs to other islands. Tana wanted tortoise shells from the Solomons in exchange for its pigs; Eromanga desired *nunpuri* shells from New Caledonia; Espiritu Santo and Eromanga received pigs, shells, tortoise shells, and whales' teeth in exchange for sandalwood (Shineberg 1966).

Another product in demand in China was the sea cucumber (also called trepang or beche-de-mer), which the Chinese valued both as a food and as an aphrodisiac. This product had long been supplied by Indonesian and Philippine sailors, but European traders began to organize the trade themselves. The collecting and processing of sea cucumbers required a great deal of labor. An average-sized establishment might house some 300 people engaged in cleaning and collecting firewood to dry the sea animals. Native laborers were contracted for, working first under their own chiefs and later under European control. The influx of trade goods, including guns, in payment for sea cucumbers was probably even greater than in the sandalwood trade. Prices at Canton went as high as $90 a picul (Furnas 1947: 212).

Sandalwooding and the trade in sea cucumbers, along with intensified whaling, contributed greatly to the distribution of firearms throughout the South Seas. Where powerful local chiefs gained control of the new weapons, they found themselves equipped with greatly enhanced military potential. Thus, European trading spurred the rise, on a number of islands, of small states headed by powerful chiefs equipped with European armament.

On Hawaii, control of favorably located beaches permitted Kamehameha, a nephew of the Hawaiian paramount, to acquire a store of weapons in the 1790s and to use these first to conquer several rival chiefdoms and then to displace the rightful successor to the kingships. By 1804 Kamehameha commanded 600 muskets, 14 small cannon, 40 swivel guns, and 20 sailing vessels (Furnas 1947: 121). His son and heir further consolidated the kingship by abolishing the system of traditional taboos through which the priesthood could have challenged the emerging centralization of power (Webb 1965; Davenport 1969).

In Tahiti the young chief Tu used European guns, obtained in exchange for pigs sold to the prison colonies of New South Wales, to set himself up as King Pomare. His son, Pomare II, consolidated the new kingship by allying himself with English missionaries and converting his people forcibly to Christianity.

Five thousand guns were introduced into Fiji between 1828 and 1835, and probably an equal number between 1842 and 1850, in the wake of the sea cucumber trade. This wealth in guns prompted the rise of the polity of Bau, when a chief called Cakobau was able to monopolize the importation of firearms (Ward 1972: 110–111). Similar war leaders arose in the Solomon Islands and in the New Hebrides (Docker 1970: 23–42).

The Portuguese pioneered the sea route into Asian waters, and Dutch, English, and French companies and private traders soon followed in their wake. Unable to penetrate the mainland directly, the Europeans consolidated points of entry along the Asian coasts and proceeded to envelop the littoral of the continent in a web of long-distance traffic and commerce. To feed the burgeoning trade, various regions along the sea routes began to specialize in the production of commodities to exchange for other commodities. Some products, above all Chinese tea, generated an especially intense demand. To pay for tea, otter skins from the Northwest Coast of North America, sea cucumbers and sandalwood from the Pacific, silver from America, and Indian raw cotton and opium all began to flow toward China in a gigantic escalation of mercantile activity. At the same time, the increase in water-borne commerce had repercussions in distant hinterlands, where it reduced the overland caravan trade, diminished the importance of caravan emporia, and altered the balance of power between pastoral and sedentary populations.

While in most of Asia European mercantile activity remained closely tied to its medium, the sea, one trade organization—the English East India Company—charted a different course for itself. It took over the political and economic inheritance of the land-based Mughal power, changing its role from that of a trading company to a political sovereign. Once established, sovereignty passed to the English Crown. English rule had profound consequences for Indian society. Land and tax reforms abrogated the hierarchies of tribute takers that had formed the Mughal order, and replaced them with echelons of landed proprietors. The elites of locally and regionally dominant castes were converted into landowning entrepreneurs, required to raise money for taxes and prompted to do so by producing cash crops. The character of relations among landowners, village servants, and dependent laborers was altered, in turn. While the cultural forms of obligation and dependency among castes were maintained and even intensified, these relationships served increasingly to mobilize labor for the production of agricultural commodities.

Within the structure of the British Empire as a whole, India came to play a crucial role. Throughout the period of British rule, India paid a colonial tribute to defray English expenses incurred during the conquest and during the defeat of the Great Mutiny, and to cover the costs of English administration in India. Plunder accumulated in the wars of the eighteenth century created great English fortunes. Revenues obtained in Bengal were of a scale sufficient to finance the expanding trade with the Orient, obviating the annual transfer of bullion from England. Indian opium opened China to foreign trade and reversed the flow of species from Europe to Asia. The English sold fine Indian textiles in Europe, Africa, and Indonesia, aiding in the accumulation of money-begetting money in the home country.

With the installation of the capitalist mode of production in England (chapter 9), industrial capital moved to dominate mercantile wealth, also drawing India into its expanding orbit. English machine-made textiles invaded the Indian market, to the detriment of Indian handicrafts. In the mid-nineteenth century, railroad building in India furnished a major outlet for English capital, spurring iron and steel production in England and opening a market for English coal on the subcontinent. Thereafter, the export of Indian agricultural commodities and machine-made Indian cottons to international markets helped balance British trade deficits with the industrializing nations of Europe and the United States. Indian surpluses enabled England to create and maintain a global system of free trade. Had England been forced to ban imports from the United States and Germany and to compete with them in foreign markets, American and German industrialization would also have been significantly slowed. Thus, "Asia in general, but India and China in particular, far from being peripheral to the evolution of the international economy of the time, was in fact crucial" (Latham 1978: 70). Under English domination, India became a key foundation of the emerging worldwide capitalist edifice.

Power loom weaving in a Manchester cotton mill. Line engraving by T. Allom, J. Carter, and J. Tingle, c. 1835. (The Granger Collection, New York)

Part Three
Capitalism

From the fifteenth century on, European soldiers and sailors carried the flags of their rulers to the four corners of the globe, and European merchants established their storehouses from Vera Cruz to Nagasaki. Dominating the sea-lanes of the world, these merchants invaded existing networks of exchange and linked one to the other. In the service of "God and profit," they located sources of products desired in Europe and developed coercive systems for their delivery. In response, European craft shops, either singly or aggregated into manufactories, began to produce goods to provision the wide-ranging military and naval efforts and to furnish commodities to overseas suppliers in exchange for goods to be sold as commodities at home. The outcome was the creation of a commercial network of global scale.

During three and a half centuries of European expansion, Spain and Portugal divided between them the South American continent. England and France laid hold of the Antilles and planted them with sugar cane. England and France also contended for control of the eastern seaboard of North America, disputing each other for the access routes to the Great Lakes and beyond. In the Old World, in contrast, the Europeans moved inland only rarely, as when the Portuguese penetrated Angola and when the English came into control of the Indian subcontinent. For the most part, the European sea traders in Asia and Africa preferred to seize and hold the major sea-lanes, and to tap the wealth of the continents through their control of vital ports.

At the same time, the growth of European commerce encountered its own limits and contradictions. Merchants strove to ensure their control of sources of cheap supply through a variety of monopolies and constraints on trade. They were aided in this by their rulers, who hoped to increase their own exchequers while decreasing those at the disposal of their opponents. Mercantile activity, enhanced and strengthened by the protection of the state, greatly enlarged the flow of commodities, but it remained largely within defined channels, hedged about by a carapace of privileges and prerogatives. Even where merchants had begun to mobilize artisans and cottage producers to make goods available for sale through purchasing arrangements or through the putting-out system, only rarely did they bring laborers directly into owner-supervised establishments. They preferred instead to reap the benefits of commodity circulation, while delegating the risks of production to the direct producer. Thus, as Dobb has phrased it, the "relations of economic dependence between individual producers or between producers and merchant was not directly imposed by the necessities of the act of production itself, but by circumstances external to it" (1947: 260).

Before capitalist relations could come to dominate industrial production, a set of related changes was required to guarantee the new order. The state had to be transformed from a tributary structure to a structure of support for capitalist enterprise. Tributary relationships, embodied in monopolies of all kinds, cut into the reproductive capacity of capital and had to be abrogated. The officialdom of the state apparatus had to be made responsive to the needs of capital accumulation by removing state control over productive resources and by reducing the hold of tributary overlords over the machinery of the state. At the same time, state investment had to be redirected toward the creation of an infrastructure of transportation and communication that could benefit capital without demanding excessive outlays from it. There was a need for new legal codes, protecting rights of private property and private accumulation, on the one hand, and enforcing new forms of the labor contract, on the other. State intervention had to be mobilized also to break down intra-state barriers to the movement of capital, machines, raw materials, and labor. Finally, state assistance and subsidies were often necessary to protect nascent industries against external competition, or to open up new markets abroad.

The breakthrough from mercantile domination to the capitalist mode of production was achieved in England in the second half of the eighteenth century. Spurred by capitalist investment, a series of linked inventions established the predominance of production by machine, first in textile production and later in the construction of railroads. The example of England was soon followed by other countries in Europe and America. Rising industrial production demanded raw materials and foodstuffs for the new "workshops of the world." While industrial production under capitalist auspices transformed the industrializing areas, equally powerful forces unleashed concomitant changes in the lives of people in the supply zones of the globe. The spread of the capitalist mode set in motion not only new flows of commodities but also large-scale movements of people toward the developing centers of industrial activity. The world witnessed the emergence of working classes, varying in their characteristics according to the place and time of their entry into the accumulation process. Driven by a general dynamic, capitalism yet gave rise to a variability of its own.

9 Industrial Revolution

The major vehicle for the transition to the capitalist mode of production was the textile industry of eighteenth-century England. In cloth production mercantile wealth was visibly transformed into capital, as it acquired the dual function of purchasing machines and raw materials, on the one hand, and buying human energy to power their operation, on the other. From then on, the accumulation of wealth no longer depended on the extraction of surpluses "by other than economic means," and on the marketing of surpluses by merchants. Through the purchase of machines, wealth-as-capital laid hold of technology and became proprietor of the material apparatus for the transformation of nature. By purchasing labor power, capital took command of social labor and applied it to the transformation of nature on its own terms. People had worked for wages before the installation of the capitalist mode; but now wage labor became the pivotal form of labor recruitment, and the existence of a class of laborers, necessarily dependent on wages, became the dominant factor governing the mobilization and deployment of social labor. Technology and labor power were subjected to the calculus of creating surplus value. The result was to speed up the pace of technological change and the synchronization of labor power with the requirements of technology. As Polanyi put it, "up to the end of the eighteenth century, industrial production in Western Europe was a mere accessory to commerce" (1957: 74). Now, in Marx's words, commerce became the servant of industrial production (*Cap.* III, 1967: 330, 336).

Why did this transformation happen in Europe? An answer sometimes given is that Europe was "endowed with the privilege of backwardness." Before A.D. 1000, Europe was a frontier region, marginal to the Mediterranean, to the Islamic Near East, and to the centralized states of the Orient. Political power was fragmented; power holders were weak. Relations between military-political overlords and merchants were often ambiguous and antagonistic. Lords might plunder merchants, restrict their political autonomy, or prohibit mercantile investment in land. Yet they also had a greater need for merchants to trade surpluses for strategic commodities than did the big centralized states, which could raise the gamut of needed supplies through taxation. Paradoxically, by keeping merchants from acquiring land and gaining political power, the lords of Europe also forced them to reinvest in trade, to risk their wealth in commerce rather than to invest it securely in real estate. Thus, in the interstices of weak power domains and in the intervals between them, European merchants were able to construct commercial linkages that could convert surpluses into commodities and commodities into money over wide geographic areas.

The presence of trade does not in itself lead to the emergence of the capitalist mode of production. There existed wide-ranging interarea trade in the Near East, India, and China, and even merchant-sponsored handicraft production concentrated in manufactories or dispersed in cottages in all these areas. Yet merchants in these centralized tributary polities remained strongly constrained by political rulers and dependent upon them. There might be "sprouts of capitalism," as Chinese scholars have said, but no capitalist mode of production. What is distinctive about the English case is not that merchants dealt in commodities, but that they were drawn—rapidly and irresistibly—into the realm of production.

The English Transformation

How and why did this happen, and why in England? In spite of a great deal of research, there seems as yet to be no comprehensive answer. One can, however, point to a number of possible causes for this unusual development.

In the fifteenth century, England had made the transition from raising sheep for wool to be sold abroad to the production of woolens on its own. Thereafter woolen production became England's chief manufacture. Echelons of merchants and financiers appeared in the provincial towns, drawing the product from the initial producers, supervising its processing, and speeding it on to market. The woolen trade thus gave rise to a hierarchy of commercial interests, linking London firmly with the hinterland.

Four interconnected developments followed. First, landowners increasingly turned agriculture into a business, converting land to sheep ranges, but also intensifying cultivation with new methods introduced from the continent. As Tawney put it, landowners "stood to gain much if they adapted their farming to meet the new commercial conditions. They stood to lose much if they were so conservative as to adhere to the old methods" (1967: 195).

Second, the chain of linkages between the hinterland and London not only gave rise to a multiplicity of merchant groups but also brought about a high degree of interaction and mutuality among commercial agents and tributary overlords, among merchants and landed aristocrats. In many parts of Europe, landowning nobles could not engage in trade, and merchants were barred from acquiring land. In England, merchants and landed aristocrats intermarried and interacted to an unusual degree.

Third, these merchants and landowners, in alliance, were able to turn to their advantage the peculiar status of the English "husbandmen." This status was the outcome of a characteristic paradox in English development: cultivators had won increasing freedom from tribute payments to overlords since the mid-fifteenth century, while at the the same time failing to establish freehold control over the land. By the middle of the fifteenth century, the English peasantry had won the total end of serfdom, and with it the end of labor dues and arbitrary tallages. Rent was fixed by custom, and its real value diminished as money lost its value in the course of inflation. Lords, unable to carry through a seignorial reaction that would have reinstituted and intensified serfdom, began to rationalize agricultural production through the use of financial instruments. They converted peasant land under customary tenure into leaseholds, favoring well-to-do tenants who worked the land profitably in large units. Furthermore, they burdened the peasantry with fines upon inheritance and upon confirmation of property titles. In areas where grain farming was prosperous, peasant holdings yielded to "improved" commercial agriculture. In areas where agriculture was poor and livestock keeping predominated, especially in the highlands of the North and West, the peasantry sought alternative employment in rural crafts and subsidiary activities. Thus, in some areas where peasants began to supplement their income, first by making wool cloth and later by weaving, the number of peasants paying customary rents (copyholds) even increased in the course of the sixteenth and seventeenth centuries, although on reduced holdings (Thirsk 1974). The ability to combine cultivation or herding with craft production, and—later— with wage work, also meant that couples were able to marry and produce offspring earlier than before. Yet population increases, in turn, probably fragmented landholdings further (see Tilly 1975: 404−405). There was also an increase in the number of the wholly landless. By the end of the seventeenth century, landlords held between 70 and 75 percent of the cultivable land (Brenner 1976: 63); by the 1790s the great landlords and gentry controlled 80−85 percent of the land (Mingay 1973: 25). E. L. Jones has estimated that by the end of the seventeenth century, as much as 40 percent of the English population had left the land, many going into industrial employment (quoted in Brenner 1976: 66). While "improving" landlords and their tenants thus laid the basis for a capital-intensive agriculture, it also made available to industry a labor force of mobile "free" laborers.

Fourth, successive political struggles weakened the power exercised by leading aristocrats and merchants in support of the king, giving greater freedom to the lower echelons of landholders and commercial agents in the provinces. The stage was thus set for innovative action on the local level.

The transformation of agriculture and the development of a rural population in need of full-time or part-time employment allowed merchants to extend their operations widely throughout the countryside. One way merchants expanded was by placing orders with master craftsmen in provincial towns, who then worked up the desired goods in small-scale workshops with family labor or hired hands. Another way was by entering the putting-out system, in which merchants distributed raw materials to workers to process in their own cottages, often using simple machines rented from the "putter-outer." These two systems for mobilizing labor often interdigitated, with master craftsmen engaged in one phase of the work process acting as rural factors in another. Merchants and their agents then collected the finished product and sent it to market.

Dutch and Indian Competition

This textile trade, operated under the aegis of merchant wealth, soon ran into seemingly overwhelming competition from two sources: the rival Dutch, and the artisan producers of India.

Dutch competition in the textile trade was serious. Their techniques of dying and finishing cloth were superior to those available to the English. To meet Dutch competition, the English shifted to a cheaper product. Instead of the undyed, unfinished, all-wool "old draperies" they had produced up to then, they took to the production of "new draperies"—mixtures of wool with silk, linen, or cotton—as well as lighter worsteds in which both warp and weft were of combed wool. They were able to produce these more cheaply than the Dutch, first by shifting production from urban areas into the countryside, and later by the mechanization of the textile industry. The Dutch were unable to follow suit because of prevailing high wages in both industry and agriculture (de Vries 1975: 56), and because their commerce earned much higher returns than their textile industry (see Smit 1975: 62). While Dutch labor, then, was expensive, English rural labor was cheap.

This cost advantage, however, did not operate in England's competition with the textile industry of India. India produced textiles both cheaper and technically better than any made by Europeans. Indian cottons or calicoes, so named after the city of Calicut on the Malabar coast, became the craze of Europe. Both the Dutch and the British East India companies, therefore, began to commission Indian weavers to produce calicoes for European tastes, and they began to import Indian calicoes into Europe for additional printing in European designs. Indian silks and muslins also became popular in Europe, and both companies imported them along with Indian cottons, especially from Bengal. At this point, however, the home industries resorted to political means to halt the inflow of Indian textiles. The English East India Company was

Calico printing on a wood-framed calico printing machine. Line engraving by J. Carter, c. 1835. (The Granger Collection, New York)

forbidden to import calicoes or to have then printed. At the same time, the English industry began to produce copies itself, notably fustian, a mixture of linen and cotton, which became increasingly difficult to distinguish from the Indian product. This competition in turn reinforced the mechanization of the English industry, allowing it to defeat its Asian competitors through the production of cheap machine-made cloth. At the same time, English success in using machine production to under-write "import substitution" for Asian products allowed them to stifle German and French competition around the end of the eighteenth century.

The New Entrepreneurs

As of 1760 the machines used in British cotton manufacture were still "nearly as simple as those of India" (E. Baines 1835, quoted in Rostow 1975: 126). The putting-out system through which cotton was spun and woven in innumerable cottages "evolved as an innovation in organization, without drastic change in technique" (Coleman 1973: 14). Two decades later, technological and organizational changes were in full swing. Who were the people responsible for this change?

They were not the big London merchants of Blackwell Hall, the

London cloth mart, but rather the provincial merchants and their agents or factors involved in the commercial networks of the putting-out system. These merchants and factors began to extend their supervision over the finishing stages of cloth production, its bleaching, dying, and printing, in order to obtain standardized products that could compete with cloth produced abroad. From control of finishing they moved to the production of improved yarn, either becoming producers of yarn themselves or motivating the owners of workshops to adopt new machines. We have noted that these two roles sometimes interdigitated: owners of workshops could also double as country factors for putting-out merchants. Indeed, as Chapman (1973) has shown in an analysis of the assets of a thousand textile entrepreneurs between 1730 and 1750, they were often also involved in malting, brewing, and innkeeping, in retail trade and farming, and in buying houses and real estate. These assets allowed them to accumulate some wealth and to improve their social standing, while serving as hedges against downturns in the textile market. Buildings, inns, and inn yards were easily converted into workshops and weavers' tenements, or mortgaged to obtain funds for investment. The amount of capital needed to buy the early machines and to hire labor power was initially low (between 3,000 and 5,000 pounds sterling), until the spread of Roberts's automatic mule raised costs tenfold after 1830 (Chapman 1972: 26, 30). As we shall see, when spinning became mechanized, weaving had to be transformed to keep up with the increased output of yarn. Once begun, capital expenditure in machines, raw materials, and labor power created its own operational logic, which strove to maximize surplus value through the "rational" coupling of factors of production. Thus, the very process of harnessing men to machines prompted the rise of the capitalist entrepreneur, who united in his person "the functions of capitalist, financier, works manager, merchant and salesman" (Wilson 1957: 103). Socially, this was a class of "new" men, recruited from the lower segments of the provincial middle class—"of a condition," as a contemporary put it, "between gentlemen and cottagers or peasants" (quoted in Dobb 1947: 125). From this same stratum and milieu, too, came the "engineers" and "artificers" who designed, improved, and produced the new machines, along with water wheels, steam engines, and agricultural equipment.

Initial capital for industry was largely local, raised through connections of kinship, marriage, friendship, and local acquaintance; it "did not come from institutional sources" (Perkin 1969: 80). Transactions were facilitated, however, by an instrument for granting short-term credit, the bill of exchange. The bill of exchange was a statement, sent to the debtor, of money owed for goods and services. The debtor would sign the bill to acknowledge his debt, and return it to the supplier. The supplier would endorse the bill and then use it to cover his own obligations. Toward the end of the eighteenth century, intermediaries—known as bill dealers or bill brokers—arose to facilitate and speed up these transactions. They usually dealt with the newly established country banks, forwarding bills from London to be used in industry.

Mechanization

Stocks of capital paid for machines, but the key problem in employing machinery to achieve low and competitive costs was the lack of synchronization between spinning and weaving. Spinning with the wheel was slow, while weaving was comparatively fast. The introduction of Kay's manually operated "flying shuttle" in 1733 had doubled the weaver's output by greatly increasing the speed with which the weft was thrown through the warp. Bottlenecks began to develop in the delivery of yarn to the weaving looms. Inventors thus concentrated heavily on rendering spinning more efficient and productive.

In 1770 James Hargreaves introduced the "spinning jenny," which enabled a spinner to spin several threads of fine yarn simultaneously. In 1769 Arkwright patented the water frame, which drew out the loosely twisted fibers on rollers and wound them on upright spindles in one continuous operation. In 1779 Crompton introduced his "mule," combining features of both water frame and jenny, to which steam power was applied in 1790. The new inventions produced a staggering increase in productivity. Whereas an Indian hand spinner of the eighteenth century had taken more than 50,000 hours to process 100 pounds of cotton, Crompton's mule cut the time to 2,000 hours, while power-assisted mules of around 1795 reduced this time further to 300 hours. This was also the level of performance of Arkwright's machine, which employed mostly unskilled and low-paid women and children, and which held its own in productivity until Roberts's automatic mules reduced operative time to 135 hours per 100 pounds of cotton around 1825 (Chapman 1972: 20–21). Increased productivity was also accompanied by improvement in the quality of yarn produced. This is measured by the number of hanks or skeins of fiber spun per pound of thread. It rose from 16–20 hanks spun by the hand wheel to over 300 attained by Crompton's mule at the end of the eighteenth century. The number of mule spindles thus rose from around 50,000 in 1788 to 4.6 million in 1811 (Chapman 1972: 21–22).

At the same time, mechanization also transformed the preparatory steps required by spinning. Cotton fresh from the bale had to be picked and cleaned. It had to be beaten to open the fibers, combed or brushed to disentangle them, and drawn out to lay them parallel. As these steps were brought under mechanical control, the bases were laid for coordinating the various activities required by spinning into a continuous flow of operations. In all of these machines, the application of Watt's steam engine (1764) provided the transition from manual to machine operations.

The new machines also affected the kinds of labor required to put them in motion. We have already seen that Arkwright's water frame could be operated by women and children, and it thus competed effectively with more productive machines until the turn of the century, and in some marginal areas even thereafter. The new machinery certainly increased the number of spindles that could be tended by one person. With the introduction of Roberts's automatic mule in the 1830s, one mule spinner, assisted by two or three boys, could work as many as 1,600 spindles. Mule spinning thus became a highly skilled and well-paid craft that soon had its own trade union, whose members occupied the best room in taverns—reserved by the sign "Mule Spinners Only."

Paradoxically, while spinning was mechanized, weaving remained for a long time technologically arrested. Cartwright's power loom was patented in 1785, but it did not begin to spread until forty to fifty years later, the number in use rising from 12,150 in 1820 to 85,000 in 1833. Yet the number of handloom weavers increased at the same time from 75,000 in 1795 to 250,000 in 1833 (Chapman 1972: 60). These figures bespeak several changes. First, competition with the power loom drove down wages and income earned by the handloom weavers, who rapidly lost their independence and grew increasingly impoverished and deprived (Thompson 1966: Ch. 9). This decline in wages in handloom weaving may actually have retarded the adoption of the power loom. Second, the decline in wages and status affected a population in widely scattered rural households, all the more defenseless because of this dispersion. A corollary of this, however, is that factory work in cotton actually did not become common until the 1830s. In the early 1830s the cotton handloom weavers still outnumbered all the adult workers, male and female, in the spinning and weaving mills of cotton, wool, and silk combined. Third, this new labor force manning the power looms was predominantly female and juvenile. By 1838 only 23 percent of textile factory workers were adult men (Hobsbawm 1969: 68).

The Factory

Inevitably, the dispersed organization of labor gave way to the development of a new form of productive enterprise, the factory. The idea of concentrating a large number of workers engaged in different technical operations on one site, and even in one complex of buildings, was not new. What was new, however, was the creation of such organizations under unified technical management, responsible for synchronized productive processes and for changes in production in response to changing conditions of the market. The workshops and cottages of the putting-out system had operated "in a partly immobile environment, with a fairly static technology, in the enjoyment of an actual or legal monopoly or of vast orders from non-commercial buyers, like Courts or armies" (Pollard 1965: 7).

The advent of the factory was a consequence of the limitations of the putting-out system (see Landes 1969: 55–60; Pollard 1965: 30–37; Schlumbohm 1977: 274–276). That system, in which a merchant-entrepreneur furnished the raw materials to have them processed in many small household establishments, encountered serious difficulties in sustaining and expanding the scale and scope of operations. It therefore set limits to the possible accumulation of capital. There were limits to the intensity and duration of labor where producers worked in scattered and unsupervisable economic units. This was especially true as long as industrial operations supplemented agricultural tasks, such that work in the fields could take precedence over work on spinning wheel and loom. Similarly, religious activities, kinship events, and recreation could, and did, interfere with work intensity and procedures. Furthermore, the merchant had little defense against pilfering and embezzlement of raw materials by the dispersed workers and little control over quality of output—both problems that grew increasingly serious in the course of the eighteenth century. The lack of synchronization among the different steps in the sequence of production added to the costs of transportation: when spinning was slow, the merchant-coordinator had to go in search of spinners to feed the looms; when spinning had improved through innovations, merchants had to go in search of handloom weavers. There were delays in processing and in deliveries, which slowed the turnover time of capital and left customers dissatisfied. Ever-rising large-scale trade thus encountered the limitations of a productive system divided into innumerable small workshop units, "unsupervised and unsupervisable" (Pollard 1965: 31). The answer to this contradiction was the establishment of the capitalist factory.

This new form of organizing work entailed a number of interconnected changes. First, it brought together "under one roof" as many phases of work as was feasible and profitable. Such concentration reduced the costs of supervision and transport characteristic of the putting-out system. It also increased control over the labor force, allowing the organizers of production to "subdue the refractory tempers of work-people accustomed to irregular paroxysms of diligence," as Andrew Ure, an apologist for the factory system, wrote in 1835 (1967: 16). Second, the work process became partitioned "into its essential constituents," replacing "the division of gradations of labour among artisans" (Ure 1967: 20). Third, these different phases of work came to be ranked by training and skill required, and remunerated differentially. This permitted a more efficient synchronization of work, while enhancing labor control through a division of the labor force into teams motivated by different interests. Fourth, synchronization of tasks rendered the work process continuous, maximizing the extraction of surplus value. Indeed, continuity of work became a major imperative of factory operation, as increased amounts of capital became fixed in machines. The merchant directing a putting-out system could simply halt operations when demand slackened. Under capitalist relations of production, however, depreciating machinery at rest ate directly into capital. Moreover, if machinery was not put to work when new, it might not repay its cost before becoming obsolete. The entrepreneur had become "a prisoner of his investment" (Landes 1969: 43).

The early British textile factories were faced, however, with a general unwillingness on the part of the potential laboring class to enter into factory employment. Above all, they resisted the unrelenting labor and discipline of the factories, so much at odds with earlier habits and with older customs of sociability of autonomous labor. Many early factories were modeled on penal workhouses and prisons, and indeed were manned by involuntary pauper apprentices. The identification of the factory with forced penal labor also meant that former artisans or laborers in cottage industry felt a loss of social status in moving from the relative self-determination of the cottage producer to the servitude of the industrial worker. Indeed, "as long as there was some measure of freedom of choice between cottage and factory the workman preferred the cottage" (Pollard 1965: 162). The growth of a free factory proletariat was slow, and it was resisted. Hatred of the factory system fueled, in no small part, the state of near civil war between the gentry and the common man that characterized the first part of the nineteenth century in Britain. This conflict began to abate only after mid-century, when increased stabilization of factory labor went hand in hand with a growing differentiation in the status and rewards of different positions, and factory discipline was reinforced by the spread of an ethos of work and obedience among the new working class (Pollard 1965: 186, 197; Foster 1974).

The growth of the cotton factory produced the growth of the great textile-producing centers of England. There had been great urban agglomerations before, but in the rise of the manufacturing towns of England the world witnessed a qualitative change unsurpassed in scale and speed. The great city of London, already crowded with half a million inhabitants in 1660, was not then an industrial city, but "a capital centre of trades and of distribution: of skilled craftsmen in metals and print; of clothing and furniture and fashion; of all the work connected with shipping and the market" (Williams 1973: 147). In contrast, the new industrial towns that carried forward the industrial revolution "were organized around their decisive places of work—usually a single kind of work" (Williams 1973: 154). Of these towns Manchester was both the quintessential embodiment and symbol. In 1773 it had a mere 24,000 inhabitants; by 1851—when the majority of the inhabitants of the British Isles lived in towns—its population had increased more than tenfold, to more than 250,000 people. Of these, by mid-century two out of every three inhabitants was a worker; in the nearby industrial satellite towns around Manchester this was true of nine out of ten. By that time, too, more than two-thirds of the population over twenty years of age had been born elsewhere. Of these, about 130,000 came from the surrounding counties, and some 40,000 came from Ireland. For some, the new city was "sublime as Niagara" (Carlyle), for others it was a "a new Hades" (de Tocqueville), "the entrance to hell realized" (Napier). For Friedrich Engels, it was one of the birth places of the English proletariat. People moved there "of their own free will" (1971: 135)— freed indeed to sell their labor power by the disintegration of a mode of production that had once held them fast. Now, however, they were subject to the exigencies of the capitalist mode, which threw the worker upon the labor market as a seller of labor power, only to transform his product into the very means by which the capitalist could then purchase it. Thus, the industrial cities became the sites of large labor markets in which various groups and categories—hand spinners and mule spinners, handloom weavers and power-loom operatives, men and women and children, former artisans and new immigrants—competed for available employment. These markets for labor created ongoing oppositions in turn: opposition between artisans about to be displaced by machines and the machine operatives; opposition between supervisors of production and producers; opposition between men, whose labor was more expensive, and women and children, who were remunerated at lower wages; opposition between employed and unemployed, especially during the cyclical downturns of 1826 and the 1840s; and opposition between English workers and Irish immigrants.

The conflict between English and Irish workers became especially severe with the progress of industrialization. The immigration of Irishmen into English cities grew heavy after 1800. By the 1830s Irishmen were to be found in "all of the lowest departments of manual labor" (Report on the State of the Irish Poor in Great Britain, quoted in Thompson 1966: 435). Marx wrote in 1870:

> Every industrial and commercial center in England now possesses a working class divided into two hostile camps, English proletarians and Irish proletarians. The ordinary English worker hates the Irish as a competitor who lowers his standard of life. In relation to the Irish worker he feels himself a member of the ruling nation and so turns himself into a tool of the aristocrats and capitalists of his own country against Ireland, thus strengthening their domination over himself. He cherishes religious, social and national prejudices against the Irish worker. His attitude towards him is much the same as that of the "poor whites" to the "niggers" of the former slave states of the USA. The Irishman pays him back with interest in his own money. He sees in the English worker at once the accomplice and the stupid tool of the English domination in Ireland. . . . This antagonism is the secret of the impotence of the English working class, despite their organization. [1972: 293–294]

The conflicts between English and Irish flared up occasionally during the first part of the nineteenth century, but they greatly increased in the second part. This intensification is linked to a general change in working-class politics, which shifted from a common antiestablishment Chartism during the first half of the century to greater acceptance of capitalist domination in the second. The developing trade union movement organized workers, but it also institutionalized gradations of skill, reinforced occupational hierarchies, including the supervision of female workers by males, and sought stabilization of employment and working conditions through the acceptance of upper-class educational and moral norms (see Foster 1974). At the same time, the conflicts between English workers and Irish workers intensified, fanned by anti-Catholic agitation by the Church of England, which was attempting to deny the political claims of the Irish Catholics (see Hechter 1975: 269, n.).

Cotton Exports

The production of cotton textiles thus became the major "carrier" industry of the industrial revolution under capitalist aegis in Britain. After the Napoleonic wars, says Eric Hobsbawm,

> something like *one half* of the value of *all* British exports consisted of cotton products, and at their peak (in the middle of the 1830s) raw cotton made up twenty per cent of total net imports. In a real sense the British balance of payments depended on the fortunes of this single industry, and so did much of Britain's shipping and overseas trade in general. Thirdly, it almost certainly contributed more to the accumulation of capital than other industries. [1969: 51]

Where did all that cotton go? Latin America constituted, in British eyes, one of the great untapped markets. By 1840 it absorbed 35 percent of English textile exports (Hobsbawm 1969: 147). This increase was accompanied by the spread of English trading firms in Latin America. By the second decade of the century, more than 150 such commercial houses operated in Latin America, most of them in Brazil and Argentina. Yet the market available to Latin American importers reached its limit when local domestic production proved able to compete with the British products, despite steadily falling prices for the imports. To retain a hold on the Latin American market, the British government used public funds to open credit lines for Latin American governments with British firms operating in Latin America, but this counteracted the decline in sales only in Brazil and Argentina. To compensate for losses in Latin America, British textile exporters enlarged their sales in Asia. India and China, taking only 6 percent of cotton exports after the Napoleonic wars, took 22 percent in 1840, 31 percent in 1850, and more than 50 percent after 1873. After that date, India became the main participant in this Asian trade (Hobsbawm 1969: 147).

Regions of Supply: The Cotton South

Unlike wool, which was England's first trump card in its entry into overseas commerce, and which had been produced at home, cotton had to be imported. In 1787 over half of these raw cotton imports came from

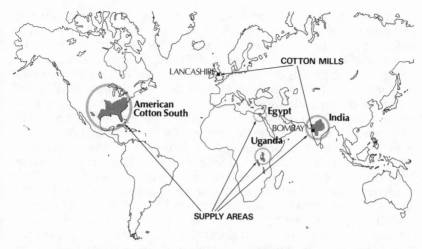

Cotton textiles in the Industrial Revolution: centers of manufacture and zones of supply.

European possessions in the West Indies. Smyrna and Turkey furnished one-quarter more. By 1807, however, more than 60 percent of all the bales that landed at London, Liverpool, and Glasgow came from England's former colony, the United States (North 1961: 41), and the United States remained the main source of English cotton thereafter. The cotton crop, in turn, became "the most important proximate cause of expansion" in the U.S. economy after 1815 (North 1961: 68). It constituted in the period between 1815 and 1860 more than half of the total value of domestic exports.

Just as spinning and weaving in England were facilitated by the technological coupling of the steam engine with spinning jennies and power looms, so cotton production in the American South was rendered possible by a machine, in this case Eli Whitney's cotton gin. Initial British demand was for Sea Island cotton, introduced to the Georgia–Carolina coast from the Bahamas in 1786. With this cotton, fibers were easily separated from the seeds by squeezing them through rollers, but restrictive climatic prerequisites kept production low. Most American cotton exported was therefore second-grade "middling Uplands." Whitney's gin, which allowed the seed to be separated easily from the sticky fibers, soon allowed a man to clean fifty pounds of Uplands in the time it had previously taken him to clean only one pound.

Cotton-growing enterprises, based on the use of slave labor, were highly organized, labor-intensive units of production. As the plantation moved westward, there was a shift from tobacco and grain growing to cotton production. This involved a growth in scale and thus an increase in the number of slaves. Only a minority of slave owners were able to keep up with this development. Most specialized cotton production came to be carried on on estates of 30 slaves or more. In the decade before the war between the Union and the Confederacy, the minimum number of slaves on an efficiently producing plantation was about 50 on the black-belt soils of Alabama and Texas, and more than 200 in the alluvial lands of the Mississippi flood plain. High intensity of labor was achieved through the assignment of labor gangs to successive specific tasks within the cycle of cultivation, in a rhythm reminiscent of industrial production. The ultimate sanction for the discipline required in these operations was, of course, force, exercised by drivers and overseers. Force was crucial to the system, for, as Fogel and Engerman (1974: 238) say, "available evidence shows that the application of force made it possible to obtain labor from slaves at less than half the price that would have had to have been offered in the absence of force."

Cotton growing with slave labor was profitable business. On the average, slave owners earned about 10 percent on the market price of their slaves, which compares favorably with the returns earned by the most successful textile firms in New England around the middle of the nineteenth century (Fogel and Engerman 1974: 70). At the same time, it must be remembered that there were many white families who owned no slaves at all, and even among slave holders almost half owned less than five slaves at a time (Bruchey 1967: 165).

Growing cotton was not the cause of slavery in the United States, but it proved an important factor in the continuance of slavery well into the nineteenth century. Underlying this continuance of slavery was the steady demand, mostly English, for cotton. From a total output of 3,000 bales of cotton in 1790, American cotton production rose to 178,000 bales in 1810, to 732,000 in 1830, and to 4,500,000 in 1860 (Fogel and Engerman 1974: 44). This growth of production was accompanied by a spread of cotton growing in space, as cotton production moved westward from the Atlantic seaboard into the Deep South along a climatic belt in which there was the minimal 200 frostless days and the amount of rainfall required by the cotton crop. The spread of cotton growing was paced by the steady advance of transportation by steamboat and railroad, which brought even more distant areas into contact with the major ports of embarkation. This expansion involved a massive relocation of people. Between 1790 and 1860, 835,000 slaves were moved—mostly from Maryland, Virginia, and the Carolinas toward Alabama, Mississippi, Louisiana, and Texas. More than two-thirds of these slaves moved between 1830 and 1860 in one of the greatest forced migrations of all times.

This slave population in North America was largely self-reproducing, in contrast to the slave populations of the West Indies. As early as 1680, Blacks born in the United States colonies made up a majority of the slave population. By the end of the American War of Independence, native-born slaves outnumbered slaves born in Africa by four to one. By 1860 all but 1 percent of slaves were native born, many of them descended from other native-born slaves in the third or fourth generation. This stands in marked contrast to the West Indies and to Brazil, where the slave population had to be replenished by continuous imports. "Of all the slave societies in the New World," says Eugene Genovese (1972: 5), "that of the Old South alone maintained a slave force that reproduced itself." The reasons for this are not wholly clear. The thesis that slaves were systematically bred for sale is called into question by research into plantation records (see Fogel and Engerman 1974: 78–86). It has been suggested that yellow fever killed off slaves in the tropical West Indies, but not on the more salubrious continent; but this would carry conviction only if the total epidemiological environment of the two areas were compared. Gutman (1976: 341–343) has pinpointed the decades immediately following 1720 as crucial in the continental shift from a West Indian-like pattern of slave mortality to self-perpetuating reproduction, and he has suggested that family formation and emerging kin networks among North American slaves played a major role in supporting further growth.

Whatever the reasons for the sustained reproduction of slaves in the United States, it follows that this population would develop its own store of experience and modes of coping, and would pass it on across the generations. Recent research (see, notably, Gutman 1976) has shown how networks of kin and fictive kin developed and functioned among the slaves, and how they were used to transmit and elaborate knowledge and beliefs based on the slave experience rather than on the requirements of the masters.

The existence of such networks, linking generations of kin and quasi-kin in space and time, also calls into question the image of the slave as a human being perfectly socialized in the patriarchal ideology of his master. Slaves learned to cope with their masters, but there is no evidence that they passively internalized the master's command as their own psychic reward. It is unlikely that force could ever be used "optimally" in such a system of labor to achieve the largest product at the lowest cost, as Fogel and Engerman have suggested (1974: 232). What was at issue between masters and slaves was not the careful calibration of "treatment" to obtain "optimal submission," but a complex and changing relationship between two classes held together by command and labor but differentiated by class organization and interest. Gutman, indeed, has suggested that "the presence of kin and quasi-kin networks within slave communities over the entire South in the 1840s and the 1850s is an important reason why the slave system remained harsh and coercive" (1976: 325). Yet within these constraints, day-to-day relationships had to be renegotiated continuously. As George Rawick (1972: 62) has said, "The relationship was a highly problematic one and required the constant creation and recreation of a day-to-day etiquette in order to help humanize social relationships that were hierarchical and based on naked power."

The Southern plantation thus involved a double tier of relationships:

the hierarchical relationships of the Big House and its slaves, and the horizontal ties of the Black community that extended beyond the plantation. The plantation unit typically comprised an overseer, usually white; drivers, usually black; slave artisans in large numbers and often highly skilled; and field hands. There were also slave house servants, although the distinction between them and the field hands might, more often than not, represent a stage in the life cycle rather than an absolute barrier—servants being drawn from the young and old, while field hands were recruited from the able-bodied young and middle-aged. There were also free Blacks, numbering about half a million in 1860, mostly concentrated in Maryland, Virginia, the Carolinas, and Louisiana. These people sometimes worked as craftsmen and laborers, especially in Louisiana, though elsewhere they were regarded with ambivalence by the plantation owners. Conversely, in the towns, slaves were often rented out for work elsewhere.

Brokers

The slaves, drivers, overseer, and owner of a plantation were only links in a chain, which also included the intermediaries who forwarded the cotton crop to its destination, and the merchants who speeded it on its

Slaves loading cotton by torchlight on the Alabama River. Engraving by W. Floyd, 1842. (Courtesy of The New York Historical Society, New York City)

way. Cotton flowed outward from the Southern states in return for credit and goods bought with credit, which flowed inward. The principal agent managing this double flow in return for a commission on sales was the factor. There were factors stationed in coastal ports, like Savanna and Charleston, and inland factors in towns such as Fayetteville, Columbia, Augusta, Macon, Atlanta, Montgomery, Nashville, Memphis, and Shreveport. These inland factors dealt directly with the larger planters, reaching the smaller planters through storekeepers in the hinterland who passed on credit in the form of advances and who received cotton. Transactions were further assisted by banks that discounted the notes of planters endorsed by their factors. As credit flowed in, cotton flowed out. Storekeepers or planters passed the cotton on to the inland factors, who negotiated with coastal factors for transshipment to Europe. Until the end of the Napoleonic wars in 1815, most of the cotton left for Liverpool from Savanna and Charleston. After that date Baltimore and, especially, New York became the main ports of transshipment across the Atlantic.

New York owed its ascendancy over the Southern cotton trade to a number of causes. In 1816 a group of entrepreneurs—most of of them Quakers connected by ties of marriage—established the Black Ball Line, which soon operated regular packet services to Europe and along the American coast. This trade began to carry cotton from Southern ports and from New York to Liverpool, returning from Europe with English manufactured goods and European immigrants. European and Northern manufactured goods would then be sent on to the South (Albion 1939). The strategic role of New York in this triangular trade was reinforced when Western grain, meat, and timber began to flow eastward over the newly completed Erie Canal, with manufactured goods, native and foreign, traveling from east to west. Another factor in the growing prominence of New York lay in the establishment there of rules prohibiting the withdrawal of goods offered for sale when bids ran low. Consequently, the city increasingly attracted buyers in search of bargains. These multiple commercial transactions, in turn, were facilitated by the development of profitable banking institutions. Finally, many cotton factors operating in the South were either New Yorkers themselves or agents of New York firms. Much of the credit advanced to Southern planters came from New York, on a scale exceeding that which Southern business houses could provide (Foner 1941: 12).

Most of the manufactured goods used in the South were supplied by the Northeast, made either at home or imported from abroad. After the end of the Napoleonic wars, the Northeast also began to employ a share of the Southern cotton in its own growing textile industry. The numbers of spindles in the region tripled between 1815 and 1831, and tripled once again between 1831 and 1860 (North 1961: 160). It was the expanding West that supplied ever larger quantities of food for the South, especially after 1816 when steamboats began to travel on the

Mississippi River. Western food also flowed increasingly northeastward with the opening of the Ohio, Erie, and Pennsylvania canals in the 1820s and 1830s. With the construction of the east-west railroads in the 1850s, largely financed by British money, Chicago became the grain elevator and "hog-butcher" of the United States. The regions composing the United States thus grew increasingly specialized and complementary in their specialization; yet within this network of interdependencies the South was clearly at a disadvantage. As soon as profits accumulated in the hands of the plantation owners, the new wealth flowed out again to pay for foodstuffs for the poorly provided estates, and to import manufactured goods—cloth and ironmongers' stock for the slaves, luxury goods for their owners.

Indian Removal

The westward expansion seemed the "American dream" come true. There appeared to be land for the taking in the North American wilderness, and agrarian democrats like Jefferson looked forward to a nation of sturdy yeomen, servants to no man through their possession of land. But, of course, this was not "a land without people for a people without land." Land was occupied and used by native American populations; and to make yeomen, these natives had first to be dispossessed. To the new settlers, land was valued for more than the crops and livestock it could sustain. Land was "the nation's most sought after commodity in the first half-century of the republic" (Rohrbough 1968: xii),its "major investment opportunity" (Rogin 1975: 81).

The major Indian political units in the Southeast were the Cherokees, in what is now Alabama, Georgia, North Carolina, and Tennessee; the Creeks, in present-day Alabama and Georgia; and the Choctaw, in Mississippi. The less numerous Chickasaw inhabited northern Mississippi, and the Seminole southern Florida. All these groups were horticulturists (with cultivation in the hands of women) as well as hunters, firmly settled upon their land and hunting ranges and unwilling to yield them to newcomers. The basic unit was the village, whose population was between 350 and 600 among the Cherokee, between 100 and as many as 1,000 among the Creek. Villages were autonomous, each with a complement of matrilineal clans, a council of elders drawn from the matrilineages, and a village chief, usually drawn from a particular matrilineage. Since clans were nonlocal and crosscut villages, there existed a mechanism for possible alliances; and in the early eighteenth century, both among the Cherokee and the Creek, villages began to form themselves into confederations. Under European pressure, often transmitted through Indian allies of the French, English, or Spanish, these confederations became increasingly centralized. Especially instrumental in this centralization was the need for defense against the expansionist Carolina colony, which raided far and wide for slaves. At the same time, relations with Europeans led to the adoption of many

European forms, including crops and livestock, as well as firearms. Some important chiefs came to be owners of cotton plantations, often worked with African slaves bought from the Europeans. A native elite developed in the late eighteenth and early nineteenth centuries. It intermarried with Europeans and was often Christianized. In the case of the Cherokee, the elite also became literate; the Cherokee script was developed in the early nineteenth century by Sequoya, who adopted the concept of writing without being literate in English (Kroeber 1948: 369).

These tribes—especially the Creek and the Choctaw—stood in the way of the expanding frontier and its primary interest, the acquisition of land for the cultivation of cotton. War with the Creek in 1813–1814 opened the first breach through which white planters moved into Alabama in the wake of rising cotton prices after the war between England and the United States in 1812. The war that Andrew Jackson conducted in 1817–1818 against the Seminoles, a Creek population that had filtered down the peninsula of Florida, not only added Florida to the United States but also closed off a sanctuary where many runaway black slaves found refuge among the native Americans.

By 1817 the idea of removing all Indians to the area west of the Mississippi—an idea already advocated by Jefferson—took hold. Under the prompting of Jackson, Indians were given the alternative of either accepting their land in commercially alienable individual allotments or of moving altogether. The campaign for removal was accompanied by a wave of intrusions into Indian lands, usually carried on with covert official support. Indian land, stock, and improvements were seized; game was killed off; Indian hunters were attacked for hunting within state lines. Indians were bribed to sell their land, and land titles were obtained through fraud. State laws were invoked to harass Indians living within their boundaries. Government agents were planted among the Indians to advocate removal, while Indian chiefs were coopted with gifts and grants of annuities to speak in favor of the policy. Missionaries and other Whites living among the Indians and opposed to removal were ordered to leave.

Removal itself was signed into law in 1830. Where Indian groups did not depart voluntarily, the army was sent in to enforce the removal order. Between 1820 and 1840, three-fourths of the 125,000 Indians living east of the Mississippi came under government removal programs; during the same period, between one-fourth and one-third of all Southern Indians lost their lives. By 1844 less than 30,000 Indians remained in the eastern United States, most of them located around Lake Superior. The entire process of forced migration was accompanied by paeans extolling the victory of civilization over savagery. The successful conclusion of the operation realized Jackson's hope that Indian land could be speedily brought "into market" (quoted in Rogin 1975: 174).

Regions of Supply: Egypt

The English textile industry imported its cotton not only from the American South but also from the eastern Mediterranean. The Levant had long raised cotton for sale in Europe, and in the nineteenth century Egypt became an important producer of cotton fibers for the European market. This Egyptian development holds a double interest. Egypt was one of the first regions of the Ottoman polity to commit itself to commercial ties with the West, and—in doing so—it became the first case of a non-European state attempting to "catch up" with the industrialization and commercialization of Europe.

This twin effort required, first, a wholesale transformation of prior political and economic relations. During the eighteenth century, power in Egypt was wielded by *mamluk*, a Turkish-Circassian elite of military bondsmen and tribute takers who bought from the Ottoman superstate the right to exact tribute from the cultivating peasantry. Egypt had entertained a lively transit trade with Europe in Yemeni coffee, but this decreased sharply toward the end of the century. The decline led to a proportionate increase in the tribute imposed on the long-suffering peasantry. Competition among the military tribute takers for power and resources further increased the burden of tribute. Still, the peasant villages managed to defend their autonomous jurisdictions over communal tenures and land transfers, and they were left free to grow whatever crops they pleased, as long as the appropriate tribute was forwarded to the mamluks by the village headmen.

This distribution of political and economic forces was altered drastically in 1803 with the advent to power of Mehemet Ali, nephew of an Ottoman vice-governor from Albania. He had grown wealthy in his homeland in the tobacco trade, and he had played an important role in leading a contingent of Albanian troops during the ousting of the French from Egypt. Mehemet Ali not only asserted his autonomy from the Ottoman polity but he broke the power of the mamluk by killing the lot of them. Although Mehemet Ali regarded Egypt as his private family domain rather than as a public trust, he recognized the need for political and economic change to meet foreign competition. Consequently, he initiated in the 1820s a program to decrease the production of grain for domestic subsistence and to increase production of the one crop that could be exported, long-staple cotton. He also launched an attempt to build industry, especially to enhance his military capability, and created an army of peasant draftees to replace his unreliable Albanian contingent. In these efforts he had the assistance of Europe's first "technocrats," the French Utopian socialist Saint-Simonians. As part of this aid, the Suez Canal was constructed under the guidance of the Saint-Simonian de Lesseps; it was completed in 1869. Peasants were also drafted in large numbers to build irrigation works and canals in order to create the hydraulic infrastructure required for cotton cultivation.

Under Mehemet Ali and his successors, peasant autonomy in growing subsistence crops was sharply curtailed in favor of mandatory cotton deliveries and forced corvées, and peasant lands were turned over to large landowners who increased cotton production. Among these land-owners was, of course, the royal family itself. Between 1818 and 1844, the land in the hands of the peasantry diminished from 85–90 percent of the total land area to 56 percent. Foreign loans incurred by the development-oriented regime led to further increases in tribute pay-ments demanded by the state, which led in turn to an ever-increasing emphasis on cotton production by laborers on large estates, as well as by sharecroppers and small owners striving to keep up with tax payments. In the process, village headmen also gained in power, both as inter-mediaries between the peasantry and the state and as moneylenders. As a result, their holdings also grew. Rising internal unrest and rebellion, coupled with the increasing inability of the state to meet its foreign debts, finally brought on foreign intervention to put down an anti-foreign military revolt. In 1882 the British took over Egypt. They rein-forced the pattern of cotton growing on large estates, thus laying the basis for the problems that were to plague Egypt in the twentieth century.

The Indian Textile Industry

In the Asian provinces of the British Empire, industrial production of textiles began to develop in the second part of the nineteenth century. This development was not an outgrowth of the highly developed Indian textile crafts of the early period of European expansion into Asia. The handicraft industry was largely destroyed by English imports into India of machine-made cloth and yarn, so that by 1840 the head of a major English firm trading in India could refer to *bandannas*, hand-printed silk handkerchiefs, as "the last of the expiring manufactures of India" (quoted in Thorner and Thorner 1962: 71). Moreover, Indian raw cotton was not favored in the English market, except when American cotton supplies were cut off; a short-staple variety, it was harder to clean and required greater attention, and hence higher labor costs, than the American long-staple varieties. Indian raw cotton, however, consti-tuted one of the major items of English exports to China. Hence cotton acreage in India expanded until there were more than 8 million acres under cotton by 1850. About half of this acreage lay in western India, within reach of the developing city of Bombay (Guha 1972, 1973). Bombay agency houses and traders, working through middlemen, ad-vanced money for cultivation to landlords in the provinces, and concen-trated the product for local use or export. The need to transport large quantities of cotton produced a "bullock cart revolution" (Guha 1972: 21), in which carts drawn by two bullocks multiplied more than sixfold the amount that could be carried by a single animal. Aided thereafter by the expansion of the Indian railroad network, cotton production came to cover 17 million acres in the last decade of the nineteenth century (Guha 1973).

The initial growth of the Indian machine-textile industry, like the expansion of cotton acreage on the subcontinent, must be understood in terms of India's role as a major English base of commerce with China. Cotton yarn and manufactures were second only to opium in items sent to China, and they were the most important after the trade in opium declined (Latham 1978: 88–90). Participation by Indian merchants in the opium and cotton trades laid the basis for the Indian fortunes that were invested in the development of the textile industry, the only industry in India that "owed its birth and development to the initiative of domestic capital and domestic entrepreneurship" (Saini 1971: 98). This autonomous development was possible because India acted as a relay station in the extraction of surpluses from China. The industry expanded until it met Japanese competition for the China market at the end of the nineteenth century. Even then the Indian textile industry continued to supply a significant proportion of the yarn employed by Japanese factories.

Bombay

The center of this new textile industry was Bombay. Originally a small settlement on one of seven islands, named after a goddess of local fishermen, it was transferred to the British Crown in 1665. In attracting settlers to the town, the English governor followed the Indian pattern of negotiating contracts between ruler and serving castes. Although its importance as a trading port was at first overshadowed by Surat and Broach, termini of the trade with the Levant, Bombay soon gained in commercial importance with the settlement of merchants from Diu and Surat and with the growth of a colony of Parsi. These were Zoroastrian artisans, merchants, and shipbuilders originally from Iran who soon enlarged their share in the lucrative trade to the east. Bombay's population increased from its initial 10,000 inhabitants to between 160,000 and 180,000 in the second decade of the nineteenth century (Morris 1965; Rowe 1973).

By 1800 Bombay had become the major port of western India, exporting opium and raw cotton to China, and importing sugar and metal goods. By mid-century it grew into the major distributing point for British manufactures in Asia, and the chief entrepot for the transshipment of raw short-staple cotton to Europe. Railroad construction after mid-century enhanced still further Bombay's role as the hub of cotton transshipment from Gujarat and Nagpur. Expectably, Indian cotton exports boomed as American supplies were cut off during the War between the States.

It was by mid-century, too, that the city became the center of the Indian cotton textile industry. The first mill, using English technology but financed by Indian—mostly Parsi—capital, went into production in 1856. At first producing only yarn, but soon engaging in weaving as well, the number of mills increased to 86 by 1900. Correspondingly, the number of laborers in the mills rose from 6,600 in 1865 to 80,000 in 1900, between a fifth and a fourth of them women.

Although Indian capital participated strongly in the founding of these mills, managerial control lay in the hands of managing agencies. Managing agents, who usually began as traders, held strategic shares in joint-stock companies and interlocking directorships within a number of different industries. They played a vital and often speculative role in developing the resources that India used to pay for foreign imports. The cotton textile industry was only one of these endeavors, and it was often "treated as a milch cow to be drained of profits" (Morris 1965: 34) to the benefit of other enterprises operated by the agencies.

Within each mill the administrative and technical staff were at first British, but soon Indians were recruited. The key figure in the organization of the mill was the "jobber," a kind of foreman charged with recruiting and supervising unskilled laborers. He wielded a great deal of power. Selecting new laborers from the shape-up at the mill gate, he could favor relatives and caste members from his village or region, unless dissuaded by an emolument or, later, kickbacks. Since he was charged with maintaining work discipline, his say in who could stay and who must go constituted another source of revenue, and often speeded up labor turnovers. At the same time, he lent money at interest to the workers, and sold them goods on commission from interested merchants. Though technically not a labor contractor, he in fact played an important role in organizing the labor market through personal ties with his followers. One surmises that preference in employment was often given to members of his own lineage or caste segment.

There was no occupational specialization by caste in the mills, with one major exception. Untouchables, constituting less than 10 percent of the labor force, were generally relegated to the performance of menial tasks. They were barred altogether from weaving, the fastest-growing and highest-paid department, on the pretext that if Untouchables sucked the yarn onto the shuttle when replacing a weft bobbin, they would pollute their ritually superior fellow workers (Morris 1965: 79).

During the nineteenth century, most laborers in the Bombay mills came from a distance of 100 to 200 miles away, from the Konkan district and the Deccan plateau south and east of Bombay. In the twentieth century, there was a marked increase of immigrant laborers from Uttar Pradesh in the north, more than 750 miles away. William Rowe, who studied such northern migrants in the 1950s, suggests that they were first recruited among Muslim cotton-carding and weaving castes (1973: 222). They settled in Bombay by place of origin and caste. In the mid-1950s such residence clusters were formed by consanguineals, but they included affines from the same caste as well. Fictive kinship, making use of the term *village brother (goan bhai)*, further strengthened the solidarity of the cluster. Clusters also had headmen who knew the city and who acted as authorities within the clusters and as representatives to the groups outside. At the same time, residential groups of higher caste status had wider kinship connections and used them to find better and better-paying jobs.

Indian textile production, with markets located mostly in Asia, represents an early example of industrial proliferation on the "periphery" of the growing industrial capitalist system. Hampered by English import duties, excise taxes, and capital exports from India, textiles nevertheless represent the one economic area in which native capital predominated. Although production expanded at first, its rate of growth began to fluctuate and to stabilize at low levels after 1890. The value of Indian textile exports, consisting mainly of yarn, fell almost by half between its high point at the end of the nineteenth century and the second decade of the twentieth. The reason for this decline was foreign competition, resulting in the loss of both the Japanese and the Chinese markets to Japan, which initiated its own textile industry after the Meiji Restoration in 1869. The Indian industry then shifted toward the production of cloth for the home market, even importing Japanese yarn after World War I (Saini 1971).

Within India, the development of the textile industry affected, in turn, the areas within which it was located. We have already seen how it gave rise to an Indian laboring class of textile workers. It also provided a stimulus to expand the acreage under cotton in India, especially in Bombay-Sind, Berar, and Hyderabad (Guha 1973), with Bombay agency houses extending credit in return for the crop. When additional cotton acreage was required, much cotton was obtained from other British possessions, especially Uganda. There the Uganda Agreement of 1900 converted lineage and clan lands to heritable freehold tenure, with the result that much of the land was monopolized by a class of about 1,000 chiefs and notables, who employed their clan brothers as share tenants in the raising of cotton (Mair 1934; Apter 1961: 122–123).

Thus, after an earlier period of political and economic destruction of much of the Indian hand-weaving artisan population, the expansion of the British Empire and its trade, notably to the East, permitted the secondary growth of a machine-based Indian textile industry with its own base of supply and labor. Even though this industrial growth was not sustained, it furnishes an early case of capitalist industrialization on the periphery, a process that greatly accelerated in the twentieth century.

Crisis and Renewed Expansion

It was in England that capitalists first took "the really revolutionary road" of transforming the means of production, and they did so in the production of cotton textiles. We have traced the development of this "carrier industry" and its impact on extra-European areas of supply, chiefly in the South of the United States and in Egypt. Yet one must keep in mind that this first launching, important though it was in spurring the economy of England and in portents for the future, was relatively modest in scale. The textile industry was only one among many industries, and the capital demanded for the construction and operation of new mills was within reach of entrepreneurs of quite modest means. At the same time, it was primarily a consumer goods industry, though it created a demand for new machines in turn. Its first success was based on rising profits, realized with relatively cheap artisan-built machinery and decreasing labor costs.

The English textile industry had seemed securely on its way when, in the second quarter of the nineteenth century, it suddenly experienced a downturn, one of the first great "structural" crises of the capitalist mode. This may have been partly the result of rising costs of machinery, causing the rate of profit to level off. It may have been in part a "realization" crisis, since low wages at home diminished the domestic market, while foreign markets seemed saturated. Whatever the reason, the period between 1826 and 1847–1848 was a period of contraction. It was accompanied, in England, by major political upheavals, as a rising tide of discontent erupted in radical agitation. This was also a time when increased numbers of migrants from the British Isles began to seek alternative homes and employment abroad (see chapter 12).

Railroad Construction

To restart the money-making engine required new infusions of capital and the development of a new industry, one capable of restoring the rate of accumulation and of tapping new markets. This industry was railroad building, with its twin satellites of steel production and coal mining. The construction of railroads had, as Dobb noted (1947: 296), "the inestimable advantage for Capitalism of being enormously capital-absorbing; in which respect they are only surpassed by the armaments of modern warfare and scarcely equalled by modern urban building."

This industry, too, had its origin in England, where the first railroad linked the Durham coal fields with the coast in 1825. At the same time, the new invention quickly spread abroad. In 1827 the Baltimore and Ohio Company received a charter for a railroad, completing seventy miles of track five years later. The inception and rapid growth of railroading in the United States was greatly affected by the infusion of English capital into American development. Its most spectacular product was the construction of the Erie Canal, begun in 1817 and completed in 1825. It linked New York with Buffalo, and through Buffalo with the West, thus making New York City the great terminus and entrepot of western trade. American railroad building was a direct consequence of this success. Other states, not to be outdone, invited English capital to finance canal building and railroad construction. English investors held at least $200 million in American securities by 1836, when the boom ended in a financial bust so complete that "the trade of three continents dwindled by a half" (Jenks 1973: 98). The inability of the American Republic to pay interest on the loans incurred "caused American stocks to join those of Portugal and Mexico and Greece in the ghettoes of finance" (Jenks 1973: 99).

By this time, however, railroad building in Britain itself offered alternative opportunities for investment. When the effects of the American bust hit England, it was discovered that the railroads built there by provincial capitalists in the 1830s were doing well and paying dividends in the 1840s. The ensuing railroad boom soon absorbed more than 60 million pounds seeking investment. Capitalization for British domestic railroads more than tripled between 1844 and 1849; railroad mileage increased nearly threefold. Steel production rose concomitantly. As "elderly men and women of small realized fortunes, tradesmen of every order, pensioners, public functionaries, professional men, merchants, country gentlemen" (Thomas Tooke, quoted in Jenks 1973: 132) poured their funds into railroad construction, the renewed upturn of the economy also silenced the mutterings of social revolt.

Railroading thus sponsored the second phase of the industrial revolution, shifting production from major reliance on cotton textiles to reliance on iron and steel. We are so accustomed to thinking of industry in terms of "heavy" industry that we may find it strange to be told by Fernand Braudel that until the beginning of the nineteenth century iron was a "poor relation" (1973b: 275–277). Before this time, metallurgical industries were important primarily in making war, flourishing when there was warfare and languishing in times of peace. In the sixteenth century, England lagged behind such iron-producing areas as the Basque country, Styria, Liège, France, Germany, and Sweden. In 1539 it produced only 6,000 tons. On the eve of the English Civil War in 1640, English production rose to 75,000 tons of iron, but in 1788 it again was only 68,000 tons.

Then, in the nineteenth century, came the great leap forward. Some of its prerequisites were technological. The big increase in production required fuel and power converters to turn heat into energy. Short of timber to provide charcoal, England turned to coal for fuel. Moreover, English ores were low grade and required power to rid them of impurities through smelting, puddling, and rolling. To furnish the power for these operations, innovators adapted the pumps used to clear flooded mines. Thereafter, the use of coal and iron turned England into the "workshop of the world."

The driving force of this transformation was the railroad. Railroad construction rose from 45,000 miles in 1840—of which 17,000 were located in Europe and 28,000 in North America—to more than 228,000 miles worldwide forty years later (Hobsbawm 1975: 54). Much of this construction was undertaken because

> organizations needed work, ironmasters orders, bankers and business organizers a project to work upon. And railway building became a service which Great Britain could dump abroad when her financial and constructing plant could not be kept employed at home. [Jenks 1973: 133–134]

British iron production reached 2.5 million tons at mid-century. British exports of railroad iron and steel more than tripled between 1845 and 1875, while exports of machinery increased more than ten times (Hobsbawm 1975: 40, 39). Financed by railway "kings" and organized by contractors, "the shocktroops of industrialization" (Hobsbawm 1975: 39) fanned out abroad to build railroads from Argentina to the Punjab. Some of this railroad building represented mere "conspicuous production," but much of it provided the infrastructure of transportation that would permit a vast increase in the transfer of goods from the sites of production overland to points of transshipment on the coast. An important aspect of this expanding movement of goods was the decline of overland freight rates, amounting in the last quarter of the nineteenth century to a decrease of more than 90 percent (Bairoch 1975: 115–119).

Shipping

Costs of ocean freight also fell dramatically in the course of the century, almost as much as the decline in overland rates. Technologically, this was made possible by improvements in sailing vessels, notably the development of the sharp-bowed, narrow-beamed American clipper ships. To these ships—Baltimore clippers, opium clippers, and tea clippers—American naval development owed much of its ascendancy in the first half of the nineteenth century. In the second part of the century, however, the British again regained naval hegemony by building clippers better adapted than their American counterparts to freighting a variety of products. In 1853 these were built with iron hulls; by 1864, with hulls of steel. Such sailing ships with metal hulls had a carrying capacity of 1,500 to 2,000 tons, making them competitive for a while with the more costly steamship.

In the end, however, the steamship won out over the sailing vessel because it possessed greater tonnage and speed. The decisive step in securing this victory was the introduction of steel boilers, which permitted the development of higher pressures and hence greater power. Whereas it took the average clipper ship of approximately 1,000 tons of cargo capacity between 120 and 130 days to make the journey from the south coast of China to London, the steamships of the Blue Funnel Line with a capacity of 3,000 tons, launched in 1865, negotiated the voyage in 77 days (Hyde 1973: 22). The steamship, first introduced in Atlantic crossings, conquered the Atlantic in the 1840s and 1850s. The use of steam-powered vessels in Asian seas was greatly encouraged by the opening of the Suez Canal in 1869. Clipper ships, however, did not disappear from the Asian seas until the last quarter of the nineteenth century. The final victory of steam over sail occurred only during the Great Depression of 1873–1894, when an overabundance of tonnage provoked a crisis of overproduction in naval craft (A. Lacroix, cited in Toussaint 1966: 212).

Construction of the Suez Canal finally cut travel time from England to eastern Asia in half. A railroad across the isthmus was begun in 1851, and in 1854 a concession for building the canal was granted to a French consortium by developing Egypt (see p. 286). France subscribed one-third of the cost and the Egyptian ruler (*khedive*) another third, with the rest of the shares intended to be sold in other countries. This last third never found buyers, and the canal had to be refinanced through private European financiers. The canal was completed in 1869, with the labor of 20,000 conscripted Egyptian fellaheen. Yet the cost of the canal and other development projects, parlayed into ever larger loans at ever higher interest rates on the advice of financial experts (see Jenks 1973: Chap. 10), eventually bankrupted the Egyptian treasury. In 1874 the British government acquired a majority of shares in the Suez Canal Company through an arrangement with the Rothschild bank, which advanced the needed money. The crushing debt imposed on Egypt put the country under financial receivership to the Anglo-French Treasury of Public Debt and committed it to annual repayments of interest thereafter. The debt was ultimately paid by the Egyptian fellaheen. When a section of the Egyptian military, supported by village sheiks, rose in revolt against the rulers who had led the country into such complete dependence on external capital, the British intervened and imposed unilateral control.

An attempt to build a western counterpart to the Suez Canal across the Isthmus of Panama began in 1879, ten years after the completion of the Suez project, again under a French company headed by the same de Lesseps. Work on the canal was initiated in 1881, primarily with Jamaican labor, but technical difficulties brought the undertaking to a halt in 1888. The project was not resumed until 1903, when the United States encouraged Panama to break away from Colombia, and received rights to the ten-mile-wide isthmus in return for a down payment in gold and annual payments "in like coin." In 1904 the United States purchased the rights to the canal from the French company; the completed canal was opened to oceangoing ships ten years later.

The growth of the English textile industry initiated a social order built upon a new mode of production. Under the governing relations of this mode, capitalists bought machines and hired laborers to set them in motion, while a new population of laborers submitted to the discipline of factory work in exchange for wages. Control of the means of production enabled capital to call up machines and labor power as required, and to arrange and rearrange them in the service of enhanced profitability. At the same time, capital could halt machines and lay off manpower in regions of low profitability, and recommence production in other regions promising higher returns. Under the conditions of the new mode, capital was able to embark on a process of continuous internal and international migration, drawing ever more groups of people into its orbit and reproducing its strategic relationships wherever and whenever it took root.

Historically, such large-scale coupling of capital with wage-dependent labor is unusual enough to lead one to ask how "free" labor ever came to develop at all. Why free labor, and not one or another form of servitude? Englishmen, like other Europeans, were familiar with penal servitude, forced employment of vagrants, pauper apprenticeships, mandatory labor in workhouses, and indenture, and could have employed any or all of these coercive mechanisms in recruiting workers for the incipient factories. The first factory masters, however, found a supply of unemployed laborers, created historically by the enclosure and clearances of land, and by the growing size of cottage families working in the putting-out system. Aided by this unusual conjuncture of factors, the English textile industry was able to employ free labor in overcoming Dutch and Indian competition.

The new industries required not merely labor power and machines but raw materials as well, and extensive regions of the world were reorganized to supply these materials to the factories. These efforts produced new regimes of labor, or greatly intensified the demands on labor in already existing systems. To feed the factories of Lancashire, slave plantations displaced native populations in the American South, while the growing demand for cotton burdened the slaves with ever-increasing exactions. In Egypt, peasant production yielded to cotton-growing large estates. To furnish cotton to the Bombay mills, millions of acres formerly in food crops were given over to cotton in western India.

When capital began to move from the manufacture of textiles into railroads, areas of raw-material supply were opened up to support the new combinations of men and machines created by the railroad era. The construction of railroads, in turn, and the development of shipping widened the area of supply and of commodity trade. Yet while the capitalist mode brought ever new populations directly and indirectly into the widening orbit of its linkages, it also subjected them to its rhythm of acceleration and advances, and deceleration and retreats. Under the new mode, incorporation brought specialization, and specialization entailed dependence on economic and political conjunctures of worldwide scope.

10 Crisis and Differentiation in Capitalism

With the mechanization of the textile industry under capitalist auspices, England entered the "really revolutionary road" toward the ascendancy of the capitalist mode of production. Expanding outward from England in the course of the ninteenth century, this mode brought the entire world under its dominance. Some areas came under its direct sway, such as North America and—after 1868—Japan. Elsewhere it enveloped and penetrated other modes, setting up capitalist enclaves with differently organized hinterlands.

The process of creating strategic bases of the capitalist mode and dependent zones of support went on in the capitalist homelands as well as abroad. This point must be stressed because it is often obscured by an uncritical use of such terms as *core* and *periphery*. Capitalist development created peripheries within its very core. The advent of industrial capitalism in England, based on mechanized weaving and spinning, caused a massive collapse of home-based crafts organized under the mercantile putting-out system. Within Britain regions able to make the transition quickly, such as West Riding and Ulster, became major industrial centers, while other regions, like the West Country, East Anglia, and southern Ireland, declined. When the end of Napoleon's continental blockade opened European markets to English textiles, European regions active in craft production fell one after another before the competition of cheaper imports. Still other areas of Europe that had produced textiles for markets overseas, especially in Latin America, yielded to English competition abroad. Ireland, Flanders and Brabant, western France, southern Spain, southern Italy, and southern and eastern Germany were especially affected by this decline. They became subsidiary or dependent regions, furnishing cheap foodstuffs, raw materials, and labor for the industrializing heartlands.

Capitalism: Mode and Market

The outcome of this process was a complex hierarchical system controlled by the capitalist mode of production, but including a vast array of subsidiary regions that exhibited different combinations of the capitalist mode with other modes. The carrier industries of the capitalist mode dominated the system, but these rested upon variable and shifting supports that were often embedded in different modes of production. Ernest Mandel (1978: 48—49) has captured the complex relationships involved in this system by defining it as "an articulated system of capitalist, semi-capitalist, and pre-capitalist relations of production, linked to each other by capitalist relations of exchange and dominated by the capitalist world market." Such a definition accomplishes at least three things. First, it draws a distinction between the capitalist mode of production and "the capitalist world market." The capitalist mode of production may be dominant within the system of capitalist market relations, but it does not transform all the peoples of the world into industrial producers of surplus value. Second, it opens up the question of how the capitalist mode relates to other modes of production. Third, it allows us to take note of the heterogeneity of the different societies and subsocieties making up the system rather than obliterating that heterogeneity in dichotomies such as "core—periphery" or "metropolis—satellite."

It should be stressed that Mandel's definition points in a direction different from the models of the capitalist system developed by A.G. Frank and Immanuel Wallerstein. Their models—implicitly in Frank's case and explicitly in the case of Wallerstein—define capitalism as a system of production for the market, propelled by the search for profit realized by nonproducing entrepreneurs who pocket the surplus of the direct producer. Both writers have therefore focused on the process of surplus transfers rather than on the mode of production under which surpluses are generated. For Wallerstein, especially, the way social labor is deployed in the production of surpluses is a secondary matter, since for him all surplus producers operating under capitalist relations of exchange are "proletarians" and all surplus takers "capitalists." These models collapse the concept of the capitalist mode of production into the concept of the capitalist world market. Furthermore, in defining capitalism as production for a market in order to earn profits, this approach identifies the expansion of Europe since the fifteenth century with the rise of capitalism in its entirety. Not only have Frank and Wallerstein thus defined the European search for wealth in the sixteenth to the eighteenth centuries as capitalism pure and simple; for them, the whole world and all its parts have become similarly capitalist since that time.

Capitalism as a mode of production is not merely economic action that "rests on the expectation of profit by the utilization of opportunities for exchange, that is on (formally) peaceful chances of profit . . . action which is, in the last analysis, oriented to profits from exchange," or disciplined "pursuit of profit, and forever renewed profit, by means of continuous, rational, capitalistic enterprise" (Weber 1958: 17). Max

Weber's definition of capitalism represents but a latter-day version of Ibn Khaldun's "search for gain" or Adam Smith's postulated "human propensity to truck and barter." No one denies that merchants seek gain. Indeed, Francesco di Marco Datini, the fourteenth-century merchant of Prato, captioned his ledgers with the motto, "In the name of God and profit" (Origo 1957). What we must be clear about, however, is the analytical distinction between the employment of wealth in the pursuit of further wealth, and capitalism as a qualitatively different mode of committing social labor to the transformation of nature.

We are dealing here with the difference between Max Weber and Karl Marx. For Marx capital was not merely a stock of wealth but a strategic financial element combined with other elements: machinery, raw materials, and labor power. This combination, in Marx's view, is not rooted in any supposed human propensity, nor in human greed. It is not universal, but particular to a time and place. It involves the historical development of indentifiable prerequisite elements and their combination over time. These elements indeed take the form of stocks of wealth, human energy, and tools. But it is precisely when a stock of wealth is able to buy human energy and set it to work with tools to produce more wealth, which can buy more human energy and tools, that wealth becomes capital. Wealth, human energy, and tools are only factors until they are combined in a relational set, a system, in which each factor acts in relation with every other. Only when the stock of wealth can be related to human energy by purchasing living energy as "labor power," offered for sale by people who have no other means of using their labor to ensure their livelihood; and only when it can relate that labor power to purchased machines—embodiments of past transformations of nature by human energy expended in the past—only then does "wealth" become "capital."

In contrast to Frank and Wallerstein, therefore, I argue that the capitalist mode of production did not come into being until the latter part of the eighteenth century. Before that time, European expansion produced a vast network of mercantile relations anchored in noncapitalist modes of production. The worldwide movement of commodities generated prices and money-begetting money, without as yet subsuming both means of production and labor power under capital. Only the conversion of means of production and labor power into factors to be bought and sold on the market created the all-embracing "self-regulating" market of the economists. After that, "the organization of labor would change concurrently with the organization of the market system" (Polanyi 1957: 75). The capitalist mode produced, at one and the same time, a new form of deploying social labor and a change from a mercantile to a capitalist market. The rise of capitalist relations of exchange is thus predicated upon the development of the capitalist mode of production, not the reverse. The enormous escalation of these relations to the level of a worldwide capitalist market was fueled by the dynamism of that newborn mode.

The Expansion of Capitalism

But what is the source of capitalism's tendency to drive incessantly beyond its own frontiers? Marx's answer was that ceaseless capital accumulation, coupled with ever-rising levels of productivity through investment in technology, produces odd and contradictory results. In the course of capitalist production, capital purchases two elements: means of production and labor power. With rising technological inputs, the proportion of capital invested in means of production would increase, while the proportion of capital invested in labor power would decrease. "Surplus" under capitalist conditions is the amount of value produced by the work force during the time it operates the means of production, beyond the time needed to obtain its wages. Thus, raising the amount of capital devoted to technological inputs lowers the relative contribution of capital invested in labor power in the total mix of capital inputs. Indeed, the surplus might rise in amount, but the *rate* of surplus production—and hence the *rate* of profits obtained—would decrease (see Sweezy 1942: 69). In this disproportion Marx saw the crucial contradiction of the capitalist mode of production. Competition requires a ceaseless investment in the growth of means of production, but that very growth threatens a decline in the *rate* of profit. When the rate falls below a certain critical point, crisis ensues.

What happens then? One consequence, which Marx stressed, is that capital becomes unproductive and even subject to destruction. Plants close, credit based on future production collapses, capital depreciates in value. At the same time, growing unemployment drives down wages. This double movement, however, causes the cycle to start anew. Capital invested in means of production would have depreciated in the course of the crisis, and labor power could be purchased at a lower cost. Hence the ratio of capital invested in means of production to capital invested in labor would now be the opposite of what it was before the crisis. Before, the increased ratio of plant to labor brought on a falling rate of profit; now, the increased ratio of labor to plant would cause the rate of profit to rise once more, and expansion would recommence. This model should not be read as an account of what actually happens in specific crises, but rather as an attempt to delineate an inherent structural imbalance in the capitalist mode, which makes it always unstable.

Marx himself noted, but did not work out, another source of crisis: the problem of realizing surplus value at the point when too much has been produced, market prices fall below value, and profit is reduced or wiped out. This "realization crisis" does not spring from the inherent tendency of the rate of profit to fall, but from an inability of capitalists to make a profit because of the inability of consumers to absorb the sum of commodities produced (see Sweezy 1942: Chap. X). Such a crisis may be the result of either competition between capitalists that causes more to be produced than can in fact be sold, or the lack of sufficient purchasing power in the hands of consumers.

Writers following Marx utilized one or another aspect of his model of the capitalist crisis to explain capitalism's tendency to expand beyond the confines of a single political system. This was a problem that engaged Marx only tangentially. He did not talk about imperialism, but about foreign trade. Indeed, the word *imperialism* does not appear in his writings, although it was in use by the 1850s. He was interested primarily in using the English case as the basis of an abstract model that would permit him to define "the law of motion" of capitalism. The search for an explanation of imperialism was, however, the main concern of some of his successors, notably Lenin and Luxemburg. Lenin's *Imperialism* was written in 1916; Luxemburg's *Accumulation of Capital* appeared in 1913.

Lenin drew on the work of the English liberal economist John Hobson, whose *Imperialism: A Study* was published in 1902. Hobson tried to account for the development of imperialism by arguing that while capital tended to accumulate in the hands of capitalists, there was not enough of a domestic market for the commodities produced; hence capital sought opportunities for new investment abroad. Behind the political and military competition of nation-states stood, according to Hobson, the economic competition of capitalists searching for opportunities to export and invest capital. But whereas Hobson's book was written to argue for the creation of greater purchasing power and of markets fed by that purchasing power at home, Lenin expanded Hobson's analysis to argue that imperialism was not a reversible variant of capitalism but rather a necessary further stage of capitalism in development. According to Lenin, capitalism had outgrown the conditions of competition among individual firms, and had entered a stage in which giant combines of financial and industrial capital concentrated production and capital accumulation in the hands of a financial oligarchy that dominated the entire economy. Possessed of amounts of capital too large to find outlets in production, these giant combines sought investment opportunities abroad. Investment in foreign areas required, in turn, a corresponding extension of political controls, and the giant combines proceeded to carve up the world into spheres of influence. Having done so, they prompted wars among the capitalist nation-states. Lenin's argument therefore connects monopoly capitalism, the need to export capital, the political seizure of colonies, and the outbreak of war among contending capitalist powers in one chain of cumulative causation.

Since Lenin wrote, some of the links in this chain of causation have been shown to operate as contingent features of particular circumstances rather than as sequential and inevitable stages. First, Lenin probably overestimated the role of monopoly in capitalism at the time he wrote. There were few capital-industry combines of consequence in the Great Britain of 1900. In Germany the banks had come to exercise control over industry rather early, but the great trusts did not arise until after the turn of the century. In the United States, the merger movement in the early years of the twentieth century led to more rather than less competition (Kolko 1963). Thus, giant combines did not grow up in the same way at the same time everywhere, nor did their growth produce uniform results.

Second, the mass of British capital exports went not so much to the colonies as to other capitalist countries—the United States, Argentina, and the British dominions of Canada, Australia, and South Africa. India received about a fifth of the capital exported. The African companies drew their funds mainly from small subscribers, not from the big banking houses (Cairncross 1953). Even in Lenin's time, capitalism showed a tendency to reinvest in already existing centers of accumulation rather than to open up frontier regions of new investment.

Third, the relation between trade and the flag was, in many parts of the world, more indirect than Lenin's analysis would suggest. England's connection with India was certainly vital to the British imperial system, and England did intervene in Egypt in 1882 in order to protect the Suez Canal lifeline to Asia. English intervention in Africa and in Malaya, however, was more frequently the result of conflicts between European traders based overseas and of local power holders competing with one another. Such local conflicts were compounded by the ever-present possibility that rival European powers would exploit the situation for their own purposes. In Latin America, indeed, the English rarely even attempted colonial rule; the seizure of Belize (British Honduras) was exceptional, and a project to take Buenos Aires was quickly abandoned. Nevertheless, intervention and seizure did often follow particular local moves in the capitalist game of expansion. Ronald Robinson has stressed the difficulties of meshing noncapitalist and capitalist social constellations. Such synchronization requires the rise of a social group of mediators or collaborators. If these collaborators are riven by conflicts among themselves, or are unable to concentrate the necessary mediating functions in their own hands, the carriers of the capitalist mode find it difficult to transact their business. Robinson thus traces imperial takeovers to "the breakdown of collaborative mechanisms in extra-European politics which hitherto had provided them with adequate opportunity and protection" (1972: 132).

Yet we must not forget that the social constellations of Europe were also unstable, although perhaps in a different way. Joseph Schumpeter, for example, thought that the great wars resulted not from capitalism as such, but from a fusion of monopolistic industry with anachronistic state machines characterized by warrior traditions. While he may have been wrong about the pacifist implications of the capitalist mode, his judgment does point to the possibility that a class of tributary overlords associated with a previous noncapitalist mode can perpetuate itself under capitalism through entry into the military or into colonial officialdom. Such a class, favoring the pursuit of war and colonial rule, could find allies among captains of industry and industrial workers, both standing to gain from an armament race or from access to cheaper raw materials, and among colonists and traders with active interests in local takeovers. Finally, there is always the possibility of a "social imperialism" that strives to unify people at home by displacing internal conflicts upon an external enemy, with tangible gains accruing to the members of a "master race" from the domination of multitudes of "wogs." The spread of imperialism and the extension of outright colonial rule thus appear to be the result of a more complex interplay of social constellations than was allowed for in Lenin's explanation.

Rosa Luxemburg's analysis is important for other reasons. For her, the real cause of the capitalist crisis lay neither in the tendency of the rate of profit to fall nor in the accumulation of capital without opportunities for investment, but rather in the tendency of the system to produce more commodities than purchasing power could absorb. Hence, she thought, capitalism could expand only by extending its markets and by selling commodities to new customers. In her view, such customers could be found only in noncapitalist economies.

Luxemburg was probably wrong in her economic diagnosis. She neglected the fact that the expansion of capitalist production is based on the tendency for production to be its own consumer—to produce ever more means of production in order to expand production, rather than producing ever larger quantities of use values for people to consume. She also thought that worker income could not increase under capitalism; in fact, capitalist expansion increases capital investment in means of production not only in producers' industry but also in consumer industry, which raises the real value of the worker's wages. Furthermore, she offered no explanation as to where the prospective consumers in noncapitalist economies would obtain the purchasing power required to buy the commodities produced by capitalist industry.

Nevertheless, Luxemburg did point to the tendency of the capitalist mode to expand in search of new raw materials elsewhere, and in search of cheap labor to process them. Moreover, her empirical accounts are replete with examples showing that such control over raw materials and labor was frequently obtained by force, and that force was also deployed to make laboring populations buy commodities produced elsewhere. She thus showed more clearly than ever before that the expansion of the capitalist mode abroad often entailed the installation of processes of domination over noncapitalist modes. She was a forerunner of approaches that reject a focus on the capitalist nation-state as an isolated phenomenon and emphasize, instead, relations between capitalist center and dominated periphery.

Differentiation in the Capitalist Mode

While Marx constructed a model of the capitalist mode of production in its pure form, it is debatable whether he ever thought that the mode would become established identically everywhere. In *Capital* (III, 1967: 792) he wrote that the same economic base could show "infinite variations and gradations in appearance" because of "innumerable different empirical circumstances, natural environment, racial relations, external historical influences, etc." He also realized that the presence of a large peasantry could inhibit the full unfolding of the capitalist mode (*Cap*.III, 1967: 196; also, the original Ch. 6 of *Cap*.I, quoted in Mandel 1978: 45). In 1881, in a letter to Vera Zasulich, he wrote that his analysis of the capitalist mode was "expressly restricted to the countries of Western Europe" (see, especially, the draft of this letter [Marx 1942: 298–302]). It is significant that Marx wrote this at a time when he had immersed himself heavily in ethnological and agrarian-historical literature.

Lenin and Luxemburg both attempted to apply Marx's pure model to an analysis of the worldwide spread and impact of the capitalist mode between the onset of the Great Depression of 1873–1894 and World War I. Lenin focused on the need for capital exports, Luxemburg on the limitations of the home market. Both, however, were interested primarily in defining the "law of motion" that propelled the movement of the capitalist mode from its point of origin outward into other areas of the globe. They focused on the capitalist vortex as it spewed forth capital or commodities; and they visualized its effects as essentially similar everywhere, encompassing the whole world in a homogeneous field of effects.

The outbreak of the Russian Revolution of 1917 (and the subsequent failure of Germany to follow suit) made it clear that "the infinite variations and gradations in appearance," which Marx had noted, had strategic consequences for the way the postulated system worked in historic actuality. When Lenin characterized Russia as "the weakest link" in the chain of capitalist domination, he implicitly raised the question of what made some links stronger and others weaker. Trotsky, who attempted an answer, argued that this variability was produced by "uneven and combined development"—"uneven" because capitalism encountered extremely diverse conditions produced by uneven development in the past, and "combined" because capitalism had to combine with these uneven conditions in the very act of permeating them. This answer granted a measure of influence to pre-existing noncapitalist modes, and recognized that the way capitalism worked depended upon this influence. Yet Trotsky still defined capitalism as uniform in its "law of motion," and therefore uniform in its effects. What, however, if the capitalist mode generated variability and differentiation not only through its combination with other modes but also in the very course of its own operations?

We can distinguish a number of sources of differentiation. Some grow out of the mode itself. All capitalists know that the drive for higher profits demands that they invest continuously in new technology in order to maximize their means of production, but not all are able to respond equally. At every point in the ascending curve of capital accumulation, some capital aggregates grow larger, while others fall behind. Some holders of capital forge ahead; others maintain their position; still others withdraw or are eliminated from the race. The victors cash in the chips of the losers:

> the differences in the level of profit arise out of the competition of capitals and the inexorable condemnation of all firms, branches and areas which fall behind in this race and are thus forced to surrender part of their "own" surplus value to those in the lead. What is this process, other than the continual production of underdeveloped firms, branches, areas, and regions? [Mandel 1978: 85]

At every point, therefore, the capitalist mode generates distinctions between those capital aggregates employing higher ratios of capital in means of production to capital laid out in labor power and those employing lower ratios. This distinction, in turn, influences the different ways that units of capital relate to other sources of finance, technological inputs, markets, arrangements for obtaining labor power, and political influences at home and abroad.

Another source of variability is the tendency of the capitalist mode to exhibit repeated upswings and downturns of economic activity, to alternate advances in capital accumulation with retreats. In the Marxian model, these swings are seen as growing out of the contradictions of the mode itself. In his book *Late Capitalism* (1978), Ernest Mandel defines seven "long waves" in the development of the capitalist mode, from the last decade of the eighteenth century to the time of the Vietnam war. Each wave is marked off from the preceding one by a change in the rate of profit, produced in turn by changes in the ratio of capital invested in means of production to capital invested in labor power. Each time capital was invested in novel technology, the higher amount of capital invested in plant, as against capital invested in labor, resulted in an acceleration of the rate of profit. This was true of the first phase of industrialization (1793–1825), which marked the replacement of crafts by artisan-produced machines; of the period between 1848 and 1873, when machine-made machines were introduced and railway construction boomed; of the period between 1894 and 1913, when electric machines and the combustion engine were introduced; and again between the onset of World War II and 1966, when capital was invested heavily in war industry, which then spun off postwar electronic industries.

Each phase of acceleration in the rate of profit was followed by a phase of deceleration. Thus, the upturn of the industrial revolution was followed by a period of depression between 1826 and 1847, which involved a "realization crisis" resulting from the shrinking of markets for industrial products. The halcyon period of machine-made machines and massive railroad building between 1848 and 1873 gave way to the

Great Depression of 1873–1894. This downturn was marked by a growing export of capital and by efforts to reduce the costs of raw materials. Its political manifestation was intensified competition among rival European powers for spheres of influence and for access to raw materials abroad. The brief boom of 1894–1913 reaped the harvest of the preceding period's capital exports and enhanced raw material production, and labor productivity increased sharply through the introduction of a new technology. The boom ended, however, with World War I and the economic and political disruption that followed (1914–1939). Only World War II and the technological revolution afterward rescued the system from depression and set off a new phase of expansion in the rate of profit.

This periodization of capitalist development demonstrates that the impact of the capitalist mode is not the same in all phases. The mode varies in its requirements at different times, and thus also in the demands it places on different world areas.

Another source of differentiation lies in the fact that precapitalist patterns of mercantile wealth sometimes survive under capitalism. Historically and developmentally, money-begetting money turned into capital when it assumed the function of capital in production. In this sense, capital is an offspring of stockpiled mercantile wealth. Yet in changing its function, money-as-capital accomplished what money-begetting money had been unable to achieve: the capacity to affect and regulate the quantity and quality of social labor embodied in commodities.

Mercantile activity had sought profit in buying cheap and selling dear, what is generally known as nonequivalent or unequal exchange. To this end, merchants obtained goods in a number of ways. In the fur trade, the trader advanced valued goods such as guns and blankets, receiving furs in return. In the spice trade, the Dutch East India Company exchanged European goods or fine cloth made in India for spices that native overlords obtained as tribute. In the case of slave-produced sugar, the merchant advanced means of production in the form of slaves and processing equipment, as well as European commodities, receiving sugar from the planter in return. In all these cases, merchants used money and goods bought with money to gain a lien on production, but they remained outside the process of production itself. They implanted their circuits of exchange in other modes of deploying social labor, using a mixture of force and sales appeal to obtain collaboration and compliance. That collaboration and compliance, however, were unstable, and subject to renegotiation when the local ally increased his demands, took his trade to a competitor, or refused to cooperate altogether. The merchant was always dependent on his own state to back up his claim. At the same time, he was obliged to sweeten the disposition of his trade partner so as to perpetuate their unequal exchange.

With the establishment of the capitalist mode in England and its borderlands, industrial capital seized control of commodity production at home; it thus attached the domestic terminus of the mercantile circuit to a new productive base. As the capitalist mode spread to other areas, it affected, in turn, the foreign terminus of the merchant's operations. This was increasingly true as the development of new machinery demanded ever larger and more secure deliveries of commodities from abroad. During the nineteenth century, then, industrial capital gradually deprived the merchants of their autonomy, turning them into agents of capital rather than actors on their own behalf. Yet this process worked unevenly during different phases of capitalist expansion and in different parts of the world. Merchants acting as agents of the growing textile industry sought markets in Latin America during the first quarter of the nineteenth century, but the subsequent economic downturn led them to seek new outlets in Africa and Asia. During the phase of railroad construction, mercantile activity intensified, but the depression that followed put the merchants under heavy pressure. The great demand for raw materials at this time led to the establishment of capitalistically operated plantations and mines in several parts of the world. In these areas merchants were either pushed to the edge of the new sector of industrial agriculture and mining, or else were forced to aggregate their resources in large commercial-industrial cartels, such as the English and French companies trading in West Africa.

Mercantile activity and accumulation, however, remained significant in many world regions that were influenced by the advances of the capitalist mode but not engulfed directly by machine production or "factories-in-the-field"—regions that lay along the forward edges of capitalist expansion or between its advancing salients. Such regions included the hinterlands of the British Empire outside of its "white" colonies and major raw-material-producing areas; the interior of Latin America beyond the belt of coastal plantations; the edges of American and Canadian advance across the North American continent; and the islands of the Pacific. In these areas advancing merchants created commodity frontiers and labor frontiers. They carried to these zones goods from the industrial centers, exchanging them for local products or advancing them in order to contract laborers for plantations or mines.

In these regions, initial mercantile penetration often enabled groups to continue in the kin-ordered or tributary mode through the nineteenth century and even into the twentieth. Occasional exchanges could reinforce a group's ability to cope with its environment and to defend itself against encroachment by outsiders. Increasing exchange, however, gradually undermined the autonomy of the local group. As long as the sphere of exchange relations remained restricted, the native trade partner and the outside merchant could be equals in exchange, each proffering goods desired by the other. But as the sphere of exchange widened, the native producers tended to become clients of the trader rather than symmetrical partners. As they grew more dependent on the merchant for instruments of production such as guns, ammunition, steel traps, and metal tools, as well as for items of consumption such as manufactured goods and even food, they came to depend increasingly on the wider capitalist market. They confronted a gradual reduction in their ability to control their means of production, especially as widening exchange eroded their ability to reproduce these means through the mechanisms of kinship or power. Similarly, tributary elites, drawn into dependence on goods produced under capitalist auspices, found themselves under pressure to intensify tributary labor and to redirect it toward commercial production. Labor recruiters who exchanged money or commodities for labor power set in motion changes in the ties linking the laborers to their kinsmen or overlords. Under such circumstances, local resources and services tended to become commodities, increasingly subject to transactions operating outside the preexisting modes.

Such frontier perimeters were thus gradually drawn into the capitalist market and connected indirectly with the industrial bases of the capitalist mode of production. In this process, the merchants became caught up in a contradiction. As advance agents of the market in frontier zones, they enjoyed a measure of antonomy that they often translated into local or regional dominance. As market relations grew more intense, however, their increasing need for capital and commodities tied them more closely to the metropolitan centers of production and distribution. At the same time, their temporary local monopolies often dissolved under the impact of widened competition.

Some frontier regions that served as sources of occasional labor were in time reshaped into permanent reservoirs of ready labor. Such regions included the catchment areas for contract laborers in India and China during the nineteenth century, the "native reserves" created in Africa toward the end of the nineteenth century, and the supply zones of migratory labor around the Mediterranean in the twentieth century. Historically, these regions formed parts of states that had been defeated by military force, or that had been sidetracked in the course of European expansion. Such regions became organized to nurture and provision labor until needed, and to maintain it after its productive years. One part of the population was mobilized for wage labor outside the zone of supply, while their families and kin would remain in the reserves, sustaining themselves through a combination of household production for subsistence and commodity production for sale. The flow of wages and remittances coming into the zone from outside, together with commodities produced within, underwrote the emergence of mercantile intermediaries who linked the labor reserve to its capitalist matrix.

Differentiation: The State

A major reason for differentiation within the capitalist mode is that capitalist development is carried forward by politically separate and distinct states. To understand this aspect of the mode, we must first ask, with Ber Borochov,

> why, on the one hand, the capitalistic system appears as international, and destroys all boundaries between tribes and people and uproots all traditions, while on the other hand, it is itself instrumental in the intensification of the international struggle and heightens national self-consciousness. [1937: 160]

In an earlier chapter (2) we defined the state in the capitalist mode as an apparatus installed to maintain and further the strategic relationships governing the capitalist deployment of social labor. The capitalist state exists to ensure the domination of one class over another. Yet in each state this function is executed differently, and with different consequences.

There are historical reasons for this. The capitalist mode did not come to dominance all at once. It was incubated in older, tributary arrangements, and it expanded only fitfully and gradually to occupy wider social terrain. Each new cohort of capitalists encountered other preexisting classes rooted in varied tributary arrangements. Each emerging capitalist society also differed from others in the background of its working class, and in the speed and intensity with which this class developed. Such variability in class "mix" was further amplified by the different ways that capitalist classes assumed dominance. In their rise to power, English industrialists entered into an alliance with "improving landlords." In the course of German industrialization, the captains of industry joined the East Elbian plantation owners, or Junkers, in a pact of "steel and bread." In the United States, the issue of who was to dominate the state led ultimately to the war between the Union and the Confederacy, ending in a defeat for the class forces represented by the South.

Once such internal wars were settled, the problem of class domination assumed the guise of politics, of "who gets what when" within the framework of class rule. Such politics again differ from state to state. Politics under capitalism involves, first of all, conflicts among segments of the capitalist class itself. While all capitalists share a common interest in class domination, individual groups of capitalists are in fact often at loggerheads, driven by divergent short-run interests. These conflicts may even grow to a point where they threaten the state. Different segments of the capitalist class will also enter into alliances with segments of other classes, including segments of the developing working class. Since the characteristics of all these classes are variable from state to state, the nature of both intraclass and interclass conflicts and alliances will also vary. This variability, working over time, cumulatively shapes the form and function of the state apparatus.

Still another source of differentiation among capitalist states lies in the manner that each capitalist cohort entered into capital accumulation abroad. The earlier expansion of European merchants abroad had created networks of commercial influence and power in different areas of the world. Some cohorts of expanding capitalists were able to take advantage of these mercantile networks and to transform them into resources for their own accumulation. Each time a capitalist state assumed control of an area, moreover, it also altered the terms of entry for later competitors. Thus England, in making the first breakthrough into the capitalist mode, was also able to capitalize on the commercial network created by British traders, gaining strategic advantages in access to markets and raw materials and denying such advantages to later competitors, such as France and Germany.

England's success, in turn, changed the course of political development for its competitors. The hegemonic expansion of England and its capitalist class evoked the consolidation of national states among all her rivals. Such consolidation sought to improve each capitalist society's control over its own "conditions of production" by strengthening the power of the state. Policies to support capitalist expansion were adopted—to protect infant industries against English competition, to develop an infrastructure of transport and communication responsive to national needs, to set up centralized investment and banking, to create national systems of labor discipline and state-sponsored education, and to develop a war-making potential. Whereas England undertook capitalist development with a "cheap" state that was still able to delegate many functions of domination to local power holders, later competitors had to build strong and expensive states to stay in the competitive race.

All states, cheap or expensive, require funds to pay for state services. Such funds are usually raised through taxes or through public loans that are repaid out of taxes. Taxes are collected by deductions on wages or by transfers of surplus value from capitalists to the state. Such deductions or transfers of surplus value are managed variably by different states, with differential results for their citizens. All, however, serve to accumulate a fund of "indirect surplus value" (O'Connor 1974: 39–42) that is managed by the state apparatus. This fund can then be used to generate additional industrial development, especially in war-related industries, favoring one segment of the capitalist class against others; or it can be dispensed in social services or in price-support programs of various sorts that favor certain classes or class segments. Once again, issues of class domination are translated into politics. The variable outcomes of conflicts over "who gets what when" add to the differentiation of capitalist states. Although we are speaking here primarily of the initial development of the international state system under capitalism during the nineteenth century, it is not amiss to point out that these state functions, based on the accumulation of indirect surplus value, were enormously enlarged in the twentieth century—especially after 1930—under the impact of depression, social dislocation, and war.

11 The Movement of Commodities

During the latter part of the nineteenth century, production under capitalism took a great leap forward, escalating the demand for raw materials and foodstuffs and creating a vastly expanded market of worldwide scope. Whole regions became specialized in the production of some raw material, food crop, or stimulant. Some of these regional specializations had been established earlier under mercantile aegis, as in the case of the sugar-producing areas of the Caribbean. Others grew up in response to early capitalist development, such as the cotton-growing regions of the United States, Egypt, and India. Still others were entirely new. Regional emphasis on a monocrop or single raw material product demanded, in turn, that other areas raise crops to feed the primary producers, or furnish labor power to the new plantations, farms, mines, processing plants, and transport systems. Through the expanding commitment to the production of commodities, changes on the level of the world market had consequences at the level of household, kin group, community, region, and class.

To understand how people were forced or drawn into this market requires cognizance of the market not only as a means for the exchange of goods and services but also as a set of "mechanisms of social articulation" (Mintz 1959a: 20). Goods and services produced for a market are commodities; as commodities, they can be compared and exchanged without reference to the social matrix in which they were produced. As we have noted, commodity exchange long preceded the rise of the capitalist mode of production, as merchants placed into exchange commodities produced under tributary or kin-ordered modes. Each commodity embodies a fraction of the social labor expended to transform nature to human purposes, social labor that has been mobilized under the governing relations of a mode of production. With the unfolding of capitalism, ever larger quantities of such commodities entered a market where they encountered and competed with commodities produced under other modes. Under the growing worldwide predominance of capitalism, the market was transformed into an arena of articulation and conflict between contending modes of production, expressed in the exchange of their diverse commodities. Capitalism did not always abrogate other modes of production, but it reached and transformed peoples' lives from a distance as often as it did so directly.

The development of industrial capitalism did not move in a smooth ascending line. Phases of advance in capital accumulation gave way to downturns; periods of optimistic expansion were followed by periods of uncertainty and gloom. Each phase of advance opened up new theaters of operation and new zones of supply. Each downturn challenged the dominant course of capital investment and raised the specter of contracting markets, as in Latin America after 1825. Each phase of advance and each endeavor to stem the tide of depression had its effects on the populations caught up in the web of capitalist linkages. Sometimes the effects of capitalism were direct, the outcome of investment or disinvestment in industrial facilities, raw material supplies, or food-producing enterprises in various regions of the globe. At other times its effects were transmitted through the mechanism of the market, intensifying or diminishing the transformative impact of the capitalist mode upon other modes. Each advance brought on changes in the way social labor was organized. When advance was followed by retreat, however, a return to previous adaptations was no longer possible. For many of the peoples studied by anthropologists, such changes became especially critical during the last quarter of the nineteenth century.

The Great Depression

Only five years after the opening of the Suez Canal, with its promise of greatly enhanced commerce between Europe and Asia, capitalist expansion experienced another major downturn. Railroad construction had pulled capitalism out of the slump of 1826–1847, and it had fueled renewed development in the years between 1848 and 1873 through a big spurt in the production of iron, steel, and coal. In 1873 expansion gave way to a downturn once again. The effects of this downturn have come to be known as the Great Depression. Economic historians disagree on the generality of the phenomenon, noting that it was not equally widespread and intense everywhere. Some scholars have even denied its occurrence altogether. Yet a major change occurred in the pace and nature of capitalist accumulation, a change still reverberating into our time. The Great Depression ushered in a new phase in the encounter between capitalism and the rest of the world. During this phase a militant capitalism encroached ever more intensively on the social arrangements predicated upon tributary or kin-ordered modes of production. It did so by drawing resources and labor power organized in different ways into a larger system dominated and permeated by capitalist productive relations. Within this system, the subsidiary parts were forced or motivated to become producers of specialized commodities, all grown and marketed under the directives of the central process of capital accumulation.

Several factors underlay this shift of gears in capitalist development. The rate of profit declined as real wages increased in Europe and the costs of raw materials went up in other parts of the world. Capital investment to finance renewal of the means of production, in order to cut these rising costs, came about only slowly. It is possible that the stock of capital then available was not sufficient to finance a rapid shift from the technology of the steam engine to a new technology based on the internal combustion engine and turbine, driven by oil or electricity. The new chemical industry was similarly in its infancy.

The industrial slowdown had a geographical and political aspect. It was steam-driven English industry that slowed down, while the United States and Germany gradually expanded their industries on the new technological foundations. Britain lost its predominance as the workshop of the world. By 1870 it possessed only a quarter of the world's steam power and produced less than half the world's steel (Hobsbawm 1969: 134). Between 1880 and 1890 U.S. steel production overtook Britain's; within another decade German steel production had overtaken the British as well (Barratt Brown 1970: 82). Britain's "satanic mills" still glowed in Birmingham and Sheffield; its bank—The Old Lady of Threadneedle Street—was still the hub of worldwide financial transactions; and Britannia "still ruled the waves." Yet Britain was no longer the industrial leader of the world; it was merely one of a number of industrializing countries.

The Great Depression was thus a crisis in capitalist accumulation because it affected the country that had fueled the process and changed its relationship to the rest of the world. It initiated a crisis in British hegemony. Thereafter it was less Britain's own industrial capacity that underwrote its continued influence than the returns on past successes. What kept Britain abreast of international competition was its control over India. Indian cotton and textiles, sold in ever-increasing quantities to the United States, on the European continent, and to Japan, furnished surpluses for the imperial system. Indian trade in cotton and textiles rose in the second half of the nineteenth century from $4 million to $50 million. Even more important were the so-called "home charges," the tribute levied on India to defray the costs of British administration and the interest payable on debts incurred by the colonial British government of India, which rose from 70 million to 225 million pounds sterling in the last quarter of the century (Barratt Brown 1970: 85). The flow of these sums maintained British predominance as a financial center, but the staff of international leadership passed to others.

At the same time, a major shift occurred in European agricultural production. European agriculture was subjected suddenly to massive imports of American and Russian wheat, which led to a precipitous fall in agricultural prices. American expansion into the plains and Russian cultivation of the southeastern steppe increased supplies of wheat, while improved transportation—because of the construction of railroads and the expansion of steamship and sailboat travel across the Atlantic—caused a rapid decline in transportation costs. The cost of carrying a quarter of wheat, or eight bushels, from Chicago to Liverpool averaged eleven shillings in 1869–1879, but fell below three shillings in 1902 (Bagwell and Mingay 1970: 75). This shook the foundations of European agriculture and intensified the outward flow of migrants to the Americas (see chapter 11).

The outcome was that the several capitalist nation-states of Europe embarked upon an intense search for new investments and markets in a period of declining opportunities. They found themselves in fierce competition with one another for control of regions that could provide cheap raw materials and labor. In the United States and Russia the same impetus fueled expansion, colonization, and consolidation across entire continents. Rising discontent at home and intensifying competition abroad, in turn, unleashed drives for expansion by political means—the politics of imperialism. These politics sought to unite disaffected and contending classes at home through a common struggle for colonies or spheres of influence abroad, while giving the "mother country" privileged access to markets and resources. The Great Depression spurred the extension of European sovereignty abroad. Africa was carved up; new colonies were established in Asia; the Pacific was colonized. The European powers during this period of economic stagnation tripled their territorial acquisitions abroad. Capitalist accumulation was thus restored, albeit haltingly. Taking advantage of the new means of transportation available in the last quarter of the nineteenth century, capital entered into the development of "tropical" agricultural products and raw materials for European markets.

Regional Specialization

The advent of new crops and new products significantly altered the relations between regions on the same continent and relations between entire continents. Some regions specialized in producing foodstuffs or industrial raw materials; others processed the raw materials, consumed the food grains or meat, and sent back manufactured goods. We have already seen how Britain became dependent on American and—later—Egyptian and Indian supplies of cotton. The cotton-producing areas, in turn, became so specialized in producing their major cash crop that they had to be supplied with food and manufactures from elsewhere. Britain, which had fed itself and even exported an agricultural surplus in the eighteenth century, was at the end of the nineteenth century dependent on foreign supplies for four-fifths of its wheat and two-fifths of its meat (Woodruff 1971: 12). The American Cotton South came to depend almost entirely on Northern manufactures and Western wheat. Regional specialization was not confined to food grains, meat, and cotton. To provide tropical products like sugar, tea, coffee, or rubber in bulk, entire world areas were turned into sugar, tea, rubber, or coffee plantations. Since plantation production was heavily concentrated on one or two cash crops, the labor force had to be sustained in turn by producers who could furnish foodstuffs and other required commodities. In the Asian context it was rice rather than wheat that supplied the basic staple for maintenance of the labor force, and the expansion of plantation agriculture therefore went hand in hand with an expanding production of rice, destined for riceless areas. Still other regions of the world came to specialize not in crops or industrial activities, but in the production of laborers for agriculture and industry. While common bonds were forged between these areas under the aegis of industrial capitalism, their involvement with one another in fact led to divergence, and to a continuing reorganization of social relations and cultural patterns within each area.

When Adam Smith and David Ricardo had envisaged a growing worldwide division of labor, they had thought that each country would freely select the commodities it was most qualified to produce, and that each would exchange its optimal commodity for the optimal commodity of others. Thus, in Ricardo's example, Britain would send Portugal its textiles, while Britons would consume Portuguese wines in turn. What this vision of free commodity exchange omits are the constraints that governed the selection of particular commodities, and the political and military sanctions used to ensure the continuation of quite asymmetrical exchanges that benefited one party while diminishing the assets of another.

Choice in the growing system of interrelationships was rarely free. In the majority of cases it was imposed by force, or by constraints stemming from market domination by more powerful participants. Coercion or constraint—whether through outright political takeover of a colony or through economic domination alone—were of the essence of the process; they were not epiphenomena. Moreover, once a region was included in the circuits of capital, the requirements of accumulation were such that it had to reorganize its factors of production to intensify capital growth, or else fall under the wheels of the chariot of progress. In capitalist agriculture this led either to the growth of highly capitalized "factories in the field," or to the growth of small-scale specialized producers whose operations were dictated by cash-product markets. At the same time, the very process of accumulation stripped other areas of access to means of production, hence "freeing" them to become vendors of labor power to third parties.

In this chapter we shall examine the ways that some agrarian and pastoral products came to be produced on plantations or on small holdings, and we shall illustrate some of the ways these new forms of production affected the participating populations. In the next chapter, we will look more closely at the worldwide development of working classes, which manned the new industries and agricultural enterprises thrown up by accumulating capital in the course of its ever-intensifying reproduction.

Commercial Agriculture: Plantations

In agriculture, the main instruments of capitalist expansion in the nineteenth century were the plantation and the specialized cash-crop-producing small farm. A plantation can be defined formally as a capital-using unit employing a large labor force under close managerial supervision to produce a crop for sale. The labor force usually works in labor gangs that carry out the repetitive and physically demanding tasks under the watchful eye of foremen who enforce the required sequence and synchronization of tasks. Plantation agriculture therefore takes on something of the order and drill of an army, which led Edgar T. Thompson to characterize it as "military" agriculture. Its aim is to produce one or two crops for the market. That specialization is a source at once of its strength and of its weakness. The organization can respond to increases in market demand; but it is also highly vulnerable to economic downturns.

Plantations tend to be large in size, achieving economies of scale by devoting as much of their resources as possible to the cultivation of a single crop. Large-scale production requires large-scale processing. The bulk product must be moved from the fields to a processing center; the processed crop must be stored until it can be taken to market. The combined functions of organizational control, processing, and storage create the plantation center, which becomes a post of command, walled off from surrounding fields and workers' barracks. Where the plantation, with its novel forms and functions, is set up in the midst of an already inhabited countryside, it appears as an "enclave" driven into an alien environment. Where plantations are formed on the edge of older settlements, they constitute an expanding "frontier." They are in fact the outposts of one mode of production in the midst of other modes. The relation between the plantation and the forms of production predicated on these other modes is usually antagonistic. The plantation is an invader, and its successful expansion is the fruit of successful invasion.

Up to the end of the eighteenth century, plantations had been created mainly in the Americas and on a few islands in the Indian Ocean. They were worked primarily with slave labor imported from Africa, which they consumed in great quantities. In 1807, however, Britain abolished the slave trade, followed soon after by the United States, France, and the Netherlands. In 1833 Britain went further, outlawing slave labor entirely in its various possessions around the world.

Why slave trading and slavery were abolished in the first decades of the nineteenth century admits of no easy answer. It is true that the profits in slaving were on the decrease (see Craton 1974: 113). It is also evident that the planter class of the British Caribbean sugar islands, once the financial cynosure of the expanding empire, was seriously weakened in the last quarter of the nineteenth century. French competition, based on exploitation of slave labor in Saint Domingue, together with rising sugar imports from Bengal, had lowered sugar prices. Warfare with the United States and then with France had disrupted relations with the North American colonies, and had brought on hunger and inflation in the islands. On some islands cane production appears to have reached the limits of productivity. During the Napoleonic wars, too, continental Europe took up the production of sugar by raising sugar beets, and it was soon to become a formidable competitor of cane-grown sugar. Beset by debts, the British planters in the Caribbean experienced a real "crisis of the planter class" (see Ragatz 1928).

Yet the shift from slave labor to other forms of labor control within the British orbit must be understood not only in terms of internal British development but also in terms of the changing international system of which Britain formed a part. Under the rising hegemony of industrial capitalism, there was a growing preference for the use of free labor over slavery. It must be noted, however, that slavery continued in the United States, and it even intensified in Brazil and Cuba in the course of the nineteenth century. Brazil did not abolish slavery until 1871, and Cuba, with its rising output of sugar produced by burgeoning factories in the field, not until 1886. The former slaves in Jamaica withdrew from the plantations to take up subsistence agriculture on their own plots. Yet Brazil still imported close to 1,900,000 slaves between 1811 and 1870, and Cuba another 550,000. The end of slave trading and slave labor in one part of the world led to its continuation and even intensification in another part. One of the areas that continued to use slave labor was the American Cotton South, now the major producer of the strategic raw material for the expanding capitalism in Britain. The rise of industrial capitalism thus rested on the maintenance of slavery in another part of the world, even though that slavery was no longer dependent on the continuation of the slave trade.

Another aspect of the shift away from slavery within the British orbit was that the Napoleonic wars placed in Britain's hands control of much of the tropical world outside the Caribbean. Whereas much of Britain's wealth before the wars had come from the Caribbean, after the wars British manufacturers could begin to look forward to a "new" empire. This empire would not be based on the coerced labor of a few islands, but on export of manufactured products to Asia and Africa, and on import of tropical products from them. New kinds of ocean transport would carry these commodities across oceans made secure against slavery by the British navy. In consequence, slavery in the British sugar islands was sacrificed to expanding plantation agriculture and to cash cropping by small producers in other parts of the world. As a result of the reorientation of British interests, therefore, slave-grown sugar from the British Caribbean declined in relative importance as a source of capital accumulation, and other kinds of cash crops grown in other parts of the world gained in significance.

In the course of the nineteenth century, agriculture on plantations underwent a major change—away from estates capitalized with the financial resources of planter families and of merchants who advanced needed commodities against the crop, and toward highly capitalized, corporate "factories in the field," in which all the factors of production, including labor, were determined by the play of the ever-enlarging capitalist market. The "fall of the planter class" was not confined to the Caribbean; it was worldwide (Beckford 1972: 102–110). The privileged relationships between planter and merchant had to give way to the free flow of liquid capital. To maximize capital accumulation and to lower labor costs, capital had to be allowed to flow freely toward forms and branches of agriculture capable of intensification and expansion, and away from those hampered by superannuated technology, limiting organization, and an immobile labor supply.

In one plantation area after another, the planter class—possessed of limited access to capital and wedded to outmoded patterns of production—failed to make the transition. Metropolitan corporations acquired their assets and transformed plantation technology and organization under corporate control, with capital pumped in from London, Paris, New York, or Hamburg. Giant producing and distributing organizations, such as the United Africa Company, United Fruit, Harrisons and Crosfields, Brooke Bond, the *Compagnie Française de l'Afrique Occidentale*, and the *Société Commerciale de l'Ouest Africain*, came to dominate entire branches of economic activities and entire countries. Both plantation agriculture and small-scale cash-crop production thus became subject to financial and commercial controls from distant centers.

Commercial Agriculture: Cash-Cropping Small Farms

The nineteenth century also witnessed, within Europe as in other parts of the world, an increase and development of cash-crop production on smaller land holdings. Put in general terms, peasants became farmers. In Europe this was accomplished in two ways. One way was by freeing the peasantry economically and politically from tributary obligations to a class of overlords, enabling the peasants to employ their land and labor as market factors of production. It was a gradual process, operating in phases and stages, and one that moved from west to east, beginning in France in 1789, reaching the Austro-Hungarian dominions after 1848, and victorious in Russia with the emancipation decrees of 1861. The second way of moving the peasantry toward specialized cash-crop production was by severing the connection between subsistence farming and household craft production under the putting-out system. As craft production under merchant control gave way to capitalist industry, the poorer peasant-artisans were forced to give up cultivation and to move toward sources of industrial employment, leaving their luckier or wealthier neighbors to engross their land and to employ it to grow specialized crops for the market. It goes without saying that this was not an even process taking place everywhere at the same time. In some areas it took several generations to complete. In the end, however, tributary modes and the operations of mercantile wealth existing alongside them were abrogated, and a new kind of agricultural producer was set free to respond to the inputs of the market.

As we shall see, such developments also occurred in areas outside of Europe, notably in West Africa and Southeast Asia. Capitalist expansion was forwarded both by small holders and by plantation agriculture; yet these were but agents on the ground, so to speak, for holders of capital in corporations or agency houses elsewhere. The expansion of commercial agriculture involved the development of a multitiered structure of capital inflows, local production and sale, and capital outflows. We shall follow the growth and spread of some crops and products, and sketch out some of the ways that this growth and spread affected the lives of populations "on the ground." These developments and their effects, however, were but local episodes of a gigantic global process of capital accumulation.

Commodity Production: Foodstuffs

Especially important in the new worldwide agricultural specialization were food grains, particularly wheat in Europe and America and rice in Asia, specialized livestock production, and plantation food crops such as bananas.

Wheat

We have already noted how much Great Britain came to depend on imports of grain crops to provide for the "workshop of the world." Three areas stand out in the specialized production of wheat for export in this period. The first was the American Midwest and West, where cultivators advanced into the Great Plains and made inroads on the tough grasses of the area with the deep plow and the mechanical reaper. The first shipment of wheat sent eastward—seventy-eight bushels— reached Chicago in 1838, but the great increase in grain production came after the war between the Union and the Confederacy. It was then that railroad construction and the advent of the tramp steamer made overseas exports increasingly profitable.

The inland march of the railroads first prompted the creation of great "bonanza" wheat farms worked with migratory wage labor. In the 1880s, however, these failed, to be replaced with farms operated by households—households equipped with agricultural machinery. Steam threshers appeared in the 1830s, mechanical reapers in the 1850s, the combined harvester-thresher in the 1880s. With this machinery it became possible for a two-male household, such as that constituted by a father-son team, to carry on successful wheat farming on 200-acre farms. These were not peasants aiming at subsistence, but commodity producers buying their means of production in the market and selling their product into a market in turn (Friedmann 1978).

American wheat, sold in Europe at lower prices than the domestic product, brought on a crisis in European peasant agriculture, sending a migrant stream of ruined peasants to seek new sources of livelihood in the burgeoning Americas. Ironically, many of them made the journey westward on the same ships that carried to Europe the wheat that proved their undoing.

The East German Junkers responded to the grain crisis by replacing their permanent tenant-laborers with migratory wage workers. The tenants had worked on the Junker estates in return for rights to a cottage, a plot to farm on their own, pasture for their cows, and a share of the harvest. They now lost these rights; many of them emigrated (Walker 1964: 184–190). To replace them, the Junkers brought in seasonal Polish agricultural workers who could be paid low wages. These wages were kept low by a Junker-backed state policy aimed at inhibiting the growth of independent Polish-owned farms in the area (Weber 1979; Gerschenkron 1943).

In the 1880s Argentina was added to the great wheat producers of the world. As of 1870 it still imported wheat from abroad, but by the end of the century it was one of the world's main exporters. European immigrant colonists, tenant farmers, and harvest laborers pushed the wheat frontier westward until it reached its limit at the line of minimum rainfall.

Western Europe, in turn, was fed by a third wheat-producing area, southern Russia, where wheat grown on the steppe tripled between 1831 and 1860. Ninety percent of this wheat was exported through the port of Odessa, where world prices began to set levels for the entire Russian region (Lyashchenko 1949: 367). In contrast to the rest of European Russia, moreover, the Russian steppe developed patterns of wage labor in agriculture, replacing serfdom on estates farmed increasingly with machinery.

Rice

While wheat poured into the European peninsula from Russia and the Americas, rice became a vital export crop in South and Southeast Asia. In 1855 Britain seized Lower Burma, the delta region of the Irrawaddy River, where about a million acres stood under rice. Between 1855 and 1881 that acreage increased ninefold. The primary producers were peasants, many of them new immigrants from the dry country of Upper Burma. Production was financed by the great rice mills in Rangoon and

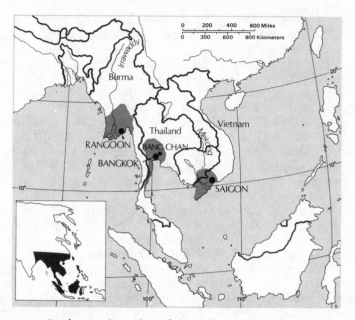

Southeast Asia: regions of rice production for export.

Bassein through a rural network of moneylenders. Most of these were members of the Chettiar caste from Madras who displaced Burmese moneylenders. Peasant indebtedness, spurring additional increases in rice production, was intensified further by loans from Burmese and Chinese shopkeepers—loans made to finance consumption, life-cycle ceremonies, and theatrical (*pwe*) performances. In Burma about half of the rice raised for export went to India; a quarter went to the plantations of Ceylon and Malaya, which had begun to specialize in the production of tea and rubber; and a quarter fed the sugar colonies of Mauritius and the West Indies. Much of this Burmese rice was consumed by Indian indentured laborers working on estates overseas, and the boats carrying these laborers to their destination also bore the rice that fed them.

Thailand, similarly, began to produce rice for export, though on a smaller scale than Burma. Here the rice mills were in Chinese hands, and it was the Chinese who expanded into the rural districts as middlemen and moneylenders. Rice growing expanded especially in Thailand's central plain. One of the settlements founded around mid-century was Bang Chan, northeast of Bangkok, which a century later was studied by Lauriston Sharp and the Cornell Thailand Project (Sharp et al. 1953; Sharp and Hanks 1978; Hanks 1972). The settlement developed in response to the construction of the Saen Saeb Canal: thirty-four miles long, it linked the eastern plain with the Chao Phraya River on which Bangkok is located. Built initially for military reasons, the canal opened up the region for the Bangkok market. The people who settled in Bang Chan were a medley of Hainanese Chinese intermarried with Thai, Muslim Malay prisoners of war from the south, Laotian prisoners of war from the northeast, and freed slaves from Bangkok. The local Buddhist temple, which imparts identity to the settlement cluster, was built around 1891 by a river trader of Chinese origin from the village where the canal and the Mae Nam join. Rice cultivation for the market increased especially in the third quarter of the century, and it had become fully dominant by the onset of World War I.

Bang Chan has acquired importance in the anthropological literature as a diagnostic case of a "loosely structured social system," a concept originally developed by John Embree (1950) to characterize Thai society. The study of Bang Chan concluded that "the exceptionally amorphous, relatively unstructured character of all Thai society is clearly reflected in the undifferentiated social organization of Bang Chan" (Sharp et al. 1953: 26). This view provoked a good deal of debate about models of Thai social structure. It led Jack Potter (1976) to propose an alternative model of a number of "structural elements" that "generate" Thai rural communities. Yet the features of Bang Chan that led to its characterization as "loosely structured"—like the features of other Thai villages caught up in the rice economy in other ways—must be understood not merely as a social structure of a certain kind but as the outcome of the expansion of commodity production.

The third Asian region producing rice for export was Cochinchina, the southern delta region of Vietnam, occupied by the French in 1861. To a large extent, this region is a product of French hydraulic engineering—work carried out to produce large quantities of rice for export. Most of the rice was produced on large estates worked by tenants. The area planted in rice doubled between 1880 and 1900, while rice exports (funneled through Saigon) nearly tripled in that period. Much of this rice was shipped to China by way of Hong Kong; this trade came to be handled largely by Chinese.

Meat

With the onset of the industrial revolution, meat consumption in Europe, which had earlier been at a relatively high level, decreased markedly. The advent of the railroad and steamboat, however, prompted the development of new "livestock frontiers." By 1860 there were new sources of meat for European and American tables.

The best known of these frontiers is the American "Wild West," which became one of the world's "cattle kingdoms" after the end of the war between the Union and the Confederacy. Great herds of half-wild and unbranded cattle roamed the open range of southern Texas before the war. Cessation of the conflict brought on a sudden spurt in the demand for meat, turning heretofore useless range stock into a marketable commodity. This turn of events initiated the great cattle drives, with "cowboys" guiding the herds toward the railheads from which trains sped the animals on their way to the slaughterhouses of the East. These mounted wageworkers consisted in part of Anglo-Americans, in part of Mexicans, in part of American Blacks who had gone out West after the end of slavery. The technology of the cattle business derived from the technology of Mexican pastoralism.

Although the days of the cowboy have become enshrined in popular American mythology, they lasted no more than a quarter of a century. Moreover, the West never furnished more than a third of all the cattle produced in the United States. The grazing of semiferal cattle on the open range was only an episode in the growth of a cattle industry that soon made its peace with the advancing cultivators by turning to tame blood cattle raised intensively on carefully fenced ranches.

The North American cattle industry developed as an adjunct to the packing houses of Chicago, St. Louis, and Kansas City; so also, cattle raising developed on the Argentine *pampa* as an adjunct to the packing houses of Buenos Aires. On this grassy steppe, cattle gone wild had first been hunted for hides, and later to provide salted meat for the slave plantations of Brazil. An industrial Argentine cattle industry did not develop until the last quarter of the nineteenth century, however, when it became possible to freeze meat and transport it cheaply to European markets, especially Britain. It was British capital that built and fueled most of the Argentine railroads, provided the blooded stock, fenced the ranches with barbed wire, built the freezer lockers required to freeze the fresh-killed meat, and provided the refrigerator ships that

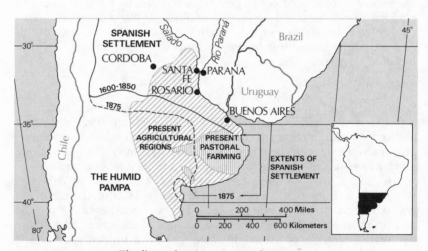

The livestock-raising region of Argentina.

took the meat across the Atlantic. "By the end of the nineteenth century," says George Pendle (1963: 141), "the *pampa* had been tamed, organized, and virtually harnessed to the economy of Great Britain." The expansion of the Argentine cattle industry was secured in three interrelated phases. First, the horse riding Araucanians of the grasslands were defeated and destroyed militarily. Second, the semi-independent cattle hunters of the pampa, the gauchos, were deprived of their autonomy. Wire fencing reduced the numbers of men needed to keep animals within ranch boundaries. The gaucho became a hired ranch hand. Third, production on ranches and agricultural estates was synchronized. The estates, now leased to Spanish and Italian immigrants, provided in rotation wheat for export and alfalfa for the cattle ranches.

A third area where a livestock industry developed was Australia. Here sheep had been raised for their exportable wool since the first quarter of the nineteenth century on ranges won from their aboriginal occupants. When the gold rush of the mid-century drained the sheep range of available labor, the sheep lords rationalized their production through the use of mounted boundary riders and through the introduction of New World techniques of fencing and other innovations. The Australian sheep ranges, however, remained separate from the agricultural regions that rimmed the periphery of the continent. The Australian sheep increased in number from 8 million at mid-century to 70 million by the end of the century.

In the last quarter of the century, Australian cattle keeping also expanded inland. Sheep and cattle came to compete increasingly for vegetation and water with the kin-ordered aboriginal population. This drew aborigines and Europeans into inevitable conflicts. Some groups, like the Ngadidji and Aranda, were simply overrun by the pastoralists. Others, like the Walbiri, who lived outside the grazing areas, kept their autonomy for a while, until the younger men began to work as hired hands on pastoral stations and were soon followed by others. Mervyn Meggitt noted that in the mid-1950s the Walbiri had made use of their increased leisure, freed from the stringent demands of food collecting by the transition to wage work, to intensify their social and ceremonial activities (1962: 333).

Bananas

Bananas are not staples in a class with grains and meat; yet the development of banana plantations, stimulated by the commercial upswing of the nineteenth century, affected wide areas, especially Central America. The plant had originally been introduced into the Americas by Spaniards from the Canary Islands during the first years of the Conquest. It had spread widely as a staple crop among both primitive and peasant populations in the tropical lowlands. In the 1870s it became a plantation crop. In 1871 a railroad promoter from the United States, engaged in constructing railroads in Costa Rica, began to experiment in commercial banana production to provide freight for his railroad. Out of these experiments grew the United Fruit Company, incorporated in 1889.

In the course of thirty-five years, the Company produced approximately 2 billion bunches of bananas on its own far-flung estates in Costa Rica, Panama, Honduras, Colombia, and Ecuador. Geographic dispersal enabled the Company to offset political pressures in any one host country. Dispersal also allowed it to take advantage of suitable environments in different locations, thus reducing the chance that floods, hurricanes, soil depletion, and plant diseases could bring production to a halt in any one of them. To further reduce these risks, the Company acquired a great deal more land than it could use at any one time, to hold as a reserve against the future. In some areas it formed relationships with local cultivators who grew bananas and then sold them to the Company.

Such was the case on the northern coast of Colombia in the floodplain at the base of the Sierra Nevada de Santa Marta (see Partridge 1979). This area—drained, irrigated, and intensively cultivated by the Tairona in pre-Hispanic times (see chapter 2)—was only sparsely settled after the Spanish conquest decimated the native population. Until the last quarter of the nineteenth century, the land was either in extensive livestock estates or was used by swidden cultivators who resided in scattered hamlets and raised crops for subsistence and occasional sale. The lifeways of these settlers form the backdrop of *One Hundred Years of Solitude* by the Colombian novelist Gabriel García Márquez, who synthesized the experience of several settlements in his portrayal of the imaginary town of Macondo. In the 1870s Colombian entrepreneurs opened up the area with the construction of a railroad, a drainage canal, and irrigation ditches. Colombian planters initiated banana production soon afterward, sending the stalks to market in New York. In 1896 the United Fruit Company bought the railroad and acquired land south of the Colombian holdings to build up its own irrigation district. The Company's control of land transport, shipping, and marketing soon rendered the Colombian planters dependent upon it, requiring them to synchronize their productive processes with those of the United Fruit plantations and to sell their fruit through the Company. Labor contractors recruited plantation workers and oversaw the actual labor process. Workers were paid a small daily cash wage and scrip for purchases at the plantation commissary. García Márquez's novel poignantly describes some of the changes wrought by wage labor in the life of the local population, and their culmination in the bloody strike of 1928.

While most workers on the Colombian banana estates were recruited locally, in Central America the Company favored workers from the English-speaking islands of the Caribbean, especially Jamaica. The Company encountered difficulty in attracting people from the adjacent highlands to work in the tropical lowlands. The English-speaking West Indians not only could communicate with the North American plantation staff but, more importantly, they were wholly dependent on the Company while in its employ abroad and thus more manageable than native workers. The islanders could also be laid off when the Company abandoned cultivation in one area in favor of another. The role of West Indian workers on United Fruit plantations gradually diminished, as host governments exerted pressure against the importation of foreign workers and native populations became more familiar with wage work on the coast.

One group of Central Americans who became workers on the Company's Panama plantations were the Guaymí. This Chibcha-speaking population had retreated from the Spanish Conquest into the sanctuary provided by the rugged mountain country of western Panama, and there they preserved their kin-based corporate landholding groups. In the 1930s, increasing numbers of Guaymí began to combine shifting cultivation in their home province with periodic stints of wage labor for the Company. Growing ever more dependent on wages and store-bought commodities, they would be hard hit in the 1960s when the Company began to mechanize, replacing men with machines. Philip Young (1971) has seen in this deprivation the main cause of the nativist millenarian movement, Mama Chi, that developed among the Guaymí at that time.

Industrial Crops

Rubber in America

An industrial tree crop that became important during the nineteenth century was rubber. It became a prime industrial material after the discovery of vulcanization in 1839, and it was used first in the manufacture of raincoats, shoes, bicycle tires, condoms, and other household articles. Then it came to be used for railroads, in engineering, and as insulation in the new electrical industries. Finally, at the end of the century, it became a major raw material for the automobile industry.

Until 1900 Brazil was the only producer of rubber; it increased its production from a mere 27 tons in 1827 to an annual average of 20,000 tons in the last decade of the century (Poppino 1968: 140–141). The primary producers were at first Amazonian Indians and Luso-Brazilian cultivators on the Amazon. Later, laborers from the Brazilian Northeast (the so-called *flagelados*) were brought in to collect rubber under contract. They were impelled to seek a new source of livelihood in the tropical forest by the general economic decline of the sugar industry in the Northeast, the former heartland of the Brazilian economy. In more immediate terms, they were victims of the great drought that assailed the region between 1877 and 1880, and that may have been responsible for the death by starvation of some 200,000 people. A similar number moved into Amazonia in the last decades of the century (Furtado 1963: 143–144). The town described by Charles Wagley (1953) under the name of Itá owes its origin to the advent of such Northeastern migrants in 1880.

Rubber Gatherers: Mundurucú

How Amazonian Indians reacted to the introduction of the rubber trade is well exemplified by the people who called themselves Weidyénye ("our people"), but who are more widely known under the name given them by their Parintintín enemies—Mundurucú—after a species of ant. The Luso-Brazilians first met up with them in the late eighteenth century, when they raided other Indians and white settlers in the lower Amazon Valley. The Mundurucú and the intruders became allies, an alliance in which Mundurucú males and females took different roles. The women began to produce manioc for the frontiersmen. The men, though initially hostile, joined their new allies as mercenaries in warfare

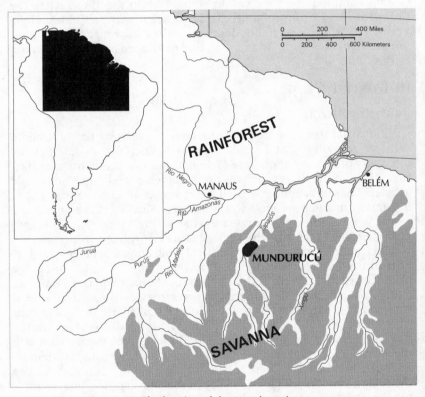

The location of the Mundurucú.

against the Mura Indians (who inhabited the area between the Amazon and the Rio Negro) and the Cawahíwa on the upper Tapajós. The Luso-Brazilians employed the Mundurucú to raid for slaves among these populations, to suppress local uprisings, and to put down general rebellions—such as the Revolution of the Cabanas in 1835, an uprising of local Whites, Afro-Brazilians, and Mura and other Indians.

The increase in manioc production, carried on by the women, and the expansion of long-distance warfare, carried on by the men, not only gave rise to an intensified division of labor between the sexes but also affected Mundurucú patterns of residence and descent. When Robert Murphy went to study the Mundurucú in the 1950s, they represented an ethnographic anomaly. They combined patrilineal reckoning of descent with matrilocal residence. Kroeber (1952: 213) had written that he "did not know of such a society, and should expect is occurrence to be rare." Murphy, moreover, found that the Mundurucú had acquired this unexpected combination by changing from an earlier pattern of patrilineality and patrilocality—a change thought by some anthropologists to be so unlikely that the obstacles to it were "well-nigh insuperable" (Murdock 1949: 217). Murphy showed how the Mundurucú had made this shift.

Until the early nineteenth century, the Mundurucú had lived in villages, each centered upon a single patrilineage that recruited women in marriage from other patrilineal villages through the rules of patrilocal residence. Each patrilineage symbolized its unity through the possession and ritual use of sacred trumpets embodying the ancestral spirits that were kept in a "men's house." With the advent of the manioc trade based on female production, however, the rule of marriage became matrilocal, which had the effect of maintaining the unity and continuity of the female-centered domestic task force. Instead of women moving to their husbands' villages upon marriage as before, men now moved to their wives' places of residence. The men in any given village were recruited from a number of different patrilineages, which were no longer anchored locally. The men's house of the village thus no longer served only one patrilineage, but became a common male clubhouse and "barracks." The sacred trumpets ceased to symbolize the distinctiveness of patrilineages. Rather, they began to stand for the unity of the men's house, emphasizing its translocal military potential.

Rubber tapping brought on still another transformation of Mundurucú social organization. Before the advent of the rubber trade, Mundurucú villages were usually located on high, savannahlike ground. In the dry season of each year, the villagers would descend to the river to fish. With the growing demand for rubber, however, they began to tap wild trees in the gallery forests along the river's edge, exchanging the latex they gathered for metal goods, clothing, and even food. Gradually, separate domestic groups set up permanent residences along the riverside, where they laid exclusive claim to tracts of forest.

Mundurucú village of Cabrua. Women drying manioc flour over a fire; men relaxing in the men's house. Photographs by Robert F. Murphy. (Courtesy of Robert F. Murphy)

Increasingly exchanging latex for commodities at the trading post, they abandoned their own crafts and became ever more dependent on the goods advanced by the trader. The Mundurucú villages, once fighting and manioc-growing units, thus dissolved into numerous small households, each linked separately to the trading post in a web of exchanges and growing debts. The trader replaced the Mundurucú chief as the pivot of local circuits of production and exchange. The rubber trader depended, in turn, on merchant houses downriver to receive the rubber and to supply him with needed commodities, while the merchant house was itself dependent upon an export-import firm for supplies and rubber sales. Thus Mundurucú, trader, merchant, and export-import firm all became linked in an expanding network of production and circulation.

Rubber in Asia

Brazilian wild rubber monopolized the world market during most of the nineteenth century. In 1876, however, Sir Robert Wickham smuggled seeds of Amazonian rubber to Kew Gardens in England, where they were acclimated and selected for planting in Malaya. After 1900 rubber production expanded rapidly in Asia, notably in Malaya. Malayan rubber plantations grew from 5,000 acres in 1900 to 1,250,000 in 1913. An

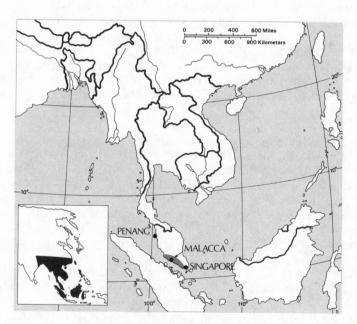

Malaya: the region of plantation rubber.

original planter class of small initial means was soon replaced by managers installed by agency houses that floated loans in London (Jackson 1968). The laborers were mostly imported from southern India. They were Tamil, working under indenture to labor contractors who hired laborers in their native villages and supervised their work in gangs on the plantation (Jain 1970).

Another rubber-producing area in southern Asia developed on the east coast of Sumatra, around Deli. In this area, the Dutch had long grown tobacco on plantations, which developed in symbiosis with the slash-and-burn agriculture of local Malay and Batak villagers. The plantation took over the labor of burning off the covering vegetation. It then raised the first crop, tobacco. When productivity decreased in the second year, the plantation opened a new field, allowing the villagers to take over the tobacco plots in order to raise food. When rubber was introduced in 1906, this symbiotic relationship came to an end. Rubber trees were a perennial crop and could not be alternated with annuals. Instead, rubber cultivation, carried on by imported Javanese and Chinese laborers, now engulfed the subsistence plots of the native population. Local villages gave way to company towns.

Plantation rubber did not remain the only source of rubber in either Indonesia or Malaya. In Indonesia, both in Sumatra and in Borneo, small holders also began to raise rubber. At first, they planted rubber in combination with food-producing swiddens, moving gradually toward greater reliance on the cash crop as market conditions and prices permitted. In Malaya, similarly, Malay cultivators came to rely on rubber production as a source of income. In a peasant village in Kelantan, studied in the late 1950s (see Downs 1967: 162–166), for instance, rubber tapping had become a source of cash income for almost three-quarters of the adult villagers. It was increasingly preferred to growing irrigated rice, in spite of the high basic value placed on rice in Malaya.

Palm Oil

A second tree crop to come into prominence during the nineteenth century was the palm. The export of palm oil from West Africa first paralleled the export of slaves, and then became the chief export of the West African forest belt with the abolition of the slave trade in the 1860s. Whereas West Africa exported a mere 1,000 tons of oil to England in 1810, palm oil exports reached an annual average of 50,000 tons between 1860 and 1900. Palm oil took the place of animal tallow in making soap, and it became increasingly important as a source of lubricants for machines. In the late nineteenth century, palm kernels also furnished oil for the manufacture of margarine and cattle feed.

The old centers of the slave trade responded to this new demand. Yet the new trade brought on major upheavals both in internal and external relations. An immediate consequence of the new trade was a "crisis of the aristocracy," namely, the warrior elites and state organizations that

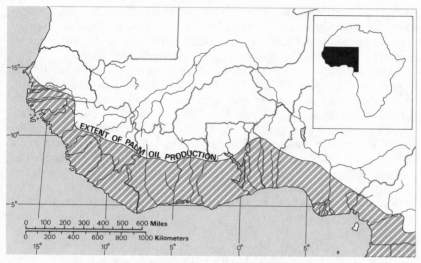

The region of palm oil production, West Africa.

had grown powerful and wealthy through the pursuit of slaving. An entity like Dahomey, wholly specialized for slave raiding and slaving, found it particularly difficult to switch over to the new commodity. There was an increase in interstate warfare for easy sources of plunder and tribute. In addition, the rulers of Dahomey and the chiefs of the Yoruba attempted to produce palm oil on plantations worked by slaves. The Asante state expanded its production and sale of kola nuts to the Hausa in the north in order to make up for the decline of slaving; but at the same time Fante middlemen on the coast were escaping the Asante grip by themselves producing palm oil for the new market. Old elites found their incomes threatened. The canoe houses of the Niger delta disintegrated; former slaves asserted their independence in order to take part in the new trade; and there were repercussions in disorders among slaves. The production of palm oil was also a business that could be entered by small cultivators if they could gain access to oil palms on the lands of their descent group or ward division and mobilize the labor of their households (see Uchendu 1965).

In contrast to the slave trade, in which African middlemen had delivered the slaves to the coast for transshipment, the palm oil trade prompted European wholesalers to establish direct contact with the producers or with their representatives in the African hinterlands. In turn, a new commercial elite of Africans, many of them ex-slaves educated in European religious missions, took over the import trade previously handled by the slave traders. The dual development of European palm oil merchants and African importers was aided by the spread of European all-purpose money in place of the iron, copper, and cowrie currencies used previously. This diminished the exchange of European goods for slaves or for African products, and it put palm oil export and commodity imports on a cash-and-carry basis.

This interplay of contending forces was profoundly affected by the Great Depression of 1873. Prices for palm oil products declined; profit margins decreased. Former aristocrats of the slave trade, new African middlemen, European wholesalers, and African producers all confronted diminished opportunities and sharply increased competition for scarcer resources. "Not surprisingly," notes A. G. Hopkins, "there was a fierce struggle in the late nineteenth century as each party sought to control the local market and dictate terms to the other" (1973: 154). The European merchants called for law and order, a call often supported by colonial officials, whose reputation was tied up with the expansion of European-based commerce. The Europeans wanted to rationalize commerce and transportation still further by expanding railroads inland; the former ruling class saw this, correctly, as the final spike driven through their declining power. To add to the embroilment, the various European powers competed with one another, each supported by a mercantile contingent hoping for privileged access to a controlled market.

The result was the entry of European troops, the conquest of the inland kingdoms of Asante, Dahomey, Oyo, and Benin, the destruction of the Aro and their Great Oracle, and the establishment of European domination. In West Africa, the expansion of imperial European rule was undertaken by imperial officials who were perhaps not fully conscious of any economic imperatives. The dialectic of forces was complex, and the resulting disorder invited political and military intervention. Yet the disorders were economic in their basic causes, and the intervention was economic in its consequences.

Stimulants

Among the panoply of products destined for consumption in the industrializing areas, a few are clearly not staple foodstuffs or industrial products but rather stimulants. Already significant during the period of Europe's initial overseas expansion, such commodities as tea, coffee, cocoa, sugar, tobacco, and even opium recur so often in the roster of imports and exports during the latter nineteenth century that some scholars have even begun to speak of their role as the "Big Fix."

The popularity of these stimulants is not easily explained. It may be that they are pharmacologically addictive, answering to certain biochemical propensities of the human body. In that sense they would not be unique, but would form part of a wider set of stimulants in human use, including the West African kola nut, the betel nut of South and Southeast Asia, the maté of Argentina, and the coca of the Andes. These other products remained of only regional interest, however, and did not enter the circuits of worldwide traffic, in contrast to the products popularized in the course of the industrial revolution. It has been suggested that these stimulants of the industrial era were favored because they provided quick energy in a period when more intense and prolonged performance was demanded from the human body. Some of them provided carbohydrates and energy, without at the same time rendering the body inefficient, as would alcohol. Thus, "tea time" and "coffee breaks" fitted better into the new industrial schedule of work than libations of gin or rum would have. Still, these latter continued to be drunk in considerable quantities, despite the great efforts of a growing temperance movement.

We should perhaps not look to the physiological properties of various stimulants as the final explanation, but rather view their increasing use as part of a general reshaping of consumption patterns. There were major changes of diet in the eighteenth and nineteenth centuries, many of them nutritionally for the worse (Braudel 1973b: 129–130; Hobsbawm 1967: Chaps. 5, 7). There was less access to peasant produce, and especially to meat, with the decline of small producers supplying local markets. There was greater demand for a few bulk products for the growing agglomerations of population in cities and industrial centers. Yet there were also new patterns of sociability and communication, such as those provided by coffeehouses and teashops. New class-based norms for where, when, and how to eat developed, in turn setting up new standards for cultural emulation in societies undergoing rapid social and cultural change. With these new patterns, the consumption of alkaloids, theobromides, sugars, and even "tranquilizers" made rapid progress in all social classes. Purveying the new products, in its turn, "European enterprise accumulated considerable savings by the provision of low-cost foods and substitutes to European working classes" (Mintz 1979b: 61).

Sugar

First among the stimulants was still sugar—an indispensable additive to sauces and pastry, as well as a sweetener for innumerable cups of tea, coffee, and cocoa. Although the supremacy of sugar cane as a source of sugar had been challenged, first by the rebellion of the slaves in French St. Domingue (Haiti) and by the abolition of slavery in British Jamaica, and later by the diffusion of the sugar beet in temperate Europe, it never lost out completely and once again expanded in acreage after the third decade of the nineteenth century.

In the British orbit, this renewed rise took place with the aid of a new labor supply, namely, indentured laborers from the East Indies. The island of Mauritius in the Indian Ocean, won from the French in 1815, was the first British colony to benefit from the arrival of these new recruits to the labor force, and it took first place among the new sugar producers. It was followed by Trinidad, which Britain captured from

Spain, and Guyana, taken from the Dutch. In the second half of the century, Indian indentured laborers began to work in the cane fields in Fiji (1850) and in Natal, South Africa (1860), while Melanesians, mostly from the New Hebrides, were impressed or contracted for work in Queensland, Australia (1863), as well as in Fiji (1864).

The forcible recruitment of Melanesians, or "blackbirding," affected large numbers of men. Between 1863 and 1907, 61,000 Melanesians were taken to Queensland alone, of whom fewer than 45,000 returned (Docker 1970: 274). On many islands, blackbirding aided the careers of local labor recruiters or hunters of men. One such was Kwaisulia on the island of Sulu Vou. Kwaisulia had signed up to work in Queensland and had returned home in the 1880s. Drawing on his local network, he provided the blackbirders with labor recruits, for which he received arms and ammunition, dynamite, kerosene, medicines, hardware, and building materials (Docker 1970: 130–138). This wealth then enabled Kwaisulia to enlarge the scale of his operations. In other areas the local end of the trade was not controlled by monopolists. Blackbirding meant, however, the advent of guns, leading to an increase in raiding and fighting and to the decimation of the local population.

Beginning in 1830, the Dutch, too, undertook to expand sugar production—in Indonesia, especially in Java, under a system known as the Culture System (Dutch *Cultuurstelsel*, meaning "cultivation system") (see Geertz 1963). The culture system demanded that villagers pay goverment taxes in crops rather than in money. Designed to elicit and increase the production of all tropical crops, it was most successful in the case of sugar and coffee. These became the two major export crops of the Dutch East Indies. Sugar, an annual, could be raised on the same land as the irrigated rice of the Javanese villagers. By allocating one-fifth of village lands to the production of sugar, the Dutch sugar estates acquired at one and the same time a suitable land base and a labor force resident in villages and available seasonally for labor in the cane fields. Independent production of sugar by Javanese smallholders was discouraged, but the customary workings of the Javanese village were reinforced. These villages, where labor reproduced itself by ever intensifying the cultivation of irrigated rice, thus functioned efficiently as labor reserves for the sugar operations.

In 1870 new legislation transferred the responsibility for making the system work from the government to private enterprises. The law continued to maintain village integrity by protecting village titles to land, but it now granted ownership of cane plantings to private holders. Soon after, when these newly created planters experienced financial shipwreck, their rights passed to Netherlands-based companies, which successfully combined the sugar estates with large capital-intensive processing facilities. Labor in sugar continued to be drawn from the wet-rice-growing villages, but management of each new mill and of the cane lands associated with it passed entirely into the hands of European personnel.

The Rise of the Capital-intensive Plantation

The Dutch transformation of the East Indian sugar estate from a unit dependent primarily on massive use of labor to a unit organized around a capital-intensive sugar mill illustrates the worldwide "fall of the planter class." The planter, drawing on merchant capital and delivering his cash crop to pay for it, could not marshall the financial and technical resources required to raise transportation, labor operations, and processing to the higher level required by ever-increasing capital accumulation. In sugar production, this stepped-up requirement involved large new outlays for land, processing equipment, and a transportation infrastructure, creating "factories in the field." Simultaneously, financial control of the undertaking shifted from merchant houses to joint-stock or limited-liability companies, and still later to corporate capital.

This transformation occurred in the Caribbean as well as in Indonesia. It was especially massive in Cuba, where sugar production intensified in the second half of the century, intensifying the exactions of slavery in turn. In Cuba, as in Puerto Rico, American intervention in the local effort to separate the islands from Spain created the conditions for the replacement of planters' capital with corporate capital brought in from the United States.

Sidney Mintz (1974: Chap. 4) has traced in detail the transformation

Cutting and loading sugar cane at Las Canas, one of Cuba's technologically most advanced sugar estates during the second half of the nineteenth century. Sketch by Walter Yeager, 1880. (Courtesy of the New York Historical Society, New York City)

of such a plantation on the south coast of Puerto Rico. Before slavery was abolished in 1873, Hacienda Vieja drew on a labor supply of landless freemen forced to work by coercive labor legislation, in addition to their supply of slaves. The plantation, owned by a single family, was small, usually falling into the range of 100 to 400 acres. A fourth of the land was in sugar cane; the rest was in pasture and subsistence plots used to feed the laborers. Fields were worked with hook-type plows; fertilizer other than animal droppings was unknown; and irrigation, necessary for cultivation on this dry coast, was limited. The sugar-processing machinery was old-fashioned, and the sugar produced was crude. When slavery was abolished, the plantation changed over to the use of free labor, paid wages, and granted subsistence plots where workers raised their own food. Available capital, however, was too limited to make possible the transition to more modern agricultural and processing technology.

This transition came only a quarter of a century later, with the North American occupation. The plantation was sold to a mainland corporation, which now aggregated the older plantations into one large complex of "tributary farms" centered upon a giant processing mill. Cultivation was expanded to engulf subsistence plots and pasture range alike, turning the whole region into a continuous belt of burgeoning cane. Irrigation and swamp drainage were expanded; fertilizer was introduced. Subsistence plots disappeared, and work—now paid as piecework—was remunerated in wages in the form of tokens exchangeable for commodities at a company store. Within a short time, the labor force of the area was transformed from a population of laborers paid largely in kind into a full-fledged rural proletariat.

Coffee

Coffee drinking reached Europe through contacts with the Near East. Originally native to Ethiopia, it was drunk in Aden by the end of the fifteenth century. In spite of frequent prohibitions, it became popular throughout the lands of the Ottoman polity in the course of the sixteenth century. It spread through Europe along with the institution of the coffeehouse in the late seventeenth century. At first the only source of the bean was the hinterland of the town of Al Mukhá (Mocha) in Yemen, but by 1712 the Dutch were planting coffee shrubs in Java. In 1833 there were more than a million coffee trees in Java; by mid-century 300 million (Geertz 1963: 66). Coffee produced on Dutch estates and by Indonesian small holders soon became the Dutch East Indies' major export crop.

Production, however, dipped severely between 1880 and 1890, when the fungus of the coffee blight hit the orchards. It recovered thereafter, with a shift in species from *arabica* to *robusta*, both on estates and on peasant-owned swiddens in the Outer Islands, but it had by then lost first place to sugar as the main export crop. In the meantime, a decade of crop destruction in Java had provided the opportunity for enlarged production in Brazil.

Coffee had reached Brazil early in the eighteenth century, but it had been grown wholly for domestic consumption. The slave rebellion in French-held St. Domingue (Haiti) brought on an increase in coffee prices, which in turn stimulated a rise in Brazilian coffee exports. Coffee produced on slave plantations rapidly became Brazil's leading agricultural export, in spite of a decline in coffee prices. The employment of unremunerated slave labor in fact compensated for the fall in returns. To expand production further, however, confronted Brazil with a serious manpower problem (see Furtado 1963: Chaps. 21, 22). The African slave trade had been halted, while Brazil's internal supply of slaves failed to reproduce itself. Moreover, slavery was, for various reasons, finally abolished in 1888. Moving labor from the precarious swidden subsistence sector into plantation agriculture would have undermined the food economy without guaranteeing an increase in the available labor force. Some Brazilians already envisaged the importation of Asians when agricultural difficulties and the decline of the textile industry in southern Italy unleashed a stream of European migrants into Brazil. A million and a half European immigrants came to Brazil between 1880 and 1890, most of them Italians, and large numbers became laborers on the rapidly expanding coffee *fazendas* of São Paulo. By the end of the century, Brazil was able to supply three-quarters of the world's coffee.

Although Brazil came to dominate the world coffee market, other areas entered coffee production as well. Among these was Central America, specifically the Mexican state of Chiapas and Guatemala. Here the spread of commercial coffee production was materially aided by legislation (Mexico, 1856; Guatemala, 1877) that abolished communal jurisdiction over land. This legislation did away with the legal armature that had permitted corporate native American communities to survive and to stabilize themselves in the face of repeated attempts to seize their resources and tap their labor supply (see chapter 5). Land was now to be owned privately and to be made subject to purchase, sale, and pawning. This allowed non-Indians to buy up unregistered land and to foreclose mortgages of Indian debtors. By the mid-nineteenth century, the Tzeltal- and Tzotzil-speaking communities surrounding San Cristóbal Las Casas in Chiapas had already lost most of their territorial base, except for a small remnant of heavily overutilized communal land. In 1869 the Tzeltal, in fact, rose in rebellion against this diminution of their resources under external pressure. In the 1870s, however, coffee was introduced on foreign-owned estates, and many Indians were encouraged to settle in the new coffee areas. After World War I, the planters further increased their labor supply by engaging temporary workers from the highland communities through the use of cash advances. This system of advances made wage labor the major source of income for

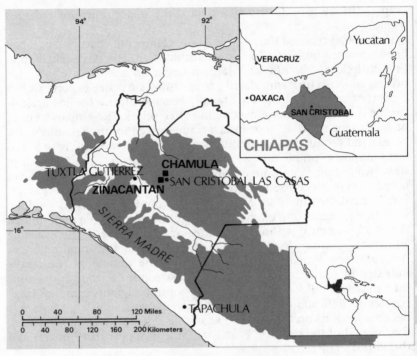

Chiapas, Mexico.

many highland dwellers who, between stints of labor, would return to their communities to farm small subsistence plots (Wasserstrom 1977, 1978). Once again, we see the development of a system whereby plantations producing a cash product and subsistence-oriented "labor reserves" came to exist side by side.

More recently, during World War II, Mexican landowners in the lowland Grijalva basin expanded their production of foodstuffs, notably corn, in response to advantageous prices in the national capital. They did this by renting unused or untapped land to Zinacanteco tenants to clear and cultivate, thus maintaining property rights over the land while obtaining a ready work force. The more successful Zinacanteco renters, in turn, hired wage laborers from Chamula to maximize their output, or they employed other members of their community to recruit and organize work crews on their behalf

Zinacantan, Chamula, and other Tzeltal- and Tzoltzil-speaking communities in the vicinity of San Cristóbal Las Casas in highland Chiapas have been studied intensively by American anthropologists since the 1940s. Most of these studies have dealt with them either as "tribal" survivors of the ancient Maya, maintained in relative isolation from outside contact, or as parts of a colonial Hispanic society preserved in encapsulated form within a modernizing Mexico. Tzeltal and Tzotzil, along with other Native Americans in Central America, however, were drawn early into the networks of mercantile expansion (see McLeod 1973), and they have participated actively since the nineteenth century in the commercial coffee and corn economy of the area and in the politics of the Mexican state. These involvements, in turn, have altered their agricultural adaptation, changed their class structure, and affected their political and ceremonial organization. Their continuing identity as inhabitants of "Indian" communities is thus not a corpus of unchanged traditions maintained in unbroken fashion from a distant past. It is, rather, the outcome of a multitude of interrelated and often antagonistic processes set in motion by capitalist development.

Tea

Tea became, of course, coffee's main competitor in providing alkaloid stimulants to the world. The first historically reliable reference to tea is in a Chinese source dating from the fourth century A.D., but it was not until the eighth century that it was given its own character, *ch'a*, in the script, and became sufficiently important economically to be taxed by the state. Portuguese missionaries were perhaps the first Europeans to report on tea, and the Dutch sea merchants introduced the brew to Europe. By the middle of the seventeenth century, it had become a popular drink in the Netherlands and France; during the last third of the century it became the predilect drink of English court circles. At this time it still came entirely from China. During the first quarter of the eighteenth century, tea replaced silk as the main item loaded on British ships trafficking along the China coast. It was soon drunk not only in the British Isles but also in the American colonies. There it constituted the third largest import, after textiles and ironwares, until Sam Adams's rebel band—clumsily disguised as Indians—initiated the American War of Independence by feeding a recently arrived consignment of tea to the fish of Boston harbor.

From 1840 on, tea began to be raised in quantity in Assam, where the bush grew wild, and in various parts of India where it was planted. Yet until the opening of the Suez Canal, Indian teas furnished only a fraction of the world's supply of tea. After the opening of the canal, the steamboat won out over the clipper ship in loading and transporting tea, and Indian "black" teas became dominant commercially over the green teas of China.

In Ceylon, tea plantations spread with astonishing rapidity throughout the uplands in the 1870s, to a great extent at the expense of the Kandyan Sinhalese peasantry. A large amount of village common land was turned into royal land and then sold to planters. In 1848 coffee had covered some 60,000 acres, held by 367 plantations, but when the coffee blight struck in 1868, the planters switched to tea. By 1903 more than 400,000 acres had been planted with tea shrubs (Royal Kandyan Peasantry Commission, quoted in Yalman 1971: 20, n. 10). The effect was to restrict the Sinhalese peasantry to the precincts of their irrigated rice villages, and to curtail their ability to open slash-and-burn fields in their land reserves.

Tea cultivation is enormously labor consuming. With each acre bearing between 3,000 and 5,000 bushes (each bush furnishing between five and eight ounces of tea), twenty to forty harvesters are needed per acre per day. To obtain the needed labor, the planters imported Tamil-speakers from South India into Ceylon. These "India Tamil," who differ from the much older "Ceylon" or "Jaffna" Tamil of the north and east coasts, today number close to a million people, as compared with some 2 million upland Kandyan Sinhalese. The socioeconomic opposition between the India Tamil and the surrounding Sinhalese peasantry has been exacerbated by linguistic and religious differences. The Sinhalese speak an Indo-European language, the Tamil are Dravidian-speakers; the Sinhalese are Buddhists, the Tamil Hindus. These differences, in turn, have fueled open conflicts between the Sinhalese cultivators and the Tamil plantation proletariat.

Cocoa

Cocoa was originally a Mesoamerican crop. In the course of the seventeenth century, the Dutch took it to the island of São Tomé in the Gulf of Guinea off the West African coast. In 1879 an enterprising Ga-speaker carried the seed from the neighboring island of Fernando Po to the Akwapim Ridge, above the city of Accra on the Gold Coast of present-day Ghana. By the 1890s cocoa was grown on the Akwapim Ridge in place of the palm products that suffered a decline in prices after 1885. Cocoa could be adopted readily: no new tools were required; drying and fermenting the beans were simple processes; and only at harvest time was there a requirement for large inputs of labor. The financial skills required for producing and marketing the new crop were also present. We have seen (chapter 7) that West Africans had acquired a great deal of knowledge and sophistication in the mechanics of commerce. The cultivators who launched themselves into cocoa production were acquainted with the mechanisms of money and credit. Some had been involved in trade in the past; others had tried their hands at collecting wild rubber for sale.

To obtain land on which to raise cocoa, the new growers negotiated land sales with the chiefs in control of surplus land in Akim Abuakwa. In buying this land, the new occupants neatly combined the new ways of land acquisition with older patterns of group organization. Patrilineal populations, like the Krobo, formed nonkin "companies" or land-buying clubs that bought land in severalty, assigning separate strips to company members. The matrilineal Aburi and Akropong bought land for their matrilineage (*abusua*), allocating land in usufruct to lineage

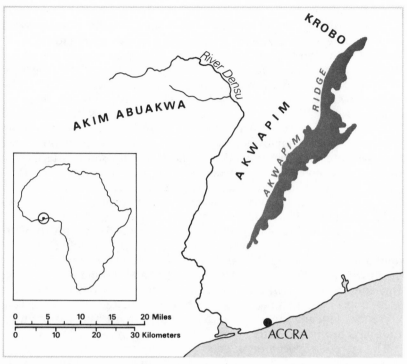

Cocoa-growing and ethnic affiliation, Ghana and Ivory Coast.

members. Usually the original settlers maintained the cohesion of their starting nucleus, including its political subordination to a local village chief.

The cocoa producers first farmed in the vicinity of their home village, growing trees until these reached maturity. With the proceeds from their original cocoa stands, they then opened up a new belt of cocoa production, bringing in share tenants and their families to cultivate and harvest, generally in return for a third of the crop. Laborers—usually Ewe and others from east of the Volta River—were also hired to weed the land between harvests. In time, people with accumulated capital would buy land "forward" and stake others to the purchase of new outlying stands of cacao, or else they would take over lands relinquished by cultivators unable to compete.

By 1911 Ghana was the world's major producer of cocoa, a commodity dear to every worshiper of chocolate candy. Expanded production favored owners of larger holdings who worked the land with sharecroppers and seasonal wage laborers, over households employing family labor only. Thus, over time, increased cocoa growing differentiated the population into classes of farmers and laborers (Hill 1963).

Cocoa growing spread rapidly throughout West Africa—northward to the Asante, eastward to the Yoruba of Nigeria, westward to the Ivory Coast. On the Ivory Coast, it was not introduced by African cultivators but rather was initiated by the French colonial government, in the hope of developing a new source of commercial wealth and taxation. The people brought into cocoa cultivation here were not, as in the Ghanaian case, pioneer cultivators on a settlement frontier, but were members of hierarchically organized African states under French colonial control. These states had been formed by the Agni, a warrior population related to the Asante. They had moved into what is now the southeastern Ivory Coast in the seventeenth century, forming two states, Ndenié in the north, Sanwi in the south. Each of these states was organized around a king who delegated power to village and matrilineal chiefs. The population was divided into tribute takers and tribute producers. The tribute takers were made up of the royal family (matrilineal descendants of the first Agni chiefs) and several strata of chiefs, including warriors appointed to the chiefship and chiefs of immigrants and of splinter groups. The producers of tribute—in labor and in kind—were either free members of Agni matrilineages or slaves who were usually descendants of populations conquered by the Agni. Rights to use the land were matrilineally inherited, with succession to usufruct passing from mother's brother to sister's son.

The advent of cocoa production on the Ivory Coast put this system under stress. First of all, lineage heads with overrights to land began to depress lineage mates to the status of laborers and to engross the profits produced by the new crop. This caused schisms within lineages. Second, matrilineal succession to rights came into conflict with the pattern whereby cocoa cultivation was carried out by patrilocal working groups. New heirs to land often found themselves in conflict with the people actually working it, either as sharecroppers (*abusan*) or as pieceworkers. Matrilineal succession to rights meant that a son could not inherit the land in which he had invested his labor; nor could he be certain that his uncle would provide him with a comparable holding. Third, foreigners—Diula, Baoulé, or Mossi—applying for use rights to Agni lineage lands found themselves at odds with the Agni chiefs granting such rights. The newcomers wanted to pass on their newly developed holdings to their own sons, but they soon found themselves beset by demands from their matrilineally organized landlords. Often successful in their cocoa-growing ventures, moreover, they sought status equal to that of the Agni, who considered themselves—as victorious warriors—superior to all foreigners. Finally, the increasing need for money and capital placed power in the hands of wealthy merchants, moneylenders, and cocoa planters. This caused the possession of wealth to override kinship connection and status distinctions based on the Agni/non-Agni polarity. Furthermore, the new wealthy elite, comprising both Agni and non-Agni, built up ties with outsiders who connected Agnidom with the circuits of capital in Abidjan and beyond. These outsiders were usually Diula or Lebanese merchants. A wholly different set of social relationships was thus superimposed on Agni society, with resulting conflicts between classes and ethnic groups.

Opium

Among the crops that grew increasingly important in the nineteenth century was opium. We have already seen that it played a major role in English trade with China. The Chinese state fought in vain to stem the increase of opium production within China and the importation of "foreign mud" from outside. Smoking opium was prohibited in 1729. A further edict, in 1800, banned smoking, growing, and importing opium. This, however, proved merely a stimulus to smuggling and to local production in the Chinese provinces of Szechwan and Yunnan. Finally, the Chinese defeat in the Opium War of 1839–1842 with Britain opened up China to unlimited imports of Indian opium. In 1858 the Chinese government recognized its inability to control the British-sponsored trade by signing an agreement that put a small tax on opium imports. At the same time, internal opium production increased spectacularly after 1860, competing effectively with the foreign product. By the 1880s Szechwan province was harvesting an estimated 10,000 tons of raw opium a year, and Yunnan province began to export opium to Southeast Asia.

Opium production and smuggling also became a mainstay in the economy of the hill people inhabiting the mountainous area between the Chinese border and the Southeast Asia lowlands. Among these were the Hmong ("Meo" or "Miao") and the Iu Mien ("Yao" or "Man"), who had been gradually driven out of China since the late seventeenth century. They now began to take up production of the resin-bearing flower on their own. In the 1890s opium was being produced in Thailand and in northeastern Burma, where a British observer saw "miles of slopes covered with the poppy" (J. Scott, quoted in McCoy 1972: 65). Among most of the hill dwellers of Southeast Asia—Hmong, Iu Mien, Akha, Lahu, Lisu—opium has since become the major cash product.

Since the Yunnan variety of the opium poppy grows best above altitudes of 3,000 feet, it is usually grown on higher ground above dry rice swiddens, or else it is rotated on swidden fields with maize as the alternate crop planted each year. Declining production on swidden fields leads to migration about every five years. In order to secure suitable terrain in competition with other groups, people draw on wide-ranging kinship ties and the backing of their ethnic category.

Opium production requires a great deal of labor. Not only must land be cleared but fields must be continuously weeded and thinned. Once the flower petals fall, the exposed capsules must be tapped. They must be carefully scored to allow the resin to flow, and the congealed resin

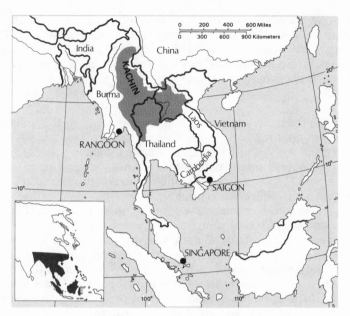

Zones of opium poppy, Southeast Asia.

must then be scraped off and packaged. This work must, of course, be synchronized with other tasks of cultivation of rice, maize, or vegetables. The high demand for labor is met by family members and sons-in-law who are expected to perform bride service. Households also exchange labor, and laborers are sometimes hired for work other than the delicate operations of tapping. These hired laborers are often addicts of other ethnic categories, who are paid in part with opium for their own use. Success in opium production thus depends on a man's ability to attract sufficient labor, and a man gains by having many children and sons-in-law. Raising numerous children and multiplying sons-in-law, in turn, hinge upon success in manipulating the marriage market and the flow of bridewealth. Success in poppy growing and in expanding kinship ties brings a man political influence, which he enhances further by offering costly feasts on behalf of household and lineage spirits.

The role of opium as a key economic factor in the lives of the hill people bears upon the case of the Kachin, who occupy the hill areas of northeastern Burma. These people have become significant in anthropological studies as a result of the path-breaking work of Edmund Leach (1954). Leach was one of the first British social anthropologists to go beyond the static structuralism advocated by Radcliffe-Brown to depict Kachin social structures as a reversible process of oscillation between a hierarchical model of chief-follower relations, called *gumsa*, and an egalitarian model of organization, called *gumlao*. The hierarchical gumsa model represented a Kachin approximation to the theocratic kingship of the valley Shan. Yet it was inherently unstable, since it lacked an economic base in lowland irrigation agriculture and a political base in a theocratic state. Instead, it was anchored in a system in which patri-lineages were ranked as wife-givers to wife-takers. This system was continuously threatened by schisms, as siblings became rivals for the same chiefship position or as sons-in-law refused to have their bride service turned into more permanent and coercive forms of dependence. Gumsa hierarchy was thus inherently subject to breakdown, giving rise to fission and to new groups organized on more egalitarian gumlao lines. Yet gumlao would again give way to gumsa as aspirants for the Shan-like chiefship began to expand their roles as "thigh-eating chiefs."

This interpretation, which locates the cause of Kachin differentiation in the inherent contradictions in their social organization, has been challenged by Jonathan Friedman (1975). In Friedman's alternative model, the causative mainspring for gumlao revolt is a combination of political-economic features. With slash-and-burn cultivation yielding diminishing returns, groups giving valuables in bride payment to wife-givers fall into debt, a condition they solve by fission. Conversely, the successful conversion of valuables into merit-making feasts to spirits allows some Kachin segments to acquire more wives and followers, enabling them to achieve greater renown and influence.

When the constellations of gumsa and gumlao are placed in a wider historical context, however, it becomes clear that gumlao revolts repre-sent historically recent reactions to changes that affected the Kachin hills in the late nineteenth century, and that they are not the invariable outcomes of gumsa status emulation and claims on the labor services of affines.

This history has been analyzed in a recent paper by Nugent (1980). Until the last quarter of the nineteenth century, Kachin chiefs were all gumsa. They grew opium with the aid of slaves, and controlled deposits of amber, serpentine, and jade—indeed, furnishing since the early eighteenth century most of the jade of China (Leach 1954: 290). Above all, they levied tolls on the extensive and lucrative Chinese carrying trade between China and Burma, and the income from these tolls constituted the major source of power for the leading gumsa chiefs in the late nineteenth century (Leach 1954: 237). The gumsa chiefs were sought after as allies by the English advancing across Assam, by the Burmese striving to contain the British advance, and by the Chinese traders running their caravans between Yunnan and Burma. The ability of Kachin chiefs to emulate the Shan *saohpas* was thus based on their control of slave labor, trade, and arms supplied by the political powers competing in the area.

This favored situation was increasingly undermined during the sec-ond half of the nineteenth century. Revolts in Yunnan and Shan rebellions against the disintegrating Burmese state brought about the decline of the carrying trade between China and Burma. English interference in Burmese affairs led to the annexation of Lower Burma in 1852, the seizure of Upper Burma in 1886, and wars of pacification against Shan and Kachin until 1891. With the exception of the Triangle area north of Myitkyina, which was not pacified until the 1920s, English administration severely curtailed the power and influence of the Kachin gumsa chiefs. Their domains were broken up, and each village under its own chief was treated as a distinct political entity. Slaves were set free, lessening chiefly participation in the production of opium. Chiefs were no longer allowed to charge tolls from passing caravans—their main source of income in the nineteenth century—and were forbidden to exact tribute from neighboring Shan communities. The forcible reduction of chiefly power by the English completed the decline of the thigh-eating chiefs initiated by the drying up of the China–Burma border trade. Gumlao revolts began to appear as the power of the gumsa chiefs waned. Thus, these revolts are better understood as a reaction to the weakness rather than the growing strength of the chiefs.

The revolts took place, moreover, against the background of opium production. As Maran La Raw has noted, the gumlao "deviation from *gumchying gumsa*, the traditional, original Kachin ideal model, has coincided with their progressively greater reliance on upland opium-poppy (cash-crop) cultivation, in place of subsistence upland-rice agriculture" (1967, I: 138–139; see also Leach 1954: 26). In raising opium, the Kachin were also raising money, since opium has always served, and continues to serve, as general-purpose money among the populations of the hills. Indeed, it plays a part in the manipulations of bride wealth important in gaining status and power. Leach mentions a case in which a man who had grown rich in trading opium paid entirely in opium a bride price set formally in cattle, silver, opium, and rifles (1954: 151, n. 66). It seems likely that the consolidation of wealth created by continued opium production underwrites the rise of new gumsa chiefs, primarily dependent on growing, selling, and smuggling opium. This seems to have occurred in the Wa States of Burma, where successful opium growers have modeled themselves on wet-rice producers of the plains, have adopted Buddhism, and have become known as Hill Shans (Tai Loi).

Gold and Diamonds

Plant and livestock products were not the only kinds of commodities that entered the world market in large quantities during the nineteenth century. There were also ores, such as tin from Malaya and copper from Chile. In 1866 diamonds were discovered in the territory of the Afrikaaner (Boer) Orange Free State in southern Africa, followed by the discovery of gold on the Witwatersrand in Transvaal twenty years later.

By 1874 there were already 10,000 Africans employed in the diamond mines, and ten years after the gold strike 97,000 were working in the gold mines. By 1910 the number of African miners had risen to 255,000; in 1940 it stood at 444,000.

In South Africa, European settlement had opened up a frontier not unlike that of North America. The initial European settlement in the area was on the Cape, a provisioning station opened up in 1652 by the Dutch East India Company for its Asian trade. From this station the initial Dutch settlers had fanned out to drive back and destroy the food-collecting San (Bushmen) and to reduce the pastoral Khoi-Khoi (Hottentot) to servitude, appropriating at the same time their fat-tailed sheep and their cattle.

Further expansion northward brought the Europeans into contact with Bantu-speaking populations, whom they drove back in stages until they reached the Fish River by 1775. There the frontier stayed for fifty years, a perimeter determined by the distance to the Capetown cattle market. After a sizable contingent of British settlers arrived in 1820 on the lower Fish River at Albany Bay, however, the frontier began to move again, this time unleashing conflicts over cattle and pasture between Boers and groups of Bantu-speaking Xhosa. With these encounters pressures built up in the area between the Fish River, to the south, and Portuguese-held Delagoa Bay, to the north.

This area was occupied by small Nguni chiefdoms, each built up around a chief, his patrilineage, and other patrilineages linked by descent or alliance. The Nguni military and hunting organization, focused on the figure of the chief, would fragment with the breakup of one chiefly domain and re-form around another, in a continuing process of fission and renewed alliance. During the last quarter of the eighteenth century, three chiefly clusters won out over the rest; in the first decade of the nineteenth century, one of these clusters, the Mthetwa, came to dominate the others, in part through the military prowess of its chief Dingiswayo, in part perhaps through trade connections with the Portuguese on the coast. Dingiswayo replaced the military and hunting organizations that owed loyalty to subchiefs by militarizing the age grades of his people. He also adapted a hunting technique—the surround by pincer movement ("the horns")—to warfare. After Dingiswayo's death, Shaka, the leader of a minor allied clan known as Zulu, usurped the Mthetwa chiefship and built a still larger Zulu polity, successfully organizing it for warfare using Dingiswayo's age-grade organization and tactics. Shaka also enhanced the shock value of the Zulu troops by introducing the *assagai*—a short stabbing spear—which he may have invented and, in any case, which he ordered the Zulu blacksmiths to produce.

The formation of the Zulu state furnishes a more dynamic example of cultural transformation than is usually available to anthropologists. Dingiswayo and Shaka responded to changes in the field of political

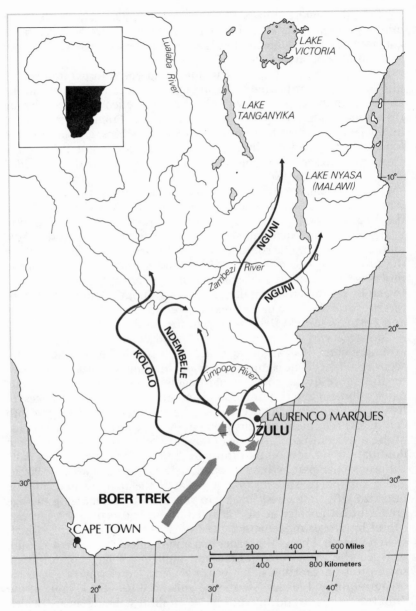

Expansion and migration in southern Africa.

forces around them by constructing a new political entity. In doing so, they drew on patterns of organization familiar to them from the past, but they altered these patterns radically in the process. These changes undermined the particularistic interests of the locally based patrilineage, while at the same time consolidating its manpower in a powerful military machine. Thus, Dingiswayo forbade the circumcision schools that had united the members of related homesteads under the jurisdiction of their chief's son. Whereas the previous military organization had brought together kinsmen drawn from neighboring homesteads under the command of their local chiefs, Dingiswayo militarized the age sets. This use of the age sets assigned successive generations of the same lineage and compound to different regiments, and focused their loyalty upon the kingship. Each regiment was given special dress and cowhide shields of a distinctive color. Shaka reinforced the role of the regiments by setting up parallel organizations for women. Men were forbidden to marry until the age of forty, and then they were assigned by regiment to take wives from the corresponding female unit.

Shaka also assumed all responsibility for magic in Zululand. He took over all rainmaking functions himself, expelling rival rainmakers; he forced medicine men to teach him their cures; and he made all verdicts in sorcery cases subject to royal confirmation. Fortifying the Zulu kingship still further, he centered the annual first-fruits and war ritual upon the figure of the king and upon the line of his royal ancestors. The annual ceremonial became a show of strength and unity by the assembled army. "The traditions of the Zulu royal lineage became the traditions of the nation; the Zulu dialect became the language of the nation; and every inhabitant, whatever his origins, became a Zulu, owing allegiance to Shaka" (Thompson 1969: 345). This transformation exhibits in stark form the ways that rituals were manipulated in a process of state making set in motion by the expanding frontiers of European settlement.

Zulu expansion between the beginning of the century and 1836, in turn, propelled other populations centrifugally in all directions, in many instances leading to the creation of new political clusters. Thus, the Kumalo clan of the Nguni first established dominance over neighboring Tswana and Sotho, and then overran populations across the Limpopo River in Zimbabwe-Rhodesia to form the Ndebele (Matabele) macrocluster. The Makololo clan moved northward into the Zambezi Valley to dominate Barotse and to become the Kololo. The Dlamini from Delagoa Bay established dominion over the Nguni and Sotho of northern Swaziland to form the Swazi macro-cluster. Other clusters, such as the Basuto of Lesotho, were formed out of refugee splinter segments of other groups. The Ngwato cluster, of present-day Botswana, was similarly compounded from a nuclear group of Western Sotho-speakers, to which were added elements of Tswana, Northern Sotho, Shona, Rotse, Kubam, Subia, Herero, and Bantuized San (Schapera 1940). The Zulu-initiated *difaqane*, or forced migration, thus created many new political clusters that had not existed before the nineteenth century—and which now are described in the anthropological literature as "tribes" or "primitive states."

The British conquered the Cape in 1795 and began to settle along the coast after the second decade of the nineteenth century. This settlement, in turn, sent the Dutch cultivators and pastoralists (*boers*) on their *trek* or migration inland, where they established the independent republics of the Transvaal and the Orange Free State in 1852 and 1854, respectively. Dutch and British both advanced against Africans in the so-called Kaffir wars against the Xhosa (1835, 1847, 1851) and against the Basutho (1858, 1865–1866, 1867–1888). These wars destroyed the pastoral basis of Xhosa life and reduced the Xhosa to servitude and squatter tenancy on European-owned farms. Millenarian movements in the 1850s—in which cattle were slaughtered to bring on the hoped-for state of purification and abundance, as well as disaster for the whites and their allies-further weakened Xhosa ability to resist. The Zulu were still strong enough to defeat the British at Isandhlwana, but they lost the final battle five months later at Ulundi. With this loss, the Zulu army ceased to exist. Thereafter, despite frequent war and rebellion, one African population after another was brought under European control—including the Basuto and Tswana in the 1880s and the Swazi in the 1890s.

The pacification of the African populations accompanied the growth of the mining industry in South Africa, an industry based on the use of African labor (see chapter 11). Within five years after the discovery of diamonds in Griqualand, diamond exports reached the value of £1.6 million per annum. During the hundred years following, no less than £700 million worth of diamonds were recovered in this part of the world. In the eighty years after the discovery of gold in 1886, the South African gold mines yielded £6,000 million worth. Both kinds of mining demanded large agglomerations of capital, especially when surface "dry diggings" gave way to mining in depth; gold mining, in addition, required expensive installations to recover gold from the immense but low-grade deposits. De Beers Consolidated Mines Ltd. was founded by Cecil Rhodes; it was named after one of the first mine sites at Kimberley, near a farm owned by a Boer called De Beer. Rhodes bought the farm for $18,000 (Gunther 1953: 553). It is now a syndicate of seven named companies, which controls diamond production and marketing. Gold mining is controlled by seven giant interlocking corporations, two of the largest—De Beers and Anglo-American—in the hands of the same family.

The Great Depression of the late nineteenth century initiated an unprecedented expansion in commodity flows among all parts of the

Zulu attack on the 80th regiment at Intombi River during the final British drive to capture the Zulu capital at Ulundi. Wood engraving based on a sketch by Lt. L. W. R. Ussher, 1879. (The Granger Collection, New York)

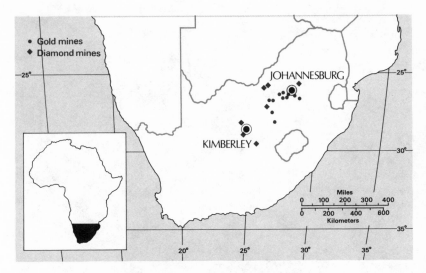

The mining regions of South Africa.

globe. Each of the commodities that served capitalist development— food products, industrial crops, stimulants, gold, diamonds—entered into a growing stream, each one broadening and intensifying its currents. We have looked at a few such commodities of import to some of the peoples who make up the anthropological record. There were many others, their accelerated movements graphed in the transactions of the world's financial markets.

Commodity production and marketing, of course, were not new. The world before 1400 was already heavily crisscrossed by the pathways of mercantile exchange within and between tributary societies, as well as between such societies and kin-ordered groups. Many populations were drawn into commodity production to supply this trade long before the advent of the European sea merchants. European expansion, however, created a market of global magnitude. It incorporated pre-existing networks of exchange and created new itineraries between continents; it fostered regional specialization and initiated worldwide movements of commodities.

The growth of capitalism brought about a qualitative change not only in the regnant mode of production but also in the commercial networks connected with it. These networks now served the process of capitalist accumulation, which not only multiplied commodities in order to beget more money but generated capital to buy machines, raw materials, and labor power in order to expand production and hence to accumulate more capital. The independence and autonomy of commercial exchange was abrogated, for the rate of profit was no longer determined solely by regional discrepancies in price (which allowed merchants to buy cheap and sell dear), but by the process of production itself.

The "people without history" were now drawn into a system that harnessed the world's resources to the cause of capital accumulation. Yet this does not mean that all the productive arrangements for supplying commodities to the market became capitalist. Following Mandel, the capitalist world economy is an articulated system of capitalist and noncapitalist relations of production, linked by relations of exchange that are dominated by capitalist accumulation (see p. 297). At any given time, some sectors and regions of this system are central and strategic to its operation, while others occupy auxiliary or marginal positions, providing commodities or labor power to the center. Over time, the distribution of central and secondary regions may change, as the demands of capital accumulation elevate auxiliary segments to a position of centrality or relegate previously central segments to marginality.

While the central sectors and regions are governed directly by the productive relations of the capitalist mode, social arrangements built up in the kin-ordered or tributary modes may be tolerated, maintained, or even reinforced in auxiliary and marginal areas. When this occurs, it is under conditions of severely limited political and economic autonomy. First, the societies in question must yield up their substantive sovereignty and their ability to deploy arms in the pursuit of their independent interests. Second, they gradually relinquish the capacity to reproduce their social networks and hierarchies without participation in the capitalistically dominated market. Their people, as commodity producers and laborers, become part of the reserve army of capitalism, mobilizable during periods of advance, released back to their reservations or enclaves during periods of retreat. In one population after another around the world, peoples' lives were thus reshaped to correspond to the dictates of the capitalist mode.

12 The New Laborers

The essence of capital is its ability to mobilize social labor by buying labor power and setting it to work. This requires a market in which the capacity of human beings to work can be bought and sold like any other commodity: buyers of labor power offer wages, which sellers accept in return for a commodity, their own labor. The market creates a fiction that this buying and selling is a symmetrical exchange between partners, but in fact the market transaction underwrites an asymmetrical relationship between classes. Through that transaction, workers are paid back a portion of the product of their own labor in the form of wages, relinquishing the remainder as surplus value to the capitalist class.

The working classes, entering industry or plantation agriculture under the aegis of the capitalist mode of production, constituted a new phenomenon in the world, a novelty well understood by many observers in the nineteenth century. The appearance of these working classes furnished a hidden agenda of modern history and social science, but scholars moved only hesitantly toward a recognition of their role in creating new kinds of societies. Their emergence upon the stage of history prompted fear of mass irruption and social disorder, as well as exaggerated hopes of imminent social renewal. For historians primarily concerned with the actions of the powerful, the new working classes had no history, only an anti-history. For social scientists who defined sociology primarily as a "moral" science, the newly emerging "masses" spelled rootlessness and anomie. For humanists concerned with upholding the higher achievements of the Human Spirit, the proletariat conjured up the image of Ostrogoths already stabling their horses within the confines of the City. For revolutionaries, the working classes embodied the promise of social transformation, the "new men" providing the antithesis to Civilization.

Even when social scientists began to examine these new men more closely, they treated them mainly as social problems—problems created by a severance from their roots through detribalization or immigration—rather than as social actors in their own right, responding to new conditions. Even labor historians concentrated at first on the history of labor organizations and labor movements; that is, they were more interested in efforts to transcend a condition than in delineating that condition itself. Research thus concerned itself mainly with what was absent—conditions and characteristics that had once been and no longer were, or conditions yet to come. Less was said of what was present, the relational matrix and content of working class existence. Only recently have some social historians moved toward the writing of a processual and relational history for the working classes, much as a history has begun to be written for the populations supposedly arrested upon some timeless plateau of evolution. In fact, the two branches of history are but one. The trajectories of the "people without history" on the various continents of the globe dovetail and converge within the larger matrix created by European expansion and the capitalist mode of production.

Labor Markets

In the course of the nineteenth century, industrialization and the introduction of large-scale cash cropping in agriculture went on apace. As capital flowed toward new areas of opportunity and into new branches of activity, it massed machines into ever larger aggregates, and brought ever new battalions of workers into the growing industrial army. Manufacture—production in which "the pace was set by men and not machines" (Landes 1969: 121)—yielded increasingly to "machinofacture," in which the machine set the pace of work. Political economies were refashioned, social ties rent and rearranged, and people moved from areas of supply to areas of demand.

Many indices trace the increases in the scale of output and reflect the growing demand for industrial labor. From the beginnings of industrialization in the second half of the eighteenth century, world steam power reached an estimated 4 million hp in 1850, and about 18.5 million only twenty years later. The production of coal, strategic in the growth of industrialism, stood at 15 million tons per annum in 1800, at 132 million tons in 1860, and at 701 million tons in 1900. World production of ferrous minerals rose from 1 million metric tons in 1820 to 65 million in 1910. Inanimate energy produced from coal, lignite, petroleum, natural gasoline, natural gas, and water power amounted to 1.1 milliard megawatt-hours in 1860, 6.1 milliard in 1900, 21 milliard in 1950 (Cipolla 1962: 48, 49, 51; Woodruff 1971: 9). Railway trackage increased from 332 km. in 1831 to more than 300,000 km. in 1876; steamship tonnage went from 32,000 tons in 1831 to 3.3 million tons in 1876 (Hobsbawm 1975: 310). Ports around the world bulged with the output of plantations, destined for transshipment to Europe and America.

The units of production increased in size, accelerating the demand for labor. The average cotton mill in Lancashire in the 1820s employed between 100 and 200 hands; but in the Oldham of 1851 one-third of the cotton workers were already employed in mills of more than 250 hands (Chapman 1972: 26; Foster 1974: 91). By 1841 more than half of the Oldham miners were in mines using more than 200 workers. Much larger aggregates of laborers appeared early, too, and became more common over the years. Thus, in 1815−1816 Robert Owen employed 1,600−1,700 hands at New Lanark (Chapman 1972: 32). In 1849 the largest iron plant in the United Kingdom, at New Dowlais, had more than 7,000 workers (Landes 1969: 121). There were only 72 workers in the Krupp works at Essen in 1848, but nearly 12,000 by 1873; at Le Creusot in France, the Schneider company employed 12,500 workers in 1870, more than half the people in town (Hobsbawm 1975: 213). Similarly, plantation agriculture demanded laborers, leading to aggregations of some 2,000 on one plantation in coastal Peru and of several thousands on estates in Java.

The new labor regime inaugurated by the capitalist mode endowed the capitalist entrepreneur with great flexibility in meeting the opportunities and requirements of growth. Under the kin-ordered mode, kinsmen cannot be hired or fired. A tributary overlord must exercise military force or a functional equivalent to expand or decrease the number of surplus producers under his jurisdiction. Even the slave owner is restricted in his ability to manipulate his labor supply, for he must protect his investment in slaves by feeding them during times when they do not labor. In contrast, capitalist entrepreneurs can hire and fire laborers or vary their wages in response to changing circumstances. Alterations in the rate of profit occasion changes in the supply and in the remuneration of labor, and hence fluctuations in the size and the character of labor markets. Intensified accumulation opens up new sectors of the labor market, or expands old ones; decelerating accumulation narrows work opportunities, or shifts them to regions of lower labor costs. As changes in capital accumulation occur, the consequent changes in the demand for labor alter, in turn, the conditions for the emergence and stabilization of different working classes.

Under capitalism, entrepreneurs can also vary their use of labor in relation to machinery, calling up additional laborers to man the available machines or reducing the size of their wage fund by substituting machines for human labor. In its continuous drive for accumulation, the capitalist mode of production has tended historically to increase the ratio of capital invested in plant and raw materials to capital paid out for labor power. Industrial units that use machines to enlarge the scale of production, while diminishing the labor cost per unit produced, have tended to replace industrial units with a higher ratio of labor power to plant. This trend, however, is neither linear over time nor general at any moment. At any point in time, competition among capitalists yields a distribution of industries, of branches of industries, and of enterprises within industries, marked by very different mixes of capital. Thus, industrial units that rely more on machines and raw materials than on labor power will always coexist with and confront industrial units that place a greater reliance on labor power.

Special circumstances may indeed favor enterprises with a high-labor, low-machine mix. For example, unskilled and low-paid women and children, using the older Arkwright technique of roller spinning in plants endowed with an abundant supply of water, could compete for a time with the more productive mule spinners (Chapman 1972: 20–21). A similar situation held in the delayed reaction of textile manufacturers on the European continent to English competition (Landes 1969: Chap. 3). Sometimes it may be efficient and profitable for entrepreneurs working with a high machine-to-labor ratio to delegate phases of the work process to firms operating at a lower level. Increases in the scale of plants and firms, intended to lower production costs per unit of output, may actually reach a critical point where unit production costs remain unchanged or even go up. Such critical points are not merely the outcome of mechanical processes of growth but are closely related to factors of concentration, location, management, labor discipline, and demand. It is thus possible for industries with a capital ratio that favors machines over labor power to spawn industries of lower organic composition.

This variation among industrial units with different capital ratios affects the labor market, producing variation in the quantitative and qualitative demand for labor. The result is that the labor market is "segmented" or "differentiated," not homogeneous (Gordon 1972). At any moment in time, branches of industry with a high capital ratio of plant to labor power will demand a high level of skill and formal or on-the-job training, pay relatively high wages and status rewards, and aim for stability of their labor force, while branches of industry with a lower capital ratio of plant to labor power will lower wages, disregard status rewards, de-emphasize skill and training requirements, and make use of an unstable or rotating labor force. Segments of the labor market—and the workers answering to the demands generated in these various segments—thus come to be ranked hierarchically with respect to one another, with a "labor aristocracy" garnering higher rewards in income and prestige at the top, and with workers receiving low wages in unstable employment at the bottom. Such a hierarchy may characterize a given industrial location; it may describe the contrasts between industrial regions connected with different branches of industry; and it may hold internationally, ranking labor forces engaged in different kinds of industrial employment in different countries and continents.

The distribution of capitals and labor markets, and the resulting differentiation of the labor force locally, regionally, nationally, and internationally, are never fixed and stable. Just as the vanguard of industrial entrepreneurs may fall by the wayside in the course of competition, so the labor aristocracy of yesteryear may be replaced by machines to become a redundant part of the labor force tomorrow. The history of technological change under capitalism is replete with examples of skilled labor suffering "de-skilling" (Burawoy 1979; Warner and Low 1947). At the same time, working-class cohorts located in one region may be thrown into the ranks of the semiemployed and unemployed "industrial reserve army" by capital movement to other regions. The decline of the New England textile industry because of plant and capital relocation to the southern United States after World War II, as well as the more recent relocation of manufacturing activity to areas of cheaper labor power like Taiwan, Hong Kong, and Korea, offers a present-day illustration of a process continuously repeated under the aegis of the capitalist mode.

Working Classes

When the term *working classes* first emerged around 1815, it took the form of a plural, describing a plurality of classes. Indeed, although the development of working classes everywhere "reproduces" the general relation of labor to capital, the characteristics of particular working classes show wide variation. They differ in origin, in point of entry into the labor force, in composition, and in the ways they relate to other groups and social categories.

Differences of origin may place varying resources at the disposal of new working classes. An artisan group such as the glassblowers of Carmaux in southwestern France embarked on a different working-class career than the miners of the same region. The glassblowers were descendants of a corporation of skilled migratory craftsmen with wide-ranging "cosmopolitan" connections. The miners were the descendants of a smallholding peasantry, with local roots and local speech, who doubled as miners during the agricultural off-season. As they lost their land, they became increasingly dependent upon industrial mining, which leveled out differences of skill and status among them (Scott 1974; Trempé 1971). The German working classes contained a very high percentage of skilled artisans; the Russian working classes recruited heavily among the sons and daughters of the peasantry (Walker 1971; Moore 1978; Lyashchenko 1949). Some countries drew their working classes mostly from within their national territories; others, like the United States, built up their labor force mainly by importing different ethnic groups and categories from abroad.

The particular circumstances surrounding working-class recruitment enhance working-class variability still further. An "old" working class will show different characteristics from "new" ones. The English working class, subdivided into a multiplicity of "trades" and recruited into plants of relatively small size, developed in response to market demands very unlike those that faced the new Russian working class of the late nineteenth century (Gordon 1941), the Chinese working class of the first decades of the twentieth century (Chesneaux 1962), or the Bemba entering the Rhodesian copper mines in the 1920s (Epstein 1958).

Working classes vary also in their composition. A large part of the labor force recruited into the English textile mills of the first phase of industrialization consisted of women, children, and pauper apprentices. The millhands of early New England were primarily young, unmarried women. The labor force of the Bombay mills that opened up after 1850, in contrast, was made up largely of adult married males. Working classes differ, further, in the location, geographical range, and supportive capacity of the social ties that underwrite their maintenance and reproduction. In the English mill towns around 1850, the constituent units of the working class were nuclear or stem families, which coped with the problems of survival by sending women and children to work, or by aggregating ("huddling") into larger domestic groups. In the textile center of Oldham, one-third of the mothers of children eleven years and under went to work, as did a quarter of the children themselves. Many families clustered together in shared accommodations (Foster 1974: 96–99). At the same time, people in the mill towns strove to maintain ties with kinsmen in the countryside, often with an eye toward maximizing mutual advantages (see Anderson 1971: 999). In contrast to the English case, in India textile workers left their wives and children with their joint families in the home villages, returning later to let other family members take their places at work (Morris 1960). Elsewhere, working class experience involved only a phase of the life cycle. For instance, it was mainly the unmarried daughters of pioneer cultivators who were recruited for work in the New England textile mills. Their wages allowed farming families to stay in the area, and the women returned to these families at marriage. In South Africa, such shuttling during the life cycle was written into the labor contract itself. Workers were brought to the mines from the different "tribal" reservations and compelled to return there when their contracts expired; thus, the development of a permanent resident working class was inhibited. Among immigrants to the United States between 1879 and 1918, males outnumbered females roughly two to one. The factors of distance and travel costs inhibited return migration, and the majority of immigrants remained in the New World; even so, over 30 percent of the new immigrants after the 1880s returned to Europe (Rosenblum 1973: 72–73, 126).

The characteristics of a working class are thus determined not only by the wage nexus but also by ties of kinship, locality, and association, spanning the distance between villages and towns of origin and the new neighborhoods of industrial locations. There are connections to parents and siblings, fiancés, wives and children back home; to kinsmen in the new place of residence; to labor bosses, emigrant agents, moneylenders, priests; to friends, neighbors, fellow workers, relationships formed in boardinghouse, taverns, and union halls; to comembers of parish sodalities, burial societies, and kite-flying clubs. Working classes are not "made" in the place of work alone; they are the outcome of many links that extend into the larger society. It is this wider web of connection that also determines working class politics—the ability of particular working classes to challenge employers and governments, to organize associations, labor unions, and party organizations, and to improve the conditions of their work and lives.

Urbanization

The development of working classes was intimately related to the accelerated growth of cities after 1800 and the massive increase in size, density, and heterogeneity of urban populations. In 1600 only 1.6 percent of Europe's population lived in cities of 100,000 inhabitants or more; in 1700 the figure was 1.9 percent; in 1800, 2.2 percent. Britain, the pioneer country of industrialization, led in urbanization. In 1801 about one-tenth of the population of England and Wales lived in cities of 100,000 and larger. By 1840 that percentage had doubled; by the end of the century it had doubled again. "By 1900 Britain was an urbanized society" (Davis 1965: 43). Embarking on industrialization somewhat later than Britain, other countries of Europe soon followed a parallel course of urban expansion.

The movement of population toward large, dense urban centers that were connected with large-scale industry reversed an earlier trend. During the two centuries from 1600 to 1800, the diffusion of the putting-out system had disseminated islands of "industrialization before industrialization" throughout the countryside. During this period, the proportion of Europeans living in cities of over 20,000 people did not grow significantly, and may well have declined, despite substantial overall population growth (Tilly 1976). Population had shifted from larger centers toward smaller towns and the countryside, probably because of the increased entry of agricultural laborers and artisans into rural cottage industries. After 1800 capitalist industrialization pulled people in the opposite direction, and in turning the rural areas into catchment basins for industrial labor, it also worked to deindustrialize the countryside.

The shift toward increased urban concentration was not merely quantitative but also entailed a qualitative change in the mechanisms allocating people to space and activities. The older centers of political administration, of trade, or of symbolic communication were now transformed into pivots of the new mode of production. Machinofacture gave rise to new factory towns like Manchester and Essen, and surrounded existing cities with a ring of industrial districts. The development of financial services and the needs of business communication supported the growth of business districts with banks, offices, and clubs. The burgeoning working classes were housed in working-class neighborhoods or districts, characterized by the large-scale construction of multifamily tenements or "rental barracks." Port facilities were built, and railroad tracks, yards, and stations transformed the urban landscape. Beyond the industrial districts, working-class neighborhoods, and freight yards, the captains of industry and commerce erected new mansions and country villas.

Labor on the Move

To meet the increasing demand for labor power, labor began to flow from regions where people were underemployed, or displaced from agriculture or cottage industries, toward regions of heightened industrial or agricultural activity. The subsequent growth and expansion of capitalism evoked massive relocations of human populations as people carried their labor and resources from areas where they were redundant or obsolete to new key areas of accumulation. This is not to say that population movements always occur in response to upswings and downturns of demand. Labor is often held fast by constraints, and governments are not always willing to allow their subjects to emigrate. Sometimes population movements precede rather than follow an upswing in economic activity, the increased supply of laborers pushing down wages and favoring investment. Nevertheless, capitalism has generally found laborers when and where it needed them, and migratory movements have carried labor power to market all across the globe.

In treating the subject of migration, social scientists usually distinguish "internal" from "international" migration, or contrast "intracontinental" and "intercontinental" flows of population. Movements over great physical distances or across politically demarcated borders create special problems of logistics and communication, both for the migrants and for the recipient populations. Yet the size of the social and cultural gap between origin and destination is not determined by physical distance or political boundaries. Nor should we prejudge the degree of estrangement experienced by the migrant by applying an ahistorical measure of national identity. The nineteenth century was, in Europe, a century of nation building—a century of economic and political incorporation, of linguistic standardization, and of the creation, imposition, and diffusion of hegemonic cultural patterns. These processes had been set in motion by the beginning of the century, but they had not yet run their course. Inhabitants of the same national polity were often still divided by barriers of linguistic and cultural incomprehension. These internal barriers between town and country, between classes, and between regions were not different in kind from those that faced the migrant in external or intercontinental movement.

It is an error to envisage the migrant as the bearer and protagonist of a homogeneously integrated culture that he either retains or yields up as a whole. We have learned enough about cultural patterns to know that they are often internally contradictory and, at the same time, able to combine with patterns drawn from other cultures. It is no more difficult for a Zulu or a Hawaiian to learn and unlearn culture than it is for a Pomeranian or a Fukien Chinese. What is significant for the migrant is the position he is placed in, in relation to other groups, on arrival. That placement determines which of his prior resources he can apply and which new ones he must acquire.

The migrant's position is determined not so much by the migrant or his culture as by the structure of the situation in which he finds himself. Under the capitalist mode of production, this structure is created by the relation of capital to labor in its particular spatial and temporal operation, that is, the structure of the labor market. People may move for religious, political, ecological, or other reasons; but the migrations of the nineteenth and twentieth centuries were largely labor migrations, movements of the bearers of labor power. These labor migrations, of course, carried with them newspaper editors to publish papers for Polish miners or German metalworkers, shopkeepers to supply their fellow migrants with pasta or red beans, religious specialists to minister to Catholic or Buddhist souls, and others. Each migration involved the transfer to the new geographical location not only of manpower but also of services and resources. Each migratory wave generated, in turn, suppliers of services at the point of arrival, whether these were labor agents, merchants, lawyers, or players of percussion instruments.

In the development of capitalism, three waves of migration stand out, each a response to critical changes in the demand for labor, each creating new working classes. The first of these waves was associated with the initial period of European industrialization. Beginning in England, these initial movements toward capitalist industry covered only short distances, since industrial development was itself still localized and limited. Thus, in the cotton town of Preston in Lancashire, where roughly half the population consisted of immigrants in 1851, over 40 percent had come less than ten miles from their birthplaces and only about 30 percent had come more than thirty miles. Fourteen percent of all immigrants had been born in Ireland, however, and came to Preston as part of the rising tide of Irish immigration in the 1840s (Anderson 1971: 37). Localized as such movements were, they made Lancashire the most urbanized county in Britain by the middle of the nineteenth century, with more than half the people of the county living in fourteen towns with populations of more than 10,000 (Anderson 1971: 32).

Belgium followed Britain in the movement of workers from the countryside, as the industrial towns of the Walloon-speaking southern provinces burgeoned in the 1820s. In the 1830s the Prussian provinces of Westphalia, Rhine, Berlin, and Brandenburg initiated their industrial expansion, attracting a large-scale flow of population from Prussia's eastern agricultural regions (Milward and Saul 1977: 44–46). This flow intensified greatly in the last quarter of the century, as dependent cultivators were displaced by the consolidation and mechanization of the large Junker estates.

While the first wave of labor migration under capitalism carried people toward the industrial centers within the European peninsula, a second flow sent Europeans overseas. An estimated 50 million people left Europe permanently between 1800 and 1914. The most important destination of this movement was the United States, which between 1820 and 1915 absorbed about 32 million immigrants, most of them of European origins (Rosenblum 1973: 70). This influx of people provided the labor power that underwrote the industrialization of the United States.

A third wave of migration carried contract laborers of diverse origins to the expanding mines and plantations of the tropics. This flow represents a number of developments, such as the establishment of a migratory labor force for the South African mines, the growth of the trade in Indian and Chinese contract labor, and the sponsored migration of Italian laborers to the coffee regions of Brazil. These movements not only laid the basis for a large increase in tropical production but also played a major part in creating an infrastructure of transport and communication, prerequisites for a further acceleration of capitalist development.

The United States

While Britain, Belgium, and Germany recruited their working classes largely through internal and intracontinental migration, the United States imported its working class by sailboat and steamship. Such reliance on immigrant labor, of course, predates the onset of industrialization in the United States. We have discussed the forced movement of Africans to the New World, including the area that was to become, under the impact of British textile development, the Cotton South. European migration before the American War of Independence also included many people who accepted the temporary bondage of indenture in the hope of establishing themselves in the New World; these indentured laborers may have comprised as many as two-thirds of all early migrants. Later in the eighteenth century, there came a quarter of a million Scotch-Irish, transplanted first from the Scottish Lowlands to Ulster, and then forced by rack-renting and rising tithes to abandon Ulster for America. Another group that came in the eighteenth century were Scottish Highlanders, displaced by sheep or driven by rising rents; they were led by their "tacksmen," heads of cadet lines of the chiefly *clann*, who acted as intermediaries between chief and commoners (see Fox 1976: 112–113). Another quarter of a million migrants arrived from southwestern Germany, an area of impoverished and parcelized agriculture. Mass immigration into the United States, however, began only after the cessation of the Napoleonic wars.

In the 1820s, 151,000 immigrants came to the United States; in the decade of the 1830s, the number tripled to 599,000. It increased again to 1,713,000 in the 1840s, and to 2,314,000 in the 1850s (Jones 1960: 93).

The main factors pushing these people out of Europe were the spread of industrial capitalism and the commercialization of agriculture. As industrial capitalism spread, it displaced artisans and destroyed the domestic putting-out system. Transformations in agriculture burdened Irish and southwestern German cultivators with increased rents, mortgages, and indebtedness, and drove Scottish, English, and Scandinavian cultivators off the land to make way for sheep or cattle. In the period between 1820 and 1860, therefore, the main contingents of immigrants came from Ireland (2 million), southwestern Germany (1.5 million), and the British Isles (750,000). Of course, the United States was not the only target of such migrations. Between 1818 and 1828, 250,000 Germans settled in southern Russia. Others went to Brazil, while Irishmen settled in Canada and the Maritime Provinces, or sought new homes in Australia. In the United States, the advent of the new immigrants speeded up capitalist industrialization. "Neither the factory system," says Maldwyn Jones, "nor the great canal and railroad development of the period could have come into existence so quickly without the reservoir of cheap labor provided by immigration" (1960: 132). The role of the Irish immigrants, who quickly developed a new monopoly on unskilled labor in construction work and factory employment in this period, in fierce competition with American Blacks, proved especially important in this regard.

More Englishmen, Swedes, and Germans from east of the Elbe arrived between 1860 and 1890. Again, many of them were displaced agriculturalists driven off the land by the disintegration of English, Swedish, and German wheat production between 1865 and 1875, a result of the importation of low-priced American and Russian grain. The Great Depression also affected German and English coal mining, iron and steel production, and textiles; miners, metalworkers, spinners, and weavers came to seek employment in the New World. The cultivators among them could take advantage of land grants offered by the advancing railroads and by the midwestern and western states and territories.

Around 1890 the area of migrant supply shifted from northern and western Europe to southern and eastern Europe. The new immigrants were largely displaced peasants and agricultural laborers from southern Italy, the Austro-Hungarian empire, and the Balkans. In addition, there were Poles, Jews, and Volga-Germans from the Russian empire; Russians themselves migrated mostly to Siberia. The newcomers quickly replaced their predecessors in a number of industrial locations and occupations. The coal miners in Pennsylvania had been largely of British or German origin before 1890, but after that time they were mainly Poles, Slovaks, Italians, and Hungarians. Whereas the New England textile mills had been manned primarily by French-Canadians, English, and Irish, the new textile workers were Portuguese, Greeks, Poles, and Syrians. In the garment trades, Russian Jews and Italians took over from Germans, Czechs, and Irish.

Italian immigrants on their way to Ellis Island, c. 1905. (The Granger Collection, New York)

This large-scale influx of European labor had a marked influence on the direction of American technological development. During the first half of the nineteenth century, capitalist entrepreneurs were faced with a relative shortage of labor. There was land available to those who wanted to farm, and there were opportunities for artisan employment, both of which attracted newcomers away from industrial work. Wages were relatively high for all categories of workers. This appears to have fostered the development of labor-saving devices and their early introduction into industry (Habakkuk 1962). The later influx of industrially unskilled workers from southern and eastern Europe, in turn, favored the further development of machinery and of rationalized processes of production that did not rely on mechanical skills. In 1908 the U.S. Immigration Commission noted that the new migrants were often drawn into highly capitalized industries, despite their lack of skills:

> As a consequence their employment in the mines and manufacturing plants of the country has been made possible only by the invention of mechanical devices and processes which have eliminated the skill and experience formerly recognized in a large number of occupations. [quoted in Rosenblum, 1973: 76].

Most of the foreign-born workers entered the unskilled, lower-paid levels of industrial occupations. While their new employment yielded remuneration substantially higher than they would have earned in Europe, the combination of mechanization and unskilled immigrant labor permitted American entrepreneurs to keep wages down (Douglas 1930; Rees 1961). Without the Italian, Slav, Greek, Portuguese, French-Canadian, and Russian Jewish workers who furnished the bulk of the labor for the leading American industries by 1900, the industrial expansion that took place between 1880 and 1900 would not have been possible (Jones 1960: 312).

Labor for the Mines: South Africa

We have seen (chapter 11) that at about the same time the United States moved toward full industrialization, a takeoff into capitalist development also took hold in southern Africa. There, diamonds and gold were discovered in the last third of the nineteenth century, in the areas north of the Orange and Vaal rivers. The core area of South African development shifted correspondingly to these inland areas. At first diamonds and gold were both mined by surface diggers. Sometimes particular tasks were contracted to White entrepreneurs who organized work gangs. While some Africans paid the license fees needed to become full-time diggers, by 1876 the higher-paid skilled jobs were monopolized by White diggers (Welsh 1971: 181), and African laborers were contracted only for short periods of about three months. By 1892 the skilled workers had formed a trade union to defend their position against any attempt of management to lower labor costs by using African laborers or by sponsoring further immigration from England.

War between Britain and the Afrikaaners for political control of South Africa disrupted mining operations between 1899 and 1902, and cut the available working force in half. By 1906, however, the mines were again in full production, with a labor force of 18,000 Whites, 94,000 Africans, and 51,000 Chinese indentured servants (Houghton 1971: 15). In 1907 there was a strike of White skilled workers who opposed management plans to increase Chinese immigration and to replace White with Black labor. It was broken when unemployed Afrikaaners were brought in as strikebreakers. The lasting outcome, however, was the repatriation of Chinese miners and a reinforcement of the color bar in employment.

Most of the White miners, as of 1912, came from outside South Africa—from Britain, Australia, the United States, and elsewhere. These Whites made up the skilled labor force. The Africans, in contrast, were unskilled migratory workers, on contracts from six to eighteen months' duration, who received a tenth of the wages paid to the Whites.

The idea of employing Africans as temporary laborers became established in the first decade of mining. In the 1880s it was combined with the notion of confining Africans to residential compounds for their contractual period. This practice took root first in the Kimberley diamond mines, in part to stop the illicit sale of diamonds by African miners to dealers, in part to control desertion. This "closed" compound has remained a feature of the diamond mines ever since. Local traders initially protested the company stores set up by the mining companies for their shut-in work force. When the gold mines adopted the compound system somewhat later, compounds were set up in an "open" rather than "closed" form to meet the objections of local storekeepers (Welsh 1971: 180).

From the beginning, the mining industry had attracted workers from as far away as Nyasaland and Mozambique, as well as from South Africa itself. In the second decade of the twentieth century, the mines began to rely increasingly on the import of temporary contract laborers from the so-called Native Reserves. The Reserves consisted of territories set aside specifically for African occupancy. They were formed from a land area that consisted of about 13 percent of the total territory of the Union of South Africa, as well as the area of the British "protectorates" of Bechuanaland (now Botswana), Basutoland (now Lesotho), and Swaziland. These areas were expected to furnish the migratory labor for the mines, while providing basic subsistence for the families of the migrants and for old people. The institution of the Native Reserves, however, formed only one component of a larger system of labor control, which involved simultaneously the organization of an African labor supply for white farmers and the denial to Africans of permanent legal residence in towns and cities. The Land Act of 1913 assigned those Africans remaining on White-owned land to the farm owners as "labor tenants." These tenants owed farmers stated amounts of labor in exchange for permission to reside on their land. This labor allowed the White farmers to expand the commercial production of food crops (notably maize) to provision the growing mines and cities, while at the same time it curtailed cash-crop sales by African cultivators living on the Reserves. This enhanced White-owned commercial agriculture and inhibited the growth of a cash-cropping African peasantry, confining the Reserves to production for subsistence only. The institution of Reserves had the effect of lowering the wages paid in the mines, since the mine owners were able to pay African labor at rates below subsistence, while the Land Act inhibited the movement of labor from White farms to towns.

Still another cornerstone in the policy of labor control was the "pass" laws, which required Africans to carry residential permits, lodgers' permits, certificates from their employers, and curfew passes, and which allowed the state to move Africans deemed supernumerary from one location to another. These laws made free movement impossible. Further laws made desertion of employment and breaches of discipline criminal offenses. The effect of these laws was to inhibit the growth of a stable African working class in towns—a class able to make demands on the economic and political system—and to force urban Africans back on their ties with their Reserves. Simultaneously, White workers were granted advantages in access to supervisory positions and in remuneration, resulting in a segmented labor market maintained by political means.

Since World War II, South African industrial development beyond mining has greatly speeded up, drawing ever larger numbers of black South African laborers into industrial employment other than mining. In response, the mining companies have intensified their search for cheap migratory labor beyond the confines of South Africa, as in Malawi and Mozambique. This policy has served to keep wages low for unskilled labor, both in the mining sector and in the industrial sector outside the mines.

Labor for the Planters: East Indians

While Britain, northwestern continental Europe, and the high South African *veld* were importing labor to man the new industrial machinery, other regions of the world were seeking new sources of agricultural labor. The "old" areas of plantation agriculture, most of them growing sugar cane, had lost their supply of slave labor with abolition. On some of the small islands of the Caribbean, such as Barbados and St. Kitts, the freed slaves had no alternative but to work for their former masters. But on the larger islands like Trinidad and Jamaica, and in the mainland sugar colony of Guyana (then Demarara), the ex-slaves could and did take up land beyond the confines of the plantation, and they resisted further work on the old estates. Facing potential ruin, the planters began to agitate for new sources of labor. Sometimes the British inter-cepted slave ships going to Brazil, nominally freed the slaves, and then sent them to the West Indian sugar islands (Furtado 1963: 135).

These proved to be only stopgap measures. To the cry for replacement of the old labor supply was soon added the demand for more and more labor as the scale of commercial agriculture expanded. Beyond the old sugar areas, there were sometimes political reasons for importing laborers. In Malaya, for example, the British decided to maintain intact the Malay peasantry and its tributary relationship with village headmen and ruling nobles. The need for plantation labor was therefore met through the organized migration of indentured laborers from India and of contract labor from China.

Whereas Chinese labor came to be utilized primarily in mining and construction work, Indian indentured labor was deployed mainly in plantations, specifically plantations located within the British empire. Already under the Mughals groups of men had taken service as bearers and on ships, and by the end of the eighteenth century there were Indian laborers—hired for periods of two to three years—in all the ports of Southeast Asia. Yet the great stimulus for the development of what Tinker (1974) has called "the second slavery" came with the abolition of the slave trade in 1808 and the sudden need for cheap and tractable labor, especially on the sugar-producing plantations of the tropics.

Guyana asked for Indian laborers, as did Jamaica and Trinidad from 1836 on. (At present, East Indians make up more than 50 percent of the population in Guyana, about 40 percent in Trinidad, and about 2 per-cent in Jamaica.) East Indian labor migration to Mauritius began in 1835; by 1861 East Indians constituted about two-thirds of the popu-lation of the island. In 1860 the tea plantations in Assam and Bhutan began to compete for migrants, and between 1870 and the end of the century 700,000—750,000 laborers were recruited for work there. The demand for East Indians in Fiji began in 1879; today, Indians there outnumber native Fijians. After the 1870s Ceylon became a main area of demand; in the 1880s, Burma; after the turn of the century, Malaya. Natal in South Africa began importing East Indian contract labor for its sugar plantations around 1870. All together, Tinker estimates, "over a million Indian laborers went overseas to tropical plantations in the forty years before 1870; though the figure could be as high as two million" (1974: 114−115).

When the English first began to recruit laborers for their indigo plantations in Bihar and for service in Calcutta, they drew heavily on the *dhangar*, or hill-dwelling populations, of the Chota-Nagpur plateau, such as the Santals, Munda, and Oraons. These hill people were also significant among the indentured servants sent to Mauritius and Guy-ana immediately after the end of slavery. In the 1870s they took part in the migration to the tea plantations of Assam and Bhutan. After the dhangar, labor recruiters turned to the populations of the "presidency towns" of Bombay, Madras, and Calcutta. In the 1840s Bihar became a province for recruitment, as Bihari in the army were replaced by Brahmans and Rajputs of Oudh. Then South India became a main recruiting ground, so much so that all South Indians overseas came to be called Malabars. Tamil-speakers made up most of the laborers for Ceylon, Burma, Malaya, and Natal. As of 1945 the population of East Indian origin in Burma was about a million, with 750,000 in Ceylon, 750,000 in Malaya, 300,000 in Mauritius, 100,000 in Fiji, 300,000 in Trinidad and Guyana, and 100,000 in Natal.

A complex delivery system developed to carry on this trade in indentured servants. At the apex of the business in India stood an elite of subagents. These usually belonged to middleman minority groups, such as Jews, Armenians, Indian Christians, and Eurasians. The subagent would send out a recruiter (called an *arkatia* or *arkati*) who was knowledgeable about local conditions. He either contacted prospects directly or worked through local gang bosses or recruiters. In the South, such a local gang boss came to be known as a *kangani*, from *kankani*, the Tamil word for headman. By the middle of the century, a kangani often managed a team of labor recruits through *silara*, agents loyal to him. Recruiting was done by offering advances, which the recruit used to settle debts, give a going-away feast, and purchase his ticket. All the obligations incurred had to be worked off at the point of arrival. Unhappily, arrival at the final destination was not assured. In the 1850s nearly one out of six passengers to the Caribbean died on the three- to four-month journey.

During the century following 1830, such Indian districts as Thanjavur in Madras province (called Tanjore by the British) were reorganized to meet the exigencies of the Indian labor trade (Gough 1978). In the 1830s the British government began to restore Thanjavur's irrigation system, which had been destroyed during the conquest. By mid-century three-quarters of Thanjavur's cultivated area was irrigated and turned over to rice production. Irrigated rice made up nearly 70 percent of the district's exports in 1841—1842 and more than 80 percent by 1868—1869, most of it going by sea to the plantation dependencies of Ceylon, Malaya, and Mauritius. At the same time, British rule wrought major changes in land tenure and in labor arrangements in Thanjavur. Lands were gradually allocated as private property to the individual households of the village managerial caste. The new landowners were empowered to negotiate private rental agreements with tenants, to dismiss unwanted dependents, and to hire casual wage labor at will, instead of the former practice of dealing collectively with village servants and tenants. These changes intensified emigration. The majority of the million or so people who left Thanjavur between 1830 and 1930 were Untouchables or members of non-Brahmin lower castes of the peasantry. Three-quarters were men, the others young women. Producing labor power and rice for export, Thanjavur became in effect "a human and nutritional service station for British plantations" (Gough 1978: 42).

Labor for the Planters: Europeans

Another major source of agricultural labor was European. We have already made mention of the Polish workers who began to replace German tenant-laborers on the Junker estates of eastern Germany after 1870. In the coffee belt of Brazil, the end of slavery also created a labor crisis. It proved impossible to tap the labor of Luso-Brazilian small-scale cultivators, most of whom were held fast in relationships of dependency upon local landlords and other powerholders. For a time, some Brazilian political leaders harbored plans to bring in indentured "Asiatics." Finally, the problem was solved by importing Italian laborers. The government paid for their voyage, and the local planter advanced a year's wages and a subsistence plot, thus subsidizing "free" Italian labor.

The Italian emigration was prompted largely by the crisis of agriculture within Italy beginning in the 1870s (see Schneider and Schneider 1976: 120–125). The sale of public-domain land and church holdings had created a situation in which large landowners were able to add to their holdings, while small cultivators were being squeezed out by falling prices for agricultural products. This price decline was in considerable part the result of competition from Russian and American wheat. The increasing flood of manufactured goods also disrupted local handicrafts, while the phylloxera blight destroyed vineyards. Wealthy landowners began to move their liquid wealth into industry (see Mack Smith 1969: 159), but smallholders and laborers could escape the squeeze only by moving elsewhere, either seasonally, temporarily, or permanently.

At first, in the 1860s, Italians took up work in France, Switzerland, Germany, and Austria-Hungary, but only 16,000 emigrated permanently in that decade. In the 1870s the stream of permanent emigration grew to 360,000, with some 12,000 now going to Argentina and Brazil. Then, between 1881 and 1901, the number of permanent emigrants rose sixfold to more then 2 million. In all, more than 4 million left Italy permanently between 1861 and 1911. The majority came from southern Italy, where the agricultural crisis hit most heavily. Four-fifths were agricultural laborers and construction workers (Sereni 1968: 353). In the 1800s and 1890s South America was the major target of migration: three times as many went to Brazil and Argentina as went to the United States. By 1901, however, the trend was reversed. In the first decade of the twentieth century, more than twice as many went to the United States as to South America; in the second decade, more than three times as many. By that time, however, the new labor supply had permitted Brazil's coffee planters to lay the basis for rapid industrial growth, with the Brazilian government paying the transportation costs for the new work force.

Rio Claro, Brazil

The changeover from slave labor to labor by immigrant workers on the Brazilian coffee plantations has been studied by Warren Dean in one county about 150 miles north of São Paulo (Dean 1976). In the eighteenth century the county of Rio Claro was still *boca do sertão*, a mouth of the backlands opening upon the wilderness beyond. It came to be inhabited by squatters who grew subsistence crops on swiddens and raised pigs to supplement the meat obtained from game; a few sold their hogs and tobacco. By the 1830s, however, two-thirds of the land had passed into the hands of plantation owners, merchants, officials, and urban professionals, either through land grants or through purchase for speculation. The displaced squatters moved farther into the wilderness, encroaching on the territories of native Tupian groups. In the resulting conflicts, they absorbed the fury of native American attacks; they attacked in turn, thus interposing a barrier between the Tupi and the developing plantations.

The first crop raised on the plantations of Rio Claro was sugar, which was usually grown by planters who owned processing mills. Their labor force was made up of African slaves, dependent laborers who settled on the plantations (*agregados*), squatters still in the area who turned to wage work to supplement their subsistence product, and floating laborers hired by the job (*camaradas*).

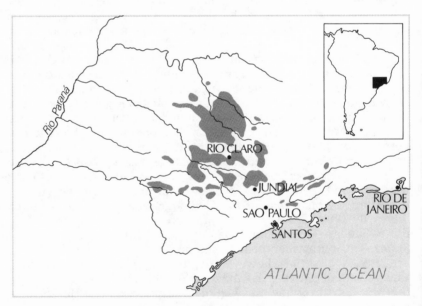

Coffee plantations, São Paulo region.

In the 1840s coffee was introduced into the area, and by 1859 2.6 million coffee trees had been planted in the county. The money for growing coffee came from reinvested sugar profits or from English and German exporters who made their homes in Santos, the port of São Paulo. The initial planting of trees was handled by contractors owning slaves. The planter then took over the groves and worked them with his own slaves; he also had to buy the expensive machinery required for hulling. The high cost of land, slaves, and equipment favored concentration, and by 1860 eleven growers accounted for more than 60 percent of the coffee produced. Although coffee became the major crop, the plantations never became entirely specialized. They grew their own food, raised their own draft animals, and maintained their own artisans, although they bought manufactured goods in town.

Coffee production rose steadily, reaching its zenith in 1901. Expansion was aided by the construction of a railroad connecting the county with the port of Santos; financing came from the local planters and from British investors. The coffee was sold to brokers who were sometimes related to the planters by kinship or marriage. With the passage of time, the planters themselves moved to São Paulo, leaving the supervision of their plantations in the hands of hired administrators.

Although the African slave trade had been declared illegal in 1835, more than half the agricultural labor force in Rio Claro still consisted of slaves in the 1870s. The use of slaves was declining in other parts of Brazil, but in Rio Claro it actually expanded as planters brought slaves from less prosperous regions and entrepreneurs with slave gangs still engaged in planting. Nevertheless, the slave population did not reproduce itself. Infanticide was common and infant mortality from other causes very high. Slaves also ran away regularly, giving employment to professional slave catchers. After mid-century, when most of the slaves had been born in Brazil and the labor force had become more homogeneous, the slaves grew increasingly rebellious.

To replenish their labor supply, the planters began to look to immigrants. Some planters in Rio Claro had already experimented with the introduction of Portuguese, German, and Swiss indentured laborers in the 1840s and 1850s. In 1857 there were more than a thousand such workers in Rio Claro. The experiment failed, however, when the Europeans protested their working conditions through their consular representatives. The planters were thus forced back on the labor of their slaves, even though slave prices rose steadily for the next twenty years and the costs of control also rose.

After abolition in 1888, the planters turned to the importation of Italian laborers. The state supported this practice by financing the passage of men and their families from Europe to Santos. The newcomers were hired as families, and they worked under the direction of the male head of the household. Contracts were on an annual basis, extending from harvest to harvest. Wages were paid according to the hoe work required and the quantity of coffee harvested. Houses were provided rent-free, and workers were allowed to buy at plantation stores, receiving advances against work performed. They could also grow subsistence crops for themselves, although this created conflicts between workers and planters, who feared that the home garden tended to diminish attention to the coffee trees. At the end of each contractual period, there was a considerable amount of movement as workers sought employment on more productive estates.

While much of the work on the plantations passed into the hands of such immigrants, about half the trees continued to be tended by Brazilian tenant laborers (colonos) or gang laborers hired by the job. Gang labor by unmarried Italians or by freedmen was contracted out; it remained important in such tasks as clearing, planting, and fencing.

The advent of wage labor caused major changes in the class structure of the town. Only about 10 percent of the immigrant colonos bought land themselves, generally with subsidies from the state, which had an interest in stabilizing the immigrant population. The remainder either returned home or joined the proletariat of the town. The increased flow of cash provided by wages intensified commerce. This brought new merchants to town, who then invested their profits in purchasing land. The freedmen were generally depressed into the ranks of casual laborers, along with the descendants of squatters remaining in the area. The Italian immigration thus created an "ethnic" stratification of the population, subsidized to a considerable extent by the state on funds that derived originally from the exploitation of Brazilian labor.

Little was done to maintain the productivity of the coffee trees. As productivity decreased, the coffee frontier moved farther inland, and planters and camaradas moved inland with it. The town remained behind, with its new middle class of merchants and professionals and its depressed proletariat, to be engulfed gradually by the urban sprawl of São Paulo.

The Trade in Chinese Labor

China proved to be another source of labor for the outside world. In Southeast Asia there had been Chinese before the European expansion. Moslem Chinese of mixed Han, Persian, Arabic, and Central Asian origins, called Hwei or Hui, moved into the southwestern Chinese borderlands during the Mongol period of the thirteenth and fourteenth centuries; many carried on the overland trade to southern Asia. Chinese trading colonies also settled in the islands at this time. In the fifteenth century, however, the Chinese state throttled foreign commerce and created an unpopulated no-man's-land along the coastal fringe in order to prevent foreign contacts with the Han population. This stemmed out-migration. Nevertheless, Chinese laborers were exported by the Portuguese through Macao, while the Dutch East India Company captured Chinese along the China coast in order to populate its headquarters town of Batavia (Dermigny 1964, I: 831).

The conclusion of treaties at the end of the Opium War in 1842 removed the barrier to emigration and permitted foreign entrepreneurs to tap the Chinese labor market directly through the establishment of the "coolie" trade. Political disorders and economic crises in China, such as the Taiping rebellion, drove many to accept labor contracts abroad. Soon a sophisticated apparatus of traders grew up to facilitate this movement. If an entrepreneur wanted Chinese laborers for use in Malaya, he could contact a "coolie broker" in Singapore or Penang. The coolie broker, in turn, issued the orders for labor to "eating-house" keepers in Swatow, Amoy, Hong Kong, or Macao. The eating-house keepers then contacted "headmen" (*khah-taus*), who recruited laborers on the village level. Laborers either paid for their own transportation or else indentured themselves to a "credit-ticket" broker who paid the cost of their travel.

The laborers who had paid their own fare could move about freely in search of work after arrival. The "unpaid passengers," however, were in debt to the broker and indentured to him for the duration of their debt. In Malaya, such indentured arrivals were housed in depots, where they were guarded by "depot keepers" employed by the coolie broker. Coolie brokers and depot keepers usually held positions in powerful secret societies, which also furnished the depot guards. The secret societies developed a dual function in the context of the labor trade. They maintained social control and coercion over the dependent Chinese population, while at the same time they defended the interests of the Chinese enclave against the dictates and strategies of local governments. The depot system lasted in Malaya until the onset of World War I in 1914.

Singapore

One of the great hubs of this Chinese labor migration was Singapore. Singapore provides an apt example of the ways that the labor trade fitted into the other activities of a major port and commercial center in Asia.

Singapore had been founded in 1819, when England received rights to the site—then inhabited by a few Malay and Chinese fishermen. By 1900 the city had 229,000 inhabitants—two-thirds of them Chinese, the remainder Malays—drawn mainly from the Malay peninsula but also from the island archipelago as far east as Borneo and the Philippines.

The surrounding population was also largely Malay. This population was organized in the tributary mode and divided into a number of kingdoms. Each kingdom was headed by a monarch drawn from a royal line and confirmed in office by a hierarchy of territorial, district, and local chiefs of aristocratic descent. At the base of the hierarchy was the village, inhabited by Malay peasantry, or *ra'ayat*. Tribute in kind and labor flowed from the village, through the village headman (*penghulu*) and the hierarchy of nobles, toward the royal capital, which was usually located strategically near the mouth of the polity's principal river. In extending their sovereignty over the Malay states, the British made a political decision to preserve the Malay social order with as little change as possible, in return for an annual quitrent. As a result, "the great bulk of Malays remained locked within the framework of a traditional society which was changing only slowly" (Roff 1967: 122).

Yet change it did, and largely through the agency of the great commercial city that had been created in its midst. When Chinese planters began to grow cash crops such as pepper and gambier (an astringent extracted from a plant and used in medicine, tanning, and dyeing) on Singapore Island, the Malay rulers welcomed further immigration by Chinese planters and cultivators in order to tap a welcome source of new revenue. After 1850 they also sponsored the movement inland by Chinese tin-mining companies. Soon the Singapore hinterland became a battlefield between rival coalitions of local Malay chiefs, Chinese tin miners, and Chinese merchants engaged in financing and supplying both chiefs and miners. The resulting rivalries undermined the edifice of indirect rule promoted by the British, inviting direct British intervention.

From 1867 on, Singapore became a pivot of the British efforts to govern in the peninsula, using British officials, Malay adjutants, and Chinese and Tamil clerks. The British also managed the agency houses charged with handling the European-based trade. Alongside the European traders stood the Chinese merchants, headed by the prestigious Baba families and closely interlinked through kinship ties. As non-Malays they were barred from any access to the formal positions of political authority, but they held much of the real power over capital and men in the city. They advanced money to planters and miners. They managed the labor trade through which workers were funneled to the tin mines of Perak and Selangor and to the plantations. They dominated the powerful secret societies that controlled the immigrant laborers and offered protection and assistance in return for loyalty and service (see Freedman 1960: 33). The British, in turn, used the heads of these secret societies as "captains of the Chinese" to control the Chinese population, until the secret societies themselves accumulated too much power and were declared illegal in 1889. Their place was taken by associations based on common dialect or surname, patterned on the regional associations found in China and fulfilling similar functions of support and welfare. These associations also functioned as religious bodies. In the setting of Singapore, they both embodied the anti-Manchu political stance of the secret societies and offered unorthodox religious expression of individual needs through spirit-medium cults.

Capital in the city thus flowed mainly through British and Chinese hands, while most of the labor was furnished by Chinese. In this city planted in their midst, the Malays were relegated to a minor role. A few held political office. A number—Bugis from Celebes, Dyaks from Borneo, and Minankabau from Sumatra—were traders dealing with the archipelago. There were a few religious teachers and mosque officials. The largest number were engaged in low-yield occupations: policemen, watchmen, drivers, servants, office runners, street hawkers, and small shopkeepers in the Malay quarter. When rubber growing became prominent at the beginning of the twentieth century, this too passed into the hands of Indian laborers, with the Malays in Singapore relegated to marginal and interstitial jobs. In the countryside the Malay cultivator, although protected in his political rights, fell victim through growing indebtedness to an army of non-Malay rice millers, rubber marketing agents, village shopkeepers, and moneylenders.

Chinese Labor: Other Destinations

Malaya was not the only destination of Chinese labor. Some 90,000 indentured Chinese laborers were sent to Peru between 1849 and 1874, mostly through Macao, to replace Hawaiians who had died working in the guano beds (Stewart 1951: 74). Some of these Chinese were assigned to work in the cotton fields of coastal Peru when demand for cotton rose in the wake of the scarcity created by the war between the Union and the Confederacy. Others were employed in railroad construction.

Another 200,000 Chinese were sent to California between 1852 and 1875 (Campbell 1923: 33), where they were employed in fruit growing and processing, in panning for gold, and in building railroads. In the 1860s some 10,000 to 14,000 Chinese laborers built the Central Pacific Railroad of California, which by 1885 linked the West Coast with eastern Utah and thus completed the transcontinental railroad. Five thousand more workers were taken from Hong Kong to Victoria to build the Canadian Pacific Railroad, which opened up the gold placer beds of British Columbia.

In California the movement of Chinese labor was controlled by merchant-brokers who hired out the laborers as needed, while retaining control over them through the operations of secret societies (see Dillon 1962; Lee 1965). The secret societies, in turn, were interlinked with the so-called Six Companies, named for their districts of origin in Kwantung province and patterned after the regional associations that developed in China during the Manchu Ch'ing regime (Ho 1966). As in Singapore, the Six Companies defended Chinese interests in an antagonistic environment. At the same time, they exercised control over the Chinese population on the West Coast. The Pacific Steamship Company cooperated with them by agreeing not to allow any man to return to China who had not cleared his debts. After the cessation of the labor trade, the Six (later Seven) Companies continued as political, educational, and welfare associations of the Chinese community in the United States.

Gold was discovered not only in California and British Columbia but also in Australia (1853). By 1854 there were 2,000 Chinese miners in the Australian gold fields, with 42,000 there by 1859. Other areas also entered the Chinese labor trade. Cuba contracted for 800 Chinese in 1847, and for some 8,000 to 15,000 in 1852. Between 1856 and 1867, 19,000 Chinese left Hong Kong under contract, of whom 6,630 went to the British West Indies (mostly Guyana), 4,991 to Cuba, 2,370 to Bombay in India, 1,609 to Dutch Guiana, and 1,035 to Tahiti, Hawaii, and other Pacific islands (Campbell 1923: 130, 150).

In addition to Chinese laborers who stayed abroad only until their contracts expired, there were also migrants who went in search of permanent settlement. One of the major areas of such settlement was Southeast Asia, where the Chinese population in the 1970s was more than 12 million (McEvedy and Jones 1978: 166). Early migrant groups were often traders who in time formed a mercantile aristocracy, such as the Babas of Malacca and the Peranakans of Indonesia. Later comers frequently had to contend for power with the earlier arrivals.

Often Chinese merchants would, in their new homeland, build up a dependable following by calling on kinsmen or people from the same home region in China. In employment, close kin were preferred to more distant kin, more distant kin to speakers of the same Chinese dialect, members of the same dialect category to other Chinese, and Chinese to non-Chinese (Jeromin 1966: 53). Such a following, built up on kin or quasi-kin ties, would engage in many different activities, often centering around operations that connected the primary producers in the hinterland with Western commercial enterprises. Chinese were widely active as middlemen, to the point where Indonesians began calling them *bangsa tengah*, "the middle race." Chinese merchants also advanced the credit necessary to oil the circuits of commerce. "The native peasant is in debt to the Chinese trader, the trader to the wholesaler, the wholesaler to the export-import firm. Debt obligations connect all the steps of trade with each other" (Jeromin 1966: 75). Unsurprisingly, these middleman and credit functions have often made the Chinese creditor-merchant the target of political attack and persecution in Southeast Asia, where their position has often been compared to that of the Jews in Eastern Europe.

The Chinese laborers, too, faced hostility from workers in the areas to which they were brought. In 1882 the United States passed the Chinese Exclusion Act under pressure from the Knights of Labor, who had even insisted on the ejection of Chinese from the laundry business. The anti-Chinese agitations that broke out on the West Coast of the United States were not merely a California problem but part of an emergent racism in the United States (see Hune 1977: 48–50). Restrictions on Chinese immigration constitute merely one phase in a larger movement to divide employment opportunities along racial lines. Similar efforts at excluding the Chinese were made in Australia after their employment in the gold fields came to an end, and in South Africa, where 43,296

Chinese contract laborers worked on the Rand in 1904, only to be repatriated in 1907 (Campbell 1923: 187).

Ethnic Segmentation

A hallmark of the industrial and plantation complexes constructed under capitalist auspices all around the world has been the juxtaposition of groups of different social and cultural origins. Societies based upon such complexes, plantation dependencies in particular, have sometimes been labeled "plural societies" (Furnivall 1939, 1942, 1948). This term was intended to convey their internal disjunction into distinctive social and cultural segments. The disparate segments, juxtaposed in the marketplace, were seen as being held together by power exercised by a dominant segment, the European minority. An underlying assumption was that the segments would cannibalize each other as soon as sovereign power were removed; European rule was thus necessary to contain the conflicts inevitably generated by diversity. The Caribbean and Southeast Asia furnished salient examples of such pluralism.

This view is misleading in that it grants explanatory power to social and cultural heterogeneity. Rather, this heterogeneity must itself be located in the organization of the labor process. The diverse groups brought together did, of course, make use of distinctive cultural forms to build ties of kinship, friendship, religious affiliation, common interest, and political association in order to maximize access to resources in competition with one another. Such activity, however, cannot be understood without seeing it in relation to the ways different cohorts of the working class were brought into the process of capitalist accumulation.

Emphasis on the distinctiveness of such cohorts leads, moreover, to a false contrast of heterogeneous "plural" societies with the supposedly homogeneous societies of Europe. It is not true that cultural uniformity eased the way to state making and nation formation in Europe. The difficulties of integrating the regional divisions of France and of turning "peasants into Frenchmen" (Weber 1976); the problems posed by the centrifugal propensities of "invertebrate Spain" (Ortega y Gasset 1937); the obstacles encountered in turning the inhabitants of multiple cities and provinces into "Italians" (Mack Smith 1969); the forging of the individualized and reluctant "home towns" of Germany into one *Reich* (Walker 1971); and the enduring divisions of Britain between its Celtic fringe and "Sassenach" core (Hechter 1975), and between its classes, divided into "two nations" (Disraeli 1954)—all call into question any simple opposition of plural heterogeneity and European homogeneity.

The "plural societies" of the plantation dependencies do not constitute a special type of society. They are historically and geographically specific instances of the general tendency of the capitalist mode to create a "disposable mass" of laborers out of diverse populations, and to then throw that mass into the breach to meet the changing needs of capital. In all such instances, the mode re-creates the basic relation between capital and labor power. At the same time, it re-creates the heterogeneity of the labor force produced. It does so in two ways: by ordering the groups and categories of laborers hierarchically with respect to one another, and by continuously producing and re-creating symbolically marked "cultural" distinctions among them.

We have noted earlier that shifts in the ratio of capital expended on plant to capital paid out in wages produce segmentation in the labor market. The workers filling positions in the more privileged segments of that market enjoy higher pay and better working conditions than those entering the lower segments; they are also better able to defend and augment their perquisities through union organization and political influence. In contrast, the workers in the lower segments are directly exposed to the downward pressure on their wages and conditions of work exerted by unemployed labor. In a wider perspective, not only are they worse paid and less secure in their jobs than the more advantaged echelons of the working class but they also buffer the upper echelons against direct job competition by the "reserve army," whether that labor reserve is national or international.

The opposing interests that divide the working class are further reinforced through appeals to "racial" and "ethnic" distinctions. Such appeals serve to allocate different categories of workers to rungs on the scale of labor markets, relegating the stigmatized populations to the lower levels and insulating the higher echelons from competition from below. Capitalism did not create all the distinctions of ethnicity and race that function to set off categories of workers from one another. It is, nevertheless, the process of labor mobilization under capitalism that imparts to these distinctions their effective values.

In this regard, distinctions of "race" have implications rather different from "ethnic" variations. Racial designations, such as "Indian" or "Negro," are the outcome of the subjugation of populations in the course of European mercantile expansion. The term *Indian* stands for the conquered populations of the New World, in disregard of any cultural or physical differences among native Americans. The term *Negro* similarly serves as a cover term for the culturally and physically variable African populations that furnished slaves, as well as for the slaves themselves. Indians are conquered people who could be forced to labor or to pay tribute; Negroes are "hewers of wood and drawers of water," obtained in violence and put to work under coercion. The two terms thus single out for primary attention the historic fact that these populations were made to labor in servitude to support a new class of overlords. Simultaneously, the terms disregard cultural and physical differences within each of the two large categories, denying any constituent group political, economic, or ideological identity of its own.

Racial terms mirror the political process by which populations of whole continents were turned into providers of coerced surplus labor. Under capitalism these terms did not lose their association with civil-disability. They continue to invoke supposed descent from such sub-jugated populations so as to deny their putative descendants access to upper segments of the labor market. "Indians" and "Negroes" are thus confined to the lower ranks of the industrial army or depressed into the industrial reserve. The function of racial categories within industrial capitalism is exclusionary. They stigmatize groups in order to exclude them from more highly paid jobs and from access to the information needed for their execution. They insulate the more advantaged workers against competition from below, making it difficult for employers to use stigmatized populations as cheaper substitutes or as strikebreakers. Finally, they weaken the ability of such groups to mobilize political influence on their own behalf by forcing them back into casual employ-ment and thereby intensifying competition among them for scarce and shifting resources (see Bonacich 1972: 555–556).

While the categories of race serve primarily to exclude people from all but the lower echelons of the industrial army, ethnic categories express the ways that particular populations come to relate themselves to given segments of the labor market. Such categories emerge from two sources, one external to the group in question, the other internal. As each cohort entered the industrial process, outsiders were able to categorize it in terms of putative provenience and supposed affinity to particular seg-ments in the labor market. At the same time, members of the cohort itself came to value membership in the group thus defined, as a quali-fication for establishing economic and political claims. Such ethnicities rarely coincided with the initial self-identification of the industrial recruits, who first thought of themselves as Hanoverians or Bavarians rather than as Germans, as members of their village or parish (*okolica*) rather than as Poles, as Tonga or Yao rather than as "Nyasalanders." The more comprehensive categories emerged only as particular cohorts of workers gained access to different segments of the labor market and began to treat their access as a resource to be defended both socially and politically. Such ethnicities are therefore not "primordial" social rela-tionships. They are historical products of labor market segmentation under the capitalist mode.

The process by which new working classes are simultaneously cre-ated and segmented has continued down to the present. It has followed the general rhythm of capitalist accumulation, which spurred the devel-opment of new labor markets as it intensified and then narrowed the demand for labor as it slackened. Accumulation slowed with the de-rangement of international markets in the wake of World War I, but it regained momentum between 1919 and 1926, when the introduction of automatic conveyor systems lowered the cost of durable consumer goods such as automobiles and electrical applicances. The process of accumulation then stagnated and collapsed, recovering only with the vast increase in military expenditures initiated by World War II and with the rebuilding of plants destroyed by the war.

This last phase of accumulation saw the introduction of automation guided by electronic machines ("continuous process technology"). Automated units of production have grown into larger complexes of automated plants and fields of related activities around them (Nehnevajsa and Frances 1959: 397). These complexes are increasingly manned by workers who no longer intervene directly in the process of production, but whose primary function is to ensure the smooth operation of the automated machines. An automated factory requires new operational teams composed of an elite of skilled workers and a supporting cast of personnel engaged in simplified routines of maintenance. Automation thus creates a specialized demand for laborers with appropriate skills, while at the same time reducing the size of that demand.

Only a minority of plants, however, have been able to automate profitably. The rest must seek to maximize profits in other ways, ranging from partial automation to primary dependence upon cheap labor power. Continued reliance on processes of production in which labor still plays a significant part is characteristic not just of "light" industries such as textile production or semiautomated food processing. Even the electronics industry, producing the strategic means for controlling automation, remains highly labor-dependent, with labor accounting for about half of its costs of production (C. Freeman, quoted in Mandel 1978: 206). Thus, capital continues to seek areas of redundant labor supply and lower labor costs, and creates new working classes through its demand for cheaper labor. Since 1960, for example, over forty top-ranked industrial firms moved from the northeastern United States to the South, where wages were 20 percent below the national average and only a minority of the labor force belonged to unions (NACLA-East Apparel Project 1977: 2). More American capital has moved south of the Rio Grande into Mexico's border region, while American, German, and Japanese capital has taken advantage of low labor costs in the "Little Japans" of Hong Kong, Singapore, South Korea, and Taiwan.

This migration of capital has given rise to an industrial pattern of combining high technology in some phases of production with labor-intensive manual production in other phases. Standardization of parts, electronic monitoring of production, and data processing have permitted the labor process to be fragmented between automated parent plants and labor-dependent assembly plants located in low-wage areas. The reduction of the labor force in automated plants is thus accompanied by the growth of new working classes in so-called "export platforms," located primarily along the shores of eastern and southeastern Asia and along the littoral of the Caribbean in the Americas.

Capital has migrated not only toward more labor-dependent industry but also toward the new and different sectors of production generated by the expansion of consumerism after World War II. This phenomenon—supported by the expansion of consumer credit and stimulated by advertising—has shifted many activities previously carried out in households to industrial and commercial enterprises, and has greatly increased the demand for industrially produced or processed commodities. This growth of consumer-oriented industries and services has been accompanied by a concomitant demand for labor, especially low-wage labor, which has been met largely by new working populations. Large-scale industrial food processing, in turn, has given rise to renewed capital investment in agriculture, the resulting "agribusiness" enterprises combining high-cost machinery and scientific inputs with intensive manual operations by low-cost migratory labor.

The period since World War II has thus intensified the recruitment and employment of working classes on an international scale. Some 11 million "temporary workers" from the Mediterranean region were at work in the booming industrial centers of West Germany, France, Switzerland, and the Benelux countries in the late 1960s (Castles and Kosack 1973), while West German industry drew on the influx of 10 million refugees from the European East. In the United States, the labor market was partly restructured by the northward movement of Afro-Americans displaced from the rapidly mechanizing South; by a nearly threefold increase in the number of working women between 1950 and 1970; and by the immigration of laborers from Mexico and the Caribbean. The oil-producing countries of the Middle East began to import a working class recruited among Egyptians, Palestinians, and Indians. Labor migration has also grown apace in Africa and Latin America. In 1950 100,000 Mossi were migrating seasonally from Upper Volta to the plantations of the Ivory Coast; in 1965 there were almost a million. In 1968 Ghana attracted 2.3 million foreigners, most of them coming to work in the cocoa orchards (Amin 1973a: 52−53, 68). About a million rural Colombians have moved to neighboring oil-rich Venezuela; another 60,000 have entered Ecuador to take jobs in the new petroleum enterprises there (Chaney 1979: 205).

Capitalist accumulation thus continues to engender new working classes in widely dispersed areas of the world. It recruits these working classes from a wide variety of social and cultural backgrounds, and inserts them into variable political and economic hierarchies. The new working classes change these hierarchies by their presence, and are themselves changed by the forces to which they are exposed. On one level, therefore, the diffusion of the capitalist mode creates everywhere a wider unity through the constant reconstitution of its characteristic capital-labor relationship. On another level, it also creates diversity, accentuating social opposition and segmentation even as it unifies. Within an ever more integrated world, we witness the growth of ever more diverse proletarian diasporas.

Afterword

This book has asked what difference it would make to our understanding if we looked at the world as a whole, a totality, a system, instead of as a sum of self-contained societies and cultures; if we understood better how this totality developed over time; if we took seriously the admonition to think of human aggregates as "inextricably involved with other aggregates, near and far, in weblike, netlike connections" (Lesser 1961: 42). As we unraveled the chains of causes and effects at work in the lives of particular populations, we saw them extend beyond any one population to embrace the trajectories of others—all others.

Ultimately, these chains of causation and consequence encompassed whole continents, and brought together the Old World and the New. In bringing about this global conjuncture, a signally important role fell to Europe—a small peninsula off the landmass of Asia. We took the year A.D. 1400 as a reference point in time, to exhibit the nature of that expansion. The world of 1400 was already burgeoning with regional linkages and connections; but the subsequent spread of Europeans across the oceans brought the regional networks into worldwide orchestration, and subjected them to a rhythm of global scope.

Drawn by these forces into convergent activities, people of diverse origins and social makeup were driven to take part in the construction of a common world. They included the European sea merchants and soldiery of various nationalities, but also native Americans, Africans, and Asians. In the process, the societies and cultures of all these people underwent major changes. These changes affected not only the peoples singled out as the carriers of "real" history but also the populations anthropologists have called "primitives" and have often studied as pristine survivals from a timeless past. The global processes set in motion by European expansion constitute *their* history as well. There are thus no "contemporary ancestors," no people without history, no peoples— to use Lévi-Strauss's phrase—whose histories have remained "cold."

To demonstrate the global interconnections of human aggregates is one task; to explain the development and nature of these connections, however, is another. I have taken the position that no understanding of these connections is possible unless it is grounded in the economic and political conditions that generated and maintained these connections. To explicate the material underpinnings of these linkages, I have drawn freely on concepts taken from the storehouse of Marxian ideas. I have taken from Marx the basic notion that social life is shaped by the ways human beings engage nature through production. I have also utilized the Marxian labor theory of value, the distinction between mercantile and industrial capital, and the idea of long waves of capitalist development. I have striven to treat these concepts as intellectual tools, not as ultimate verities; their utility resides in their explanatory adequacy.

I have placed special analytic weight on a concept intended to reveal the key relationships through which social labor is brought to bear upon nature—the mode of production. In this usage "production" is not synonymous with work; a mode of production is not the same thing as a system of technology. Nor is a mode of production identical with a "society." The idea of society centers upon the social alignment of groups; the idea of mode of production aims at identifying the forces that guide those alignments. To speak of a mode of production, therefore, draws attention to the ways in which human beings confront their world in order to modify it in their favor, and focuses on the dynamic consequences of that confrontation. I do not use the term *relationship* to indicate co-occurrence or co-variation of perceived characteristics of elements, an occurrence itself empty of consequences. I think of relationships as possessing force: relationships subject human populations to their imperatives, drive people into social alignments, and impart a directionality to the alignments produced. The key relationships of a mode of production empower human action, inform it, and are carried forward by it. As Marx said, men make their own history but not under conditions of their own choosing. They do so under the constraint of relationships and forces that direct their will and their desires.

Each mode of production gives rise to a characteristic conjunction of social groups and segments, a conjunction that embodies its dynamic and reproduces the conditions for its proliferation. Each mode also creates its own characteristic fissures and oppositions. The kin-ordered mode is predicated upon oppositions between those who "belong" and those who do not, and engenders distinctions of gender, rank, and privilege favoring some kin over others. The tributary mode sets tribute takers against the producers of tribute and gives rise to military and political competition both within and between the contending classes. The capitalist mode acts to accumulate capital through the hiring of labor power, but it is marked by the cyclical alternation of labor mobilization and labor displacement; each intake of labor power uproots some prior adaptation, while each sloughing off of labor power creates a new cohort of the disemployed. Since the key relationships governing the mobilization of social labor differ for each mode, and since each mode produces its own disjunctions, the encounter of different modes spells contradictions and conflicts for the populations they encompass.

To envisage human aggregates interconnected in time and space, yet responding to the forces generated by various modes of production, impels us to think in more processual ways about the notion of society. "Societies" emerge as changing alignments of social groups, segments, and classes, without either fixed boundaries or stable internal constitutions. Each mode, in the compass of its influence, generates conjunctions of groups and classes that serve its requirements under given historical and geographical circumstances. These requirements change, as do the resulting alignments. Where different modes of production intersect, the conjunctions of groups will bear the mark of the interplay of forces. Therefore, instead of assuming transgenerational continuity, institutional stability, and normative consensus, we must treat these as problematic. We need to understand such characteristics historically, to note the conditions for their emergence, maintenance, and abrogation. Rather than thinking of social alignments as self-determining, moreover, we need—from the start of our inquiries—to visualize them in their multiple external connections.

Such a view of the connectedness of human aggregates also demands that we rethink the concept of culture. We need to remember that the culture concept came to the fore in a specific historical context, during a period when some European nations were contending for dominance while others were striving for separate identities and independence. The demonstration that each struggling nation possessed a distinctive society, animated by its special spirit or culture, served to legitimate its aspirations to form a separate state of its own. The notion of separate and integral cultures responded to this political project. Once we locate the reality of society in historically changing, imperfectly bounded, multiple and branching social alignments, however, the concept of a fixed, unitary, and bounded culture must give way to a sense of the fluidity and permeability of cultural sets. In the rough-and-tumble of social interaction, groups are known to exploit the ambiguities of inherited forms, to impart new evaluations or valences to them, to borrow forms more expressive of their interests, or to create wholly new forms to answer to changed circumstances. Furthermore, if we think of such interaction not as causative in its own terms but as responsive to larger economic and political forces, the explanation of cultural forms must take account of that larger context, that wider field of force. "A culture" is thus better seen as a series of processes that construct, reconstruct, and dismantle cultural materials, in response to identifiable determinants.

Nearly fifty years ago Robert Lowie distinguished between "matter-of-fact usage" and "secondary interpretations" or "rationalizations" (1937: 138−139). The distinction is still useful. Even the simplest food-collecting group deploys an impressive array of objects, customs, and knowledge in its dealings with the world, together with a body of instructions for their use. This constitutes the matter-of-fact level of cultural phenomena. On another level, such instrumental forms—objects, acts, and ideas—appear as elements in cultural codes, which purport to define their place in the relations of human beings to one another, and of human beings to the surrounding world. Instructions about the instrumental use of cultural forms are synchronized with communications about the nature and praxis of the human situation. This is the level of interpretation, rationalization, or ideology, of assumptions and perspectives defining a particular view of the human lot. These communications are more than denotative and logical; they are often somatic, kinesthetic, affective, and aesthetic as well.

Anthropologists have called particular combinations of such matter-of-fact usages and ideological rationalizations "cultures," dealing with them as if they possessed an inherent coherence over time. Yet the association of matter-of-fact instruments with communications about their wider import is by no means automatic and self-evident. Meanings are not imprinted into things by nature; they are developed and imposed by human beings. Several things follow from this. The ability to bestow meanings—to "name" things, acts, and ideas—is a source of power. Control of communication allows the managers of ideology to lay down the categories through which reality is to be perceived. Conversely, this entails the ability to deny the existence of alternative categories, to assign them to the realm of disorder and chaos, to render them socially and symbolically invisible. Once things are named, moreover, power is required to keep the meanings so generated in place—names must, as the Chinese say, be "rectified." Sanctions must be used to defend the categories of ideological discourse against possible challenges. The construction and maintenance of a body of ideological communications is therefore a social process and cannot be explained merely as the formal working out of an internal cultural logic. The development of an overall hegemonic pattern or "design for living" is not so much the victory of a collective cognitive logic or aesthetic impulse as the development of redundancy—the continuous repetition, in diverse instrumental domains, of the same basic propositions regarding the nature of constructed reality.

If ideology-making is social in nature, it follows that the processes through which ideologies are constructed take place in historic time and under definable circumstances. The ability to project symbolic universes may well be located in the structure of the human brain, driven—according to Lévi-Strauss—to resolve the irresolvable contradiction between Nature and Culture. Lévi-Strauss notwithstanding, however, this contradiction is dealt with not in pure thought alone ("myth thinking man"), but in the active transformation of nature through the social labor of human beings. Contrary to those who believe that Mind follows an independent course of its own, I would argue that ideology-making does not arise in the confrontation of Naked Man thinking about Naked Nature; rather, it occurs within the determinate compass of a mode of production deployed to render nature amenable to human use.

Each mode of production entails essential distinctions among human beings. The social oppositions engendered by these distinctions constitute the forcing ground for the construction of ideologies. In the kin-ordered mode, the key distinction between kinsmen by descent and by affinity is variously symbolized as ties of blood, bone, or fertilizing spirit. The tributary mode's primary antithesis is phrased as that between tribute-taking "children of the Sun," "descendants of the gods," "blue bloods," or "white bones," and tribute-producing "commoners," "black bones," or "black-haired people." The primary antithesis is then compounded by further differentiation among the various grades within each category. The capitalist mode's basic opposition between owners of means of production and working hands is legally and politically sanctified, and is conjugated by additional discriminations, such as "white-collar" and "blue-collar" workers.

Ideologies codify these distinctions not merely as instrumental aspects of social relations, but as grounded in the essence of the universe—in the nature of nature, the nature of human nature, and the nature of society. In kin-ordered societies the distinctions of descent and affinity are anchored in the workings of super-nature. In tributary societies the differences in basic social categories are conceptualized as an aspect of cosmic hierarchies, and myth and ritual as well as force are deployed to maintain the proper orchestration between Earth and Heaven. In societies dominated by the capitalist mode, distinctions of essence appear in the Calvinist notion that God rewards virtue and that the successful are virtuous, or in the idea that Nature awards the palm of success to winners in natural selection. Poverty is thought to demonstrate lack of worth and failure in natural selection to merit assignment to base occupations.

Yet each mode at the same time generates characteristic contradictions that appear in both behavior and thought. In the kin-ordered mode, some kinfolk emerge as "more equal than others," and lesser kin confront the real limits of kin-based assistance. A social world divided into insiders and outsiders, moreover, creates the problem of strangers and orphans. In the tributary mode, the continuing clashes of interest between tribute takers and tribute payers engender not only social opposition but also ideological concerns about what constitutes "right action" or "commensurate justice," as opposed to "wrong action" and "injustice." Thus tributary social orders, in enforcing divine hierarchies, may yet face rebellion to right the injustices caused by such enforcement.

In the capitalist mode the regnant ideology assumes the equality of all participants in the market, in the face of basic distinctions in political and economic power between capitalists and workers. While all social actors are defined as participants in commodity exchange, the mode is structurally dependent upon the "unequal factor endowment" of owners of capital and sellers of labor power. Ideology-making thus transmutes the distinction between classes into distinctions of virtue and merit. Success is demonstrated by the ability to acquire valued commodities; hence, inability to consume signals social defeat. Since the mode alternates continuously between labor mobilization and abandonment, however, it also continuously reproduces an opposition between virtuous consumers and the disvalued poor. Just as the tributary mode gives rise to both class opposition and rebellions to right injustice, so the capitalist mode spawns both labor discontent and ideological movements to change the definitions of virtue and demerit.

Ideology may mediate contradictions, but it cannot resolve them. Alternative systems of ideas and ideologically charged behavior are continuously generated by the operations of the modes themselves. They are produced in the interplay of groups and classes that use ideological alternatives to define their place in the field of force generated by a mode of production. The alternatives take various forms, expressing both the relatedness of groups and classes within a given mode and their opposition. They may appear as different accents or connotations imputed to the same communicative code by social actors occupying distinct points of vantage. They may take shape in ideas and practices that sound a systematic counterpoint to the mainstream of communication. They may even develop into heterodox visions of reality, carrying with them a threat of rebellion against the prevailing order. Such connotations, counterpoints, and heterodoxies, moreover, remain but rarely confined within a single social constellation or society; cults, religions, or political movements all tend to overleap boundaries and to convey ideological alternatives to audiences beyond the frontiers.

There is thus an economic and political side to the formation of idea-systems, and idea-systems, once produced, become weapons in the clash of social interests. Sets of ideas and particular group interests, however, do not exist in mechanical one-to-one relationships. If a mode of production gives rise to idea-systems, these are multiple and often contradictory. They form an "ecology" of collective representations, and the construction of ideology takes place within a field of ideological options in which groups delineate their positions in a complex process of selection among alternatives. This process of inclusion and exclusion is not only cognitive; it also involves the exercise of power. To sustain ideological hegemony, the defenders of orthodoxy must carry their message into an ever larger number of instrumental domains, while curtailing the ability of subaltern groups to advance viable alternatives. Where redundancy falters and ideology-making fails, the deficit may be made up by force.

It has been an argument of this book that we can no longer think of societies as isolated and self-maintaining systems. Nor can we imagine cultures as integrated totalities in which each part contributes to the maintenance of an organized, autonomous, and enduring whole. There are only cultural sets of practices and ideas, put into play by determinate human actors under determinate circumstances. In the course of action, these cultural sets are forever assembled, dismantled, and reassembled, conveying in variable accents the divergent paths of groups and classes. These paths do not find their explanation in the self-interested decisions of interacting individuals. They grow out of the deployment of social labor, mobilized to engage the world of nature. The manner of that mobilization sets the terms of history, and in these terms the peoples who have asserted a privileged relation with history and the peoples to whom history has been denied encounter a common destiny.

Bibliographic Notes

This book incorporates the findings of various disciplines, and ranges widely in historical time and geographical space. In such a work the author owes his readers an account of his sources, together with the reasons for their selection. The body of the text includes reference only for quantitative information, quotations, and points upon which there might be dispute. In this essay I present the larger body of materials on which this book is based. My intent is not to cite all the works I have consulted, but rather to indicate those that most significantly shaped my theoretical understandings and most directly contributed to my education in each subject matter. Since this book is the cumulative outcome of many experiences and research efforts, the discussion of my sources is to some extent also an intellectual autobiography.

1. Introduction

Criticism of the social sciences for excessive specialization, professional myopia, and a neglect of history is not new. Sociologist Robert S. Lynd wrote *Knowledge for What?* in 1939, and a critique of sociological method in "The Science of Inhuman Relations" in 1949. C. Wright Mills advocated a renewal of sociology throughout his career, and Alvin Gouldner was a major intellectual critic of the field until his death in 1981. In trying to understand the development of social thought, I have found most useful the masterful trilogy by H. Stuart Hughes (1958, 1966, 1975). Leon Bramson has provided insight into the conservative basis of sociology in his too little-known *Political Context of Sociology* (1961).

Political science has lost its generalizing thrust since it forsook political sociology and a concern with economics for "behavioral" studies. The influence of scholars like V. O. Key, Jr., who combined micro-studies (such as his 1949 *Southern Politics*) with an interest in the state apparatus, seems to have been swept away by a concentration on small-group politics and attitude surveys. The recent work by Charles Lindblom (1977), which compares the economic performance of different political systems, is quite unique. The most vital work on politics recently has come from historically minded sociologists, such as Barrington Moore, Jr. (1966, 1978), Charles Tilly (1975), Ellen K. Trimberger (1978), and Theda Skocpol (1979). Political theory has been greatly illuminated by C. B. Macpherson's *Political Theory of Possessive Individualism* (1962) and by the works of Nicos Poulantzas (especially *Political Power and Social Change*, 1973), whose promise was cut short by his suicide in 1979. A useful overview of "recent theories of the capitalist state" can be found in Bob Jessop (1977).

Anthropology has been slower than sociology to take a critical look at its basic assumptions. An early attack on functionalism and its implications by Dorothy Gregg and Elgin Williams (1948) presaged later criticisms, but its effects were neutralized by its style of argument and by the wrath unleashed against it by both Kroeber and Radcliffe-Brown. The next major critical voice to be heard was that of Peter Worsley, first in the little-read appendix to his *Trumpet Shall Sound* (1957), then in "The Analysis of Rebellion and Revolution in British Social Anthropology" (1961). In the early 1960s J. R. Hooker raised questions about anthropology in Africa (1963), and Jacques Maquet wrote critically about "Objectivity in Anthropology" (1964). Within American anthropology it was Kathleen Gough who first asked, in 1967, why the discipline seemed to "bypass the most crucial problems of world society" (1968: 138). Thereafter there was an outpouring of self-consciously critical discussions, such as Dell Hymes, ed., *Reinventing Anthropology* (1969), Talal Asad, ed., *Anthropology and the Colonial Encounter* (1973, and Jean Copans, ed., *Anthropologie et impérialisme* (1975), to name only a few. The search for viable alternatives, however, has been slow. Two interesting attempts, from very different perspectives, are Worsley's *Third World* (1964) and Darcy Ribeiro's *Civilizational Process* (1968).

Since Karl Marx's name is such a bugaboo, it is important to focus on his ideas rather than on the polemics surrounding them. Vernon Venable's *Human Nature: The Marxian View* (1945) is, to me, still the best all-round introduction to the subject. Bertell Ollman's "Philosophical Introduction" to his book *Alienation* (1976) offers a useful entry into Marxian philosophical ideas. Alfred Schmidt's *Concept of Nature in Marx* (1971) is rewarding but difficult. I have learned a great deal about the development of Marx's ideas from Franz Mehring's biography of Marx (1935). Alvin Gouldner's *Two Marxisms* (1980) is a good introduction to the contradictions in Marx's own thought and to the subsequent variants in Marxism that incorporate one or another aspect of that thought. Eric J. Hobsbawm has written perceptively on "Karl Marx's Contribution to Historiography" (1973).

Anthropologists may wish to turn to Eleanor B. Leacock's introduction to the 1972 edition of Friedrich Engels's *Origin of the Family, Private Property and the State*, to Maurice Godelier's "Dead Sections and Living Ideas in Marx's Thinking on Primitive Society" (1977), and to the well-written book by James W. Wessman, *Anthropology and Marxism*

(1981). Marx's own ethnological researches have been edited and brought into publication by Lawrence Krader (1972).

2. The World in 1400

The effort to write a world history as a process of cultural connections, or to understand culture in global terms, is not new in anthropology. I came into the field when V. Gordon Childe's *What Happened in History* (1946) was required reading, and graduate education included an obligatory immersion in Kroeber's rewritten *Anthropology* (1948). Ralph Linton's *Tree of Culture* (1955), based on his lectures and bereft of references, is also in that tradition, which seems to be alive in anthropology today only among archaeologists. Within the field of history, there are prodigious universal historians such as Arnold Toynbee, whose view of history as a march toward salvation, however, will persuade only believers. Much more helpful for anthropologists is William McNeill's *Rise of the West* (1963), which attempts to portray human history as linkages and interconnections, challenging the civilizational monads of a Spengler or a Toynbee.

My penchant for seeing Europe and Asia synoptically traces back to the influence of Joseph Strygowski, whose lectures and exhibits on the Eurasian animal style were much discussed during my childhood in Vienna. Owen Lattimore's *Inner Asian Frontiers of China* (1951) offered a stimulating general view of nomad-cultivator interaction, as did his later collection of essays (1962).

In trying to understand nomad-cultivator relations around the Mediterranean region, I have benefited by Altheim (1954, 1960), as well as by von Barloewen (1961). Frederick J. Teggart's *Rome and China* (1939) is an interesting work; an example of early cliometrics, it also reveals the limitations of mechanical quantification.

My major source on the political history of Asian nomadism has been René Grousset's *Empire of the Steppes* (1970). The anthropology of this cultural type owes a great deal to Lawrence Krader, especially his papers on social organization (1955), ecology (1957), and polity (1958). It is clear that one should not regard the role of the pastoral nomads as an independent prime mover of political history, but view it rather in relation to the ecology, exchange systems, and power structure of the settled areas. On this, see Lacoste (1974) and Lees and Bates (1974).

I have had a long-standing interest in the history and development of the Islamic world (see Wolf 1951; 1969: Chap. 5). A great deal of what I know I learned from teaching on Mediterranean cultures jointly with William D. Schorger at the University of Michigan from 1961 to 1971. The standard treatises on Islam are listed in readily available bibliographies, but I would single out Marshall G. S. Hodgson's three-volume *Venture of Islam* (1974). This work has been criticized for its idealist bias, a charge that can be laid at the door of most treatments that emphasize the normative character of Islam. It does, however, deal with the Islamic world in all its geographic and temporal dimensions, and it avoids many of the ethnocentric biases of other Western writers. Its major short-coming is its lack of grounding in social and economic history—a weakness, once again, that is general among writers on Islam. For a trenchant critique of much of the writing on the Islamic world, see Bryan Turner's *Marx and the End of Orientalism* (1978).

Apart from a few scattered essays of an earlier time, the social and economic history of Islam is only now beginning to be written. The salient efforts include the volumes edited by M. A. Cook (1970), Charles Issawi (1966), and, especially, Abraham Udovitch (1980). Useful discussions of technology and production are Andrew Watson's "Arab Agricultural Revolution" (1974) and Richard Bulliet's *Camel and the Wheel* (1975). On relations between town and country, see Ira M. Lapidus's collection, *Middle Eastern Cities* (1969), especially the essay by Lapidus himself. The writers on Islamic history who pay special attention to social and economic aspects include Claude Cahen (1955, 1957, 1959, 1965) and S. D. Goitein, who has dealt with the rise of Near Eastern artisans and bourgeoisie (1956–1957, 1964). Some day we will have a better understanding of the wide-ranging trade connections of the Islamic world. Heyd (1885) and Lybyer (1915) remain classics; there is much information in Robert Lopez and Irving Raymond's collection on Mediterranean trade (1955); and D. S. Richards has edited a useful book on Islam and the trade of Asia (1970). Udovitch has written a splendid book on commercial law in medieval Islam (1970), and Maxime Rodinson's *Islam et capitalisme* (1966) is replete with insights and information.

On early Ottoman history, Wittek (1957) is indispensable, especially if read in conjunction with Werner (1966). Halal Inalcik's *Ottoman Empire* (1973) is a valuable contribution by a Turkish historian; I would also call attention to his "Capital Formation in the Ottoman Empire" (1969). Most challenging are the recent papers by Çağlar Keyder on Ottoman disintegration (1976) and by Huri Islamoğlu and Keyder, "Agenda for Ottoman History" (1977).

The exploration of African prehistory constitutes an exciting research frontier. A useful overview of the subject is Roland Oliver and Brian Fagan's *Africa in the Iron Age* (1975). J. D. Fage and Oliver had edited a selection of major papers from the *Journal of African History* under the title, *Papers in African Prehistory* (1970). Oliver's own paper in that volume, on "The Problem of Bantu Expansion," however, must yield first place in an exposition of this subject to D. W. Phillipson's "Spread of the Bantu Languages" (1977), on which I have relied. Vansina, Mauny, and Thomas (1964), as well as McCall (1969), explore the possibilities and difficulties facing the historian in Africa.

We now know something about the extensive networks of exchange that linked many parts of Africa. E. W. Bovill's *Golden Trade of the Moors*

(1968) deals with trans-Saharan trade; this is a revised version of a book that he wrote in 1933, *Caravans of the Old Sahara*. Lars Sundstrom's *Exchange Economy of pre-Colonial Tropical Africa* (1974) is a welcome reprint of a little-known book published in Sweden. Also valuable is Mauny (1961). Ivor Wilks (1962) stresses east-west trade routes, as well as north-south connections. A collection edited by Claude Meillassoux (1971) contains relevant information, but it deals mostly with nineteenth-century trade. On West Africa as the leading supplier of gold to the international economy between the eleventh and the seventeenth centuries, see Braudel (1972: 462–475) and Hopkins (1973: 82).

The politics of the Sudan have been discussed by Nehemia Levtzion and by Abdullahi Smith in Ajayi and Crowder, eds., *History of West Africa* (1972). Levtzion deals with the states of the Western Sudan before 1500, Smith with those of the Central Sudan. Daniel McCall (1971) has written on Islamization in this area in the eleventh century. Jack Goody (1971) illuminates state formation in Africa through comparisons with state-formation processes in Europe and Asia; but see also the critique by Emmanuel Terray (1973).

The volume edited by Robert Rotberg and H. Neville Chittick on *East Africa and the Orient* (1975) makes one think about connections across the Arabian Sea and the Indian Ocean. G.S.P. Freeman-Grenville's *Medieval History of the Coast of Tanganyika* (1962) and Chittick's paper on "The Coast Before the Arrival of the Portuguese" (1972) provide the archaeological background of coastal settlement. Roger Summers has been interested in defining and dating the archaeological sequences at Zimbabwe; see his book *Zimbabwe* (1963) and his later "Rhodesian Iron Age" (1970). K. R. Robinson has written on "The Archaeology of the Rozwi" (1966). D. P. Abraham has pioneered the combined study of Portuguese records and African oral traditions in several articles (1961, 1962, 1966). Also useful are Edward Alpers's discussion of "The Mutapa and Malawi Political Systems" (1968) and S. G. Mudenge on "The Role of Foreign Trade" (1974).

My perspective on India was shaped early in my graduate-school days by a paper by Paul Rosas, "Caste and Class in India" (1943), and later by Frederic K. Lehman's ambitious doctoral thesis, *Anthropological Parameters of a Civilization* (1957). Bernard S. Cohn's *India: The Social Anthropology of a Civilization* (1971) is excellent. I have also learned something from K. S. Shelvankar's little book on *The Problem of India* (1943), and a great deal from an article by P. C. Joshi (1970), who argues against the uniformity and unchangeability of traditional India.

Like everyone who has studied India, I have tried to comprehend caste. The literature on the topic is labyrinthine, and the reader is not always sure there is light at the end of the tunnel. There are those who locate the cohesive forces holding the caste system together in ideology, in an underlying structure or postulate of ritual purity and pollution. The major statement of this position is Louis Dumont's *Homo Hier-*

archicus (1970). Others, whose approach I find more persuasive, hold "that caste systems are held together by power, concentrated in certain groups, more than by consensus" (Berreman 1979: 112). That power plays an important role in maintaining caste distinctions and caste positions was made abundantly clear in M. N. Srinivas's paper, "The Dominant Caste in Rampura" (1959), and in F. G. Bailey's books, *Caste and the Economic Frontier* (1957) and *Tribe, Caste, and Nation* (1960). The systemic nature of this power emerged for me from Eric Miller's demonstration that royal power was the linchpin of the system in his "Caste and Territory in Malabar" (1954); from the discussion of the conflict between priestly and political power in J. C. Heesterman's "India and the Inner Conflict of Traditions" (1973); and from Chandra Jayawardena's explanation of "The Disintegration of Caste in Fiji Rural Society" (1971).

At the same time, one should not conclude that caste is merely epiphenomenal. Caste categories involve notions of corporate membership, common descent, and endogamy, even when subcastes and caste sections merge or separate according to context and situation (Béteille 1969: 157), or when castes as a whole change their social positions (see Sinder 1964; Silverberg 1968). Morton Klass (1980) has plausibly traced the rise of the caste system to a process of differentiation of originally equivalent corporate groups. Claude Meillasoux (1974) has offered a model of the caste system based on such differentiation in access to means of production, although he slights the ideological element in the determination of which group gets what. Joan Mencher's "The Caste System Upside Down" (1974) clarifies the position of the Untouchables.

I conclude that the caste phenomenon is tied up intimately with power and control of economic resources, but that the corporate nature of descent-based groups must be taken into account in trying to understand the workings of the Indian system of classes within a field of power. The model for such an approach, for me, is Richard G. Fox's *Kin, Clan, Raja, and Rule* (1971); I have relied heavily on this brilliant study.

My reading on China began with Owen and Eleanor Lattimore's *Making of Modern China* (1944) while I was in the army during World War II. I subsequently encountered two remarkable books: Karl Wittfogel's *Wirtschaft und Gesellschaft Chinas* (1931) and Owen Lattimore's *Inner Asian Frontiers* (1951). During my graduate studies I learned much from Morton Fried, who was then laying the basis for his renowned courses on China and the Chinese periphery, first offered in 1950. Fried also introduced me to the ethnic complexities of the Southwestern Chinese frontier; see his "Land Tenure, Geography and Ecology" (1952). Wolfgang Eberhard's writings, now synthesized in *A History of China* (1977), as well as Mark Elvin's notable *Pattern of the Chinese Past* (1973), provided a different perspective in their emphasis on cumulative, noncyclical changes in Chinese development. Elvin offers an especially dramatic account of Han expansion into the Chinese South. My discussion of trends in Chinese land tenure draws on Étienne Balazs's "Evolution of Landownership in Fourth- and Fifth-Century China" and "Landownership in China from the Fourth to the Fourteenth Century," both included in a book of his essays (1964); Denis Twitchett's *Land Tenure and the Social Order in T'ang and Sung China* (1962); and chapters 6 ("Manorialism without Feudalism") and 15 ("The Disappearance of Serfdom") of Elvin's *Pattern of the Chinese Past.* Elvin has also influenced my view of Chinese mercantile activity, together with W. E. Wilmott, ed., *Economic Organization in Chinese Society* (1972). Trade connections with the Arab world are discussed by Jitsuzo Kuwabara in the work "On P'u Shou-keng" (1928–1935). I first became aware of Chinese contacts with Africa through J.J.L. Duyvendak's *China's Discovery of Africa* (1949).

In early graduate work in anthropology I read on the ecology of Southeast Asia: E.C.J. Mohr's *Tropical Soil Forming Processes* (1933) and *Soils of Equatorial Regions* (1944); Pierre Gourou's *Les paysans du delta tonkinois* (1936); and Karl Pelzer's *Pioneer Settlement in the Asiatic Tropics* (1945). At that time, various writings by Robert von Heine-Geldern, Anj. Thomassen a Thuessink, and B.H.M. Vlekke furnished a spotty and conjectural view of early culture history. The situation has much improved since then, through such works as J. C. van Leur's *Indonesian Trade and Society* (1955); George Coedès's *Les peuples de la Péninsule Indochinoise* (1962) and *Les états hindouisés d'Indochine et d'Indonésie* (1964); Paul Wheatley's *Golden Khersonese* (1961) and his fine essay on the change from reciprocity to redistribution (1975); and the books by O. W. Wolters on *Early Indonesian Commerce* (1967) and *The Fall of Śrīviyaya in Malay History* (1970).

D.G.E. Hall's *History of South-East Asia* (1968) offers a sound general introduction to the history and politics of the area. I have also found useful the systematized ethnographic information in Lebar, Hickey, and Musgrove, eds., *Ethnic Groups of Mainland Southeast Asia* (1964), as well as Kunstadter, ed., *Southeast Asian Tribes, Minorities, and Nations* (1967). An enduring contribution to the understanding of this area is Harry J. Benda's 1962 essay, "The Structure of Southeast Asian History," which calls for systematic attention to major social, economic, and political relationships. It is included, together with his other essays, in a volume published to honor that gifted author after his death (Benda 1972).

The study of cultural development in the New World owes a debt to Julian Steward for his part in moving American archaeology toward a concern with ecology and socioeconomic processes. I cut my anthropological eyeteeth on the *Handbook of South American Indians*, which Steward edited (1946–1959). A synoptic version of this seven-volume work is available in Steward and Faron (1959). Steward's paper, "American Culture History in the Light of South America" (1947), has been an aid to me in thinking comparatively about native American ethnology. I found very useful the papers in Jennings and Norbeck, eds., *Prehistoric Man in the New World* (1963) and in Meggers and Evans, eds., *Aboriginal Culture Development in Latin America* (1963); Gordon R. Willey's two-volume *Introduction to American Archaeology* (1966, 1971); and William T. Sanders and Joseph Marino's *New World Prehistory* (1970).

The "paleosociology" of the Andean and sub-Andean areas is illuminated in John V. Murra, *Formaciones económicas y políticas del mundo andino* (1975); Betty J. Meggers, *Ecuador* (1966); and Gerardo Reichel-Dolmatoff, *Colombia* (1965). On the site of Buritaca, see *Colombia Today* (1979). Donald Lathrap, in *The Upper Amazon* (1970), emphasizes the relationship of the Andean and Amazonian zones, a topic that is likely to hold some surprises in the future. The archaeology of Isthmian America is ably reviewed by Olga R. Linares (1979). Mary Helms has written a fine book on *Ancient Panama: Chiefs in Search of Power* (1976).

For Mesoamerica, on which I have written earlier (Wolf 1959), I have made use of William T. Sanders and Barbara J. Price, *Mesoamerica: The Evolution of a Civilization* (1968); Pedro Carrasco et al., *Estratificación social en la Mesoamérica prehispanica* (1976); and Carrasco and Johanna Broda, eds., *Economía, política e ideología en Mesoamérica* (1977).

Gordon F. Ekholm and Gordon R. Willey together edited the fourth volume of the *Handbook of Middle American Indians*, entitled *Archaeological Frontiers and External Connections* (1966), in which J. Charles Kelley deals with Mesoamerica—Southwest connections and James B. Griffin discusses the relation of Mesoamerica to the Eastern United States. See also Charles Di Peso, *Casas Grandes* (1974). On the prehistory of the Eastern United States, see Joseph R. Caldwell's *Trend and Tradition* (1958) and "Eastern North America" (1962); Melvin L. Fowler's "Agriculture and Village Settlement in the North American East" (1971); and James A. Brown's "Spiro Art and Its Mortuary Contexts" (1975).

3. Modes of Production

This book makes extensive use of the concept of "mode of production," but in a more eclectic fashion than some of its current advocates. An introduction to the concept can be gained from Bridget O'Laughlin's "Marxist Approaches in Anthropology" (1975), Jonathan Friedman's "Marxism, Structuralism and Vulgar Materialism" (1974), and Chapter 6 of Wessman (1981). Readers should be aware, however, that the concept of the mode of production has achieved its current salience only recently, through the fusion of Marxism and structuralism in France. It thus represents a particular variant of Marxian thought and not its totality.

Marx and Engels themselves used the term *Produktionsweise* quite freely and often ambiguously. They distinguished a number of "generic types of productive systems" (in Venable's terms). They sometimes wrote as if they saw the succession of such systems—primitive communism, Asiatic society, slaveholding society, feudalism, capitalism, and socialism—as evolutionary stages. At other times, they arranged these generic types bilineally, visualizing one line of evolution moving from primitive communism to the Asiatic mode, and another line from primitive communism to capitalism on the Western European model. Eric J. Hobsbawm has examined some of the issues involved in his "Introduction" to Marx's *Precapitalist Economic Formations* (1964), which embodies a part of the long-untranslated and unknown *Grundrisse*. Orthodoxy after Marx and Engels tended to favor a unilineal evolutionary model in which each generic type of productive system gave rise, in turn, to a higher stage. Soviet interpretations, especially under Stalin, tended to favor a worldwide universal sequence—slaveholding society, feudalism, capitalism, and socialism—in order to lend ideological legitimacy to Soviet socialism as a rightful successor to its feudal and capitalist predecessors.

The attempts of French structuralists (notably Louis Althusser and Étienne Balibar in philosophy and Maurice Godelier in anthropology) to define and analyze modes of production as structures or systems in their own right, without reference to questions of evolution, transition, or history, needs to be understood as a reaction against the accepted orthodoxy. These attempts have contributed clarity to the discussion, as well as a good deal of sophisticated Gallic logic chopping.

I have learned much from the structuralists; at the same time, I see limitations in their approach. Since they believe that Marx was a systems theorist before his time, one who used Hegelian language because he could not speak Althusserian, they have eliminated the Hegelian dialectic in Marx. This does away with Marx's interesting (and, to me, valuable) effort to build a philosophy of internal relations, in favor of a mechanistic systems approach that deals with elements-in-relation instead of elements-of-relation (see Ollman 1976: Part I). The structuralists, moreover, have endowed the structure or system with an absolute teleology ("structural causality"), which moves people as carriers of the system but leaves no room for human consciousness or history. In their anthropology they consequently show a tendency to collapse all culture and cultural diversity into the elements of the mode of production. Furthermore, they reify the mode of production concept into timeless essences, which are then allowed to reproduce themselves or conjugate ("articulate") with one another without reference to historical time or circumstance.

I have adopted the mode of production concept as a way of thinking about relationships, not as God's truth. The concept cannot account for everything, nor is it the solution to all theoretical problems. I favor it in this work because it allows us to move away from mechanical, linear causalities; but I am not prepared to embrace the Rube Goldberg-like theoretical constructions of articulated sectors, levels, moments, and instances that are often only complicated rephrasings of the time-hallowed notion of "function."

Those interested in delving deeper into the relevant literature should read Althusser and Balibar, *Reading Capital* (1970), especially Part III, and Godelier's *Rationalité et irrationalité en économie* (1966). A book edited by David Seddon, *Relations of Production* (1974), offers a convenient selection of writings in English translation by French structuralist anthropologists; however, Seddon's introduction misleads in suggesting that Marxist approaches in anthropology originated at the École Normale Superieure in Paris in the 1960s. Those able to read German will find Irmgard Sellnow's *Grundprinzipien einer Periodisierung der Urgeschichte* (1961) an interesting contribution from a different tradition. Barry Hindess and Paul Q. Hirst, acting as the *enfants terribles* of Marxian social science in Britain, "out-Althusser" Althusser in their "Introduction" to *Pre-capitalist Modes of Production* (1975). They are infuriating in their insistence that no fact exists without theory, and in their resolute denial of history in constructing their modes of productions; but their extremism provides a standard against which others can test their own ideas. An informed, angry critique of the entire structuralist enterprise is provided by E. P. Thompson in *The Poverty of Theory* (1978).

Some of my insights into how the capitalist mode operates derive from the experience of growing up among textile workers in the German-Czech borderland of northern Bohemia in the Depression years of the 1930s. My interest in an alternative economics was whetted by John Strachey's *Nature of the Capitalist Crisis* (1935), which I read in 1939. When I attended Queens College in New York, I became acquainted with institutional economics through reading Dixon and Eberhardt (1938). Two outstanding books dealing with Marxian economics are Paul M. Sweezy's *Theory of Capitalist Development* (1942) and Ernest Mandel's *Marxist Economic Theory* (1968). Since 1968, the *Review of Radical Political Economics* has proved a lively and productive source of high-quality publications on economic and political subjects. The Rosetta stone of analysis is, of course, Karl Marx's *Capital*; I have used the 1977 Vintage/Random House edition for Volume I and the 1967 International Publishers edition for Volume III.

The concept of a "tributary mode of production" has been used by Samir Amin in a number of his writings, such as *Le développement inégal* (1973), especially Chapter 1 on precapitalist formations. But the concept is foreshadowed by Marx in a discussion, in the *Grundrisse*, of the possible outcomes of conquest (*Gr.* 1973: 97). The Japanese historian Jiro Hayakawa, writing in the mid-1930s, equated the tributary mode of production with the Asiatic mode (see Shiozawa 1965). Ion Banu, historian of philosophy at the University of Bucharest, similarly identified Asiatic and tributary social formations (1967).

The notion of a distinctive Asiatic mode of production stems from the writings of the classical economists: Adam Smith, James Mill, Richard Jones, and John Stuart Mill. Marx developed the concept in a number of writings, notably the *Grundrisse*, but with varying emphases, stressing sometimes the hydraulic underpinnings of Asiatic societies, sometimes the presence of village communities acting in support of a god-king who represents their undifferentiated unity. The pioneer attempt to use the concept operationally in the analysis of a hydraulic society is Wittfogel's masterly *Wirtschaft und Gesellschaft Chinas* (1931). Wittfogel continued to be the main protagonist of the idea after the advent of Stalinism rendered its discussion impermissible in the Soviet Union and elsewhere in the member parties of the Communist International. Soviet Marxism-Leninism evidently felt threatened by the critical stance toward state managerial bureaucracies that the concept implied; by the possibility that it could be used to characterize Soviet society as "Asiatic"; and by the implication that sociocultural evolution might be multilineal rather than unilineal, and thus might demand multilineal and heterodox political responses and strategies rather than uniform and orthodox ones. The renewed interest in the concept after Stalin's demise seems to be the result of efforts on the Left to chart multilineal, nationally differentiated roads to socialism. Among writings pointing in that direction are those by the redoubtable East German historian of the Near East and classical antiquity, Elisabeth Charlotte Welskopf (1957); the French historian of the Orient, Jean Chesneaux (1964); the French anthropologist Maurice Godelier (1965); and the Hungarian historian of Oriental literature, Ferenc Tökei (1966). Useful works dealing with the issues posed by the concept are Wittfogel's *Oriental Despotism* (1957), especially chapter 9; the volume of collected papers, *Sur le 'mode de production asiatique,'* published by the Centre d'Études et de Recherches Marxistes (1969); Lawrence Krader's *Asiatic Mode of Production* (1975); the critical chapter 4 in Hindess and Hirst (1975); and Irfan M. Habib's "Examination of Wittfogel's Theory of Oriental Despotism" (1969). Jonathan Friedman's *System, Structure and Contradiction* (1979) suggests the possible development of Asiatic state forms out of pre-existent kin-ordered "conical clan" structures, and encourages one to think of rank-ordered and kin-based, feudal, and Asiatic formations as transformations of one another.

An introduction to the issues posed by feudalism and to the relevant bibliography is the article "Feudalism" by Joshua Prawer and Shmuel N. Eisenstadt in the *International Encyclopedia of the Social Sciences* (1968). The classic work on the topic remains Marc Bloch's *Feudal Society* (1961), first published in 1939–1940 at the beginning of the war from which its author would not return. The Centre d'Études et de Recherches Marxistes has published a volume of papers, *Sur le féodalisme* (1971), in which René Gallissot questions why the weak, short-lived, and peripheral Northwest European feudalism should serve as the type case for feudalisms everywhere. Heide Wunder has brought together an interesting collection of papers by West and East German authors, *Feudalismus* (1971), which includes a helpful introduction by Wunder. The publisher did not, however, receive permission to reprint Otto Hintze's important essay on "Wesen und Verbreitung des Feudalismus" (1929). This paper first encouraged me to think of feudalism as a phase within a larger mode. It treats feudalism as a recurrent, but not universal, constellation or syndrome, which can occur either in the course of state formation or as a result of political devolution and breakdown. The East German scholars included in the Wunder volume treat feudalism as a mode of production, as do Hindess and Hirst (1975: Chap. 5). Among the East Germans, Bernhard Töpfer (Wunder 1971: Chap. 7) is the most concerned with feudalism as particular outcomes of multilineal processes; in contrast, Hindess and Hirst are prevented by their extreme structuralism from asking questions about the cross-cultural temporal and geographic occurrence and variability of their postulated mode. Also important for its discussion of feudal "rationality" and the role of commerce in a feudal system is Witold Kula's economic theory of the feudal system (1970).

My construction of a kin-ordered mode was prompted by diverse influences. Among these were Paul Kirchhoff's "Principles of Clanship in Human Society," written originally in 1935 but not published until 1955 (reprinted 1959), along with Morton H. Fried's reworking of Kirchhoff's ideas in his "Classification of Corporate Unilineal Descent Groups" (1957). A second source was the essays of Claude Meillasoux, especially "Essai d'interprétation du phénomène économique" (1960), "From Reproduction to Production" (1972), and "The Social Organization of the Peasantry" (1973). A third influence was Marshall Sahlins's notion of the contradiction between the domestic level and kinship (see, especially, his *Stone Age Economics*, 1972: Chaps. 2 and 3). A fourth was Janet Siskind's excellent "Kinship and Mode of Production" (1978), which links the basic elements of kinship and marriage to the division of labor between the sexes. The complexities of kinship as a symbolic construct were brought home to me by David M. Schneider's "What is Kinship All About?" (1972).

On the contradictory role of the chief within the kinship order, and on the transition from kinship to classness, see Kirchhoff (1959), Fried (1957, 1960), Sahlins (1960; 1972: 130–148, 204–210), Ruyle (1973), and Webster (1975, 1976).

The question of how modes of production articulate with one another has been raised by Pierre-Philippe Rey's *Les alliances de classes* (1976), the essay on articulation included in that volume having been circulated in mimeographed form since 1969. Barbara Bradby's article, "The Destruction of Natural Economy" (1975), represents a lucid and important contribution. Aidan Foster-Carter's "Can We Articulate Articulation?" (1977) discusses some of the relevant literature and its problems.

4. Europe, Prelude to Expansion

To explain Europe's peripheral position in relation to the Levant after the fall of the Roman Empire requires one to ask first just who and what fell. A useful introduction to diverse views on the problem is the booklet edited by Mortimer Chambers, *The Fall of Rome* (1963). A sophisticated recent appraisal of the question is Perry Anderson's *Passages from Antiquity to Feudalism* (1978). There clearly was a political collapse in the western half of the empire, but a simultaneous diffusion of Roman patterns throughout the rural areas; on this point, see Heichelheim (1956). One must also remember that while Western Rome fell, Eastern Rome survived for another thousand years. The major work on Byzantium is Georg Ostrogorsky's *History of the Byzantine State*, but Anderson's discussion of Byzantium (1978: 265−293) cites much new literature. My concept of the Byzantine-Viking pincer that contained Europe to the west is based on my reading of Archibald Lewis's splended *Naval Power and Trade in the Mediterranean, 500−1100* (1951) and *The Northern Seas* (1958), as well as Gwyn Jones's *History of the Vikings* (1968), which treats the Viking connections to the east (Part 2, Chap. 4).

There is need for further detailed study of the trade in European slaves to the East, where until the tenth century they constituted a major article of commerce. On Byzantine slavery, see Hadjinicolaou-Marava (1950); on the slaving activities of the Al-Radhaniyya in the ninth century, Lopez and Ramond, *Medieval Trade* (1955: 31−32, 115); on Viking trade in slaves to the Islamic world, see the chilling account of Ibn Fadlan, in Togan (1939); on the Venetian slave trade, Lane's *Venice* (1973: 69). Charles Verlinden's *L'esclavage* (1955) is the major source on the slave trade through the ports of the Black Sea. Iris Origo documents the presence of large numbers of such Eastern slaves in Tuscany in the fourteenth and fifteenth centuries (1955).

On the development of the Italian city-states, see Robert Reynolds's *Europe Emerges* (1961); Gino Luzzatto's *Economic History of Italy* (1961), which includes much pertinent bibliography; and Robert Lopez's booklet on the commercial revolution of the Middle Ages (1971). The entire subject of the Crusades requires re-examination. Reynolds offers useful comments on European expansion in the Mediterranean in "The Mediterranean Frontiers, 1000−1400" (1957). Heyd (1885) remains a key source for the commercial activity connected with the eastward religious-political thrust. The renewed European movement beyond the frontiers of the peninsula after 1400 should be seen as a response to the so-called "crisis of the fourteenth century." This crisis is well discussed by Leopold Génicot in his contribution to the *Cambridge Economic History of Europe* (1966), which includes an extensive bibliography. Immanuel Wallerstein offers a particularly clear presentation of the issues posed by the crisis in his *Modern World-System* (1974: 21−28). Rodney Hilton (1951) argues that there was a general crisis of feudalism. He sees the roots of the crisis in the inability of the feudal system to increase production without stepping up the level of tributary extraction from the peasantry, and in the peasant revolts that engulfed Europe in response to heightened exploitation.

Portuguese development is well covered in A. H. Oliveira Marques's *History of Portugal* (1972). My sources for the discussion of the Portuguese abroad include: Charles R. Boxer, *The Portuguese Seaborne Empire* (1973*a*); Bailey W. Diffie and George D. Winius, *Foundations of the Portuguese Empire* (1977); and Vitorino Magalhães Godinho's two-volume work on the global economic aspects of the discoveries (1963 – 1965).

My views on Spain have been shaped by Ángel Palerm's article "El industrialismo y la decadencia" (1949). Indispensable are Jaime Vícens Víves's *Economic History of Spain* (1969) and his *Approaches to the History of Spain* (1970), as well as John H. Elliott's *Imperial Spain 1469–1716* (1966). Palerm also introduced me to Ramón Carande's *Carlos V y sus banqueros* (1943, 1949). I learned much from Ruth Pike's account of the Genoese role in the opening of the New World (1966). I have consulted—but am overawed by—Huguette and Pierre Chaunu's eight-volume study of the Spanish and Spanish-American economies, *Séville et l'Atlantique* (1955 – 1959). E. J. Hamilton's *American Treasure* (1934), a book much discussed and much criticized, remains the classic work on the impact of American silver on the Spanish economy.

On the development of the Dutch Republic, I read Pieter Geyl's book, *The Revolt of the Netherlands* (1932), while still in college. Historical geography, such as the work of C. T. Smith (1967), is useful in locating the Low Countries within the developing European economy. Virginia Barbour (1963) on seventeenth-century Amsterdam, and Charles Boxer (1973*b*) and George Masselman (1963) on Dutch overseas expansion, allow one to connect internal and external developments. I have found helpful the symposium on Britain and the Netherlands edited by J. S. Bromley and E. H. Kossman (1964, 1968), especially the contributions (in Vol. II) by J. G. van der Dillen on the role of Amsterdam and by J. D. Roorda on the ruling classes of seventeenth-century Holland. Jan de Vries (1974) has stressed the high level of specialization achieved by the Netherlands, and has argued that Dutch success in making the most of the "Renaissance" technology of windmills, canals, wood mechanisms, and peat fuel inhibited the capacity of the Netherlands to move in the direction of industrial capitalism and proletarianization (de Vries 1975).

It is not easy to grasp the continuous threads in French development, perhaps because few books on French history escape the impact of the revolutionary rhetoric of 1789. As an anthropologist, I am impressed with the diversity of the nation, pulled into concordance by the force of its political and ideological center at Paris. This impression has been heightened by reading Edward W. Fox (1971) on the geographic divisions within France; Charles Tilly's analysis of the *Vendée* rising against the revolution (1964); and the fine, unpublished doctoral dissertation by Harriet Rosenberg (1975) on the development of underdevelopment in the Alpine Queiras. The growth of hegemonic France has been clarified for me by Henri Sée (1937), by Barrington Moore (1966), and by Theda Skocpol (1979). Marc Bloch's *French Rural History* (1970) deals with the development of the French agrarian base and its many variations, and offers counterpoints with the course of English agricultural development. I have found convincing François Crouzet's comparison of economic growth in France and England during the eighteenth century (1967). Cobban (1964), Hobsbawm (1962), and Kemp (1971) all wrestle with the paradoxical character of the French Revolution— bourgeois but noncapitalist, even anticapitalist.

For an understanding of medieval England I have relied on Doris Stenton's *English Society in the Early Middle Ages* (1952), Marion Gibbs's *Feudal Order* (1949), and Joseph Strayer's insightful *On the Medieval Origins of the Modern State* (1970). These works elucidate the apparent paradox of the early political unification of the realm and its simultaneous delegation of legal and political activities to locally based groups and categories of people. S. T. Bindoff's *Tudor England* (1966) shows how the Tudor dynasty was able to consolidate its rule upon the ruins of the English aristocracy, brought on by its internecine War of the Roses after withdrawal from the Hundred Years War with France. Rodney Hilton's book on the decline of serfdom (1969) and, especially, Robert Brenner's trenchant article on "Agrarian Class Structure and Economic Development" (1976) throw light on the contradiction between the political gains of the English peasantry and its weakening grip on economic resources. Alan MacFarlane (1979) deals with many of the same issues, but he takes the idealist view that English individualism led to the development of private property in land rather than looking to the condition of the English peasantry to explain its individualism. The separation of English cultivators from the land is well treated, I think, by Richard Tawney's *Agrarian Problem in the Sixteenth Century* (1967), Moore's *Democracy and Dictatorship* (1966: Chap. 1), and William Lazonick's paper on enclosures (1974). Lazonick properly argues that scholars such as T. S. Ashton, J. D. Chambers, and G. Mingay, who claim that the separation of people from the land improved their chances of employment, do so from the perspective of a developed capitalism rather than from the evidence of the period in which the capitalist system was first installed. Sylvia Thrupp deals with *The Merchant Class of Medieval London* in the fourteenth and fifteenth centuries (1962), while Ralph Davis summarizes his many papers on the trade abroad in *English Overseas Trade 1500–1700* (1973). The subsequent development of England is well covered in Maurice Dobb's *Studies in the Development of Capitalism* (1947), in Christopher Hill's *Reformation to Industrial Revolution* (1967), and in Charles H. Wilson's *England's Apprenticeship* (1965).

Wilson has also written a fine book on English-Dutch rivalry, *Profit and Power* (1957). Both Moore (1966) and Wallerstein (1974) make perspicacious use of the voluminous literature on the class alliances and fissions of England from the sixteenth to the eighteenth centuries.

In gaining an overview of European overseas expansion, I have drawn on a number of writers. Wallerstein, as always, provides information and insight. Andre Gunder Frank's *World Accumulation* (1978) details the global scope of the stockpiling of mercantile wealth, although he calls capitalist what I would, with Marx, treat as "the prehistory of capital." I have learned a great deal from Oliver C. Cox's *Foundations of Capitalism* (1959), even though I part company with him when he traces the roots of capitalist development back to the Italian city-states. Frédéric Mauro furnishes a temporal frame for European expansion between 1600 and 1870 (1967), and provides a useful model of "intercontinental" economic connections from 1500 to 1800 (1961). John H. Parry has written on the establishment of European hegemony between 1415 and 1715 (1966) and on European overseas empires in the eighteenth century (1971).

5. Iberians in America

Since I first began to read and write on Iberian America in the 1950s, research has opened up new sources of information and novel interpretations. It is now clear, after the work on silver mining by Peter J. Bakewell (1971), D. A. Brading (1971), and Brading and Cross (1972), that there was little or no relation between the massive decline of the native American population and the level of silver production. It now also seems that while the seventeenth century was a period of depression for the Iberian mother countries, the colonies prospered, although in contradictory ways. One of the important sources of this prosperity was contraband. This suggests that much of world history needs to be rewritten in light of what is now politely called "the informal economy." Further research on areas beyond the main centers of colonial government has also revealed unexpected variation and interesting differences. The organization and functioning of the hacienda now also seem more variable than they once did. See, on this point, Magnus Mörner (1973) and the volume on *Haciendas, latifundios y plantaciones* brought together by Enrique Florescano (1975).

I have found valuable the two volumes by James Lang on Spain and England in the Americas (1975) and on Portuguese Brazil (1979). These works, by a historical sociologist with a firm grounding in economic realities, focus on the different kinds of states created by European colonization. Other productive general treatises are Stein and Stein (1970), which views Latin America through the optic of dependency theory; Carmagnani (1975), specifically useful for its discussion of trade and economic rationality; and the provocative essays compiled by

Florescano (1979), including one that has been especially important for my own thinking, Palerm's "Sobre la formación del sistema colonial." There now exists a growing body of work by anthropologically informed historians and historically informed anthropologists on particular populations and regions. To name the most important, there is Charles Gibson's now classic work on the colonial Aztecs (1964); William Taylor's book on Oaxaca (1972); Murdo MacLeod on Central America (1973); Juan and Judith Villamarín on Colombia (Juan Villamarín 1972, 1975; J. and J. Villamarín 1979); James Lockhardt on the first century of the Spanish conquest of Peru (1968, 1972); Karen Spalding on colonial Indian society in Peru (1967, 1972); Frederick Bowser on slavery in Peru (1974) and William Frederick Sharp on slavery in the Chocó (1976); Michael Craton and James Walvin on a Jamaican plantation (1970); and Manuel Moreno Fraginals on the Cuban sugar mill (1978).

6. The Fur Trade

The development of the fur trade runs like a thread of blood and gold through the history of North America. Anthropological ethnohistory has now begun to converge with the research of social and economic historians to produce a clearer picture of the ways that the expanding trade involved local populations and was affected by them in turn.

One of the most useful books I have come by for understanding the historical encounters of different populations in North America during the colonial period is Gary Nash's *Red, White, and Black* (1974). Some good standard works on the fur trade are those by Murry Lawson (1943), E. E. Rich (1959), Paul Phillips (1961), and especially Harold Innis (1956, a revised edition of a 1930 classic). Useful papers dealing with the trade appear in several collections, among them the contributions to two conferences (American Fur Trade Conference, 1967; Bolus, ed., 1972); two special issues of the *Western Canadian Journal of Anthropology*, in 1972, and in 1976, under the editorship of Bishop and Ray; and a volume edited by Hauptman and Campisi (1978). Eleanor Leacock and Nancy Lurie have brought together a number of case histories of *North American Indians in Historical Perspective* (1971), some of them dealing explicitly with the effects of the trade.

On the Northeastern populations, Alfred Bailey wrote in 1937 a general account of *The Conflict of European and Eastern Algonkian Cultures 1504–1700* (1969). Leacock (1954), writing on the Montagnais, was the first to detail the impact of fur trapping on the organization of family hunting territories. Francis Jennings (1976) has dealt with the European invasion of the Atlantic coast, concentrating specifically on New England. The Iroquois have played an important part in American anthropology, as they have in American history, but informed synoptic treatments of Iroquois development, such as Quain (1937) and Fenton

(1971), are rare. Volume V of the new *Handbook of North American Indians*, dealing with the Northeast (Trigger 1978), synthesizes the results of Iroquois research by William N. Fenton, Elizabeth Tooker, Anthony Wallace, and others; it also contains an unparalleled bibliography. George Hunt (1940), Allen Trelease (1960), and Barbara Graymont (1972) have illuminated the external political involvements of the Iroquois. On the Huron there is now the truly outstanding work by Bruce Trigger, *The Children of Aataentsic* (1976); see also the review by Fenton (1978).

Great Lakes ethnography is covered in traditional fashion in Kinietz (1965), but our new understandings of the Ojibwa and their neighbors owe everything to Harold Hickerson and, more recently, to Charles Bishop. I have relied on Hickerson (1960, 1962a) for the interpretation of the Feast of the Dead and the Midewiwin, and also on his *Southwestern Chippewa* (1962b) and his fine ethnohistory, *The Chippewa and Their Neighbors* (1970). I have drawn on Bishop (1976) for a discussion of the development of the northern Ojibwa. Peckham (1970) is a study of Pontiac's revolt by a historian. The Indian role in the trade of the Hudson Bay Company has been examined by Arthur Ray (1974). There are fine papers on subarctic hunters and trappers by Edward Rogers, Richard Slobodin, and June Helm in the volumes edited by David Damas (1969a, 1969b).

The literature on Plains Indians is rich, exciting, and uneven. Perhaps the best overview of Plains adaptation is provided by Symmes Oliver's "Ecology and Cultural Continuity" (1974). H. Clyde Wilson (1963) has analyzed Plains pastoralism, and Frank Secoy's doctoral dissertation (1953) is a masterful account of the emergence of Plains social, political, and military organization. Edward Bruner (1961) has looked at Mandan development in connection with the growth of trade, and Preston Holder (1970) has outlined the contradictions produced by fully specialized horse pastoralism within Plains horticultural societies. Two contributions deal specifically with the external linkages of Plains groups: Oscar Lewis's monograph on the effects of the fur trade on the Blackfoot (1942), and Joseph Jablow's fine *Cheyenne in Plains Trade Relations, 1795–1840* (1951). The spread of slave raiding in the Southwest is discussed by L. R. Bailey (1966); its wider implications still need to be defined. The changed logistics of the fur trade, with its expansion from the Great Lakes toward the drainage of the Saskatchewan, only became clear to me after reading Robert Merriman, *The Bison and the Fur Trade* (1926). On the Red River métis, an interesting source is Joseph Howard's *Strange Empire* (1952); see also McHugh (1972) and Hickerson (1956).

Philip Drucker's little book on *The Indians of the Northwest Coast* (1963) remains a useful introduction full of insight. Erna Gunther (1972) has gathered together the reports—most of them not easy to come by—of early European travelers to the region. The *Noticias de Nutka* of 1792 by the Spanish naturalist José Mariano Moziño is now available in translation (1970). Robin Fisher (1977) offers an account of the contacts between native Americans and newcomers over time.

Joyce Wike completed an outstanding thesis on the maritime trade and its effects at Columbia University in 1947, when I was in my first year of graduate studies there. All her later papers (1952, 1957, 1958*a*, 1958*b*) have proven invaluable. Wayne Suttles and the scholars he has influenced have deepened our understanding of regional ecology; an article on environmental and cultural variability in the Northwest Coast area (1960) exemplifies his approach. Abraham Rosman and Paula Rubel's study of potlatching (1971) fruitfully examines the role of gift exchange in succession and marriage. For me, the ecological approach of Suttles and the structuralist approach to group relations of Rosman and Rubel are complementary rather than opposed. I have also used the work of Frederica De Laguna on the Yakutat Tlingit (1972); Kalervo Oberg on the Chilcat Tlingit (a 1933 dissertation, published in 1973); Viola Garfield on the Tsimshian (1939); "Bella Coola" McIlwraith on the Bella Coola (1948); Philip Drucker on the Nootka (1951); Helen Codere (1950, 1961) and Irving Goldman (1975) on the Kwakiutl; and June Collins on the Skagit (1974). I have always thought that Goldman's paper on the Alkatcho Carrier (1940), a contribution to Linton's volume on acculturation among North American Indians, was a small masterpiece.

My interest in the Russian fur trade goes back to childhood, when I read stories of the Russian explorer Arseniev and Dersu the Trapper, along with *The Last of the Mohicans* and *Winnetou*. Coming into anthropology, I was intrigued by the seemingly apocryphal story about the fish-eating horses of the Yakuts; James Gibson (1969: 191) provides bona fide evidence that they were real. Robert Kerner's *The Urge to the Sea* (1942) is a basic source on Russian expansion and fur trading. John Baddeley's book on *Russia, Mongolia, and China* (1919) contains a copy of the 1673 map from the *Remezoff Atlas*. Raymond Fisher (1943) covers the Russian trade between 1500 and 1700; Mark Mancall (1971) is informative about the trade with China until 1728; and Clifford Foust (1961, 1969) deals with the Chinese segment of the trade in the eighteenth century. E. E. Rich, in "Russia and the Colonial Fur Trade" (1955), sheds light on the international linkages of the trade. James R. Gibson (1969) touches on much Siberian ethnology in showing how the fur trade was provisioned in Russia's Asiatic maritime provinces. Some of the effects of the trade on the Yakuts are discussed in Nelson Graburn and B. Stephen Strong's *Circumpolar Peoples* (1973).

7. The Slave Trade

As an adolescent I read Leo Frobenius's *Kulturgeschichte Afrikas* (1933); I remained fascinated by it long afterward, while growing increasingly suspicious of its conjectural history and subjective interpretations of "cultural morphology." Reading Robert Stevenson's book on *Population and Political Systems in Tropical Africa* (1968) first persuaded me that a real history of African societies was possible, and that the results of such a history would alter the perspectives developed by social anthropologists working in Africa. The book, which in criticizing functionalist demography also criticized functionalist anthropology, has been both challenged (see Goody 1973) and successfully defended (Harris 1979: 306–307). Since about 1960, there has been an upsurge of writings on African history, much of it truly excellent and deserving of a wide audience.

The question of whether slavery in Africa antedates the arrival of the Europeans or was a phenomenon largely generated by European demand for coercible labor is a difficult one that requires further research. Igor Kopytoff and Suzanne Miers (1977) argue that African slavery represents but an extension of the quest to augment rights over persons, a drive at the root of African systems of kinship and marriage. In their view, slavery allowed kin groups to increase their scope by adding persons who did not have the backing of a corporate group of kin; the opposite of slavery is thus not "freedom," but "belonging." Mary Douglas argues in the same direction in her valuable paper on pawning (1964). Various researchers have also pointed out—properly so—that rights over slaves and the rights of slaves varied greatly from society to society.

It would be erroneous, however, to conjure up a vision of an Africa wholly composed of egalitarian kin groups. Tributary states and kin-ordered societies in the process of stratification existed before 1400, as did the trade in African slaves across the Sahara and the Indian Ocean. Much more needs to be learned about slavery in the Islamic world, from the eighth century on. Raymond Mauny (1961: 379) and Tadeusz Lewicki (cited in Hopkins 1973: 82, n. 11) both suggest that slave exports across the Sahara involved millions of people. The sustained European demand for slaves certainly intensified enslavement and furnished the structural impetus for the growth of slave-raiding aristocracies and states. Some other contributions to the elucidation of slavery in Africa are Meillassoux (1975) and Watson (1980).

For a grasp of the slave trade in West Africa, I turned to Philip Curtin on Senegambia (1975), Walter Rodney on the Upper Guinea Coast (1970), Kwame Daaku on the Gold Coast (1970), and Kwame Arhin (1967) and Ivor Wilks (1967, 1975) on the development of Asante. Peter Morton-Williams's paper on the role of trade in shaping the policies of Asante and Oyo (1969) provided major insights, as did I. A. Akinjogbin on the linked development of Oyo and Dahomey (1972). Both Morton-Williams (1964, 1965, 1967, 1969) and Robin Law (1975) were helpful for my understanding of Oyo, while Akinjogbin (1967, 1972) added to what I had learned earlier about Dahomey from Melville Herskovits (1938), Stanley Diamond (1951), and Karl Polanyi (1966). Peter Lloyd (1954, 1965, 1968), as well as William Bascom (1969) are important sources for the Yoruba kingdoms; R. E. Bradbury has written on Benin (1957, 1964). The literature on the Niger Delta is rich and full of surprises. In addition to G. I. Jones (1963) and K. O. Dike (1956) on trade and politics in the Delta region, there is Robin Horton's social history of New Calabar (1969), A. J. Latham on *Old Calabar 1600–1891* (1973), and Richard N. Henderson's *The King in Every Man* (1972) on Onitsha Ibo. David Northrup is informative about Ibo trade (1972), and Simon Ottenberg is excellent on oracles and intergroup relationships among the Ibo (1958).

For Central Africa, Jan Vansina's *Kingdoms of the Savannah* (1968) provides a pioneering effort and the basis for further research. Also important are his papers on long-distance trade routes in Central Africa (1962) and on the origin of the Congo kingdom (1963). The great archives of Lisbon and Rome will undoubtedly yield still unsuspected riches, but Jean Cuvelier and Louis Jadin have begun to collect the Roman documents on the Congo. Their *L'Ancien Congo* (1954) furnishes the basis for Georges Balandier's account of Congo history in *Daily Life in the Kingdom of the Congo* (1968). I have relied heavily on Kajsa Ekholm's insightful structural study (1977), which relates matriliny to political relations based on the circulation of prestige goods. For Angola, I read David Birmingham's *The Portuguese Conquest* (1965) and *Trade and Conflict* (1966), as well as his thoughtful re-evaluation of some earlier interpretations (1972). Joseph C. Miller's works on the *Mbundu States in Angola* (1975) and on "The Slave Trade in Congo and Angola" (1976) made me wish that I had read him long ago. Vansina's *Kingdoms* also provided a basis for understanding the Luba-Lunda expansion, along with Jean-Luc Vellut's "Notes sur le Lunda" (1972). Ian Cunnison deals with the eastern marches of Lunda expansion (1956, 1957, 1961), and Malyn Newitt discusses *Portuguese Settlement on the Zambesi* (1973). Andrew Roberts's *History of the Bemba* (1973) places this group firmly in the context of the expanding trade in slaves and ivory.

Figures on slave exports from Africa are drawn from Philip Curtin's *The Atlantic Slave Trade, a Census* (1969).

8. Trade and Conquest in the Orient

European penetration into Asian waters must be understood as a continuation of past European involvements with Asia. J. Innis Miller (1969) offers a detailed treatise on the Roman-Asian spice trade. The book by Lopez and Raymond on trade in the Mediterranean (1955) includes a great deal of information about European commercial dealings in Asia. Lopez, in his little book on *The Commercial Revolution of the Middle Ages* (1971), speaks of the "explosion of Italian trade" from Greenland to Peking. The Islamic expansion into southern and Southeast Asia is sketched out in Hall's *History of South-East Asia* (1968, Chap. 10) and discussed in Wertheim (1973: 13). C.G.F. Simkin (1968) deals with the "traditional" trade of Asia before the advent of the Europeans. The first part of Carlo Cipolla's book on European overseas expansion (1970), on "guns and sails," offers an excellent introduction to the naval and military logistics of European sea-borne commerce. Niels Steensgard (1973) is masterly on the impact of that commerce on the continental caravan trade of Asia.

For an understanding of Portuguese expansion in Asia, I have drawn on Godinho (1969), Boxer (1948, 1953, 1973a), T'ien-tse Chang (1934), and Diffie and Winius (1977). On Dutch expansion I have consulted Masselman (1963), Boxer (1973b), Kristof Glamann (1958), and especially M.A.P. Meilink-Roelofz (1962).

The agrarian system of Mughal India was first described in detail by W. H. Moreland (1963, first pub. 1929), but Irfan Habib has added greatly to our knowledge of it with his recent *Agrarian Systems* (1963). Habib stresses commercialization and class conflict; he has also discussed the prevalent money economy in a paper on "Banking in Mughal India" (1960), included in Raychaudhuri's *Contributions*. Howard Spodek emphasizes the role of independent merchants and moneylenders, among other urban-based social segments, in his "Rulers, Merchants and Other Groups" (1974). Percival Spear offers an excellent introduction to the governing structure of the Mughal realm in his contribution to the volume edited by Leach and Mukherjee (1970).

The role of the English in India is illuminated by Philip Woodruff's two-volume *The Men Who Ruled India* (1964). This work is enjoyable and useful, as long as one balances its celebration of the British raj against other works, such as Romesh Dutt's *Economic History of India* (1960), originally published in 1901, and Ramkrishna Mukherjee's appraisal of the English East India Company (1958). A new economic history of India by Indians is represented in the two volumes of essays edited by Ganguli (1964) and Raychaudhuri (1960). Morris D. Morris and Burton Stein have written a helpful bibliographic essay on Indian economic history (1961); Morris's own attempt to evaluate positively Indian industrialization and commercialization in the nineteenth century has been reprinted, together with critical comments by Japanese and Indian economists, in the *Indian Economic and Social History Review* (see Morris 1963). The papers in Leach and Mukherjee (1970) portray various Indian mercantile and governmental elites. J. H. Broomfield's excellent article on "Regional Elites" (1966) offers insight into the rise and succession of such elites under British rule. Spear delineates the lifestyle adopted by the English in India in his book *The Nabobs* (1963).

Bernard S. Cohn has given us several fine studies on the effects of British rule at the local level in northern India. I have drawn on his discussions of legal change (1959, 1961) and on his analyses of the interplay of political systems in the Benares region (1960, 1962). For information on English-held Madras, I have used Holden Furber

(1970). Kathleen Gough (1978) deals with the changes initiated in Thanjavur.

My understanding of how British control of India related to the commercial penetration of China has benefited greatly from the large-scale, exciting, Braudel-like work of Louis Dermigny, *La Chine et L'Occident* (1964). This book also gave me a sense of the importance of clandestine trade and politics along the South China coast in the sixteenth and seventeenth centuries. Bromley and Kossman have compiled a useful set of papers on Dutch-English relations and competition (1964, 1968).

There are many books on the opium trade. Michael Greenberg points out that trade in opium was "probably the largest commerce of the time in any single commodity" (1951: 104). Frederic Wakeman depicts the resulting social disorders in his excellent *Strangers at the Gate* (1974). John Fairbank's *Trade and Diplomacy on the China Coast* (1953) has become a classic statement on the subject for the nineteenth century.

A wholly satisfactory account of commodity trade and cultural encounters in the Pacific seems to have escaped me. Oliver (1961) and Dodge (1976) provide good introductions. Two books by historians—H. E. Maude (1968) and R. Gerard Ward, ed. (1972)—furnish more detailed accounts of certain trades. Ward's collection contains his own essay on the bêche-de-mer, or trepang, trade (pages 91–123). The implications of this trade for relationships between Malay fishermen and Australian aborigines is dealt with by C. C. MacKnight (1972); but I remember an earlier treatment of the subject by W. Lloyd Warner in his book on the Murngin (1958, original ed. 1937, especially Appendix 1). Dorothy Shineberg has written on the sandalwood trade in Melanesia (1966, 1967); she is also the author of a perceptive paper on the difficulty of using musketry in the wet tropics (1970). J. C. Furnas's *Anatomy of Paradise* (1947) is useful for Hawaii. Webb (1965), Levin (1968), and Davenport (1969) all explore why Hawaii abolished its complex taboo system, an event that Kroeber had ascribed to "cultural fatigue" (1948: 403–405).

9. Industrial Revolution

Many authors have questioned the uniqueness of the period beginning around 1750, suggesting either that *the* industrial revolution was but one industrial revolution among many, or that it was simply a phase in an ongoing cumulative process. I have nevertheless adopted the term *industrial revolution* in this chapter, because it indicates a qualitative change both in the forces and in the relations of production. This view is based on Maurice Dobb (1947) and Paul Mantoux (1928); both the titles and the substance of Polanyi's *Great Transformation* (1944) and David Landes's *Unbound Prometheus* (1969) carry the same conviction. I learned a great deal from Kriedte, Medick, and Schlumbohm (1977), which builds on Franklin Mendels's concept of proto-industrialization (1972). The section by Schlumbohm (pages 194–257) dealing with the limitations of the putting-out system was especially useful. I think these authors have a sound analytic grasp of the phenomena involved, although Pierre Jeannin (1980) has taken them to task for underestimating the variability caused by geographic and social differentiation.

Dobb (1947) and Hobsbawm (1962, 1969, 1975) provided the guiding threads of my presentation; but I have also consulted Lampard (1957), Flinn (1966), and Hartwell (1970) for differing perspectives. The social background of the first factory masters is now fairly well understood, especially through the work of S. D. Chapman (1967, 1973), on whose findings I have relied. Harold Perkin (1969) offers a sociologically oriented discussion of English society in the century after 1780; see also Thompson (1978).

In explicating the development of cotton manufactures, the "carrying industry" of the industrial revolution, I drew on knowledge accumulated in my own patriline, in the textile trades for generations. My basic sources included Mantoux's *Industrial Revolution* (1928), A. P. Wadsworth and Julia de L. Mann's classic *The Cotton Trade and Industrial Lancashire* (1931), Mann's *Cloth Industry* (1971), and the valuable booklet by S. D. Chapman (1972). On factory organization and management, I read Sidney Pollard (1965) and Reinhard Bendix (1956), and benefited from the insistence by Bowles and Gintis that "authority at the point of production must be used to *evince* worker behaviour not guaranteed by the wage labour contract" (1977: 177).

A now-classic work dealing with the growth of the English working class has been written by E. P. Thompson (1966). Duncan Bythell (1969) deals specifically with the handloom weavers, from a point of view opposed to Thompson's. To gain an acquaintance with the growing literature on working-class recruitment, families, and kinship ties, I read Neil Smelser (1959), who stresses the continuity between domestic work and factory employment, as well as his (to me, convincing) critics, Michael Edwards and R. Lloyd-Jones (1973); Arthur Redford (1926) on labor migration; and Michael Anderson (1971) and David Levine (1977) on family transformation among increasingly proletarianized cultivators and artisans. John Foster's *Class Struggle and the Industrial Revolution* (1974) is an excellent study of the developing working-class communities in three English towns, including Oldham. Steven Marcus, in *Engels, Manchester, and the Working Class* (1974), presents a sympathetic view of Engels as an interpreter of the new capitalist industrialism.

Since 1960 many outstanding works on Black slavery and the American Cotton South have appeared. I have steered away from the moralistically tinged literature on race relations and concentrated instead on empirically-based historical studies, such as those by Eugene Genovese (1966, 1969), Edmund Morgan (1975), Robert Fogel and Stanley

Engerman (1974), Edgar Thompson (1975), and Gavin Wright (1978), in order to better understand the relation between slavery and plantation agriculture. I think rather better of Fogel and Engerman than many of their critics for raising important questions, and have relied on them for quantitative information, although I would not agree with some of their conclusions. I have drawn on Bruchey, ed., *Cotton and the Growth of the American Economy* (1967), as well as Moore (1966: Chap. 3), Dowd (1956), North (1961), and Bruchey (1965), to place Southern cotton production within the larger context of the developing economy of the United States. To get a sense of "the world the slaves made," I turned to Genovese (1972), Herbert Gutman (1976), John Blassingame (1972), and George Rawick (1972). Sidney Mintz and Richard Price (1976) offer a useful approach to Afro-American culture patterns, and Gutman (1976: Chap. 8) suggests how such patterns might have been generated.

The literature on the native American populations of the southeastern United States is rich and suggestive, although uneven. John Swanton (1946) and Charles Hudson (1976) provide ethnological overviews. William Willis (1980) draws on archaeological and ethnohistorical evidence to discuss the formation of native multicommunity systems. On the interaction between European settlers and native American groups in the seventeenth and eighteenth centuries, I found Verner Crane (1956) and David Corkran (1962, 1967) helpful. G. Foreman's *The Five Civilized Tribes* (1934) and R. S. Cotterill's *The Southern Indians* (1954) have become standard sources. Fred Gearing's *Priests and Warriors* (1962) analyzes Cherokee society and politics. Gary Nash (1974: Chap. 10) offers a summary statement of Creek and Cherokee social and political change, and discusses Indian strategies in the face of the encroachment of Whites. More needs to be learned about the enslavement of Indians in the Southeast, building on the work of Lauber (1913) and Winston (1934); about the interaction of Africans, Indians, and Whites (Willis 1963, 1970); and about the enslavement of Blacks among Indian populations (Willis 1955; Perdue 1979). William Sturtevant has written on Indian-Spanish relations (1962), and has published an excellent article on the development of the Seminole, "Creek into Seminole" (1971). I have also benefited from an unpublished manuscript on the Southeast by Gerald Sider, based on his doctoral thesis (1970). The question of Indian removal is treated in Debo (1941). I have drawn on Michael Rogin (1975) for historical information about the role of Andrew Jackson in the forcible displacement of the native Americans from the region, without relying in any way on Rogin's psychohistorical interpretation.

On the topic of Egypt, I used Alan Richards's brilliant analysis of Egypt's separation from the Ottoman Empire, the attempt of Muhammad Ali to set in motion an autonomous process of modernization, and the gradual conversion of Egypt to the production of cotton, in "Primitive Accumulation in Egypt, 1798–1882" (1977). E. R. J. Owen (1969) deals specifically with the role of cotton in the Egyptian economy, and Gabriel Baer (1962) details the displacement of the peasantry by cotton-growing large estates. Elsewhere, Baer (1969: Chaps. 2, 3) sketches the dissolution of the Egyptian village community and the growing power of the local sheikhs who became landowners. David Landes (1958) has studied the impact of international finance on Egypt, a topic explored earlier by Leland Jenks in a splendid chapter, "Bankrupting the Near East," in his *Migration of British Capital to 1875* (1973, first pub. 1927).

On the British cotton trade, Michael Edwards (1967) deals with the development of the trade; D.C.M. Platt (1973) provides information on the limitations of Latin America as a market for cotton goods; and Peter Harnetty (1972) discusses the relation between Lancashire and the Indian market. Morris D. Morris (1965) has written a major work on the development of the Bombay cotton mills and the growth of their labor force; Morris's essay on "The Recruitment of an Industrial Labor Force in India" (1960) provides interesting comparisons with labor-force recruitment in England and America. Amalendu Guha (1972, 1973) was my major source on Indian production of raw cotton between 1750 and 1901. Richard Schermerhorn (1978: 268–272) discusses the background of the Parsi business elite involved in the cotton industry and trade. The impact of cotton growing on Uganda is delineated in Lucy F. Mair's *An African People in the Twentieth Century* (1934) and David Apter's *Political Kingdom of Uganda* (1961). Cotton production is also a theme in Beverly Gartrell's doctoral dissertation on British officials in Uganda (1979).

The role of railroad construction in restarting the engine of capital accumulation is dealt with convincingly in Jenks (1973: Chap. 5); both Dobb and Hobsbawm acknowledge their debt to him. Daniel Thorner (1950) has written on railroad building in India, and George Taylor's *Transportation Revolution* (1951) is an outstanding contribution to the economic history of the United States. William Woodruff discusses the role of land and maritime transport in unifying the world in a chapter entitled "The Conquest of Distance" (1966: Chap. 6). The development of transport and trade in the Far East is examined by Francis Hyde (1973). Both Bairoch (1975) and Latham (1978) discuss the decline of transportation costs in the second half of the nineteenth century.

10. Crisis and Differentiation in Capitalism

While I am persuaded by Marx's argument that the process of capitalist accumulation entails a tendency for the rate of profit to decline, I also think that Otto Bauer (1907), Paul Sweezy (1942), and Ernest Mandel (1978) are correct in arguing that particular crises may be set off by a variety of causes and may issue in a variety of responses. Crisis may be endemic, but the form of crises and the manner of their resolution are variable and contingent. I find convincing Mandel's argument (1978:

Chap. 1) that Marx's theory of the capitalist crisis was intended to explain why capitalism, with all its inherent tendencies toward chaos, could function at all.

In contrast to the position of Lenin (1939), Luxemburg (1922), and also Sternberg (1929), I would argue that aggressive warfare, imperialism, colonialism, and neocolonialism are contingent and not structural phenomena. Roger Owen and Bob Sutcliffe (1972) have brought together a useful reader on different theories of imperialism and on the different imperialist strategies pursued by various European nations. I find the recent attempt by Giovanni Arrighi (1978) to develop a structural model for analyzing and predicting these various responses to be full of insights, but overly "Cartesian" and typological. For me, two facts stand out. First, England secured its dominion over world trade in the nineteenth century through imperialism and colonialism in India, while exercising only indirect "neocolonial" influence in Latin America; on the crucial economic role of India, see Barratt Brown (1970) and Latham (1978). Second, the success of the first capitalist nation altered the conditions encountered by nations launched into capitalist development later, a point first raised explicitly by the "first National Socialist," Friedrich List (1789–1846), and later by Alexander Gerschenkron (1962: Chap. 1). While the competition between capitalist cohorts, segments, or fractions may be structural, moreover, there is no inherent reason why such competition ought to involve nations rather than city-states, regions, or multinational firms.

The division of the competitive arena among a number of rivalrous nation-states is one of the moot points of Marxian analysis. We can now see, more clearly than was possible in the nineteenth century, that nations and nation-states may be but historical products, built up over time and perhaps withering away in the face of new, transnational processes. I know of no fully satisfactory argument that can explain why a particular form of "thick" state is essential or even functional for capitalist accumulation during strategic phases of its growth, or why the historic articulation of classes requires the development of just this kind of political-economic apparatus. There remains valuable ore to be mined on this question in Otto Bauer's wrongly maligned *Nationalitätenfrage* (1907), as well as in Karl Deutsch's *Nationalism and Social Communication* (1966). I have tried my own hand at explanation in a paper available only in Spanish (Wolf 1953). Some progress in comprehending what the capitalist state *does* has been achieved by Nicos Poulantzas (1968, 1978) and by James O'Connor (1974).

On changes of phase in capitalist development, I have used Mandel's discussion of "long waves" in *Late Capitalism* (1978: Chap. 4). I also accept, in general terms, his explanation of the phenomenon, although I am mindful of the criticisms of it (e.g., Rowthorn 1976). Mandel, like many others, continues the tradition of Nikolai D. Kondratieff, an economist and statistician who headed the Moscow Business Conditions Institute between 1920 and 1928 but who disappeared in the subsequent Stalinist purges. Kondratieff formulated his hypothesis in 1919–1921. A paper by him in Russian appeared in 1925, was translated into German in 1926, and translated once again into English for a special issue of *Review* devoted to "Cycles and Trends" (Kondratieff 1979). Schumpeter used the Kondratieff concept in *Business Cycles* (1939). Walt W. Rostow's discussion of Kondratieff cycles (1978) coincides with Mandel's interpretation from an opposed political position (see Wallerstein 1979: 665). Hans Rosenberg, in his *Grosse Depression* (1967), uses the concept to interpret the multifaceted German reaction to the Great Depression in the last third of the nineteenth century.

11. The Movement of Commodities

In tracing the flow of particular products from production to market, my intention was to bring together three aspects usually dealt with separately: the imperatives deriving from the requirements of capital accumulation; the ecological implications of collecting or raising a given crop or extracting a given substance; and the consequences for the people whose labor is mobilized for these endeavors. Particular commodities were included in the discussion because these commodities were quantitatively significant in world markets; because economists, economic geographers, or historians had paid some attention to the transformations wrought by the large-scale production of these commodities; and because anthropologists had something to say about the populations caught up in these transformations.

My discussion of plantations owes much to an interest shared by Sidney Mintz and me in the dialectic between plantations and peasantries, an interest that goes back to our common participation in Julian Steward's study of Puerto Rico; see Steward et al. (1956: Chaps. 7, 9), as well as the reappraisals of the study in Duncan, ed. (1978), especially William Roseberry's contribution. Among our various writings on the topic are those by Mintz on the plantation type (1959*b*), on peasantries in the Caribbean (1961, 1979*a*), and on "the definition of peasantries" (1973); by Wolf on subcultures and classes in plantation systems (1959) and on peasantry in general (1966); and by Wolf and Mintz on different kinds of large estates (1957). Edgar Thompson has made major contributions to an understanding of plantation agriculture, and his many writings on the subject are now collected in one volume (1975). Also useful are Lloyd Best's model of the "pure plantation economy" (1968) and George Beckford's book on the plantation as a source of underdevelopment (1972).

Among the many studies of peasant marketing by anthropologists, I have been especially influenced by Mintz's attempt to understand market systems as "mechanisms of social articulation" (1959*a*). For me, the market is constituted by relations between classes, not by households acting as "market agents." In contrast to neoclassical economic theory, which treats the initial factor endowments of households as givens and argues that competition in the market sorts them according to the relative efficiency with which they employ these factors, I accept Edward Nell's contention that "markets distribute income according to relative power" (1973: 95). Nell's juxtaposition of the opposing paradigms of orthodox neoclassical economics and what he calls "Classical-Marxian" economics is superlatively clear and concise.

On wheat production in North America, I consulted Paul Gates's *Prairie Frontier* (1973), the now-classic book by Walter Webb on *The Great Plains* (1931), and Charles Kraenzel's *Great Plains in Transition* (1955). Especially helpful was the brilliant paper by Harriet Friedmann on "World Market, State, and Family Farm" (1978). James Scobie (1964) has written an excellent history of wheat production in Argentina. Junker wheat farming has been discussed by Max Weber (1979) and by Alexander Gerschenkron (1943). On commercial grain farming in Russia, I relied on Peter I. Lyashchenko's economic history (1949) and on a paper by Patricia Herlihy on the role of Odessa in the grain export trade (1972). The development of rice production in Burma is well discussed by Michael Adas in *The Burma Delta* (1974). On Thailand, see Lucian Hanks's *Rice and Man* (1972); on Vietnam, Charles Robequain's *Economic Development* (1944) and the historically oriented chapter 2 in Robert Sansom's *Economics of Insurgency* (1970).

My understanding of the growth of livestock production after 1860 owes a great deal to Arnold Strickon's paper on "The Euro-American Ranching Complex" (1965), which compares the western United States and Argentina. Webb (1931) is again indispensable for understanding cattle herding in North America, as is E. S. Osgood's *Day of the Cattleman* (1957). Joe Frantz and Julian Choate (1955) have written on the myths and realities of the American cowboy, a topic that demands further inquiry; on Black cowboys, see Durham and Jones (1965). Strickon's paper and his dissertation (1960) are most useful on Argentina, as is Tulio Halperin-Donghi's reinterpretation of Sarmiento's polarity of Civilization and Barbarism in his *Aftermath of Revolution* (1973: Chap. 3). On Australia I read the volume edited by G. Greenwood (1955), which contains a very good paper by Ronald Hartwell on the "pastoral ascendancy." I have also benefited by comments in Rosecrance (1964) and in Burt (1957) on the political implications of Australian pastoralism.

The literature on banana cultivation is strong with regard to business and company history; much less attention has been paid to the fate of affected local populations. I have drawn on Charles Kepner and Jay Soothill's *Banana Empire* (1935), Kepner's *Social Aspects of the Banana Industry* (1936), Charles Wilson's *Empire in Green and Gold* (1947), and Watt Stewart's biographical study of Minor C. Keith, the founder of the United Fruit Company (1964). Michael Olien (1970) discusses the role of Black populations, with specific reference to Costa Rica.

There are a great many works on sugar. Some that were of special importance for my understanding of the issues involved were Noel Deerr's voluminous *History of Sugar* (1949); Fernando Ortiz's *Cuban Counterpoint* (1947); Mintz's writings on sugar plantations in Puerto Rico (especially 1956, 1974); Solomon Miller's study of sugar plantations in coastal Peru (1967); and Clifford Geertz's discussion of the interdigitation of plantation-grown sugar and subsistence rice fields in Java (1963). Mintz's "Time, sugar and sweetness" (1979*b*) marks an interesting new departure into the question of the cultural dynamics of diet.

A practical guide to coffee production and marketing that contains much information is William Ukers's *All About Coffee* (1935). Case studies of coffee-growing regions include my doctoral thesis on highland Puerto Rico (Steward et al. 1956: Chap. 7), William Roseberry's fine work on Andean Venezuela (in press), and the excellent historical account of southern Brazil by Warren Dean (1976) described in chapter 12. Alain Dessaint, in his paper on the impact of coffee production on native American communities (1962), was perhaps the first anthropologist to stress labor migration in Mesoamerica. We still need a history of the coffeehouse and its effects on European patterns of politics and sociability; Braudel's comments (1973*b*: 184—187) are suggestive. On tea drinking in England, see Forrest (1973).

In addition to the sources on the opium trade listed for chapter 8, I have relied heavily on Alain and William Dessaint for a grasp of the mechanics and consequences of opium production (A. Dessaint 1971, 1972; W. Dessaint and A. Dessaint 1975). The volumes edited by Peter Kunstadter on *Southeast Asian Tribes, Minorities, and Nations* (1967) include ethnographic data on opium raising among the hill-dwelling populations of mainland Southeast Asia. Alfred McCoy's *Politics of Heroin* (1972) traces the growth of heroin production after World War II.

I have drawn on Robert Murphy's discussion of changes wrought by rubber cultivation among the Mundurucú (1958, 1960); however, his account of early Mundurucú history has been challenged by Alcida Ramos (1978). There is need for a detailed study of the impact of the rubber trade on Amazonian populations. In the meantime, we must rely on dramatic accounts such as Richard Collier's story of the Amazon rubber barons (1968). On rubber production in Malaya, I have used G. C. Allen and A. G. Donnithorne's *Western Enterprise in Indonesia and Malaya* (1962), James Jackson's work on *Planters and Speculators* (1968), and the study of a rubber plantation by Ravindra Jain (1970). On cocoa production in West Africa, I read A. Hopkins's economic history (1973), Polly Hill's excellent book on migratory cocoa planters in Ghana (1963), and Rodolfo Stavenhagen's summary of research on the Ivory Coast (1975: Part II), which interprets much of the available French literature. Keith Hart also allowed me to read his as yet unpublished manuscript on the development of commercial agriculture in West Africa (1979). For a grasp of what transpired in South Africa, I turned to the useful historical geography by N. C. Pollock and Swanzie Agnew (1963) and to the fine two-volume *Oxford History of South Africa*, edited by Monica Wilson and Leonard Thompson (1969–1971). I greatly benefited from Benjamin Magubane's paper, "The Politics of History in South Africa" (1978). On the specific events of the Xhosa cattle killings, see Keller (1978).

12. The New Laborers

This chapter draws on several different, though convergent, sources. One of these is the "new urban sociology," which is interested in cities as loci of capital accumulation and investment, as reservoirs of labor, and as nodes of intervention by the state. Major contributions to this development are Manuel Castells's *Urban Question* (1977) and David Harvey's *Social Justice and the City* (1973). I have also benefited from Castells's discussion of trends of research in his "Urban Sociology and Urban Politics" (1975) and the literature cited there. An outstanding discussion and overview of this direction in research is Sharon Zukin's "A Decade of the New Urban Sociology" (1980). Some recent work in urban anthropology shares similar concerns; see Jack Rollwagen's review of "New Directions in Urban Anthropology" (1980).

A second body of material relevant to this chapter is provided by the new labor history. This approach is exemplified by such works as Thompson's *The Making of the English Working Class* (1966), Hobsbawm's *Labouring Men* (1964), Rolande Trempé's *Les mineurs de Carmaux* (1964), and Alan Dawley's study of Lynn, Massachusetts (1976). These scholars write a social history that tries to locate working classes in a wider and historically changing social and cultural matrix, rather than focusing only on working-class or labor organizations. A programmatic statement of the approach is given in Georges Haupt's paper, "Why the History of the Working-Class Movement?" (1978). For an overview of this trend in the United States, see David Brody on "The Old Labor History and the New" (1979). In anthropology, there was an early move in this direction by Godfrey Wilson, the embattled head of the Rhodes-Livingstone Institute, 1938–1941. What Wilson called "detribalization" in *The Economics of Detribalization* (1941–1942) was none other than the process of working-class formation in the Rhodesian Copper Belt. On Wilson and his attempt to effect "a marriage of Marx and Malinowski," see the evenhanded account by Richard Brown (1973).

A third inspiration for this chapter was the new literature on migration. The older work on the subject dealt with migration primarily as the collective outcome of attempts by individuals or groups to better their life chances, and sought explanations for their success or failure in the cultural processes of assimilation or pluralism. The new research on migration attempts to see it in international terms, as the result of political and economic changes in the "sending" societies as well as of shifts in the demand for labor on the part of the "recipient" societies. Among the contributions that have been especially helpful to me are Marios Nikolinakos's attempt to develop a general theory of migration in "late" capitalism (1975), together with Teodor Shanin's critique of this study (1978); Saskia Sassen-Koob's papers on migrant and immigrant labor (1978, 1981); and Alejandro Portes's "Migration and Underdevelopment" (1978). Some interesting comments from an anthropological viewpoint appear in Anthony Leeds's article on "Women in the Migratory Process" (1976). A successful attempt to apply the perspectives of the new approach to the particular case of Puerto Rico can be found in the volume by the History Task Force (1979).

A fourth research direction I drew on is the work on labor market segmentation. This concept first appeared in Clark Kerr's "Balkanization of Labor Markets" (1954), but it has since been elaborated in various writings. The most significant for me were David Gordon's *Theories of Poverty and Underemployment* (1972) and the book on *Labor Market Segmentation* edited by Edwards, Reich, and Gordon (1975). Edna Bonacich (1972) has made an innovative attempt to relate the "split-labor market" to issues of ethnic antagonism. This general approach, which takes account of changing labor markets and shifting group placement within them, avoids the static and confining model of a hierarchy of occupations serving as niches for supposedly stable, culturally marked groups.

Among publications on migration to the United States, I found most helpful Maldwyn Jones's book on *American Immigration* (1960) and Gerald Rosenblum's *Immigrant Workers* (1973). I also learned from Shirley Hune's *Pacific Migration to the United States* (1977). The main source for the Chinese labor trade is still Persia Crawford Campbell's *Chinese Coolie Emigration* (1923). Hugh Tinker, in *A New System of Slavery* (1974), deals with the Indian labor trade; I have also drawn on Kathleen Gough's account of the impact of the trade on Thanjavur (1978).

In reading on South Africa, I returned to S. H. Frankel (1938) on capital investment and to the section on southern and eastern Africa by H. J. Simons in Linton, ed., *Most of the World* (1949), both of which I had first read in graduate school. The book Simons later coauthored with Ruth Simons, *Class and Color* (1969), also proved useful. Benjamin M. Magubane has written a fine work on the *Political Economy of Race and Class* (1979); see also the interesting review by David Kaplan (1979). The chapters by D. Hobart Houghton and by David Welsh in the *Oxford History of South Africa* (Wilson and Thompson, eds., 1971: Vol. II) are informative, and two articles in the collection edited by Palmer and Parsons (1977), Martin Legassick on the shift from mining to industry and Colin Bundy on the Transkei peasantry, are most valuable. Charles Van Onselen, who is also the author of a book on African mine labor in

Southern Rhodesia (1976), has written on the creation of the dual Black and White labor force on the Rand (1979), and Francis Wilson (1972) has dealt specifically with labor in the gold mines. Harold Wolpe (1972) and Michael Burawoy (1976) both discuss, from somewhat different perspectives, the interdigitation of labor reserves and mining locations so characteristic of southern and central African development under capitalist auspices.

The section of this chapter on Rio Claro in Brazil is based on Warren Dean's historical study (1976). William Roff (1967), dealing with Malay nationalism, and Maurice Freedman on Chinese migrants (1960), offer information and insight into Singapore.

The concept of "plural societies" was first proposed by J. S. Furnivall in writings on Indonesia and Burma (1939, 1948), and elaborated by M. G. Smith, especially in his *Plural Society in the British West Indies* (1965). The literature on the concept and its uses has grown large; a convenient entry into the relevant problematic, with bibliography, is the volume edited by Leo Despres, *Ethnicity and Resource Competition in Plural Societies* (1975).

Afterword

The Afterword represents an attempt to rethink the anthropological culture concept in the light of the Marxian notion of ideology and of the sociology of knowledge. The gamut of writers on the subject range from Friedrich Engels, August Thalheimer, Franz Borkenau, Antonio Gramsci, Louis Althusser, and Stuart Hall on the Marxian side to sociologists of knowledge who trace their lineage to Max Weber and Wilhelm Dilthey. Georg Lukács, Lucien Goldmann, and Karl Mannheim have combined the two traditions, albeit in different ways. Talal Asad, Steve Barnett and Martin Silverman, Maurice Bloch, Stephan Feuchtwang, Jonathan Friedman, Maurice Godelier, and Joel Kahn have variously used the Marxian concept of ideology in anthropological discussions.

The concept of ideological alternatives or variants, produced within and between societies, informs the work of Claude Lévi-Strauss; but Lévi-Strauss sees the relation of Nature and Culture as passing directly through the human mind. I hold that thought is mediated by the prevailing mode of production. The concept of hegemony derives from the writings of Antonio Gramsci. Raymond Williams (1973) has brilliantly elaborated the notion of alternative and oppositional forms. The concept of differential accents appears in Vološinov (1973), that of counterpoints in Willem Wertheim (1974). I continue to believe that the human sciences cannot do without a conception of culture. I think of the present discussion as a contribution to an ongoing debate on how the concept can be recast in the light of new understandings.

Bibliography

ABRAHAM, D. P. 1961. Maramuca: An Exercise in the Combined Use of Portuguese Records and Oral Tradition. Journal of African History 2: 211–245.
—— 1962. The Early Political History of the Kingdom of Mwene Mutapa (850–1589). In Historians in Tropical Africa: Proceedings of the Leverhulme Inter-Collegiate History Conference Held at the University College of Rhodesia and Nyasaland, 1960. Pp. 61–92. Salisbury: International African Institute.
—— 1964. Ethno-History of the Empire of Mutapa, Problems and Methods. In The Historian in Tropical Africa. Jan Vansina, R. Mauny, and L. V. Thomas, eds. Pp. 104–121. London: Oxford University Press.
—— 1966. The Roles of the 'Chaminuka' and the Mhondoro-Cults in Shona Political History. In The Zambezian Past. Eric T. Stokes and R. Brown, eds. Pp. 28–46. Manchester: Manchester University Press.
ABUN-NASR, JAMIL M. 1971. A History of the Maghrib. Cambridge: Cambridge University Press.
ADAMS, ROBERT MCC. 1965. Land Behind Baghdad: A History of Settlement on the Diyala Plain. Chicago: University of Chicago Press.
ADAS, MICHAEL 1974. The Burma Delta: Economic Development and Social Change on the Rice Frontier, 1852–1941. Madison: University of Wisconsin Press.
AJAYI, J. F. ADE, and MICHAEL CROWDER, eds. 1972. History of West Africa, Vol. 1. New York: Columbia University Press.
AKINJOGBIN, I. A. 1967. Dahomey and Its Neighbors, 1708–1818. Cambridge: Cambridge University Press.
—— 1972. The Expansion of Oyo and the Rise of Dahomey 1600–1800. In History of West Africa, Vol. 1. J. F. Ade Ajayi and Michael Crowder, eds. Pp. 304–343. New York: Columbia University Press.
ALBION, ROBERT G. 1939. The Rise of New York Port, 1815–1860. New York: Scribner's.
ALLEN, G. C., and A. G. DONNITHORNE 1962. Western Enterprise in Indonesia and Malaya. London: Allen & Unwin.
ALPERS, EDWARD 1968. The Mutapa and Malawi Political Systems. In Aspects of Central African History. Terence O. Ranger, ed. Pp. 1–28. Evanston, IL: Northwestern University Press.
ALTHEIM, FRANZ 1954. Gesicht vom Abend und Morgen. Frankfurt a.M.: Fischer Bücherei.
—— 1960. Zarathustra und Alexander. Frankfurt a.M.: Fischer Bücherei.

ALTHUSSER, LOUIS, and ÉTIENNE BALIBAR 1970. Reading Capital. New York: Pantheon Books.

AMERICAN FUR TRADE CONFERENCE 1967. Selected Papers of the 1965 American Fur Trade Conference. St. Paul: Minnesota Historical Society.

AMIN, SAMIR 1973a. Neo-Colonialism in West Africa. Harmondsworth: Penguin Books.

―――― 1973b. Le dévéloppement inégal. Paris: Les Éditions de Minuit.

ANDERSON, MICHAEL 1971. Family Structure in Nineteenth Century Lancashire. Cambridge: Cambridge University Press.

ANDERSON, PERRY 1974. Lineages of the Absolutist State. London: New Left Books.

―――― 1978. Passages from Antiquity to Feudalism. London: Verso.

ANSTEY, ROGER 1977. The Profitability of the Slave Trade in the 1840s. In Comparative Perspectives on Slavery in New World Plantation Societies. Vera Rubin and Arthur Tuden, eds. Pp. 84–93. Annals of the New York Academy of Sciences, Vol. 292. New York: New York Academy of Sciences.

APTER, DAVID E. 1961. The Political Kingdom of Uganda: A Study in Bureaucratic Nationalism. Princeton, NJ: Princeton University Press.

ARHIN, KWAME 1967. The Structure of Greater Ashanti (1700–1824). Journal of African History 8: 65–85.

ARRIGHI, GIOVANNI 1978. The Geometry of Imperialism: The Limits of Hobson's Paradigm. London: New Left Books.

ASAD, TALAL, ed. 1973. Anthropology and the Colonial Encounter. London: Ithaca Press.

BADDELEY, JOHN F. 1919. Russia, Mongolia, and China. 2 vols. London: Macmillan.

BAER, GABRIEL 1962. A History of Landownership in Modern Egypt. London: Oxford University Press.

―――― 1969. Studies in the Social History of Modern Egypt. Publication of the Center for Middle Eastern Studies, No. 4. Chicago: University of Chicago Press.

BAGWELL, PHILIP S., and G. E. MINGAY 1970. Britain and America 1850–1939: A Study of Economic Change. New York: Praeger.

BAILEY, ALFRED G. 1969. The Conflict of European and Eastern Algonkian Cultures 1504–1700: A Study in Canadian Civilization. Toronto: University of Toronto Press. (First pub. 1937.)

BAILEY, F. G. 1957. Caste and the Economic Frontier. Manchester: Manchester University Press.

―――― 1960. Tribe, Caste, and Nation. Manchester: Manchester University Press.

BAILEY, L. R. 1966. Indian Slave Trade in the Southwest: A Study of Slave-taking and the Traffic in Indian Captives from 1700–1935. Great West and Indian Series, Vol. 32. Los Angeles: Westernlore Press.

BAIROCH, PAUL 1975. The Economic Development of the Third World Since 1900. Berkeley, Los Angeles, London: University of California Press.

BAKEWELL, PETER J. 1971. Silver Mining and Society in Colonial Mexico: Zacatecas, 1546–1700. Cambridge: Cambridge University Press.

BALANDIER, GEORGE 1968. Daily Life in the Kingdom of the Congo From the Sixteenth to the Eighteenth Century. New York: Pantheon Books.

―――― 1970. The Sociology of Black Africa: Social Dynamics in Central Africa. New York: Praeger.

BALAZS, ÉTIENNE 1964. Chinese Civilization and Bureaucracy. New Haven, CT: Yale University Press.

BANU, ION 1967. La formation sociale 'tributaire.' Recherches Internationales à la Lumière du Marxisme, No. 57–58. Special number: Premières sociétés des classes et mode de production asiatique. Pp. 251–253. Paris: Éditions de la Nouvelle Critique.

BARBOUR, VIOLET 1963. Capitalism in Amsterdam in the Seventeenth Century. Ann Arbor: University of Michigan Press.

BARLOEWEN, WOLF-DIETRICH VON 1961. Abriss der Geschichte Antiker Randkulturen. Munich: Oldenbourg.

BARRATT BROWN, MICHAEL 1970. After Imperialism. New York: Humanities Press.

BARRETT, WARD J., and STUART B. SCHWARTZ 1975. Comparación entre dos economías azucareras coloniales: Morelos, México y Bahía, Brasil. *In* Haciendas, latifundios y plantaciones en América Latina. Enrique Florescano, ed. Pp. 532–572. Mexico City: Siglo Veintinuno Editores.

BASCOM, WILLIAM 1969. The Yoruba of Southwestern Nigeria. New York: Holt, Rinehart & Winston.

BAUER, OTTO 1907. Die Nationalitätenfrage und die Sozialdemokratie. Marx-Studien, Vol. 2. Max Adler and Rudolf Hilferding, eds. Vienna: Volksbuchhandlung Ignaz Brand.

BEAN, RICHARD 1974. A Note on the Relative Importance of Slaves and Gold in West African Exports. Journal of African History 15: 351–356.

BECKFORD, GEORGE L. 1972. Persistent Poverty: Underdevelopment in Plantation Economies of the Third World. New York: Oxford University Press.

BENDA, HENRY J. 1972. Continuity and Change in Southeast Asian History. Yale University Southeast Asian Studies Monograph Series, No. 18, New Haven, CT: Yale University Southeast Asian Studies.

BENDIX, REINHARD 1956. Work and Authority in Industry: Ideologies of Management in the Course of Industrialization. New York: Wiley.

BERREMAN, GERALD 1979. Caste and Other Inequities. Meerut, India: Folklore Institute.

BERTIN, JACQUES, SERGE BONIN, and PIERRE CHAUNU 1966. Les Philippines et le Pacifique des Ibériques, XVIe–XVIIe–XVIIIe siècles, Construction Graphique. Paris: École Pratique des Hautes Études, VIe Section, S.E.V.P.E.N.

BEST, LLOYD A. 1968. Outlines of a Model of Pure Plantation Economy. Social and Economic Studies 17: 282–326.

BÉTEILLE, ANDRÉ 1969. Castes: Old and New. Bombay: Asia Publishing House.

BINDOFF, S. T. 1966. Tudor England. The Pelican History of England, Vol. 5. Harmondsworth: Penguin Books.

BIRMINGHAM, DAVID 1965. The Portuguese Conquest of Angola. London: Oxford University Press.

——— 1966. Trade and Conflict in Angola: The Mbundu and Their Neighbors Under the Influence of the Portuguese 1483–1790. Oxford: Clarendon Press.

——— 1972. The African Response to Early Portuguese Activities in Angola. *In* Protest and Resistance in Angola and Brazil. Ronald Chilcote, ed. Pp. 11–28. Berkeley, Los Angeles, London: University of California Press.

BISHOP, CHARLES A. 1976. The Emergence of the Northern Ojibwä: Social and Economic Consequences. American Ethnologist 3: 39–54.

BISHOP, CHARLES A., and ARTHUR J. RAY, eds. 1976. The Fur Trade and Culture

Change: Resources and Methods. Special Issue. Western Canadian Journal of Anthropology 6 (1).

BLASSINGAME, JOHN 1972. The Slave Community: Plantation Life in the Antebellum South. New York: Oxford University Press.

BLOCH, MARC 1961. Feudal Society. 2 vols. Chicago: University of Chicago Press. (First pub. in French 1939—1940).

———— 1970. French Rural History: An Essay on Its Basic Characteristics. Berkeley, Los Angeles, London: University of California Press. (First pub. in French 1931.)

BOAS, FRANZ 1921. Ethnology of the Kwakiutl Based on Data Collected by George Hunt. 35th Annual Report of the Bureau of American Ethnology. Pt. 2. Pp. 795—1481. Washington, DC.

BOLUS, MALVINA, ed. 1972. People and Pelts: Selected Papers of the Second North American Fur Trade Conference. Winnipeg, Manitoba: Peguis.

BONACICH, E. 1972. A Theory of Ethnic Antagonism: The Split-Labor Market. American Sociological Review 5: 533—547.

BOROCHOV, BER 1937. Nationalism and the Class Struggle: A Marxian Approach to the Jewish Question. New York: Poale-Zion.

BOVILL, E. W. 1968. The Golden Trade of the Moors. New York: Oxford University Press. (First ed. 1933, as Caravans of the Old Sahara.)

BOWLES, SAMUEL, and HERBERT GINTIS 1977. The Marxian Theory of Value and Heterogeneous Labour: A Critique and Reformulation. Cambridge Journal of Economics 1: 173—192.

BOWSER, FREDERICK P. 1974. The African Slave in Colonial Peru 1524—1650. Stanford, CA: Stanford University Press.

BOXER, CHARLES B. 1948. Fidalgos in the Far East, 1550—1770; Fact and Fancy in the History of Macao. The Hague: M. Nijhoff.

———— 1953. South China in the Sixteenth Century, Being the Narratives of Galeote Pereira, Fr. Gaspar da Cruz, O.P.Fr. Martín de Rada, O.E.S.A., 1550—1575. London: Hakluyt Society.

———— 1973a. The Portuguese Seaborne Empire 1415—1825. Harmondsworth: Penguin Books.

———— 1973b. The Dutch Seaborne Empire 1600—1800. Harmondsworth: Penguin Books.

BRADBURY, R. E. 1957. The Benin Kingdom and the Edo-Speaking Peoples of South-western Nigeria, Ethnographic Survey of Africa: Western Africa, Pt. 13. London: International African Institute.

———— 1964. The Historical Uses of Comparative Ethnography: Data with Special Reference to Benin and Yoruba. In The Historian in Tropical Africa. Jan Vansina, R. Mauny, and L. V. Thomas, eds. Pp. 145—160. London: Oxford University Press.

BRADBY, BARBARA 1975. The Destruction of Natural Economy. Economy and Society 4: 127—161.

BRADING, D. A. 1971. Miners and Merchants in Bourbon Mexico 1768—1810. Cambridge: Cambridge University Press.

———— 1977. The Haciendas as an Investment. In Haciendas and Plantations in Latin American History. Robert G. Keith, ed. Pp. 135—140. New York: Holmes & Meier.

BRADING, D. A., and HARRY E. CROSS 1972. Colonial Silver Mining: Mexico and Peru. Hispanic American Historical Review 52: 545—579.

BRAMSON, LEON 1961. The Political Context of Sociology. Princeton, NJ: Princeton University Press.

BRAUDEL, FERNAND 1972. The Mediterranean and the Mediterranean World in the Age of Philip II, Vol. 1. New York: Harper & Row.

———— 1973*a*. The Mediterranean and the Mediterranean World in the Age of Philip II, Vol. 2. New York: Harper & Row.

———— 1973*b*. Capitalism and Material Life 1400–1800. New York: Harper & Row.

BRENNER, ROBERT 1975. England, Eastern Europe, and France: Socio-Historical Versus Economic Interpretation. *In* Failed Transitions to Modern Industrial Society: Renaissance Italy and Seventeenth Century Holland. Frederick Krantz and Paul M. Hohenberg, eds. Pp. 68–71. Montreal: Interuniversity Centre for European Studies.

———— 1976. Agrarian Class Structure and Economic Development in Pre-Industrial Europe. Past and Present, No. 70: 30–75.

BRODY, DAVID 1979. The Old Labor History and the New: In Search of an American Working Class. Labor History 20: 111–126.

BROMLEY, J. S., and E. H. KOSSMANN, eds. 1964. Britain and the Netherlands. Groningen: Wolters.

———— 1968. Britain and the Netherlands in Europe and Asia. London: Macmillan.

BROOMFIELD, J. H. 1966. The Regional Elites: A Theory of Modern Indian History. *In* Modern India: An Interpretative Anthology. Thomas R. Metcalf, ed. Pp. 60–70. London: Macmillan.

BROWN, JAMES A. 1975. Spiro Art and Its Mortuary Contexts. *In* Death and the Afterlife in Pre-Columbian America. Elizabeth P. Benson, ed. Pp. 1–32. Washington, DC: Dumbarton Oaks Research Library and Collections, Trustees for Harvard University.

BROWN, JUDITH K. 1975. Iroquois Women: An Ethnohistoric Note. *In* Toward an Anthropology of Women. Rayna Rapp Reiter, ed. Pp. 235–251. New York: Monthly Review Press.

BROWN, RICHARD 1973. Anthropology and Colonial Rule: Godfrey Wilson and the Rhodes-Livingstone Institute, Northern Rhodesia. *In* Anthropology and the Colonial Encounter. Talal Asad, ed. Pp. 173–197. London: Ithaca Press.

BRUCHEY, STUART W. 1965. The Roots of American Economic Growth 1607–1861: An Essay in Social Causation. New York: Harper & Row.

BRUCHEY, STUART W., comp. and ed. 1967. Cotton and the Growth of the American Economy: 1790–1860, Sources and Readings. New York: Harcourt, Brace and World.

BRUNER, EDWARD M. 1961. Mandan. *In* Perspectives in American Indian Culture Change. Edward H. Spicer, ed. Pp. 187–227. Chicago: University of Chicago Press.

BULLIET, RICHARD 1975. The Camel and the Wheel. Cambridge: Harvard University Press.

BUNDY, COLIN 1977. The Transkei Peasantry, c.1890–1914: Passing Through a Period of Stress. *In* The Roots of Rural Poverty in Central and Southern Africa. Robin Palmer and Neil Parsons, eds. Pp. 201–220. Berkeley, Los Angeles, London: University of California Press.

BURAWOY, MICHAEL 1976. The Functions and Reproduction of Migrant Labour: Comparative Material from Southern Africa and the United States. American

Journal of Sociology 81: 1050–1087.
—— 1979. The Anthropology of Industrial Work. Annual Review of Anthropology 8: 231–266.
BURT, A. L. 1957. If Turner Had Looked at Canada, Australia, and New Zealand When He Wrote about the West. *In* The Frontier in Perspective. Walker D. Wyman and Clifton B. Kroeber, eds. Pp. 60–77. Madison: University of Wisconsin Press.
BYTHELL, DUNCAN 1969. The Handloom Weavers: A Study in the English Cotton Industry During the Industrial Revolution. Cambridge: Cambridge University Press.
CAHEN, CLAUDE 1955. L'histoire économique et sociale de l'orient musulmane médiéval. Studia Islamica 3: 93–116.
—— 1957. Les facteurs économiques et sociaux dans l'ankylose culturelle de l'Islam. *In* Classicisme et déclin culturel dans l'histoire de l'Islam. Pp. 195–207. Paris: Besson et Chantemerle.
—— 1959. Mouvements populaires et autonomisme urbain dans l'Asie musulmane de moyen-âge. Arabica 5: 225–250; 6: 25–56, 233–265.
—— 1965. Quelques problèmes concernant l'expansion économique musulmane jusqu'au XIIe siècle. *In* Occidente e l'Islam nell' alto medioevo, Vol. 1. Pp. 391–432. Spoleto: Centro Italiano di Studi sull' alto Medievo.
CAIRNCROSS, A. K. 1953. Home and Foreign Investment, 1870–1913. Cambridge: Cambridge University Press.
CALDWELL, JOSEPH R. 1958. Trend and Tradition in the Prehistory of the Eastern United States. American Anthropological Association, Memoir 88.
—— 1962. Eastern North America. *In* Courses Toward Urban Life: Archaeological Considerations of Some Cultural Alternatives. Robert J. Braidwood and Gordon R. Willey, eds. Pp. 288–308. Viking Fund Publications in Anthropology, Vol. 32. Chicago: Aldine.
CAMPBELL, MAVIS C. 1977. Marronage in Jamaica: Its Origin in the Seventeenth Century. *In* Comparative Perspectives on Slavery in New World Plantation Societies. Vera Rubin and Arthur Tuden, eds. Pp. 389–419. Annals of the New York Academy of Sciences, Vol. 292. New York: New York Academy of Sciences.
CAMPBELL, PERSIA CRAWFORD 1923. Chinese Coolie Emigration to Countries Within the British Empire. Studies in Economics and Political Science, London School of Economics, Monograph No. 72. London: P. S. King and Son.
CARANDE Y THOBAR, RAMÓN 1943. Carlos V y sus banqueros. Madrid: Revista de Occidente.
—— 1949. La Hacienda real de Castilla. Madrid: Sociedad de Estudios y Publicaciones.
CARMAGNANI, MARCELLO 1975. L'America latina dal '500 a oggi: Nascita, espansione e crisi di un sistema feudale. Milan: Feltrinelli.
CARRASCO, PEDRO, et al. 1976. Estratificación social en la Mesoamérica prehispánica. Mexico City: SEP-INAH.
CARRASCO, PEDRO, and JOHANNA BRODA, eds. 1977. Economía, política e ideología en Mesoamérica. Mexico City: Editorial Nueva Imagen.
CASTELLS, MANUEL 1975. Urban Sociology and Urban Politics: From a Critique to New Trends of Research. Comparative Urban Research 3: 7–13.
—— 1977. The Urban Question. London: Edward Arnold. (First ed. in French 1972).

CASTLES, STEPHEN, and GODULA KOSACK 1973. Immigrant Workers and Class Structure in Western Europe. London: Oxford University Press.

CENTRE D'ÉTUDES ET DE RECHERCHES MARXISTES 1969. Sur le 'mode de production asiatique.' Paris: Éditions Sociales.

——— 1971. Sur le féodalisme. Paris: Éditions Sociales.

CHAMBERS, MORTIMER, ed. 1963. The Fall of Rome: Can It Be Explained? European Problem Studies. New York: Holt, Rinehart & Winston.

CHANEY, ELSA M. 1979. The World Economy and Contemporary Migration. International Migration Review 13: 204–212.

CHANG, T'IEN-TSE 1934. Sino-Portuguese Trade from 1514 to 1644. Leiden: Brill.

CHAPMAN, S. D. 1967. The Early Factory Masters: The Transition to the Factory System in the Midlands Textile Industry. Newton Abbot: David and Charles.

——— 1972. The Cotton Industry in the Industrial Revolution. Studies in Economic History prepared for the Economic Historical Society. London: Macmillan.

——— 1973. Industrial Capital Before the Industrial Revolution: An Analysis of the Assets of a Thousand Textile Entrepreneurs c.1730–50. In Textile History and Economic History: Essays in Honour of Miss Julia de Lacy Mann. N. B. Harte and K. G. Ponting, eds. Pp. 113–137. Manchester: Manchester University Press.

CHAUNU, HUGUETTE, and PIERRE CHAUNU 1955–1959. Séville et L'Atlantique 1504–1650. 8 vols. Vol. 1, Paris: Lib. Armand Colin. Vols. 2–8, Paris: S.E.V.P.E.N.

CHAUNU, PIERRE 1960. Les Philippines et le Pacifique des Ibériques (XVIe, XVIIe, XVIIIe siècles). Introduction Méthodologique et indices d'activité. Ports-Routes-Trafics, Vol. 11. Paris: S.E.V.P.E.N.

CHEONG, W. E. 1965. Trade and Finance in China: 1784–1834; a Reappraisal. In Les grandes voies maritimes dans le monde, XV-XIXe siècles: Rapports présentés aux XIIe Congrès International des Sciences Historiques par la Commission Internationale d'Histoire Maritime. Pp. 277–290. Paris: Biblioteque General de l'École Pratique des Hautes Études, VIe Section.

CHESNEAUX, JEAN 1962. Le mouvement ouvrier Chinois de 1919 à 1927. École Pratique des Hautes Études-Sorbonne, Sixième Section: Sciences Économiques et Sociales, Le Monde d'Outre-Mer Passé et Présent, Première Série, Études XVII. The Hague: Mouton.

——— 1964. Le mode de production asiatique: quelques perspectives de recherches. La Pensée, No. 114: 47–53.

CHILDE, V. GORDON 1946. What Happened in History. New York: Penguin Books.

CHITTICK, H. NEVILLE 1972. The Coast Before the Arrival of the Portuguese. In Perspectives on the African Past. Martin A. Klein and G. Wesley Johnson, eds. Pp. 93–106. Boston: Little, Brown.

CIPOLLA, CARLO M. 1962. The Economic History of World Population. Baltimore: Penguin Books.

——— 1970. European Culture and Overseas Expansion. Harmondsworth: Penguin Books.

COBBAN, ALFRED 1964. The Social Interpretation of the French Revolution. Cambridge: Cambridge University Press.

CODERE, HELEN 1950. Fighting with Property: A Study of Kwakiutl potlatching and Warfare, 1792–1930. American Ethnological Society, Monograph No. 18. New York: J. J. Augustin.

—— 1961. Kwakiutl. *In* Perspectives in American Indian Culture Change. Edward H. Spicer, ed. Pp. 431–516. Chicago: University of Chicago Press.

COEDÈS, GEORGE 1962. Les peuples de la Péninsule Indochinoise. Paris: Dunod.

—— 1964. Les états hindouisés d'Indochine et d'Indonésie. Paris: E. de Bocard.

COHEN, YEHUDI A. 1969. Ends and Means in Political Control: State Organization and the Punishment of Adultery, Incest, and Violation of Celibacy. American Anthropologist 71: 658–687.

COHN, BERNARD S. 1959. Some Notes on Law and Change in North India. Economic Development and Cultural Change 8: 79–93.

—— 1960. The Initial British Impact on India: A Case Study of the Benares Region. Journal of Asian Studies 19: 419–424.

—— 1961. From Indian Status to British Contract. Journal of Economic History 21: 613–628.

—— 1962. Political Systems in Eighteenth Century India: The Benares Region. Journal of the American Oriental Society 82: 312–320.

—— 1971. India: The Social Anthropology of a Civilization. Englewood Cliffs, NJ: Prentice-Hall.

COLEMAN, D. C. 1973. Textile Growth. *In* Textile History and Economic History: Essays in Honour of Miss Julia de Lacy Mann. N. B. Harte and K. G. Ponting, eds. Pp. 1–12. Manchester: Manchester University Press.

COLLETTI, LUCIO 1973. Marxism and Hegel. London: New Left Books. (First pub. in Italian 1969.)

COLLIER, RICHARD 1968. The River That God Forgot: The Dramatic Story of the Rise and Fall of the Despotic Amazon Rubber Barons. New York: Dutton.

COLLINS, JUNE MCCORMICK 1950. Growth of Class Distinctions and Political Authority Among the Skagit Indians During the Contact Period. American Anthropologist 6: 331–342.

—— 1974. Valley of the Spirits: The Upper Skagit Indians of Western Washington. American Ethnological Society, Monograph No. 56. Seattle: University of Washington Press.

COLOMBIA TODAY 1979. La Ciudad Perdida—Major Colombian Archaeological Find. Colombia Today 14 (4). New York: Colombian Information Service.

COOK, M. A., ed. 1970. Studies in the Economic History of the Middle East. New York: Oxford University Press.

COPANS JEAN, ed. 1975. Anthropologie et imperialisme. Paris: François Maspéro.

CORKRAN, DAVID H. 1962. The Cherokee Frontier: Conflict and Survival, 1740–1762. Norman: University of Oklahoma Press.

—— 1967. The Creek Frontier, 1540–1783. Norman: University of Oklahoma Press.

COTTERILL, R. S. 1954. The Southern Indians: The Story of the Civilized Tribes Before Removal. Norman: University of Oklahoma Press.

COX, OLIVER C. 1959. The Foundations of Capitalism. London: Peter Owen.

CRANE, VERNER W. 1956. Southern Frontier, 1670–1732. Ann Arbor: University of Michigan Press.

CRATON, MICHAEL 1974. Sinews of Empire: A Short History of British Slavery. Garden City, NY: Anchor Books, Doubleday.

CRATON, MICHAEL, and JAMES WALVIN 1970. A Jamaican Plantation: The History of Worthy Park 1620–1970. Toronto: University of Toronto Press.

CROUZET, FRANÇOIS 1967. England and France in the Eighteenth Century: A Comparative Analysis of Two Economic Growths. *In* The Causes of the Industrial Revolution in England. Richard Hartwell, ed. Pp. 139–174. London: Methuen.

CUNNISON, IAN 1956. Perpetual Kinship: A Political Institution of the Luapula Peoples. Human Problems in British Central Africa 20: 28–48.

———— 1957. History and Genealogies in a Conquest State. American Anthropologist 59: 20–31.

———— 1961. Kazembe and the Portuguese, 1789–1832. Journal of African History 2: 61–76.

CURTIN, PHILIP D. 1969. The Atlantic Slave Trade, a Census. Madison: University of Wisconsin Press.

———— 1975. Economic Change in Precolonial Africa: Senegambia in the Era of the Slave Trade. Madison: University of Wisconsin Press.

———— 1977. Slavery and Empire. *In* Comparative Perspectives on Slavery in New World Plantation Societies. Vera Rubin and Arthur Tuden, eds. Pp. 3–11. Annals of the New York Academy of Sciences, Vol. 292. New York: New York Academy of Sciences.

CUVELIER, JEAN, and LOUIS JADIN 1954. L'Ancien Congo d'après les archives romaines (1518–1640). Institut Royal Colonial Belge (Brussels). Section des Sciences Morales et Politiques, Mémoires, Vol. 36. Brussels: Académie Royale des Sciences d'Outre-Mer.

DAAKU, KWAME YEBOA 1970. Trade and Politics on the Gold Coast 1600–1720: A Study of the African Reaction to European Trade. Oxford: Clarendon Press.

DAMAS, DAVID, ed. 1969a. Contributions to Anthropology: Band Societies. Proceedings of the Conference on Band Organization, Ottawa, 1965. National Museums of Canada Bulletin No. 228. Anthropological Series No. 84.

———— 1969b. Contributions to Anthropology: Ecological Essays. Proceedings of the Conference on Cultural Ecology, Ottawa, 1966. National Museums of Canada Bulletin No. 230. Anthropological Series No. 86.

DAVENPORT, WILLIAM 1969. The 'Hawaiian Cultural Revolution': Some Political and Economic Considerations. American Anthropologist 71: 1–20.

DAVIDSON, BASIL, with F. K. BUAH and J. F. ADE AJAYI 1966. A History of West Africa to the Nineteenth Century. Garden City, NY: Anchor Books, Doubleday.

DAVIS, DAVID BRION 1966. The Problem of Slavery in Western Culture. Ithaca, NY: Cornell University Press.

DAVIS, KINGSLEY 1965. The Urbanization of the Human Population. Scientific American 213: 41–53.

DAVIS, RALPH 1954. English Foreign Trade, 1660–1700. Economic History Review 7: 150–166.

———— 1962. English Foreign Trade, 1700–1774. Economic History Review 15: 285–299.

———— 1973. English Overseas Trade 1500–1700. London: Macmillan.

DAWLEY, ALAN 1976. Class and Community: The Industrial Revolution in Lynn. Cambridge, MA: Harvard University Press.

DEAN, WARREN 1976. Rio Claro: A Brazilian Plantation System, 1820–1920.

Stanford, CA: Stanford University Press.

DEBO, ANGIE 1941. The Road to Disappearance. Norman: University of Oklahoma Press.

DEERR, NOEL 1949–1950. The History of Sugar. 2 vols. London: Chapman and Hall.

DE LAGUNA, FREDERICA 1972. Under Mount Saint Elias: The History and Culture of the Yakutat Tlingit. 3 parts. Smithsonian Contributions to Anthropology, Vol. 7. Washington, DC: Smithsonian Institution Press.

DERMIGNY, LOUIS 1964. La Chine et l'Occident: Le commerce a Canton au XVIIIe siècle, 1719–1833. 3 vols. + album. Ports-Routes-Trafics, Vol. 18. École Pratique des Hautes Études, VIe Section, Centre de Recherches Historiques. Paris: S.E.V.P.E.N.

DESPRES, LEO A., ed. 1975. Ethnicity and Resource Competition in Plural Societies. World Anthropology: An Interdisciplinary Series. The Hague: Mouton.

DESSAINT, ALAIN Y. 1962. Effects of the Hacienda and Plantation Systems on Guatemala's Indians. América Indígena 22: 323–354.

——— 1971. Lisu Migration in the Thai Highlands. Ethnology 10: 329–348.

——— 1972. The Poppies Are Beautiful This Year. Natural History 81: 31–37, 92–96.

DESSAINT, WILLIAM Y. and ALAIN Y. DESSAINT 1975. Strategies in Opium Production. Ethnos, Nos. 1–4: 153–168.

DEUTSCH, KARL W. 1954. Political Community at the International Level: Problems of Definition and Measurement. Doubleday Short Studies in Political Science. Garden City, NY: Doubleday.

——— 1966. Nationalism and Social Communication: An Inquiry into the Foundations of Nationality. Cambridge, MA: MIT Press. (First pub. 1953).

DIAMOND, STANLEY, 1951. Dahomey: A Proto-State in West Africa. Ph.D. dissertation, Department of Anthropology, Columbia University.

DIFFIE, BAILEY W., and GEORGE D. WINIUS 1977. Foundations of the Portuguese Empire 1415–1580. Europe and the World in the Age of Expansion, Vol. 1 (Series). Minneapolis: University of Minnesota Press.

DIKE, K. ONWUKA 1956. Trade and Politics in the Niger Delta, 1830–1885. Oxford: Clarendon Press.

DILLON RICHARD 1962. The Hatchet Men: The Story of the Tong Wars in San Francisco's Chinatown. New York: Coward-McCann.

DI PESO, CHARLES 1974. Casas Grandes: A Fallen Trading Center of the Gran Chichimeca. 3 vols. Dragoon, AZ: Amerind Foundation; Flagstaff, AZ: Northland Press.

DISRAELI, BENJAMIN 1954. Sybil, or The Two Nations. Harmondsworth: Penguin Books. (First pub. 1845.)

DIXON, RUSSELL A., and E. KINGMAN EBERHARDT 1938. Economic Institutions and Cultural Change. New York: McGraw-Hill.

DOBB, MAURICE 1947. Studies in the Development of Capitalism. New York: International Publishers.

DOBYNS, HENRY F. 1963. An Outline of Andean Epidemic History to 1720. Bulletin of the History of Medicine 37: 493–515.

DOCKER, EDWARD WYBERGH 1970. The Blackbirders: The Recruiting of South Sea Labour for Queensland, 1863–1907. Sydney: Angus and Robertson.

DODGE, ERNEST S. 1976. Islands and Empires: Western Impact on the Pacific and East Asia. Minneapolis: University of Minnesota Press.

DOUGLAS, DAVID C. 1969. The Norman Achievement, 1050–1120. Berkeley and Los Angeles: University of California Press.

DOUGLAS, MARY 1964. Matriliny and Pawnship in Central Africa. Africa 34: 301–313.

DOUGLAS, PAUL 1930. Real Wages in the United States: 1890–1926. Boston: Houghton Mifflin.

DOWD, DOUGLAS F. 1956. A Comparative Analysis of Economic Development in the American West and South. Journal of Economic History 16: 558–574.

——— 1974. The Twisted Dream: Capitalist Development in the United States Since 1776. Cambridge, MA: Winthrop.

DOWNS, RICHARD 1967. A Kelantanese Village of Malaya. *In* Contemporary Change in Traditional Societies, Vol. 2. Julian H. Steward, ed. Pp. 107–186. Urbana: University of Illinois Press.

DRUCKER, PHILIP 1951. The Northern and Central Nootkan Tribes. Bureau of American Ethnology, Bulletin 144.

——— 1963. Indians of the Northwest Coast. American Museum Science Books. New York: Natural History Press. (First pub. 1955).

DUMONT, LOUIS 1957. Une sous-caste de l'Inde du Sud. The Hague: Mouton.

——— 1970. Homo Hierarchicus: An Essay on the Caste System. Chicago: University of Chicago Press. (First pub. in French 1966.)

DUNCAN, RONALD J., ed. 1978. Social Anthropology in Puerto Rico. Special issue. Revista/Review Interamericana 8: 3–64.

DURHAM, PHILIP, and EVERETT L. JONES 1965. The Negro Cowboys. New York: Dodd, Mead.

DUTT, ROMESH CHUNDER 1960. The Economic History of India. 2 vols. Classics of Indian History and Economics. New Delhi: Publications Division, Ministry of Information and Broadcasting, Government of India. (First pub. 1901).

DUYVENDAK, J. J. L. 1949. China's Discovery of Africa. London: Probsthain.

EBERHARD, WOLFGANG 1977. A History of China. Berkeley, Los Angeles, London: University of California Press. (First pub. in German 1948).

EDWARDS, MICHAEL M. 1967. The Growth of the British Cotton Trade 1780–1815. Manchester: Manchester University Press.

EDWARDS, MICHAEL M., and R. LLOYD-JONES 1973. N. J. Smelser and the Cotton Factory Family: A Reassessment. *In* Textile History and Economic History: Essays in Honour of Miss Julia de Lacy Mann. N. B. Harte and K. G. Ponting, eds. Pp. 304–319. Manchester: Manchester University Press.

EDWARDS, RICHARD, MICHAEL REICH and THOMAS E. WEISSKOPF, eds. 1972. The Capitalist System. Englewood Cliffs, NJ: Prentice-Hall.

EKHOLM, GORDON F., and GORDON R. WILLEY, eds. 1966. Archaeological Frontiers and External Connections. Handbook of Middle American Indians, Vol. 4. Robert Wauchope, general ed. Austin: University of Texas Press.

EKHOLM, KAJSA 1978. External Exchange and the Transformation of Central African Social Systems. *In* The Evolution of Social Systems: Proceedings of a meeting of the Research Seminar in Archaeology and Related Subjects, Institute of Archaeology, London University. Jonathan Friedman and Michael J. Rowlands, eds. Pp. 115–136. London: Duckworth.

ELIAS, NORBERT 1939. Über den Prozess der Zivilisation. 2 vols. Basel: Haus zum Falken.

ELLIOTT, J. H. 1966. Imperial Spain 1469–1716. New York: Mentor Books, New American Library.

———— 1970. The Old World and the New 1492–1650. Cambridge: Cambridge University Press.

ELVIN, MARK 1973. The Pattern of the Chinese Past. London: Eyre Methuen.

EMBREE, JOHN F. 1950. Thailand, A Loosely Structured Social System. American Anthropologist 52: 181–193.

ENGELS, FRIEDRICH 1971. The Condition of the Working Class in England. W. O. Henderson and W. H. Chaloner, transl. and eds. Oxford: Basil Blackwell. (First pub. in German 1845.)

ENGLER, ROBERT 1968. Social Science and Social Consciousness: The Shame of the Universities. In The Dissenting Academy. Theodore Roszak, ed. Pp. 182–207. New York: Vintage Books.

EPSTEIN, A. L. 1958. Politics in an Urban African Community. Manchester: Manchester University Press.

FAGE, J. D., and R. A. OLIVER, eds. 1970. Papers in African Prehistory. Cambridge: Cambridge University Press.

FAIRBANK, JOHN K. 1953. Trade and Diplomacy on the China Coast: The Opening of the Treaty Ports, 1842–1854. 2 vols. Cambridge, MA: Harvard University Press.

FAIRBANK, JOHN K., EDWIN O. REISCHAUER, and ALBERT M. CRAIG 1973. East Asia: Tradition and Transformation. Boston: Houghton Mifflin.

FALS BORDA, ORLANDO 1976. Capitalismo, hacienda y poblamiento en la Costa Atlántica. 2d revised edition. Bogotá: Editorial Punta de Lanza.

FEINMAN, GARY 1978. The Causes of the Population Decline in Sixteenth Century New Spain. Paper written for Ethnology and Ethnography of Mesoamerica, U 732.02. Program in Anthropology, Graduate Center, City University of New York.

FENTON, WILLIAM N. 1971. The Iroquois in History. In North American Indians in Historical Perspective. Eleanor B. Leacock and Nancy O. Lurie, eds. Pp. 129–168. New York: Random House.

———— 1978 Huronia: An Essay in Proper Ethnohistory. American Anthropologist 80: 922–935.

FEUCHTWANG, STEPHAN 1975. Investigating Religion. In Marxist Analyses and Anthropology. Maurice Bloch, ed. Pp. 61–82. Association of Social Anthropologists, Studies No. 2. London: Malaby.

FIELDHOUSE, D. K. 1967. The Colonial Empires: A Comparative Survey from the Eighteenth Century. New York: Delacorte Press.

FINER, SAMUEL E. 1975. State- and Nation-Building in Europe: The Role of the Military. In The Formation of National States in Western Europe. Charles Tilly, ed. Pp. 84–163. Princeton, NJ: Princeton University Press.

FISHER, RAYMOND H. 1943. The Russian Fur Trade, 1550–1700. University of California Publications in History, Vol. 31. Berkeley and Los Angeles: University of California.

FISHER, ROBIN 1977. Contact and Conflict: Indian-European Relations in British Columbia, 1774–1890. Vancouver: University of British Columbia Press.

FLINN, M. W. 1966. The Origins of the Industrial Revolution. New York: Barnes & Noble.

FLORESCANO, ENRIQUE, ed. 1975. Haciendas, latifundios y plantaciones en América Latina. Simposio de Roma, org. por CLACSO. Mexico City: Siglo Veintiuno Editores.

———— 1979. Ensayos sobre el desarrollo económico de México y América Latina (1500–1975). Mexico City: Fondo de Cultura Económica.

FOGEL, ROBERT W., and STANLEY L. ENGERMAN 1974. Time on the Cross: The Economics of American Negro Slavery, Vol. 1. Boston: Little, Brown.

FONER, PHILIP S. 1941. Business and Slavery: The New York Merchants and the Irrepressible Conflict. New York: Russell and Russell.

FOREMAN, G. 1934. The Five Civilized Tribes. Norman: University of Oklahoma Press.

FORREST, DENYS 1973. Tea for the British: The Social and Economic History of a Famous Trade. London: Chatto and Windus.

FORTES, MEYER 1953. The Structure of Unilineal Descent Groups. American Anthropologist 55: 17–41.

FOSTER, JOHN 1974. Class Struggle and the Industrial Revolution: Early Industrial Capitalism in Three English Towns. New York: St. Martin's Press.

FOSTER-CARTER, AIDAN 1977. Can We Articulate Articulation? New Left Review, No. 107: 47–77.

FOUST, C. M. 1961. Russian Expansion to the East Through the 18th Century. Journal of Economic History 21: 469–482.

———— 1969. Muscovite and Mandarin: Russia's Trade with China and Its Setting, 1727–1805. Chapel Hill: University of North Carolina Press.

FOWLER, MELVIN L. 1971. Agriculture and Village Settlement in the North American East: The Central Mississippi Valley Area, a Case History. *In* Prehistoric Agriculture. Stuart Struever, ed. Pp. 391–403. Garden City, NY: Natural History Press.

FOX, EDWARD 1971. History in Geographic Perspective: The Other France. New York: W. W. Norton.

FOX, RICHARD G. 1971. Kin, Clan, Raja, and Rule: State-Hinterland Relations in Preindustrial India. Berkeley, Los Angeles, London: University of California Press.

———— 1976. Lineage Cells and Regional Definition in Complex Societies. *In* Regional Analysis, Vol. 2. Carol A. Smith, ed. Pp. 95–121. New York: Academic Press.

FRANK, ANDRE GUNDER 1966. The Development of Underdevelopment. Monthly Review 18: 17–31.

———— 1967. Sociology of Development and Underdevelopment of Sociology. Catalyst (Buffalo), No. 3: 20–73.

———— 1978. World Accumulation 1492–1789. New York: Monthly Review Press.

FRANKEL, S. H. 1938. Capital Investment in Africa. London: Oxford University Press.

FRANTZ, JOE B., and JULIAN E. CHOATE, JR. 1955. The American Cowboy: The Myth and the Reality. Norman: University of Oklahoma Press.

FREEDMAN, MAURICE 1960. Immigrants and Associations: Chinese in Nineteenth-Century Singapore. Comparative Studies in Society and History 3: 25–48.

FREEMAN-GRENVILLE, G. S. P. 1962. The Medieval History of the Coast of Tanganyika. London: Oxford University Press.

FRENCH, DAVID 1961. Wasco-Wishram. *In* Perspectives in American Indian Culture Change. Edward H. Spicer, ed. Pp. 337–430. Chicago: University of Chicago Press.

FRIED, MORTON H. 1952. Land Tenure, Geography and Ecology in the Contact of Cultures. American Journal of Economics and Sociology 11: 391–412.

———— 1957. The Classification of Corporate Unilineal Descent Groups. Journal

of the Royal Anthropological Institute 87: 1−29.
—— 1960. On the Evolution of Social Stratification and the State. *In* Culture in History. Stanley Diamond, ed. Pp. 713−731. New York: Columbia University Press.
—— 1966. On the concepts of 'tribe' and 'tribal society.' Transactions of the New York Academy of Sciences, (Ser. 2) 28: 527−540.
—— 1967. The Evolution of Political Society: An Essay in Political Anthropology. New York: Random House.
—— 1975. The Notion of Tribe. Menlo Park, CA: Cummings.
FRIEDMAN, JONATHAN 1974. Marxism, Structuralism and Vulgar Materialism. Man 9: 444−469.
—— 1975. Tribes, States, and Transformation. *In* Marxist Analyses and Social Anthropology. Maurice Bloch, ed. Pp. 161−202. Association of Social Anthropologists, Studies No. 2. London: Malaby Press.
—— 1979. System, Structure and Contradiction: The Evolution of 'Asiatic' Social Formations. Social Studies in Oceania and South East Asia, No. 2. Copenhagen: The National Museum of Denmark.
FRIEDMANN, HARRIET 1978. World Market, State, and Family Farm: Social Bases of Household Production in the Era of Wage Labor. Comparative Studies in Society and History 20: 545−586.
FROBENIUS, LEO 1933. Kulturgeschichte Afrikas: Prolegomena zu einer historischen Gestaltenlehre. Zurich: Phaidon-Verlag.
FURBER, HOLDEN 1970. Madras Presidency in the Mid-Eighteenth Century. *In* Readings on Asian Topics: Papers Read at the Inauguration of the Scandinavian Institute of Asian Studies 16−18 September 1968. Kristof Glamann, ed. Pp. 108−121. Scandinavian Institute of Asian Studies Monograph Series, No. 1. Lund: Studentlitteratur.
FURNAS, J. C. 1947. Anatomy of Paradise: Hawaii and the Islands of the South Seas. New York: William Sloane Associates. (First pub. 1937).
FURNIVALL, J. S. 1939. Netherlands India: A Study of Plural Economy. Cambridge: Cambridge University Press.
—— 1948. Colonial Policy and Practice: A Comparative Study of Burma and Netherlands India. London: Cambridge University Press.
FURTADO, CELSO 1963. The Economic Growth of Brazil: A Survey from Colonial to Modern Times. Berkeley and Los Angeles: University of California Press.
GANGULI, B. N., ed. 1964. Readings in Indian Economic History: Proceedings of the First All-India Seminar on Indian Economic History, 1961. London: Asia Publishing House.
GARFIELD, VIOLA E. 1939. Tsimshian Clan and Society. University of Washington Publications in Anthropology, Vol. 7, No. 3. Seattle: University of Washington Press.
GARTRELL, BEVERLY 1979. The Ruling Ideas of a Ruling Elite: British Colonial Officials in Uganda, 1944−52. Ph.D. dissertation, Program in Anthropology, Graduate School, City University of New York, New York.
GATES, PAUL W. 1973. Landlords and Tenants on the Prairie Frontier: Studies in American Land Policy. Ithaca, NY: Cornell University Press.
GEARING, FRED 1962. Priests and Warriors: Social Structures for Cherokee Politics in the 18th Century. American Anthropological Association, Memoir 93, Vol. 64, No. 5, Pt. 2.
GEERTZ, CLIFFORD 1963. Agricultural Involution: The Processes of Ecological

Change in Indonesia. Berkeley and Los Angeles: University of California Press.

GÉNICOT, LEOPOLD 1966. Crisis: From the Middle Ages to Modern Times. *In* The Cambridge Economic History of Europe, Vol. 2: The Agrarian Life of the Middle Ages. M. M. Postan, ed. Pp. 660–741. Cambridge: Cambridge University Press.

GENOVESE, EUGENE D. 1966. The Political Economy of Slavery: Studies in the Economy and Society of the Slave South. New York: Pantheon Books.

——— 1969. The World the Slaveholders Made: Two Essays in Interpretation. New York: Pantheon Books.

——— 1972. Roll, Jordan, Roll: The World the Slaves Made. New York: Pantheon Books.

GERSCHENKRON, ALEXANDER 1943. Bread and Democracy in Germany. Berkeley and Los Angeles: University of California Press.

——— 1962. Economic Backwardness in Historical Perspective. New York: Praeger.

GEYL, PIETER 1932. The Revolt of the Netherlands (1559–1609). London: William and Norgate.

GHIRSCHMAN, ROMAN 1954. Iran, from the Earliest Times to the Islamic Conquest. Harmondsworth: Penguin Books.

GIBBS, MARION 1949. Feudal Order: A Study of the Origins and Development of English Feudal Society. London: Cobbett Press.

GIBSON, CHARLES 1964. The Aztecs Under Spanish Rule: A History of the Indians of the Valley of Mexico 1519–1810. Stanford, CA: Stanford University Press.

GIBSON, JAMES R. 1969. Feeding the Russian Fur Trade: Provisionment of the Okhotsk Seaboard and the Kamchatka Peninsula 1639–1856. Madison: University of Wisconsin Press.

GLAMANN, KRISTOF 1958. Dutch Asian Trade, 1620–1740. The Hague: M. Nijhoff.

——— 1971. European Trade 1500–1750. *In* The Fontana Economic History of Europe, Vol. 2: 1500–1700, The Sixteenth and Seventeenth Centuries. Carlo M. Cipolla, ed. *separatum*. London: Fontana.

GODELIER, MAURICE 1965. La notion de mode de production asiatique. Temps Modernes 20: 2002–2027.

——— 1966. Rationalité et irrationalité en économie. Paris: François Maspéro.

——— 1977. Dead Sections and Living Ideas in Marx's Thinking on Primitive Society. *In* Perspectives in Marxist Anthropology. Maurice Godelier, ed. Pp. 99–124. Cambridge Studies in Social Anthropology, No. 18. Cambridge: Cambridge University Press. (First pub. in French 1973.)

GODINHO, VITORINO MAGALHÃES 1963–1965. Os descobrimentos e a economia mundial. 2 vols. Lisbon: Editoria Arcádia.

——— 1969. L'économie de l'empire Portugais aux XVe et XVIe siècles. École Pratique des Hautes Études, VIe Section, Centre de Recherches Historiques. Paris: S.E.V.P.E.N.

GOITEIN, S. D. 1956–1957. The Rise of the Near Eastern Bourgeoisie in Early Islamic Times. Cahiers d'histoire mondiale 3: 583–604.

——— 1964. Artisans en Méditerranée orientale au haut Moyen Age. Annales 15: 847–868.

GOLDMAN, IRVING 1940. The Alkatcho Carrier of British Columbia. *In* Acculturation in Seven American Indian Tribes. Ralph Linton, ed. Pp. 333–389. New York: Appleton-Century.

—— 1975. The Mouth of Heaven: An Introduction to Kwakiutl Religious Thought. New York: Wiley.

GOODY, JACK 1971. Technology, Tradition, and the State in Africa. London: Oxford University Press.

—— 1973. British Functionalism. In Main Currents in Cultural Anthropology. R. Naroll and F. Naroll, eds. Pp. 185–215. New York: Appleton-Century-Crofts.

GORDON, DAVID M. 1972. Theories of Poverty and Underemployment: Orthodox, Radical, and Dual Labor Market Perspectives. Lexington, MA: Lexington Books, D.C. Heath.

GORDON, MANYA 1941. Workers Before and After Lenin. New York: Dutton.

GOUGH, KATHLEEN 1968. World Revolution and the Science of Man. In The Dissenting Academy. Theodore Roszak, ed. Pp. 135–158. New York: Vintage Books

—— 1978 Agrarian Relations in Southeast India, 1750–1976. Review 2: 25–53.

GOULDNER, ALVIN 1980. The Two Marxisms. New York: Seabury Press.

GOUROU, PIERRE 1936. Les paysans du delta tonkinois. Paris: Éditions d'art et d'histoire.

GRABURN, NELSON H. H., and B. STEPHEN STRONG 1973. Circumpolar Peoples: An Anthropological Perspective. Pacific Palisades, CA: Goodyear.

GRAHAM, GERALD S. 1970. A Concise History of the British Empire. London: Thames and Hudson.

GRAYMONT, BARBARA 1972. The Iroquois in the American Revolution. Syracuse, NY: Syracuse University Press.

GREENBERG, MICHAEL 1951. British Trade and the Opening of China 1800–42. Cambridge: Cambridge University Press.

GREENFIELD, SIDNEY M. 1977. Madeira and the Beginnings of New World Sugar Cane Cultivation: A Study in Institution Building. In Comparative Perspectives on Slavery in New World Plantation Societies. Vera Rubin and Arthur Tuden, eds. Pp. 536–552. Annals of the New York Academy of Science, Vol. 292. New York: New York Academy of Sciences.

GREENWOOD, G., ed. 1955. Australia: A Social and Political History. New York: Praeger.

GREGG, DOROTHY, and ELGIN WILLIAMS 1948. The Dismal Science of Functionalism. American Anthropologist 50: 594–611.

GROUSSET, RENÉ 1970. The Empire of the Steppes: A History of Central Asia. New Brunswick, NJ: Rutgers University Press. (First pub. in French 1939).

GUHA, AMALENDU 1972. Raw Cotton of Western India: Output, Transportation and Marketing, 1750–1850. Indian Economic and Social History Review 9: 1–41.

—— 1973. Growth of Acreage Under Raw Cotton in India 1851–1901—A Quantitative Account. Artha Vijñāna 15: 1–56.

GUNTHER, ERNA 1972. Indian Life on the Northwest Coast of North America as Seen by the Early Explorers and Fur Traders During the Last Decades of the Eighteenth Century. Chicago: University of Chicago Press.

GUNTHER, JOHN 1953. Inside Africa. New York: Harper & Brothers.

GUTMAN, HERBERT G. 1973. Work, Culture, and Society in Industrializing America, 1815–1919. American Historical Review 78: 531–587.

—— 1976. The Black Family in Slavery and Freedom, 1750–1925. New York: Pantheon Books.

HABAKKUK, H. J. 1962. American and British Technology in the Nineteenth Century: The Search for Labour-Saving Inventions. Cambridge: Cambridge University Press.

HABIB, IRFAN 1960. Banking in Mughal India. *In* Contributions to Indian Economic History, Vol. 1. Tapan Raychadhuri, ed. Pp. 1–20. Calcutta: Mukhopadhyay.

———— 1963. The Agrarian System of Moghul India 1556–1707. New York: Asia Publishing House.

———— 1964. The Structure of Agrarian Society in Mughal India. *In* Readings in Indian Economic History: Proceedings of the First All-India Seminar on Indian Economic History, 1961. B. N. Ganguli, ed. Pp. 37–43. London: Asia Publishing House.

———— 1969. An Examination of Wittfogel's Theory of Oriental Despotism. *In* Studies in Asian History: Proceedings of the Asian History Congress, New Delhi, 1961. K. S. Lal, ed. Pp. 378–392. London: Asia Publishing House.

HADJINICOLAOU-MARAVA, ANNE 1950. Recherches sur la vie des esclaves dans le monde byzantin. Athens: L'Institut Français.

HALL, D.G.E. 1968. A History of South-East Asia. 3d revised edition. London: Macmillan.

HALPERIN-DONGHI, TULIO 1973. The Aftermath of Revolution in Latin America. New York: Harper & Row.

HAMILTON, E. J. 1934. American Treasure and the Price Revolution in Spain 1501–1650. Harvard Economic Studies, Vol. 42.

HANKS, LUCIEN M. 1972. Rice and Man: Agricultural Ecology in Southeast Asia. Chicago and New York: Aldine and Atherton.

HARNETTY, PETER 1972. Imperialism and Free Trade: Lancashire and India in the Mid-Nineteenth Century. Vancouver: University of British Columbia Press.

HARRIS, MARVIN 1972. Portugal's Contribution to the Underdevelopment of Africa and Brazil. *In* Protest and Resistance in Angola and Brazil. Ronald H. Chilcote, ed. Pp. 210–223. Berkeley, Los Angeles, London: University of California Press.

———— 1979. Cultural Materialism: The Struggle for a Science of Culture. New York: Random House.

HART, KEITH 1979. The Development of Commercial Agriculture in West Africa. Discussion paper prepared for the United Nations Agency for International Development.

HARTWELL, R. M., ed. 1970. The Industrial Revolution. New York: Barnes & Noble.

HARVEY, DAVID 1973. Social Justice and the City. Baltimore: Johns Hopkins University Press.

HAUPT, GEORGES 1978. Why the History of the Working-Class Movement? Review 2: 5–24.

HAUPTMAN, LAURENCE M, and JACK CAMPISI, eds. 1978. Neighbors and Intruders: An Ethnohistorical Exploration of the Indians of Hudson's River. Canadian Ethnology Service, Paper 39. National Museum of Man Mercury Series. Ottawa: National Museums of Canada.

HAYS, HOFFMAN R. 1975. Children of the Raven: The Seven Indian Nations of the Northwest Coast. New York: McGraw-Hill.

HECHTER, MICHAEL 1975. Internal Colonialism: The Celtic Fringe in British National Development 1536–1966. Berkeley, Los Angeles, London: University of California Press.

HEESTERMAN, J. C. 1973. India and the Inner Conflict of Traditions. Daedalus, Winter: 97–113.

HEICHELHEIM, FRITZ H. 1956. Effects of Classical Antiquity on the Land. *In* Man's Role in Changing the Face of the Earth. William L. Thomas, ed. Pp. 165–182. Chicago: University of Chicago Press.

HELMS, MARY 1976. Ancient Panama: Chiefs in Search of Power. Austin: University of Texas Press.

HEMMING, JOHN 1978. Red Gold: The Conquest of the Brazilian Indians. Cambridge: Harvard University Press.

HENDERSON, RICHARD N. 1972. The King in Every Man: Evolutionary Trends in Onitsha Ibo Society and Culture. New Haven, CT: Yale University Press.

HENIGE, DAVID 1977. John Kabes of Komenda: An Early African Entrepreneur and State Builder. Journal of African History 18: 1–19.

HERLIHY, PATRICIA 1972. Odessa: Staple Trade and Urbanization in New Russia. Paper presented at the Symposium "Italian, Russian and Balkan Cities," 87th Meeting of the American Historical Association, New Orleans, December 29th, 1979.

HERSKOVITS, MELVILLE J. 1939. Dahomey, an Ancient West African Kingdom. 2 vols. New York: J. J. Augustin.

HEYD, W 1885. Histoire du commerce du Levant au Moyen-Age. 2 vols. Leipzig: Otto Harrassowitz.

HICKERSON, HAROLD 1956. The Genesis of a Trading Post Band: The Pembina Chippewa. Ethnohistory 3: 289–345.

—— 1960. The Feast of the Dead Among the Seventeenth Century Algonkians of the Upper Great Lakes. American Anthropologist 62: 81–107.

—— 1962a. Notes on the Post-Contact Origin of the Midewiwin. Ethnohistory 9: 404–423.

—— 1962b. The Southwestern Chippewa: An Ethnohistorical Study. American Anthropological Association, Memoir 92. Menasha, WI: American Anthropological Association.

—— 1970. The Chippewa and Their Neighbors: A Study in Ethnohistory. New York: Holt, Rinehart & Winston.

HILL, CHRISTOPHER 1949. The English Revolution and the State. The Modern Quarterly 4: 110–128.

—— 1967. Reformation to Industrial Revolution, 1530–1780. The Making of English Society, Vol. 1. New York: Pantheon.

HILL, POLLY 1963. Migrant Cocoa Farmers in Southern Ghana: A Study in Rural Capitalism. Cambridge: Cambridge University Press.

HILTON, RODNEY 1951. Y eut-il une crise générale de la feodalité? Annales 6: 23–30.

—— 1969. The Decline of Serfdom in Medieval England. London: Macmillan.

HINDESS, BARRY, and PAUL Q. HIRST 1975. Pre-Capitalist Modes of Production. London and Boston: Routledge & Kegan Paul.

HINTZE OTTO 1929. Wesen und Verbreitung des Feudalismus. Akademie der Wissenschaften, Berlin, Philosophisch-historische Klasse, Sitzungsberichte. Pp. 321–347. (Reprinted *in* Die Welt als Geschichte 4: 157–190, 1938. Reproduced in part in English transl. *in* Lordship and Community in Medieval Europe. Fredric Cheyette, ed., 1968. New York: Holt, Rinehart & Winston.)

HISTORY TASK FORCE, CENTRO DE ESTUDIOS PUERTORRIQUEÑOS 1979. Labor Migration Under Capitalism: The Puerto Rican Experience. New York: Monthly Review Press.

HO, PING-TI 1965. The Introduction of American Food Plants into China. American Anthropologist 57: 191–201.

——— 1966. The Geographical Distribution of hui-kuan (Landsmannschaften) in Central and Upper Yangtze Provinces. Tsing Hua Journal of Chinese Studies 5: 120–152.

HOBSBAWM, ERIC J. 1962. The Age of Revolution: Europe 1789–1848. London: Weidenfeld & Nicolson.

——— 1967. Labouring Men: Studies in the History of Labour. New York: Anchor Books, Doubleday.

——— 1969. Industry and Empire. Harmondsworth: Penguin Books.

——— 1973. Karl Marx's Contribution to Historiography. *In* Ideology in Social Science. Robin Blackburn, ed. Pp. 265–283. New York: Vintage.

——— 1975. The Age of Capital 1848–1875. New York: Scribner's.

HOBSBAWM, ERIC J., ed. 1964. Karl Marx. Precapitalist Economic Formations. New York: International Publishers.

HODGSON, MARSHALL G. S. 1974. The Venture of Islam. 3 vols. Chicago: University of Chicago Press.

HOLDER, PRESTON 1970. The Hoe and the Horse on the Plains: A Study of Cultural Development Among North American Indians. Lincoln: University of Nebraska Press.

HOOKER, J. R. 1963. The Anthropologist's Frontier: The Last Phase of African Exploitation. Journal of Modern African Studies 1: 455–459.

HOPKINS, A. G. 1973. An Economic History of West Africa. London: Longman Group.

HORTON, ROBIN 1969. From Fishing Village to City-State: A Social History of New Calabar. *In* Man in Africa. Mary Douglas and Phyllis M. Kaberry, eds. Pp. 37–58. London: Tavistock.

HOUGHTON, D. HOBART 1971. Economic Development, 1865–1965. *In* The Oxford History of South Africa, Vol. 2: South Africa 1870–1966. Monica Wilson and Leonard Thompson, eds. Pp. 1–48. New York and Oxford: Oxford University Press.

HOWARD, JOSEPH K. 1952. Strange Empire, a Narrative of the Northwest. New York: Morrow.

HU, HSIEN CHIN 1948. The Common Descent Group in China and Its Functions. Viking Fund Publications in Anthropology, No. 10. New York: Wenner-Gren Foundation for Anthropological Research.

HUDSON, CHARLES M. 1976. The Southeastern Indians. Knoxville: University of Tennessee Press.

HUDSON, CHARLES M., ed. 1971. Red, White and Black: Symposium on Indians in the Old South. Southern Anthropological Society Proceedings, Series No. 5. Athens, GA: Southern Anthropological Society (distributed by University of Georgia Press).

HUGHES, H. STUART 1958. Consciousness and Society: The Reorientation of European Social Thought 1890–1930. New York: Random House.

——— 1966. The Obstructed Path: French Social Thought in the Years of Desperation, 1930–1960. New York: Harper & Row.

——— 1975. The Sea Change: The Migration of Social Thought, 1930–1965. New York: Harper & Row.

HUNE, SHIRLEY 1977. Pacific Migration to the United States: Trends and Themes in Historical and Sociological Literature. RIIES Bibliographic Studies, No. 2. Washington, DC: Research Institute on Immigration and Ethnic Studies,

Smithsonian Institution.

HUNT, GEORGE T. 1940. The Wars of the Iroquois: A Study in Intertribal Trade Relations. Madison: University of Wisconsin Press.

HUNTINGTON, SAMUEL P. 1968. The Bases of Accommodation. Foreign Affairs 46: 642–656.

HUTCHINS, FRANCIS G. 1967. Illusion of Permanence: British Imperialism in India. Princeton, NJ: Princeton University Press.

HUTTON, JOHN H. 1951. Caste in India, Its Nature, Function and Origins. 2d edition. New York: Oxford University Press.

HYDE, FRANCIS E. 1973. Far Eastern Trade, 1860–1914. The Merchant Adventurers Series. New York: Harper & Row/Barnes & Noble.

HYMES, DELL, ed. 1969. Reinventing Anthropology. New York: Pantheon.

INALCIK, HALAL 1969. Capital Formation in the Ottoman Empire. Journal of Economic History 29: 97–140.

―――― 1973. The Ottoman Empire: The Classical Age, 1300–1600. New York: Praeger.

INIKORI, J. E. 1977. The Import of Firearms into West Africa, 1750–1807: A Quantitative Analysis. Journal of African History 18: 339–368.

INNIS, HAROLD A. 1956. The Fur Trade in Canada: An Introduction to Canadian Economic History. 2d revised edition, by Mary Q. Innis. Toronto: University of Toronto Press. (First pub. 1930.)

ISLAMOĞLU, HURI, and ÇAĞLAR KEYDER 1977. Agenda for Ottoman History. Review 1: 31–55.

ISSAWI, CHARLES, ed. 1966. The Economic History of the Middle East 1800–1914. Chicago: University of Chicago Press.

JABLOW, JOSEPH 1951. The Cheyenne in Plains Trade Relations 1795–1840. American Ethnological Society Monograph, No. 19. New York: J. J. Augustin.

JACKSON, JAMES S. 1968. Planters and Speculators: Chinese and European Enterprise in Malaya. Kuala Lumpur: University of Malaya Press.

JACOBS, WILBUR R. 1972. Dispossessing the American Indian: Indians and Whites on the Colonial Frontier. New York: Scribner's.

JAIN, RAVINDRA K. 1970. South Indians on the Plantation Frontier in Malaya. New Haven, CT: Yale University Press.

JAYAWARDENA, CHANDRA 1971. The Disintegration of Caste in Fiji Rural Society. *In* Anthropology in Oceania: Essays Presented to Ian Hogbin. L. R. Hiatt and C. Jayawardena, eds. Pp. 89–119. San Francisco: Chandler.

JEANNIN, PIERRE 1980. La protoindustrialisation: développement ou impasse. Annales 35: 52–65.

JENKS, LELAND R. 1973. The Migration of British Capital to 1875. New York: Harper & Row/Barnes & Noble. (First pub. 1927.)

JENNINGS, FRANCIS 1976. The Invasion of America: Indians, Colonialism, and the Cant of Conquest. New York: W. W. Norton.

JENNINGS, JESSE D., and EDWARD NORBECK, eds. 1963. Prehistoric Man in the New World. Chicago: University of Chicago Press.

JEROMIN, ULRICH 1966. Die Überseechinesen: Ihre Bedeutung für die wirtschaftliche Entwicklung Südostasiens. Ökonomische Studien, Vol. 12. Stuttgart: Gustav Fischer.

JESSOP, BOB 1977. Recent Theories of the Capitalist State. Cambridge Journal of Economics 1: 353–373.

JONES, G. I. 1963. The Trading States of the Oil Rivers. London: Oxford University Press.

JONES, GWYN 1968. A History of the Vikings. New York: Oxford University Press.

JONES, MALDWYN ALLEN 1960. American Immigration. Chicago: University of Chicago Press.

JORDAN, WINTHROP D. 1968. White over Black: American Attitudes Toward the Negro, 1550–1812. Chapel Hill: University of North Carolina Press.

JOSHI, P. C. 1970. Social Change in Traditional India. *In* Neue Indienkunde— New Indology, Festschrift Walter Rubin zum 70. Geburtstag. Horst Krüger, ed. Pp. 287–306. Berlin: Akademie Verlag.

KAPLAN, DAVID 1979. Toward a Marxist Analysis of South Africa: Review of Bernard Makhosezwe Magubane, The Political Economy of Race and Class in South Africa. Socialist Review 9: 117–137.

KEA, R. A. 1971. Firearms and Warfare on the Gold and Slave Coasts from the Sixteenth to the Nineteenth Centuries. Journal of African History 12: 185–213.

KELLER, BONNIE B. 1978. Millenarianism and Resistance: The Xhosa Cattle Killing. Journal of Asian and African Studies 13: 95–111.

KELLEY, J. CHARLES 1966. Mesoamerica and the Southwestern United States. *In* Archaeological Frontiers and External Connections. Gordon F. Ekholm and Gordon R. Willey, eds. Pp. 95–110. Handbook of Middle American Indians, Vol. 4. Robert Wauchope, general ed. Austin: University of Texas Press.

KEMP, TOM 1971. Economic Forces in French History. London: Dobson Books.

KEPNER, CHARLES D., JR. 1936. Social Aspects of the Banana Industry. New York: Columbia University Press.

KEPNER, CHARLES D., JR., and JAY H. SOOTHILL 1935. The Banana Empire. New York: Vanguard Press.

KERNER, ROBERT J. 1942. The Urge to the Sea: The Course of Russian History. The Role of Rivers, Portages, Ostrogs, Monasteries, and Furs. New York: Russell and Russell.

KERR, CLARK 1954. The Balkanization of Labor Markets. *In* Labor Mobility and Economic Opportunity. E. Wight Bakke, et al. Pp. 92–110. New York: Wiley.

KEY, V. O. 1949. Southern Politics in State and Nation. New York: Knopf.

KEYDER, ÇAĞLAR 1976. The Dissolution of the Asiatic Mode of Production. Economy and Society 5: 178–196.

KINIETZ, W. VERNON 1965. The Indians of the Great Lakes 1615–1760. Ann Arbor: University of Michigan Press. (First pub. 1940).

KIRCHHOFF, PAUL 1959. The Principles of Clanship in Human Society. *In* Readings in Anthropology, Vol. 2. Morton H. Fried, ed. Pp. 260–270. New York: Thomas Y. Crowell.

KLASS, MORTON 1980. Caste: The Emergence of the South Asian Social System. Philadelphia: Institute for the Study of Human Issues.

KLEIN, A. NORMAN 1969. West African Unfree Labor Before and After the Rise of the Atlantic Slave Trade. *In* Slavery in the New World. L. Foner and E. D. Genovese, eds. Pp. 87–95. Englewood Cliffs, NJ: Prentice-Hall.

KOENIGSBERGER, H. G. 1971. Estates and Revolutions: Essays in Early Modern European History. Ithaca, NY: Cornell University Press.

KOLKO, GABRIEL 1963. The Triumph of Conservatism: A Reinterpretation of American History, 1900–1916. Glencoe, IL: The Free Press.

KONDRATIEFF, N. D. 1979. The Long Waves in Economic Life. Review 2: 519–562.

KONETZKE, RICHARD 1971. América Latina II: La época colonial. Historia Universal Siglo XXI. Madrid and Mexico City: Siglo XXI. (First pub. in German 1965).

KOPYTOFF, IGOR, and SUZANNE MIERS 1977. African 'Slavery' as an Institution of Marginality. *In* Slavery in Africa: Historical and Anthropological Perspectives. Igor Kopytoff and Suzanne Miers, eds. Pp. 3—81. Madison: University of Wisconsin Press.

KOSAMBI, D. D. 1969. Ancient India: A History of Its Culture and Civilization. New York: Meridian Books—World Publishing Company.

KRADER, LAWRENCE 1955. Principles and Structures in the Organization of the Steppe-Pastoralists. Southwestern Journal of Anthropology 11: 67—92.

———— 1957. Culture and Environment in Interior Asia. *In* Studies in Human Ecology. Ángel Palerm, et al. Pp. 115—138. Social Science Monographs III. Washington, DC: Pan American Union.

———— 1958. Feudalism and the Tatar Polity of the Middle Ages. Comparative Studies in Society and History 1: 76—99.

———— 1975. The Asiatic Mode of Production: Sources, Development and Critique in the Writings of Karl Marx. Assen: Van Gorcum.

KRADER, LAWRENCE, ed. 1972. The Ethnological Notebooks of Karl Marx (Studies of Morgan, Phear, Maine, Lubbock). Assen: Van Gorcum.

KRAENZEL, CHARLES F. 1955. The Great Plains in Transition. Norman: University of Oklahoma Press.

KRIEDTE, PETER, HANS MEDICK, and JÜRGEN SCHLUMBOHM 1977. Industrialisierung vor der Industrialisierung: Gewerbliche Warenproduktion auf dem Land in der Formationsperiode des Kapitalismus. Veröffentlichungen des Max-Planck-Instituts für Geschichte 53. Göttingen: Vandenhoek and Ruprecht.

KROEBER, ALFRED L. 1948. Anthropology. New York: Harcourt Brace.

———— 1952. Basic and Secondary Patterns of Social Structure. *In* The Nature of Culture. Pp. 210—218. Chicago: University of Chicago Press. (Article first pub. 1938).

———— 1952. The Nature of Culture. Chicago: University of Chicago Press.

KUBLER, GEORGE 1946. The Quechua in the Colonial World. *In* Handbook of South American Indians, Vol. 2: The Andean Civilizations. Julian H. Steward, ed. Pp. 331—410. Bureau of American Ethnology, Bulletin 143. Washington, DC: Smithsonian Institution.

KULA, WITOLD 1970. Teoria economica del sistema feudale. Turin: Einaudi. (First pub. in Polish 1962.)

KUNSTADTER, PETER, ed. 1967. Southeast Asian Tribes, Minorities, and Nations. 2 vols. Princeton, NJ: Princeton University Press.

KUWABARA, JITSUZO 1928—1935. On P'u Shou-keng, a Man of the Western Regions Who Was the Superintendent of the Trading Ships Office in Ch'uanchou Towards the End of the Sung Dynasty, Together with a General Sketch of Trade of the Arabs in China During the T'ang and Sung Eras. Memoirs of the Research Department of the Toyo Bunko, No. 2: 1—79; No. 7 (1935): 1—102.

LACOSTE, YVES 1974. General Characteristics and Fundamental Structures of Medieval North African Society. Economy and Society 3: 1—17.

LAMPARD, ERIC R. 1957. Industrial Revolution: Interpretations and Perspectives. Service Center for Teachers of History, Publication No. 4. Washington, DC: American Historical Association.

LANDES, DAVID 1958. Bankers and Pashas: International Finance and Economic

Imperialism in Egypt. Cambridge: Harvard University Press.

———— 1969. The Unbound Prometheus: Technological Change and Industrial Development in Western Europe from 1750 to the Present. Cambridge: Cambridge University Press.

LANE, FREDERICK C. 1973. Venice: A Maritime Republic. Baltimore: The Johns Hopkins University Press.

LANG, JAMES 1975. Conquest and Commerce: Spain and England in the Americas. New York: Academic Press.

———— 1979. Portuguese Brazil: The King's Plantation. New York: Academic Press.

LAPIDUS, IRA M. 1969. Muslim Cities and Islamic Societies. *In* Middle Eastern Cities. Ira M. Lapidus, ed. Pp. 47–79. Berkeley and Los Angeles: University of California Press.

LAPIDUS, IRA M., ed. 1969. Middle Eastern Cities. Berkeley and Los Angeles: University of California Press.

LAROUI, ABDALLAH 1976. The Crisis of the Arab Intellectual: Traditionalism or Historicism? Berkeley, Los Angeles, London: University of California Press.

LATHAM, A. J. H. 1973. Old Calabar 1600–1891: The Impact of the International Economy Upon a Traditional Society. Oxford: Clarendon Press.

———— 1978. The International Economy and the Underdeveloped World 1865–1914. London: Croom Helm.

LATHRAP, DONALD 1970. The Upper Amazon. London: Thames and Hudson.

LATTIMORE, OWEN 1951. Inner Asian Frontiers of China. 2d edition. New York: American Geographic Society. (First pub. 1940.)

———— 1962. Studies in Frontier History: Collected Papers 1928–1958. London: Oxford University Press.

LATTIMORE, OWEN, and ELEANOR LATTIMORE 1944. The Making of Modern China. Washington, DC: The Infantry Journal.

LAUBER, ALMON W. 1913. Indian Slavery in Colonial Times Within the Present Limits of the United States. New York: Columbia University Press.

LAW, ROBIN 1975. A West African Cavalry State: The Kingdom of Oyo. Journal of African History 16: 1–15.

LAWSON, MURRY G. 1943. Fur: A Study in English Mercantilism, 1700–1775. University of Toronto Studies, History and Economics Series, Vol. 9. Toronto: University of Toronto Press.

LAZONICK, WILLIAM 1974. Karl Marx and Enclosures in England. Review of Radical Political Economics 6: 1–59.

LEACH, EDMUND R. 1954. Political Systems of Highland Burma: A Study of Kachin Social Structure. Cambridge: Harvard University Press.

———— 1961. Rethinking Anthropology. London School of Economics Monographs on Social Anthropology, No. 22. London: Athlone Press.

LEACH, EDWARD R., and S. N. MUKERJEE, eds. 1970. Elites in South Asia. Cambridge: Cambridge University Press.

LEACOCK, ELEANOR B. 1954. The Montagnais 'Hunting Territory' and the Fur Trade. American Anthropological Association Memoir 78. Menasha, WI: American Anthropological Association.

———— 1972. Introduction. *To* Frederick Engels, The Origin of the Family, Private Property, and the State. Pp. 7–67. New York: International Publishers.

LEACOCK, ELEANOR B., and NANCY O. LURIE, eds. 1971. North American Indians in Historical Perspective. New York: Random House.

LEBAR, FRANK M., GERALD C. HICKEY, and JOHN K. MUSGROVE, eds. 1964. Ethnic Groups of Mainland Southeast Asia. New Haven, CT: Human Relations Area Files Press.

LEE, CALVIN 1965. Chinatown, U.S.A. Garden City, NY: Doubleday.

LEEDS, ANTHONY 1976. 'Women in the Migratory Process': A Reductionist Outlook. Anthropological Quarterly 49: 69−76.

LEES, SUSAN H., and DANIEL G. BATES 1974. The Origins of Specialized Pastoralism: A Systemic Model. American Antiquity 39: 187−193.

LEGASSICK, MARTIN 1977. Gold, Agriculture, and Secondary Industry in South Africa, 1885−1970; from Periphery to Sub-Metropole as a Forced Labour System. In The Roots of Rural Poverty in Central and Southern Africa. Robin Palmer and Neil Parsons, eds. Pp. 175−200. Berkeley, Los Angeles, London: University of California Press.

LEHMAN, FREDERIC K. 1957. Anthropological Parameters of a Civilization: The Ecology, Evolution and Typology of India's High Culture. 2 vols. Ph.D. dissertation, Department of Anthropology, Columbia University, New York.

LEKACHMAN, ROBERT 1976. Economists at Bay. New York: McGraw-Hill.

LENIN, V. I. 1939. Imperialism: The Highest State of Capitalism. Little Lenin Library, Vol. 15. New York: International Publishers. (First pub. in Russian 1917.)

LE ROY LADURIE, EMMANUEL 1977. Occitania in Historical Perspective. Review 1: 21−30.

LESSER, ALEXANDER 1961. Social Fields and the Evolution of Society. Southwestern Journal of Anthropology 17: 40−48.

LEUR, JACOB CORNELIS VAN 1955. Indonesian Trade and Society: Essays in Asian Social and Economic History. The Hague and Bandung: W. van Hoewe.

LEVIN, STEPHANIE SETO 1968. The Overthrow of the *Kapu* System in Hawaii. Journal of the Polynesian Society 74: 402−430.

LEVINE, DAVID 1977. Family Formation in an Age of Nascent Capitalism. New York: Academic Press.

LEVTZION, NEHEMIA 1972. The Early States of the Western Sudan to 1500. In History of West Africa, Vol. 1. J. F. Ade Ajayi and Michael Crowder, eds. Pp. 120−157. New York: Columbia University Press.

LEWIS, ARCHIBALD R. 1951. Naval Power and Trade in the Mediterranean, 500−1100. Princeton, NJ: Princeton University Press.

———— 1958. The Northern Seas: Shipping and Commerce in Northern Europe, A.D. 300−1100. Princeton, NJ: Princeton University Press.

LEWIS, OSCAR 1942. The Effects of White Contact Upon Blackfoot Culture: With Special Reference to the Role of the Fur Trade. American Ethnological Society, Monograph No. 6. New York: J. J. Augustin.

LINARES, OLGA T. 1979. What Is Lower Central American Archaeology? Annual Review of Anthropology 8: 21−43.

LINDBLOM, CHARLES E. 1977. Politics and Markets: The World's Political Economic Systems. New York: Basic Books.

LINTON, RALPH 1955. The Tree of Culture. New York: Knopf.

LLOYD, PETER C. 1954. The Traditional Political System of the Yoruba. Southwestern Journal of Anthropology 10: 235−251.

———— 1965. The Political Structure of African Kingdoms. In Political Systems and the Distribution of Power. Michael Banton, ed. Pp. 25−61. Association of Social Anthropologists, Monograph No. 2. London: Tavistock Publications.

———— 1968. Conflict Theory and Yoruba Kingdoms. In History and Social

Anthropology. I. M. Lewis, ed. Pp. 25–61. Association of Social Anthropologists, Monograph No. 7. London: Tavistock Publications.

LOCKHART, JAMES 1968. Spanish Peru, 1532–1560: A Colonial Society. Madison: University of Wisconsin Press.

—— 1972. The Men of Cajamarca: A Social and Biographical Study of the First Conquerors of Peru. Austin: University of Texas Press.

LOPEZ, ROBERT S. 1971. The Commercial Revolution of the Middle Ages, 950–1350. Englewood Cliffs, NJ: Prentice-Hall.

LOPEZ, ROBERT S., HARRY A. MISKIMIN, and ABRAHAM UDOVITCH 1970. England to Egypt, 1350–1500: Long-Term Trends and Long-Distance Trade. *In* Studies in the Economic History of the Middle East from the Rise of Islam to the Present Day. Michael A. Cook, ed. Pp. 93–128. London: Oxford University Press.

LOPEZ, ROBERT S., and IRVING W. RAYMOND 1955. Medieval Trade in the Mediterranean World, Illustrative Documents Translated with Introduction and Notes. New York: Columbia University Press.

LOVE, THOMAS F. 1977. Ecological Niche Theory in Sociocultural Anthropology: A Conceptual Framework and an Application. American Ethnologist 4: 27–41.

LOWIE, ROBERT H. 1920. Primitive Society. New York: Boni and Liveright.

—— 1937. The History of Ethnological Theory. New York: Rinehart.

LUXEMBURG, ROSA 1922. Die Akkumulation des Kapitals. Ein Beitrag zur ökonomischen Erklärung des Imperialismus. Berlin: Vereinigung Internationaler Verlags-Anstalten. (First pub. 1913).

LUZZATTO, GINO 1961. An Economic History of Italy from the Fall of the Roman Empire to the Beginning of the Sixteenth Century. London: Routledge & Kegan Paul.

LYASHCHENKO, PETER I. 1949. History of the National Economy of Russia to the 1917 Revolution. New York: Macmillan. (First pub. in Russian 1939.)

LYBYER, A. H. 1915. The Ottoman Turks and the Routes of Oriental Trade. Economic History Review 30: 577–588.

LYND, ROBERT S. 1939. Knowledge for What? Princeton, NJ: Princeton University Press.

—— 1949. The Science of Inhuman Relations. The New Republic 121: 22–24.

MCCALL, DANIEL F. 1969. Africa in Time-Perspective. New York: Oxford University Press.

—— 1971. Islamization in the Western and Central Sudan in the Eleventh Century. *In* Aspects of West African Islam. Daniel F. McCall and Norman R. Bennett, eds. Pp. 1–30. Boston University Papers on Africa, Vol. 5. Boston: African Studies Center, Boston University.

MCCOY, ALFRED W., with CATHLEEN B. READ and LEONARD P. ADAMS II 1972. The Politics of Heroin in Southeast Asia. New York: Harper & Row.

MCEVEDY, COLIN, and RICHARD JONES 1978. Atlas of World Population History. Harmondsworth: Penguin Books.

MACFARLANE, ALAN 1979. The Origins of English Individualism: The Family, Property and Social Transition. New York: Cambridge University Press.

MCHUGH, TOM, with VICTORIA HOBSON 1972. The Time of the Buffalo. New York: Knopf.

MCILWRAITH, T. F. 1948. The Bella Coola Indians. 2 vols. Toronto: University of Toronto Press.

MACKNIGHT, C. C. 1972. Macassans and Aborigines. Oceania 42: 283–321.

MACK SMITH, DENIS 1969. Italy: A Modern History. (2d revised edition.) Ann Arbor: University of Michigan Press.

MACLEOD, MURDO J. 1973. Spanish Central America: A Socioeconomic History, 1520–1720. Berkeley, Los Angeles, London: University of California Press.

MCNEILL, WILLIAM H. 1963. The Rise of the West: A History of the Human Community. Chicago: University of Chicago Press.

MCPHERRON, ALAN 1967. On the Sociology of Ceramics: Pottery Style Clustering, Marital Residence, and Cultural Adaptations of the Algonkian-Iroquoian Border. *In* Iroquois Culture, History and Prehistory: Proceedings of the 1965 Conference on Iroquois Research. Elizabeth Tooker, ed. Pp. 101–107. Albany: State Education Department, University of the State of New York, and New York Museum and Science Service.

MACPHERSON, C. B. 1962. The Political Theory of Possessive Individualism: Hobbes to Locke. Oxford: Clarendon Press.

MAGUBANE, BERNARD M. 1978. The Politics of History in South Africa. Notes and Documents No. 11/78. New York: Centre Against Apartheid, Department of Political and Security Council Affairs, United Nations.

―――― 1979. The Political Economy of Race and Class in South Africa. New York: Monthly Review Press.

MAIR, LUCY P. 1934. An African People in the Twentieth Century. London: Routledge.

MANCALL, MARK 1971. Russia and China: Their Diplomatic Relations to 1728. Cambridge, MA: Harvard University Press.

MANDEL, ERNEST 1968. Marxist Economic Theory. 2 vols. New York: Monthly Review Press (First pub. in French 1942.)

―――― 1978. Late Capitalism. London: Verso. (First pub. in German 1972.)

MANN, JULIA DE LACY 1971. The Cloth Industry in the West of England from 1640 to 1880. Oxford: Clarendon Press.

MANTOUX, PAUL 1928. The Industrial Revolution in the Eighteenth Century: An Outline of the Beginnings of the Modern Factory System in England. London: Jonathan Cape.

MAQUET, JACQUES J. 1961. Une hypothèse pour l'étude des feodalités africaines. Cahiers d'études africaines 2: 292–314.

―――― 1964. Objectivity in Anthropology. Current Anthropology 12: 419–430.

MARAN LA RAW 1967. Towards a Basis for Understanding the Minorities in Burma: The Kachin Example. *In* Southeast Asian Tribes, Minorities, and Nations, Vol. 1. Peter Kunstadter, ed. Pp. 125–146. Princeton, NJ: Princeton University Press.

MARCUS, STEVEN 1974. Engels, Manchester, and the Working Class. New York: Random House.

MARX, KARL 1942. The Marx-Zasulich Correspondence. The New International, November: 298–302 (Dated 1881.)

―――― 1967. Capital: A Critique of Political Economy. Vol. 3: The Process of Capitalist Production as a Whole. New York: International Publishers. (First pub. in German 1894.)

―――― 1972. Ireland and the Irish Question: A Collection of Writings. New York: International Publishers.

―――― 1973. Grundrisse: Foundations of the Critique of Political Economy, Rough Draft. Martin Nicolaus, transl. London: Allen Lane. (Manuscript written in 1857–1858; first pub. in German 1939.)

———— 1977. Capital: A Critique of Political Economy. Vol. 1. David Fernbach, transl. Marx Library. New York: Vintage-Random House. (First pub. in German 1867.)

MASSELMAN, GEORGE 1963. The Cradle of Colonialism. New Haven, CT: Yale University.

MATHEW, GERVASE 1963. The East African Coast Until the Coming of the Portuguese. *In* The History of East Africa, Vol. I. Roland Oliver and Gervase Mathew, eds. Pp. 94–127. Oxford: Clarendon Press.

MAUDE, H. E. 1968. Of Islands and Men: Studies in Pacific History. Melbourne: Oxford University Press.

MAUNY, RAYMOND 1961. Tableau géographique de l'ouest africain au Moyen Age, d'après les sources ecrites, la tradition et l'archéologie. Mémoires de l'Institut Français d'Afrique Noire, No. 61, Dakar.

MAURO, FRÉDÉRIC 1961. Toward an 'Intercontinental Model': European Overseas Expansion Between 1500–1800. Economic History Review 14: 1–17.

———— 1967. L'expansion européenne (1600–1870). Paris: Presses Universitaires de France.

MEGGERS, BETTY J. 1966. Ecuador. New York: Praeger.

MEGGERS, BETTY J., and CLIFFORD EVANS, eds. 1963. Aboriginal Culture Development in Latin America: An Interpretive Review. Smithsonian Miscellaneous Collections, Vol. 146. Washington, DC: Smithsonian Institution.

MEGGITT, MERVYN J. 1962. Desert People: A Study of the Walbiri Aborigines of Central Australia. Sydney: Angus and Robertson.

MEHRING, FRANZ 1935. Karl Marx, the Story of His Life. New York: Covici, Friede.

MEILINK-ROELOFSZ, M.A.P. 1962. Asian Trade and European Influence in the Indonesian Archipelago Between 1500 and About 1630. The Hague: M. Nijhoff.

MEILLASSOUX, CLAUDE 1960. Essai d'interpretation du phénomène économique dans les sociétés traditionelles d'auto-subsistence. Cahiers d'Études Africaines, No. 4: 38–67.

———— 1972. From Reproduction to Production: A Marxist Approach to Economic Anthropology. Economy and Society 1: 93–105.

———— 1973. The Social Organization of the Peasantry: The Economic Basis of Kinship. Journal of Peasant Studies 1: 81–90.

———— 1974. Are There Castes in India? Economy and Society 2: 89–111.

MEILLASSOUX, CLAUDE, ed. 1971. The Development of Indigenous Trade and Markets in West Africa. London: Oxford University Press.

———— 1975. L'esclavage en Afrique Précoloniale. Paris: François Maspéro.

MENCHER, JOAN 1974. The Caste System Upside Down: Or the Not So Mysterious East. Current Anthropology 15: 469–494.

MENDELS, FRANKLIN F. 1972. Proto-Industrialization: The First Phase of the Industrialization Process. Journal of Economic History 32: 241–261.

MERRIMAN, ROBERT O. 1926. The Bison and the Fur-Trade. Departments of History and Political and Economic Science in Queen's University, Bulletin 53, Kingston, Ontario.

MEYEROWITZ, EVA L. R. 1951. The Sacred State of the Akan. London: Faber and Faber.

MILLER, ERIC 1954. Caste and Territory in Malabar. American Anthropologist 56: 410–420.

MILLER, J. INNIS 1969. The Spice Trade of the Roman Empire, 29 B.C. to A.D. 641. Oxford: Clarendon Press.

MILLER, JOSEPH C. 1973. Requiem for the 'Jaga.' Cahiers d'Études Africaines 13: 121–149.

——— 1975. Kings and Kinsmen: Early Mbundu States in Angola. London: Oxford University Press.

——— 1976. The Slave Trade in Congo and Angola. In The African Diaspora: Interpretive Essays. Martin L. Kilson and Robert I. Rotberg, eds. Pp. 75–113. Cambridge, MA: Harvard University Press.

MILLER, SOLOMON 1967. Hacienda to Plantation in Northern Peru: The Processes of Proletarianization of a Tenant Farmer Society. In Contemporary Change in Traditional Societies, Vol. 3: Mexican and Peruvian Communities. Julian H. Steward, ed. Pp. 133–225. Urbana: University of Illinois Press.

MILWARD, A., and S. B. SAUL 1977. The Development of the Economics of Continental Europe. Cambridge, MA: Harvard University Press.

MINGAY, G. E. 1973. English Landed Society in the Eighteenth Century. London: Routledge & Kegan Paul.

MINTZ, SIDNEY W. 1956. Cañamelar: The Subculture of a Rural Sugar Plantation Proletariat. In The People of Puerto Rico. Julian Steward, et al. Pp. 314–417. Urbana: University of Illinois Press.

——— 1959a. Internal Market Systems as Mechanisms of Social Articulation. In Intermediate Societies, Social Mobility, and Communication. Proceedings of the 1959 Annual Spring Meeting of the American Ethnological Society. Verne F. Ray, ed. Pp. 20–30. Seattle: University of Washington.

——— 1959b. The Plantation as a Socio-Cultural Type. In Plantation Systems of the New World. Ángel Palerm and Vera Rubin, eds. Pp. 42–49. Social Science Monographs VII, Pan American Union. Washington, DC: Pan American Union.

——— 1961. The Question of Caribbean Peasantries: A Comment. Caribbean Studies 1: 31–34.

——— 1973. A Note on the Definition of Peasantry. Journal of Peasant Studies 1: 91–106.

——— 1974. Caribbean Transformation. Chicago: Aldine.

——— 1979a. Slavery and the Rise of Peasantry. Historical Reflections 6: 215–242.

——— 1979b. Time, Sugar and Sweetness. Marxist Perspectives 2: 56–73.

MINTZ, SIDNEY W., and RICHARD PRICE 1976. An Anthropological Approach to the Study of Afro-American History: A Caribbean Perspective. Philadelphia: ISHI.

MOHR, E. C. J. 1933. Tropical Soil Forming Processes and the Development of Tropical Soils with Special Reference to Java and Sumatra. Peking: National Geological Survey of China.

——— 1944. The Soils of Equatorial Regions. Ann Arbor, MI: Edwards Brothers.

MOORE, BARRINGTON, JR., 1966. Social Origins of Dictatorship and Democracy: Lord and Peasant in the Making of the Modern World. Boston: Beacon Press.

——— 1978. Injustice: The Social Bases of Obedience and Revolt. White Plains, NY: M. E. Sharpe.

MORELAND, W. H. 1963. The Agrarian System of Moslem India. Bombay: Oriental Book Reprint Corporation. (First pub. in 1929.)

MORENO FRAGINALS, MANUEL 1978. El ingenio: complejo económico social cubano del azúcar. 2 vols. La Habana: Editorial de Ciencias Sociales.

MORGAN, EDMUND S 1975. American Slavery—American Freedom: The Ordeal of Colonial Virginia. New York: W. W. Norton.

MÖRNER, MAGNUS 1973. The Spanish American Hacienda: A Survey of Recent Research and Debate. Hispanic American Historical Review 53: 183−216.

MORRIS, MORRIS D. 1960. The Recruitment of an Industrial Labor Force in India, with British and American Comparisons. Comparative Studies in Society and History 2: 305−328.

―――― 1963. Towards a Reinterpretation of Nineteenth Century Indian Economic History. Journal of Economic History 23: 606−618. (Reprinted with critical comments by Toru Matsui, Bipan Chandra, and T. Raychaudhuri, Indian Economic and Social History Review, 1968: 1−100, 319−388.)

―――― 1965. The Emergence of an Industrial Labor Force in India: A Study of the Bombay Cotton Mills 1854−1947. Berkeley and Los Angeles: University of California Press.

MORRIS, MORRIS D., and BURTON STEIN 1961. The Economic History of India: A Bibliographic Essay. Journal of Economic History 21: 179−207.

MORTON-WILLIAMS, PETER 1964. The Oyo Yoruba and the Atlantic Slave Trade, 1670−1830. Journal of the Historical Society of Nigeria 3: 24−45.

―――― 1965. The Fulani Penetration into Nupe and Yoruba in the Nineteenth Century. In Political Systems and the Distribution of Power. Michael Banton, ed. Pp. 1−24. Association of Social Anthropologists, Monograph No. 2. London: Tavistock Publications.

―――― 1967. The Yoruba Kingdom of Oyo in the Nineteenth Century. In West African Kingdoms in the Nineteenth Century. Daryll Forde and Phyllis Kaberry, eds. Pp. 36−69. London: Oxford University Press.

―――― 1969. The Influence of Habitat and Trade on the Polities of Oyo and Ashanti. In Man in Africa. Mary Douglas and Phyllis Kaberry, eds. Pp. 79−98. London: Tavistock Publications.

MOZIÑO, JOSÉ MARIANO 1970. Noticias de Nutka: An Account of Nootka Sound in 1792. American Ethnological Society, Monograph No. 50. Seattle: University of Washington Press.

MUDENGE, S. I. 1974. The Role of Foreign Trade in the Rozvi Empire: A Reappraisal. Journal of African History 15: 373−391.

MUKHERJEE, RAMKRISHNA 1958. The Rise and Fall of the East India Company: A Sociological Appraisal. Berlin: VEB Deutscher Verlag der Wissenschaften.

MUKHERJEE, S. N. 1970. Class, Caste and Politics in Calcutta, 1815−38. In Elites in South Asia. E. R. Leach and S. N. Mukherjee, eds. Pp. 38−78. Cambridge: Cambridge University Press.

MURDOCK, GEORGE P. 1949. Social Structure. New York: Macmillan.

MURPHEY, RHOADS 1977. The Outsiders: The Western Experience in India and China. Ann Arbor: University of Michigan Press.

MURPHY, ROBERT F. 1958. Matrilocality and Patrilineality in Mundurucú Society. American Anthropologist 58: 414−434.

―――― 1960. Headhunters' Heritage: Social and Economic Change Among the Mundurucú Indians. Berkeley and Los Angeles: University of California Press.

MURRA, JOHN V. 1972. El control 'vertical' de un máximo de pisos ecológicos en la economía de las sociedades andinas. In Iñigo Ortiz de Zúñiga, visitador, visita de la provincia de León de Huánuco en 1562, Vol. 1. John V. Murra, ed. Pp. 427−476. Documentos para la Historia y Etnología de Huánuco y la Selva

Central. Huánuco, Peru: Universidad Hermilio Valdizán.

────── 1975. Formaciones económicas y políticas del mundo andino. Lima: Instituto de Estudios Peruanos.

NACLA-East Apparel Project, North American Congress for Latin America 1977. Capital on the Move: An Overview. NACLA's Latin American and Empire Report 11: 2−3.

NASH, GARY B. 1974. Red, White, and Black: The Peoples of Early America. Englewood Cliffs, NJ: Prentice-Hall.

NEHNEVAJSA, JIRI, and ALBERT FRANCES 1959. Automation and Stratification. *In* Automation and Society. Howard B. Jacobson and Joseph S. Roucek, eds. Pp. 394−415. New York: Philosophical Library.

NEKICH, SANDRA 1974. The Feast of the Dead: The Origin of the Indian-White Trade Ceremonies in the West. Western Canadian Journal of Anthropology 4: 1−20.

NELL, EDWARD 1973. Economics: The Revival of Political Economy. *In* Ideology in Social Science: Readings in Critical Social Theory. Robin Blackburn, ed. Pp. 76−95. New York: Vintage Books/Random House.

NEWELL, WILLIAM H. 1974. Comment on "The Caste System Upside Down," by Joan P. Mencher. Current Anthropology 15: 487−488.

NEWITT, MALYN D. D. 1973. Portuguese Settlement on the Zambesi: Exploration, Land Tenure and Colonial Rule in East Africa. New York: Africana.

NIKOLINAKOS, MARIOS 1975. Notes Towards a General Theory of Migration in Late Capitalism. Race and Class 17: 5−17.

NORTH, DOUGLASS C. 1961. The Economic Growth of the United States 1790−1860. Englewood Cliffs, NJ: Prentice-Hall.

NORTHRUP, DAVID 1972. The Growth of Trade Among the Igbo Before 1800. Journal of African History 13: 217−236.

NUGENT, DAVID 1980. Closed Systems and Contradiction: The Kachin In and Out of History. Manuscript, files of the author, Department of Anthropology, Columbia University, New York.

OBERG, KALERVO 1973. The Social Economy of the Tlingit Indians. American Ethnological Society, Monograph No. 55. Seattle: University of Washington.

O'CONNOR, JAMES 1974. The Corporations and the State: Essays in the Theory of Capitalism and Imperialism. New York: Harper & Row.

O'LAUGHLIN, BRIDGET 1975. Marxist Approaches in Anthropology. Annual Review of Anthropology 4: 341−370.

OLIEN, MICHAEL D. 1970. The Negro in Costa Rica: The Role of an Ethnic Minority in a Developing Society. Developing Nations Monograph Series, No. 3. Winston-Salem, NC: Overseas Research Center, Wake Forest University.

OLIVEIRA MARQUES, A. H. DE 1972. History of Portugal. 2 vols. New York: Columbia University Press.

OLIVER, DOUGLAS L. 1962. The Pacific Islands. Revised edition. Cambridge, MA: Harvard University Press.

OLIVER, ROLAND A. 1970. The Problem of Bantu Expansion. *In* Papers in African Prehistory. J. D. Fage and R. A. Oliver, eds. Pp. 141−156. Cambridge: Cambridge University Press.

OLIVER, ROLAND A., and BRIAN FAGAN 1975. Africa in the Iron Age, 500 B.C. to A.D. 1400. London: Cambridge University Press.

OLIVER, ROLAND A., and J. D. FAGE 1962. A Short History of Africa. New York: New York University Press.

OLIVER, SYMMES C. 1974. Ecology and Cultural Continuity as Contributing Factors in the Social Organization of the Plains Indians. *In* Man in Adaptation: The Cultural Present. 2d edition. Yehudi A. Cohen, ed. Pp. 302–322. Chicago: Aldine.

OLLMAN, BERTELL 1976. Alienation. 2d edition. Cambridge: Cambridge University Press.

ONSELEN, CHARLES VAN 1976. Chibaro: African Mine Labour in Southern Rhodesia 1900–1933. London: Pluto Press.

——— 1979. The World the Mineowners Made: Social Themes in the Economic Transformation of the Witwatersrand, 1886–1914. Review 3: 289–302.

ORIGO, IRIS 1955. The Domestic Enemy: The Eastern Slaves in Tuscany in the 14th and 15th Centuries. Speculum 30: 321–366.

——— 1957. The Merchant of Prato, Francesco Di Marco Datini, 1335–1410. London: Jonathan Cape.

ORLOVE, BENJAMIN 1977. Integration Through Production: The Use of Zonation in Espinar. American Ethnologist 4: 84–101.

ORTEGA Y GASSET, JOSÉ 1937. Invertebrate Spain. New York: W. W. Norton. (First pub. in Spanish 1921.)

ORTIZ, FERNANDO 1947. Cuban Counterpoint: Tobacco and Sugar. New York: Knopf. (First pub. in Spanish in 1940.)

OSGOOD E. S. 1957. The Day of the Cattleman. Chicago: Phoenix Books.

OSTROGORSKY, GEORG 1957. History of the Byzantine State. New Brunswick, NJ: Rutgers University Press. (First pub. in German 1940.)

OTTENBERG, SIMON 1958. Ibo Oracles and Intergroup Relations. Southwestern Journal of Anthropology 14: 295–317.

OTTERBEIN, KEITH F. 1964. Why the Iroquois Won: An Analysis of Iroquois Military Tactics. Ethnohistory 11: 56–63.

OWEN, E. R. J. 1969. Cotton and the Egyptian Economy 1820–1914: A Study in Trade and Development. Oxford: Clarendon Press.

OWEN, ROGER, and BOB SUTCLIFFE, eds. 1972. Studies in the Theory of Imperialism. London: Longman.

PALERM, ÁNGEL 1949. El industrialismo y la decadencia. Presencia (Mexico City), Nos. 5–6: 38–80.

——— 1979. Sobre la formación del sistema colonial: apuntes para una discusión. *In* Ensayos sobre el desarrollo económico de México y América Latina (1500–1975). Enrique Florescano, ed. Pp. 93–127. Mexico City: Fondo de Cultura Económica.

PALMER, ROBIN, and NEIL PARSONS, eds. 1977. The Roots of Rural Poverty in Central and Southern Africa. Berkeley, Los Angeles, London: University of California Press.

PARRY, J. H. 1966. The Establishment of the European Hegemony 1415–1715: Trade and Exploration in the Age of the Renaissance. 3d revised edition. New York: Harper Torchbooks/Harper & Row.

——— 1971. Trade and Dominion: The European Overseas Empires in the Eighteenth Century. London: Weidenfeld & Nicolson.

——— 1973. The Spanish Seaborne Empire. Harmondsworth: Penguin Books.

PARTRIDGE, WILLIAM L. 1979. Banana County in the Wake of the United Fruit: Social and Economic Linkages. American Ethnologist 6: 491–509.

PECKHAM, HOWARD H. 1970. Pontiac and the Indian Uprising. New York: Russell and Russell. (First pub. 1947.)

PELZER, KARL 1945. Pioneer Settlement in the Asiatic Tropics: Land Utilization and Agricultural Colonization in Southeast Asia. American Geographical Society, Special Publication No. 29. New York: American Geographical Society.

PENDLE, GEORGE 1963. A History of Latin America. Baltimore: Penguin.

PERDUE, THEDA 1979. Slavery and the Evolution of Cherokee Society 1540–1866. Knoxville: University of Tennessee Press.

PERKIN, HAROLD J. 1969. The Origins of Modern English Society 1780–1880. Toronto: University of Toronto Press.

PHILLIPS, PAUL C. 1961. The Fur Trade. 2 vols. Norman: University of Oklahoma Press

PHILLIPSON, D. W. 1977. The Spread of the Bantu Language. Scientific American 286: 106–114.

PIKE, RUTH 1966. Enterprise and Adventure: The Genoese in Seville and the Opening of the New World. Ithaca, NY: Cornell University Press.

PIRENNE, HENRI 1937. Economic and Social History of Medieval Europe. New York: Harcourt Brace. (First pub. in French 1933.)

PLATT, D. C. M. 1973. Latin America and British Trade, 1806–1914. The Merchant Adventurers Series. New York: Harper & Row/Barnes & Noble.

POLANYI, KARL 1957. The Great Transformation: The Political and Economic Origins of Our Time. Boston: Beacon Press. (First pub. 1944.)

———— 1966. Dahomey and the Slave Trade. American Ethnological Society, Monograph No. 42. Seattle: University of Washington Press.

POLLARD, SIDNEY 1965. The Genesis of Modern Management: A Study of the Industrial Revolution in Great Britain. Cambridge, MA: Harvard University Press.

POLLOCK, N. C., and SWANZIE AGNEW 1963. An Historical Geography of South Africa. London: Longmans.

POPPINO, ROLLIE 1968. Brazil: The Land and People. London: Oxford University Press.

PORTES, ALEJANDRO 1978. Migration and Underdevelopment. Politics and Society 8: 1–48.

POTTER, JACK M. 1976. Thai Peasant Social Structure. Chicago: University of Chicago Press.

POULANTZAS, NICOS 1973. Political Power and Social Classes. London: New Left Books. (First pub. in French 1968.)

———— 1978. Classes in Contemporary Capitalism. London: Verso. (First pub. in French 1974.)

PRAWER, JOSHUA, and SHMUEL N. EISENSTADT 1968. Feudalism. *In* International Encyclopedia of the Social Sciences, Vol. 5. David Sills, ed. Pp. 393–403. New York: Macmillan and Free Press.

QUAIN, BUELL 1937. The Iroquois. *In* Cooperation and Competition Among Primitive Peoples. Margaret Mead, ed. Pp. 240–281. New York: McGraw-Hill.

RAGATZ, LOWELL J. 1928. The Fall of the Planter Class in the British Caribbean, 1763–1833. New York: Century.

RAMOS, ALCIDA R. 1978. Mundurucú: Social Change or False Problem? American Ethnologist 5: 675–689.

RANDLE, MARTHA C. 1951. Iroquois Women, Then and Now. Bulletin of the Bureau of American Ethnology, No. 149: 167–180.

RANGER, TERENCE O., ed. 1968. Aspects of Central African History. Evanston, IL: Northwestern University Press.

RAWICK, GEORGE P. 1972. From Sundown to Sunup: The Making of the Black Community. Contributions in Afro-American and African Studies, No. 11. Westport, CT: Greenwood.

RAWSKI, EVELYN SAKAKIDA 1972. Agricultural Change and the Peasant Economy of South China. Harvard East Asian Series, No. 66. Cambridge, MA: Harvard University Press.

RAY, ARTHUR J. 1974. Indians in the Fur Trade: Their Role as Hunters, Trappers and Middlemen in the Lands Southwest of Hudson Bay 1660–1870. Toronto: University of Toronto Press.

RAYCHAUDHURI, TAPAN, ed. 1960. Contributions to Indian Economic History, Vol. 1. Calcutta: Firma K. L. Mukhopadhyay.

REDFORD, ARTHUR 1976. Labour Migration in England, 1800–1850. 3d edition. Manchester: Manchester University Press. (First pub. 1926.)

REES, ALBERT 1961. Real Wages in Manufacturing: 1890–1914. Princeton, NJ: Princeton University Press.

REICHEL-DOLMATOFF, GERARDO 1961. The Agricultural Basis of the Sub-Andean Chiefdoms of Colombia. *In* The Evolution of Horticultural Systems in Native South America: Causes and Consequences. A Symposium. Johannes Wilbert, ed. Pp. 83–100. Supplement Publication No. 2, Antropológica. Caracas: Sociedad de Ciencias Naturales La Salle.

——— 1965. Colombia. New York: Praeger.

REY, PIERRE-PHILIPPE 1976. Les alliances de classes. Paris: François Maspéro.

REYNOLDS, ROBERT L. 1957. The Mediterranean Frontiers, 1000–1400. *In* The Frontier in Perspective. Walker D. Wyman and Clifton B. Kroeber, eds. Pp. 21–34. Madison: University of Wisconsin Press.

——— 1961. Europe Emerges. Madison: University of Wisconsin Press.

RIBEIRO, DARCY 1968. The Civilizational Process. Washington, DC: Smithsonian Institution Press.

RICH, E. E. 1955. Russia and the Colonial Fur Trade. Economic History Review 7: 307–328.

——— 1959. History of the Hudson's Bay Company 1670–1870. 2 vols. London: Hudson's Bay Record Society.

RICHARDS, ALAN R. 1977. Primitive Accumulation in Egypt, 1798–1882. Review 1: 3–49.

RICHARDS, CARA B. 1957. Matriarchy or Mistake: The Role of Iroquois Women Through Time. *In* Cultural Stability and Cultural Change. Proceedings of the 1957 Annual Spring Meeting of the American Ethnological Society. Verne F. Ray, ed. Pp. 36–45. Seattle: American Ethnological Society, University of Washington.

RICHARDS, D. S., ed. 1970. Islam and the Trade of Asia: A Colloquium. Oxford: Bruno Cassirer; Philadelphia: University of Pennsylvania Press.

RICHARDS, W. 1980. The Import of Firearms into West Africa in the 18th Century. Journal of African History 21: 43–59.

ROBEQUAIN, CHARLES 1944. The Economic Development of French Indo-China. London: Oxford University Press. (First pub. in French 1939.)

ROBERTS, ANDREW D. 1973. A History of the Bemba: Political Growth and Change in North-eastern Zambia Before 1900. Madison: University of Wisconsin Press.

ROBINSON, K. R. 1966. The Archaeology of the Rozwi. *In* The Zambezian Past: Studies in Central African History. Eric T. Stokes and R. Brown, eds. Pp. 3–27.

Manchester: University of Manchester Press.

ROBINSON, RONALD 1972. Non-European Foundations of European Imperialism: Sketch for a Theory of Collaboration. *In* Studies in the Theory of Imperialism. Roger Owen and Bob Sutcliffe, eds. Pp. 118–140. London: Longman.

RODINSON, MAXIME 1966. Islam et capitalisme. Paris: Éditions du Seuil.

RODNEY, WALTER 1970. A History of the Upper Guinea Coast. Oxford: Clarendon Press.

ROFF, WILLIAM R. 1967. The Origins of Malay Nationalism. New Haven, CT: Yale University Press.

ROGERS, EDWARD S. 1969. Band Organization Among the Indians of Eastern Subarctic Canada. *In* Contributions to Anthropology: Band Societies. Proceedings of the Conference on Band Organization, Ottawa, 1965. David Damas, ed. Pp. 21–50. National Museum of Canada Bulletin No. 228, Anthropological Series No. 84. Ottawa: National Museums of Canada.

ROGIN, MICHAEL P. 1975. Fathers and Children: Andrew Jackson and the Subjugation of the American Indian. New York: Knopf.

ROHRBOUGH, MALCOLM J. 1968. The Land Office Business: The Settlement and Administration of American Public Lands, 1789–1837. New York: Oxford University Press.

ROKKAN, STEIN 1975. Dimensions of State Formation and Nation-Building: A Possible Paradigm for Research on Variations Within Europe. *In* The Formation of National States in Western Europe. Charles Tilly, ed. Pp. 562–600. Princeton, NJ: Princeton University Press.

ROLLWAGEN, JACK 1980. New Directions in Urban Anthropology: Building an Ethnography and an Ethnology of the world system. *In* Urban Life: Readings in Urban Anthropology. George Gmelch and Walter P. Zenner, eds. Pp. 370–382. New York: St. Martin's Press.

ROSAS, PAUL 1943. Caste and Class in India. Science and Society 7: 141–167.

ROSEBERRY, WILLIAM 1978. Historical Materialism and *The People of Puerto Rico*. *In* Social Anthropology in Puerto Rico. Special issue. Robert Duncan, ed. Revista Interamericana (San Germán, Puerto Rico) 8: 26–36.

ROSECRANCE, RICHARD N. 1964. The Radical Culture of Australia. *In* The Founding of New Societies. Louis Hartz, ed. Pp. 275–318. New York: Harcourt, Brace and World.

ROSENBERG, HANS 1967. Grosse Depression und Bismarckzeit: Wirtschaftsablauf, Gesellschaft und Politik in Mitteleuropa. Veröffentlichungen der Historischen Kommission zu Berlin beim Friedrich-Meinecke-Institut der Freien Universität Berlin, Vol. 24; Publikationen zur Geschichte der Industrialisierung, Vol. 2. Berlin: Walter de Gruyter.

ROSENBERG, HARRIET G. 1978. The Experience of Underdevelopment: Change in a French Alpine Village from the Old Regime to the Present. Ph.D dissertation, Departments of Anthropology and History, University of Michigan, Ann Arbor.

ROSENBLUM, GERALD 1973. Immigrant Workers: Their Impact on American Labor Radicalism. New York: Basic Books.

ROSMAN, ABRAHAM, and PAULA RUBEL 1971. Feasting with Mine Enemy: Rank and Exchange Among Northwest Coast Societies. New York: Columbia University Press.

ROSTOW, WALT WHITMAN 1960. The Stages of Economic Growth: A Non-Communist Manifesto. Cambridge: Cambridge University Press.

———— 1975. How It All Began: Origins of the Modern Economy. New York: McGraw-Hill.

———— 1978. The World Economy: History and Prospect. Austin: University of Texas Press.

ROTBERG, ROBERT I., and H. NEVILLE CHITTICK, eds. 1975. East Africa and the Orient: Cultural Syntheses in Pre-Colonial Times. New York: Africana.

ROTHENBERG, DIANE 1976. Erosion of Power: An Economic Basis for the Selective Conservatism of Seneca Women in the Nineteenth Century. Western Canadian Journal of Anthropology 6: 106–122.

ROWE, JOHN H. 1957. The Incas Under Spanish Colonial Institutions. Hispanic American Historical Review 37: 155–199.

ROWE, WILLIAM L. 1973. Caste, Kinship, and Association in Urban India. *In* Urban Anthropology. Aidan Southall, ed. Pp. 211–249. New York: Oxford University Press.

ROWTHORN, BOB 1976. Late Capitalism. New Left Review, No. 98: 59–83.

RUSSELL, JOSIAH C. 1958. Late Ancient and Medieval Populations. Transactions of the American Philosophical Society, Philadelphia, Vol. 43, No. 3.

———— 1972. Medieval Regions and Their Cities. Bloomington: Indiana University Press.

RUYLE, EUGENE 1973. Slavery, Surplus, and Stratification on the Northwest Coast: The Ethnoenergetics of an Incipient Stratification System. Current Anthropology 14: 603–631.

SAHLINS, MARSHALL D. 1960. Political Power and the Economy in Primitive Society. *In* Essays in the Science of Culture in Honor of Leslie A. White. Gertrude E. Dole and Robert L. Carneiro, eds. Pp. 390–415. New York: Thomas Y. Crowell.

———— 1972. Stone Age Economics. Chicago: Aldine-Atherton.

SAHLINS, MARSHALL D., and ELMAN R. SERVICE, eds. 1960. Evolution and Culture. Ann Arbor: University of Michigan Press.

SAINI, KRISHAN G. 1971. A Case of Aborted Economic Growth: India, 1860–1913. Journal of Asian History 5: 89–118.

SANDERS, WILLIAM T., and JOSEPH MARINO 1970. New World Prehistory. Englewood Cliffs, NJ: Prentice-Hall.

SANDERS, WILLIAM T., and BARBARA J. PRICE 1968. Mesoamerica: The Evolution of a Civilization. New York: Random House.

SANSOM, ROBERT L. 1970. The Economics of Insurgency in the Mekong Delta of Vietnam. Cambridge, MA: MIT Press.

SANTAMARÍA, DANIEL J. 1977. La propiedad de la tierra y la condición social del indio en el Alto Perú, 1780–1810. Desarrollo Económico: Revista de Ciencias Sociales (Buenos Aires, Argentina) 17: 253–271.

SASSEN-KOOB, SASKIA 1978. The International Circulation of Resources and Development: The Case of Migrant Labour. Development and Change 9: 509–545.

———— 1981. Notes Towards a Conceptualization of Immigrant Labor. Social Problems, 29: 65–85.

SAUER, CARL O. 1966. The Early Spanish Main. Berkeley and Los Angeles: University of California Press.

SCHAPERA, ISAAC 1940. The Political Organization of the Ngwato of Bechuanaland Protectorate. *In* African Political Systems. Meyer Fortes and E. E. Evans-Pritchard, eds. Pp. 56–82. London: Oxford University Press.

SCHERMERHORN, RICHARD A. 1978. Ethnic Plurality in India. Tucson: University of Arizona Press.
SCHLUMBOHM, JÜRGEN 1977. Produktionsverhältnisse—Produktivkräfte—Krisen in der Proto-Industrialisierung. *In* Industrialisierung vor der Industrialisierung: Gewerbliche Warenproduktion auf dem Land in der Formationsperiode des Kapitalismus. Peter Kriedte, Hans Medick, and Jürgen Schlumbohm, eds. Pp. 194–257. Veröffentlichungen des Max-Planck-Instituts ür Geschichte 53. Göttingen: Vandenhoeck & Ruprecht.
SCHMIDT, ALFRED 1971. The Concept of Nature in Marx. London: New Left Books.
SCHNEIDER, DAVID M. 1972. What Is Kinship All About? *In* Kinship Studies in the Morgan Centennial Year. Priscilla Reining, ed. Pp. 32–63. Washington, DC: Anthropological Society of Washington.
SCHNEIDER, JANE 1977. Was There a Pre-Capitalist World System? Peasant Studies 6: 20–29.
SCHNEIDER, JANE, and PETER SCHNEIDER 1976. Culture and Political Economy in Western Sicily. New York: Academic Press.
SCHUMPETER, JOSEPH 1939. Business Cycles: A Theoretical, Historical and Statistical Analysis of the Capitalist Process. 2 vols. New York: McGraw-Hill.
SCOBIE, JAMES R. 1964. Revolution on the Pampas: A Social History of Argentine Wheat, 1860–1910. Austin: University of Texas Press.
SCOTT, JOAN WALLACH 1974. The Glassworkers of Carmaux: French Craftsmen and Political Action in a Nineteenth-Century City. Cambridge, MA: Harvard University Press.
SECOY, FRANK R. 1953. Changing Military Patterns on the Great Plains (17th Century Through Early 19th Century). American Ethnological Society, Monograph No. 21. New York: J. J. Augustin.
SEDDON, DAVID, ed. 1974. Relations of Production: Marxist Approaches to Economic Anthropology. London: Frank Cass.
SÉE, HENRI 1937. Orígen y evolución del capitalismo moderno. Mexico City: Fondo de Cultura Económica. (First pub. in French 1926.)
SELLNOW, IRMGARD 1961. Grundprinzipien einer Periodisierung der Urgeschichte. Berlin: Akademie Verlag.
SERENI, EMILIO 1968. Il capitalismo nelle campagne (1860–1900). Turin: Einaudi.
SERVICE, ELMAN R. 1962. Primitive Social Organization: An Evolutionary Perspective. New York: Random House.
——— 1968. War and Our Contemporary Ancestors. *In* War: The Anthropology of Armed Conflict and Aggression. Morton H. Fried, Marvin Harris, and Robert F. Murphy, eds. Pp. 160–167. Garden City, NY: Natural History Press.
SHANIN, TEODOR 1978. The Peasants Are Coming: Migrants Who Labour, Peasants Who Travel, and Marxists Who Write. Race and Class 19: 277–288.
SHAPIRO, SEYMOUR 1967. Capital and the Cotton Industry in the Industrial Revolution. Ithaca, NY: Cornell University Press.
SHARP, LAURISTON, and LUCIEN M. HANKS 1978. Bang Chan: Social History of a Rural Community in Thailand. Ithaca, NY: Cornell University Press.
SHARP, LAURISTON, HAZEL M. HAUCK, KAMOL JANLEKHA, and ROBERT B. TEXTOR 1953. Siamese Rice Village: A Preliminary Study of Bang Chan, 1948–1949. Bangkok: Cornell Research Center.
SHARP, WILLIAM FREDERICK 1976. Slavery on the Spanish Frontier: The Colom-

bian Chocó 1680–1810. Norman: University of Oklahoma Press.

SHARROCK, SUSAN R. 1974. Crees, Cree-Assiniboines, and Assiniboines: Interethnic Social Organization on the Far Northern Plains. Ethnohistory 21: 95–122.

SHELVANKAR, K. S. 1943. The Problem of India. Harmondsworth: Penguin Books.

SHINEBERG, DOROTHY 1966. The Sandalwood Trade in Melanesian Economics, 1841–65. Journal of Pacific History 1: 129–146.

―――― 1967. They Came for Sandalwood: A Study of the Sandalwood Trade in the South-West Pacific 1830–1865. Carlton: Melbourne University Press.

―――― 1970. Guns and Men in Melanesia. Journal of Pacific History 5: 61–82.

SHIOZAWA, KIMIO 1965. Les historiens japonais et le mode de production asiatique. La Pensée, No. 122: 63–78.

SIDER, GERALD M. 1970. The Political History of the Lumbee Indians of Robeson County, North Carolina: A Case Study of Ethnic Political Affiliations. Ph.D. dissertation, Department of Anthropology, New School of Social Research, New York.

SILVERBERG, JAMES ed. 1968. Social Mobility in the Caste System in India. Comparative Studies in Society and History: Supplement III.

SIMKIN, C. G. F. 1968. The Traditional Trade of Asia. London: Oxford University Press.

SIMONS, H. J. 1949. Race Relations and Policies in Southern and Eastern Africa. *In* Most of the World: The Peoples of Africa, Latin America, and the East Today. Ralph Linton, ed. Pp. 271–330. New York: Columbia University Press.

SIMONS, H. J., and R. E. SIMONS 1969. Class and Colour in South Africa. Harmondsworth: Penguin Books.

SINDER, LEON 1964. Caste Instability in Moghul India. Seoul: Chung-ang University.

SINHA, SURAJIT 1962. Status Formation and Rajput Myth in Tribal Central India. Man in India 42: 35–80.

SISKIND, JANET 1978. Kinship and Mode of Production. American Anthropologist 80: 860–872.

SKOCPOL, THEDA 1979. States and Social Revolutions: A Comparative Analysis of France, Russia, and China. Cambridge: Cambridge University Press.

SMELSER, NEIL J. 1959. Social Change in the Industrial Revolution: An Application of Theory to the British Cotton Industry. Chicago: University of Chicago Press.

SMIT, J. W. 1975. Holland: Comment. *In* Failed Transitions to Modern Industrial Society: Renaissance Italy and Seventeenth Century Holland. First International Colloquium 1974. Frederick Krantz and Paul M. Hohenberg, eds. Pp. 61–63. Montreal: Interuniversity Centre for European Studies.

SMITH, ABBOT E. 1947. Colonists in Bondage: White Servitude and Convict Labor in America, 1607–1776. Chapel Hill: University of North Carolina Press.

SMITH, ABDULLAHI 1972. The Early States of the Central Sudan. *In* History of West Africa. J. F. Ade Ajayi and Michael Crowder, eds., Vol. 1. Pp. 158-201. New York: Columbia University Press.

SMITH, C. T. 1967. An Historical Geography of Western Europe Before 1800. Praeger Advanced Geographies. New York: Praeger.

SMITH, M. G. 1965. The Plural Society in the British West Indies. Berkeley and

Los Angeles: University of California Press.

SNOW, DEAN 1976. Abenaki Fur Trade in the Sixteenth Century. Western Canadian Journal of Anthropology 6: 3–11.

SOUTHALL, AIDAN W. 1953. Alur Society: A Study in Processes and Types of Domination. Cambridge, MA: W. Heffer.

SPALDING, KAREN W. 1967. Indian Rural Society in Colonial Peru: The Example of Huarochiri. Ph.D. dissertation, Department of History, University of California, Berkeley.

—— 1974. De indio a campesino: Cambios en la estructura social del Perú colonial. Lima: Instituto de Estudios Peruanos.

SPEAR, PERCIVAL 1963. The Nabobs: A Study of the Social Life of the English in Eighteenth Century India. London: Humphrey Milford/Oxford University Press.

—— 1970. The Mughal Mansabdari System. *In* Elites in South Asia. E. R. Leach and S. N. Mukherjee, eds. Pp. 1–15. Cambridge: Cambridge University Press.

SPODEK, HOWARD 1974. Rulers, Merchants and Other Groups in the City-States of Saurashtra, India, Around 1800. Comparative Studies in Society and History 16: 448–470.

SRINIVAS, M. N. 1959. The Dominant Caste in Rampura. American Anthropologist 61: 1–16.

—— 1961. Social Change in Modern India. Berkeley and Los Angeles: University of California Press.

STAVENHAGEN, RODOLFO 1975. Social Classes in Agrarian Societies. Garden City, NY: Anchor Press/Doubleday.

STEENSGARD, NIELS 1973. Carracks, Caravans, and Companies: The Structural Crisis in the European-Asian Trade in the Early 17th Century. Monograph Series, Vol. 17. Copenhagen: Scandinavian Institute of Asian Studies.

STEIN, STANLEY J., and BARBARA STEIN 1970. The Colonial Heritage of Latin America. Oxford: Oxford University Press.

STENTON, DORIS M. 1952. English Society in the Early Middle Ages (1066–1307). 2d revised edition. Pelican History of England, Vol. 3. Harmondsworth: Penguin Books.

STERNBERG, FRITZ 1926. Der Imperialismus. Berlin: Malik.

STEVENSON, ROBERT F. 1968. Population and Political Systems in Tropical Africa. New York: Columbia University Press.

STEWARD, JULIAN H. 1947. American Culture History in the Light of South America. Southwestern Journal of Anthropology 3: 85–107.

STEWARD, JULIAN H., ed. 1946–1959. Handbook of South American Indians. 7 vols. U.S. Bureau of American Ethnology, Bulletin 143. Washington, DC: U.S. Government Printing Office.

—— 1956. The People of Puerto Rico: A Study in Social Anthropology. Urbana: University of Illinois Press.

STEWARD, JULIAN H., and LOUIS G. FARON 1959. Native Peoples of South America. New York: McGraw-Hill.

STEWART, WATT 1951. Chinese Bondage in Peru: A History of the Chinese Coolie in Peru, 1849–1874. Westport, CT: Greenwood Press.

—— 1964. Keith and Costa Rica: The Biographical Study of Minor Cooper Keith. Albuquerque: University of New Mexico Press.

STRACHEY, JOHN 1935. Nature of the Capitalist Crisis. New York: Covici Friede.

STRAYER, JOSEPH R. 1970. On the Medieval Origins of the Modern State.

Princeton, NJ: Princeton University Press.

STRICKON, ARNOLD 1960. The Grandsons of the Gauchos: A Study in Subcultural Persistence. Ph.D. dissertation, Department of Anthropology, Columbia University, New York.

—— 1965. The Euro-American Ranching Complex. *In* Man, Culture, and Animals. Anthony Leeds and Andrew P. Vayda, eds. Pp. 229–258. American Association for the Advancement of Science, Publication 78. Washington, DC: American Association for the Advancement of Science.

STURTEVANT, WILLIAM C. 1962. Spanish-Indian Relations in Southeastern North America. Ethnohistory 9: 41–94.

—— 1971. Creek into Seminole. *In* North American Indians in Historical Perspective. Eleanor B. Leacock and Nancy O. Lurie, eds. Pp. 92–128. New York: Random House.

SUMMERS, ROGER 1961. The Southern Rhodesian Iron Age. Journal of African History 2: 1–13.

—— 1963. Zimbabwe: A Rhodesian Mystery. Johannesburg: Nelson.

—— 1970. The Rhodesian Iron Age. *In* Papers in African Prehistory. J. D. Fage and R. A. Oliver, eds. Pp. 157–172. Cambridge: Cambridge University Press.

SUNDSTROM, LARS 1974. The Exchange Economy of Pre-Colonial Tropical Africa. New York: St. Martin's Press. (Reprint of The Trade of Guinea, 1965).

SUTTLES, WAYNE 1960. Variation in Habitat and Culture in the Northwest Coast. Akten des 34. Internationalen Amerikanisten-Kongresses, Vienna. Pp. 522–537. Horn, Vienna: Ferdinand Berger.

SWANTON, JOHN R. 1946. The Indians of the Southeastern United States. U.S. Bureau of American Ethnology Bulletin 137. Washington, DC: U.S. Government Printing Office.

SWEEZY, PAUL M. 1942. The Theory of Capitalist Development: Principles of Marxian Political Economy. New York: Oxford University Press.

TAWNEY, R. H. 1967. The Agrarian Problem in the Sixteenth Century. New York: Harper & Row. (First pub. 1912.)

TAYLOR, GEORGE ROGERS 1951. The Transportation Revolution 1815–1860. The Economic History of the United States, Vol. 4. New York: Rinehart.

TAYLOR, WILLIAM B. 1972. Landlord and Peasant in Colonial Oaxaca. Stanford, CA: Stanford University Press.

TEGGART, FREDERICK J. 1939. Rome and China: A Study of Correlations in Historical Events. Berkeley and Los Angeles: University of California Press.

TENG, SSU-YÜ, and JOHN K. FAIRBANK 1961. China's Response to the West: A Documentary Survey 1839–1923. Cambridge, MA: Harvard University Press.

TERRAY, EMMANUEL 1973. Technologie, état et tradition en Afrique. Annales 28: 1331–1338.

—— 1975. Classes and Class Consciousness in the Abron Kingdom of Gyaman. *In* Marxist Analyses and Social Anthropology. Maurice Bloch, ed. Pp. 85–135. Association of Social Anthropologists, Studies No. 2. London: Malaby Press.

THIRSK, JOAN 1974. The Disappearance of the English Peasantry. Paper presented at the Peasant Seminar, Centre of International and Area Studies, University of London, March 15. Mimeographed version P.74/37.

THOMPSON, EDGAR T. 1975. Plantation Societies, Race Relations, and the South: The Regimentation of Populations. Durham, NC: Duke University Press.

THOMPSON, E. P. 1966. The Making of the English Working Class. New York: Vintage Books.

——— 1978*a*. Eighteenth-Century English Society: Class Struggle Without Class? Social History 3: 133–165.

——— 1978*b*. The Poverty of Theory and Other Essays. New York and London: Monthly Review Press.

THOMPSON, LEONARD 1969. Cooperation and Conflict: The Zulu Kingdom and Natal. *In* The Oxford History of South Africa, Vol. 1: South Africa to 1870. Monica Wilson and Leonard Thompson, eds. Pp. 334–390. New York and London: Oxford University Press.

THORNER, DANIEL 1950. Investment in Empire: British Railway and Steam Shipping Enterprise in India, 1825–1849. Philadelphia: University of Pennsylvania Press.

——— 1964. Agricultural Cooperatives in India: A Field Report. London: Asia Publishing House.

THORNER, DANIEL, and ALICE THORNER 1962. Land and Labour in India. Bombay: Asia Publishing House.

THRUPP, SYLVIA L. 1962. The Merchant Class of Medieval London (1300–1500). Ann Arbor: University of Michigan Press.

TILLY, CHARLES 1964. The Vendée: A Sociological Analysis of the Counterrevolution of 1793. New York: Wiley.

——— 1975. Food Supply and Public Order in Modern Europe. *In* The Formation of National States in Western Europe. Charles Tilly, ed. Pp. 380–455. Princeton, NJ: Princeton University Press.

——— 1976. Sociology, History, and the Origins of the European Proletariat. Center for Research on Social Organization, Working Paper No. 148. Ann Arbor: University of Michigan.

TILLY, CHARLES, ed. 1975. The Formation of National States in Western Europe. Princeton, NJ: Princeton University Press.

TINKER, HUGH 1974. A New System of Slavery: The Export of Indian Labour Overseas 1830–1920. London: Oxford University Press.

TITIEV, MISCHA 1943. The Influence of Common Residence on the Unilateral Classification of Kindred. American Anthropologist 45: 511–530.

TOGAN, A. ZEKI VALIDI 1939. Ibn Fadlan's Reisebericht. Abhandlungen für die Kunde des Morgenlandes (Leipzig) 24 (3).

TÖKEI, FERENC 1966. Sur le mode de production asiatique. Paris: Centre d'Études et de Recherches marxistes. (First Hungarian ed. 1965; first German transl. 1969.)

TÖPFER, BERNHARD 1974. Zu einigen Grundfragen des Feudalismus. Ein Diskussionsbeitrag. *In* Feudalismus. Heide Wunder, ed. Pp. 221–254. Munich: Nymphenburger Verlagshandlung.

TOUSSAINT, AUGUSTE 1966. History of the Indian Ocean. Chicago: University of Chicago Press.

TRELEASE, ALLEN W. 1960. Indian Affairs in Colonial New York: The Seventeenth Century. Ithaca, NY: Cornell University Press.

TREMPÉ, ROLANDE 1971. Les mineurs de Carmaux. Paris: Éditions Ouvrières.

TRIGGER, BRUCE G. 1976. The Children of Aataentsic: A History of the Huron People to 1660. 2 vols. Montreal: McGill-Queen's University Press.

TRIGGER, BRUCE, ed. 1978. Handbook of North American Indians, Vol. 5: The Northeast. Washington, DC: Smithsonian Institution.

TRIMBERGER, ELLEN K. 1978. Revolution from Above: Military Bureaucrats and Development in Japan, Turkey, Egypt, and Peru. New Brunswick, NJ: Transaction Books.

TURNER, BRYAN S. 1978. Marx and the End of Orientalism. Controversies in Sociology, No. 7. London: Allen & Unwin.

TURNER, VICTOR 1967. The Forest of Symbols: Aspects of Ndembu Ritual. Ithaca, NY: Cornell University Press.

TWICHETT, DENIS 1962. Land Tenure and the Social Order in T'ang and Sung China. Inaugural Lecture, November 28th, 1961. London: School of Oriental and African Studies, University of London.

UCHENDU, VICTOR C. 1965. The Igbo of Southeast Nigeria. New York: Holt, Rinehart & Winston.

UDOVITCH, ABRAHAM L. 1970. Partnership and Profit in Medieval Islam. Princeton, NJ: Princeton University Press.

UDOVITCH, ABRAHAM L., ed. 1980. The Islamic Middle East, 700−1900: Studies in Social and Economic History. Princeton, NJ: Princeton University Press.

UKERS, WILLIAM H. 1935. All About Coffee. 2d edition. New York: Tea and Coffee Trade Journal Company.

URE, ANDREW 1967. The Philosophy of Manufacturers or, an Exposition of the Scientific, Moral, and Commercial Economy of the Factory System of Great Britain. Reprints of Economic Classics. New York: Augustus M. Kelley. (First pub. 1835.)

VANSINA, JAN 1962. Long Distance Trade-Routes in Central Africa. Journal of African History 3: 375−390.

───── 1963. Notes sur l'origine du royaume du Congo. Journal of African History 4: 33−38.

───── 1968. Kingdoms of the Savanna. Madison: University of Wisconsin Press.

VANSINA, JAN, R. MAUNY, and L. V. THOMAS, eds. 1964. The Historian in Tropical Africa. London: Oxford University Press.

VASILIEV, L. S., and I. A. STUCHEVSKII 1967. Three Models for the Origin and Evolution of Precapitalist Societies. Soviet Review: A Journal of Translations 8: 26−39.

VELLUT, JEAN-LUC 1972. Notes sur le Lunda et la frontière Luso-Africaine (1700−1900). Études d'Histoire Africaine 3: 61−166.

VENABLE, VERNON 1945. Human Nature: The Marxian View. New York: Knopf.

VERCAUTEREN, FERNAND 1967. The Circulation of Merchants in Western Europe from the 6th to the 10th Century: Economic and Cultural Aspects. *In* Early Medieval Society. Sylvia L. Thrupp, ed. Pp. 185−195. New York: Appleton-Century-Crofts.

VERLINDEN, CHARLES 1955. L'esclavage dans l'Europe médiévale. Vol. 1: Peninsule Ibérique, France. Bruges: De Tempel.

VÍCENS VIVES, JAIME 1969. Economic History of Spain. Princeton, NJ: Princeton University Press. (First pub. in Spanish 1955.)

───── 1970. Approaches to the History of Spain. Revised edition. Berkeley, Los Angeles, London: University of California Press. (First pub. in Spanish 1952.)

VILLAMARÍN, JUAN A. 1972. Encomenderos and Indians in the Formation of Colonial Society in the Sabana de Bogotá, Colombia: 1537−1740. Ph.D. dissertation, Department of Anthropology, Brandeis University, Waltham, Mass.

───── 1975. Haciendas en la Sabana de Bogotá, Colombia, en la época colonial: 1539−1810. *In* Haciendas, latifundios y plantaciones. Enrique Florescano, ed. Pp. 327−345. Mexico City: Siglo XXI Editores.

VILLAMARÍN, JUAN, and JUDITH E. VILLAMARÍN 1975. Indian Labor in Mainland Colonial Spanish America. University of Delaware Latin American Studies

Program Occasional Papers and Monographs, No. 1. Newark: University of Delaware Latin American Studies Program.

——— 1979. Chibcha Settlement Patterns Under Spanish Rule 1537–1810. *In* Social Fabric and Spatial Structures in Colonial Latin America. Dellplain Monograph Series in Latin American Studies, Vol. 1. David J. Robinson, ed. Pp. 25–84. Syracuse, NY: Department of Geography, Syracuse University.

VOLOŠINOV, VALENTIN N. 1973. Marxism and the Philosophy of Language. New York and London: Seminar Press. (First pub. in Russian 1930.)

VRIES, JAN DE 1974. Dutch Rural Economy in the Golden Age, 1500–1700. New Haven, CT: Yale University Press.

——— 1975. Holland: Commentary: *In* Failed Transitions to Modern Industrial Society: Renaissance Italy and Seventeenth Century Holland. First International Colloqium 1974. Frederick Krantz and Paul M. Hohenberg, eds. Pp. 55–57. Montreal: Interuniversity Centre for European Studies.

WADSWORTH, A. P., and JULIA DE LACY MANN 1931. The Cotton Trade and Industrial Lancashire, 1600–1780. Manchester: Manchester University Press.

WAGLEY, CHARLES 1953. Amazon Town: A Study of Man in the Tropics. New York: Macmillan.

WAKEMAN, FREDERIC, JR. 1974. Strangers at the Gate: Social Disorder in South China 1839–1861. Berkeley, Los Angeles, London: University of California Press.

——— 1975. The Fall of Imperial China. New York: Free Press.

WALKER, MACK 1964. Germany and the Emigration, 1816–1885. Cambridge, MA: Harvard University Press.

——— 1971. German Home Towns: Community, State, and General Estate 1648–1871. Ithaca, NY: Cornell University Press.

WALLACE, ANTHONY F. C. 1970. The Death and the Rebirth of the Senecas. New York: Knopf.

WALLERSTEIN, IMMANUEL 1974. The Modern World-System: Capitalist Agriculture and the Origins of the European World-Economy in the Sixteenth Century. New York: Academic Press.

——— 1979. Kondratieff Up or Kondratieff Down? Review 2: 663–673.

WANG, YÜ-CH'ÜAN 1936. The Rise of the Land Tax and the Fall of Dynasties in Chinese History. Pacific Affairs 9: 201–220.

WARD, R. GERARD 1972. The Pacific Bêche-de-Mer Trade with Special Reference to Fiji. *In* Man in the Pacific Islands. R. Gerard Ward, ed. Pp. 91–123. Oxford: Clarendon Press.

WARD, R. GERARD, ed. 1972. Man in the Pacific Islands. Oxford: Clarendon Press.

WARD, W.E.F. 1966. A History of Ghana. London: Allen & Unwin.

WARNER, W. LLOYD 1958. A Black Civilization: A Social Study of an Australian Tribe. Revised edition. New York: Harper & Row. (First pub. 1937.)

WARNER, W. LLOYD, and J. LOW 1947. The Social System of a Modern Factory. New Haven, CT: Yale University Press.

WASHBURN, WILCOMB E., ed. 1964. The Indian and the White Man. Documents in American Civilization Series. New York: Anchor Books.

WASSERSTROM, ROBERT 1977. Land and Labour in Central Chiapas: A Regional Analysis. Development and Change 8: 441–463.

——— 1978. Population Growth and Economic Development in Chiapas, 1524–1975. Human Ecology 6: 127–143.

WATROUS, STEPHEN D. 1966. John Ledyard's Journey Through Russia and

Siberia 1787–1788. The Journal and Selected Letters. Madison: University of Wisconsin Press.

WATSON, ANDREW M. 1974. The Arab Agricultural Revolution and Its Diffusion, 700–1100. Journal of Economic History 34: 8–35.

WATSON, JAMES L., ed. 1980. Asian and African Systems of Slavery. Oxford: Basil Blackwell.

WEBB, MALCOLM C. 1965. The Abolition of the Taboo System in Hawaii. Journal of the Polynesian Society 74: 21–39.

WEBB, WALTER P. 1931. The Great Plains. New York: Grosset's Universal Library.

WEBER, EUGEN 1976. Peasants into Frenchmen: The Modernization of Rural France 1870–1914. Stanford, CA: Stanford University Press.

WEBER, MAX 1958. The Protestant Ethic and the Spirit of Capitalism. New York: Scribner's. (First pub. in German 1904–1905.)

———— 1968. On Charisma and Institution Building: Selected Papers. Shmuel N. Eisenstadt, ed. Chicago: University of Chicago Press.

———— 1979. Developmental Tendencies in the Situation of East Elbian Rural Laborers. Economy and Society 8: 177–205. (First pub. in German 1894.)

WEBSTER, DAVID 1975. Warfare and the Evolution of the State: A Reconsideration. American Antiquity 40: 464–470.

———— 1976. On Theocracies. American Anthropologist 78: 812–828.

WEIGAND, PHIL C. 1978. La prehistoria del estado de Zacatecas: una interpretación. Zacatecas No. 1: 203–248.

WELSH, DAVID 1971. The Growth of Towns. In The Oxford History of South Africa, Vol. 2: South Africa 1870–1966. Monica Wilson and Leonard Thompson, eds. Pp. 172–243. New York and Oxford: Oxford University Press.

WELSKOF, ELISABETH CHARLOTTE 1957. Die Produktionsverhältnisse im Alten Orient und in der Griechisch-Römischen Antike. Berlin: Akademie Verlag.

WERNER, ERNST 1966. Die Geburt einer Grossmacht—Die Osmanen: Ein Beitrag zur Genesis des türkischen Feudalismus. Forschungen zur Mittelalterlichen Geschichte, No. 13. Berlin: Akademie Verlag.

WERTHEIM, W. F. 1973. Dawning of an Asian Dream: Selected Articles on Modernization and Emancipation. Antropologisch-Sociologisch Centrum van de Universiteit van Amsterdam, Afd. Zuid-en Zuidoost Azie, Publication No. 20.

———— 1974. Evolution and Revolution: The Rising Waves of Emancipation. Harmondsworth: Penguin Books.

WESSMAN, JAMES W. 1981. Anthropology and Marxism. Cambridge, MA: Schenkman.

WESTERN CANADIAN JOURNAL OF ANTHROPOLOGY 1972. Special Issue on the Fur Trade. Vol. 3, No. 1.

WHEATLEY, PAUL 1961. The Golden Khersonese: Studies in the Historical Geography of the Malay Peninsula Before 1500 A.D. Kuala Lumpur: University of Malaya Press.

———— 1975. Satyānrta in Suvarnadvīpa: From Reciprocity to Redistribution in Ancient Southeast Asia. In Ancient Civilizations and Trade. Jeremy A. Sabloff and C. C. Lamberg-Karlovsky, eds. Pp. 227–283. Albuquerque: University of New Mexico Press.

WHEELER, MORTIMER 1955. Rome Beyond the Imperial Frontiers. Harmondsworth: Penguin Books.

WIKE, JOYCE 1947. The Effects of the Maritime Fur Trade on Northwest Coast

Indian Society. Ph.D. dissertation, Department of Anthropology, Columbia University, New York.

—— 1952. The Role of the Dead in Northwest Coast Culture. *In* Indian Tribes of Aboriginal America. Proceedings of the 29th International Congress of Americanists, Vol. 3. Sol Tax, ed. Pp. 97–103. Chicago: University of Chicago Press.

—— 1957. More Puzzles on the Northwest Coast. American Anthropologist 59: 301–317.

—— 1958a. Social Stratification Among the Nootka. Ethnohistory 5: 219–241.

—— 1958b. Problems in Fur Trade Analysis: The Northwest Coast. American Anthropologist 60: 1086–1101.

WILBUR, CLARENCE M. 1943. Slavery in China During the Former Han Dynasty, 206 B.C.–A.D. 25. Field Museum of Natural History, Publication 525, Chicago.

WILKS, IVOR 1962. A Medieval Trade Route from the Niger to the Gulf of Guinea. Journal of African History 3: 337–341.

—— 1967. Ashanti Government. *In* West African Kingdoms in the 19th Century. Daryll Forde and P. M. Kaberry, eds. Pp. 206–238. Oxford: Oxford University Press.

—— 1975. Asante in the Nineteenth Century: The Structure and Evolution of a Political Order. London: Cambridge University Press.

WILLEY, GORDON R. 1966. An Introduction to American Archaeology, Vol. 1: North and Middle America. Englewood Cliffs, NJ: Prentice-Hall.

—— 1971. An Introduction to American Archaeology, Vol. 2: South America. Englewood Cliffs, NJ: Prentice-Hall.

WILLIAMS, ERIC 1944. Capitalism and Slavery. Chapel Hill: University of North Carolina Press.

WILLIAMS, RAYMOND 1973a. The Country and the City. New York: Oxford University Press.

—— 1973b. Base and Superstructure in Marxist Cultural Theory. New Left Review, No. 82: 3–16.

WILLIS, WILLIAM S., JR. 1955. Colonial Conflict and the Cherokee Indians 1710–1760. Ph.D. dissertation, Department of Anthropology, Columbia University, New York.

—— 1963. Divide and Rule: Red, White, and Black in the Southeast. Journal of Negro History 48: 157–176.

—— 1970. Anthropology and Negroes on the Southern Colonial Frontier. *In* The Black Experience in America. James C. Curtis and Lewis L. Gould, eds. Pp. 33–50. Austin: University of Texas Press.

—— 1980. Fusion and Separation: Archaeology and Ethnohistory in Southeastern North America. *In* Theory and Practice: Essays Presented to Gene Weltfish. Stanley Diamond, ed. Pp. 97–123. The Hague: Mouton.

WILMOTT, W. E., ed. 1972. Economic Organization in Chinese Society. Stanford, CA: Stanford University Press.

WILSON, CHARLES H. 1957. Profit and Power: A Study of England and the Dutch Wars. Cambridge: Cambridge University Press.

—— 1965. England's Apprenticeship, 1603–1763. London: Longmans, Green.

WILSON, CHARLES MORROW 1947. Empire in Green and Gold. New York: Henry Holt.

WILSON, FRANCIS 1972. Labour in the South African Gold Mines, 1911–1969. African Studies 6. Cambridge: Cambridge University Press.

WILSON, GODFREY 1941–1942. The Economics of Detribalization in Northern Rhodesia. Rhodes-Livingstone Papers No. 5 (Part I, 1941) and No. 6 (Part II, 1942). London: Oxford University Press, for the Rhodes-Livingstone Institute.

WILSON, H. CLYDE 1956. A New Interpretation of the Wild Rice District of Wisconsin. American Anthropologist 58: 1059–1064.

——— 1963. An Inquiry into the Nature of Plains Indian Cultural Development. American Anthropologist 65: 355–369.

WILSON, MONICA, and LEONARD THOMPSON, eds. 1969–1971. The Oxford History of South Africa. 2 vols. Vol. 1: South Africa to 1870 (1969); Vol. 2: South Africa 1870–1966 (1971). New York and Oxford: Oxford University Press.

WINSTON, SANFORD 1934. Indian Slavery in the Carolina Region. Journal of Negro History 19: 431–440.

WITTEK, PAUL 1957. The Rise of the Ottoman Empire. London: Royal Asiatic Society.

WITTFOGEL, KARL A. 1931. Wirtschaft und Gesellschaft Chinas, Erster Teil: Produktivkräfte, Produkts- und Zirkulations-Prozess. Schriften des Instituts für Sozialforschung an der Universität Frankfurt a.M. Vol. 3. Leipzig: C. L. Hirschfeld.

——— 1957. Oriental Despotism. New Haven, CT: Yale University Press.

WOLF, ERIC R. 1951. The Social Organization of Mecca and the Origins of Islam. Southwestern Journal of Anthropology 7: 329–356.

——— 1953. La formación de la nación. Part I. Ciencias Sociales 4: 50–62.

——— 1959. Specific Aspects of Plantation Systems in the New World: Community Sub-cultures and Social Class. In Plantation systems in the New World. Angel Palerm and Vera Rubin, eds. Pp. 136–146. Social Science Monograph No. 7. Washington, DC: Pan American Union.

——— 1966. Peasants. Foundation of Modern Anthropology Series. Englewood Cliffs, NJ: Prentice-Hall.

——— 1969. Peasant Wars of the Twentieth Century. New York: Harper & Row.

WOLF, ERIC R., and SIDNEY W. MINTZ 1957. Haciendas and Plantations in Middle America and the Antilles. Social and Economic Studies 6: 380–411.

WOLPE, HAROLD 1972. Capitalism and Cheap Labour-Power in South Africa: From Segregation to Apartheid. Economy and Society 1: 425–456.

WOLTERS, O. W. 1967. Early Indonesian Commerce: A Study of the Origins of Śrīviyaya. Ithaca, NY: Cornell University Press.

——— 1970. The Fall of Śrīviyaya in Malay History. London: Lund Humphries.

WOODRUFF, PHILIP 1964. The Men Who Ruled India. 2 vols. New York: Schocken Books.

WOODRUFF, WILLIAM 1966. The Impact of Western Man, a Study of Europe's Role in the World Economy: 1760–1960. London: Macmillan.

——— 1971. The Emergence of an International Economy 1700–1914. In The Fontana Economic History of Europe, Vol. 4: The Emergence of Industrial Societies. Carlo Cipolla, ed. separata. London: Fontana.

WORSLEY, PETER 1957. The Trumpet Shall Sound: A Study of 'Cargo' Cults in Melanesia. London: Macgibbon and Kee.

——— 1961. The Analysis of Rebellion and Revolution in British Social Anthropology. Science and Society 21: 26–37.

———— 1964. The Third World. London: Weidenfeld & Nicolson.

WRIGHT, GARY A. 1967. Some Aspects of Early and Mid-Seventeenth Century Exchange Networks in the Western Great Lakes. Michigan Archaeologist 13: 181–197.

WRIGHT, GAVIN 1978. The Political Economy of the Cotton South: Households, Markets, and Wealth in the Nineteenth Century. New York: W. W. Norton.

WUNDER, HEIDE, ed. 1971. Feudalismus. Munich: Nymphenburger Verlag.

YALMAN, NUR 1971. Under the Bo Tree: Studies in Caste, Kinship, and Marriage in the Interior of Ceylon. Berkeley, Los Angeles, London: University of California Press.

YOUNG, PHILIP D. 1971. Ngawbe: Tradition and Change Among the Western Guaymí of Panama. Illinois Studies in Anthropology, No. 7. Urbana: University of Illinois Press.

ZUKIN, SHARON 1980. A Decade of the New Urban Sociology. Theory and Society 9: 575–601.